The evolving world of work in the enlarged EU

The evolving world of work in the enlarged EU

Progress and Vulnerability

Edited by François Eyraud
and Daniel Vaughan-Whitehead

International Labour Office Geneva

ISBN 978-92-2-119547-4 (printed version)
ISBN 978-92-2-119548-1 (web .pdf version)

ILO descriptors: conference paper, labour market, labour flexibility, labour relations, working conditions, conditions of employment, employment security, Croatia, EU countries. 13.01.2

First published 2007

Cover: designed by C. McCausland (ILO Geneva)

Contents

List of Contributors

Iskra Beleva
Senior Research Fellow, Institute of Economics, Bulgarian Academy of Science, Sofia.

Rune Holm Christiansen
Researcher, Oxford Research A/S, Copenhagen; Masters student on working conditions, Roskilde University, Department of Environment, Technology and Social Studies.

Emma Cronberg
Researcher, Oxford Research A/S; Masters student at Copenhagen Business School, Market analysis and international business.

Lenka Dokulilová
Researcher, Research Institute for Labour and Social Affairs, Prague.

François Eyraud
ILO, Executive Director, Turin Training Centre.

Vojmir Franičević
Professor of Economics and Political Economy, University of Zagreb.

Damian Grimshaw
Professor of Employment Studies and Director of the European Work and Employment Research Centre, Manchester Business School, University of Manchester.

Akima Hamandia
Scientific consultant for various national and international organisations.

János Köllő
Senior Researcher, Institute of Economics, Hungarian Academy of Sciences, Budapest.

Renata Kyzlinková (Vašková)
Senior researcher, Research Institute for Labour and Social Affairs, Prague.

Jenny Lundberg
Analyst, working and employment conditions, Oxford Research A/S, Copenhagen.

Lorrie Marchington
Research Associate, European Work and Employment Research Centre.

Philippe Méhaut
Senior researcher, Institute of Labour Economics and Industrial Sociology
(LEST), Aix en Provence.

Rafael Muñoz de Bustillo Llorente
Professor of Economics, University of Salamanca.

Beáta Nacsa
Lecturer in Labour Law, Eötvös Loránd University, Budapest.

Maj Pagh Petersen
Researcher, Oxford Research A/S, Copenhagen; Masters' student at
Copenhagen Business School, International Human Resource Management.

Henrik Stener Pedersen
Research Manager, Oxford Research A/S, Copenhagen.

Stéphane Portet
Senior Lecturer in Social Sciences, Ecole des Hautes Etudes en Sciences
Sociales (EHESS), Paris.

Alina Surubaru
PhD student in Economic Sociology, Ecole Normale Supérieure, Cachan.

Karolina Sztandar-Sztanderska
Doctoral student, Institute of Sociology, Warsaw University.

Vassil Tzanov
Senior Research Fellow, Institute of Economics, Bulgarian Academy of
Science, Sofia.

Daniel Vaughan-Whitehead
Senior Adviser, ILO, Conditions of Work and Employment Programme
(TRAVAIL), Geneva.

List of Abbreviations

AT	Austria
BE	Belgium
BG	Bulgaria
CY	Cyprus
CZ	Czech Republic
DK	Denmark
DE	Germany
EE	Estonia
EL	Greece
ES	Spain
FI	Finland
FR	France
HR	Croatia
HU	Hungary
IE	Ireland
IT	Italy
LT	Lithuania
LU	Luxembourg
LV	Latvia
ML	Malta
NL	Netherlands
PL	Poland
PT	Portugal
RO	Romania
SE	Sweden
SK	Slovakia
SL	Slovenia
UK	United Kingdom

EU-15	former 15 Member States of the European Union
EU-25	former 25 Member States of the European Union (before the entry of Bulgaria and Romania on 1 January 2007)
NM-10	10 new Member States of the European Union

1. Employment and working conditions in the enlarged EU: Innovations and new risks

François Eyraud and Daniel Vaughan-Whitehead

1.1 INTRODUCTION

The need to emphasize job creation and economic growth more strongly is one of the main policy conclusions of the mid-term review of the Lisbon strategy. While significant employment creation is expected from reaching the Lisbon employment targets, other developments are expected to generate economic growth. These include the consolidation of an open market of goods in an enlarged EU-25, the liberalization of services and a progressive improvement in human capital, as well as research and development. Because it is also clearly foreseen that economic growth cannot be sustainable – and employment creation cannot remain a long-term process – if it is not also based on strong education and social policies.

In this perspective the present chapter is aimed at providing a first assessment of the dynamics of the world of work in the EU. However, the analysis here will not address the question of employment and the efficiency of the policies undertaken to fight unemployment per se but instead the impact of the policies implemented by governments, enterprises and social partners on employment quality. At the same time, while presenting facts on working conditions in general, we will focus our analysis on non-standard working conditions in order to identify the trends that may create or reinforce vulnerability for certain categories of worker. This well suits the new Lisbon target of creating "more and better jobs" (European Commission, 2005a) and the EU contributions to the implementation of the ILO's Decent Work Agenda in the world (European Commission, 2006a).

In section 1.2 we present a first picture of the main trends in working and employment conditions. In sections 1.3 and 1.4, we identify the structural problems that such trends may create or reinforce and how these structural problems could lead to the increased vulnerability of certain groups or types of worker and thus threaten the overall sustainability of the policies with regard to social cohesion. Finally, in section 1.5 we look at the effects of the policies implemented by governments and social partners in these areas.

1.2 FACTS ABOUT FLEXIBILITY OF WORKING CONDITIONS

The aim of this section is to map how standards in working conditions have developed in recent times in a number of different areas. There will appear a number of striking differences between countries, which indicates that some countries have preferred one form of flexibility over others.

Flexibility at firm level – or, to be more precise, action taken by employers to adapt working conditions to the perceived requirements of competitiveness – concerns four areas above all: (i) length and adaptability of employment contracts, (ii) working time arrangements, (ii) organizational changes and (iv) labour cost containment.

Greater diversity in employment contracts

Whether for the purpose of adapting production to market fluctuations, reducing labour costs or for other economic reasons, most employers' federations have been pleading for more flexible labour contracts. The first significant change has been a diversification of non-standard employment contracts: fixed-term contracts, part-time work, employment through interim agencies and – a category which deserves particularly careful analysis – self-employment. It should be stressed that the use of non-standard contracts is certainly not limited to private firms. In many countries the public sector is the main user, particularly in health care and education. Indeed there are negative as well as positive aspects of the development of these forms of labour contracts. They will be examined in section 1.3. In the following section we will focus on presenting the main trends.

The growth of *fixed-term contracts* occurred in the EU-15 in the early 1990s; only in the last few years have they begun to increase in most of the 10 new Member States and three candidate countries, a process which apparently is not yet over, as shown in Figure 1.1, referring to the period 1998–2005.

While open-ended contracts remain most common, the rise of fixed-term contracts affects the majority of countries. However, in certain countries open-ended contracts can be more flexible than fixed-term ones. This is the case in Hungary where small and medium-sized enterprises prefer to have open-ended contracts which are easier and cheaper to terminate in some cases

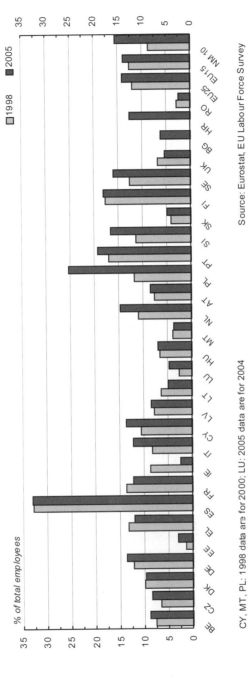

Figure 1.1 Employees on fixed-term contracts in Member States, 1998 and 2005

than fixed-term contracts (chapter 8). However, in most countries fixed-term contracts are used to achieve greater flexibility. As a percentage of total employment, fixed-term employment increased from 12.1 per cent in 1998 to 14.2 per cent in 2005 in the EU-25, becoming even more widespread in the 10 new Member States, with a percentage of 15.6 compared to 14.0 in the EU-15. The most noticeable increases occurred in Poland (from 11.9 per cent of total employees to 25.5), Portugal (from 17.2 to 19.5 per cent), Sweden (from 12.9 to 16.2 per cent) and the Netherlands (from 11.1 to 14.8 per cent). Conversely, some countries displayed decreases, in particular Ireland (from 8.8 to 2.5 per cent) and the United Kingdom (from 7.0 to 5.5 per cent). A few countries presented a percentage of fixed-term contracts well above the average in 2005 (EU-25: 14.2 per cent): the Netherlands (14.8 per cent), Sweden (16.2 per cent), Slovenia (16.8 per cent), Finland (18.1 per cent), Portugal (19.5 per cent), Poland (an exception with Slovenia among the eastern members with 25.5 per cent) and the well-known case of Spain, with 33.3 per cent. In 2005, 54.6 per cent of Spanish employees under 30 were on fixed-term contracts.

Clearly, young workers in the EU-25 are most affected by fixed-term contracts: in 2005, 30.7 per cent of employees under 30 were on fixed-term contracts as against 9.1 per cent for employees over 30. The proportion of workers under 30 in the EU-15 has risen slightly (from 26.9 per cent in 1998 to 30.8 per cent in 2005), while the percentage of those over 30 has increased more significantly (+28.5 per cent between 1998 and 2005). In the 10 new Member States not only is the share of young workers under 30 already similar (29.9 per cent in 2005) but it has increased by more than 50 per cent since 1998 (from 14.6 per cent). This will be analysed in more detail in section 1.3. Finally, in the EU-25 women are more likely to be on a fixed-term contract than men.

It is also worth mentioning the development of *project-based contracts* where the employees are hired only for the duration of the project. In Sweden, this type of employment has doubled since 1990.

Another form of temporary work particularly worth taking into consideration is *agency work*. Unfortunately, the quality of the data enabling us to analyse the trends in this area is not fully satisfactory, as not all agencies are included.[1] However, Table 1.1, based on CIETT statistics, provides some interesting indications.

Agency work is most prevalent in the United Kingdom, then in Luxembourg, the Netherlands and France, followed by Belgium, Denmark and Finland. Indeed, there appears to be some symmetry between resort to this

---

1. For a more detailed analysis of the statistical shortcomings, see European Foundation for the Improvement of Living and Working Conditions (2002).

Table 1.1 Agency workers as percentage of total workforce, 2000 and 2004

	AT	BE	FI	FR	DK	DE	EL	IE	IT	LU	NL	PL	PT	SE	UK	ES
2000	–	–	–	2.10	0.30	0.87	–	1.38	–	–	4.50	–	–	0.96	4.7	0.96
2004	1.38	2.00	1.20	2.10	1.20	1.00	0.1	–	0.63	2.50	2.50	0.22	0.90	1.00	5.00	0.80

Source: CIETT.

type of job and fixed-term contracts: the United Kingdom has a high level of agency work but a relatively low rate of fixed-term contracts. Similarly, the decrease in agency work in the Netherlands could be related to the increase in the use of fixed-term contracts. In the same vein, agency work is not important in Spain but it has the highest rate of fixed-term employees. However, many other factors should be taken into consideration to explain these differences, one of them being the flexibility of labour law regarding termination of employment.

As for fixed-term contracts, agency work could be a port of entry to the labour market with a view to a more permanent contract. In Sweden, for instance, some government surveys indicate that around 60 per cent of those hired through an interim agency end up getting employment at the interim agency's customer company. The rate is below 50 per cent in the United Kingdom and estimated at 30 per cent in France (chapter 6; chapter 13). It is also true that being a "regular" agency work employee could be a choice: this is estimated to affect 20–25 per cent of employees in France. However, in most cases temporary agency contracts are concentrated in unattractive, low-skilled jobs.

Temporary agency work is still a new form of employment in most eastern European Member States. It is often considered that this is due to the use of other forms of irregular contract and particularly "self-employment" (employment on the basis of civil contracts rather than employment contracts). However, agency work is on the rise and this explains government regulation of the matter (see section 1.4).

This regulation is particularly welcome as temporary agencies can vary greatly. In Germany, for example, our case studies show that firms create their own temporary agencies (see chapter 7). In the United Kingdom a new form of temporary agency called "gangmasters", which specialize in recruiting foreign labour for British companies, has been on the rise (see chapter 13). With appropriate regulation this could be seen as a positive trend since this type of manpower is often brought into European countries by illegal means.

Part-time contracts may provide another source of flexibility. In some countries they have been developed as a flexible arrangement to improve the labour market situation, as in the Netherlands.

Part-time work has increased in most EU countries, rising from 15.8 per cent of total employment in 1998 (EU-25 average) to 18.4 per cent in 2005 in the EU-25 (Figure 1.2). However, differences remain high among countries. Part-time work remains poorly developed in all the new EU Member States. The main reason is still the low wage level: workers are keen to work as many hours as possible to improve their income and living standards.[2] On the employers' side, this type of flexibility is not yet integrated into work organization. Only a slight increase can be noted over the period in these countries. Undoubtedly, the Netherlands is by far the biggest user of part-time work, accounting for 46.0 per cent of employment in 2005. Furthermore, the percentage has increased drastically, from 36.6 per cent in 1998. Most Northern Europe countries exhibit a high percentage (above 20 per cent): the United Kingdom, Sweden, Germany, Austria, Denmark and Belgium. Apart from the Netherlands, the biggest increases have been in Luxembourg (+8.2), Belgium (+6.2), Germany (+5.8) and Austria (+5.2). It is interesting to note the exception of Ireland, which registered a significant decrease in part-time work (from 16.7 to 12.8 per cent).

Although the proportion of men working part time has increased (EU-15: 5.2 per cent in 1995 to 7.7 per cent in 2005; 7.4 per cent in EU-25 in 2005), particularly in the service sector, women constitute the majority of part-time workers and their share is increasing (EU-15: 31.3 to 36.5 per cent; 32.6 per cent in the EU-25 in 2005). We should also note that the percentage of young workers is rising (18.4 per cent of employees aged 15–29 were on part-time contracts in 2005 as against 16.3 per cent in 2000) maintaining, though to a lesser extent, the gender pattern. In the service sector of the EU-15 in 2005, males aged 15–29 represented 19.3 per cent (10.2 per cent of all males) and their female colleagues 33.2 per cent (38.1 per cent of females as a whole).

These increases have accompanied the growth of the service sector, and particularly activities such as hotels and restaurants, personal services, and so on, which are well suited to the segmentation of working time.

Indeed, part-time work may be a positive and individual choice, mainly for the purpose of finding a better balance between work and family. In some cases, however, it is imposed. Figure 1.3 presents trends in the proportion of part-time workers who would have preferred to work full time.

Given the sharp difference between the 10 new Member States and the EU-15, we must analyse them separately. In both cases, however, we can observe an increase in the percentage of "involuntary" part-time workers. In Bulgaria, the rate is close to 70 per cent. It also affects specific sectors. This is the case in France where involuntary part-time work, which could be considered as underemployment, is particularly concentrated in the retail and the household

---

2. Thus confirming the peculiar nature of part-time work in these countries, already identified in EC Industrial Relations Report 2004 (European Commission, 2004).

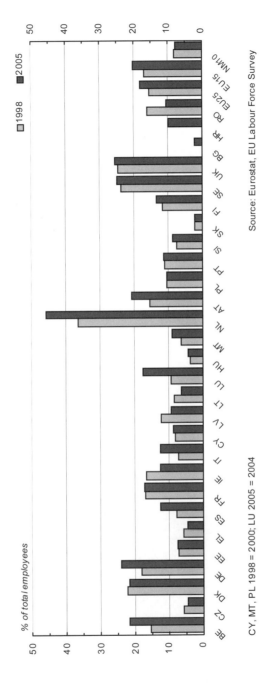

Figure 1.2 Part-time employment in EU Member States, 1998 and 2005

Innovations and new risks

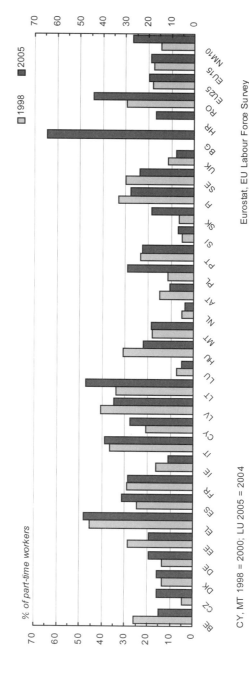

Figure 1.3 Proportion of persons working part time because they could not find a full-time job, EU Member States, 1998 and 2005

service industries, and in Sweden where it is concentrated in the health care sector (chapter 12). The increases do not necessarily affect the countries with the highest rates of part-time workers. On the contrary, the numbers of dissatisfied part-time workers are very low, and decreasing, in the Netherlands and the United Kingdom. This is probably due to the particular nature of part-time contracts in these countries, for instance, involving students who are unwilling to work more hours. However, in other countries the rate of dissatisfaction is quite high. Unsurprisingly, this is the case in many eastern European EU countries for the reasons given above, but also in countries like Finland, France, Germany, Greece, Italy, Spain and Sweden. Increases in the rate of dissatisfaction could be observed particularly in Spain and Italy, but also in Germany and Denmark.

Germany has developed an extreme form of part-time work called the "mini-job"; and although not part-time, we should also mention "stand-by" contracts where employees are put on "stand-by" and work only when there is a need for extra work. The number of such arrangements grew from 40,000 in 1990 to almost 145,000 in 2005 (Nelander and Goding, 2005).

Finally, *self-employment* is a very heterogeneous category. The self-employed can be employers (self-employed with employees) or individual workers under a self-employment contract (self-employed without employees). The latter category has partly become a flexible form of employment to which enterprises are increasingly having recourse. It is also a type of employment encouraged by some governments to help the unemployed get a job – particularly the young unemployed – as an alternative to salaried employment. However, this category of self-employment can be quite precarious. The problem is to identify such workers statistically. Obviously this category is more likely to be present among the self-employed without employees. Globally, it has increased slightly but steadily over the last decade, representing 10.3 per cent of total employment in 2005 in the EU-25. However, quite large variations may be observed among countries; and these are not due to variations in agriculture, which generally accounts for the major part of the self-employed without employees.

Two sectors are particularly worth scrutinizing for our purposes: manufacturing and personal services. Manufacturing is the sector in which "false self-employment" is most likely to be found among the category of self-employed without employees. Although the proportion is not high, we find large increases in the Czech Republic, Estonia, Latvia and Slovakia, but also in Italy, the United Kingdom, Austria and Luxembourg. More moderate increases can also be observed in Germany and Ireland. This is not to say that all the increases are due to false self-employment. The specific industrial structures of the countries concerned are also relevant. However, case studies show that this type of self-employed are often regular employees who have been asked by their employer – mainly to avoid social contributions and taxes – to shift from a regular employment contract to a self-employment contract. This is also the case in construction, which in many countries represents the second largest proportion of self-employed without employees after agriculture. Table 1.2 presents particularly sharp increases in the proportion of self-employed without employees.

Table 1.2 Self-employed without employees as a percentage of total employed in construction, 1998 and 2004

	CZ	EE	IT	NL	SK	UK	RO
1998	18.5	5.8	16.4	6.9	9.0	29.5	6.4
2004	31.1	12.8	24.3	11.4	23.9	31.0	13.1

The concerns of the Commission regarding this problem were expressed in a recent report on free movement of workers across the enlarged EU: "The problem of persons posing falsely as self-employed workers to circumvent the law should be dealt with by Member States" (European Commission, 2006b; see also Vaughan-Whitehead, 2005).

Alternatively, they may be former employees who have been made redundant, or unemployed workers who had no choice but to become self-employed. Probably this also applies to self-employed persons without employees working in the personal services branch. They have increased in number in most countries, with particularly noticeable increases in Italy, Latvia, the Netherlands and Slovakia. The increase is also steady in Germany and the United Kingdom. We also find some in the business services sub-sector: the percentage of self-employment without employees rose from 13.3 per cent in 1998 to 15.8 per cent in 2004 in the EU-15, but fell in the eastern EU countries.

Our analysis is confirmed if we look at the self-employed without employees by occupation. We can safely say that the self-employed status of low-skilled manual workers is dubious. Interestingly, their share is increasing in most new Member States, and particularly in Latvia (from 6.2 per cent of total self-employment without employees in 1998 to 13.5 per cent), but also in Germany, Spain, the Netherlands, Austria, Finland, Sweden and the United Kingdom. This is also true of other occupations such as skilled workers or professionals and technicians.

Although this does not represent a major phenomenon, the trend is steady and defines a population of workers at risk. In some cases, the self-employed are quite happy with their status, which gives them more autonomy, but to the detriment of other working conditions, such as irregular income, stress and excessive hours. In many cases, however, self-employment is more a survival strategy than a job seeking strategy. From this point of view, it has been found that self-employment in Spain follows a counter-cyclical pattern: increasing during recessions and decreasing when growth occurs. It could be that some workers become self-employed when they cannot find a job in the labour market (see chapter 11). A recent study came to the conclusion that the self-employed in Spain are more at risk of impoverishment (Mercader-Prats, 2005).

This review of non-standard contracts shows how difficult it is to evaluate precisely the percentage of precarious workers. We have also seen that the situation is quite diverse among the EU-27 countries. However, the increasing trends in all dimensions of non-standard contracts indicate that while it concerns a minority of workers, quantitatively as well as structurally, it has become a major feature of the labour market. In the next section we will examine the impact it could have in the long run.

Longer and more atypical working hours

Working time is undoubtedly an area in which there are still some differences between the EU-15 and the new Member States and three candidate countries: all employees (either part-time or full-time) seem to be working, on average, more hours in the latter countries. Working time in the EU-25 seems to be characterized by great diversity.

When we take the figures for all employees, in 2005 all 12 new Member States were above the EU-15 average (37.3 hours a week) and the EU-25 average (37.8), especially the Czech Republic, Poland and Latvia. The two new southern members (Cyprus and Malta) are also characterized by a longer working week. The same is true of Bulgaria, Croatia and Romania. The increase from 15 to 25 Member States did not significantly change the EU average, however (from 37.3 to 37.8 in 2005). Moreover the highest number of weekly working hours – 43.2 hours – is found in Greece.

The difference is particularly striking for women, however: while men in the new EU Member States seem to be working up to two hours more, women work on average 6 hours more (38.7 hours for women in the 10 new EU Member States compared to 32.5 for women in the EU-15). Since Figure 1.4 includes all employees this huge difference in the number of working hours between the EU-15 and the 10 new Member States in relation to women could be explained mainly by the much lower incidence of part-time work in these countries, where women have to work long hours and full time in order to maintain the family. Interestingly, there do not seem to be major differences in average working hours for self-employed men, who work longer than other employees in both EU-15 and new Member States, whilst self-employed

Figure 1.4 Average hours usually worked by men and women, 2000 and 2005

women were found to work many more hours in the new EU Member States. Again, this difference could be due to the combination of self-employment and part-time work in the older EU Member States.

The picture is only slightly different when we take into account the figures on working time of those only working full time. Greece remains in first place, but with Austria (44.3 hours a week) not far behind, followed by Poland (43.3), the United Kingdom (43.2), the Czech Republic and Slovenia (42.9), Latvia (42.8), Cyprus and Spain (42.4) (see Figure 1.5). Although a few of the new EU Member States have a much higher number of working hours – but in the end not many more than in the EU-15 – the average for the new Member States (41.9) is comparable to that in the EU-15 (41.8). This is partly due to a slight increase in working hours in the EU-15 (from 41.7 in 2000 to 41.8 in 2005) – notably through the greater use of overtime – but also a rapid catching-up process in the new EU Member States that has been achieved mainly through changes in national labour laws – for example, a reduction in the maximum weekly working time in Poland from 42 to 40 hours between 2001 and 2003 – mainly to fall into line with the EU working time directive. Average working time decreased significantly in some new Member States from 1998 to 2005, for instance by two hours in the Czech Republic and Slovakia.

More generally, we can observe that between 2004 and 2005, 10 countries out of the former EU-15 experienced an increase in their weekly working time. In contrast, only two out of the 12 new EU Member States have experienced a – very moderate – increase, Lithuania and Slovakia.

The figures also show a percentage of employees working more than 50 hours a week that is much higher in the new EU Member States. According to Paoli et al. (2002), in 2001, 79 per cent of workers in the 12 candidate countries (that is, the 12 new Member States) – compared to 48 per cent of workers in the EU-15 – were found to work more than 40 hours a week on average. More recent evidence from case studies seems to confirm this long working time in the new EU Member States, and this is also observed in the candidate countries (Vaughan-Whitehead, 2005). In Croatia, for instance, according to national survey results, self-reported average weekly working hours stand at 45.5, with 75 per cent working in excess of 40 hours, 22 per cent more than 50 and 6 per cent more than 60.

There is also good reason to believe that in the context of a strong informal economy – something that characterizes most new and future EU Member States – official statistics on working time clearly undervalue the real number of working hours, especially since the extension of working hours has become a way of coping for both employers and employees. On the employers' side it is a way of responding to peak periods of activity with the same manpower: in this way they limit the payment of social security contributions

Innovations and new risks

Figure 1.5 Usual average hours worked by full-time employees, 2000 and 2005

and avoid costly hiring/firing procedures. From the employees' side accumulating the number of hours during the week has become the main way of increasing low basic wages and of obtaining the supplementary means necessary for family survival. It is mainly low wages that impel workers to accumulate extra working hours. However, longer working hours are often due not to the employees' wishes but to the employers' requirements. As an example, 30 per cent of extra working time is involuntary in Poland and thus does not correspond to a free choice on the employees' side.

New organizational arrangements requiring new working practices

Technological developments and the forces of globalization seem to be transforming demands on workers, such as new forms of organization that require a higher degree of flexibility, lean production, just-in-time, client-oriented activity, job rotation and quality control. New forms of organization of production such as human resource management (HRM), but also a new type of trading relationship between subcontractors and main entrepreneur tend to be replacing the traditional employer–employee relationship. Linked to fierce cost-saving objectives, these trends can lead to the intensification of work and an increase in workload. In Germany, for example – but also in many other countries – car suppliers are complaining about the pressure applied by car producers to reduce their costs.

One of the most characteristic processes is the recourse to *shift work* that has been expanding not only in manufacturing but also in services and agriculture. One employee in five in 2004 reported being usually involved in shift work in the EU-25. This global average masks important differences by country but also by sector of activity – although less by gender. We may observe, first, greater recourse to shift work in the new EU Member States and candidate countries (nearly double that in the EU-15, 33 and 19 per cent respectively), which may reflect the delocalization of the manufacturing activities of multinational companies in these emerging market economies: more than 50 per cent of manufacturing and 70 per cent of exports in some of these countries seem to come from foreign investors within the framework of their strategy of using these new markets and lower-labour-cost economies as platforms for exports to feed EU markets.

The countries with the highest levels of shift work (in both industry and services) are Poland, Croatia, Slovenia, Slovakia and the Czech Republic. In Poland, 40.6 per cent of women and men in industry and 37 per cent of men and 27 per cent of women in services are affected by shift work. The figures for Croatia are 31 per cent for both sexes in industry and 36 per cent for men and 33 per cent for women in services, and for Slovenia they are 30.9 and 31 per cent for women and men in industry, and 31 and 29 per cent in services. More than one third of male and female employees in industry (slightly less in services) are also working within the framework of this work organization in the Czech and Slovak Republics, with foreign investment being more concentrated in the automobile industry. In Latvia, shift work affects services more, with 26 per cent of male and 22 per cent of female workers involved.

Shift work affects fewer people in agriculture (8 per cent in the EU-25) but is much more common for women and a widespread phenomenon in countries like the Czech Republic, where 31 per cent of women in agriculture work shifts.

The trend towards shift work is on the increase in the new EU Member States. For instance, in Slovenia the proportion of female workers in shift work in industry increased by 5 percentage points between 2000 and 2004. In contrast, in Finland it has decreased everywhere except for women in services.

Shift work does not seem to have expanded only in new EU Member States since it is also booming in Portugal (it has doubled in industry and services both for males and females), but also in Greece and Austria. It has increased slightly in the United Kingdom, Denmark and Belgium, whilst it has decreased in France and Sweden. In the countries where the phenomenon had not yet developed extensively before 2000 it has since increased significantly, as in Sweden. In the countries where the process had already reached high levels in industry by 2000, it has slightly decreased since then but has tended to expand in the service sector. This is the case in Austria, for instance, where shift work has been increasing significantly in services, the highest rates being found in the health and social care sector (35.5 per cent), followed by hotels and restaurants (27.2 per cent). This means that women, who dominate in these two service sectors, are particularly affected by shift work, a finding that is confirmed by the rate of progression of shift work in services in most countries.

In the new EU Member States the most striking increase in shift work is in industry. This is also a direct consequence of production and sales in the manufacturing sector that require just-in-time production and large-scale operations with 24-hour working and immediate adaptation of the production process to demand. At the same time, atypical employment has also been on the rise in new services occupations demanding a more educated workforce, such as consultancy and IT. Demand for flexible services is also rising together with changes in consumer expectations and will certainly spread to other occupational areas. These are the reasons why atypical employment has risen but also why today it is more widely distributed in the labour market. It also explains the rapid development of unsocial hours that are increasingly needed both in manufacturing and services.

It is obvious that this expansion of shift work practices is influencing working conditions such as working rhythms – often more intense in companies that have implemented shift work – and working hours, that may be fewer because shared among different shifts. Shift work – especially for those doing their shift at night – also often leads to more difficulties in reconciling work and family since it is often combined with an increased number of unsocial hours on Saturday or Sunday, or both.

The increased recourse to shift work has also often led to a parallel development of *weekend work*: the countries with a greater number of unsocial hours are often those with more recourse to shift work (Figure 1.6).

Unsocial hours are clearly the most developed in agriculture, followed by services and industry. In 2005 they were the most developed in Slovakia, Malta, Estonia, but also in Austria, Denmark, and France. Since 2000 they have increased the most in Slovakia, Austria, the Czech Republic, France and Italy. They have also slightly increased in Slovenia, Croatia, Spain, Belgium and Portugal. The issue – and in particular working on Sunday – has recently been placed at the centre of public debate in Croatia and Slovenia, in which not only political but also religious representatives have been directly involved.

Night work (Figure 1.7) is often developed alongside shift work, which generally involves night shifts. Night work is well developed in both industry and services in the Slovak Republic (more than 15 per cent of employees) and in the United Kingdom (13 per cent), though with country specificities. Night work clearly affects more men in the United Kingdom – and France – while women in industry are also affected in Slovakia, Malta, Finland and Estonia. There thus seems to be a significant variety in terms of trends between the 27 EU countries which goes well beyond the differences expected between new and older EU members.

Significant diversity between countries is also observed in terms of *flexible working time* – another aspect of flexibility – in terms of both scope and categories concerned.

In Finland and in Sweden, for instance, 50 per cent of establishments with more than 10 employees reported flexible working time arrangements; in the three southern countries Greece, Portugal and Cyprus, however, such arrangements are implemented in only 10 to 15 per cent of establishments. In terms of the percentage of employees covered by such arrangements, they vary from more than 20 per cent in Finland, Sweden, Denmark, Germany, France and the United Kingdom to less than 10 per cent in Greece, Spain, Italy, Luxembourg and Portugal. This type of arrangement is still very rare in new EU Member States – as well as in future EU Member States – where the classical full-time working arrangement prevails, with significant overtime either paid or unpaid.

Innovations and new risks

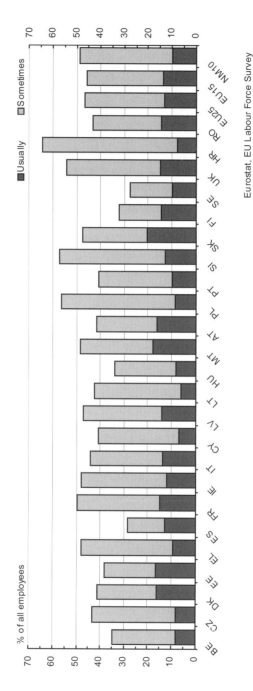

Figure 1.6 Proportion of employees working both Saturday and Sunday, 2005

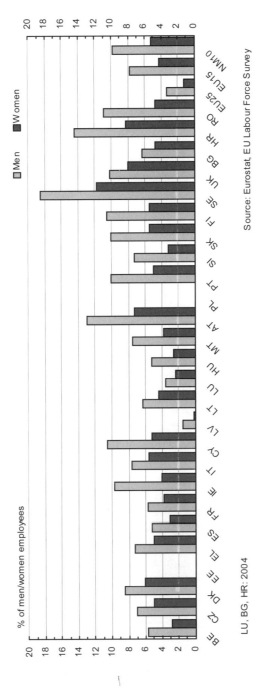

Source: Eurostat, EU Labour Force Survey

Figure 1.7 Proportion of employees usually working at night, men and women, 2005

One in five employees had flexitime in 2001; that is, they could schedule their daily working hours beyond or below their contractual number of hours within certain limits. Credit hours can be accumulated – for instance, by means of a working time account – and can be deducted as days of leave. The categories of worker concerned may also vary by country and by sector. While men generally use flexitime more frequently in France, Ireland and Finland, women were generally found to be more likely to use flexitime overall. In some sectors, such as banking, flexitime is more prevalent among highly skilled, non-manual workers, while in other sectors it can also be applied in technical or manual occupations.

Interestingly a recent survey carried out in May 2004 by the Dublin Foundation among 21,000 managers in 21 European countries reveals that 61 per cent report higher job satisfaction among employees resulting from the introduction of flexible working time arrangements. The managers – 54 per cent – also report better adaptation of working hours to the workload, lower absenteeism – reported by 27 per cent – and also a reduction in paid overtime (mentioned by 22 per cent). However, we may also note that the percentage of employees able to determine their own work schedule – that is, without formal restrictions – remains rather limited (generally much less than 10 per cent of employees), something that may also limit the effect on productivity. In many cases, flexible working time has been found to cause people to work more. At the same time, the percentage of employees working irregular work schedules seems to have increased in many countries, as in Denmark where it increased from 8 to 11 per cent between 1990 and 2000.

Moreover, not all employees seem to have benefited equally from access to flexible working time schemes. In Denmark they have been applied more to men than to women, and young people seem to have the most limited opportunities for planning their own work schedules. Paradoxically, in Denmark the employees with the most flexible working time were found to be single fathers, but also single women without children. This shows that this type of scheme could also be better adapted to the categories most in need of such flexible arrangements. Similarly, a dual system seems to be developing in Germany with a general reduction in working time for regular employees – following formal collective agreements on reduced working hours in most sectors – while the working hours of employees under more atypical contracts (temporary and self-employment) have been dramatically extended.

As seen above, *stand-by work* has also been developing, a form of working which gives employees no control whatsoever, not only over their working schedule but also their employment schedule since both are decided by the company. Although it affects a small minority of workers on average (less than 2–3 per cent) it has been increasing in some countries, in particular the Netherlands where it affects 2.5 per cent of men and 6 per cent of women, and

Sweden (2.5 and 4.5 per cent, respectively); this form of working has increased rapidly in Sweden over recent years, as indicated previously (see Chapter 12). Similarly, in Austria today it affects 5 per cent of all employees, and is much more frequent in sectors such as hotels and restaurants and community, social and personal services, where it reaches almost 10 per cent.

New health and safety issues

The intensification of workload together with the growth of the service sector may explain to a great extent the shift in the pattern of health and safety at work. Recent studies (Halldén, 2005) have shown that the changes accompanying new ways of organizing work have, in many cases, increased work intensity.[3] The increased intensity of work will obviously have direct effects on *health and safety*. In most EU Member States we can observe a common trend: a fall in the number of fatal and serious occupational accidents, generally due to better prevention and information at enterprise level. At the same time, the number of accidents remains high in a number of other countries, such as Spain and France.[4] It should also be mentioned that health and safety risks are most pronounced in the new Member States and candidate countries where enterprises have so far not always found the necessary funds to put into practice the general EC framework and the myriad detailed directives to which their governments have subscribed. In Croatia, for instance, according to a survey in 2005, the process of harmonization seems to be complete for eight EC directives in this area, while a further five are expected to be completed during 2006, compared to the list of 26 directives yet to be implemented.

Accidents or work illness, however, are more widely extended across sectors, with notably an increase in the number of accidents in the service sector. At the same time, we also observe a dramatic increase in the number of psychosocial illnesses due to stress and a poor psychosocial environment. In Denmark, the number of cases increased from 3 per cent of total occupational diseases in 1996 to 16 per cent in 2003. The reasons for this are diverse and linked to other things besides work, although the prevalence of stress is

---

3. Work intensity is rather complex to identify, however, and even more complex to assess statistically. There are different sources of intensification: one is pace of work, that is, working rhythms; another concerns the quantitative demands or workload resulting from a large number of assignments and deadlines. A rapid pace of work does not necessarily involve many deadlines. Finally, one should also try to identify qualitative aspects such as motivation, relations between colleagues, teamwork, and so on.

4. There seems to be significant underreporting in this area, as suggested by a recent Danish study that indicates a level of underreporting as high as 50 per cent. The level of underestimation in France is estimated at around 20 per cent.

thought to be also closely linked to the new ways of organizing work. The difficulty of balancing private and working life also plays a major role. Working time flexibility may help to resolve the dilemma but could also be a worsening factor when employees have a limited say in work organization. Obviously the risk is high for precarious and/or unprotected workers.

Containment of labour costs

Like employment flexibility, wage containment is often considered a part of policies aimed at maintaining or boosting employment. Wage moderation has been seen as an important ingredient in success. In Spain, for instance, wage moderation, backed by the two major Spanish trade union federations, is seen by many analysts as one of the key elements behind the huge employment growth. The same logic explains concessionary bargaining.

As for flexible working time, whether at the central level as in Ireland or in the process of the decentralization of collective bargaining, there are many examples of concessionary bargaining moderating, freezing or even decreasing wages. Even in Denmark, where concessionary bargaining is limited, there are examples of major wage concessions: for example, for SAS Ground Service in February 2005 or in one of the Tulip Slaughter Houses in Ringster in December 2004, where 300 workers had to accept wages 15 per cent below the industry level to keep their jobs.

Are these trends confirmed by the data? Figure 1.8 presents the increases over the period 2000–2004.

It appears that the highest increases are found in the NM-10 where wages were the lowest. In the other countries wage rises have been quite moderate, particularly in Germany, whereas wage rises in the United Kingdom and Finland have been above the EU-15 average. There is no great difference among the main sectors; increases (but not levels) are only slightly higher in private services.

However, having the highest wage increases does not necessarily mean that the country concerned is a high-wage economy. Taking the usual definition of low wages (wages under 60 per cent of the average wage), Figure 1.9 presents countries according to the percentage of low-wage workers. The majority of low-wage economies (above 30 per cent of employees paid a wage under 60 per cent of the average wage) are in the NM-10, with the exceptions of Portugal and the United Kingdom (32.2 per cent), whereas the highest wage economies (under 15 per cent) are from the EU-15: Denmark, Italy, Belgium, Finland and Sweden. Average wages are found in countries from all over the European Union.

Size of establishment is believed to be crucial, with wages in small firms supposedly lower. The reality is more complex. The positive relationship

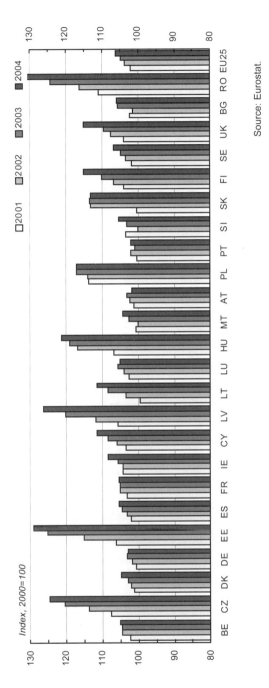

Figure 1.8 Index of gross wages in real terms in EU Member States, 2000–2004

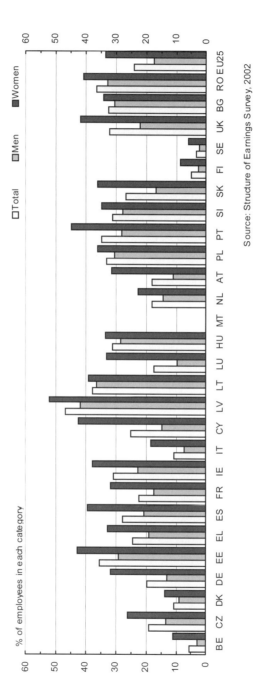

Figure 1.9 Employees on low wages in EU Member States, 2002

between size of firm and wage level (the bigger the firm, the higher the wages, and vice versa) applies clearly in manufacturing in all EU countries, for both males and females. However, the situation is quite different in services.[5] Whether for men or women, the optimum company size appears to be 250–499 employees. It should also be noted that variations are wider in manufacturing than in services. Unsurprisingly, wages are lower in services and even lower for women. In manufacturing, for all countries, on average the highest wage that women can get in enterprises of over 1,000 employees corresponds to the wages paid to men working in firms of 50–249 employees. In services, the pattern is even worse in the EU-15 where women's wages never catch up with men's wages, whatever the size of company. The pattern is less discriminatory in the NM-10 where an overlap exists between men and women, even if it is always in favour of men.

Table 1.3 Average hourly earnings in enterprises of different sizes, 2002

	Manufacturing				Services			
	EU-15		EU-10		EU-15		EU-10	
	M	W	M	W	M	W	M	W
1–9	91	75	81	79	88	69	83	69
10–49	100	80	100	82	100	76	100	81
50–249	116	88	120	90	108	79	112	89
250–499	128	98	132	102	114	84	118	89
500–999	133	104	152	121	112	81	115	84
1000+	144	117	174	134	106	75	105	80

Note: Base – men's earnings in enterprises with 10–49 employees=100.

Source: Eurostat, Structure of Earnings Survey, 2002.

The vulnerability of part-time wages is also worth considering. It is interesting to note that men working part time in manufacturing are in a rather good position. The hourly rate is higher for a part-time worker than for a full-time one. In the EU-25 in 2002, taking 100 as the index for full-time employees,[6] the hourly wage index for a part-time worker[7] was 122.6. In contrast, the figures for women are 100 and 92.6, respectively. The pattern is quite different in the service sector. For both men and women, working part time reduces

---

5. Eurostat's SES covers only the three main sub-sectors of the service sector: NACE-G (wholesale and retail trade; repair of motor vehicles and personal goods, etc.), NACE-H (hotels and restaurants) and NACE-K (real estate, renting and business activities).

6. Working between 160 and 170 hours a month.

7. Working less than 100 hours a month.

the hourly rate but relatively more for men than for women. In absolute and hourly terms, however, part-time female workers earn less than full-time female workers but also less than part-time male workers. In all cases, being a part-time female worker entails wage vulnerability.

Along the same lines, the gender pay ratio, while improving during the last decade, seems to have reached a kind of glass ceiling. In Sweden, for instance, the ratio is frozen at about 82 per cent. Germany, Spain, Slovakia and the United Kingdom are among the most discriminatory economies.[8] Obviously, the above results showing the high proportion of women among low-paid workers explain this trend.

1.3 IDENTIFYING STRUCTURAL DRAWBACKS

The trends in working conditions that have just been described define what is and will be the work regulation pattern. Taken individually they are not enough to say what impact they have on job quality. It is essential to identify the context in which working conditions occur in order to identify the dynamic which puts workers at risk. This is the purpose of this section.

Poor long-term prospects

The basic reasoning behind the flexibilization of labour contracts is that by making hiring and firing easier, it helps the unemployed (and particularly the medium/long-term unemployed, young people and ageing workers) to find a job more easily. Even short-term experience acquired through a series of precarious jobs may facilitate access to more secure jobs. This policy may be effective and we have seen in section 1.2 that it can be a stepping-stone for more regular employment. However, it can also be a dead end. The main risk with temporary contracts is that they may constitute a trap that undermines the long-term employability of these categories of worker. This is the potential drawback that is analysed in this section.

In most countries, temporary jobs, whatever the type of contract, are low-skilled jobs. In Hungary, the majority of fixed-term jobs are semi-skilled or unskilled and the proportion is rising: 69.7 per cent of fixed-term jobs were unskilled in 2001, 81.1 per cent in 2003. Similarly, in the Czech Republic temporary work is concentrated among the lowest-skilled tasks and attracts less qualified workers, of whom 20 per cent are in the age group 20–24 and 25 per cent above 55. In addition, while traditionally restricted to a few sec-

---

8. The ratios in 2002 were: 73.4, 72.6, 67.7, 75.2 (EU-25: 76.9) in manufacturing.

tors, such as retail or agriculture, it is now tending to spread to all economic activities. In Germany, the rise of temporary work has mainly occurred in the low-qualified segment of the labour force (Jahn and Rudolph, 2002). In addition, fixed-term contracts have been used for the temporary replacement of workers – and this also affects the public sector. It is interesting to note that in Denmark, according to a recent study (Tüchsen et al., 2002), many temporary jobs are the result of the leave-of-absence schemes facilitated by the government, which benefit permanent workers

The same is true of temporary agency work. In France, such work is highly concentrated among low-skilled blue-collar and young workers, and while fixed-term contracts can be used as a screening device for hiring, they also more often end in unemployment. Similarly, in the United Kingdom agency jobs are mostly found in low-to-middle skilled occupations, such as clerks, secretarial staff, routine operatives, numerical clerks and despatch workers. The following quote from an employee working at a call centre at a large telecommunications firm is illustrative: "No disrespect to them, I could not do that job. It's so boring ... They are agency workers probably because it is so mind-numbingly boring ... Telecomco probably know they wouldn't be able to employ anybody on a permanent contract to do it" (Ward et al., 2001).

With such low-skilled jobs it is difficult for these categories of workers to acquire enough qualifying experience to find better jobs. The difficulty is made worse by the fact that the length of fixed-term contracts is generally very short. In 2005 in the EU-25, 42.4 per cent of fixed-term contracts were for fewer than six months and the percentage is even increasing (from 35.2 per cent in 1998 to 43.7 per cent in 2005 in the EU-15).

Although the situation varies, the percentage of workers on very short contracts is increasing in most countries. In addition, when temporary contracts do serve as a stepping-stone, it is primarily educated workers who are affected, while for workers with less education and for women, temporary contracts are often a dead-end. The poor quality of this type of job therefore reduces the chances of already vulnerable persons even more.

Such a pattern may become a structural dimension of the labour market as enterprises may institutionalize the use of fixed-term contracts in their work organization structure. Studies in the United Kingdom (Grimshaw and Carroll, 2006) suggest that during the late 1990s employers reduced the scope of their internal labour market (characterized by relatively secure and well paid jobs) and shifted many jobs to the secondary labour market, entailing in many instances the contracting of temporary workers from employment agencies. In other words, by allocating the lowest-skilled tasks to temporary workers, they have denied them the opportunity to increase their skills by on-the-job training and have trapped them in a low-skilled-jobs cycle. This is also true of formal training given by enterprises. In most EU countries temporary workers have much less access to training. A recent study has shown that in the EU-15 enterprises invest less in training for temporary workers (Nienhüser and Matiaske, 2006). More generally, internal labour markets are leaving less and less opportunity for workers to enter these more regulated markets (see chapter 6).

Inequality in working conditions

Non-standard jobs that often deny long-term prospects have other drawbacks in terms of conditions of employment that call into question their social and economic sustainability. The issue is a serious one, as job creation is mainly occurring in the sectors that tend to have poor working conditions; retail, hotels and restaurants, other service activities and domestic staff.[9] Not only is the share of temporary workers the highest, but wages are also comparatively low. In Spain, for instance, four sectors (restaurants, retail, real estate and construction), where the average wage is significantly under the average national wage, account for 62 per cent of total salaried employment creation (see chapter 11). Therefore, the employment recovery of the Spanish economy has been based to a large extent on low-quality jobs. That means that the proportion of low-paid workers may increase in the future and pose serious problems of sustainability.

In the same vein, it should be noted that in many countries the public sector is characterized by both low wages and precarious employment, particularly in education and health care. In addition, the subcontracting of some public services to the private sector could lead to a situation where such outsourcing may affect mainly low-skilled activities, transferring low-paid jobs from a traditionally protected sector to a more flexible one. This has happened in the United Kingdom where the government has speeded up the practice of contracting out low-skilled services to lower-paying private sector firms. On top of the inadequacy of the wages themselves, this process may enshrine low wages as a permanent and growing feature of the labour market, which is a more worrying phenomenon.[10]

Non-payment of wages is also a serious problem in some countries. This is particularly the case in Poland. A report published by the Polish national labour inspectorate reveals that two out of three companies examined are still not paying their employees correctly. It seems that the situation has

---

9. In these sectors, over the period 2000–2005, job growth in the EU-25 was: +0.7, +2.8, +2.4 and +6.2. Job growth was negative in most of the other sectors.

10. However, this tendency could be contained. A new agreement in the British health care sector has committed the government to provide funds of up to £75 million to private sector firms to match pay rates agreed in the public sector wage agreement (Grimshaw and Carroll, 2006).

improved since 2002 in terms of non-payment of wages but has deteriorated as regards the level of payment. More companies pay below the minimum wage (EIRR, Feb. 2005: 19; see also ILO, 2006: 369). What makes this situation quite worrying is that those primarily affected are workers from poorly developed areas.

In the first section we noted an increase, varying among EU countries, in non-standard working time and work organization practices. These trends, which are not new but are consolidating, are largely linked to the working-practices flexibility required by the enlarged economic environment. More specifically, these trends involve an increasing or high number of additional hours of work, shift and night work, unsocial hours and other flexible working time arrangements. Their main impact can be observed in two areas: health and safety, and work and family.

Working time flexibility, in whatever form, could generate new *health and safety* risks, undermining the progress made on traditional work accidents. From this point of view, certain trends in social dialogue may contribute to modifying the overall context of work organization. This could be the case with the development of more decentralized agreements on flexibility, which could become more constraining for workers. Take, for example, the new two-year collective agreement reached in the construction sector in Sweden on 9 November 2005, in exchange for a pay increase. It introduced more work flexibility by introducing the possibility for employers to agree schedules of work directly with individual workers or teams. However, the union refuses to go further in terms of individualizing working relations (particularly regarding wage negotiations), which would indeed impose high pressure and stress on workers. Similarly in the Netherlands, draft legislation approved in late 2005 proposes to grant more responsibility for working conditions and the achievement of health and safety goals on the shop floor to employers and employees. The trade unions oppose this because they fear such new regulations will progressively replace existing – more central and protective – regulations governing working conditions. A similar risk exists when companies subcontract risky tasks to small subcontracting firms, where social dialogue does not exist and working conditions are much more permissive.

These new risks, however, as indicated above, should be analysed not only in relation to work but also in conjunction with constraints on private life. Flexible working time may be the best but also the worst arrangement. In Austria, interestingly, 45 per cent of employees were found to work in the evening, at night or during the weekend. In some sectors it is the rule rather than the exception, as in the hotels and restaurants sector (79.3 per cent), education (65 per cent), wholesale and retail (58.7 per cent) and other community, social and personal service activities (57 per cent). However, a high rate of respondents report that they had no difficulties with these working time arrangements (European Foundation for Improvement of Living and Working Conditions, 2005). In other countries, however, the uncertainty linked to this type of arrangement produces stress and an inability to balance work and private life. It is thus important not to reach definite conclusions on their effects on work and family balance. In other countries, especially in new Member States where these rhythms seem to be much more intense and less planned in advance, with less regular shifts, the effects seem to be much more detrimental to a work and family life balance. Conversely, in the Czech Republic, when applying for jobs people often consider the best work schedule to fit their family constraints rather than those which best fit their qualifications and experience (see chapter 4). The way flexible work, or shift work, is organized can thus make all the difference in terms of work and family life balance, workers' satisfaction and thus productivity.

The same conclusion is reached if we consider the most popular form of working time flexibility, part-time work. It is true that part-time work is in many instances an individual choice made to maximize the well-being of the household. It is interesting to note that it does not yet seem to be an alternative in the new or future EU Member States, where part-time work is very poorly developed and where women are found not to work fewer hours.[11] In a context of high unemployment and very low wages women seem to be obliged to accumulate working hours in order to sustain the family. It is only in the public sector and in certain activities in the tertiary sector that women manage to work less and thus have more flexibility in reconciling work and family life.

However, we have also seen that part-time work can the worst arrangement when it leads to discriminatory and dead-end jobs. This may hit women in particular who, mostly in the EU-15 countries, are in part-time jobs which offer no prospects. One example among others is the British economy which is suffering from a "hidden brain drain" due to the very low pay and poor career prospects for part-time workers, who are predominantly female, a process that could lead to significant productivity losses. While the United Kingdom has a high rate of part-time arrangements women working part time were found to earn 40 per cent less per hour than men working full time. Not only is part-time work generally low-paid but it is also of poor quality, with the exception of a limited supply of higher-paid part-time senior jobs. Part-timers were also found to have little access to training and career development opportunities. As a result most part-timers were found to work well below their potential, leading to a "huge waste of talent" that would apply to some 5.6 million part-time workers or about a fifth of the entire British working

---

11. Compared to the EU-15 where working hours are less for women than for men.

population. Twenty per cent of those reporting working under their potential also indicated that they had not found any part-time job that could use their skills, qualifications or experience, and nearly a fifth feel held back because career opportunities with their current employer are limited.[12] Chapter 13 shows that part-time work tends to be strangely marginalized and associated with an accumulation of bad characteristics.

Working time flexibility, then, in the context of new work organization systems and taking into account the current economic trends that reinforce the growth of certain types of job, can produce severe drawbacks, damaging workers and the quality of jobs. This is why it is essential when designing and implementing employment policies that due consideration be given to the qualitative aspect of jobs. In the following section we will try to identify at which stage and under which circumstances low-standard working conditions put workers at risk.

1.4 VULNERABILITY: LONG-TERM TRAPS FOR SOME GROUPS

From the above analysis we can see that there are clearly some risks that may put workers in more uncertain or vulnerable situations. While certain risks can neutralize each other, there are also some risks that can accumulate, rendering it more difficult for the categories concerned to cope with them. When some risks are frequently accumulated by some categories of worker they may be channelled along "vulnerability or risk vectors", with the result that such workers are in danger of remaining in a long-term exclusion situation or trap. We must therefore insist on the need to distinguish between individual risks and accumulated risks or vulnerability vectors.

Individual risks not always determinant

From our analysis of the labour market we can distinguish between different types of risk with regard to employment and working conditions that may threaten workers. The risks can be of a very different nature.

First, we saw how the efforts of governments and social partners combine in a general collective attempt to boost employment and reduce unemployment. We would consider the greatest risk as *remaining excluded from the labour market* because this often leads more quickly to social exclusion. Easier labour market entry and exit must therefore be ensured.

---

12. According to the recent report *Britain's hidden brain drain*, Equal Opportunities Commission, London, 2005.

However, we have seen that another type of risk is becoming widespread, namely *employment insecurity*, notably through the multiplication of short-term contracts, self-employment with a higher risk of being fired, and so on.

Other risks are more associated with working conditions per se, such as being paid low wages, or being asked to work a greater number of working hours or unsocial hours or in stressful working rhythms, or being confronted by greater health and safety problems (work accidents or diseases, and so on). We should also add the risk of employees not having equal and adequate access to training facilities, not to mention access to direct participation channels or social dialogue and collective agreements that may obviously influence all other conditions at work.

The above developments can in turn lead to another type of risk, outside the work environment but as a direct consequence of it, namely greater difficulties in *reconciling work and family life* with possible consequences outside the economic area, for instance in social and demographic terms.

The above-mentioned individual risks have sometimes changed both in nature and in scope. They often affect the same – most vulnerable – categories of worker, but also may affect new profiles of worker as well.

*1) First of all, **traditional categories** considered most vulnerable remain under continuous exposure to the above identified risks.*

Clearly, *women* are more affected by the low-wages phenomenon mentioned in section 1.2 (in the EU-25, 33.8 per cent of women are low paid as against 17.4 per cent of men), as are young workers (in the EU-25, 40.4 per cent of workers under 30 are low paid, as against 19.3 per cent of workers above 30).[13] They are also often overrepresented among atypical forms of employment. In Denmark, for instance, women with lower-level education are among those most reliant on interim work agencies that are also associated with lower pay and poorer access to training and collective agreements. At the same time, men were found to be more at risk in terms of long working hours, stress at work and unsocial hours.

Young people remain and are increasingly a category at risk. We have seen in section 1.2 that they are particularly exposed, for example, to precarious labour contracts and low wages. Measures taken to secure employment may further harm their working conditions. As an example, the Volkswagen agreement of November 2004 – agreed under pressure to reduce labour costs in the face of international competition – proposes among other things provisions on wage reductions for the newly hired. While the aim of this process is obviously not to affect the current workers of the enterprise it clearly weakens an

---

13. All the following figures are from the Structure of Earnings Survey, 2002.

already fragile category that is most affected by future recruitment, namely young workers.

The temporary work contracts mentioned in section 1.2 mainly affect young employees under 30: 52.5 per cent of them are under such contracts in Spain, 44.1 per cent in Poland and 43.7 per cent in Slovenia. The percentage of younger workers with this status has doubled since 1998 in these countries. It is also to be noted that young women seem to be more affected than young men by this form of employment contract, especially in Slovenia, where 51 per cent of women under 30 are affected compared to 38 per cent of their male colleagues of the same age, but also in Finland (48 per cent for women and 32 per cent for men), Sweden (45 per cent versus 33 per cent), and even Cyprus (22 per cent against 14 per cent). The opposite seems to be true for Lithuania (13 per cent for men compared to 5 per cent for women) but also Latvia and Estonia. This may be because of the more permanent nature of employment contracts in the public sector where there is a higher proportion of women than men.

Older people are also more at risk. First, they continue to face discrimination in recruitment because they are considered to be more expensive in terms of labour costs.[14] They also often have more problems in coping with changes in organization, labour markets and conditions of work. Increased requests for lengthened working time, more unsocial hours or greater mobility may affect their work and productivity. They may be placed in particular forms of atypical employment contracts, as in Germany where the government introduced a new form of contract for those above 50 years of age. Physical conditions at work also impact directly on their employment, and often on their decision to retire, as shown in the United Kingdom and Sweden (Humphrey et al., 2003). Moreover, contrary to what is sometimes thought older workers also face great problems in reconciling work and family life, although they do not have much access to work and family policies. Due to increased life expectancy older workers may have to provide care for elderly parents or ill spouses. They also have to provide childcare to grandchildren when the costs or availability of childcare is problematic for adult parents. For example, in Poland 12 per cent of economically active women and men aged 55–59 provide childcare, with similar statistics being reported in other EU-25 countries (Avramov and Maskova, 2003).

The age group most at risk, however, can change according to specific country conditions. For instance, in Hungary – as in Romania – the category most threatened by lay-offs remains workers in their 40s, since the employment of young workers continues to be subsidized and older workers are protected.

---

14. See the results of the 57th Eurobarometer survey of 15 European Union countries in Marsh and Sahin-Dikmen (2003).

In some countries barriers to entry into the labour market are particularly strong for *minority groups*. In Hungary, Slovakia and many other new and future EU Member States the Roma are primarily affected. In Croatia, the risks are more acute for Serbs – who have no access to state or regional administration – and Roma, but also war veterans and the disabled. In Bulgaria *ethnic minorities* such as Roma and ethnic Turks have a much lower level of employment security and problems in terms of health and safety protection (Beleva, 2006).

Immigrants also appear to be discriminated against in the world of work. In Sweden, for instance, there is a strikingly high percentage of working poor among the self-employed, who are dominated by immigrants who have great difficulties finding a place in the regular Swedish labour market. Many immigrant workers do not have a choice other than to adopt self-employed status, unless they manage to enter the Swedish labour market through interim agency work.

Lower-educated workers are also more at risk, as seen in the previous section. This is the case, for instance, with regard to interim agency work: while a "freelancer" – for instance, an IT consultant or even a nurse whose qualifications are in demand – can navigate with ease in a job market that offers a diversity of opportunities (although also bringing stress and burnout risks) the low-skilled temporary worker is often compelled to accept less favourable conditions and is thus more vulnerable. In the Czech Republic it has been shown that uneducated people scarcely participate in further training offered by firms.

2) At the same time, we also can identify **new types of vulnerable workers** *often associated with new types of risks.*

A major new risk in some new market economies in Central and Eastern Europe is related to *restructuring and privatization*. These have led to massive lay-offs and thus increased both insecurity of employment and the unemployment risk. This has affected in particular young people, older people, and also women – a process that partly explains why the employment rates of women have decreased in these countries more than for men in the course of the transition.

This process in some cases has also hit *new categories of employees*, especially in sectors most affected by the opening of their country to international markets. Consider the example of the high-level scientists working for the Croatian pharmaceutical company Pliva who were the first victims of the change in strategy decided by the company in order to survive new international competition. Henceforth the focus will be more towards generics than fundamental research into new molecules.

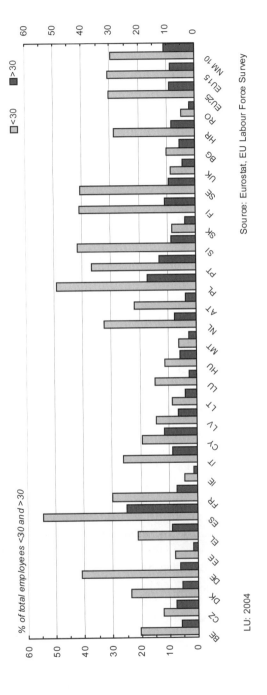

Figure 1.10 Employees on fixed-term contracts by age group in EU Member States, 2005

No doubt, increased competition within the EU-25 and globalization generally have affected new categories of employees, too. We could also mention the white-collar employees of Hewlett-Packard France who in 2005 were most affected by the restructuring and lay-off programme. More generally, we can observe increasing stress on managers and white-collar workers in the EU-25 that may become a determinant risk if it starts to affect their mental and physical health. Some case studies in this volume (Denmark, for example) also report that such higher work intensity is reducing this category's ability to follow training programmes, although they are clearly at an advantage in this respect vis-à-vis unskilled workers.

Conditions of work and forms of employment have also deteriorated in some countries for *teachers and employees in the health sector* – many of them in the public sector – who are victims of increased stress at work and where there is not always appropriate funding for improving working conditions. This process is particularly acute in the new EU Member States, such as Hungary, Estonia, Latvia and Lithuania, but also Bulgaria and Romania. It has brought about a high emigration potential among health employees. Conditions of work for this category of worker – for instance, hospital attendants – have also deteriorated in older EU Member States, such as the United Kingdom or France. More generally, employees in services – as we saw in previous sections – seem to be increasingly confronted by different types of risk. In France, as elsewhere, night work (cleaning teams, and so on) and unsocial hours over the weekend (in supermarkets and other shops) are the most frequent. Moreover, it is often in services that there is the highest proportion of working poor (cleaning or other services to households or elderly and disabled people, and so on). Although these jobs cannot be relocated they are becoming more and more precarious (see Chapter 6).

Subcontracting, which often brings lower working conditions, is also a process that merits particular attention, especially where it is practised on a large scale, as in Romania. More than 90 per cent of Romania's production in clothing results from subcontracting for both large multinational groups and small foreign enterprises (see chapter 10). A similar process is also observed in Bulgaria, not only in textiles but also in wood processing, and especially for women in certain towns on the border between Turkey and Greece working for generally foreign-owned companies under very difficult conditions.

We could also include among the new risks those that are affecting potential victims of *industrial relocation* who are put under pressure to engage in greater work intensity and harder working conditions, while also facing significant employment insecurity. This risk is present in all EU Member States as well as future Member States, such as Croatia. Significant relocation further east is already affecting the automobile and electronics industries in Hungary. Similarly, a few foreign-owned textile companies have already moved out of Romania further east, for instance to Ukraine.

New regions may also be at risk. This is typically the case for Eastern Germany (the former GDR) where employees not only suffer from lower wages and poorer working conditions – these differences being clearly observed in the contents of their respective collective agreements and with quality of life being directly affected – but also have to face significant restructuring, including industrial relocation (sometimes a few kilometres across the border to one of the new EU Member States) and thus greater unemployment and social exclusion risks. Increased regional differentials in the new and future new Member States, despite their sustained economic growth, is also worrying, suggesting possible dual economic development. In Poland, for instance, the areas most affected by both unemployment and low living standards are the same – the west and north of the country – as those affected in the early transition, that is, 15 years ago, indicating a durable phenomenon of regional fragmentation. Unemployment, for instance, is 40 per cent in the commune of Lobeski (Zachodniopomorske) compared to 6.3 per cent in Warsaw. The growth of atypical employment contracts does not seem to have changed anything with regard to such differentials.

*3) We must emphasize, however, that the **above risks are not enough in themselves** to bring about vulnerability.*

The case of *low pay* is particularly illustrative: individual factors are not enough to make someone a low-paid worker. A young highly educated worker with a temporary contract can get a reasonably high wage. Similarly, the United Kingdom, where the percentage of temporary contracts is relatively low, has one of the highest percentages of low-paid workers. Conversely, Sweden with a high rate of temporary contracts shows a small percentage of low-paid workers. Therefore, the vulnerability trap is not a one-entry track.

Moreover, certain risks can compensate for other risks, with the final outcome being more favourable for workers. In the United Kingdom, 2.1 million people reported that they "are doing lower-skilled work than they are capable of because it is less demanding and stressful than jobs they have had in the past" (UK Equal Opportunities Commission, see note 12 above). In this specific case the risk of over-stress has been neutralized through a new job that may, however, bring new types of risk, such as lower pay and inadequate training opportunities. The outcome seems fair enough when it is the choice of the employees themselves. In most cases, however, employees do not really have the opportunity to choose. In other cases, long working time is compensated by higher wages.

Other examples illustrate how one risk can drive out another. While it is true that the *self-employed*, for instance in Denmark – especially in construction, agriculture, services and retail – are more affected by more difficult working conditions (lower pay, less access to training, and also much longer working time with an average week of more than 50 hours, involving greater stress, health consequences and work/life balance problems) their psycho-social work environment was found to be more satisfactory as they report more variation in the tasks performed.

Similarly, in Sweden interim agency work has led many immigrants to accept adverse working conditions but has nevertheless allowed them to integrate in the labour market, thus reducing their risk of remaining unemployed.

In some new small service businesses in new and future EU Member States, high wages (that is, a lower risk of low wages) are associated with high employment insecurity (that is, unemployment risk). Highly qualified young workers generally get very good jobs and are well paid but suffer from very high stress and are obliged to often change jobs (high mobility is demanded).

Vulnerability vectors leading to social exclusion

While some of the above-mentioned risks can neutralize each other – and thus may not be determinant – other risks can be accumulated, rendering it more difficult for the categories concerned to cope with them. This may plunge these workers into a situation of long-term social exclusion where they remain trapped along what we may call "vulnerability vectors". Below we try to provide examples of some of the risks or combinations of risks that may bring about entry to such vicious circles, as well as describing the groups of workers who may be most affected.

Low pay clearly represents a possible entry into a vulnerability vector. We have seen, for instance, that women are more affected by low wages. This should be analysed together with the huge differences that exist between permanent and temporary workers, women being overrepresented among the latter category of contracts. Particularly striking differences are to be found in Germany (78.5 per cent low paid among temporary workers as against 15.7 per cent among permanent workers), but also in high-wage economies, such as Denmark (36.5 and 8.0 respectively), while the gaps are much less wide in low-wage economies. For example, differences are respectively 43.6 and 31.5 per cent in the United Kingdom and 37 and 30.7 per cent in Hungary.

Indeed, wage precariousness factors are cumulative, the worst pattern being for young women with temporary contracts. Education can then act as an additional discriminatory factor: in the EU-25, 31.7 per cent of low-paid workers are low-educated, while the figure for the better educated is 6.8 per cent, the gap being again generally much smaller in high-wage economies.

A specific risk facing women is also related to the combination of low pay and part-time work. Obviously, part-time work may be a voluntary choice made by a household whose overall income is sufficient. In this case, low pay may be discriminatory but does not put the workers at risk. In Sweden, living standards increased by 25 per cent between 1995 and 2004, despite a significant rise in part-time workers. However, we have seen that the rate of involuntary part-time work is quite high. If this feature is associated with the increasing rate of divorce, women workers may become highly vulnerable. Studies and statistics show that poverty mainly hits single mothers. As a matter of fact, in Sweden again, the number of mono-parental households has increased by 30 per cent during the last decade, 80 per cent being single mothers. Single mothers have lower living standards than single fathers (–18 per cent) and cohabiting parents (–32 per cent). In this perspective, low pay and part-time jobs – especially when combined with other adverse features – may lead to severe unsustainable societal problems. Families with a high number of children are also at greater risk, for instance in Poland, the United Kingdom and elsewhere in the EU-25 (*Economie et Statistiques*, 2005: 60). Older people are also often caught in a vulnerability vector. In Portugal older people seem to be more at risk of becoming working poor, especially if their children, once they have reached adulthood, do not contribute to increase their household income (*Economie et Statistiques*, 2005: 63).

We have seen that *atypical employment* can constitute a stepping stone into the labour market and thus represent an essential tool for escaping from vulnerability and social exclusion. On the other hand, it can also represent entry into a vulnerability vector when combined with other adverse conditions. For young workers, for instance, atypical employment seems to influence not only their wage levels – particularly low – but also several family-related matters. For instance, the combination of low wages and irregular work contracts often prevents them from having access to decent housing. This in turn may lead to exclusion or at least induce them to postpone the creation of a family. It is against such vicious circles – rather than only against the peculiar form of fixed-term contracts for young workers proposed by the government, the CPE (*contrat premier embauche*) – that many students in France took to the streets in 2006. In Spain, the high and continuously increasing emancipation rate (the age at which the young leave their parents' household) is due not only to the increase in the duration of university studies but also to the precarious conditions of young people in the labour market. In fact, in Spain – where there is a high rate of working poor among young people – it has become a major way of avoiding or limiting social exclusion. It is noteworthy that in Spain the risk of poverty is the strongest for young self-employed, sometimes more than for unskilled blue-collar workers or even the unemployed.

Migrant workers may also be the victims of interim work agencies. The number of such agencies has rapidly multiplied with the arrival of a migrant labour force, especially in those countries which have decided to open their borders earlier to workers from the new EU Member States – such as the

United Kingdom, Ireland and Sweden – and they have also led this group of newcomers into a combination of adverse working and living conditions. In the United Kingdom we have seen the rapid growth of so-called "gangmasters" specializing in providing a large number of workers from Central and Eastern Europe, or from further afield, to large companies in the United Kingdom, usually for lower wages; they also often supply accommodation for the newcomers, often in miserable conditions.[15]

Difficulties encountered by women with regard to *reconciliation of work and family life* may also be determinant. In some new Member States tougher labour markets seem to be one major cause of women's lower employment rates. In a context of high unemployment, with men ready to accumulate long hours for low wages, the new employers of private businesses became more and more reluctant to employ women who might leave to have children and thus not only interrupt their activity but also claim maternity leave and benefits. In some cases women who want to remain in the labour market do not have any other choice than postponing – sometimes by a few years – their first maternity until they feel more secure about their type of employment contract. This is especially the case since they are found to have more difficulties than previously in reintegrating in the labour market after maternity leave. In the case of self-employment, maternity leads directly to dismissal.

In fact, while in 2005 the employment rate of women without a child under 6 was rather similar – and even slightly higher – in the 10 new EU Member States compared to the EU-15 – 73.7 per cent compared to 72.9 per cent – this rate drops dramatically to 49 per cent as soon as women have a child under 6, compared to 60 per cent in the EU-15. In Hungary it falls as low as 33 per cent (less than half thus remain in a job), and in the Czech Republic and Slovakia to 35 and 36 per cent respectively. The rate in Malta is particularly low (28.6) but must be compared with an initial situation where the initial employment rate of women is very low (41 per cent before a child under 6). The situation is much better in Slovenia, however, where the employment rate of women is relatively the same with or without a child under 6, a situation also found in Portugal, the Netherlands and, to a lesser extent, in Belgium, France and Lithuania.

If employment rates are lower in the new EU Member States it is less because of the number of children – employment rates of women with children are higher than in the EU-15 – than the presence of a child under 6. This indicates that women can continue working when their children are of school age. They are prevented from working by children under 6, either because of

---

15. See, for instance, the 21 Chinese cocklepickers who died at Morecombe Bay because the gangmasters didn't take care or were simply ignorant of the tides and the extremely dangerous conditions: http://news.bbc.co.uk/1/hi/england/4582470.stm

a lack of crèche facilities or because of the difficulties mentioned earlier of reintegrating in the labour market after maternity, or both. The poor development of part-time work and flexible working arrangements in these countries is also important.

These developments run counter to the current need to increase fertility rates that have fallen to alarming levels. The new EU Member States have fertility rates (below 1.3) even worse than those in the other EU countries (1.5).

Apart from the demographic implications the vulnerability traps identified above can have significant *social effects*. The casualization of the employment relationship, together with greater pressure overall to keep wages and labour costs at the lowest possible level, have combined with other societal developments – such as housing, a deteriorating family situation, an increase in the number of single parents, and so on – to put many workers in a situation of social exclusion, with the consequent increase in the size of the working poor.

However, the issue has to be tackled in all its complexity. We have seen, for instance, that low wages do not necessarily put workers at risk, while representing a potential port of entry to vulnerability traps. As a matter of fact, low wages do not, alone, make a worker poor. Unfortunately, there are no recent data on the impact of low wages on poverty. Nevertheless, a report on the subject published in 2004 estimated that in 1995 the share of low-wage workers among the working poor was 37 per cent in the EU-13.[16] At the same time, factors other than wages are playing a role, such as the size and total income of the household. However, low wages do matter in explaining poverty, as do periods in unemployment (that is, breaks linked to insecure employment contracts).

1.5 THE GOVERNANCE DILEMMA: BOOSTING EMPLOYMENT LEVEL VS EMPLOYMENT QUALITY

No doubt governments have played a central role in encouraging flexibility measures at enterprise level, generally with the aim of boosting employment and reducing unemployment. Several examples show the central role of governments in this process. Social partners have also been active at all levels, national, branch and enterprise, depending on the country. The well-known law–collective bargaining shuttle has been particularly effective in some countries. In France, implementation of the new law on the 35-hour working week has enriched enterprise collective bargaining. Similarly, in the Czech

---

16. European Foundation (2004), p. 33 – Finland and Sweden excluded.

Republic the new proposal on working time accounts is demanding negotiated agreements between the social partners, especially since the negotiated agreement can double the reference period.

However, the emphasis put on job creation has also led to an increase in the number of low- or very low-quality jobs. This is not to say that government, employers or trade unions disregard job quality but rather that maintaining or improving job quality may come under another logic than the one which encourages job creation through flexibility.

In this section we will review the main trends in labour market policies and collective bargaining and their role in the design of current working conditions in order to evaluate whether the current regulatory model could address the main challenges of the European world of work.

Facilitating exit and entry...

Many governments in the EU in their attempts to fight unemployment have partly "deregulated" their labour markets, promoting different forms of atypical employment: temporary work, part time, self-employment, and so on. While this may lead to increased insecurity for workers concerning their future contractual relationship with the enterprise it may also lead to better security if this policy is effective in ensuring low unemployment rates. The best example – as usual – is Denmark, which has taken a series of measures to increase rotation between jobs by removing obstacles to hiring and firing employees. This has not led to job insecurity because it has been based on a solid active safety net (the so-called "flexicurity" system).

The pace, focus and depth of reforms aimed at introducing more flexibility have been quite disparate among countries. For instance, the length of the probationary period after recruitment is quite diverse: from an average of 12 months in the United Kingdom, and 9 to 12 (depending on category) in Denmark, to 1 to 2 months in France and even 1 to 2 weeks in Italy. Spain achieved flexibilization of the labour market early in the 1990s. Germany has also promoted, notably through financial and tax incentives but also through labour market deregulation, recourse to new employment forms: temporary work, including very short-term, one-off jobs – so-called mini-jobs – self-employment and part-time work.

More recently, France also decided to abandon its protective armoury of labour legislation in order to facilitate entry and exit from the labour market. A new law has been passed to encourage a new type of two-year contract (the so-called *"contrat nouvelle embauche"*) for enterprises with less than 20 employees. A similar contract for young people (*contrat premier emploi*) has also been envisaged, but has provoked fierce opposition. The government as an employer has also played a direct role in the development of these types of contract by offering many temporary employment contracts through its public works schemes for young unskilled workers and long-term unemployed. It should be recalled that, in many countries, the public sector is a major user of fixed-term contracts.

All these measures are aimed at enhancing job creation and reducing unemployment. Action in other areas has also taken place with the same purpose. This was the case in France with the new legislation on the reduction of weekly working time to 35 hours – implemented to boost "employment-sharing" – which, despite a number of drawbacks, seems to have successfully increased employment.[17] Interestingly, some enterprises and employers' organizations have attempted to bring back longer working time – though without seeking withdrawal of the legislation – while small and medium-sized enterprises have so far managed to remain outside its scope.

Increases in working time are occurring in many other countries, mainly among the EU-15. This is justified by international competition and as a means of maintaining employment. There is more flexibility concerning maximum working hours, with new legislation, for instance, in Austria, France, and Germany which makes it possible to increase such limits. Despite the high number of working hours in Greece, a draft law was submitted by the government in July 2005 that seeks to reduce the cost of overtime and introduce more flexible working time – especially by lengthening the possible number of daily hours, previously limited to eight. The trade unions have opposed this draft law precisely because of these two major changes with regard to existing workers' rights. Decentralization of social dialogue also contributes to greater individual flexibility on working time. Even in a country like Denmark – which is known to have high coverage of collective agreements (75 per cent of the labour force), the lowest working hours, behind France and Germany, and the most central collective agreements (national and sectoral) – there is a trend toward decentralized local bargaining, despite the 37-hour week, allowing many more hours, generally a 40–45 hour week for different groups of employees. The shortage of labour that is expected to emerge soon in Denmark, following very low unemployment and shortages already observed in some sectors and occupations, will also certainly lead to greater demand from employers to lengthen the working week even further.

Government measures regarding retirement are also having an impact on the labour market for the oldest workers. After having encouraged early retirement in the restructuring process, most governments have radically changed direction, promoting postponement of the retirement age in order to cope with the consequences of an ageing society and the problem of financing pension and social security systems. Similarly, the debate is fierce in Denmark about

---

17. The number of new jobs created is generally estimated at 300,000. See chapter 6 on France.

the reform of the early retirement scheme. So far, the success of these policies has been very limited. Regarding ageing, it is also interesting to note that Germany intends to introduce a two-year probationary contract to help older workers in long-term unemployment to get a job.

However, governments and social partners have not moved in only one direction – encouraging more flexible forms of employment – but also in the other, that is, limiting the risks associated with these employment forms.

...while limiting the excesses of "flexibilization"

In the United Kingdom, often quoted as an example of labour market deregulation, the government recently had to legislate in order to better monitor and control the activities of the so-called gangmasters (specialized in the deployment of overseas workers), as well as the whole interim agency world. Interim agency work has been heavily regulated in most countries. This is the case in the Czech Republic which introduced a law in 2004 protecting temporary workers in particular from the non-payment of social and health insurance; Germany implemented its first legislation on the matter in 1972. In the EU-15, the principle of non-discrimination against this category of workers is in force in countries such as Finland, France, Greece, Italy, Austria, Portugal and Spain. Indeed, the social partners have played a major role in elaborating collective agreements in what has become a "sub-sector". This is the case, for instance, in Denmark where increased regulation of temporary agency work has been elaborated through collective bargaining. A major issue regarding temporary work (and more generally all precarious employment) has been addressed in Austria: training. A collective agreement concerning temporary agency work was introduced in 2005 with a provision facilitating permanent training for temporary workers in personal healthcare activities.

Action has also been taken against false self-employment status, in particular in the NM-12. Indeed, it is prohibited by law but quite widespread in Hungary – for instance, for truck drivers, security guards and journalists or in the building industry. It is also the case in the Czech Republic in several branches of the service sector. In these countries, as in others, measures have been taken to reinforce labour inspections and sanctions. Undeclared work is also an area where government policy has been active. The case of Bulgaria deserves particular attention. The country has managed to drastically reduce the number of employees without any form of contract (from 115,800 workers in 2000 to 73,400 in 2005 – see chapter 2).

Finally, many countries have tried to regulate the use of fixed-term contracts before and after the 1999 EU Directive on the matter. Spain, for instance, has tried to limit the scope – and excesses – of short-term contracts through three reforms of the labour law in 1994, 1997 and 2001. Polish law restricts the use of successive fixed-term contracts but requires also that the employers inform temporary workers about vacant permanent posts in their enterprises. However, the data presented above show that legislation has had an uneven impact on the extent of these employment contracts. Interestingly, some collective agreements have been very innovative. This is the case, for example, in Spain where the problem of fixed-term contracts is particularly acute. A national agreement has been concluded for 40,000 employees in Spain's telemarketing sector, providing more security on a wide range of working conditions. It is stated, for instance, that the total number of structural staff on fixed-term contracts should not exceed 40 per cent of the permanent workforce. As for operational staff, who are more likely to be on fixed-term contracts, the agreement stipulates that at least 30 per cent of operational staff should be employed on open-ended contracts.

However, agreeing on specific provisions for temporary workers may be of dubious benefit for some unions who can claim, as was the case in the Spanish example, that it contributes to formalizing inequalities in employment conditions and pay in a specific sector of activity. As a matter of fact, agreements on job security are generally taking the form of concessionary bargaining introducing more flexibility in working time, work organization or wages in favour of maintaining or increasing the number of jobs. Agreements of the Spanish type directly addressing the question of job contracts are less usual. This is nevertheless a serious problem for the union movement. A recent study by the Finnish Institute on Employees found that one important factor in the decrease of union membership in Finland is the fact that young people have difficulty finding a permanent job (UIMM, 2005: 18).

Finally, the data show that working conditions for women are particularly affected by family constraints. Alongside greater flexibility, governments have also tried to ensure a better *work and family life balance* through legislation on, for instance, parental leave, following EU directives in this regard. Legislation has also tried to avoid that working part time leads to lower standards in term of conditions of employment and, particularly, wages and social benefits. Conversely, Danish law states that an employer cannot fire an employee who refuses to accept a part-time job. Measures regarding extended welfare services and especially childcare facilities, which have been implemented in most countries, could also greatly help the flexibility of the labour market. Work and family issues have been widely studied by the European Union and the OECD,[18] for instance, but we have no room here to develop

---

18. Among the most recent publications, see European Commission (2005b) and the OECD series "Babies and bosses. OECD Recommendations to help families balance work and family life".

the matter. To conclude, it may be added that the number of collective agreements specifically focused on this issue is still limited but increasing.

We have seen that a key issue is training. The question is whether national training policies compensate for the lack of training opportunities (whether on-the-job or formal) that afflicts temporary workers, undermining their chances of getting a more long-term job.

Governments have generally accompanied flexibility of the kind that leads to more employment rotation with significant training programmes, although in recent years the relevance of current training practices and arrangements has been called into question. Even in Denmark, where the upgrading of the labour force is identified as a central precondition for maintaining the Danish welfare system, training within companies has diminished in recent years and has neglected less-skilled workers. In that country, however, unemployed people have relatively good access to national training facilities (see chapter 5). Spain is among the lowest investors in training programmes – only 25 per cent of employees receive training – and it does not seem to have played a central role in government employment policy. Germany's renowned vocational training system is also under threat. In 2005, the number of vocational training seekers increased by 0.6 per cent, whereas the number of training positions offered within the vocational training system decreased by 9.3 per cent. The situation of vocational training is even more worrying in the former GDR. In 2004 every fifth jobseeker in the former West Germany and every second job seeker in the former GDR was without any vocational training. This situation obviously does not help them to increase their chances in the labour market, while also impeding future efforts to find a higher quality job. Unpredictable economic fluctuations, together with the cost of training, explain the reluctance of enterprises to offer training positions.

However, some countries have tried to cope with this situation. In 2004, the German government agreed with the social partners on a three-year National Pact for Training which has contributed to drastically reducing the surplus of vocational training applicants.[19] In France, a national agreement and a new law introduced in 2003 and 2004, respectively, tried to stimulate training by increasing the employers' training levy. However, the most significant measure is the establishment of an "individual right to training". Employers still decide on the content of the training, ensuring that it fits enterprise needs. Training takes place during normal working hours. In addition, the reform has introduced individual training leave, allowing employees granted such leave to decide on the content of the training.[20]

---

19. Sachverständigenrat zur Begutachtung der gesamtwirtschaftlichen Entwicklung (2005): Die Chance nutzen? Reformen mutig voranbringen, *Jahresgutachten* 2005/06.

20. For a more detailed summary of the reform, see chapter 6.

It is still the case that those who suffer the most from insufficient training are the categories of worker who need it most: the low-educated, women, immigrants and temporary workers (OECD, 2003).

Balancing wage moderation and wage equity

The government plays a role in the wage-fixing process. Its intervention was definitely stronger during the inflationary period. However, in the current period, wage moderation is still encouraged, notably through wage policy in the public sector. Nevertheless, wage regulation by government as well as by the social partners is today more focused on such issues as discrimination and low wages. As for employment flexibility, wage containment is often considered a part of policies aimed at boosting employment. The same logic explains concessionary bargaining.

Like precarious contracts, low pay may be temporary for a young worker starting a career whether on a fixed-term or a permanent contract. From this point of view government setting of a specific minimum wage for young workers for a limited period of time to facilitate their recruitment is sometimes considered as a positive measure to boost employment. The story is quite different for workers trapped in low-paid jobs. Low pay is in any case an indicator of low-quality jobs whose consequences in terms of vulnerability should be analysed differently depending on the characteristics of particular jobs.

In this context, the minimum wage appears to be one of the most important income policy tools (Eyraud and Saget, 2005).

Table 1.4 shows that minimum wages have increased in most countries over the period. Progression has been particularly high in new EU Member States and candidate countries, with the exception of Poland in the more recent period. This sharp increase follows the very restricted early years of transition during which it was used as a tool to keep all social expenditure under control (Standing and Vaughan-Whitehead, 1995), with the minimum wage remaining at a very low proportion of the average wage.

However, the percentage of workers covered by the minimum wage shows that its role in protecting low-paid workers is quite variable among countries. Only in France, Latvia and Romania is a significant proportion of workers directly affected by minimum wages. In the other countries its impact on low wages seems more limited. However, it does protect very low wages, as shown by the British case where a national minimum wage was introduced in 1999. As a result, the share of employees on very low pay (defined as less than half median earnings) fell from 12.0 per cent to 9.6 per cent between 1998 and 2004 (see chapter 13).

For women the change was especially significant, with a drop of nearly one quarter (18 to 14 per cent). This explains why the minimum wage is also used

Table 1.4 Minimum wages in Europe, 1995–2004

	Change of MW in %			% of full-time workers on MW		
	1995/98	1998/2001	2001/04	Total	Men	Women
BE	+2.0	+6.1	+6.1	–	–	–
CZ	+20.4	+88.7	+34.0	2.0	1.2	3
EE	+41.4	+45.7	+55.9	6.4***	5.5***	7.3***
EL	+21.4	+11.3	+18.4	–	–	–
ES	+8.4	+5.9	+13.4	0.8	0.6	1.1
FR	+8.7	+6.1	+6.1	15.6	–	–
IE	–	–	+17.3	3.1	2.7	3.9
LV	+50.0	+42.9	+33.3	13.6***	13.1***	14.1***
LT	+21.0	+3.3	+16.0	12.1	–	–
HU	+59.8	+105.1	+32.5	8.0	9.5	6.4
MT	+14.0	+8.5	+9.6	1.5	1.7	0.9
NL	+6.6	+12.7	+7.2	2.2***	1.7***	4.1***
PL	+47.7	+61.4	–10.7	4.5	4.2	4.8
SI	+38.9	+38.5	+34.0	2.0	–	–
SK	+7.7	+62.9	+46.5	1.9	–	–
UK	–	+13.9*	+18.3	1.8	1.6	2.1
BG	–	–	+37.9	5.1**	6.1**	4.2**
RO	+13.0	+62.9	+35.3	12.0***	11.4***	12.8***

Notes: * 1999–2001; ** 2002; *** 2003; – = not available.

as a tool against wage discrimination. As more women than men are likely to have a low or very low wage, increases in minimum wages benefit women more than men, reducing discrimination at the low levels of the wage scale.

Indeed, other measures have been taken by governments and social partners to fight gender discrimination. Many new laws and collective agreements on equal pay have been implemented in the Member States. However, the data show that more remains to be done.

'The main problem with these policies is that they remain fragmented and disconnected, and do not address the relations between adverse working conditions that create what we call "vulnerability". For instance, bad working conditions are often worst where collective bargaining itself is weakest. Policy action should thus be more focused on proposing a package of measures to fight the different sources of vulnerability.

The weaknesses of collective bargaining regulation

A few examples illustrate the adaptation of the traditional system of collective bargaining to the new trends in the labour market.

In Sweden, one of the most publicized examples is the case of the Latvian construction firm which did not sign up to the collective agreement for the Swedish construction industry. The firm was therefore legally able to fix lower labour standards for its employees, including lower wages. The same has happened in countries not applying statutory minimum wages, such as Denmark and Germany.

The Swedish example shows that the traditional labour protection system does not always meet new challenges. In particular, the absence of a national system of minimum wages allows enterprises to "legally" introduce lower standards for workers coming from the eastern part of the European Union. Other types of protection exist. In Sweden, the Latvian case cited above has, for example, pushed the white-collar union of salaried, technical and clerical workers and the engineering industry employers' federation to negotiate an agreement at the branch level which, among other things, requires that "the union be informed of the employment conditions offered to new immigrants at the point when work permits are sought from the immigration authorities" (EIRR, July 2005: 16). The German answer has been based on the EU Directive on posted workers, introducing statutory minimum wages in certain sectors, in particular construction, as well as the recent extension to the service sector. In this country, the Posted Workers Act has been extended to address the problem of wage dumping. The recent ferries dispute in Ireland is also illustrative of the trend: a company wanted to replace 543 seafarers with cheaper labour from eastern EU countries. Finally, an agreement was signed imposing the payment of at least the Irish minimum wage (EIRR, January 2006: 9).

We have given a few examples of *social dialogue* where decentralization of collective bargaining may have an indirect negative impact on vulnerable workers. However, the weaknesses of collective-agreement coverage lead more often to serious drawbacks for working conditions. Taking the case of wages, in a country like Germany, where extension is not as widely used as in Finland or Italy, the proportion of workers covered by branch agreements in retail, for example, is 55 per cent (Euronline, 2005: 15). In Sweden and Denmark collective agreements are not as protective for temporary contract workers – especially those working through interim agencies – which explains the lower wages, longer working time and poorer conditions in general. At the same time, working under individual contracts or working longer and irregular hours (often at home if self-employed, or at night) also diminishes these workers' participation in social dialogue. Furthermore, temporary workers' coverage by collective agreements in Germany does not impede adverse conditions for such atypical workers, something that also sheds light on the vulnerability of the trade unions with regard to the interests of such categories of worker.

The trend is even more striking in new and future EU Member States where low coverage of collective bargaining and low development of social dialogue, at both branch and enterprise level, explain to a large extent the low standard of working conditions. In particular, serious drawbacks in the implementation of all EU regulations on health and safety continue to prevail. There is thus a need not only for social dialogue but also for the necessary actors to interact in the new market environment.

CONCLUSION

This volume identifies a number of drawbacks in the world of work in the EU, confirmed by the recent (2005) European Working Conditions Survey (European Foundation for the Improvement of Working and Living Conditions, 2007). It thus seems essential for policy-makers, as well as economic and social actors, to pay more attention to such trends, and especially the vulnerability vectors, as well as to the conditions that may constitute possible entry to such longer-term vulnerability. We have also seen that one way of better addressing the issue may be to pay more attention to quality of employment, particularly long-term prospects, and also to working conditions as a whole – that is, not only wages or working time but other issues such as reconciliation of work and family life – as well as the way they interact within the framework of workers' careers and life prospects.

Finally, it should again be emphasized that employment creation is occurring mainly in less-regulated sectors, such as retail, personal services, and so on, which affect mainly young workers. It is therefore for this age group, which represents our future, that the problems are most acute.

A multidimensional approach is therefore required to address all the elements of work in an interactive fashion, including in terms of policy making. Implementation should be participatory in nature, involving all those concerned, who could make a valuable contribution. This is urgently needed not only better to capture, but also better to master the new world of work that is emerging in the new European and international context. At a time when we are emphasizing the need to strengthen the European economy and society through its knowledge base and lifelong learning, access to training – and more generally to better quality jobs – for a significant proportion of the working population remains a serious concern, especially in relation to other employment and working conditions, to which policy-makers and economic and social actors (notably employers and trade unions) should be giving priority.

REFERENCES

Avramov, D., and M. Maskova. 2003. *Active ageing in Europe*. Strasbourg: Council of Europe.

Economie et Statistiques. 2005. *Les approches de la pauvreté à l'épreuve des comparaisons internationals*, 384, INSEE.

Euronline. 2005. *Minimum wages in Europe*. European Foundation.

European Commission. 2004. *Industrial relations in Europe 2004*, Brussels.

————. 2005a. Working together for growth and jobs – A new start for the Lisbon Strategy, Communication from President Barroso to the Spring European Council, European Commission, COM (2005) 24, 2 February 2005.

————. 2005b. *Reconciliation of work and private life*. Directorate-General for Employment, Social Affairs and Equal Opportunities.

————. 2006a. Communication from the Commission to the Council, the European Parliament, the European Economic and Social Committee and the Committee of the Regions: Promoting decent work for all. CEE, Brussels, 24 May 2006, CM(2006) 249.

————. 2006b. *Report on the Functioning of the Transitional Arrangements Set Out in the 2003 Accession Treaty*.

European Foundation for Improvement of Living and Working Conditions. 2002. *Temporary agency work in the European Union*, Dublin.

————. 2004. *Working poor in Europe*, Dublin.

————. 2005. *Working time flexibility in Austria*, Dublin.

————. 2007. *Fourth European working conditions survey*, Dublin.

European Industrial Relations Review (EIRR) (various issues) February 2005, p. 13; July 2005, p. 16; January 2006, p. 9.

Eyraud, F., and C. Saget. 2005. *The fundamentals of minimum wage fixing*. Geneva: ILO.

Grimshaw, D., and M. Carroll. 2006. Adjusting to the National Minimum Wage: constraints and incentives to change in six low paying sectors. *Industrial Relations Journal*, 37 (1): 22–47.

Halldén, K. 2005. Globalization, work intensity and health inequalities: A cross-national comparison, in I. Lundberg (ed.), *Work and social inequalities in health in Europe*.

Humphrey, A., P. Costigan, K. Pickering, N. Stratford and M. Barnes. 2003. *Factors affecting the labour market participation of older workers*. UK Department for Work and Pensions Research Report No. 200.

ILO (International Labour Organization). 2006. Report of the Commission of Experts on the Application of Conventions and Recommendations. Geneva.

Jahn, E.J., and H. Rudolph. 2002a. Zeitarbeit? Teil I: Auch für Arbeitslose ein Weg mit Perspektive, IAB Kurzbericht No 20 from 28.8.2002.

————. 2002b. Zeitarbeit? Teil II: Völlig frei bis streng geregelt: Variantenvielfalt in Europa, IAB Kurzbericht No. 21 from 29.8.2002. Bundesanstalt für Arbeit.

Marsh, A., and M. Sahin-Dikmen. 2003. *Discrimination in Europe*.

Mercader-Prats, M. 2005. La pauvreté menace les jeunes espagnols au moment où ils s'émancipent. *Economie et Statistique*, INSEE, nos. 283, 384–385, pp. 75–89.

Nelander, S., and I. Goding. 2005. *Anställningsformer och arbetstider*. ILO.

Nienhüser W., and W. Matiaske. 2006. Temporary agency work in 15 European countries. *Industrial Relations Journal* (January): 64–77.

OECD. 2003. *Employment Outlook*. Paris.

Standing, G., and D. Vaughan-Whitehead (eds). 1995. *Minimum wages in Central and Eastern Europe: From protection to destitution*. Budapest: Central European University Press.

UIMM. 2005. *Social International* (December).

Vaughan-Whitehead, D. (ed.). 2005. *Working and employment conditions in new EU Member States: Convergence or diversity*. Geneva: ILO.

Ward, K., D. Grimshaw, J. Rubery and H. Beynon. 2001. Dilemmas in the management of temporary work agency staff. *Human Resource Management Journal*, 11 (4): 3–21.

2. Bulgaria: Towards a better balanced world of work?

Iskra Beleva and Vassil Tzanov

2.1 INTRODUCTION

The purpose of this chapter is to identify the main trends in the condition of employment and the interaction between employment status, wages, working time and work intensity, safety and health, access to training, reconciliation of work and family life, and social dialogue and workers' participation during the transition period, particularly the period after 2000. The study is based on relevant national statistics and four case studies carried out in the first semester of 2006 and focusing on the employment conditions of some vulnerable groups.

The main conclusion of our study is that, after a period of deep transformation of economic regulations and actors and a significant deterioration in working conditions, the main trends since 2000 have been towards improvement and more positive interactions between the various areas of working conditions. This improvement has been influenced to a considerable extent by the stable macroeconomic environment, accompanied by the implementation of a new legal framework and an improvement in institutional capacity and efficiency. International experience and assistance in the preparation of Bulgaria's EU membership has also had a positive impact on the rules and conditions of work. Nevertheless, there are still areas where imbalances exist and further efforts are needed.

Positive trends have been identified in relation to labour contracts. More employed people have shifted from the informal to the formal sector and thus work on labour contracts – which means higher social insurance, guaranteed wages and health insurance. These positive trends have resulted from improvements in labour legislation and better monitoring of its implementation. Meanwhile, dynamic growth in the number of people hired on temporary labour contracts indicates greater flexibility of labour relations, more opportunities for combining several jobs and more opportunities for choosing between working time and family time.

Table 2.1 Working and employment conditions, Bulgaria

Element	Item	Trends	Risks/Exposed groups
Employment status and contracts	Legalized employment	Increasing level of legalized employment	
	Non-legal employment	Decreasing	Agriculture
	Temporary employment	Increase of 54 per cent for 2001–05	Hotels and restaurants, trade, young people, people 65+
	Self-employed	Stable	Heterogeneous, most at risk from employment insecurity, long working hours, higher labour intensity
Wages	Real wages	Slight increase in real wages	
	Low wages	Increase in minimum wage	Three economic branches: textiles and clothing; leather processing; hotels and restaurants
	Wage inequality	No long-term trend. Increase in differentiation has been monitored over the last five years, but it does not exceed previous levels	Women
Working time and work organization	Part time	Increasing	Young people
	Long weeks and long hours	Case studies show an increasing trend	Services and trade
	Flexible working time	Increasing	
Work intensity	Measured by output per worked hour	Increasing at macro-level	Construction
Safety and health	Unfavourable microclimate	Increasing	Manufacturing, mining and quarrying
	Noise	Increasing	
	Dust	Increasing	
	Toxicity	Increasing	
	Vibration	Increasing	
	Lighting	Increasing	
	Stress	Increasing	Managers, teachers

Element	Item	Trends	Risks/Exposed groups
Safety and health (*cont.*)	Physical load Work-related sickness Accidents at work	Increasing Increasing Decrease in 1999–2003	Manufacturing, mining and quarrying
Access to training	Depends on technological and management changes	Low level, covers about 3 per cent of employed people per year	
Work and family	Postponed childbirth Postponed marriages Women's exclusion from labour market Incentives for reconciliation	Increased Increased Increased Not high	Poor women, women from minorities, less educated women
Social dialogue and workers' *participation*	Wage bargaining Social dialogue at branch level Social dialogue at company level	Understanding by social partners of need to gradually increase minimum wage; new social pact for economic and social development by 2009, signed on 26.09.06 Need to intensify social dialogue at branch level Problems at company level	 Need to expand trade union influence in low-wage sectors Trade unions not in a position to exert effective pressure to improve working conditions (including wages)

Real wages are growing at a lower rate than labour productivity, however. This imbalance between wages and labour productivity indicates inadequate bargaining at firm level. The relatively weaker position of trade unions in social dialogue is expressed in the low labour wage level, the deterioration of the work environment and the increase in work-related illness. Increasing labour intensity is an additional factor contributing to the deterioration of employed people's health. Practical changes in the work environment towards healthier and better working conditions are being implemented slowly, although the legislation is in place and the institutional network has been established. Preventive measures for protection of the employed are insufficiently developed.

Positive trends in terms of working time and labour organization have also been observed. The provision of more legal opportunities for working time flexibility enables workers to better balance work with their personal needs. At the same time, however, low wages forces most people to substitute leisure time with more work and this has a negative effect on their health. Workers often voluntarily ignore working time limits and labour protection by doing extra work. Labour intensification in a number of cases happens in hidden form and is not paid.

Training as a component of working conditions is underdeveloped. This is no doubt a negative feature and indicates the still low degree of technological innovation and the employers' unwillingness to invest in human resources. Most workers have to invest in their own career development, particularly in the private sector and in small and medium-sized enterprises. Some groups of employed are particularly isolated from training, mainly self-employed people in agriculture and traditional services.

The dynamics of working conditions indicates contradictory developments. Some areas are characterized by more balanced and steadily increasing development, while others demonstrate significant collapses as a result of the general economic environment and the deep structural reforms that still cannot be overcome.

The study identified differences among employed people. Branch specifics are a determining factor. Workers' age also affects the evaluation of working conditions. The case studies carried out with some groups at risk – teachers, employees in the banking sector and textiles, as well as with employment office mediators – confirmed the differences in working conditions and revealed some specific problems.

2.2 EMPLOYMENT STATUS – GREATER LEGITIMACY AND SOCIAL SECURITY

The dynamics of employment in terms of different labour contracts in the period 2000–05 indicates positive trends in relation to the number of employees whose main job is under a labour contract (Figure 2.1).

Figure 2.1 Employees by type of labour contract, Bulgaria, 2000–05

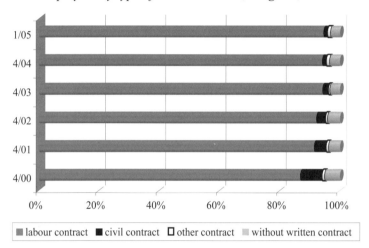

Source: LFS.

The positive trends towards greater employment legitimacy and social security according to the type of labour contract result from a number of changes in labour legislation (Labour Code) in the middle of 2002 and intensified monitoring on the part of the General Labour Inspectorate. These two factors significantly improved the behaviour of private employers where most violations were registered. As a result, the proportion of employed persons on labour contracts in the private sector increased.

This change in behaviour on the part of private employers is also a consequence of the relatively stable and improved business environment since 1998. This has consolidated the private sector which is now better able to plan its employment needs and even employees' career development.

However, a number of sectoral imbalances are being monitored in light of this general positive trend. The agricultural sector appears to be the one with the most precarious employment: 18.3 per cent of all workers are without a contract, about 60 per cent of all those working without a contract in Bulgaria as a whole.

The prevalence of people without or with only low education among the employed without a labour contract is also characteristic. In 2005 people with lower secondary (10.7 per cent) or primary or lower education (18.9 per cent) prevailed among workers without labour contracts. These are usually workers hired in sectors with low labour productivity or with low wages, such as textiles and services. Our case study in the textile industry confirms this conclusion.

Within the last five years *temporary and permanent contracts* have developed differing trends. Temporary employment has increased greatly (by 69 per cent) compared to only 16 per cent in the case of permanent employment (Table 2.2).

Table 2.2 Temporary and permanent jobs, Bulgaria, 2001–05 ('000)

	Permanent job	Temporary job	Not classified	Total
Dec. 2001	1 937.5	88.6	237	2 263.2
4Q 2005	2 252.5	149.4	152.3	2 554.2
2005/2001	**116.2%**	**168.6%**	**0.64%**	**112.8%**

Source: LFS.

We identified the following profiles of temporarily employed people:

*   More females than males.
*   Predominantly in the private sector.
*   One case study asserts that mainly young people, older people and single people work under temporary contracts (University for National and World Economy, 2005).
*   There is a significant number of employed people who do not mention the period of their contract (third column in Table 2.2; it underlines the great number of people who do not know what type of contract they have – the number of such persons is even higher than the number of people in temporary employment); among them males outnumber females by two to one. The majority are engaged in the private sector (96 per cent of total).

As regards job security/insecurity and its trends we can say the following:

*   There are positive trends in terms of labour legitimacy: more employed people have labour contracts. This means security of income (at least at a minimum level), and social and health insurance. However, employment

on temporary labour contracts is increasing more dynamically. This obviously indicates more flexible behaviour on the part of employers who are resorting more to legal employment but using temporary labour contracts to pre-empt business downturns when lay-offs might be called for. In this sense there is less security of employment in the long run.

• Non-standard forms of employment are insufficiently developed. However, information on seasonal employment, and so on, is very limited. Some self-employed or hired family workers work at the margins of legalized employment in terms of the availability/unavailability of labour contracts, as well as in terms of social insurance and good working conditions. It could be assumed that this category of employed have unregulated working time to a greater extent.

2.3 WAGES – POSITIVE TRENDS BUT STILL TOO LOW

Incomes policy throughout the 1990s could be characterized as restrictive, with weakening or strengthening of restrictions at various times. The restrictions were first imposed in the whole economy, to be then only applied in the public sector, centred around a tax-based incomes policy. As a result of this real wages fell by about 52 per cent between 1990 and 2005. Wage policy has changed in recent years, with a view to stimulating the economy. By using the available instruments the government aims to promote higher wages in accordance with productivity increases. This policy has so far had a positive influence on real wage dynamics.

However, the positive trend of real wages in the last eight years has fallen behind GDP and labour productivity. While in 2005 real GDP reached the 1990 level, real wages had fallen behind by about 48 per cent. This is due to the inadequacy of bargaining as an instrument of promoting workers' interests. Bargaining is absent in the private sector, particularly in the small and medium-sized enterprises which comprise 99 per cent of all enterprises in Bulgaria. The young people interviewed, who work mainly in such enterprises, confirmed this fact fully.

Real wage dynamics differ by sector and in terms of different forms of ownership. For example, case studies (banking and textiles) indicate that in enterprises with private participation real wage dynamics and levels are much higher compared to the national average. Despite this, wages in the private sector are officially lower than in the public sector. The differences are possibly due to non-declaration of actual wages in this sector (employers declaring only the minimum wage to avoid the payment of taxes and social contributions). Wages in reality are lower in the public sector than in the private sector – and particularly in science, education and health care – but employment security is relatively high there compared to other sectors in terms of type of labour contract and duration.

The state influences working conditions by ensuring a minimum wage for people on employment contracts. Real minimum wage dynamics in the last ten years indicate an increasing trend. The growth since 2000 is particularly strong, reaching the 1995 level. In 2005 the nominal minimum wage increased significantly (25 per cent), which is a continuation of the growing trend in real terms.

This growth in recent years is the result of the changed incomes policy. The government aims to affect not only a limited number of workers but wages overall. The minimum wage increase may push up other wages. At the same time, there have been pressures – for instance, from the IMF – for fewer rigidities in the wage structure, recommendations which have led to the removal of wage bonuses for accepting bad health and safety conditions. The abolition of seniority bonuses was similarly requested by the IMF but met fierce and successful opposition from the trade unions.

In September 2006 a tripartite agreement was reached on wage policy that represents a major step forward in this area. It provides a more comprehensive wage and incomes policy strategy. There was an agreement on annual negotiations for wages, taking into account inflation, productivity increases, changes in taxation policy and the competitiveness of the economy. At national level the social partners will negotiate an index for wage increases, which will be recommended at the lower levels.

Some economic sectors and activities are particularly affected by low wages, such as processing (textiles and clothing, leather), agriculture and hotels and restaurants. Wages in textiles and tailoring are about 60 per cent of the national average. This is due to a number of circumstances. First, the sector comprises mainly small and medium-sized enterprises with foreign participation established in border regions with poor infrastructure and high unemployment. Second, wages in such firms are determined on the basis of individual bargaining, as in many cases contracts are not concluded. Third, the greatest violations of labour legislation and working conditions take place in SMEs. The reasons for low wages in hotels and restaurants are similar, with mainly seasonal workers, often without labour contracts.

The following conclusions can be drawn on the basis of the survey results:

•   Restrictions on real wage growth have been reduced by the removal of the tax-based incomes policy and the linkage between the minimum wage and other payments.
•   Real wages in Bulgaria have increased in recent years but wages are still below the pre-transition level.
•   Wages are not closely linked to GDP dynamics.

- There are increasing wage differentials; workers in the processing industry (textiles, clothing and leather) and the service sector (hotels) have the lowest wages, alongside some vulnerable groups, such as women and people with a low education.
- The role of bargaining in wage formation is not sufficiently developed. It does not occur in a number of sectors or in SMEs. In sectors with bargaining, the role of trade unions is weak and not effective enough to link wage dynamics to labour productivity.

2.4 WORKING TIME AND WORK ORGANIZATION – CHANGES TOWARDS MORE FLEXIBILITY

The main changes in working time in Bulgaria in recent years are related to its restructuring and the increase in flexible employment forms. These changes result from the need to adapt job demand and supply under conditions of economic restructuring, as well as from the need to create more employment opportunities, particularly for people who prefer flexible working time or part-time work. According to surveys, about 65 per cent of the employed have normal working time (day-time work, eight-hour working day), about 25–28 per cent work two or more shifts and 7 per cent have flexible working time (European Foundation, 2005a: 7).

The public debate on working time reflects the search for compromise solutions between the employers and the trade unions concerning changes resulting from: economic dynamics and restructuring; the financial restrictions at macro- and micro-level resulting from the currency board arrangement in Bulgaria; the harmonization of labour legislation with the EU *acquis*. In this sense it is difficult to say what role is played in the debate by the need for more free time, better balancing of work and family life and greater international competitiveness. Perhaps they all influence the behaviour of employers and employees in the formation of labour demand and supply at the micro-level. Legislative changes in this direction mostly reflect changes in the direction of greater flexibility and freedom of choice.[1]

---

1. So, for example, the changes in the Labour Code introduced in 2004 allow the introduction of extended working time by the employer, but total weekly duration cannot exceed 48 hours (40 hours for employees with reduced working time). The extended working day cannot exceed 10 hours (for employees with reduced working time – up to 1 hour over reduced working time). There are also additional legal norms concerning people whose working time is calculated for a certain period. The duration of their working day cannot be over 12 hours, and weekly duration cannot exceed 56 hours. It is forbidden for mothers with children below the age of 3 to work extra hours or night shifts, although this can be waived if the employee agrees in writing. If employees whose working time is calculated on a daily basis work extra hours, they are entitled to compensation amounting to 24 hours in the following week, to be determined by the employer.

Full-time employment increased in the period 2001–05 from 2,407,000 to 2,796,400 (LFS). This is of course positive in terms of wage income. Meanwhile there is still potential for further increases since 68 per cent of those who work part time do so because there is a lack of full-time employment. Women predominate in this category, as does the private sector (University for National and World Economy, 2005).

The statistical information indicates that – in compliance with the legislation – the average duration of working time varies around 41 hours. For men in the public sector it is 40.9 hours, and for women 39.4 hours. In the private sector average weekly working time is slightly higher, at 41.8 hours (men), and 40.9 hours (women). Part-time workers worked on average 20.3 hours per week (2005), and within the studied period the trend is relatively stable (21.0 average working hours per week in 2001).

The majority of part-timers do it because of the lack of full-time employment: in 2005 among the 56,100 part-timers 38,400 were in that situation (LFS).

Nevertheless, flexible working time seems not to be a preference for either employers or employees. Employers are subject to restrictions on offering limited working hours to employees and part-time employment did not contribute significantly to reducing labour costs. That is why in the "Supplementary memorandum on economic and financial policies" agreed between the Bulgarian government and the World Bank (2005) the Bulgarian government declared an intention to "make working conditions more flexible, to increase working time flexibility by raising the legal limits on maximum working hours, lengthening calculation periods and expanding the reasons for work outside regular hours" (p. 9).

At the other extreme, the data on extra working time indicate that, compared with 1999, in 2004 more people worked 40–49 hours, 50–59 hours and even 60 and more hours (men predominated). An international comparative study on working conditions in 28 EU countries (EU Member States plus Bulgaria, Romania and Turkey) shows that, in terms of people working 48 or more hours per week (European Foundation, 2003a: 29), people in Bulgaria worked more extra hours than those in the old EU Member States but fewer than those in the new Member States (Eurobarometer data for 2001). In a case study on the retail trade the effects of extra working hours were reported as follows: for 13.5 per cent of respondents the extra working hours increased their incomes; for 35.2 per cent the extra working hours resulted in decreased leisure time; 30.9 per cent reported that they felt more tired; and 46.8 per cent declared that the extra working hours negatively affected their family life, as well as limiting the time available for training and qualification.

The data indicate a certain stability in the structure of employment by hours worked during 2003–05. Employees on 40–49 hours worked per week formed the largest group in 2004, at 80.7 per cent. This is an important finding that shows the concentration of the labour force on long hours. More women worked 40–49 hours than men. Part-time employed people (1–19 hours) made up only 1.3 per cent of total employment in the second half of 2005, confirming the limited extent so far of this employment form.

A number of international studies confirm that the majority of employed people in Bulgaria worked 35–47 hours (62 per cent) and part-time work was very limited in comparison with the EU-25 (European Foundation, 2003b). From a gender point of view more women (67 per cent) have a normal working day (59.7 per cent of men), although women are more likely than men to work two shifts (15 per cent compared to 9.6 per cent) or three shifts (4.7 per cent compared to 3.9 per cent). Work on a 12- and 24-hour basis is more typical for men, as is flexible working time and "on call" work. Shift work is characteristic of young people – 52 per cent – and the oldest workers – 55 per cent (University for National and World Economy, 2005: 39).

In summary:

- The restructuring of working time in the transition period could be said to have broken up the prevalent time model for employment (eight hours a day, five days a week), providing legal opportunities for more flexible employment forms, although they are still not widespread.
- The legally regulated opportunities for working time flexibility enable people to have more than one job – the relatively low wages are also a factor in this. At the same time, working longer hours leads to physical and psychological overburdening and affects the health of employed people.
- Accepted norms on working time duration are being violated by employers in various covert ways: non-payment of compensation for extra work, cutting of obligatory breaks during working time, and so on.
- Attempts to intensify labour by increasing the pace of work are degrading working conditions and adversely affecting workers' health.

2.5 HEALTH AND SAFETY INDICATORS DETERIORATING

Trends in relation to risk factors (climate; noise; physical burden; dust; toxic substances; lighting; vibrations and ionising radiation) rose over the two years 2002–03; in 2003, 36.1 per cent of the employed worked in such conditions compared with 20 per cent in 2002 (Figure 2.2).

In light of the increasing share of workers in unfavourable working environments the Ministry of Health's *Report on the health of the nation at the beginning of the twenty-first century* shows a rising trend in registered sickness at work, from about 400 cases per year in 2000 to about 950 in 2003.

Figure 2.2 Unfavourable factors in the working environment, Bulgaria, 2002–03

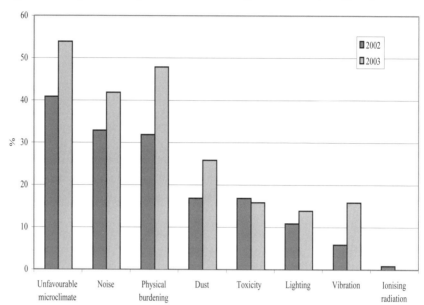

Source: Data of the Central Labour Inspectorate based on 27,081 monitored enterprises with 1,091,920 employees, in *Report on the health of the nation at the beginning of the twenty-first century*, Ministry of Health (August 2004).

National data indicate that during 1999–2003 accidents at work and loss of working days as a result of labour incidents decreased (*Statistical Yearbook 2004*, NSI, p. 96). These statistics contradict the conclusions made in the report by the Ministry of Health, however, which indicate that, along with the increase in sickness at work, the overall morbidity rate and absence from work are increasing as a result of high morbidity rates in socially significant ailments, such as heart and respiratory illnesses.

Risk in terms of working conditions and health naturally depends on the branch in which workers are employed. In addition:

• According to Central Labour Inspectorate data for 2005, 44 per cent of workers are at increased risk of a deterioration in their hearing. In this group people aged 45–55 years and with length of service over 10 years are particularly at risk.
• People working in small and medium-sized enterprises are exposed to a higher degree of risk related to noise because there is no regular monitoring of the working environment for the purpose of eliminating health risk factors.

- In Bulgaria 25.4 per cent of workers suffer from stress at work according to Eurobarometer (2002), compared to 17 per cent in the EU-25. This results from the high degree of uncertainty stemming from relatively high unemployment. The fear of losing one's job encourages compromise regarding working conditions, working time duration and other factors that have a negative impact on health. A national survey indicates that 48.3 per cent of people working in unfavourable conditions do so due to the lack of alternatives and 22.1 per cent in return for better wages (University of National and World Economy, 2005: 179).
- Work organization and work atmosphere are also stress factors. The above-mentioned survey indicates that 46.6 per cent of the employed suffer stress due to the nature of their work; 33.5 per cent consider relations with customers as stressful (in services), 23.7 per cent define relations with their colleagues as stressful, while relations with superiors are stressful for 35.6 per cent.
- Changes in working conditions show better results for women than for men. During the period 1990–2000 the working environment for men deteriorated in relation to: intensity of work rhythm; increased monotonous manual work with repeated operations; an increase in painful postures in the work process; carrying of heavy burdens; increased vibrations; noise over the permitted level; and inhalation of hazardous substances.
- Although better trends were monitored for women they have also experienced a deterioration in working conditions in some areas, including increased work intensity due to fast rhythm of work, carrying of heavy burdens, work at higher temperatures, work with hazardous substances, and so on. Increased weekend work is also greater for women (29.8 per cent compared to 16 per cent for men).
- Breaks during work are not monitored: 44 per cent of women and 40 per cent of men declare that they work without breaks, according to the above-mentioned national survey.
- Measures against sickness at work, which are obligatory for employers, are much reduced. According to the above-mentioned survey on working conditions and working time, over the previous three years almost half of those interviewed (48.5 per cent) had undergone a medical examination, 28.1 per cent only once and only 12.1 per cent twice. Only 6.2 per cent of the employed had been examined over three times.

2.6 TRAINING – STILL NOT A KEY PRIORITY

Training is a key factor in improving quality of employment, a major objective of the Lisbon Strategy. This aspect of employment is even more impor-

tant in Bulgaria because the economic restructuring during the transition period caused significant changes in labour demand regarding qualifications and
occupations. Nevertheless, in 2002 only 33 per cent of companies in Bulgaria
country engaged in training and in 2004 this share was even lower, at about
20 per cent. The proportion of the employed who get training is relatively
small – only 15 per cent on average over the last five years – but the trend is

*Figure 2.3 Share of participants in CVT or IVT by size of enterprise,
Bulgaria, 2000–04*

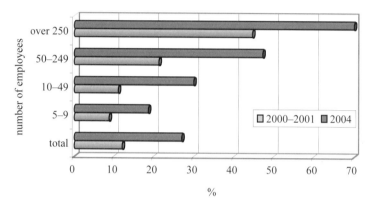

Source: NSI, *Continuing vocational training*, Sofia (2004), p. 75.

increasing, as seen in Figure 2.3. Training involves mostly learning though
gaining more experience in the job.[2]

Greater interest in vocational training has been demonstrated in recent
years (Figure 2.3). The total number of participants in CVT (continuing vocational training) courses in 2000–01 represented 11 per cent of all employed
people. This increased to 14 per cent in 2004.

Vocational training includes CVT courses or other forms of continuing
training, as well as initial vocational training (IVT). In 2000–01 only 14 per
cent underwent it, mainly in mining, financial intermediation and public
administration. In 2004, 27 per cent of enterprises provided different forms of
training, of which 11 per cent was CVT.

---

2. Conclusions are based on NSI surveys of continuing vocational training within Eurostat
CVTS2 in 2000, and national monitoring in 2001 and 2003. The 2003 survey includes 44,890
enterprises in 24 economic activities and 1.6 million employees. The results of the survey present
the situation in 2002 related to training within firms, forms of training, number of people involved
in training, duration of training, expenditure, and so on. The last survey is from June–July 2005
and reports data for 2004. The sample covers 53,060 firms.

Other forms of training (instruction, classes, self-learning, conferences, workshops, seminars) were used by 12 per cent of enterprises in the period 2000–01 and 24 per cent in 2004; initial vocational training was organized by 5 per cent of enterprises in 2000–01 and 4 per cent in 2004.

Enterprises preferred external training courses: the number of enterprises choosing this form was twice the number of those choosing internal courses.

Men received most training (60 per cent in 2000–01 and 55 per cent in 2004). The proportion of employees from private enterprises was twice that of employees from the public sector. By branch, participants from manufacturing dominated, followed by transport, storage, communication and public administration; on the other hand, agriculture, construction, hotels and restaurants and education had an insignificant number of participants.

Of those who underwent training in 2004 managerial staff dominated: 83 per cent of all enterprises that provided training did so for this occupational group, followed by technical and skilled staff (52 per cent) and last were the unskilled employed (14 per cent).

Training included courses on technical and production issues (18 per cent); finance and accounting (11 per cent); foreign languages (6 per cent); marketing (9 per cent); computer skills (10 per cent); and administration (10 per cent).

As far as unemployed people are concerned, their training is part of active labour market policy. Data on these activities are collected by the National Employment Agency and we shall cite this agency's annual reports. It must be pointed out that, depending on the programme, training often accompanies employment under specific Active Labour Market programmes. For the period January–September 2006 labour offices organized 1,268 courses for unemployed people, which is significantly more than the same period in the previous year (902 courses). Labour offices also organized training courses for employed people (247 in 2005) (Employment Agency, 2005). The number of participants increased in 2005 compared to 2004 but as a percentage of the total number of unemployed people it was still insignificant (less than 1 per cent).

2.7 WORK VS FAMILY LIFE: THE PRIORITY OF WORK

The radical changes in economic conditions and social values in the transition period significantly transformed the behaviour of employees in relation to work and family life compared with the pre-transition period. Strong competition for jobs and career development caused both men and women in Bulgaria to pay less attention to family life and family responsibilities. Meanwhile, Bulgarians became poorer during the transition period, with inevitable ramifications for their motivation and such decisions as starting a family.[3] According to a case study from 2001 women rank income and housing conditions among the main factors determining their behaviour in terms of work and family life. Due to economic reasons and unemployment 23.3 per cent postponed the birth of their first child, 46.4 per cent a second child and 31.3 per cent a third child. A more focused question on work and births showed that 65.2 per cent of women did not consider work as a factor influencing birth decisions. However, 9.8 per cent declared that their employer had imposed limitations related to marriage or birth when they engaged these women (University of National and World Economy, 2005: 186).

High unemployment and uncertainty boosted the importance of economic factors in people's priorities, particularly young people. A number of changes in family status also occurred, reflecting ways of combining labour and personal life. Young people prefer co-habiting with a partner without marriage, the birth of the first child is postponed and the raising of children by a single parent is becoming frequent. For example, since 1989 the share of unmarried people over the age of 30 has increased significantly. The marriage coefficient declined from 6.9 per thousand in 1990 to 3.7 per thousand in 2002 (Bulgarian Academy of Sciences, 2005: 7). The postponement of marriage leads to an increase in average birth age and reinforces negative reproductive behaviour. The number of extramarital births has increased: their relative share grew from 12.4 per cent in 1990 to 25.8 per cent in 1995 and 42.9 per cent in 2002. The reasons for declining reproductiveness are mostly related to limited resources, lack of housing and low wages. The postponement of childbirth is to a smaller extent related to preferences for higher education or career development. This indicates that the economic factors connected with low living standards and poverty limit family reproduction. One case study points out that for 73.8 per cent of the families interviewed the family decision on the birth of a child and the number of children they would like to have strongly depends on family living standards.[4] The share of working poor, according to one study, indicates a relative share of 7.6 per cent of all poor people in Bulgaria in 2003. The reasons for the working poor phenomenon described in this study are low qualifications (23.5 per cent of the working poor are low qualified); employment status (70 per cent of the working poor are self-employed or unpaid family workers); sector of activity (9.1 per cent of agricultural workers are working poor, as well as 8.3 per cent of manufacturing and construction workers) (NSI, 2006: 71).

---

3. The poverty rate varied from 5.5 per cent in 1995 to 36 per cent in 1997 and 11.7 per cent in 2001 (World Bank, 2002).

4. The marriage coefficient presents contracted marriages per 1,000 population (Bulgarian Academy of Sciences, 2005: 7).

With a view to encouraging female participation in employment some policy decisions were taken to improve reconciliation of work and family life: for example, since 2004 parental leave has been transferable to the father and grandparents if they are insured for all risks. Another important thing is stricter monitoring of discrimination – for example, according to a survey 2 per cent of women aged up to 35 years old reported that they were fired because of pregnancy (Bulgarian Academy of Science, 2001: 6). Young mothers are not favoured by employers because they more frequently take leave, for example to care for sick children.

Employed women usually combine childcare with household labour. In 2001–02 women had more time for childcare and childrearing compared to 1988. This means that women stayed at home longer and took more care of children, while men concentrated more on work and provision of income. According to survey data, in 2004 women in Bulgaria spent four hours per day on childcare and housework (National Statistical Institute Survey, 2004: 357).

The conditions for combining work and family life changed considerably during the transition. On the one hand, the participation of women in the labour market requires more effort due to the highly competitive environment. On the other hand, there is not enough favourable social infrastructure to support child raising and to alleviate household labour. Opportunities for better combination of work and family commitments through flexible working time are still underdeveloped but in any case low living standards and low wages reduce the demand for them.

2.8 SOCIAL DIALOGUE – LOW IMPACT ON WORKING CONDITIONS

Industrial relations in Bulgaria, including the bargaining system, have a number of features which distinguish them from traditional centralized and decentralized systems. It could be defined as national-centralized: the main characteristic features[5] indicate that it is not typically centralized because there is no clear dependence and subordination of decisions made at lower level;[6] on the other hand, the existence of the national level makes it different from decentralized systems. The particular bargaining levels have different degrees of development. Branch bargaining is least developed. The system operates in practical terms at national and company level. The consultative character of

5. For a detailed description see Beleva and Tzanov (2001), pp. 47–49.

6. The observance of the agreements regarding the minimum wage is an exception. The minimum wage is obligatory as a minimum limit for the lowest levels. The agreements for the parameters of the mechanism for additional taxation of funds for wages had the same effect.

bargaining at national level and the fact that there is bargaining at company level mean that the industrial relations system is similar to a decentralized system.

Collective bargaining in Bulgaria covers all workers in the state sector, no matter what their trade union affiliation. This is due to the fact that the law allows bargaining to also cover non-trade union members. Social dialogue is not widespread in the private sector. It exists mostly in large companies where trade union organizations were preserved after privatization. All indications are that there are no trade union organizations in newly established medium-sized and large companies.

Collective bargaining does not have much effect on wage dynamics. This finding is confirmed by two facts. First, real wages are little protected against inflation and have declined significantly throughout the period. The insufficient connection between wages and labour productivity is the main problem in bargaining. In the state sector this is to a great extent due to the application of regulatory mechanisms which are insufficiently related to production. Second, the incomes of people on the minimum wage are little protected. Up to 2003 the minimum wage was around 35–38 per cent of the average wage, a relatively low percentage compared to more developed European countries. Besides this, in most companies the minimum wage is negotiated at national level regardless of financial capacity. Low wages for low-qualified workers imply greater employment uncertainty as they can be easily substituted by external workers.

The lack of compensation for workers for increased labour intensity could be largely explained by the low effectiveness of social dialogue at company level or even the absence of such dialogue. This aspect of working conditions is underdeveloped in the bargaining process. Along with protection at the workplace and employment and wages, the trade unions should also include adequate compensation for increased labour intensity in negotiations with employers.

The main conclusions about the role of social dialogue in working conditions may be summarized as follows:

- There is an understanding on the part of the social partners regarding the gradual need to increase the minimum wage. Practice in recent years confirms this finding. The employers' fears that low-qualified workers would have to be laid off due to an increase in the minimum wage have not been realized.
- There are bargaining problems at company level. The trade unions are not in a position to exert effective pressure to improve working conditions (including wages) especially in the private companies and SMEs. They cannot negotiate wages in accordance with labour productivity.

• There is a need to intensify social dialogue at branch level and to extend trade union influence in low-wage sectors. The establishment of trade union organizations in these sectors will improve working conditions and wages.

CONCLUSION: SOURCES OF RISK AND VULNERABILITY

In this chapter, based on the available information, we have tried to present development trends in working conditions, and the interaction between them and the most vulnerable groups. We have found positive trends in legalizing employment and increasing job security with regard to employment contracts. There is increasing flexibility in working time restructuring since more people are becoming engaged in part-time work. We have also identified that the real wage increase has been relatively modest. There is an increasing trend in additional employment (second or multiple jobs). Access to training is also trending upwards, although the level of participants in different forms of training is very low compared with other EU countries.

Working conditions have deteriorated in recent years with regard to indicators of health and safety, leisure time and reconciliation of family and work.

Vulnerabilities depend on the sources of risk. In terms of working conditions these sources are: sector of employment; gender; age; level of education; qualifications and occupation; and family status. In Bulgaria the risk of vulnerability in most cases has cumulative effects: for example, a combination of sources of risk. Thus, women were identified as a risk group because of the concentration of their employment in low-paid branches – textiles or public services with state constraints on wage increases, for example, teachers. Women are a vulnerable group because of their difficulties reconciling work and family life, deteriorating health status, and so on. Our study also identified young people as a vulnerable group, who have difficulties concerning working conditions, employment contracts, temporary employment and working time duration, since most of them are employed part time, work overtime and have less social security because of their employment in the informal sector. The lack of professional experience is also a factor pushing young people to accept compromises in working conditions, level of pay, and so on. Meanwhile, employed young people suffer more from stress, long working hours, less leisure time and postponement of family life. People employed in construction, manufacturing, mining and quarrying suffer because they work in more unsafe and less healthy conditions. Low-paid branches such as agriculture, textiles and hotels, also figure in this connection. Less-educated people make up the bulk of employees in textiles, agriculture, construction and services; they also predominate in the informal sector (and the majority of them are Roma). Self-employed people are also a group at risk of vulnerability if they have a small business in services or agriculture, have little education, and so on.

The types of vulnerability risk are changing as the economy globalizes, and alongside the introduction of new forms of work organization, dynamic changes in labour demand regarding qualifications, and so on. In this respect the Bulgarian economy is facing all kinds of risks from population ageing, labour force migration, deterioration of quality of the labour force, and so on.

Increasing flexibility in the labour market could also be a factor increasing vulnerability. There is a trade-off between employment stability and flexibility. The increase in temporary employment reduces stability but increases flexibility. The study could not identify whether part-time workers tend to combine their basic job with a second job, or work only as part-time workers for other reasons, for example, reconciliation of family life and work, because there is a lack of relevant statistics. The study found that younger people, people in the age group 65+ and women prevailed in part-time employment or in work without a labour contract.

With regard to the working poor (estimated at 8 per cent but probably higher) the relatively modest increase in wages is a risk factor for poverty. People with little education engaged on the minimum wage, as well as people in low-paid branches, as already mentioned, are among the most at risk groups from this point of view.

Relatively low wages are an incentive for additional employment (second or multiple jobs), leading to decreased leisure time and family time and over-burdened workers. This increases workers' health problems: for example, stress and exhaustion. The relatively low wages press people to work overtime or undertake jobs with unsocial working time, which additionally stresses their family and social life.

Relatively high unemployment and existing skill mismatches pressed some vulnerable groups (people with low education) to continue compromising on working conditions in favour of paid or even unpaid work. Particularly instructive examples come from case studies in hotels and restaurants and trade.

Although the trend regarding access to training is upward, training is not among the priorities of employers and employees. This follows from insignificant technological investment and renovation. Only certain groups of employees participate in different forms of training and retraining, mainly in more advanced economic activities, such as financial intermediation, electricity, gas and water supply, and public administration. Within active labour market programmes unemployed people are to some extent integrated in training and retraining, but as a percentage of the total number of unemployed people the share is low – 8.3 per cent in 2004.

Social dialogue at enterprise level does not press employers effectively to improve working conditions. Within the bargaining process the trade unions are still weak and unable to influence employers to link wages with productivity, although this would be possible without reducing employment.

REALITY AT ENTERPRISE LEVEL: CASE STUDIES

Bulgaria Case Study 1: Teachers' world of work

Introduction: A difficult financial and social context for teachers

Education accounts for about 6 per cent of overall employment in Bulgaria. Due to the reforms in the education system in the last ten years there is a declining trend in terms of employment and working conditions. The ongoing reforms are connected with insufficient funding, while the system is also over-regulated, and there are social conflicts and poor working conditions. Women account for the bulk of employees. In the first part of the study we identified them as an employment risk group due to low wages, poor working conditions, few job opportunities and difficult reconciliation of work and family life. Meanwhile, work in the education sector, particularly for teachers, is characterized by its high intensity.

In February 2006 teachers in Bulgaria declared a national strike, demanding higher wages and the maintenance of existing jobs. Tensions have accumulated due to delayed reforms and the poor quality of education, which is generally reckoned to be deteriorating. There are problems with children dropping out of school, and the poor attainment of primary and secondary school graduates. A number of problems related to the financing of the system were mentioned, as was the capacity of the system to respond to the increasing need to build a knowledge-based society.

Security of employment but over-regulation?

Labour contracts are predominantly permanent, covering 99 per cent of employees. At the school we looked at, only eight people are employed on a temporary labour contract, substituting people who are temporarily absent from work. One-year contracts are given to persons being employed for the first time. After the expiry of this initial year the contract may be renewed or terminated; 10 per cent of employees are hired on civil contracts – these are lecturers receiving honoraria and two teachers who are not in full-time employment according to the usual criteria (mainly foreign language teachers). One teacher teaches two subjects.

The state regulation of employment in the education system gives rise to a number of problems:

- The lack of correspondence between the start of the school year and the financial year does not allow an immediate response to the need for teachers (depending on the number of students).
- The use of civil contracts is limited due to the way in which planning is

carried out for the school year, not to mention low wages for additional hours (BGN 3.40 or EUR 1.7 per hour.)

- Staff are selected on the basis of open competition. However, staff certification is absent and teachers hired on permanent contracts are difficult to dismiss. This creates problems if the wrong person is hired.
- Limited opportunities for "on call" employment, particularly when teachers are unable to work due to sudden illness.

High degree of social security

The teacher and trade union chairman we interviewed said there was a high degree of job security. Teachers are secure in their jobs because there is a very good working environment, the number of schoolchildren is increasing and relations between the director, the trade union and the teachers are very good. When conflicts arise the three parties jointly seek reasonable solutions.

This school is not characterized by high staff turnover and, despite the low wages, the overall environment of understanding and mutual support promote staff stability. However, when younger teachers find a better-paid job they often leave the teaching profession.

Adding seniority bonuses to relatively low basic wages

Supplement for length of service is 1 per cent for one year of service. For people with long service this supplement may form up to 25 per cent of the wage. Additional work over and above the norm is paid for as lecture hours (BGN 3.40 or EUR 1.7), a very small sum.

Low number of working hours but faster working rhythms

Working time is determined on the basis of a norm of 648–720 school hours per year. It is worked over five days per week, with an average commitment of 17–20 hours per week. Lesson preparation and extra-curricular work constitute an additional burden above the regular hours, however. Additional hours are often required for school competitions, checking of written work, and so on, usually at weekends. The extra work is not paid. It is difficult to evaluate labour intensity, although teaching is unquestionably highly intensive labour. Not all teachers have a separate workplace. However, a risk evaluation has been carried out in the school and budgetary funds for medical assistance are planned.

High health risks: Between stress and physical pain

The main health problems affecting teachers are stress, overburdening of the throat and working with computers (particularly for computer science teachers, of course). Another health problem is related to the general environment, which, for example, presents risks due to contact with many people, particularly during periods of viral infections. The general impression is of increasing teacher absences due to illness, as well as permanent breakdowns in health, particularly for those with greater length of service. This trend confirms the conclusion in the report that sickness at work is increasing and the general health of employees in Bulgaria is deteriorating.

Difficult work–family balance along with stressful teaching rhythms
The main compromises made when choosing a teaching career are difficult to evaluate. It is creative work often carried out with high motivation. Thus teachers who love their work compromise in terms of low wages and sometimes poor working conditions, but above all in terms of the rather intense and stressful teaching burden.

Easy, but not always effective, access to training
Access to training and qualifications is related to length of service. However, teachers are in principle able to engage in various forms of professional improvement. For example, in the 2005/06 school year almost all teachers attended computer science courses organized by the Ministry of Education. Course duration was one month and it was funded by the PHARE Programme. The usual system for improving qualifications is courses organized by the Teacher Training Institute. However, the teachers do not rate the quality of training in this system highly. Teachers do not have problems accessing training and receive diplomas for successfully completed training. Various national and international projects involving exchange of experience with similar schools in Bulgaria and abroad are considered very successful. However, bureaucracy and administration have been mentioned as obstacles to project work.

Social dialogue developed but ineffective regarding wages
The employees in this educational institution have a collective agreement, which is part of the branch contract of the teachers' trade union. The collective agreement is amended only when there are radical changes in working or employment conditions. Almost 90 per cent of the employees are covered by this agreement. The wage formation of education-system employees is laid down in a Ministry of Education Regulation and depends on length of service, qualifications and workload within regulated annual norms. Average teachers' pay is BGN 382 a month: 56 per cent receive wages above the national average. The non-teaching staff receive significantly less than the national average (75 per cent).

The three persons interviewed were unanimous about the good cooperation between the administration and the trade union organization and that there was goodwill to seek ways of resolving occurring or potential conflicts.

Meanwhile, those interviewed stated that the unsuccessful national teachers' strike at the beginning of 2006 made trade union members lose faith in the power of the teachers' trade union to protect their interests, for example, by fighting for wage increases.

The employers (the director who represents the municipality as main employer) have little leeway in this area because the school does not have its own funds with which to launch initiatives. The practice is to free mothers with small children and older women from early morning or late afternoon lessons and to let them choose the most convenient time for lessons.

Conclusion

This survey confirmed some of the lessons outlined in the first part of the report, while others were not confirmed. In particular, the world of work for teachers is characterized by a number of contradictory features. The positive ones include relatively stable employment – contracts are mostly permanent and full time; the high degree of employment security; relatively easy access to training; and the well developed social dialogue; while the negative features are related to the high labour intensity and risks to teachers' health; and difficulties in reconciling family and work.

Teachers' risks of vulnerability follow mainly from high intensity and fast work rhythms. Another risk factor is the low wages due to limited school budgets within the highly restrictive state budget.

Some of the positive aspects of teachers' world of work are not effective enough: the survey results indicated a higher degree of access to qualifications and education than the trends outlined in the first section of the report. However, the quality of training remains a problem because it does not correspond to the teachers' expectations and requirements.

Teachers as a group are quite homogeneous and the differences among schools are insignificant.

Considering the strategic importance of education for the country and the quality of human capital the main policy recommendations should focus on: (a) further improvement of the legal basis, since a number of legislative provisions impede more flexible employment, as well as the remuneration of overtime; (b) increasing the flexibility of the system with regard to its administration, such as forms of contracts; (c) better coordination of the management of the system – head teachers and the local authorities; (d) developing policies for better reconciliation of family life and work since recent policies are limited in this respect, although there is an understanding and a willingness to help; (e) the teaching profession is *sui generis* and often the motives for going into it go beyond what would normally be categorized as working conditions – they may be expressed in terms of a compromise between professional devotion and wages and working conditions.

Bulgaria Case Study 2: The difficult transition of the textile industry

Why the textile industry?

The textile branch was selected for a specialized survey based on the results of a statistical analysis. According to these results this branch has a relatively high level of health risk related to working conditions, employees are mainly women, less educated, and wages are below the national average.

Background

We visited a textile company to gather more information on employment structures and working conditions. The textile company is located in the city of Kyustendil, a relatively large city 100 km to the west of Sofia. The company was established in 1968. It manufactures yarns for manual and machine knitting for the domestic and international markets. By 1980 the company employed 2,500 people and was one of the largest companies in this area on the Balkan Peninsula. Privatization started in 1990 and was completed in 1994–5 when 30 per cent of the company's shares were purchased through mass privatization and 67 per cent by individual stakeholders. This was an example of so-called "worker–manager" privatization.

Nowadays the company employs 450 people, of whom 400 are women. Shopfloor workers number 300, administrative staff 30, and auxiliary staff, such as drivers, maintenance technicians, and so on, 20. The company also employs about 50–60 people who are placed in appropriate work due to health reasons. Their employment is protected by a law encouraging the employment of this group of people; companies are obliged to hire up to 6 per cent of their total employment from this group.

Since 2000 company policy has been directed towards reducing employment because productivity is lower than competing companies in the domestic market and companies offering yarns from Turkey and China. The company manufactures 150 tons of yarn per month and works at one-third of capacity. The average wage is low: BGN 180, compared to other companies in this branch whose higher productivity permit an average wage of BGN 280.

Positive features of work: secure jobs, additional pay, low labour intensity.

Concerning the positive aspects of working conditions we must say that, although employment has been significantly reduced, at present employees feel secure about their jobs. Labour contracts are permanent and full-time. Temporary labour contracts are given to newly employed workers and the term is from 3 to 6 months. It is worked in shifts: a four-shift arrangement is practised in the winter months and a three-shift arrangement in the summer months. Working time for people transferred to appropriate work due to health reasons is reduced in compliance with the legal regulations. The company does not use other types of labour contract because it is afraid that the Central Labour Inspectorate may sanction it. The trade union organizations at the company also confirm that job security is relatively high, although wage levels and regular wage payments are less safe.

Some additional payments can be considered as compensation for the low wages and this is positive: food vouchers are provided and work above the fixed quota is paid in accordance with the Labour Code. For older workers the supplement for length of service (7–8 per cent) is about BGN 20–30. Nightwork brings a wage supplement of 5 per cent. Both workers and trade unions declared that labour intensity is not high. Breaks of 15 minutes are regularly observed.

Negative features of the work: low wages; poor work organization; poor health and safety conditions; lack of training; weak social dialogue.

As already pointed out, the negative features of working conditions prevail. The poor working conditions result in relatively high staff turnover: about 10 people per month, generally voluntarily. Wages include a component based on labour norms and an adjustment coefficient. The low level of wages in textiles and their trends have been presented in detail in Part 1 of this study. According to the chair of the trade union there have been periods when the company did not pay wages regularly or sent people home on unpaid leave. The company's director said that work organization is a problem and the company is unable to improve it.

Two trade union organizations operate in the company. They bargain on staff expenditure, including expenditure on food and transport because 60 per cent of the employees are from nearby villages. The workers declared they would like to have more dialogue with the management regarding the company's financial status, the allocation of profits and incentives that might be used to raise labour productivity.

Although the workers and trade unions acknowledge that labour intensity is not high, an increase would not be acceptable, according to the union chairman. On the other hand, everybody accepts the need for new work organization. It was suggested that failure so far is due to the lack of management will.

As far as workers' health is concerned, there are hazardous conditions connected with dyes, noise and dust from the production process. The company has a medical unit. Periodical medical examinations are performed, although in many cases the workers do not meet the recommendations for health protection: for example, no anti-noise devices are used for noise protection. Absences due to illness are increasing, although the director believes that some are not the result of real illness.

One worker suggested that working conditions could be improved by providing special facilities for women. Air conditioning should also be installed because the temperature in the summer is very high.

Staff training includes internal company training: people starting work are trained by experienced workers. Medium-level staff do not receive training because there is no training organization.

The reconciliation of family duties – and particularly the raising of children – with work is a real challenge for women. They rely to a great extent on the assistance of their husbands or relatives.

Considering the positive and negative features of working conditions in this factory it could be said that in this particular case the transition has caused more negative than positive effects. The main reasons for this are unsuccessful privatization and poor management.

The main reasons that provoke vulnerability based on poor working conditions are external economic factors and internal organizational weaknesses. According to the company's director the main problems are that the import of yarn is free of customs duties – this makes imported products more competitive – and the lack of support from the state and branch organizations. There is a need to exchange experiences with other companies and apply better forms of work organization. However, they do not receive any assistance in this from the association of textile manufacturers, including in relation to the new standards which will come into force after EU accession. According to the workers, work coordination among different units is not good and this impedes production.

About the internal problems that create vulnerability the opinions of the manager and of the workers and trade unions differ: the manager points to workers transferred to a more appropriate job for health reasons as a problem for the company. The management would like the state to pay for hiring them. The training of staff and the absence of young people in the company were further problems raised in the interview. We were informed that active labour market programmes – particularly qualification – are rather short in duration and do not provide an opportunity for longer and systematic training of employees. According to the workers and trade unions the lack of social dialogue and poor coordination are among the problems that create risks and vulnerability.

Conclusion: Are there any prospects of improving working conditions?
As already pointed out above, the vulnerability in this factory is driven by the accumulated effect of unfavourable external and internal factors. Also, there is no agreement among the main actors – management, trade unions and workers – about the risk factors: they outlined different aspects of the problems. This means that each participant in the company sees the problems and seeks ways of solving them. However, such solutions have so far not been found. The reason for this is the lack of dialogue and of a will towards new and modern forms of management and work organization. The problems of

the sector are extremely difficult for all companies involved. External competition is very aggressive and there is something in the idea that the state
should develop a clearer policy for the development of this branch. There is
considerable scope for informing companies about changes and ways of
adapting textile production to European and international markets. State assistance is also needed for better company management through the active education of top management. More efforts are needed to reach an agreement
about the internal factors that cause vulnerability and ways of overcoming
them, starting with better dialogue among managers, trade unions and workers. The improvement of work organization and creating healthier and safer
work conditions could be the focus of social dialogue. It must be said that textile workers all over the world are at risk regarding working conditions
because of the nature of the production process. Meanwhile, this is a branch
with low productivity and high labour intensity, as well as being quite risky in
terms of health and safety conditions. The Bulgarian textile industry is not an
exception in this respect, although there are some factories (mainly international) where working conditions are relatively better regarding wages. In any
case, the search for better solutions should be the focus of all institutions in
charge of working conditions and particularly the branch trade unions.

Bulgaria Case Study 3: Better working conditions in the internationalized banking sector

Looking for good examples
We included the banking sector in our study in order to present good practices
that reflect not only the better financial conditions of banks, but also their
management of working conditions.

Influence of international markets but also innovative internal policy
The bank in question is the second largest in terms of capital and the third
largest in terms of assets. The bank emerged as a result of the first successful
bank privatization in Bulgaria, completed in mid-1997. In July 2000, the
National Bank of Greece paid US$ 207 million for the stakes in UBB of
Bulgaria's largest bank, Bulbank, EBRD, CIBC Oppenheimer Corp and
Jodrell Enterprises Ltd, which amounted to a total of 89.9 per cent. The EBRD
retained 10 per cent in the Bulgarian bank but sold its stake to the Greek bank
for US$ 27 million under a call option exercised in July 2004. In May 2002,
the bank launched BGN 15 million worth of three-year, fixed coupon corporate bonds on the Bulgarian stock exchange. In July 2004, UBB issued a BGN
40 million five-year mortgage bond issue, which bears a 6.625 per cent annual coupon and was successfully placed. The international rating agency

Standard & Poor's rates UBB at BB+ with a stable outlook, while Fitch has put the long-term credit rating of the bank at BBB– with a stable outlook.

The bank is number two in terms of corporate and retail business, with one million retail accounts and 60,000 corporate customers. The bank is most advanced in terms of internal restructuring and the implementation of best banking practices and standards in all key banking areas. This is one of the most modern and innovative Bulgarian banks with a leading position in electronic banking (Internet, PC, phone, GSM), corporate and retail business and the introduction of new products.

The branch network includes 123 branches countrywide, located in the major cities, as well as in some towns with economic potential.

The following officials were interviewed in semi-standardized interviews for the purposes of the case study: the human resources director, the chairman of the trade union and a bank employee.

Permanent and motivated employees a definite asset

The employees number about 2,100, of whom about 900 are employed in the central office in Sofia and the rest in bank branches throughout the country. This staff level has remained relatively stable over the last two years. It is projected to increase in the future due to the opening of new branches throughout the country. The staff is relatively young, with an average age of 37.

Employment is organized on the basis of different kinds of labour contract but mainly permanent labour contracts on a full-time basis. The bank offers six-month probationary contracts for newly hired employees. After this period the contracts are transformed into permanent ones. In some cases "study" contracts are offered, with a duration of 15 days.

Other forms of flexible contract emerging

International experience regarding the use of flexible forms of contract is very useful for increasing the efficiency of employment. Leased staff, a form of employment that this bank practises, is an interesting form of labour relations that is not very popular but can be used more widely. Civil contracts are used in legal services since this is the most efficient form for such activities. From this point of view (efficiency) the bank has also outsourced some activities. Temporary labour contracts are used during the summer holidays when pensioners, former bank employees, are hired while bank staff are on holiday. This is an efficient form of employment for both sides – the bank, since it can rely on qualified temporary workers, and the pensioners, who receive additional income. The bank also has summer internship programmes and students who do well may be hired.

The average duration of service is eight years. The bank has been in existence since 1993. Staff turnover is under 6 per cent and is generally voluntary.

The motives for this are usually higher paid work available elsewhere (although the average wage in the banking sector is above the national average) or possibilities for faster progress in the hierarchy (some people preferred faster career prospects, while at the bank they have to move step by step up the hierarchy).

Different time schedules according to activity – stressful in some departments
Working time duration for most staff is eight hours per day, five days a week. The people working these schedules are relatively few in number and working conditions are laid down in additional working agreements. Extra labour is required in some departments, such as information technology, repair and communication because these departments work beyond the bank's working time. This work is additionally remunerated. A bank employee told us that in hectic periods working time can be 10–12 hours. Employees may be compensated for this longer working time through leave or in agreement with the manager.

The bank recruits staff through internal competition for vacancies and thus ensures staff development. The bank also works with two private mediation agencies, one in Sofia and the other in Plovdiv, which monitor the labour market all over the country, selecting and supplying staff in compliance with the bank's requirements. The bank maintains a relatively rich database of applicants for work.

Work organization and intensity follow modern banking practices. The work in the bank's branches is particularly intensive, demanding and strenuous, especially in the units that work directly with clients. The quality of work requirements is increasing continuously, together with the number of products and services offered. Modern software is used and this requires heightened employee attention and increases their stress, particularly when they work with BGN and foreign currency.

Safety and health risks closely monitored
Working conditions in terms of employees' health are relatively good compared to the national average and are continuously improving. The bank has its own work medical unit which carries out the legally required evaluations of risk in the workplace. Standards for furniture, equipment and working conditions comply with the legal requirements, and the working conditions groups and the trade union perform additional monitoring. The bank's officials have life insurance and work accident insurance. Medical treatment and care are provided under a contract with a specialized clinic. The work does entail some risk of eye illnesses and particular attention is paid to this. Analyses of staff sickness are drafted on an annual basis and relevant recom-

mendations made for improving conditions and the health of the bank's employees.

A bank employee (among whom women predominate) we interviewed thought that working conditions might be improved: the central office has relatively old computer equipment and the air-conditioning system does not manage to ventilate the premises properly

Although safety and health conditions are relatively good, new health risks are emerging due to modern ITCs: people reported eye problems, headaches and orthopaedic pains due to the sedentary work. It might be considered that the new risks define new categories of vulnerable workers, who use modern technology and are highly qualified.

An emphasis on qualifications and training

Access to training and qualifications is promoted through annual training programmes. In 2005 all bank employees underwent internal and external forms of training. The total number trained was 4,088 people. Many bank employees are studying on Masters programmes both in Bulgaria and abroad. There are also long-term specializations in banking: seven people have passed two-year specializations and 19 people six-month specializations in the last two years. Short-term specialized seminars lasting 1–3 days are also often held. Internal banking training covers all staff at branches, and introductory training for new employees is obligatory. Foreign language training for certain positions is also actively performed.

Bonuses and wages linked to performance

Wages are above the national average and the average in private banking. The wage structure includes one-third flexible wages related to performance. Basic wages are determined on the basis of a scale, rules and the relevant system for basic wages. The gross wage is agreed on the basis of a bonus system.

There are also social payments – Christmas bonuses, individual benefits, and so on.

Wage growth is planned over a three-year period. Evaluations are made through certification of employees and their development in the hierarchy is promoted.

Social dialogue the way of setting disputes

Social dialogue is very well developed. It involves management and the trade union, in which 90 per cent of the employees participate. The collective agreement is part of the social dialogue, renewed every two years. Consultation is the main way of settling labour disputes. Changes in the area of labour relations are agreed in advance. The chairman of the trade union stated that their demands are moderate and comply with the collective agreement. Staff expenditure, contracted with the employer, varies from 8 per cent to 12.5 per cent of total expenditure. Subject to the collective agreement are the number of staff in relation to the introduction of new work organization and work technologies. They usually agree on employment restructuring without the need for lay-offs. The trade unions participate in setting training and qualifications policy, as well as policy on healthy working conditions.

Work and family life balance a company priority
The reconciliation of work and family life is encouraged through programmes and additional payments for marriage and childbirth. Additional social benefits are granted in case of financial problems related to the health of employees' children. Despite this, the high labour intensity, the stressful environment and the extra hours (although paid) disturb the balance between work and family life. This is a particular problem for women, who, as already pointed out, predominate among bank staff.

Conclusion: the lessons of this good example
This study is focused on the good practice that international experience transfers to Bulgaria. Although this good example is in one, quite specific sector, it encourages the perception that good working conditions could be achieved in all sectors of the economy. It is only to some extent a matter of the funds needed to improve working conditions. It is more a matter of the will and of innovative thinking on the part of managers, trade unions and employees. This example shows that the workforce can be used more efficiently by means of more flexible contracts and working time organization, and with effective social dialogue. It also shows that by investing in health prevention measures and training the firm gains qualified and more competitive staff, reduces labour turnover and increases productivity. At the same time, modern working conditions clearly create new risks of vulnerability: for example, more stressful conditions, higher labour intensity, less leisure time and difficulties reconciling family and work. This means that further efforts are needed to overcome these new risks and to attain a more balanced world of work.

Bulgaria Case Study 4: Mediation services – a vulnerable activity in increasing demand

The role of private mediation services in Bulgaria
Private employment offices supplement the mediation services provided by the employment offices of the National Employment Agency. The website of the National Employment Agency (NEA) provides a list of private employment offices licensed by the NEA. Private employment offices may provide:

mediation services for seeking jobs nationally (206 in number); mediation services for seeking jobs abroad (125 in number); and mediation services in particular branches, such as maritime (57 in number). The number of firms providing mediation services has increased. The NEA has registered 81 new firms. In 2005, 65,352 people registered as jobseekers, of whom 26,075 were women, 24,383 young people, and 30,032 people with a university education. The number of people who were placed in a job was 13,535, of whom 3,936 were women, 4,395 young people and 5,226 people with a university education. The majority of people – 71 per cent – were placed nationally.

Our case study includes an interview with a manager of a private mediation company. Employment mediation is the main activity of the company. It also engages in additional activities related to the operation of training centres for qualifications based on individual training. The company has operated in this branch for over 10 years and has served over 3,000 people. The average number of people placed in work is about 600 people a year. It has annual framework contracts with companies which oblige it to be active in employment mediation and to follow the contract's provisions.

Sources of vulnerability and risks for workers placed by mediation services, but also for employers
The sources of vulnerability are connected with the extent to which the mediation services manage to match employers' demand for skills/knowledge and jobseeker supply. Those seeking work often present skills which do not correspond to their real abilities, while for the employer it is important what the jobseekers are actually able to do. Thus the employment mediator often has to substitute people provided to the employer within three months according to the signed contract. The opposite situation is also a source of vulnerability: for example, when the employer breaks the rules, requests extra knowledge or skills, or extra working hours, or pays less than the contracted wage, and so on.

Another source of vulnerability is that private employers (who are the major clients of the mediation service) still do not have enough experience in working with employment mediators. Thus the private mediator has to guide them when formulating requirements. Subject to bargaining are wages, working conditions, social security contributions, working time, leave, and so on. There are a number of sources of vulnerability and risks for those who obtain work through these mediation services.

Legal basis supposed to prevent vulnerability still wanting
The Employment Promotion Law and the Regulation for its implementation describe the contents and measures of the services provided in employment mediation. They include the following:

- Active jobseekers whose profiles match available vacancies are directed to the relevant employers right away.
- Assessment of realization of potential and an Action Plan with a clear schedule are prepared for unemployed persons not placed in the labour market within a month. Concrete measures and services are included in the Action Plan, developed by the employment mediator in coordination with the client. The Action Plan is in writing and approved by the NEA executive director. The unemployed are obliged to follow the employment mediator and the Action Plan recommendations, visit schedule, terms and approved actions.
- Jobseekers receive information on available vacancies from the LODs' information boards. Employers' names and addresses are not found there; this information is published on the NEA website.

Work in private mediation services includes the same stages and might be conditionally divided in the following way:

- Work with the unemployed or people who want to find a better job;
- Work with employers to gather vacancies and organization of meetings between employers and jobseekers.

Further improvement of legal norms could focus on increasing the flexibility of mediation services regarding job placement, but also on increasing responsibility for outcomes. Too much bureaucracy complicates the present institutional system. Simplifying roles, duties and responsibilities, as well as the licensing regime, could increase the efficiency of private mediation services and thus reduce vulnerability.

The risk of vulnerability for mediators
These risks come from the way relations between private mediators and state institutions are regulated, as well as from the financial environment in which private mediators work.

The private employment offices are licensed every two years and this is considered additional bureaucracy and an obstacle to smooth operations because, besides the payment for obtaining the license, the process is also connected with excessive documentation and bureaucratic procedures. Thus although it was proposed to have only initial licensing and, if lapses were found, companies would be sanctioned or deprived of their license, this proposal was not considered. The private employment offices seeking work abroad have an association which represents their interests. Cooperation with state institutions is not secure. Private mediators submit quarterly information to the National Employment Agency about the number of persons who have sought mediation services and the number of people placed in work, broken down by different profiles. The indicators and profiles of the required information are often changed and this represents an additional burden on private mediators.

A second problem is that private employment offices are entitled to 25 per cent of the first wage in the case of a successful work placement and this is one of their major sources of income. This percentage was abolished at the beginning of 2006 as the service became free of charge for jobseekers; however, the private employment offices have not been compensated by the state.

The difficulties faced by private employment offices include the fact that people seeking new jobs or the unemployed after registration or declaring an interest in finding work do not show subsequent interest. This means that the private mediators have to find them and encourage them to attend interviews, and so on. In many cases the clients of private employment offices are unemployed, socially vulnerable people, that is, people seeking a solution to their other social problems. Jobseekers also do not have a clear view of what they want from the employment mediator and cannot properly present their working career. From this point of view the work of private mediators is very intensive and stressful – it is not unknown for them to work 15–16 hours a day. Work with people from ethnic minorities and people with criminal records also creates problems and even may require cooperation with the police.

Another interesting feature of private mediators is that more people who are employed are turning to mediation services to find a better job. The leading motive for young people is work with prospects, and for older people wages, working conditions, social insurance and job security.

Contact with employers includes the signing of a contract after the mediator has been to the employer to find out precisely what kind of workers the employer is seeking, monitoring working conditions and evaluating the extent to which the employer is seriously seeking employees and how it is treating people hired via its mediation.

The prospects for mediation services
The prospects are controversial:

• On the one hand, mediators are optimistic because of the increasing number of employers turning to private mediation services. Meanwhile, in some cases employers from competing companies want to use private mediation services to get information about their competitors, placing their own employees in competitor companies.
• On the other hand, the transformation of services from paid to free of charge (since 2006) will decrease profits and might stimulate them to reshape their activities or even exit from this activity.

- The present upward trends in labour demand may also have contradictory effects on mediation service prospects: on the one hand, the higher demand for labour increases the chances of job placement without mediation services; on the other hand, as already pointed out, more and more employed people are turning to mediation services looking for a better paid job.

Bearing in mind the already described risks of vulnerability as reported by mediators and with regard to the prospects of mediation services we may draw the following conclusions:

- There is a need to increase the efficiency of mediation services to improve the balance between labour demand and supply. While bargaining in relation to jobs the mediation services should pay more attention to working conditions. Since employers have insufficient experience in seeking workers and particularly in precisely formulating their requirements, mediation services could be of help in these processes. In order to better match labour demand and supply, mediators have to increase the motivation of jobseekers to cooperate. They can do that by offering better packages of services, including different ways of increasing their employability. The concentration of mediation services on the training and qualification of jobseekers is a visible short-term prospect in Bulgaria.
- There is a need to improve the partnership between state institutions and private mediation services with a view to reducing administration and bureaucracy and increasing cooperation and mutuality. From this point of view private mediation services could be financially supported by the state, depending on the efficiency of their work.

REFERENCES

Aro, P., and P. Repo. 1997. *Trade union experience in collective bargaining in Central Europe*. Geneva: ILO.

Beleva, I., and V. Tzanov. 2001. *Labour market flexibility and employment security in Bulgaria*, Employment paper, 2001/30, Geneva: ILO.

Bulgarian Academy of Sciences. 2001. *Social demographic survey*, Institute for Demographic Studies.

——. 2005. *Demographic developments in Bulgaria*. Sofia.

Cazes, S., and A. Nesporova. 2004. Labour markets in transition. *Employment Outlook*, OECD.

Centre for Demographic Studies, Bulgarian Academy of Sciences. 1997. *Women in the private sector and their demographic situation*.

Doklad za zdraveto na najiata v nachaloto na 21 vek. 2004. Ministry of Health (August).

Doklad za rsultatite ot izvarjeni proverki na Glavna Inspektia po truda. http://git.mlsp.government.bg/Bul/Doclad_shum.html.

Employment Agency. 2005. *Information bulletin*, MLSP.

European Foundation for the Improvement of Living and Working Conditions. 2003a. *Working conditions in an enlarged Europe*.

——. 2003b. *European quality of life survey*.

——. 2005a. *National Working Conditions Survey*. Bulgaria.

——. 2005b. *Working and living in an enlarged Europe*. Luxembourg.

Labour Force Surveys, 1994 to 2005.

Labour Code, State Gazette 52/2004.

NSI, *Statistical Yearbook, 2000–2004*.

——. 2004. *Prodaljavajo profesionalno obuchenie*.

——. 2005. *Prebroiava na naselenieto*, tom 6, kniga Budjet na vremeto na naselenieto. Promenite v Kodeksa na tuda ni priobjavat kam Evropa, V. Mrachkov, *Trud i Pravo* (11): http://trudipravo.bg/mats/trp/2004/1/mat/htm

——. 2006. *Bulgaria: the challenge of poverty*.

Supplementary Memorandum on Economic and Financial Policies. 2005.

Tomev, L. 2000. *Rabotnoto vreme na targovskite obekti – ikonomicheski, sojialni I trudodvd-pravni aspeki*. Sofia: KNSB.

Universitet za najionalno i svetovno stapanstvo. 2005. *Vremeto za trud I usloviata na trud*. [University for National and World Economy. 2005. Working time and labour conditions], Sofia.

World Bank. 2002. *Poverty in Bulgaria*. Washington.

3. Croatia: Between EU normalization and persistent hard reality

Vojmir Franičević*

3.1 INTRODUCTION: LABOUR MARKET DEVELOPMENTS

Employment and working conditions in Croatia have developed under the impact of demographic and structural changes, transition-related reforms, war and state building in the first decade of transition; and political and economic progress, regional stabilization and EU association processes in the second. This "great transformation" has been characterized by major economic, democratic, institutional and social "deficits" (Franičević and Bićanić, 2004). The effect on the population was dramatic, including employees or those seeking employment, and in relation to work and workers' rights.

By the end of the 1990s and into the 2000s Croatia had embarked on the path of democratic consolidation and economic growth with good prospects of EU integration. The second decade has brought "normalization" (economic and political), yet in many respects only "nominal". Labour market and work trends during the 2000s reflect this. Improvements have been registered in terms of many indicators; the EU accession process is greatly contributing to that, particularly when it comes to legal and/or institutional developments. Yet, many "hard realities" of the real world of work established in the 1990s have hardly changed.

* I very much want to acknowledge the contribution to preparing parts of an early draft of this report of Prof. Dr. Mirjana Dragičević. I thank Ms Sanja Mudrić of the University of Rijeka who helped me with LFS data, as did Ms. Tihana Cukina of the CBS. Space does not allow me to list the numerous colleagues, experts from ministries, public institutions, and trade unions who helped me with data, documents and their expert knowledge – to all of them I am very grateful.

Table 3.1 Working and employment conditions in Croatia

Element	Item	Trends	Risks/Exposed groups
Labour market	Employment	Slow increase, low jobs creation	Young people, discouraged, women, long-term unemployed
	Unemployment	Still high, though decreasing, increased share of long-term	Young, less educated; minorities, some regions
Employment status and contracts	Temporary employment	Increase but very slow since 2002; new openings mostly on fixed time	New entrants, young and/or less educated in particular
	Self-employment	Increased	Necessity entrepreneurs; Unofficial activities
Wages	Real wages	After catching up now slower than GDP growth	Weakened bargaining power of workers
	Wage differentials	Considerable; education pays; women earn less	Less educated, women, discrimination
	Low pay	High share of below average and 60% of average	Working poor; some sectors in particular
	Poverty risk	Lower for all employed; high for retired and unemployed	Old, unemployed and retired
Working time and work organization	Working time	Long but some decrease; long hours common	All; self-employed in particular
	Unsocial hours	High share of shift and weekend work; increase in Sunday work	Some sectors; women with small children; Sunday major issue
	Part time	Low share; in increase for women	High share of involuntary
Work intensity and stress	Intensity	Seems to be increasing; little hard data	Different groups and occupations
	Stress	On increase	Bullying became public issue; NGOs involved

Safety and health	Safety	Decreased number/rate of accidents in 2000s; recent trends unclear; in firms often low respect for it	Some sectors in particular; Implementation and enforcement deficit
	Health	Recent increase in sick leave rates; work-related diseases not in focus	All. Weak prevention and monitoring; problematic incentives
Education and training	Education	Not adapted to LM needs; low lifelong learning level	Youth, unemployed; reform –a major issue
	Training	Underdeveloped in most firms	Less educated; those with skills not in demand
Social dialogue and workers' participation	Social dialogue	Functional; but major difficulties on all levels; Firm-level dialogue dominates; sector-level dialogue underdeveloped; CA coverage less than 50%;	Non-unionized workers in private-sector firms. Problematic monitoring and enforcement of CAs
	Workers' participation	State dominates over the partners Employees' councils in larger firms – mostly formal	Employed in small firms Lacking policy support
Workers' rights protection	Institutional protection	Low credibility of rights' enforcement; low courts and state inspection capacities	All; non-unionized in particular; Reform of judicial system

Low activity and employment

Demographic trends in Croatia are unfavourable. The population is falling (from 4.499 million in 1991 to 4.195 million in 2001) and ageing (share of 65+ in total population increased from 7.4 per cent in 1961 to 16.3 per cent in 2001), and the working age population, after reaching its peak in 1991, is decreasing: in 2001 it was 66.4 per cent (Gelo et al., 2005).

The activity rate is comparatively low and falling. Despite decreasing unemployment, the share of the inactive population has risen to 50.8 per cent (CBS LFS, 2005, second half). Despite economic growth, employment rates, after reaching their lowest level in 2001 (41.5 per cent, first half), have been around 43 per cent in recent years.[1]

Paid employment dominates, but the share of self-employment is growing: from 17.6 per cent in 2000 to 22.3 per cent in 2005 (CBS LFS, 2nd half). However, only 5.2 per cent are employers: "survival entrepreneurship" still dominates. The share of private sector employment is also increasing (from 63 per cent in 2002 to 67.8 per cent in 2005) (CBS LFS, second half).

The sectoral structure of employment has changed: the share of services has increased and the main losses in employment have been in industry. In 2005 the service sector's share was 62.8 per cent, agriculture's 5.9 per cent and industry's 31.2 per cent (in 2002 the respective shares were 61.3 per cent, 7.8 per cent and 30.7 per cent) (CBS, 2005 and 2006). In parallel, there has been a relocation of employment towards small and medium-sized firms. Most new jobs – with less security for employees – have been created in SMEs. However, in the 2000s large firms' share in active enterprises' employment is increasing: from 42.1 per cent in 2000 it reached 48.1 per cent in 2005. Such trends, coupled with more stringent regulations for larger firms, have certainly contributed to a slowing down of the increase in non-standard work in the last couple of years.

Unemployment slowly decreasing

The 1990s saw a dramatic rise in unemployment: the output "shock" was strong and persistent. Apart from war, it was greatly compounded by privatization failures and restructuring (Franičević, 2002). Unemployment peaked in 2002 at 390,000, with unemployment rates reaching 22–23 per cent in 2000–02. From 2001/02 onwards, with stronger economic growth, registered and LFS unemployment rates fell to 17.9 per cent (registered) and 12.3 per cent (LFS) in 2005.

Besides a pronounced regional component,[2] unemployment has a strong structural component: (i) high and increasing share of older and long-term unemployed; (ii) high, slowly decreasing unemployment rates among the

---

1. Employment rates (employed aged 15–64, divided by total 15–64 population) in 2002–05 were 53.4, 53.4, 54.7 and 55.0. Respective numbers for men are: 60.5, 60.3, 61.8 and 61.7; for women: 46.7, 46.7, 47.8 and 48.6 (Eurostat).

2. While most of the 21 Croatian counties have above-average unemployment rates (13, ranging from 18.3 to 32.1 per cent), there are important exceptions: city of Zagreb (7.8 per cent) and Istarska county (8.0 per cent). The other six counties have 13.4 to 16.8 per cent unemployment rates. Unemployment registers particularly high rates in war-affected areas (CES, *AB 2005*, on 31 December 2005).

young; skills mismatches are present (Obadić, 2006), particularly where restructuring and new investments have generated demand for skills which is unmatched by the current or estimated medium-term supply (Crnković-Pozaić, 2006a and b). Our case studies confirm that almost all firms complain about a chronic lack of skilled workers in a number of occupations, forcing some to import skilled workers from abroad (for example, construction, shipbuilding, tourism). This points to the long-term nature of unemployment problems, but also to the need for educational and training system reforms.

Not only labour market but also institutional deficiencies

The job creation rate is comparatively very low (Rutkowski and Scarpetta, 2005). Analysts point to the detrimental effects of labour market rigidities (World Bank, 2003).

Employment protection legislation was very strict until 2003 (World Bank, 2003), particularly in relation to temporary employment and collective dismissals. With the new Labour Act (2004), collective dismissals were simplified, thus reducing employers' separation costs (ILO, 2004). However, the effects on job creation have been limited. The Croatian Employers' Association (CEA), professing to find labour markets still too rigid and fragmented, recently asked for further deregulation (Kulušić, 2006).

Employment deficit has been also caused by barriers to entrepreneurship (Franičević, 2005; World Bank, 2003). Private sector density and share of SMEs in employment are below OECD countries and CEE economies (World Bank, 2003, 131); average annual gross rate of new enterprise formation remains rather low: 2.1 per cent in 1999–2004 (Čučković and Bartlett, 2006). Restructuring has been limited, coming up against social and political barriers. Pressures towards further restructuring and privatization (of public sector and sectors with state ownership) are strong (EC, 2005), exposing many employees to the risk of job loss. As our case studies also illustrate, this is setting social dialogue a significant challenge. The enhancement of job creation capacity requires more than labour market reforms: sensible structural policies and institutional reforms are also essential.

Unemployed the most vulnerable

In general, the less educated are more exposed to the risk of unemployment. Also vulnerable are women, young people, older workers and minorities.

During the whole period, due to higher unemployment rates (14 per cent vs 11 per cent for men in 2005, CBS LFS), *women's share in the total number of registered unemployed* has been above 50 per cent and is growing (from 51.4 in 1995 to 53.4 in 2001 and to 58.6 in 2005).

Youth unemployment has remained comparatively high (33.8 per cent in 2004 and 32.0 per cent in 2005, CBS LFS), falling from the record levels of 2000–01 (above 40 per cent). The share of *long-term unemployment* in total young people's unemployment is 40.9 per cent, much higher than the EU-25 average (29.8 per cent, Eurostat), exposing young people to poverty, social exclusion and illegal activities (Mudrić, 2006). This is particularly true for those with low education or lacking in-demand skills: fundamental educational reform is a prerequisite of improving this group's position.

The employment rates of *older workers* are comparatively low, but increasing, at 32.6 per cent in 2005. Differences between males (43.0 per cent) and females (23.8 per cent) were considerable (CBS LFS data). Among the registered unemployed those aged 40+ accounted for 45.5 per cent in 2005, while those aged 50+ increased their share from 20.1 per cent in 2004 to 22.0 per cent in 2005 (CES AB, 2006). In firms making job cuts older workers are often targeted first, and restructuring has not yet come to an end.

Finally, there are some *minority groups* whose members are exposed to a high risk of unemployment and little chance of employment, with the result that they often become discouraged. This applies particularly to Roma and Serb returnees (ILO, 2004), as well as to the handicapped.

Serbs' reintegration into the labour market in areas of return is hampered by lack of business opportunities, unresolved property issues, discrimination and corruption (OSCE, 2004).

Kušan's and Zoon's (2004) report on Roma employment – some 30–40,000 live in Croatia, of whom 21,400 receive social benefits – offers a stark picture of extremely low employment, discrimination and stereotyping.

Long-term unemployment most problematic issue

Long-term unemployment rates are much higher than in the EU. In 2005 they stood at 7.4 per cent (for females: 8.4 per cent) (Eurostat-LFS; CBS LFS).

The share of the long-term unemployed in total unemployment is very high and increasing, rising from 52.4 per cent in 2000 to 58.0 per cent in 2005, and to 62.8 per cent by the end of July 2006 (registered, CES data). In July 2006, 36 per cent had been unemployed for over three years. Long-term unemployed are predominantly the unskilled, semi-skilled, those with basic schooling or three years of secondary school, accounting for 72.4 per cent of the total in 2005 (CES AB, 2006).

This is the most serious labour market problem facing Croatia and represents a kind of "road to perdition" in terms of unemployability and social exclusion (particularly for older workers, as stressed by Šverko et al., 2005).

3.2 EMPLOYMENT CONTRACTS: STALLED FLEXIBILIZATION?

The predominance of permanent contracts

Although changes in employment and working conditions were dramatic in many respects, these changes have been less radical than one might have expected. This strongly reflects the state's dominant position in the development of labour regulations, but also the high political risk of alienating organized labour, however weakened and fragmented, but still strong in large privatized firms, SOEs and/or the public sector. *All this is reflected in a slower flexibilization of labour markets, with permanent contracts and full-time jobs still strongly dominating.*

Table 3.2 Employment contracts by duration, Croatia, 2000–05

	2000	2001	2002	2003	2004	2005
Permanent contracts	90.5	88.9	87.5	88.2	87.5	87.9
Fixed-term contracts	6.6	7.8	9.7	9.6	10.4	10.1
Seasonal contracts	1.2	1.5	1.3	1.0	1.3	1.3
Specific assignment or short-term contracts	1.6	1.8	1.5	1.1	0.8	0.7
Temporary contracts	9.4	11.1	12.5	11.7	12.5	12.1

Source: CBS, Labour Force Surveys.

Between 2000 and 2005 there was an increase in temporary employment and a fall in permanent employment, but with very little change after 2002.

The temporary nature of the great majority of new contracts

However, this picture may be deceptive: (i) the share of fixed term contracts has increased; (ii) the share of permanent contracts in legal entities is slowly declining; (iii) the share of 1–6-month contracts has increased (from 39.5 per cent in 2000 to 58 per cent in 2005, CBS LFS), particularly 1–3-month fixed contracts (from 20.4 per cent in 2000 to 31.5 per cent in 2005), leading to an increased numbers of persons moving back and forth between temporary jobs and unemployment (Crnković-Pozaić, 2005); (iv) among new job openings fixed-term contracts increasingly dominate: in 2005, 141,000 were employed from the unemployment register, 85.6 per cent fixed-term (in 2004, 83.4 per cent; and in 1997, about 50 per cent) (CES data); (v) *young people are par-*

ticularly exposed to non-standard employment. While for workers over 25 the standard form of employment is still permanent – 90.8 per cent in 2005 – some 39 per cent of young people were on temporary contracts (30 per cent on fixed ones) (CBS, LFS 2nd half); (vi) finally, in the firms we visited, despite the fact that by the 2004 Labour Code fixed-term contracts (after a compromise with the unions) were discouraged as something to be used "exceptionally", almost all recent employment was fixed and/or contracted out!

Use of temporary agencies not yet extensive

Temporary agency employment is still limited but seems to be picking up; some major Croatian companies are using their services (for example, Podravka, Pliva, Atlantic). It was legalized in January 2004. Some 15 agencies are active. The strongest are Dekra (with 11 regional offices), Adecco and other international chains. Recently, press and unions reported that some 4,000 people are presently employed by TAs, 1,000 with Dekra alone; by 2008 it is expected that around 15,000 will be employed (for example, *Poslovni dnevnik*, 3.10.2006 and 9.11.2006). Employers are still not sufficiently aware of the potential benefits, according to the Dekra regional manager (*Karlovački list* 22.3.2006). Gotovac (2003) warns about a too "liberal regime and lack of supervision", and a major union confederation recently voiced deep concerns about workers' rights abuses and asked for changes in the law, as well as opening up a collective bargaining process with Dekra (Večernji list, 7.11.2006). The manager of one agency in our interview confirmed that abuses are possible: some agencies pay employees less than mandated by the law, that is, less than the user firm's minimum wage. An additional issue is temporary employment abroad. It is still the Croatian Employment Service's monopoly, but there are a lot of private agencies in the "grey zone", with little or no protection by way of employment rights (for example, on big cruisers, *Poslovni dnevnik*, 19.7.2006). In the process of EU harmonization, private agencies will be permitted too, hopefully under transparent and supervised conditions.

Part time not yet integrated into work organization

Particularly in legal entities, full-time work is still the norm: 98.2 per cent of employees are full time; the shares of part time (1.5 per cent) and short time (0.3 per cent) are very low (CBS, *SR 1307*, 2006 on 31 March 2005). The share of *part-time employment* is comparatively low, ranging mostly between 8 and 9 per cent of total employment. However, higher rates for women are noticeable, increasing significantly in 2005 (to 10 and 13.4 per cent for females, CBS LFS). Importantly, the *share of involuntary part-time* was high in 2000–05, usually higher than 40 per cent. In 2005, 17.1 per cent declared that they couldn't find full-time work (CBS LFS). This indicates that *part-time work has not yet become a widespread option* for either employers or employees. Our case studies support the observation that for most Croatian firms part-time work has not become an integral part of their work organization (exceptions include some foreign retail chains), and some of those considering it find that the necessary social conditions are not yet in place (for example, a shift system in schools, as pointed out by a major retail chain manager in our interview).

Flexibilization of the labour market has been limited so far, and employers are pressing for more. However, it is unlikely that the government, seeking re-election in 2007, will embark on moves that would dramatically increase flexibility and risk a loss of support from well protected layers of the workforce and open confrontation with the trade unions. Yet, while further flexibilization might be constrained for the time being, it can hardly be stalled forever.

It also seems that the above trends, particularly in larger firms and the public sector, may consolidate a dualization of the workforce (institutionalized through differential treatment of firms according to numbers employed), with a "core" enjoying longer tenure under permanent contracts and access to other benefits under collective agreements (due to a strong union presence and coverage), participation rights, and so on, while on the other hand the burden of adverse cyclical developments and seasonality falls on those with fixed contracts and/or on subcontractors. Some of our case studies also point in that direction. However, due to high structural risks, removal of subsidies and reforms in the public sector, the position of the "core" may easily become precarious too. Unfinished restructuring, privatization and the reform agenda may put categories at risk that have so far enjoyed high security.

3.3 WAGES: CATCHING UP BUT LOW PAY PREVAILS

Real wage recovery

After a shocking collapse of *real wages* in the early 1990s (by 64 per cent in 1991–93) real wage growth was particularly strong in the second half of the 1990s. In the years of catch-up (eased by the populist policies of the period; Franičević 2002) wages grew faster than *productivity*. From 2001 this went into reverse: real wages grew by 1.6 per cent in 2001, 3.1 per cent in 2002, 3.8 per cent in 2003, 3.7 per cent in 2004 and 1.5 per cent in 2005, while the respective GDP growth rates were higher: 4.4 per cent, 5.6 per cent, 5.3 per cent, 3.8 per cent and 4.3 per cent (CBS data; SI various years): by 2005 not only real GDP but real wages too were close to the pre-transition (that is, 1989) level. These data reflect a drastic slowing down of wage increases in the public sector. It could also be plausibly argued that the above trends in the 2000s indicate increased flexibility of labour markets but reduced labour bargaining powers in Croatia.

Wage differentials

Sectorally, differences in wage growth and average wage levels are considerable. The most important factor is *educational differences*: in 1996 the rate of return on one additional year of education was 7.6 per cent, but by 2001 it had risen to 10.5 per cent (Šošić, 2004). Education is the key factor in explaining wage variations in Croatia (Nestić, 2005).

Women's average net earnings are lower than men's. Nestić estimates, using 2003 data, that even after control for differences in education, experience and various job characteristics, employed women *at the first decile of wage distribution* earn about 10 per cent less than men, while at the ninth decile the difference is higher and their wage is 20 per cent lower. Therefore, "in high-paid jobs, women are relatively more disadvantaged than in low-paid jobs" (Nestić, 2005, 15).

More wage security but widespread low pay

Security of wage payment has increased: late payment or failure to pay are still common but much less pronounced than in the late 1990s when it was a major public issue. However, for many this *increased security* has not brought much in terms of improvement of living standards: *the share of low wages is high.*

It can be estimated that, similarly to 2004, (for full-time employed at legal entities only) in 2005 more than 60 per cent received below the average wage, and about 24 per cent below 60 per cent of the average wage.[3] *Low pay* is particularly characteristic of agriculture, fishing, retail, hotels and restaurants, construction, some services and some manufacturing sectors (textiles, leather, lumber, furniture, metal working and paper). *Many can barely cope.* The "financial situation in households" was judged "mostly bad" or "bad" by 58–59 per cent in 2005 (CBS LFS, 1st and 2nd half of year). This also explains why there is still a strong demand for longer hours and unofficial and/or unregistered work. This was frequently confirmed in our interviews.

---

3. Based on CBS data. Similarly, REGOS data on social insurance show that 63 per cent of those insured were registered on below the average gross wage in June 2006.

A *minimum wage* for full-time work is not laid down by law but determined by collective agreement (according to the minimum basis for calculation of obligatory social security contributions and applied to all employees in Croatia) (ILO, 2004). It has been rising annually, too. At present it is (gross) HRK 2,169.65 (EUR 293) per month. REGOS data on social insurance show that in June 2006 there were 17,991 workers registered on lower pay than this (that is, 1.5 per cent of the total; and a further 21,878 on the minimum wage, that is, 1.9 per cent).

Additional payments – often "hidden" or "under the table"

In the firms we visited we noted a number of important characteristics. First, *extensive use is made of overtime* as part of wage policy: both sides accept this as a way of increasing otherwise low wages, and some consider it as a bonus for good workers. Second, *use of "hidden wages" is extensive*: for example, various benefits (for example, allowances for being away from home, for difficulty of work and so on, as in the construction case study) and payments in kind. Third, *cash payments*, particularly at small firms, are common practice. A recent (unrepresentative) online survey is indicative: employers (n = 291) and employees (n = 525) think that about one third of workers' pay is "under the table" (Selectio, 2006).

Poverty risk greatest for unemployed

Being employed in Croatia is a major insurance against poverty, even on modest pay. The greatest *risk of falling into poverty* is faced by the old, the unemployed and the retired. While poverty risk overall was, in 2005, 19.9 per cent without and 17.5 per cent with incomes in kind, poverty indicators (see Table 3.3) for 2003–05 show that the *poverty risk among the employed is much lower* than among *other groups, and was falling*: from 5.6 per cent in 2003 to 4.3 per cent in 2005. It also significantly decreased for the self-employed (from 25.5 per cent to 17.0 per cent), but *remained high and was increasing for the unemployed* (34.1 per cent in 2003 and 37.3 per cent in 2005) and was *high and stable for pensioners* (22.4 per cent in 2003 and 22.5 per cent in 2005).

Not surprisingly, public surveys (for example, IDEA, 2002) show fears of poverty and unemployment as the most important personal fears and the most important public issues in Croatia.

Table 3.3 Poverty indicators, Croatia, 2003–05

	2003		2004		2005	
	With n.i.*	Without	With n.i.	Without	With n.i.	Without
Rate of poverty						
risk, %**	16.9	18.9	16.7	18.8	17.5	19.9
Men	15.8	17.7	15.1	17.0	15.9	18.1
Women	17.9	20.1	18.1	20.5	18.9	21.5
Employed	5.2	5.6	4.4	4.6	3.9	4.3
Self-employed	18.4	25.5	22.6	28.2	13.7	17.0
Unemployed	32.4	34.1	32.0	33.2	33.4	37.3
Pensioners	20.7	22.4	20.5	23.5	19.3	22.5
Relative risk of						
poverty gap, %***	21.1	24.2	22.4	25.7	22.9	24.8
70% threshold	24.6	25.7	24.3	26.1	25.5	27.4
Gini coefficient	0.29	0.30	0.29	0.31	0.29	0.31

Source: CBS (2006), *'Pokazatelji siromaštva od 2003–2005' (Poverty indicators 2003–2005)*.

Notes: * n.i. = natural income; ** percentage of persons whose equivalent net income is below the risk of poverty threshold (60 per cent of median equivalent household income); *** difference of poverty threshold income and median equivalent income of those below the threshold.

3.4 WORKING TIME: OVERTIME AND LONG HOURS ARE COMMON

Decrease in working hours: official but real too

In 1996–2004, *reported* (by firms) *working hours of employees at enterprises* were remarkably stable: about 2,100 hours per person annually. On the other hand, *overtime working hours* were very stable in 1996–99 (at 23 hours), but they rose to 29 in 2004 (CBS, *SR 1307*, 2006). This may indicate increased pressure on workers to work longer hours.

However, Labour Force Surveys show a decrease in average usual working hours for all employed from 41.7 in 1998 to 40.4 in 2005 (1st half). For full-time employees this decrease is much weaker (from 42.6 to 41.6) than for full-time self-employed (from 51.5 in 1998 to 46.5 in 2005) (CBS LFS). These trends reflect the legal reduction of the working week from 42 to 40 hours (very little change for full-time employees since 2001), but also decreased average hours for the self-employed. Despite that, the *self-employed are still working much longer hours* than employees (as our case studies also illustrate).

Overtime not always paid

The trade unions often complain that unreported, even unpaid *overtime* is very common (for example, in retail) which is also confirmed by the state inspection findings. However, while firms "supply" overtime, there is also "demand" for it on the part of the workers. Managers sometimes rely on overtime as an "incentive" offered to workers (for example, shipyard, construction, metal working). Many workers are forced but others are willing, in order to cope or reach their targets, or just to keep their job, to work overtime on a more or less permanent basis, particularly among the self-employed. This also emerged in our interviews.

Research carried out in 2002 (focusing on an intermediate and higher educated urban population sample) found that the mean number of self-reported working hours per week was 45.5 (75 per cent work in excess of 40, 22 per cent more than 50, and about 6 per cent more than 60 hours per week). The authors found that "long hours are a common experience", but "hours spent on the job are particularly high for people holding high-level jobs and those running their own businesses" (Šverko et al., 2002: 293, 296). This was supported in our interviews as well.

Many work unsocial hours, endangering work–family balance

Many are exposed to *unsocial hours*, in particular:

- The shares of those *usually* working *shifts* are comparatively high, but slightly decreasing (from above 20 per cent in 1999–2003 to 18.8 per cent in 2005, 2nd half); yet *women's shares* were considerably higher (for example, in 2005, 2nd half – 20.2 per cent vs 17.7 per cent for men).
- The share of those persons *usually working nights* is between 2.0 per cent and 2.5 per cent (for men in 2005, 2nd half, it was 2.8 per cent and for women 1.3 per cent). The share of those persons *usually working evenings* decreased to 5.1 per cent in 2004), but less for women so that women's share became higher than men's (5.7 vs 5.6 in the 2nd half of 2005).
- Many *usually work on Saturdays* (with quite stable shares, between 25 per cent and 26 per cent, although women's shares are significantly higher – in 2005 the figure was 24 per cent for men but 28.4 per cent for women), *and on Sundays* (more than 13 per cent recently). It seems that since 2000 *there has been considerable increase of Sunday work*, particularly for women, reaching a very high 17.1 per cent in the 2nd half of 2005 (most likely associated with retail sector reorganization,

that is, the entry of international and the development of domestic chains, the construction of large shopping malls at the edge of towns).

• In addition, in 2005, 27.7 per cent men and 20.2 per cent women were *occasionally* working *Sundays*; 52.9 per cent men and 37.4 per cent women *Saturdays*; 20.6 per cent men and 9.2 per cent women *nights*; and 8.5 per cent men and 5.7 women *shifts* (CBS LFS 2005, 2nd half).

Women's exposure to unsocial hours is high and, in some important respects, increasing.

In our interviews three groups emerged as having particular difficulties in keeping a good work–life balance: married women with children working Sundays, holidays and shifts; those usually working on remote sites (for example, construction workers); and the self-employed, who put in very long hours with very little free time and almost no holidays. Some managers complained of the same problem. It also emerged that *low pay* may be disruptive for balance in two ways: first, by forcing people into long hours and/or additional jobs; second, due to the frustrations inherent in being unable to realize important family and/or family members' goals.

With the retail explosion, involving the entry of multinational chains and growing consumerism, *working Sundays has become a major labour issue.* For the Union of Commerce of Croatia the preferred solution is a radical restriction of Sunday work. In this respect, it is receiving the full support of the Catholic Church which is organizing a campaign on the basis of a "culture of free Sundays" and arguments centred on dignity and "family protection" (Prenđa et al, 2004; Baloban and Črpić, 2005).

The first attempt by the trade unions and a group of (conservative) political parties was successful: by January 2004 all shops, after amendments to the Law on Commerce, were forbidden to open on Sundays, except some small ones. Six months later the Law was successfully contested before the Constitutional Court. However, the Court's decision opened the way for legitimate contestation of working Sundays, thus opening up a new round of action and debates. A new compromise solution (aiming at better protection of workers' rights) is expected to come before Parliament.

Finally, public polls show the citizens to be divided: a December 2005 online poll by Moj Posao showed 44 per cent against and 43 per cent in favour of shops opening on Sundays.

Intensity and stress on the increase?

There is no research or data base which offers a good view of trends in intensity of work. However, there is a lot of indirect and anecdotal evidence that in many occupations it has grown.

Labour productivity has been growing: in 1993–2001 by 50 per cent and in 2001–04 by 12 per cent (NVK, 2003 and 2005). However, restructuring (particularly in the first period) was predominantly "defensive", that is, productivity growth must be attributed primarily to employment cuts (NVK, 2003: 96). If the 2000s brought more aggressive restructuring, productivity growth is still not accompanied by stronger employment growth. *These trends may be indicative of growing intensity of work,* although from our interviews at hypermarkets, construction sites and hotels a picture emerges of very uneven changes in work intensity across occupations.

In addition, many believe that the *workplace has become more stressful.* A recent non-representative survey (n=474) showed that 34 per cent of people would willingly accept a lower-paid job with less stress (some report family priorities, some are "at their wit's end"); an additional 35 per cent would accept a lower-paid job on condition that the reduction did not exceed 10–25 per cent of current pay (MP, 2005).

3.5 HEALTH AND SAFETY: DEFICITS IN BOTH REGULATION AND ENFORCEMENT

A low policy priority

In 2002 the tripartite National Council for Work Protection was formed, including four independent experts. It has not had much of an impact so far, but its 2005 outline of the "National Programme for the Protection of Health and Safety at Work" (July 2005) is a sobering document on issues which are still receiving *low priority* from policy-makers and enterprises. It reveals numerous failures and weaknesses in workers' health and safety protection. *There are serious problems concerning health protection:*

- *There is no systematic follow-up of workers' health conditions exposed to specific risks.* In spite of legal requirements, only 10 per cent are regularly monitored while "specific health protection is practically unavailable to workers" (NCWR, 2005, 9).
- *Coordination is lacking* between institutions involved in implementing measures to protect workers' health; prevention and monitoring are seriously compromised by the current status of *occupational medicine* which is "completely excluded from the ... system of primary health insurance" (NCWR, 2005, 16).
- Current social security regulations don't stimulate employers to take more care: the costs of work injuries and occupational diseases are borne by contributors (that is, the employed and self-employed) (NCWR, 2005, 16).

• *The law does not recognize work-related diseases*, and the capacity for their early recognition or prevention is low. However, *systematic data are produced only for occupational diseases and work injuries. This considerably distorts perceptions of the situation*:

> There are no data on workplace influence on health degradation, except when the primary causes are occupational disease or accidents at work. When workplace hazards are a cause of invalidity (but not the basic one) the harmful influence is not registered at all. It is not known ... how much is being spent on the consequences of injuries and diseases due to harmful workplace conditions. (NCWR, 2005, 11, 12 and 14)

The low numbers on *occupational diseases* may be misleading too. There is weak enforcement of regulations and employers have low incentives to engage in prevention. There is typically a major increase in the number of occupationally sick when a firm goes bankrupt: workers claim occupational disease in order to realize their rights. The case of asbestosis, in two firms, is paradigmatic in that respect (NCWR, 2005, 12). Occupational diseases are most often diagnosed in workers exposed to harmful influence for more than 21 years (46.6 per cent); next come those with 16–20 years of exposure, at 17.2 per cent; with those with less than 6 years, at 11.2 per cent (Dečković-Vukres, 2006) – indicating weak monitoring and prevention.

Decrease in accidents but increase in sick leave

The number of accidents decreased from 24,681 in 1997 to 22,738 in 2005, with a 3.6% increase in 2005. The accident rate (per 100,000 employed) decreased too – from 1,839 to 1,568, again with a slight decrease in 2005 (Dečković-Vukres, 2006). It is hard to tell from the available information whether this is an effect of greater safety at work, and/or the effect of a shift of the labour force towards "less accident-prone" occupations.

The largest *number of accidents in the workplace* in 2005 was found in manufacturing (35.1 per cent in 2005) and construction (13.5 per cent). In 2005 there was an increase in fatal accidents from 42 to 62. Again, construction (20 per cent), manufacturing (11 per cent) and agriculture and forestry (11 per cent) dominate (Dečković-Vukres, 2005 and 2006).

The Croatian Health Insurance Institute's data on *temporary work disability* show, after some decrease in 2002–04, *a notable increase in 2005 and the first half of 2006*: with the sick leave rate rising to 3.7; the average number of days off work rising to 54,000 (and 55,000 in 2006, 1st half); and the average number of absences per employee to 11.6. This increase may be indicative of the stress employees are being exposed too, but solid research is lacking. A notable psychiatrist recently attested that *stress-related symptoms are increas-*

ingly bringing the employed into clinics (*Slobodna Dalmacija*, 28.8.2006). As the Institute data show, after musculo-skeletal disorders, mental disorders (together with work accidents) are the most common cause of sick leave.

Limited willingness of employers to observe new safety regulations

Workers' safety is regulated by the 1996 Law on Protection at Work, and related acts and norms. The development of regulations in this area is influenced by Croatia's EU association process and legal harmonization. There are a great number of EU directives on health and safety, and the process is well under way (Analiza, 2004). Out of 26 EU directives, the harmonization process has been completed for eight, and a further five are expected to be realized during 2006 (communication from government expert). For many businesses, which give these issues low priority, it may produce additional pressures – they can hardly expect to compete in the EU by cutting corners on safety and health protection.

Even when regulations are EU-harmonized*, some firms simply do not observe them* (for example, in the case of machinery and other equipment) (Analiza, 2004, 11). For example, little attention has been paid to the health implications of prolonged work with PCs and monitors; on the other hand, musculo-skeletal diseases make up 30 per cent of the total (Analiza, 2004, 13) and result in a high rate of work absences and health costs.

The employer is responsible for organizing and enforcing protection at work and the burden of proof is on him (objective responsibility), regardless of the number of employees. However, inspectors find *employers* "uninterested in assuring a satisfactory level of safety for their employees … Those working in special conditions … are not sent for preliminary and periodical health examinations … while dangerous equipment is not regularly checked … Employers and their agents are still not aware that ... they are responsible for the safety and health protection of employees." *Employees'* work and technical discipline is lacking, and employers do not enforce it in accordance with the law (SI, 2005 and 2006). *These findings were fully confirmed in the firms we visited.* In most firms safe work is not a priority even for the trade unions which focus more on wages and other rights.

Poor enforcement capacity

Fears have recently been expressed (by employers) of a regulatory overload, particularly in the case of SMEs which lack resources and the capacity to comply with the numerous regulations.

Implementation deficits are more pressing than the regulatory gaps. The number of occupational safety inspectors is insufficient, and monitoring and enforcement capacities are low. According to the law there should be 170 inspectors; in fact, there are only 89 (SI, 2006). For that reason the proportion of planned inspections, with a stronger focus on prevention, is decreasing. On the other hand, there has been an increase in mandatory inspections due to the rise in reported fatal, heavy and collective accidents at work (692 inspections in 2002, but 1,124 in 2005). This *increase* was attributed in the SI reports to an increase in economic activity often without sufficient safety measures; the absence of efficient prevention systems, including insurance systems (nowadays most costs are socialized); and a lack of education (SI, 2005 and 2006). Safety managers at some firms pointed to increased risks due to growing reliance on cooperation and subcontracting with firms whose employees are not sufficiently trained to carry out (safely) the work they are asked to perform.

The credibility of the courts is low: in 2005 inspectors submitted 1,750 misdemeanour applications for 3,483 misdemeanours; in the same year the courts issued 1,267 fines (SI, 2006). Since the courts are overburdened they often do not reach a decision in the cases brought to them by the SI before the deadline: this applied to as many as 41 per cent of 1,099 decisions received by the SI from the courts in 2005. In addition, court proceedings typically last for a couple of years, often resulting in a conditional discharge, even when consequences for workers are very grave (ibid).

Bullying yet to be recognized as a work-related problem

The influence of stressful relationships at work has recently been recognized in debates on "workplace bullying". Its victims often suffer from various psychic, emotional, physical and behavioural conditions: PTSD is often diagnosed (Jokić-Begić et al., 2003). The government Office for Gender Equality and the parliamentary Gender Equality Committee have become interested, as have a number of public health institutions.

The evidence indicates that the extent of bullying may be quite large. The new association has been approached by many victims from across the board: from cleaners to university teachers (*Vjesnik*, 25.10.2005). The 2002 field research found that between 15.4 per cent and 53.4 per cent of the sample (n=700) had experienced some sort of bullying. Men are more exposed to threats or physical assaults, women to sexual harassment (Koić et al. 2003, 16). Online research showed that among 812 persons who decided to participate, 84 per cent had been exposed to psychic abuse at work (Posao.hr, 2005).

Legal protection and public policies to deal with bullying are considered inadequate – this is one of the reasons why the establishment of a Court of Labour Disputes should be seriously considered (Bodiroga Vukobrat, 2005).

Recognizing bullying as a "work-related problem" (ibid.) and developing a network of supporting public institutions where victims will be able to find help has also been suggested. Particularly important, experts believe, is to sensitize employers to the issues involved, such as the potentially detrimental effects of bullying for productivity and efficiency.

3.6 EDUCATION AND TRAINING: A PROFOUND DEFICIT

The Croatian education system is poorly adapted to the needs of a "knowledge-based economy" (Lowther, 2004). Enrolment rates are lower than in the EU-15 (Šošić, 2004). The average number of years of education a Croatian five-year-old is expected to receive is four years below the OECD average (Babić, 2005),

Vocational education is "the most problematic" (Babić, 2005, 101). The European Training Foundation report recommends building a new governance framework for VET (with increasing capacities at local level) and curriculum reform: "most of these occupations are too narrow, the training for them is too specialized, and they hardly reflect the skill needs of employers and the requirements of a modern VET in a lifelong learning perspective" (ETF 2003, 20).

In *higher education*, the structure of enrolment is considered sub-optimal and efficiency is extremely low: "only a third of graduates get a degree" (Šošić, 2004). With the 2005 introduction of the Bologna process fundamental reform started; its impact is too early to assess.

Lifelong learning is extremely poorly developed: while in the EU-15/-25 in 2004, 11 per cent of those over 25 were taking part in some form of education and training, in Croatia it was only 2 per cent (CBS LFS). On the other hand, no incentives or funds are provided by the government (with the exception of some specific government programmes, local-level and CES programmes, Outline, 2006; HGK, 2005).

The *Croatian Employment Service* is responsible for providing training for the unemployed. But funds to realize CES plans are insufficient. In 2005 only 33.5 per cent of the amount planned by the CES was spent or just 0.06 per cent of total CES costs. The numbers are scarcely spectacular: expenditure on ALMP has been below 1 per cent of GDP, *with too little focus on training and skills development* in favour of job subsidies; altogether there is very little evidence of an integrated policy approach (Crnković Pozaić, 2006b).

Research shows that in most *enterprises* human resource management is unsatisfactory. In 2003, 334 firms were surveyed: the study found that "Croatian companies mostly invest in additional training and development of employees with university degrees"; "46.6 per cent did not invest in the further training of their employees at all"; "83.3 per cent did not invest at all in those with basic education, and 48.4 per cent neglected those with only secondary and college qualifications" (Pološki, Vokić and Frajlić, 2004, 71). In all firms we visited there were complaints about the lack of important occupations and skills, and worries about their future availability.

One effort to address these issues is the government's 2004 strategy for adult education, and the May 2006 Outline of the Law on Adult Education. It aims at building a new system of adult education based on lifelong learning (Outline, 2006). In secondary education, a state matriculation exam is being introduced, as well as VET reform. Eventually, the whole education system will be reformed in accordance with the 2005–10 Plan (Plan, 2005). However, its success will very much depend on the actors' incentives and capacities.

3.7 SOCIAL DIALOGUE AND PARTICIPATION: LIMITED INFLUENCE ON WORKING CONDITIONS

Increased flexibility of labour markets, diversification of employment status and growth of the private sector are reducing the proportion of well-protected workers. There are two major channels of employees' representation: *unions* and *employee councils*. They both remain weak.

The trade unions' too narrow focus

In 2000 five nationally representative confederations had 440,100 and in 2004 436,700 members. Together with a sixth confederation which in 2004 also met the representativeness criteria, that makes 456,800. Total union membership may be estimated at 500,000 presently. Generally, the trade union movement is still considered as "weak and fragmented", and not yet stabilized (Bocksteins and Vermuijten, 2005).

Union density is decreasing, but much more slowly than in the 1990s: it was about 40 per cent in 2005. In 1990–91 the membership rate was 60–70 per cent. Those employed in SMEs and those on temporary contracts are unlikely to become union members, and their share, together with that of the self-employed, is growing. In many firms unionization is discouraged, while unions have not been active enough in extending their membership base. Unions are more focused on protecting the rights of permanently employed workers in large unionized firms/sectors than of specific vulnerable groups (for example, young people, minorities or unemployed). Many workers and firms remain out of their reach, particularly smaller ones. However, and in spite of many weaknesses, unions have certainly influenced the evolution of labour regulations, pushing the government to accept compromises and so preventing more radical flexibilization of work relations, as employers and foreign advisors have often asked for (this is typical of the present Labour Code). Secondly, they have influenced the public, including political actors, and have made it more sensitive to numerous issues concerning protection of workers' rights, working time (Sunday work, for example), wage security, and so on. Thirdly, in highly unionized firms and sectors they have established themselves – sometimes quite successfully, often merely formally – as a legitimate partner in restructuring and privatization processes.

But the unions' capacity for collective action seems often to be less than their leaders' ability to participate in "high-level" talks, often giving rise to cynicism among the public and workers (present in our case studies too). Yet, even if it can plausibly be argued that unions' impact on working conditions has been limited, it has certainly been important. It will also be significant in coming talks on changes to the Labour Code (related to EU association) in respect of which the initial agendas of employers and unions on a number of issues are very much at odds.

Employee councils: an unused potential

Workers in firms employing at least 20 have a right to elect members of the *Employee Council* (EC). In firms employing more than 200 employees one member of the supervisory board must be a workers' representative, nominated by the EC.

There is little evidence on ECs' and even less on workers' representation on firms' controlling boards. A recent unrepresentative and unpublished survey by the Office for Social Partnership indicates that ECs' rights are realized only *partially*. When it comes to *information*, ECs are assessed more positively than *on decisions affecting the workers' situation*.

Arguably, the best results are found in firms where there is good cooperation between unions and the EC: the EC can benefit from union help and training (Miličević Pezelj, 2001).[4] However, in the presence of weak unions, the management may play the EC against the union.

Even if workers' participation is mostly reduced to formal requirements, with hundreds of thousands of workers employed in smaller firms left out, *there is potential for development*. Two surveys confirm this. *Firstly*, a 2004 representative survey[5] shows that more than 70 per cent "agree" or "very much agree" (whatever their political orientation) that some form of workers'

---

4. UATUC's Centre for Industrial Democracy offers training to members of ECs, independently of their union affiliation.

5. As part of the 2004 South East European Social Survey (not yet published).

participation would be welcome in Croatia (Sekulić, 2006). *Secondly*, ESOP programmes are quite rare: some 100 by 2004 – firms most likely to implement them are large firms with a significant proportion of small shareholders. In ESOP firms 56 per cent of managers are "satisfied" and 19 per cent "very satisfied" with the programmes' effects: 48 per cent *associate them with an increase of participation* in the firms (Tipurić, 2004).

Collective bargaining: a lot of shortcomings

The main tripartite institution is the Economic and Social Council. While some progress has been made in the 2000s it has remained too formal and has not had much real influence on working conditions. One reason is that the government clearly dominates agenda building and the other social partners (Cimeša and Marinković Drača, 2002; interviews at UATEC).

Firm-based dialogue and collective bargaining dominate. Presently, 100 collective agreements (CAs) are in force; out of this 17 are sectoral but 10 are in the public sector. Some 90 per cent of all registered CAs are at enterprise level (OSP, 2006). The number of registered CAs is increasing each year: 30 in 2000, 46 in 2002, 44 in 2004, and 57 in 2005 (OSP, 2006). However, *CA coverage* is at somewhat less than 50 per cent. In the private sector it is even lower;[6] but more than it would have been if out of seven existing sectoral CAs in the private sector six were not extended by the relevant ministerial decision and made mandatory for all firms in the sector (for example, construction, commerce, hotels and restaurants).

CA enforcement is also problematic: "implementation ... is rather weak, with monitoring and enforcement mechanisms underdeveloped" (ILO, 2004: 34). Since 2003 there has been an increase in the number of conflicts over CAs, followed by peaceful resolutions: 31 in 2003, and 105 in 2005 (60 successfully) (OSP, 2006). *Effective social dialogue* is still underdeveloped. *At the enterprise level*, it is strongest when the state, as majority owner, pursues restructuring and privatization in firms with strong unions, and when union cooperation is necessary if radicalization and heavy conflict are to be avoided (for example, shipyards or Croatian Railways). *At the sectoral level* social dialogue is particularly weak; its effects are marginal and it mostly deals with partial rights or repeats rights laid down in the Law, and very little with the major issues of the sector (Rebac, 2006; ILO 2004, 34). However, the unions are becoming more interested in sectoral social dialogue, and recently opened sectoral negotiations in a couple of sectors (for example, metal and electro, textile and leather industry) (OSP, 2006).

---

6. URSH's president, arguing for the re-introduction of the national collective agreement, claimed that some 772,000 workers were not covered by collective agreements (*Novi List*, 12.10.2005).

3.8 CONCLUSION

Available data on employment, work contracts and wages point towards the conclusion that vulnerable groups in the Croatian labour market include young and old, women and minorities – particularly those members of these groups with low and/or "wrong" education and lack of skills.

The unemployed are certainly the most vulnerable group – many have a high poverty risk. In spite of some encouraging trends (decreasing unemployment), including active policy developments, the prospects of getting a decent job are particularly dim for the older and/or long-term unemployed. As we have seen, many are facing social exclusion.

Many share *multiple vulnerabilities*: for example, young people with substandard education risk substandard employment and low pay too. On the other hand, older workers, if unemployed, risk unemployability and poverty; if employed, loss of preferred contracts, redundancies and very low pensions. Women are typically paid less than men, are more often exposed to unsocial hours and have difficulties establishing a good work–life balance; they are also more exposed to "bullying". Many in addition face considerable safety and health risks, and are exposed to overtime pressures and increased work intensity and stress. However, workers in Croatia are vulnerable to high institutional deficits and structural *uncertainties* too: there are considerable institutional deficits in the protection of workers' legal rights, while many firms face restructuring, competition and globalization pressures, which might lead to changing employment and working conditions, whether the firm is large or very small. Concerning *institutional deficits*, weak law enforcement makes all employees vulnerable to unlawful employer behaviour. The capacity of the courts to effectively protect workers' material and other rights is low: thorough reform of the judicial system and proceedings are needed, on top of the EU's demands (EC, 2005).

The labour inspectorate is understaffed – in 2004–05 inspections were carried out at no more than 3 per cent of employers. In spite of an increase in the number of misdemeanours discovered (concerning illegal employment, over time, night work and so on), the *credibility of enforcement* before the courts is again low. (SI, 2006). *Particularly vulnerable* are the increasing number of workers who cannot rely on trade union support.

Serious institutional deficits, affecting many, were identified in education and training, health and safety and employment of minorities.

Structural risks are high too. There are strong pressures to continue with restructuring and reforms: both may strongly affect employment and working conditions in some sectors and/or firms.

Privatization remains incomplete. The state still controls some firms whose future prospects are highly uncertain. Typical examples are shipyards, some firms in the agricultural sector, steel-making and tourism. All this can only lead to further differentiation of working conditions and employment status, but also consolidate segmentation trends in the Croatian labour market.

Nevertheless, in many respects *trends of the "normalization"* of labour markets and work have set in in the 2000s. This has been supported by political normalization, solid economic growth and growing credibility, coupled with associated conditionalities of EU integration. This last factor will be important in coming years, too. However, *progress in working conditions* may be undermined by *the weaknesses of actors*: that is, unions (decreasing density, fragmentation and narrow agenda) and employers' associations (low coverage, questionable legitimacy), as well as by low government capacities and particularly low credibility of enforcement (for example, health and safety, VET, law enforcement). For too many this "normalization" is merely nominal, while real employment and working conditions have remained hard or even worsened. Closing this gap, reducing the chronic "attainment deficits" Croatian workers feel concerning the most valued aspects of their jobs (from adequate pay to job security) (see Maslić et al., 2005) is a profound challenge for all actors involved in employment and labour policy.

REALITY AT ENTERPRISE LEVEL: CASE STUDIES

Introduction

The first case study is of a partially rehabilitated, internally privatized former socialist construction giant, still large, with major imbalances in its workforce. The second is of a medium-sized privatized hotel firm, owned by an investment fund, in urgent need of finding effective responses to the industry's inherent seasonality and its own inefficiencies. Finally, the third case study looks at the diverse world of self-employment, with four stories illustrating its "in between": very long hours on the one hand and personal autonomy on the other, formality vs informality, a "good life" vs sheer survival.

The cases presented here are particularly indicative or illustrative of a number of trends and issues identified in the first part of the report. Both the construction and the hotel case studies illustrate the pressures towards flexibilization faced by many (particularly under-restructured) firms and their employees: (i) trends of increasing temporary (through fixed-term and/or seasonal employment) employment and/or sub-contracting; (ii) pressures to (re)organize working time flexibly, involving a lot of overtime and unsocial hours (including the retail firm not reported here); (iii) pressures to control (labour) costs. They also illustrate the precarious position of older workers, the low paid and particularly those who might be considered "surplus to requirements". In both cases (and similarly in the shipyard we visited), vulnerability is not distributed evenly: in all firms we find groups of workers who are particularly vulnerable (to low pay, risk of losing their job or permanent contract, work–life imbalances, difficult and/or degrading working conditions). All three cases (including small installation firms) point to difficulties in devising motivating pay systems, with overtime and/or hidden payments being used as "substitutes". They also illustrate major deficits concerning training and safety, as well as typical difficulties in relation to enterprise-level social dialogue, which is functional but limited.

In addition, the third case study shows the enormous pressures on the self-employed to work very long hours and even to engage in illegal practices in order to survive, exposing them to the risk of prosecution too.[7]

---

7. Due to space limitations two cases (one a troubled shipyard facing radical restructuring or imminent liquidation; and the other a foreign retail chain with very organized work processes, strong HRM but weak unions) are not reported here.

Croatia Case Study 1: Construction industry under reconstruction

The Croatian construction industry has been experiencing a *strong recovery* after its dramatic decline in the early 1990s. Its *organization* has changed. Before 1990 large firms dominated, while in the 1990s they experienced a collapse of the market and crises, including labour force reductions. The share of small firms has increased (7,394 employ 0 to 9 workers), as has the role of subcontracting and the role of "engineering" firms which organize financing and construction. Due to the market recovery, a number of privatized socialist "giants" have become profitable operations again, with much smaller workforces, but with greater reliance on cooperation. There are 22 firms employing 255–499, and 15 employing 500+ workers (CBS, ibid.).

Construction has become characterized by: (i) *lower wages* (14 per cent below average), coupled with a lot of "cash" and "hidden" payments; (ii) *changing labour conditions*: new employment is mostly fixed term (temporary contracts' share in 2001–04 was between 15 per cent in 2004 and 19.7 per cent in 2002 – CBS LFS, 2nd half); (iii) *a lot of unregistered/underreported work*: this is particularly associated with smaller firms; (iv) *difficult working conditions*: an above-average number of injuries; a lot of pressure for long hours and reorganization of working time due to seasonal characteristics of the industry and geographical location of construction sites; and (v) *difficulties on the labour market*: a number of occupations are lacking despite the large number of unemployed construction workers (most are "too old", unable to work any more, according to the president of the Construction Union of Croatia). This is putting pressure on firms to import workers from abroad (often "black-market"), but also to engage in internal training programmes (large firms).

Trade unions are present in large firms, but the share of non-unionized workers is increasing, as is the number of workers working in non-unionized firms. There is an industry collective agreement signed in 2001, last renewed in 2005 (talks on renewal are in progress): the Construction Union president explains that the construction branch of the Croatian Employers' Association sees this as a way of controlling dumping and unfair competition. Because CEA is not representative of the industry, the application of the collective agreement has been made mandatory by the relevant ministries. For some it is an excuse to avoid firm-based negotiations on an "in-house" collective agreement (as stressed by Ana, a legal advisor to the union).

This case study presents a large privatized firm in northern Croatia, engaged in many state-financed infrastructural projects, and specializing in the construction of tunnels, viaducts, hydrotechnical projects, and so on.

T&V: back from the ashes?

T&V was founded in 1995 from the "old" T&V, one of giants of the socialist era, with a good reputation both at home and abroad. A peak in employment was reached in 1980, at 12,800. Employment started to decrease, however, due to reorganization and market slowdown: by 1990–01 only 5,400 were employed. Of these, only 1,370 workers were registered as living in Croatia; the rest were mostly from Bosnia and Herzegovina and Serbia/Kosovo. With war and the federation's break-up many left ("disappeared", as Filip, the CEO, put it; in the course of two months 1,600 Serbs returned to Bosnia and Herzegovina). When the Croat–Muslim conflict in Bosnia started, about 600 workers from Bosnia left in just one month ("one day we received a call from a site in Split – no asphalter appeared at the job!"). By 1993, T&V had 3,770 employees. Privatization, war and economic depression contributed to further decreases. The new T&V was founded in 1995, but commenced operations in 1996. After the bankruptcy of the former T&V in 1997 equipment and 1,780 workers were transferred to the "new" T&V, but so were the company's debts (some HRK 500 million, i.e. EUR 68 million). At present – 8 March 2006 – it employs 1,912 (Hrvoje, personnel department manager).

With the recovery of the market, financial results have started to improve, and the normalization of business is pronounced (CEO). Annual revenue grew: by 2003 it was higher than annual expenses. In 2005 net annual profits were HRK 2.8 million (EUR 0.38 million). However, debts to suppliers and subcontractors are high and many are suing (Ana). This is why some fear that the threat of bankruptcy is not far away (Grga, president of the CU branch at T&V).

Coping with an unbalanced workforce structure: workers under pressure

At T&V there is a *core* of 1,437 employees (75 per cent of the total) *on permanent contracts* and 475 on fixed ones. The core was largely "inherited" from the old T&V and its structure is considered by the management as *unbalanced.*

First, too large a proportion of the workers are *not directly employed in construction*. There are 205 such workers (i.e. in different support service jobs in administration, commerce, accounting, cleaning, security, and so on) at the company headquarters, and 71 at building sites: there is a "*surplus*" of about 15–20 per cent, but almost all are on permanent contracts (Hrvoje). The company hopes to achieve reductions through "natural wastage" and not through redundancies (CEO). However, it seems that low pay, characteristic of many of them, may be part of the management's policy to encourage such workers to leave the firm or retire (Ana).

Secondly, concerning the *age structure*, T&V is "too old". This is why *the issue of older workers is particularly important.* "We encourage them to retire as soon as they qualify for retirement", says the CEO (hoping thus to achieve greater flexibility in employment – based on temporary contracts and on sub-contracting). Management would like some 400 older workers, many with impaired health, to retire quietly, without any stress: "we could declare them 'unfit' for the job, but we would rather go 'slow' – first we send them home (on minimum pay), then we offer them a severance payment if they take early retirement (in accordance with the industry collective agreement)", explains Hrvoje. Until 2000 this worked well (80–100 workers retired each year). However, due to the dramatic decrease in expected pensions, since 2000 there has been increasing pressure on the kind of workers in question to remain employed as long as the law allows (Nada, president of the Independent Union at T&V). In 2005 only 20 retired. Hrvoje complains about the unions' failure to cooperate on this issue: "they insist on workers' rights to remain employed until the legal limit, but they should help the firm too".

Thirdly, new employees are predominantly employed on fixed-term contracts: 475 with good prospects of renewal, and some with a chance of landing a permanent job; the great majority of them are construction workers on building sites. The exception is engineers – being in low supply they are offered permanent contracts from the start (Hrvoje).

There is a serious lack of some important skills (bar benders, carpenters, masons, and so on). Enrolment for such occupations at secondary schools is low, and offering stipends and other benefits to encourage young people to enrol has had little result. This is why T&V *hunts* for good workers working for small firms, but also *imports* them through a long-standing cooperation agreement with a firm in Bosnia and Herzegovina, explained Hrvoje. Around 500 workers *employed by sub-contracting firms* are also working on building sites. Great care is taken to make sure they have all the necessary papers. "There has never been black work"; it is in T&V's interest to prevent unfair competition, the CEO said.

T&V organizes *internal training* (6–12 months) for some occupations, offering those attending "internal certificates": "the best among them will be taken on permanently" (CEO). Ana, who is the union's representative on the Supervisory Board, is not content: there is no systematic personnel policy at T&V and training does not receive proper attention. In 2005, she pointed out, training costs were HRK 55,000 (EUR 7,432), a mere 0.08 per cent of total expenditure!

Wage system deficiencies might lead to conflicts

Wages are considered low by many, but they are slightly above the industry average. While it is hard to have higher wages when profitability is low and pressures for modernization strong, they are *never late*, points out the CEO. However, *wages are particularly low for some categories of workers* not directly engaged in construction ("they were the same 10 years ago", Nada complained). Ana talks about "discrimination" against such workers, who are mostly female: "this is a man's business – men are preferred", and points to the lack of solidarity in the firm. Generally, she finds the wage system, including systematization of jobs, inadequate, with a lot of discretionary behaviour.

On construction sites the situation is better and "workers are content": besides wages, they are entitled to various *benefits*: for example, allowances for living away from home, working conditions and travel. Together with *overtime*, they all get HRK 5–7,000 (EUR 675–945), says Grga, who, as a qualified locksmith, spends most of his time on different sites, and adds: "people fight for sites with a lot of benefits". Workers on tunnel projects earn, with all the benefits, about HRK 7–8,000 (EUR 945–1,080), 30 per cent higher than other types of construction, says Pavle, an engineer managing a tunnel construction site I visited. Moreover, they have a year-round building season. This is why they are considered an "elite", difficult to break into (Vjekoslav, a foreman).

However, says Grga, *not all recorded overtime is paid by management* ("there is no money ... there is overreporting, they say"). For example, out of 79,000 reported overtime hours in April 2006, some 7,000 were "denied" by management – workers are not always aware of these "cuts" *due to the low transparency of payment methods* (Mira, who works in technical logistics).

Working conditions: difficult work, longer hours and a decent family life impossible

Working conditions in the construction industry are *difficult and risky*, says Zorka, a safety manager at T&V (confirmed by interviewees at the tunnel building site). Few are able to work until retirement age; most take early retirement (president of the Construction Union of Croatia). Nikola, an experienced tunnel digger, now 52, was quite pessimistic: "I don't think I'll be able to make it until full (65) retirement age". Vjekoslav, a foreman, now 48, agrees: "It will be hard to make it, but I'll have to…"

With *technological change*, less physical work is needed than before (CEO). On the other hand, there is more pressure on workers: "everything goes faster", Vjekoslav says. "Nowadays it is easier with all this mechanization, but there are fewer of us in the tunnel", adds Nikola. *Stress is common*, but it is mainly caused by shortage of time, not by technology. Due to contract terms "foremen particularly put a lot of pressure on workers" (Zorka). *Work organization* may be more of a problem than the difficulty of the work per se, adds Ozren, a tunnel digger.

Longer hours (due to reorganization of working time and overtime) *are typical*, particularly in high season. To these pressures, workers respond with demands for higher wages and benefits, and for more free time too (CEO).

Overtime is the main problem. There is too much of it (between 9 per cent and 11 per cent, according to Hrvoje, but some claim more). It is not unusual for workers in winter time to do 30 or 40 hours overtime per month, and in high season 60 to 80, sometimes more than 100. Behind this is the insufficient number of workers at construction sites, involving great pressure on workers to work long hours and skip free days (Mira).

The formal working-time schedule at T&V reflects the *high seasonality*: it ranges from 138 hours in January (there is a 7-hour working day between November and February) to 200 in June (8-hour working day March to October); on Saturdays the working day is 6 hours. There are *different working-time models*: in tunnels workers typically work 10 days on, with an 11-hour working day in two shifts (7–19, and 19–7 with a one-hour break), and then have 5 days off. When they return, they also change shifts (Pavle). It seems that workers prefer it: "you can do a lot when you are at home for five days" (Ozren, married, two children). Mirko, a bulldozer operator, who had spent the last four weeks working without a free day, complains: "Normally, I go home once a month; it is costly (only one round trip is covered by the firm) and it is not worth it". In order to avoid too large an accumulation of overtime, sometimes workers will be compensated *with a free day* (many go home on Saturday afternoon and "we tell them then to stay over Monday too, particularly if rain is expected" – Hrvoje).

Maintaining a work–life balance is very difficult indeed. Many have spent years moving around from one construction site to another. As Vjekoslav put it jokingly: "If I hadn't been sent home to 'wait' (due to bad business conditions in 1988) I would never have got married at all". The workers I talked to, all married with children, did not complain too much. However, the price may be high: "I provide my family with money, but at home I am more of a guest", says Nikola (a tunnel digger, aged 52, married, two children) bitterly.

Significant safety and health risks

The number of injuries is "below the industry average" and decreasing (110 in 2000; 76 in 2002; 61 in 2004; and 35 in 2005); legal regulations are respected, says Zorka, responsible for *safety at T&V*. Importantly, she finds the state inspector's role in putting things in order as "very helpful". Nowadays, she adds, their role is pretty much "routine": "they know us, there are no problems with us".

All workers are trained in safe working practices. Union safety representatives are helpful yet involved less than they could be, says Nada. Foremen are responsible for applying safety rules. However, *the foremen are the main problem* (Zorka): they often "turn a blind eye" and rarely sanction workers for not respecting the rules (CEO). This is precisely what I witnessed – Pavle reacted only when I noticed workers without helmets in the tunnel: "it is difficult to sanction them", he said. And sometimes foremen pressurize workers into unsafe actions, complained Mirko, recalling one such event which had put him at great risk. Injuries do happen: "most are caused by a lack of care and concentration, and a refusal to use safety equipment", explains Zorka.

Health risks abound. Mandatory health checks are being organized. Still, 40–60 people are permanently on very long sick-leave, and many are "worn down" (even before their 50s) with chronic health problems (CEO). Not surprisingly, every year 4–5 workers take a disability pension (Nada). A number of older workers (Nikola, for example) expressed concerns over their future health and their ability to go on until full retirement age.

Social dialogue: disconnection between workers and their representatives
There are *two unions at T&V*. The Construction Union of Croatia emerged out of the old socialist one. In 1990 the Independent Union was founded in opposition to the "communist one" (Grga), but relations between unions are cooperative now, Nada and Grga agree. Nowadays, each has about 400 members at the company; membership is quite stable and people join mostly looking for benefits (Nada) (for example, bank loans), but also for greater security, adds Grga. Nada, who works in the financial department, points out that the IU is not active enough in getting new members: "the problem is that construction sites are dislocated and organizing union meetings there is difficult".

Cooperation between management and unions in the 1990s was central for the firm's survival. Social dialogue is still developed and "intensive", argues the CEO. Ana, from CUC, agrees: "Social dialogue functions well, management is responsive" and still "socially sensitive". However, *there is a potential for conflict* concerning the signing of the new firm-based collective agreement. In 2003 the management cancelled ("illegally", points out Ana) the existing firm-based collective agreement, claiming that the industry one applied (Ana). For more than a year "we have failed to agree on it" (Grga). Yet Ana does not see any prospect of collective action: not only do unions not have the capacity for collective action, but there is no real basis for it: wages are being paid regularly and the industry collective agreement is respected.

While trade unions are active at the company headquarters level and interested in T&V's future, as well as in protecting workers' material rights, it seems that their impact on working and living conditions has been limited. A part of this is workers' indifference, particularly those on fixed-term contracts. Union activities seem unappreciated by workers at the construction sites: some even had harsh words for union leaders (Pavle). Vjekoslav, a member of the union, is very critical: "their work is 'zero', only pieces of pork and chicken drumsticks on discount ... I don't see them taking any care and they rarely visit us on the sites, particularly distant ones" (similarly Nikola, who is a member of another union).

Conclusion: vulnerable workers, but vulnerable T&V too

Three groups at T&V may be identified as particularly vulnerable. These are:

1. Older workers: some 400 are under pressure to retire early. Even if they work up to the legal age limit they may expect very low pensions and increased poverty risk. Due to harsh working and living conditions, many are vulnerable to deteriorating health, even disability. In case of radical restructuring they will be the prime target for lay-offs.
2. It may be expected that the number and share of those employed on fixed-term contracts will increase, as will T&V's reliance on sub-contracting, in pursuit of more flexibility. They will be particularly vulnerable to worsening market conditions: it is hard to believe that the current boom in state investment will last for long.
3. Many workers not directly involved in construction activities are vulnerable to low pay. If pressure to restructure the workforce becomes stronger, they may become a prime target, too.

Many workers face *major difficulties finding a balance between work and family life*. For many, spending years moving from one site to another makes it impossible to have a decent family life. Even good earnings can hardly compensate for that.

Privatization remains unfinished, too. If the construction boom has provided T&V with some stability, its changed ownership structure (bringing in new managers, certainly less "sensitive" to social concerns and the legacy of the "old" T&V than the current ones, and more concerned about efficiency) might have a significant impact on employees and their working conditions, as well as on social dialogue. Recent dealing in T&V shares indicates that such changes are in the making. In addition, T&V's financial results and liabilities do not make for a rosy picture. Being too dependent on state investments, and with many internal weaknesses, T&V is still not able to ensure its future in global markets. There is still a long way to go to ensure its long-term viability.

Croatia Case Study 2: How to adapt to seasonality?

Croatia is a tourist country. The tourist industry has undergone a lot of restructuring and reorganization due to the privatization of large socialist enterprises and the entry of numerous small firms, as well as foreign investors. It – Dalmatia in particular – suffered gravely from the civil war and political instabilities in the 1990s. The tourist industry is characterized by: *low wages*, *unregistered workers*, *changing working conditions*, and *major labour market difficulties, leading to increasing "importation" of workers from abroad.* Another major characteristic of the industry is its *seasonality*, which puts the pressure on for employment flexibilization. The share of fixed-term contracts is high and on the increase (7.1 per cent in 2000 rising to 15.5 per cent in 2004 – the national average in 2004 was 10.4 per cent), but the share of seasonal contracts is high, too (8.2 per cent in 2000 and 9.5 per cent in 2004; with the national average for 2004 being only 1.2 per cent) (CBS-LFS, 2nd half).

The case presented here focuses on the ways in which a privatized hotel company (particularly its largest hotel, the "Sea Star") from Dalmatia is reorganizing its labour force and work organization.

CBSH, a traditional tourist company shaken by depression and ownership changes

CBSH d.d. is located in a beautiful small town on the island of Dalmatia with a long tradition of tourism.

The company operates four hotels, four apartment blocks and one trailer camp. It has been central to the area's tourist development and provides secure employment for the islanders. A skilled local labour force is provided by the island's secondary schools. However, like many others it suffered heavily from the depression caused by the war in the early 1990s. Chronic losses and underinvestment ensued. In 1993–2005, despite the return of the tourists in the late 1990s, annual losses ranged between HRK 4.6 and 14 million (EUR 0.6–1.9 million).

After privatization in 1994, 500 small shareholders subscribed to some 30 per cent of the shares at a discount; the rest remained with the state funds. Through voucher privatization the investment funds acquired a majority – by February 2002 one of them had 79 per cent of CBSH. Lupus d.d., the fund's legal successor, now owns 85 per cent, remaining small shareholders 8 per cent, and the rest is in state hands. This has caused many worries in the town concerning the future of the hotels and local employment.

Employment status: new contracts mainly seasonal?

Two trends characterize the restructuring of employment at CBSH: (i) the decrease in the number of permanent employees, and (ii) the increase in the number of seasonally employed. Table 3.4 shows that 2005 was the first year in which the seasonally employed prevailed, a trend that continued into 2006.

Table 3.4 Employment at CBSH, 1990–2005

	1990	1992	1994	1995	1996	1998	2000	2001	2002	2003	2004	2005
Permanent Dec. 31	251	213	195	181	180	190	189	186	184	176	171	137
Seasonal	n.a.	0	32	0	87	139	160	157	138	136	137	152

In 2004 a redundancy programme was implemented due to restructuring (involving 35 workers), and the reliance on seasonal employment became a "strategic orientation". Lupus's managers firmly believe that there is overemployment of employees on permanent contracts and want to reduce it even more (Marica, a personnel manager).

Concerning permanent employees, surpluses (for example, of waiters, mostly due to organizational changes, such as the 2004 introduction of self-service around a "smorgasbord") coexist with deficits (for example, for cooks), explains Marica. A further problem is the *unfavourable age structure*. "We are old", says Dinko, a hotel manager. In 2004, 71 per cent were over 45, though in 2005, after the above-mentioned reductions, this was "corrected" to 65 per cent. Long tenure dominates: out of 137, 114 have been with the firm more than 20 years.

On the other hand, *new employment is predominantly seasonal*. Some start in May, most come in June, and the peak is in July and August. The season ends in October. Despite the low pay, many return the next season. The company uses the services of employment offices (Dinko). Seasonal employees receive a contract which terminates "at the end of the tourist season", which in practice may often lead to unfair dismissals: "you are not needed any more, don't come tomorrow" (Marica).

Lack of policy on education

While the *educational structure* is quite favourable – 109 out of 137 have secondary or higher education – very little, and not systematically, is being done by the management about further education and training. It seems that the motivation for this is low on both sides, Marica and Dinko agree. The *sustainability of the labour force* is questionable: the number of young people signing up as cooks or waiters is decreasing, Those finishing school are employed on a seasonal basis only, adds Marica, but the incentives of seasonal employees to study are much lower, while the management has little incentive to invest in their training.

Unmotivating wages: labour costs versus work quality

The new owner argues that wages are too high, yet they are below the industry average, explains Marica. For about 70 per cent of the staff the full wage (based on wage rates) is less than HRK 4,000 (EUR 540). The others receive mostly between HRK 4,000 (EUR 540) and HRK 4,500 (EUR 608). Particularly vulnerable to low pay are those who depend entirely on their wages to make a living (some 20 to 30 per cent, according to Stipe, president of the union at CBSH), and who don't accumulate enough overtime in high season. The wage system does not encourage good work. However, wages are at least paid regularly, though often with 5–10 days' delay (this is a problem, particularly for those without additional incomes, stresses Stipe). Most importantly, even if workers do not work all year round, wages are paid all year round, but reduced to a minimum for the period (so-called "waiting") not covered by overtime hours accumulated during the working season (around HRK 1,700/EUR 230). One major motivation to reduce permanent employment and substitute it with seasonal employment is the wage costs of the permanently employed, which are now above 45 per cent of total costs. However, quality of work is likely to suffer (particularly in the kitchen), adds Dinko (an experienced hotel manager).

Most interviewees find their wages insufficient ("hardly enough to survive", as Braco, a waiter, put it) and are highly dependent on other sources of income. Some occasionally moonlight (doing different occasional jobs: Stipe, electrical installation; Braco, small electrical jobs, bringing him just a couple of hundred HRK); some rent rooms or apartment(s) to tourists (like Ivka, a chambermaid, and Vicko, a chief cook, whose additional income, including agricultural work, is close to his wage), some have additional income from agriculture (like Miko, a hotel restaurant manager), and some have a plot of land (Braco). Marin, a restaurant manager, does all three. This is not that rare on the island, which has a tradition of agriculture and tourism, and booming (re)construction. Particularly vulnerable are those who depend entirely on their CBSH wage (like Nela, a waitress, who earns about HRK 3,000/EUR 405, but only HRK 1,700/EUR 230 while "waiting"), even when they enjoy higher pay, as Marica does. Vulnerability to low pay is particularly high in the winter, explains Stipe, when the hotels are closed.

Working time: conditional on the season
As explained by Marica, in January and February only management and a few others work; in March preparations for the tourist season start, involving some 100 workers; by 15 May everyone is working. By 1 October staff begin to be laid off as hotels begin to close down; in November and December annual vacations and free days are taken. Workers' pay in February and March will greatly depend on the number of overtime hours they worked in high season.

For example, the most recent *agreement on working time allocation*, signed between management and the employee council, stipulates that for 255 workers between 1 June and 31 October the average working week is 56 hours. Hours worked above 40 during that period are not considered "overtime" but transferred to the November–May period, when workers use their free days and vacations or work less than full time. However, although many do more than 60 hours per week in high season without taking free days (these are taken after the season ends), Marica and Miko explain, it is rare that anyone does enough hours to fully "cover" the annual working fund. This leads to the curious (not existing in law but quite common in the industry) institution of "waiting", which for most people lasts between 30 and 60 days. During that period they receive the minimum wage only. *There is no overtime: permanent employees at CBSH are underemployed!* For the new owner this constitutes substantial proof that a further reduction in permanent employment is needed.

Workload and intensity: unevenly distributed

Work intensity is unevenly distributed, not only through the year ("in high season you go nuts, in winter there's only lethargy…", Stipe), but among jobs. Particularly vulnerable are *chambermaids*: permanent employees are quite old, but the maids' workload has increased (Marica). Ivka, a chambermaid aged 52, complained about that: while in the 1980s there were 15 rooms each, now it is 23; particularly stressful are the days on which tourist agency guests leave/arrive, adds Lina. Additional stress is caused by low supplies of towels and linen ("guests are not always understanding", Ivka). Quality of work suffers: "cleaners and chambermaids are now mostly seasonal – local women don't want to take these jobs" (Ivka). Lack of qualified personnel affects the *kitchen* in particular: "I am under stress, it is too demanding, and there are only a couple of us who are qualified", complains Vicko (a chief cook, aged 50 – he believes he will have to take early retirement). The kitchen is built to handle 350–400 meals, but regularly more than 500, and occasionally more than 700 meals have to be prepared. On the other hand, many waiters work two shifts a day (like Nela, as do restaurant managers Marin and Miko), or face great uncertainty concerning the organization of working time ("I can't plan a day in advance", says Braco, adding, "the management's savings on labour are putting increasing pressure on me"). Two-shift work particularly hurts those living in villages (as Nela does). Miko manages the hotel's restaurants and bars and feels a lot of stress (particularly when faced with "emergencies", which are common).

Work safety: workers buying their equipment themselves

As far as *work safety* is concerned, it is not only that safety at work has a very low priority at CBSH (no one is responsible for it and there is no systematic approach, according to Miko and Stipe), among both management and employees, but my interviewees complained about not being provided with the necessary equipment (Miko), and being forced to buy it themselves. Ivka said, "We [maids] don't use gloves, it's too expensive for the firm" and her apron looked old and distressed. However, Lina uses gloves provided by the firm and pointing out that "older workers don't use them"; Braco said, "We [waiters] last received a uniform in 1996; we buy everything ourselves"). Vicko emphasizes that "seasonal workers are not trained for safe work". Stipe, who manages laundry services, complains, "women in the laundry don't have protective clothes".

Deskilling and degradation of work

Permanent employees remember with nostalgia a time when their work made them proud of their skills. The impact of work reorganization has been felt most strongly by waiters: the introduction of self-service around a "smorgasbord" in 2004 "turned us into cleaners, collecting dirty dishes from the tables" (Braco); "We lost our trade, and we are not indifferent to this", says Nela, adding "there is little we can teach young waiters nowadays". Those working in hotel restaurants and bars seem frustrated by the guests too, who "order much less than they used to" (Marin and Nela). For waiters it means much less income from tips, adds Braco (HRK 300/EUR 40 a month maximum, even in high season). On the other hand, this reorganization has imposed a much heavier workload on cooks (responsible now for bringing food to the long table and replenishing it), says Vicko, who also complains of reduced creativity. In addition, permanent employees were almost in unison in their opinion that increased reliance on seasonal work is endangering quality.

Social dialogue: powerless collective agreement and no capacity for collective action

There is one union in the firm, with 90 members (formerly there were more members, but more employees too, says Stipe, the union's president since 1993). The first firm-based collective agreement was signed in 1998 and renewed in 2003 according to the industry one. It has been respected except on provisions on "material rights" (children's gifts, Christmas and vacation bonuses, as well as bonuses for years of service): "there is no money, they say", he explains. Material rights have not been respected for years. This was confirmed in my interviews with all permanent employees (for example, Nela, 28 years at the hotel, recalls receiving her last bonus for years of service a very long time ago: for 10 years' service). Delays are also significant (more than one year) in recovering the travel costs employees are entitled to: those coming from villages (and some do so twice a day, like Nela) are particularly hard hit (Nela often walks and/or hitch-hikes: "what they give me covers about one third of the real costs").

In 2003 the union signed – under management pressure – a temporary agreement on reducing the basic wage ("due to business difficulties"), explains Miko who has been president of the Employees' Council for eight years. This has caused a significant lag in relation to the industry's basic wage. However, this "temporary measure has lasted three years", says Marica bitterly. "My wage is about HRK 400/EUR 54 lower than it should be if the industry's collective agreement was applied, and this is what we are now asking for", adds Stipe. Yet the management refuses: "There is no money". Typically, they add: "You work only seven months but receive pay for twelve – you should be happy with what you get" (Marica). However, negotiations on the basic wage are still going on.

The union is not considering collective action. There is great identification with the firm, particularly on the part of workers. Stipe explains: "I am against it, it hurts the firm and then it hurts me; we are more loyal to the firm than the owners are, and management is playing on our loyalty." Similarly, Miko: "Legally we could go on strike, but we would be hurt the most." Adds Marica: "There is no capacity for collective action, people feel that the firm is some- how their own." But another problem is fear: "Now we are too afraid, we are too old for a new start" (Nela). "It is hard to find a job on the island", adds Braco. Finally, "many have loans to repay, this is why they are silent" (Miko).

However, social dialogue is not dead at CBSH; there are some talks on wages, and surplus employment was dealt with in an orderly way: the Employees' Council was involved (Miko). Vicko is a member of the Employees' Council: "We are not satisfied, but the doors are not closed to us and we have realized some, if minimal, demands." He is not the only one who is aware of the fact that insisting on rights might lead to the loss of what is being received now. "Compromise in order to survive … is needed" (Vicko). Marica, however, thinks that workers are not considered true social partners by management; social dialogue is not active and ongoing, but confined to particular occasions.

Conclusion – what lies in the future?
CBSH is a curious mixture of old socialism and brute capitalism. Both man- agers and owners, on the one hand, and employees on the other share the same opinion: it cannot go on like this for long, the firm is poorly managed, with underinvestment, with a total absence of care for the training and education of its employees; it is hardly viable as it is. There is great uncertainty and fear for the firm's future. Without major investment in hotel renewal there is no future for CBSH. Will Lupus d.d. sell it or take a long-term interest in the tourist business, for which there are recent signs but no firm commitments (Dinko)? However, according to trends visible in many other tourist firms, radical changes in employment and working practices can only continue. Will they lead towards further flexibilization of employment and deskilling of most jobs, as is happening at CBSH, or towards product and employee upgrades (examples of both are present in Croatia)? Dependence on seasonal employ- ment may also lead to the adoption of permanent seasonal employment which would certainly increase motivation for training seasonal employees on both sides. STUH (Tourism and Services Union of Croatia) seems very interested in this. (*Seasonal employment*, on www.ssuth.hr).

Besides this general uncertainty about CBSH's future (present in many other Croatian firms), this case particularly points to the precarious position of (i) the seasonally employed and/or the low paid, particularly those who cannot increase their security and living standards through additional activities – fortunately available to many in the particular local economy; and of (ii) older workers with long tenure who are vulnerable to becoming redundant, as well as to the loss of their present status, and to very low pensions. In addition, the future for young people on the island who might consider studying for various hotel-related occupations and/or consider looking for employment in the island's hotel industry will certainly bring less security of employment than their parents enjoyed: the favoured solution to the inherent seasonality of business is temporary employment, and this is what they will most likely be looking at. Finally, typical weaknesses in social dialogue, and management's only partial respect for the collective agreement, as found in many firms in Croatia, are certainly hurting all those employed at CBSH. While their capacity for collective action is low, their loyalty to "their" firm is still surprisingly high.

Croatia Case Study 3: Individual stories in the neighbourhood – is small really beautiful?

As seen in the first part of this chapter, the *proportion of self-employed* is growing. As LFS data show, the full-time self-employed usually put in more weekly hours in their job (about 47 hours per week in 2004) than full-time employees (about 41.5). There is also a large number (although decreasing in 1998–2002, from 72,000 to 45,000 (Crnković-Pozaić, 2005)) of *multiple job holders*, many with *self-employment as a second job*, often unregistered.

A recent study (under the GEM project) of Croatian entrepreneurship shows that, besides the growth of the SME sector in terms of number of firms and total employment, the Total Entrepreneurial Activity index (TEA) is also growing, meaning that the share of those who in the last three months decided to start their own business, or who have active businesses less than 42 months, but more than 3 months old, is increasing. In 2002 it was 3.62; in 2003, 2.56; in 2004, 3.74; but in 2005, 6.11, thus moving Croatia from the bottom of the annual sample (30 or more countries) to the middle. However, the dominant contribution (which puts Croatia last among 35 countries – the only one whose TEA "necessity" is greater than its TEA "opportunity") comes from an increase in "necessity" entrepreneurship rather than in the "opportunity" kind: self-employment, in other words, is increasingly being accepted as a strategy for coping with unemployment and the difficulties of employment. On the good side, while Croatian SMEs are typically very small, the share of those who expect employment in their firms to grow over the next year is increasing (Singer et al., 2006).

The business landscape of firms serving people's everyday needs in goods and services has dramatically changed, including the mushrooming of small businesses, legal and illegal, serving local needs. Many are failing, but new ones are appearing. They tend to be strongly embedded in local communities. This case study presents a typical "neighbourhood" in an eastern Croatian town, based on four interviews carried out with owners of small businesses, only one of whom serves a larger market.

Case 1: How much can one work?

Ivan, aged 49, who completed secondary school, owns a small shop in the apartment building where he lives, selling newspapers, tobacco, stationery, toys, books and everything for school and providing photocopying services. In 1992, when he returned from the war and found his earlier job taken, he decided to strike out on his own. He had his wife's support, though she also said: "I hope you know what you're doing, you've got two children to take care of." After a "troublesome start", business picked up: in 1994 he opened another shop, but it soon closed (again, he was drafted and "there was nobody to take care of it"). Drafted for the third time, 1995 was again a difficult year: he missed the beginning of the school year when his business is normally at its best. After 1996 his business stabilized, but again it is getting "worse" due to the spread of large shopping centres and the fall in cigarette sales caused by the growth of illegal trade.

In 1995 he employed a first employee, and in 1996 a second – Nena. After one left in 2000, only one remains ("I couldn't afford two anymore"). Ivan is a very concerned employer: Nena has permanent employment, no overtime and no work on weekends; all her rights according to the industry collective agreement are respected. She receives modest but comparable pay (with all contributions paid regularly): HRK 2,680 (EUR 362), recently increased to HRK 3,100 (EUR 419). While she enjoyed two maternity leaves, Ivan was on his own, working even harder than usual. *And that is already a lot.*

The shop is open Monday to Saturday from 7.00 to 21.00, and on Sundays from 8.00 to 12.00. Normally, Ivan is there at 6.30 am to receive the newspapers and switch on the copying machines. At 7.00 he opens, between 8.00 and 9.00 is "coffee time" (while working together with Nena). Then he leaves – to make payments, visit suppliers and make new orders; at around 10.00 he eats his breakfast at the shop. At 14.00 he goes up to his apartment to have lunch and get some rest. At 15.00 Nena leaves and he is back on his own until 21.00 (sometimes longer). He works Sundays too – "because of the neighbours, so they can have their newspapers" – he is afraid of losing "loyal customers". However, he was happy during the short period when Sunday opening was forbidden and he is looking forward to having it prohibited again. But this is not all. His mother, an old but still active lady, runs a traditional family craft business, established in 1890, at a small nearby town: the business has a lot to do with the local Christian shrine. Ivan goes there to help her some 15 Sundays a year (from 15.00–20.00) and the whole day on three major holidays. When asked about annual leave, he laughed: "Not a day off in the last five years!"

Does this amount of work pay? *Hardly in monetary terms*: the shop's annual net profit (he uses an accountant) is between EUR 6,000 and EUR 7,500 – that is, between HRK 3,700 and HRK 4,600 (EUR 500–622) a month for around 90 hours' work a week. What about his *work–life balance*? Ivan has two sons: one recently graduated and is in his first job; another is still at university. Despite the fact that his wife is also employed (and works almost every Saturday), he thinks that it is worth it: "The children have grown up in a family where they have learned that you have to work hard." However, he has spent less time than he would have liked with his children.

He is overworked, "permanently tired" (worrying his friends), and recently under stress too – due to suppliers changing terms at the same time as "it is becoming increasingly difficult to sell the stuff". *Ivan still likes his job*: "I like this contact with people" (many stop by to have a chat; he is the best informed person around). However, he is considering a change: "I can't go on like this for much longer, and I don't want to"; but he is not looking to become an employee again. He is thinking of opening a used book shop instead, but "space is a problem" (a more central, and so more expensive location is needed).

Case 2: Surviving on the borderline

Milan, in his fifties, runs a video rental shop, established in 1989. Since 2000 he has been a single father of three children (two of school age, the third older but barely employable due to ill health). His former wife left a well-paid job at the hospital to start a business ("I would never have done that; I prefer paid jobs"). The early 1990s were a "golden age" for business: "pirates" who did not respect copyrights dominated. In 1992 he opened a second shop and in 1993 a third. However, only the original one is still in business: due to stricter regulation and enforcement of copyrights, costs are increasing. On the other hand, people "burn DVDs, buy burned DVDs; business is much worse than it was five years ago". This has forced him to rent out part of his business space (which he owns) for another use.

All this is reflected in his workload, which has increased. In his shop(s) he used to have young employees, employed on student contracts (through the student employment service); since 2003 he has not been able to afford this and he is on his own. This means a ten-hour working day (from 12.00 to 22.00), every day, including holidays: some 70 hours a week. Like Ivan, he has not had a day off since 2000.

His business is still dependent on combining regular, copyrighted material with pirated (50:50): "I couldn't survive without it." After some "good times", when he enjoyed high earnings (between HRK 15,000 and HRK 20,000 a month, i.e. between EUR 2,027 and EUR 2,703), in the last couple of years he has been earning much less: some HRK 3,000–4,000 (EUR 405–540) for rentals and HRK 1,000–1,500 (EUR 135–203) for selling used videos and DVDs. In addition, he receives HRK 3,000 (EUR 405) for renting the space. His earnings hardly suffice to cover all family needs – he is the sole provider. To help the family budget he formally quit the job at his firm (now registered in his brother's name) and registered as unemployed (receiving an additional HRK 1,000, i.e. EUR 135). He is working for his brother illegally.

He feels *under permanent stress*, due to both "not working according to the rules, there is always the fear of inspections", and to the pressure of family duties: *it is hard to balance work and family life.* He is doing his best: "In the morning I clean, I cook … but I can't be with them enough." His quality of life is suffering: "I am not going out, I don't see my friends…". Milan likes the job, he loves discussing movies but he feels that he is "losing his drive". He is quite depressed: "After years of the good life, I found myself threatened with poverty." He does not see a future in his shop – he is considering selling the business space and taking a paid job (but is it realistic with his age and skills?) and he dreams of getting some state-owned land and farming.

Case 3: Reaching into the underground

Joško, aged 40, is employed at a printing company. In addition, he runs an unregistered garage where he does small repairs. He is a qualified auto-electrician but after joining his present company he first requalified as a graphics technician, and then enrolled at a graphics college (both at the firm's expense).

After five years of paid work, in 1989 he opened an auto-electric repair shop. In 1998 he had to close down ("rent and other costs were too high"). Very long hours were routine, as they were for the next two years while he was a truck driver for a transport firm ("often I would do 1,500 km without a proper break"). In 2001, through a connection of his father, he landed his present job. He works shifts for seven days at a stretch, followed by two free days. However, if somebody is absent – and this often happens – he works for 15 or even more days without a day off (in May he had only one free day). He accumulates a lot of overtime (up to 80 hours): only part of it (some 40 hours) is paid, and the rest is transferred to free days, which "I can hardly ever use". He is exposed to very intensive and noisy work, with a lot of operations to perform. His starting pay was HRK 3,200 (EUR 432), rising to HRK 4,200 (EUR 568) in September 2005; with overtime it comes to HRK 4,500 (EUR

608) (including travel costs). He is repaying a loan for his current, very modest apartment: HRK 1,500 (EUR 203) per month.

However, *his pay is far from meeting the family needs*. He *urgently needs additional income*: "I have to, my wife is unemployed." When their son was born (nine years ago) his wife – a hairdresser by profession – had to close down her shop in order to take care of the boy who needed special care after the birth. He is well now, but she is registered as unemployed, doing occasional cleaning and ironing at neighbouring homes (which bring her some HRK 400–500 per month, i.e. EUR 54–68). Recently, she started working illegally in the kitchen of a neighbouring pizzeria – "the owner is happy with her, we hope she'll get legalized". When he moved to the present neighbourhood five years ago, he started doing small repairs for his neighbours and some "old" customers from the auto-electric repair business in his garage. He works there almost every day: from one to eight hours ("it depends…"), which brings him some HRK 1,000–1,500 (EUR 135–203) per month. But he also enjoys it: often he does not charge his neighbours for smaller jobs. Yet, some people are unhappy about having this kind of business in their neighbourhood: on a couple of occasions, the police were called in, but nothing happened: "It was always my mum's or my dad's, or my friend's car … they couldn't do a thing."

On average, Joško works between 65 and 70 hours a week. Due to shift work, his sleep is disturbed: "I cannot get enough, I am chronically tired, and dependent on coffee." *He is thinking of making a major change*. He is looking for a small house with its own work space out of the city. He would like to get back to auto repairs ("there will always be cars to fix…") but he does not want to rent business space again. However, his immediate future is his present employment – under his contract he must stay with the firm for the next three years: "they paid for my qualifications and training." At least for the time being, unregistered work in his garage will be his everyday routine.

Case 4: Somewhere "in-between"

C&H was founded in 1996: it installs heating and air-conditioning systems. Mladen is a mechanical engineer, aged 56. After years of working for a government ministry, and after a lot of "in-fighting", he decided to go out on his own: "It was my last chance to see what I can do with my knowledge." An important factor in his decision was that his wife has secure employment ("our insurance policy") – still, "she wanted to kill me".

The firm started with two additional employees, doing small jobs in apartments and family houses. Nowadays they number 15: 12 workers are employed directly, organized in six teams of two (one is a qualified and certified welder, another is his assistant, either fresh from school or just "trained"), there is one salesperson, assisting him in management tasks too, and one book-keeper who also performs secretarial duties.

At the beginning, everyone was employed on a permanent contract, but later shifted to fixed ones. Now six have permanent contracts (mostly skilled "craftsmen"). The increased role of fixed employment is due to the "variability" of the market and uncertainty that he will always be able to find enough business to keep everyone busy.

Working time at C&H is formally organized on the basis of an 8-hour day, 40 hours a week. However, due to the specific demands of contractors or due to the organization of construction site processes ("which we are just one part of"), overtime work, work on Saturdays, and even Sundays, is common: typically about 10 per cent of work is overtime (20 per cent in high season).

Registered wages are quite low, though a little above the national average for Mladen and his assistant (HRK 4,700/EUR 635), lower for skilled workers (HRK 4,000/EUR 540), and HRK 2,200–2,500 (EUR 297–338) for their assistants. With overtime and working Saturdays "craftsmen" can make up to HRK 6,000 (EUR 810). Part of that payment is usually *"in cash"*, that is, not registered. However, "small jobs are often paid in cash, which makes it possible to pay workers in cash too". *On average, unregistered cash payments are no more than 20 per cent above the contracted wage.* Mladen argues that C&H is atypical because in the installation business, where small firms dominate, the share of cash payments tends to be much greater. C&H is somewhere "between a small and a medium-sized firm", and thus dependent for its survival on getting contracts for larger projects where everything is done "by the book". Small jobs (typically done by very small firms) only "fill the gaps".

Very often, C&H cooperates with some larger firm (a construction or engineering firm with the contract for the whole project with an investor): out of ten contracts, only one is C&H's own. This is a significant hindrance; often "we face a construction mafia", complains Mladen (they are very late with payments, they find every possible reason to pay less than the contracted amount, they "blackmail us"). On the other hand, small firms are fighting "over the bones", "we are too small to organize ourselves". Faced with an increase in demand, Mladen employs additional workers. Usually, they are people with their own small firm or registered craftsmen – often paid "in cash" (for example, when renovating an apartment, which C&H often does, they need a plumber's services or an electrician's).

Mladen is a friendly person, he likes to develop cooperative relations with employees: "We start our day in a nearby café", he explains, "and then we first discuss daily plans: I like us all to think aloud, but mine is the last word." He believes that his employees have great esteem for his atypical managerial style. In ten years, only two have left: one started his own business ("I helped him with that, and we cooperate)", another (young one) left for better pay.

So far C&H has been financially successful, providing its employees with regular pay but its owner with little profit. Mladen is facing a major *dilemma*: either to increase employment (by three teams) and become a "larger firm doing large jobs only", or to halve current employment and do small jobs only. The irony is that by growing it is more difficult to make money "for yourself": it is "difficult to get paid", but "I don't like to offer bribes". (Offering bribes to get contracted payments for jobs done is widespread for smaller firms: such complaints are not often voiced publicly but I have often heard them made privately by small entrepreneurs.) By reducing operations, the risks are decreased and potential for cash payment is increased: with much less effort "I might have the same profit but earn more". However, while the "risks of growth are enormous", Mladen enjoys doing large complicated projects: "I am a mechanical engineer", and when the whole installation works "I am impressed with myself, this is something which pushes me forward."

Long hours have become Mladen's routine. Before, he was on a regular 8 hours; now he is at work from 8.00 to 18.00, often works at home ("after dinner", for example, making calculations), on Saturdays from 8.00–14.00 he does his paperwork, and sometimes on Sundays he goes to see a potential work site. All this has brought him *a lot of stress*. It is related "to the environment" (investors, contractors, pressure to pay taxes on time – if not, "they block my account, while I have to wait for ages to get paid for jobs done"). His heart condition has dramatically deteriorated ("80 per cent of it was the result of running a business") so that in 2005 he had heart surgery and three by-passes. Now he feels much better, but can't quit smoking.

But he is very content: "I am happy, my expectations are fulfilled". This provides him with a "normal life" and "I immensely enjoy, like a kid, the engineering part of it". He believes that he is not paying a big price in his private life. He has his family's support ("and the children are grown up"). While he is always "on the road", his wife has quite an orderly working life: this brings some conflicts: "she would like to go out in the evening, and I am 'dead tired', I prefer to stay at home."

Conclusion

While these four cases shouldn't be taken as "representative", they certainly illustrate the enormous difficulties faced by the self-employed and small firms, and the multiple vulnerabilities they typically face. Many find it problematic to meet their families' needs (as Milan and Joško do), pushing them to work very long hours (all four of them) and multiply activities (Joško), depriving them of sleep and rest (as Ivan and Joško complained), not to mention holidays with their families for whom they provide a livelihood (even a decent one, as Mladen does), but not enough of their time (Milan, a single father, in particular finds it difficult to maintain good work–life balance). They also illustrate the enormous pressure the self-employed feel from competition – where sheer survival is difficult without a lot of work (as Ivan, Milan and Mladen feel), but also without crossing the borderline of regularity and descending into unregistered (Joško) and even illegal activities (Milan and Mladen). Even if all four enjoy what they are doing, and would not prefer paid employment to self-employment (or find themselves too old to get a paid job – as Milan does) the pressure to survive is asking too much of them: some of them feel very tired (Ivan, Milan, but Joško too), under the stress (Milan and Mladen) and find their health deteriorating (Mladen), or in jeopardy (Ivan); and some are looking to change their way of life (Ivan, Joško and Milan). However, this may be very difficult to accomplish. If self-employment in Croatia is a major survival strategy, but also a source of satisfaction, for many it is a hard choice, full of risks and associated vulnerabilities.

REFERENCES

Analiza. 2004. *Analiza učinaka odredaba Direktiva EU o zaštiti na radu* [An analysis of the effects of EU directives on safety at work]. Ministry of Economy, Labour and Social Care, mimeo.

Babić, Z. 2005. Participation rates and investment in education in Croatia. *Croatian Economic Survey*, No. 8, pp. 81–105.

Baloban, S., and G. Črpić (eds). 2005. *Kultura nedjelje i dostojanstvo radnika* [The culture of Sunday and workers' dignity]. Zagreb: Centar za promicanje socijalnog nauka Crkve i Kršćanska sadašnjost.

Bocksteins, H., and S. Vermuijten. 2005. *Analysis of the role and further development of trade unions in the Balkans*. Final Report, European Commission (October).

Bodiroga-Vukobrat, N. 2005. Mobbing uvrstiti među profesionalne bolesti [To include bullying among occupational hazards] (interview), *Vjesnik* (13 March).

CBS (Central Bureau of Statistics) SR. 2006. *Zaposlenost i plaće u 2005* [Employment and wages in 2005], *Statističko izvješće* 1307. Zagreb.

CBS SY, *Statistical Yearbook*. Zagreb, various years.

CES AB, *Annual Bulletins*. Croatian Employment Service, various years.

Cimeša, M., and D. Marinković Drača. 2002. *Socijalni dijalog u Hrvatskoj* [Social dialogue in Croatia]. Research supported by the European Commission, SSSH: Zagreb (June).

Crnković-Pozaić, S. 2005. *Flexibility and security in the labour market: Croatia's experience*. Flexicurity paper 2004/1, Budapest: International Labour Office.

———. 2006a. *Croatia: trends on the labour market*. Flexicurity project. Budapest: International Labour Office.

———. 2006b. The transition countries – flexible and jobless. Presentation, at www.cepor.hr.

Čučković, N., and W. Bartlett. 2006. Entrepreneurship and competitiveness: The Europeanization of SME policy in Croatia. *Journal of Southeast European and Black Sea Studies*, 6 (4).

Dečković-Vukres, V., together with K. Rutar-Kožul and M. Hemen. 2005. *Ozljede na radu i profesionalne bolesti u Hrvatskoj 2004. godine* [Work injuries and professional diseases in Croatia in 2004]. Zagreb: Hrvatski zavod za javno zdravstvo – služba za socijalnu medicinu, Odjel za medicinu rada.

————. 2006. *Ozljede na radu i profesionalne bolesti u Hrvatskoj 2005. godine* [Work injuries and professional diseases in Croatia in 2005]. Zagreb: Hrvatski zavod za javno zdravstvo – služba za socijalnu medicinu, Odjel za medicinu rada.

European Commission. 2005. *Croatia: 2005 Progress Report* (November). Brussels.

ETF (European Training Foundation). 2003. *Initial vocational education and training in the Republic of Croatia – assessment and options for development.* Report by the international peer review team, European Training Foundation, March.

Franičević, V. 2002. Politička i moralna ekonomija hrvatske tranzicije [Political and moral economy of Croatian transition]. *Politička misao*, 39/1, pp. 3–34.

————. 2005. Poduzetništvo i ekonomski rast u hrvatskom postsocijalističkom kontekstu [Entrepreneurship and economic growth in Croatian postsocialist context], in D. Čengić (ed.), *Menadžersko-poduzetnička elita i modernizacija: razvojna ili rentijerska elita?* Zagreb: Institut društvenih znanosti Ivo Pilar, pp. 169–210.

Franičević, V., and I. Bićanić. 2004. Understanding Croatia's transformation: Dismantling, social engineering and windows of opportunity, Eighth EACES Conference EU Enlargement – What Comes After 2004?, Belgrade, 23–25 September. Mimeo 1–40 (2003 version on www.wiiw.ac.at/balkan/2ndphase.html).

Gelo, J., A. Akrap and I. Čipin. 2005. *Temeljne značajke demografskog razvoja Hrvatske: Bilanca 20. stoljeća* [Basic characteristics of demographic development of Croatia: Balance for the 20th century]. Zagreb: Ministarstvo obitelji, branitelja i međugeneracijske solidarnosti.

Gotovac, V. 2003. Izmjene i dopune zakona o radu [Changes and amendments to the Labour Act]. *Revija za socijalnu politiku*, 10 (3).

HGK. 2005. *The educational system in the Republic of Croatia.* Croatian Chamber of Economy.

IDEA. 2002. *South Eastern Europe Public Agenda Survey.* International Institute for Democratic and Electoral Assistance – International IDEA, March, 2002 (on www.idea.int/balkans)

ILO (International Labour Office). 2004. *Country review of the employment policy of Croatia.* Prepared by the International Labour Office and the Council of Europe, First Draft, November 2004.

Jokić-Begić, N., A. Kostelić-Martić and I. Nemčić-Moro. 2003. Mobbing – moralna zlostavljanja na radnom mjestu [Bullying – moral molestation in the workplace]. *Socijalna psihijatrija* [Social psychiatry], 31 (1): 25–31.

Koić, E., P. Filaković, L. Mužinić, M. Matek and S. Vondraček. 2003. Mobbing [Bullying]. *Rad i sigurnost*, 7 (1): 1–20.

Kulušić, J. 2006. *Fleksibilizacija tržišta rada* [Flexibilization of the labour market]. Presentation at Dan poduzetnika 2006. Zagreb: Hrvatska udruga poslodavaca (CEA), mimeo.

Kušan, L., and Zoon, I. 2004. *Izvještaj o pristupu Roma zapošljavanju* [Report on Roma access to employment], September, Stability Pact for South Eastern Europe. Council of Europe: European Commission.

Lowther, J. 2004. The quality of Croatia's formal education system, in P. Bejaković and J. Lowther (eds), *Croatian human resource competitiveness study*. Zagreb: Institute of Public Finance, pp. 15–27.

Maslić Seršić, D., B. Šverko and Z. Galić. 2005. *Radne vrijednosti i stavovi prema poslu u Hrvatskoj: Što se promijenilo u odnosu na 1990-te?* [Work values and job-related attitudes in Croatia: What has changed in comparison with the 1990s?]. *Društvena istraživanja*, 14 (6): 1039–54.

Milićević, P. 2001. *Socijalni dijalog u Hrvatskoj* [Social dialogue in Croatia]. SSSH. Mimeo.

Ministry of Science, Education and Sport. 2005. *Plan razvoja sustava odgoja i obra- zovanja 2005–2010* [Development plan for the education system, 2005–2010). September.

————. 2006. *An outline of the law on adult education* (May).

MP. 2005. *Less stress with 25 per cent less pay*. Online survey, December, at www.moj-posao.net.

Mudrić, S. 2006. *Tržište rada mladih i politike zapošljavanja u Republici Hrvatskoj* [Youth labour market and employment policies in Croatia]. Magistarski Rad, Zagreb: Ekonomski fakultet Zagreb.

NCWR. 2005. *Nacionalni program zaštite zdravlja i sigurnosti na radu – prijedlog nacrta programa* [National Programme for protection of health and safety at work – an outline proposal]. Nacionalno vijeće za zaštitu na radu, Zagreb, July.

Nestić, D. 2005. *The determinants of wages in Croatia: Evidence from earnings regres- sions*. 65th Anniversary Conference of the Institute of Economics, Zagreb.

NVK. 2003. *Godišnje izvješće o konkurentnosti Hrvatske 2002* [Croatia's competi- tiveness report, 2002]. Zagreb: Nacionalno vijeće za konkurentnost.

————. 2005. *Godišnje izvješće o konkurentnosti Hrvatske 2004* [Croatia's competi- tiveness report, 2004]. Zagreb: Nacionalno vijeće za konkurentnost.

Obadić, A. 2006. Influence of regional mismatch on the employment process in select- ed transition countries. *Ekonomski pregled*, 57 (1–2).

OSCE. 2004. *Return and integration*. OSCE Mission to Croatia, at www.osce.org/croa- tia

OSP. 2006. *Collective bargaining in Croatia*. Report prepared by Office for Social Partnership in Republic of Croatia, with ILO support.

Pološki Vokić, N., and D. Frajlić. 2004. Croatian labor force competitiveness indica- tors: results of empirical research, in P. Bejaković and J. Lowther (eds), *Croatian human resource competitiveness study*. Zagreb: Institute of Public Finance, pp. 61–76.

Prenđa, I., G. Črpić and B. Vuleta. 2004. Nedjelja radi čovjeka [Sunday set aside for humanity's sake]. *Veritas*, 5.4.2004, at www.veritas.com

Rebac, I. 2006. Kolektivno pregovaranje u Hrvatskoj [Collective bargaining in Croat- ia]. *Radno pravo*.

Rutkowski, J., and S. Scarpetta. 2005. *Enhancing job opportunities in Eastern Europe and the former Soviet Union*. Washington DC: The World Bank.

Sekulić, D. 2006. *Izazovi socijaldemokracije u globalizacijskim procesima i promje- nama u svijetu rada*. Round table, Social Democratic Party, Zagreb, 13 June, mimeo.

Selectio. 2006. *Istraživanje o radu na crnom*, January. In cooperation with CES, Zagreb.

SI. 2005. *Report on State Inspectorate's work in 2004*. Mimeo. Zagreb: State Inspectorate.

SI. 2006. *Report on State Inspectorate's work in 2005*. Mimeo. Zagreb: State Inspectorate.

Singer, S., N. Šarlija, S. Pfeifer, Ð. Borozan and S. Oberman Peterka. 2006. *Što čini Hrvatsku poduzetničkom zemljom? Rezultati GEM 2002–2005 za Hrvatsku* [What makes Croatia an entrepreneurial country? GEM 2002–2005 results for Croatia]. Zagreb: CEPOR.

Strategy. 2004. *Strategy on Adult Education*. Government of Republic of Croatia, November.

Šošić, V. 2004. Does it pay to invest in education in Croatia? Return to human capital investment as a factor in human resources competitiveness, in P. Bejaković and J. Lowther, *The competitiveness of Croatia's human resources*. Zagreb: Institute of Public Finance, pp. 29–46.

Šverko, B., L. Arambašić and M. Galešić. 2002. Work–life balance among Croatian employees: role time commitment, work–home interference and well-being. *Social Science Information*, 41 (2): 281–301.

Šverko, B., Z. Galić and D. Maslić Seršić. 2005. Nezaposlenost i socijalna isključenost: longitudinalna studija [Unemployment and social exclusion: a longitudinal study]. *Revija za socijalnu politiku*, 13 (1): 1–14.

Tipurić, D. 2004. Izazovi zaposleničkog dioničarstva za hrvatska poduzeća [Challenges of employee shareholding for Croatian firms], in D. Tipurić, *ESOP i hrvatsko poduzeće* [ESOPs and Croatian firms]. Zagreb: Sinergija.

World Bank. 2003. Strengthening the legal and regulatory framework for efficient labor markets. In *Croatia: Country Economic Memorandum* (July). Washington DC: The World Bank (on www.worldbank.org).

List of Abbreviations:

CEA – Croatian Employers' Association
CBS – Croatian Bureau of Statistics
CES – Croatian Employment Service
REGOS – Central Registry of Insured Persons
SI – State Inspectorate

4. Czech Republic: Increased risks alongside involuntary flexibility

Renáta Kyzlinková (Vašková) and Lenka Dokulilová

4.1 INTRODUCTION

There have been significant changes in the Czech labour market in recent years, in conjunction with restructuring of the economy. Jobs, specializations and even whole fields have disappeared; required qualifications for different jobs have changed. These structural changes in the labour market affecting both supply and demand have been accompanied by a steep rise in the unemployment rate: from 4.8 per cent in 1997 to 8.9 per cent in 2000. In 2005 the unemployment rate reached 7.9 per cent. Structural unemployment has become a serious problem in most regions in the country. On the one hand, there is a lack of qualified workers and technicians; on the other hand, young people with a general education but no experience find major difficulties when searching for a job.

Transformational changes in the economy and labour market have thus unavoidably contributed to workers' increased uncertainty. Since the end of the 1990s, companies have been forced to reduce labour costs while increasing productivity.

The Czech economy has shown dynamic growth in recent years. This growth has not been associated with the expected growth in employment rates and a significant decrease in unemployment, however. Long-term unemployment has become a sensitive social and economic problem in the Czech Republic, which among other things has its roots in relatively high social benefits for the long-term unemployed. The long-term unemployment rate increased from 0.7 per cent in 1993 to 4.2 per cent in 2005.

These changes have gone hand in hand with the development of labour legislation. The main goal of the majority of policies nowadays is to promote the basic principles of flexicurity. Flexible work organization and time are to be important elements of flexibility in the Czech labour market. The first steps towards achieving these objectives have already been taken by means of amendments of the Labour Code (effective as of 1 March 2004) and the new

Law on Employment (effective as of 1 October 2004). Moreover, the new Labour Code, which is supposed to create a more flexible environment for both employees and employers, has been passed, coming into force on 1 June 2007.

Table 4.1 Working and employment conditions in the Czech Republic

Element	Item	Trends	Risks/Exposed groups
Working and employment conditions	Membership density Bargaining level Supra-enterprise level collective bargaining	Continuous, barely reversible decline Collective bargaining at company level plays crucial role Absence of contractual partner on part of employers	Trade union representation and power under public discussion Absence of trade unions in small and medium-sized enterprises and private newly founded companies after 1989 Public sector, automobile industry, water management
Employment status and contracts	Temporary employment	New phenomenon, slightly increasing	Less skilled and less educated people, immigrants
Social bargaining and workers' participation	Fixed-term contracts Self-employment	Stable at low levels with a long-term trend Short-term decrease after new legislation[1] Remaining at a reasonable level Slight decrease after compulsory min. tax assessed[2]	Youth, less educated women Elementary occupations and service workers (shop and market sales) Enforced self-employment – building, transport and some services (business, real estate, etc.)
Wages	Real wages Low wages	Real wages annual growth: 3–6% (since 1999); After early transition significant fall. Wage inequality has been growing more slowly since 1993 than in the first years of transition Percentage of employees drawing minimum wages grew slightly	 Wage differentiation Women earn persistently lower average wages than men Unqualified and less qualified labourers; primary and secondary sector, young people aged 20 and under

Working time and work organization	Long weeks and long hours	Stable at high levels	Men, self-employed, executives and managers
	Part-time	Stable at low levels; mostly voluntary; anticipated increase	Women, the elderly
	Flexible working time	Preferred by women to reduced working hours (part-time)	Flexible working time domain of male employees
Work intensity and working rhythms	Work intensity	Increase, in terms of both pace and quantitative demands	Stress and work–life balance problems, affecting especially highly educated employees in in foreign-owned companies
Safety and health	Fatal/serious accidents	Decline	Men aged 45–55 working in construction and agriculture
	Sick leave length	Considerable increase	Low-paid sectors, self-employed
Access to training	Training in companies	Slight growth in training	Employees of small-sized enterprises, less educated persons (without school-leaving certificate), primary and secondary sector, Roma minority
Work and family	Reconcile family and working life	Slightly improving conditions. Most women still carry a double burden	Especially women working in small enterprises, workers in private companies and the self-employed
	Gender discrimination in the labour market	Still exists	Gender inequalities of access to employment, treatment at work and career advancement possibilities
New sources of vulnerability	Temporary agency work	New phenomenon	Unethical behaviour of interim agencies towards immigrants and less qualified workers
	Working conditions of foreign workers	New phenomenon after 1989	Mainly workers from Ukraine, Viet Nam and Slovakia. Client system, high work intensity, undignified working conditions, qualification devaluation
	Jobless growth	Increasing intensity and demands on labour force	Service sector, knowledge workers

Notes:
  1. Difficult to say. According to LFS in Q1 2005 there were 6.7 per cent employees working on fixed-term contracts. In Q1 2006 the number was slightly higher than 7.3 per cent.
  2. A number of inactive traders have been forced to dissolve their business since they could not afford to pay obligatory social security contributions and minimum tax transfers any more.

Harmonization of Czech legislation with EU directives has led to many benefits in terms of employment protection. Among other things, the new labour legislation lays down regulations regarding equality for men and women, protection of temporary agency workers, overtime and limits on fixed-term contracts. Another positive trend can be seen in the extended public discussion regarding corporate social responsibility, oriented not only towards the external environment but also – and this is important – inwards, towards employees. Not enough time has passed for an objective assessment of the impact of all legislative changes in the last two years, and the efforts concerning quality of working life and workforce flexibility in particular. However, it is already clear that the risk of involuntary flexibility will grow within the Czech labour market, especially among less qualified workers.

4.2 EMPLOYMENT CONTRACTS: FOR A BETTER FLEXIBILITY–SECURITY BALANCE

Low-skilled and less educated working on a temporary basis

Atypical forms of employment are quite rare in the Czech Republic. Czechs are as yet not willing to work on that basis. However, this is considered to be only one reason for Czech labour market inflexibility. For example, rigid forms of employee–employer contract relations prevent companies' flexible adaptation to the current volume of work and orders.[1]

In recent years the *proportion* of workers on *fixed-term contracts* has hovered around 9 per cent and the number of employees with fixed-term contracts rose slightly year on year to 2003.

Despite the fact that the government's goal is to promote flexible forms of employment, the Labour Code Amendment Act No. 46/2004 was designed to prevent series of fixed-term contracts with the same employee. It sets the maximum total duration of consecutive fixed-term employment contracts at two years. In the wake of this amendment the share of those working on fixed-term contracts fell from 9.3 per cent in 2004 to 8.5 per cent in 2005. The problem of repeated signing of fixed-term contracts was striking, especially among employees in health care, trade and education: moreover, teachers' contracts were often concluded only for one school year without holidays.

---

1. This problem was widely discussed at the consultation stage of the new Labour Code. A certain amount of flexibility can now be attained through the newly established "working time accounts". This new legal institution enables employers to react to current volume of work and orders by uneven distribution of working hours, providing that employees will be rewarded by a fixed monthly salary. Employees have their own accounts for working hours and wages. The law regulates the balance period which is 26 weeks (max. 52 weeks negotiated in collective agreement).

Furthermore, 17.3 per cent of employees with basic education have these non-permanent contracts. But the workers most exposed to this type of employment are *polarized by age*: almost one in five employees aged 20–24 work on a fixed-term contract. On the other hand, every fourth employee working on a temporary basis is aged over 55. This situation arises particularly due to a legislative provision enabling the employment of persons of retirement age only on temporary contracts. According to the Labour Code amendment the restriction on repeated short-term employment contracts does not apply to such cases.

Employees contracted for a limited period are also mostly concentrated in small companies of up to 10 employees, in which this type of employment contract affects 12.3 per cent of employees.

Temporary agency work as a new form of employment

Temporary agency work (TAW) can be considered a new form of employment on the Czech labour market. There was no specific legislation on agency employment until the new Employment Act came into force on 1 October 2004. The Employment Act will provide more extensive protection of employees and at the same time increase the use of temporary agency workers. In this case, employees may be contracted by multiple contracts for a limited period of time (exception to sub par. 2 of §30, Labour Code). Users may also agree with an agency the right to terminate the hire of agency employees at short notice, retaining only the number of agency employees they need. This lays employees wide open to vulnerability.

Another way in which agency employees have less protection is that they are not covered by collective agreements. According to the available information, TAW workers in the Czech Republic are not organized into *trade unions*; it is also a complex task for them to appoint their own representatives. At employment agencies, employees are mostly contracted temporarily and for a short time, therefore the minimum communication platform necessary to establish their own representatives does not exist.

Estimates based on sociological surveys indicate that *TAW workers* constitute about 1 per cent of the workforce. In general, temporary work is developing relatively quickly and the range of sectors using such workers is increasing. In practice, such workers are most frequently assigned to perform less qualified work, such as telephone operators, labourers and tradesmen.

Employment status: self-employment still at a reasonable level

Employees have suffered the biggest decrease in employment since 1993. In contrast, the *number of self-employed increased* from 9 per cent in 1993 to

15.3 per cent (2005). The most distinctive changes have been recorded amongst the self-employed without employees (almost doubling in number from 6.3 per cent to 11.6 per cent).[2]

However, since 2004 we have witnessed a slight decrease in the numbers of self-employed. This trend reflects a series of tax reforms entering into force at the beginning of 2004.

Supplementary employment still exceptional

The need to maintain two or more jobs in the Czech Republic has been falling since the beginning of the 1990s. In 1993, 5.2 per cent of employees had more than one job; since 2000 the rate has fallen to around 2.4 per cent in 2005.

An increase in the demands made on workers and insufficient part-time jobs, as well as an increase in standards of living, may be behind this development. Two thirds of additional jobs are taken by male workers. *Second jobs* tend to be *on a self-employed basis* (57.8 per cent in 2004).

4.3 WAGES: HOW TO MAKE WORK PAY?

From centrally planned economy to market economy – growing income inequality

Wage development in the Czech Republic has been fluctuating since 1993, when the independent republic was founded. The development of real wages is shown in Table 4.2. From 1999 until 2005 the situation gradually stabilized and annual growth of nominal wages was in the region of 6 per cent to 9 per cent, which represents real growth of over 2 per cent, including inflation.

Table 4.2 Development of average real wages, Czech Republic, 1993–2005

	1993	1994	1995	1996	1997	1998	1999	2000	2001	2002	2003	2004	2005
Real wages indices[*]	–	107.8	108.7	108.7	101.3	98.6	106.2	102.4	103.8	105.4	106.5	103.7	103.4

Note: * Real wages indices are set as an increase/decrease in the ratio of average nominal wage indices and consumer price indices for the same period.

Source: Czech Statistical Office.

---

2. In 1993 the Workforce Sample Survey was carried out for the first time in the Czech Republic.

The period since 1993 can be characterized in terms of a gradually declining tendency for increasing *wage differentiation*. This trend of growing income inequality is to a great extent a necessary process of transition, from the equalized remuneration in the centrally planned economy to the market economy.

Lag in the earnings of young people and women

In *economic activity* (CZ-NACE), the highest average wages are in financial intermediation, which grew rapidly in the first half of the 1990s and still maintain their lead. Above-standard growth is recorded also in wholesale and retail, repairs, transport, storage and communications and, last but not least, real estate, renting and business activities. On the other hand, the primary sector, in particular agriculture, forestry and fishing, records the lowest wage development. Wages have also grown slowly in hotels and restaurants (see Case Study 3) and partially also in construction, where the situation has now improved.

A frequently discussed problem is the low wages of some professionals, including doctors and teachers, particularly in relation to comparable incomes in other EU countries.

Wage differentiation by *age* has changed considerably as a result of the transformation from a centralized to a market economy. Whereas, prior to 1989, average wages increased with age (seniority principle), today the maximum average wage has shifted towards the intermediate generation. Another change is the relatively lower wages in the two youngest age categories but relatively higher wages in the two oldest age categories which is caused partly by the later start and finish of working careers.

The labour market position of young people up to 20 years of age deteriorated during the 1990s. By the end of the 1990s problems with employment and low wages had spread to take in also those aged 20–29. Employers are primarily interested in the most productive employees, aged 30–39 (Vlach and Baštýř, 2003). As a result, young people up to 18 years of age are more frequently threatened by poverty in the Czech Republic than in other EU countries, while age categories above 55 are considerably less at risk of poverty than elsewhere in the EU.[3]

Gender wage discrimination is also frequently talked about. According to the Labour Force Sample Survey, women persistently earn considerably lower average wages than men. In 2004 women earned 75 per cent of men's wages.

---

3. Figures valid for 2000. T. Sirovátka et al. (2005), "Monetary poverty, material deprivation and social exclusion in the Czech Republic in comparison with EU countries" (Research paper from the project "Poverty Monitoring"), Prague, RILSA – Research Centre Brno.

In terms of the highest wages, women's situation is even worse: the 5 per cent best paid women receive only 69 per cent of the wages of the corresponding group of men. Wage differentiation is least pronounced in the middle range.

Demotivational influence of the minimum wage decreasing

At present, the legal minimum wage is CZK 7,955; EUR 279 (7 July 2006).[4] In specific cases, lower rates are applied with the aim of facilitating the employment of groups at risk on the labour market. Lower rates apply to young people aged 18–21 years in the first months of employment, to juvenile employees aged 15–18 years and also to disability pension recipients.

The minimum wage recorded rapid growth between 1999 and 2002. In 2000, the minimum wage for the first time rose above the subsistence minimum. The setting of the minimum wage below subsistence serves to deter labour market entry for less qualified employees. In large families in particular it can happen that social benefits far exceed the potential income of less qualified or unqualified workers. This inevitably promotes a reliance on social benefits.

The estimated share of employees earning the minimum wage is 2–3 per cent. In small organizations[5] the share of employees earning the minimum wage is considerably higher (10 per cent; 2004). Workers on the minimum wage are particularly represented in areas in which wages are generally lower, as in agriculture, textiles and clothing, and hotels and restaurants (See Case Study 3 on hotels and restaurants). Also, women earn the minimum wage more often than men.

Especially in small enterprises, the employer frequently officially pays employees a minimum wage on the basis of which tax and social contributions are calculated, while the employees receive the rest of their wages unofficially in cash. There are no estimates about the percentage of firms doing this but in the hotels and restaurants sector it is particularly widespread (see Case Studies 1 and 3 on transport and hotels and restaurants).

In 1998–2004, the level of the minimum wage increased significantly so that it now provides an appreciably higher income than social benefits (pegged to the subsistence minimum). This income gap between subsistence minimum and statutory minimum wage has grown gradually; in 2004 the difference was 33 per cent. The basic conditions for enabling the minimum wage to carry out its protective and incentive functions have thus been created (Baštýř, 2005).

---

4. A higher minimum wage may be agreed in a company collective agreement. This option is frequently used.

5. Small organizations with less than 20 employees.

One question still to be resolved is longer term development of the minimum wage; recently minimum wage growth has substantially exceeded average wage growth, which would seem unacceptable over the longer term. The minimum wage as a proportion of gross average earnings has been growing since 1998 (22.7 per cent), reaching 37.8 per cent in 2005 (see Table 4.3).

Table 4.3 Statutory minimum wage as a proportion of the average monthly gross wage, Czech Republic, 1995–2005

	1995	1996	1997	1998	1999	2000	2001	2002	2003	2004	2005
SMW/ AMGW	0.269	0.258	0.234	0.227	0.284	0.331	0.338	0.359	0.366	0.371	0.378

Notes: SMW – statutory minimum wage; AMGW – average monthly gross wage.

Source: Ministry for Labour and Social Affairs (MPSV).

Risk of poverty – objectively measured poverty far below EU average

According to the Household Social Situation Survey 2001 (HSSD), 7.1 per cent of households live below the poverty line.[6] The rate of persons at risk of poverty remained at 8 per cent in 2003.[7]

Focusing on different categories, women are more vulnerable to poverty than men. The highest risk of poverty is faced by persons aged 18 years or under, accounting for 32 per cent of all poor persons.[8] In contrast, persons aged 55 to 64 years are at the lowest risk of poverty.

Young people in the Czech Republic (18 or under) more frequently face poverty than in the EU. The share of people under the poverty line among pensioners is only 4 per cent and is thus the lowest within the EU-25.[9] Households which in European comparison have a higher risk of poverty in the Czech Republic include single families and couples with three or more children.

Comparing the proportions of persons living in the EU under the poverty threshold, the Czech Republic comes out very favourably: while the EU average is 15 per cent, in the Czech Republic it is only 8 per cent. Also, the share of working poor is very low: only 3 per cent for the Czech Republic (compared with the EU-25's 7 per cent of working poor in 2001/2).

---

6. The poverty income threshold is set in the amount of 60 per cent of the median of equalized income per consumption unit. Calculation based on the EU methodology.

7. Eurostat: Population and Social Conditions, Living Conditions and Welfare State (20 October 2006).

8. Persons 18 and under represent more than one fifth of the population.

9. Bulletin of Czech Statistical Office 6-2005.

However, if we measure subjective income poverty and material deprivation,[10] the share of persons in the Czech Republic is high at 17 per cent, which
puts the Czech Republic among the EU countries with the highest subjectively perceived income poverty.[11]

The effectiveness of social benefits in poverty elimination is relatively
high in the Czech Republic. The success of poverty elimination as defined by
the EU is in the region of 78 per cent (Sirovátka et al., 2005).

The Czech Republic has among the lowest levels of poverty threat, deriving from relative stability of the lowest incomes and targeted social transfers.

4.4 WORKING TIME AND WORK ORGANIZATION: ALL DAY AT WORK

Working part-time – province of a vulnerable labour market group

In the Czech Republic part-time jobs are quite rare. Out of total employment
only 2.1 per cent of men and 8.5 per cent of women worked part time in 2005.
Although the importance of flexible employment forms is stressed in the
National Action Employment Plan for 2004–06, the Czech Republic lacks
sophisticated and effective programmes which could promote the growth of
flexibility and increase opportunities for part-time jobs. According to a 2000
enterprise survey (Polívka and Zamykalova, 2000) most companies (65 per
cent) have no plans to expand the supply of part-time jobs.

The inadequate supply of part-time jobs is the main reason for the low
development of this flexible type of employment. Furthermore, sociological
surveys show that *neither men nor women want to work part-time* because the
resultant income would not be sufficient and working conditions are worse
compared to those of full-timers. Within the context of harmonization of family and working life, Czech women would prefer to work under a *flexitime
system* rather than part-time. Still, the flexitime option has so far been rather
the domain of male employees (Štěpánková, 2003).

In addition, part-time employment is mostly specific to *less-qualified
employees* working for minimum wages. The profitability of such employment is further reduced by travel costs, time costs, and so on.

10. Measured based on the EUROSTAT selected indicators.

11. The contradiction in the percentage figures of an officially set poverty threshold and subjectively perceived poverty is apparently caused by a relatively even (egalitarian) distribution of
the middle and lower incomes in CR earned by a majority of inhabitants in the country. The limit
of a 60 per cent median income as a selected poverty limit is more concentrated in the lower
income zones than in the "old" countries of the EU, where the distribution of incomes is more differentiated (*Právo* 18 July 2005). Another reason for a higher share of people who feel subjectively poor in CR may also be a lower living standard compared with the EU-15 countries.

Part-time employment is clearly women's domain at present and distributed among all age groups more equally than among men. However, the main group of employees among whom part-time jobs predominate is *the elderly*, who seek to supplement their income and living standards this way. This trend is especially distinct among men; more than half of all those in part-time jobs are aged 55 or over. Health reasons are another important factor in part-time work: 22.4 per cent of men and 11.9 per cent of women aged 55 or over stated health problems as the reason for the part-time job. The second highest rate for part-time jobs among women was recorded in the 25–34 age group, the main reproductive age span in the Czech Republic. Half of these women stated that they work part time due to family responsibilities.

More detailed analysis of the LFS shows that part-time work is also more widespread among *single parents and handicapped people* than other employees (Vyhlídal and Mareš, 2006). *Underemployment* is also low in the Czech Republic: only one in seven persons working part-time wishes to work more hours a day. Overtime is quite rare for part-time employees: 97 per cent of persons with such employment stated that they had not worked overtime during the reference week.

Full-time workers – usual working hours well above statutory fixed working hours

The law lays down a working week of 40 hours, excluding meal and rest breaks. In fact, *usual working hours are notably higher*, especially among self-employed men (self-employed with employees: 55.7 hours on average; self-employed without employees: 51.4 hours on average). However, a higher number of working hours than laid down by law was recorded for employees as a whole (41.2) – only female employees come close to the legal limit (40.3). Women are mainly responsible for household and family tasks and deliberately select employment where no overtime is required. This maintains occupational gender segregation and significantly reduces women's career prospects. Unsurprisingly, those working in the private sector have a longer working week than those working in the state sector.

We find the longest average weekly working hours in construction (46.0), restaurants (43.8) (see Case Study 3), motorcars and consumer goods trading and repairs (43.4), services and agriculture (43.46). Sectoral differentiation of working time is significantly affected by the presence of the self-employed, who tend to increase the mean number of working hours in sectors in which they are well represented. In terms of *employment status* executives and managers tend to work 48.6 hours a week on average, according to LFSS.

Czechs work on average more than their colleagues in Western European countries. The few people working on a part-time basis are one reason already pointed out. Another reason why Czechs have a longer working week compared to the EU-15 is the frequency of *overtime*: in 2004, 13.4 per cent of employees worked at least one hour overtime in the reference week. In the Czech Republic overtime is still a very important part of an employee's monthly wage, especially among manual workers.

Besides those who prefer working overtime because it boosts their wages, there is still a high proportion of employees who work overtime without compensation (see Case Study 2 on retail). In 2004, 39 per cent of employees working at least one hour overtime per week did not get any compensation. The impact of *gender segregation* on overtime compensation is significant: women are more represented than men in sectors in which overtime is not compensated. While overtime was at least partly compensated for almost two thirds of men, only just over half of women receive anything. However, men generally work overtime more than women.

Working unsocial hours and its risks

Working unsocial hours usually means working evenings or Saturdays. Roughly half of employees had worked at least on occasion on Saturdays or evenings. One in five workers work at night and slightly more than one third work on Sundays (see Case Study 2 on retail).

Those exposed to working unsocial hours are mostly self-employed, middle-aged men working in mining, transport, and hotels and restaurants (see Case Studies 1 and 3 on transport and on hotels and restaurants). Self-employed people are significantly more exposed to evening and Saturday work than employees. Significant differences are also found on the basis of a gender breakdown: while women work fewer unsocial hours than men, they suffer much more than men from this type of working time organization. Dissatisfaction with unsocial working hours among women is associated to a large degree with their ability to reconcile family and working life.

Besides problems harmonizing working and family life there is an *increased health risk* and other negatives associated with working outside regular hours. The results of the survey *Working Conditions 2000* clearly indicate an increased – though subjectively declared – health risk among persons working unsocial hours. Men working unsocial hours stated more often than women that the work threatened their health and safety.

The Czech Republic is also characterized by the *very early start of the working day*, especially in manufacturing. The day tends to begin at 6 a.m.:[12]

---

12. Although it might seem it would cause families problems the reality is different. The child care system is well adapted to this early start. There is a widely used option for schoolchildren to attend pre-school care centres. School starts at 8 a.m. in the Czech Republic and these pre-school

this arrangement is not very comfortable, especially in winter when it is dark. With the arrival of foreign companies on the Czech labour market, new trends of flexible work organization have meant that the start of the working day has been put forward to a more reasonable hour; however, it remains the rule in smaller towns or villages.

Shift work and its impact on family and social life

Shift work is another mode of work organization that interferes with family life to some degree. Approximately the same proportion of women and men work shifts. Nevertheless, this work schedule, however regular, affects women more than men. Generally, 81.2 per cent employees are satisfied with shift work; however, only 77.4 per cent of women are satisfied compared to 84.4 per cent of men. The least satisfaction with multi-shift operations is shown in industries with the highest proportion of employees working shifts: manufacturing, motor vehicles and consumer goods repairs. Shift work least suits women aged 25–44, clearly because of family and work reconciliation problems (see Case Study 2 on retail).

4.5 HEALTH AND SAFETY: WILL THE NEW LAW CHANGE THE POPULARITY OF SICK LEAVE?

Occupational diseases and work accidents: positive trends

In recent years there has been a constant decline in the number of newly reported cases of incapacity for work, occupational diseases and working accidents in the Czech Republic. This trend is predominantly due to the restructuring of the Czech economy over the last 15 years. The number of enterprises in sectors with a concentration of occupations of above average safety and health risks has shrunk and there have also been shifts in the workforce from the primary sector to the service sector, which is less risky.

Nevertheless, the Czech Republic has a higher rate of secondary sector employment compared to the EU-15, which is higher-risk in terms of accidents at work.

centres usually open at 6 a.m. Kindergartens are usually open between 6:30 a.m. and 4 p.m. This system persists from the communist period when early starts were more common than today and can be inconvenient today because of their relatively early closing hours (which is particularly difficult for families living in bigger cities).

Average sick leave duration one of the highest in the EU

In the context of the Czech Republic it is crucial to assess *the average duration of work incapacity.* Recently, an increasing trend in sick leave length has been apparent among all diagnosed diseases (from 18.4 days in 1990 to 31.5 in 2005). At the same time, the growth rate is higher in the private sector and Czech-owned companies.

Employers often *deal with a lack of orders by imposing sick leave* with the aim of reducing labour costs. Therefore, the average sick-leave duration increases in regions where there is high uncertainty in the labour market. Exploitation of sick leave occurs not only amongst employers, but also among employees who seek to at least postpone dismissal by going on sick leave, so ensuring them at least short-term protection against job loss.[13] The new Law No. 187/2006 Coll. on Sickness Insurance, which came into force on 1 January 2007, tries to prevent the misuse of sick leave benefit. It has increased the direct participation of employers in providing sick leave benefits. Employers are now obliged to cover[14] two weeks of an employee's sickness.

In general, *low average sectoral wages* tend to go hand in hand with an increased incidence of work incapacity. On the other hand, workers with above average wages are sick less often or prefer to take a holiday when ill because sickness benefits provide them with very low compensation.

The current relatively long average sick leave duration is also reflected in a general indicator often used for international comparison, that is, *the average percentage of work incapacity due to disease or injury.*[15] This statistic is very unfavourable for the Czech workforce since it shows that the Czechs are top of the league in terms of time spent on sick leave compared to other European States (CZSO, 2003).

Regarding individual sectors and occupations, *health care* is among the sectors with the highest rate of diagnosed occupational diseases since 2001. High numbers of recorded disease have been caused especially by infectious and parasitic diseases and professional dermatitis. The occupational groups most affected are female nurses, then male nurses, paramedics, auxiliary staff/ cleaners and physicians. These personnel most frequently fall ill in the first four years after entering the job (Fenclová et al., 2003). Occupational illnesses

---

13. According to the Labour Code (§48 sub-par.1a), the employer shall not terminate the employment contract during a so-called protection period, which also includes periods when the employee has been declared temporarily unable to work due to illness and/or accident, provided that inability had not been caused intentionally or by drunkenness.

14. The first three days of sick leave benefit amount to 30 per cent of average daily income. From the fourth day to the fourteenth day sick leave benefit amounts to 69 per cent of average daily income.

15. Average percentage of incapacity for work = calendar days of incapacity for work x 100 / average number of sickness insured persons x number of calendar days in reference period.

in this sector represent 16 per cent of all cases. Furthermore, high numbers of occupational diseases have been reported in mineral raw materials mining, construction, metal work and textiles. As regards age, the workers most affected by occupational illness are aged 50–54.

In general, occupational illnesses and accidents at work tend to affect men more than women. However, not surprisingly, in *feminized sectors* such as health care and education, more cases are registered for women.

While women are affected more by infectious and parasitic diseases men suffer more from diseases caused by physical factors (for example, *musculo-skeletal diseases* or "MSDs"). Concerning MSDs, the data show interesting discrepancies between men and women with regard to length of work incapacity: the average number of days off for women greatly exceeds the average number of days off for men. Women are therefore affected by musculo-skeletal diseases less often, but when they are, they have a longer duration.

4.6 FURTHER TRAINING MAINLY FOR PEOPLE WITH HIGHER QUALIFICATIONS

Lifelong learning is part of the *Czech Republic's human resources development strategy*. Apart from education within the framework of the school system, emphasis is placed on further education and development of abilities to respond flexibly to the changing labour market.

The latest data on participation in informal education[16] show that 3.45 per cent of inhabitants had participated in informal education within the four weeks prior to the survey (2004). Over the previous 12 months 11 per cent of all respondents had participated.[17]

The structure of those participating in further education is influenced by a number of *factors*, above all educational attainment hitherto. The rate of participation in further education increases along with level of education. One quarter of university educated people participated in further training compared to only 5 per cent of elementary educated people. People with uncompleted elementary education did not participate in informal education at all.[18]

16. Informal education is further training which helps to upgrade the professional level after completion of formal education. Training usually takes place in a special institution or at the workplace. The necessary precondition of this type of education is the presence of a qualified instructor. Examples of informal training are language courses, computer courses, retraining programmes and also short-term training programmes and lectures.

17. The data are drawn from the Ad-Hoc Module 2003 on Lifetime Education (CZSO, 2003) and from the publication Human Resources 2003. Ad-Hoc Module 2003 distinguished between three categories of education: formal education, informal education and self-learning.

18. University education (25 per cent); secondary education finished by a school-leaving examination (15 per cent); skilled workers and secondary school graduates not having a school-leaving examination (8 per cent); elementary education (5 per cent).

The share of *women* in education was lower than that of men. The difference is probably caused by women's earlier retirement and also the period of maternity leave.

Role of enterprises in ongoing training

Further training was offered to employees by 67 per cent of companies.[19] Almost half those concerned took the opportunity. In the Czech Republic the share of companies providing employees with further training was the highest of the new EU members and slightly above average compared to the EU-15. However, a comparison of further training expenditure compared to overall labour costs is less favourable for the Czech Republic (CR: 1.9 per cent; EU-15: 2.3 per cent).

The survey also confirmed that employee training is more intense in larger companies than in small ones. Employees in small and medium-sized enterprises are also less informed concerning the type and scope of training.

Training costs are predominantly covered by the employer. Very rarely do the employees cover their own training costs.

One third of Czech companies – as already mentioned – do not provide their employees with further training. Enterprises try to justify this by saying that they tend to employ people whose existing knowledge is sufficient for the task. Other reasons include the cost of training and the adequacy of the employee's training/education prior to employment. The last and most frequently stated reason is the workload of employees.

In general, the trend in the area of further training is positive and indicates an increase. Simultaneously, however, the growth of expenditure on further training is relatively slow. In this respect, the companies would welcome an improvement in the financing of further training and possible financial incentives for development.

Roma minority and training/education

One group accumulating handicaps related to further training is the *Roma minority*. The education and qualifications of Roma lag behind the majority on a long-term basis.[20] Due to low or often no qualifications, Roma are predominantly employed as day labourers and unqualified labourers in construction and industry where there is generally a low intensity of further education.

---

19. Information on further professional training is provided by the international Continuing Vocational Training Survey or CTVS (2000).

20. Over 90 per cent of Roma have only elementary education; some have an incomplete one. Due to the language handicap, Roma children are often placed in special schools, which represents a further barrier to education.

According to estimates, only a third of working-age Roma are employed. Those who are not have the chance to participate in retraining programmes, though often they do not take it up. Even if they retrain, they are then faced with the unwillingness of employers to hire Roma on a full-time basis.

4.7 WORK AND FAMILY: LOWEST FERTILITY, AND FOR WOMEN A TWO-FOLD BURDEN

The Czech Republic has one of *the lowest total fertility rates* in Europe (1.28 in 2004). One reason for this is the more uncertain position of individuals in the labour market and the increased unemployment rate compared to the centrally planned economy. It is now also much more difficult to harmonize working life and family duties.

Double burden for Czech women

Czech women take relatively long parental leaves; they are entitled to parental benefits if they personally take care all day long of children under 4 years of age. However, most women return to work after three years and in most cases start to work on a full-time basis. The economic activity of Czech women with no children under 6 years of age is one of the highest in the EU (CZ 83.3 per cent; EU-25 73.2 per cent in 2005). The traditional family – the man as the breadwinner and the woman as the homemaker – is not very common in Czech society. However, women as mothers still bear the main responsibility for the care and upbringing of children and household management (MPSV, 2005), which virtually constitutes a "second shift" after they return from work. Most Czech employers are unable to offer women flexible working time to enable them to order their working day according to their needs. Women are very much disadvantaged in the labour market by the fact that fixed working time formulas prevail in Czech companies. According to many sociological surveys, women attribute the highest value to the family. A preference for a family over a profession thus makes women accept jobs below their level of qualifications but which are not time-consuming; in the Czech context this means working time without frequent overtime. This is one explanation of women's fewer working hours.

Do companies support the harmonization of work and family life?

Although special programmes for reconciling parental and work duties are not yet being disseminated (the absence is obvious especially in small and medium-sized enterprises) and the situation has significant room for improvement, it is apparent that in recent years such issues have been a focus of both government and non-profit organizations. Also, *some change in enterprise environments has been detected*; some progress has been made in developing equal opportunities for men and women and an environment in which family-friendly working conditions are provided.[21] Generally, flexible start and end times are the most widely used measures to improve the work/life balance in the Czech Republic. Paradoxically, however, this privilege is more frequent among men than women. Some foreign companies – the main providers of a family-friendly approach – also offer the possibility of working from home. On the other hand, companies are still afraid of investing in programmes whose effect will only be felt in the long term. This is seen as the main obstacle to the introduction of work/life balance programmes; other obstacles are factors linked to work organization (shift-work, irregular flow of orders, the nature of work in which there is heightened sensitivity to clients' needs, and so on). The option of childminding in the workplace is very rare due to various obstacles, including strict hygiene standards, administrative workload and regulations laying down, for example, the qualification criteria for staff.

4.8 CONTINUOUS DECLINE IN TRADE UNION MEMBERSHIP

The trade unions have always been one of the *strongest lobbies* in the Czech Republic. Their influence on Czech political events, the social and economic system and working conditions is undisputed (Mansfeldová, 2005). Recently, the importance and power of social dialogue in the Czech Republic could be seen when the new Labour Code (in force in January 2007) was discussed in Parliament.[22] The social partners hold strongly divergent opinions. However, employee representatives have successfully defended their claims, especially with regard to their competence in health and safety issues.

---

21. A quality survey of companies in the Czech Republic clearly shows that to the extent that companies are interested in ameliorating women's disadvantages, it is especially in the occupational field and women's working conditions, that is, discrimination against women with regard to jobseeking, wages, returning to their job after maternity or parental leave, and so on. In contrast, companies are little concerned about solving the problems of disadvantaged older women and women from ethnic minorities (Simerská, 2005).

22. In this respect, the employers confirmed the basic principles of collective negotiation, namely the right of trade unions to negotiate collectively, not only on behalf of trade union members, but also on behalf of all employees. Also, a requirement was introduced to cancel trade unions' inspection rights in the field of safety and health protection at work. Nevertheless, substantial trade union powers in the area of occupational health and safety remained unchanged in the new Labour Code. The employers also pointed to excessive powers on the part of the unions and growth in wage and other costs in the form of increasing severance pay or extra pay for work performed in hazardous and unhealthy environments.

However, the number of trade union organized employees in the Czech Republic is now *falling continuously*. The level of trade union membership in the Czech Republic can only be estimated from fragmentary sources. There are no official statistical data on the numbers of union members. Figures vary between 17 per cent and 33 per cent. We can assume that the reality might be somewhere in between. The best breeding ground for the unions is large industrial enterprises with over 250 employees. The level of trade union organization is heavily dependent on the period of employment of employees: the longer employees have been employed in a given company, the higher the probability that they will become a member of the union. Younger employees below 35 years of age are significantly less likely to be trade union members (Vašková et al., 2005)

The reputation and image of the Czech unions suffered a lot as a result of their close cooperation with the Communist Party and it is obvious that they will regain support only very slowly. However, a key role in the *decline of the trade unions* is also played by overall structural changes in society and particularly in the labour market. New production methods, growth of the share of employees working in small enterprises, increasing share of employees in services, growth of atypical and flexible jobs and a general inclination towards individualism are characteristics of Czech society over the last 15 years and at the same time factors which make the expansion of the trade union membership base very difficult (see Case Studies 1, 2 and 3).

4.9 VULNERABLE GROUPS

Traditional groups jeopardized

Taking a closer look at workers' vulnerability as it stems from the working environment described above we must first highlight the traditional jeopardized groups in the labour market, especially those whose handicaps are accumulated.

Two core characteristics of vulnerable groups in the labour market are insufficient qualifications and work experience, faced in particular by juveniles and recent school-leavers. Other characteristics are insufficient flexibility and disability, often a problem particularly of *older persons*.

In addition, overall demographic changes play a crucial role in the employability of older workers and their quality of working life. The Czech population is aging, and retirement age extension means more older people in the labour market. As a consequence, an increase of the employment rate but also the unemployment rate of older people is expected. The generally lower educational level of older people, together with generally worse health, leads

to increased vulnerability which is deepened by their restricted further training opportunities. Their unequal access to lifelong learning and requalifica-
tion can have a serious negative impact on their working life. Women with
less education are considered to be the most vulnerable group among older
persons.

Another traditional vulnerable group is *young people*. Surveys show that
Czech young people seem to be the worst off in terms of job stability since
they have the highest probability of having a fixed-term contract, working on
a fee basis, or a performance-based contract, while they have the lowest probability of a permanent job (Štěpánková, 2003).

In the Czech Republic 20 per cent of those aged 20–24 work on a fixed-
term contract. Czech young people also work more often without a contract
and it is not easy for them to enter the labour market in the first place because
of their lack of qualifications and work experience. Thus, a specific group vulnerable in the labour market is *school/college leavers* (up to 25 years of age).
There is a risk here that the initial unemployment of this group will deform
work habits and that young people will get used to living on benefits (whether
from the family or the state) and will be at risk of falling into a number of risk
groups (drugs, delinquency).[23]

Low education is the surest stepping stone to vulnerability and also serves
as an intersection among all vulnerable groups. Less educated people are
more likely to work on a temporary basis for the minimum wage.
Furthermore, employers are not interested in investing in further training for
people with low qualifications. This handicap is reinforced by the temporary
character of their employment. It has been proved that people working on
fixed-term contracts have less access to further education.

Women also belong to the traditional group of workers at higher risk of vulnerability. It often happens that women, conscious of their situation, do not
consider qualifications and experience as the most important criteria when
applying for a job: the main criterion is whether the job fits in with their time
schedule. The fact that significantly fewer women than men reported that their
employment required creative thinking and that they are also less likely to be
in jobs requiring a high degree of expertise illustrates the situation clearly.
Shorter working time, higher frequency of part-time jobs and fewer overtime
hours, which are paid at a higher rate, but also gender segregation of employ-

---

23. One handicap of school graduates is the fact that they come en masse to the labour market
and have little or no experience. The government therefore decided to reduce the minimum wage
for school leavers with no experience for a period of six months to facilitate their employment and
thereby balance the handicap resulting from lack of experience. To motivate young people to
obtain hands-on experience while studying and to motivate school-leavers to seek a job is one task
of the new employment law valid from September 2004. In order for a school-leaver to obtain
unemployment benefit they must have paid health and social insurance contributions for at least
one year. A school-leaver without prior employment is thus not entitled to the dole.

ment structure and gender pay discrimination contribute to Czech women's lower average wages. Particularly among single mothers these circumstances easily lead to precarious life situations.

Excessive work intensity for the self-employed (without employees)

The vulnerability of the self-employed emerges especially in the form of overload and insecurity. The obligatory minimum tax introduced in 2004 brought greater uncertainty into the working lives of the self-employed, especially of small traders without employees. Relatively high numbers of small tradesmen were not able to pay it and many were forced to dissolve their business. People at a higher risk of vulnerability included those who moved directly from self-employment to unemployment and this was mainly the case of older people. In addition, these people are more at risk of long-term unemployment since they are not able to cope with the stricter employee regime any more.

Extraordinarily long working hours and frequent work at unsocial hours is another disadvantage related to the working life of the self-employed. Self-employed people also suffer more than employees from not being able to reconcile family and working life.

Longer working hours and work intensity might be compensated to a certain extent by independence, flexibility and autonomy. However, a considerable number of the self-employed without employees still work in "hidden employment". These people thus accumulate only the disadvantages of self-employed status: they neither enjoy employees' rights nor perform work autonomously.

Non-existent individual performance of temporary migrant workers from the former USSR – the "client system"

After the fall of communism it was not long before economic immigration became a feature of the Czech labour market. In 2004 there were 254,294 foreigners with permanent or long-term residence permits in the Czech Republic (Leontiyeva, 2005). Estimates of illegal migrant workers are even higher. The largest proportion of economic migrants come from Slovakia and Ukraine. Ukrainian temporary migrant workers take less qualified jobs mostly in construction or agriculture. Their willingness to accept unqualified jobs often contributes to the devaluation of migrants' position in the labour market in comparison with their position in their country of origin. However, their overqualification can be considered a minor aspect of their discrimination. The main source of vulnerability of the majority of Ukrainian migrants, working both legally and illegally, is the so-called "client system". A "client" in this sense is someone who knows the rules of the destination country (Černík,

2006) and is able to guarantee protection for incoming workers. The "client" recruits using informal networks in the country of origin, negotiates jobs in the destination country, arranges visas with work permits or legal residence, transport, accommodation, catering and, last but not least, protection from organized crime. These services are paid for out of the migrant workers' wages and the "commission" on wages usually amounts to 50 per cent. In comparison with the unrestrained development of the "client system" after 1989 the situation has changed and nowadays "clients" usually have a proper licence for work intermediation. They tend to be former Ukrainian workers, but Czech clients are no longer an exception. Nevertheless, their activities are rather part of the shadow economy. Some qualitative studies have detailed the exploitation of Ukrainian workers in terms of hidden work contracts or lack of sick pay. The working conditions of illegal migrants are further violated in terms of hygiene and safety and health norms. Ukrainian migrants are sub-jected to work in very harsh conditions. Moreover, they have extremely long working hours as they receive an hourly wage and want to send home to the family as much money as possible. The "client system" is well established in the Czech labour market and looking for jobs on an individual basis is gener-ally a waste of time for Ukrainian migrant workers. In addition, the attempt to escape this "vassalship" generally means the loss of entitlement to work and, as a result, also the loss of the residence permit.

REALITY AT ENTERPRISE LEVEL: CASE STUDIES

Introduction

To describe the possible sources of vulnerability in companies three case studies were carried out. Three different companies were chosen to cover the variety of working conditions with the focus on workers' vulnerability. Company 1 is a haulage and logistics business, Company 2 operates a retail chain and Company 3 is a small pub in the capital city. From the company size point of view we can call Company 3 a micro firm, while Companies 1 and 2 are large. There are also significant differences in ownership. While Companies 1 and 3 are family firms with Czech owners, Company 2 has foreign ownership. The workforce structures are also very different: Company A is male-dominated, whereas in Company 2 women prevail. All companies must face some kind of market competition, which has – at least in the first two cases – a global character. Logistics Company A in particular currently has to cope with global competition after Czech Republic accession to the EU.

Czech Republic Case Study 1: Road transport – opportunities and risks due to EU membership

Sectoral environment: strong competition and social dumping

With accession to the European Union, Czech haulage contractors were confronted with dramatic changes in their business environment. They now face more competition and a larger and more open market. A number of Czech hauliers have realized the growing threat of competition and are trying to diversify their portfolio of services and to gain a competitive edge. Company 1 is also taking this direction, adopting a strategy of offering comprehensive logistic services. Viewed from the perspective of labour and employment statistics, the road transport sector (NACE 60.2) employs predominantly men with a secondary education without a school-leaving certificate (ISCED 3), and falling in the "Plant and machine operators" category (66 per cent in 2003). Almost all employees work on a full-time basis in the road transport sector (99 per cent in 2003) and the share of employees with fixed-term contracts is below the national average.

The road transport sector has been undervalued over a long period of time in terms of wages. The wages of road transport sector employees are below the national average.

An essential characteristic of the sector is the high number of one-man businesses without employees or businesses with the minimum number of employees (more than 90 per cent). According to the top representative of the Transport Trade Union, haulier–sole traders breach the regulations and standards most frequently. So-called "owner drivers" in particular frequently violate specified rest times as it is very hard to determine precisely when they use their vehicles for the job and when for leisure.

Collective bargaining in the road transport sector occurs both at the business and the sectoral level. About 50 per cent of employees were covered by collective agreements in 2003 in the NACE 60.2 road transport sector. At the sectoral level, the main representatives of the interests of employees are the Transport Trade Union (OSD) and DOSIA Trade Union. The bargaining partners are the Czech Transport Association (SD CR) and the Czech Association of Haulage Companies (SDP ÈR). A supra-enterprise level collective agreement has been concluded for 2006–08. The trade unions consider the conclusion of this agreement a great success, the first to be concluded in the road transport sector since 1999. Under present legislation, it is possible to extend the binding nature of the collective agreement to enterprises with the same business orientation.

The case study was prepared based on interviews with the human resources manager as a representative of higher management, two employees in lower management, three employees in the control department and in the warehouse, one employee in maintenance and five drivers. An interview was also carried out with the Vice-Chairman of the Transport Trade Union, which presented the key problems of employees in this sector.

Logistics Enterprise 1: Investing in modernization, less in people

Impressive growth and modernization reducing workers' identification with the firm

The company was established in 1990 as a limited-liability company with four owners. They started as a family haulage company with several trucks made in the Czech Republic. They managed to maintain sales growth and to meet the competition of newly privatized state-owned enterprises, and later the competition of multinational companies. The service portfolio is very diversified, comprising a courier business utilizing not only its own fleet, but also foreign hauliers, offering storage space and running authorized car repair and maintenance facilities. The company increased its fleet from 120 trucks to 160 last year. Another innovation in 2005 was internet sales of spare parts.

Growth resulted in large personnel changes which contributed to a certain destabilization of relations among workers and a decline in the identification of employees with the company.

The company employs about 320 employees, the majority drivers (200). Other employees work in the warehouse, administration, courier and maintenance services. The number of employees has doubled since 2000. The fastest increase in the workforce took place in 2005 in conjunction with a number of modernization changes. Employees are mostly men: women account only for 7.5 per cent of all employees. The age structure is polarized. The company has a very young team composed of employees aged up to 30 years, the second most frequent group, however, being drivers of over 45 years of age. With regard to the high share of drivers in the workforce, in terms of qualifications, employees with a secondary education but without a school-leaving certificate prevail.

Diverse contracts according to individual profile
The company mostly uses one-year fixed contracts. However, employment contracts are concluded for an indefinite period of time especially with quality drivers with long experience. The legal three-month probation period strangely "goes against the employers in the road transport sector", the company HR manager says. With regard to the pressure on haulage companies, the sector faces a problem of a lack of qualified and competent drivers. The situation is illustrated by the following:

> ... and they started to hire employees through ads. From the very beginning, there were very demanding conditions of selection. The drivers were hired and tested by the owners themselves. The quality of employees was the primary concern. These days, they hire everybody who applies and the drivers come and go. ... Many more experienced drivers left to go abroad or went to larger companies where they have better financial conditions. (Igor, lower management)

Apart from full-time employees, the company cooperates with a personnel agency which provides it with seasonal workers, mostly students to cover extraordinary demand peaks.

Drivers, the nomads of the labour market
The turnover of drivers is very high. Drivers could be described as nomads, not only in terms of their mobile profession but also their constantly changing position in the labour market. The HR manager says that drivers who have worked for 9–10 companies in two years are not exceptional: "The wage level is the most important thing to them, and whether they are paid on time."

Too-high flexible part of wages putting some workers at risk
The company tries to motivate its employees by combining a basic wage with a performance-based component. According to respondents, the basic component is below average. Some employees consider the combination system rather discouraging as the wages are determined by a low base and the floating part is too uncertain and accounts for a considerable part of the wage. For

instance, despatching employees, who organize the haulage for their own trucks, are compensated based on saved mileage and fuel related to standards laid down in advance.

> The colleagues who take care of their own trucks are in a bad situation. They do the same quality job, but they cannot influence oil prices or accidents and then they do not meet the target set as a standard for the month. This is reflected in their bonuses, which form a substantial part of the wage. The worst thing is that this is influenced by little things you cannot control. This, I would say, is the largest stumbling block. (Hana, dispatch controller)

For some drivers their only certainty is an amount near the minimum wage (CZK 8,000/ EUR 277). The rest of the wage is composed of several components. For vehicle maintenance (CZK 1,000 per month/EUR 37) and for compliance with the set standards on fuel consumption (CZK 3,000 per month/EUR 104), the personal bonus is CZK 1,000–2,000 (EUR 37–74). If the driver fulfils all prerequisites, his gross monthly wage is CZK 13–14,000 (EUR 450–80). The standards are unfortunately set in such a way that drivers driving older vehicles or with a heavier load can hardly keep them. Also, the personal bonus component is not very transparent and, according to the respondents, rather depends on management discretion.

A substantial part of drivers' income does not, however, result from their officially determined wage assessment, but from travel reimbursements – the boarding allowance – per diem, which is nearly double their salary.

In terms of long-term wage trends, it is possible to say that, after 1990, there was a dramatic devaluation of driving professions in general and the prestige of international haulage drivers has declined considerably.

Overtime – no compensation for drivers

The driving time and rest time laid down in the law are set by the European Agreement concerning the Work of Crews of Vehicles engaged in International Road Transport or AETR.[24] Given the wage system predominantly dependent on the boarding allowance,[25] the drivers usually have no motivation to violate the driving time and rest regulation as it is more profitable to stay abroad as long as possible. However, for companies the opposite

---

24. Regulation No. 108/1976 Coll.

25. According to the experience of drivers, there are a number of companies where compensation depends on the volume of invoiced contracts. In this case, the drivers fall in with the unlawful behaviour of the company, which does not compensate them with per diem allowances, but provides a share in the profit of the contract as another component of financial compensation. This system indirectly encourages drivers to violate the driving time regulation. If an inspection finds that the regulation has been breached, the fine is paid mostly by the company, but the driver receives penalty points and there is a risk of a driving ban in particular territories (for instance, Germany).

is the case. Most drivers have received instructions from system operators to violate the AETR regulation and to reach their destination disregarding the rest obligation.[26] In this respect, great pressure is exerted on the system operators, as the penalties for failure to deliver the shipment on time are relatively high and reflected also in their bonuses. Even the widespread "just-in-time" system encourages the drivers to violate the regulations.

It is up to the individual decision of every driver whether he obeys the system operator's suggestion to breach the rest time regulation. Older drivers in particularly are afraid of refusing because they fear loss of employment. All drivers declared that their job performance well exceeds the average weekly working hours determined by law – 40 hours a week – but the company does not compensate them for their overtime. Similarly, the company does not compensate employees in any way for time spent doing emergency service.

Increasing work intensity for all

Increasing work intensity was a subject of complaint for almost all responding employees. More work at a higher pace and a more demanding environment came mainly after the admission of the Czech Republic to the European Union, when the volume of contracts grew markedly. More work and higher costs are reflected in the growing pressure from the management to improve productivity to maintain or even increase the profit level. The increased activity of the company is reflected in the rapid growth of administrative tasks. According to the HR manager, this has been managed without the need to hire new employees.

The increased stress level in the workplace resulting from the lack of employees to perform jobs is also reflected in human interaction.

> Communications and relations with people in the workplace are much influenced by the stress level. It is a really stressful occupation and those who do not do it themselves – for instance, from higher management – think that we do not do enough. There is a lack of recognition for a job well done.[27] I believe that at present we would need at least two more people so that we could manage our job well. (Marie, forwarding controller)

The drivers also complain that since the cancellation of border inspections the work pace is higher. The stress load has also been increased by more frequent use of tandem crews in order to have trucks working full time. Most drivers do not favour this system. They often do not trust the abilities of the other

---

26. Every driver has it in his employment contract that he has to comply with this regulation.
27. The HR manager himself admits that the company does not provide feedback to employees on the quality of their work. The company planned to introduce appraisal interviews, the results of which would be reflected in the floating component of employees' pay. Obstacles exist mainly on the side of the management, however, which cannot find the time to introduce this system.

driver and, what is more, they have to share a very small space in the cabin for a relatively long period of time.

Work–life balance: things can get even worse

All drivers, without exception, complained about the difficulty of harmonizing family life and work. The sacrifice in terms of private life is immense and the likelihood that the driver's family will break up is very high, according to all respondents.

> My wife could not get used to me being at home. (Luboš, driver)

> I even work weekends in my truck. I am never at home at all. I wanted to stay at home after 6 weeks at least because I do not have any clean clothes now … I do not even know how my children are growing up. (Josef, driver)

Drivers' contact with their families will be even more restricted after the launch of a new European regulation which reduces maximum weekly driving time from 74 hours to 56 hours: this simply means that orders will require more time to be delivered. The responses of the drivers to this change emphasize the positive but also the very real negative features of the regulation: "Drivers who are predominantly paid by invoices and by mileage will lose out, but for me it will be good. Here in the company it will be good, too, but I will hardly be at home" (Jiří, driver).

In addition, employees in most head office departments (dispatch, warehouse and servicing) face another serious problem: interference by the job in leisure and private life which is not financially compensated. The servicing department manager identified this problem as the most significant disadvantage of his job.

> A telephone call at half past midnight four days in a row is nothing exceptional. My wife is bothered most. I come home at half past ten from my shift, go to sleep and a telephone call wakes me up and then again at half past six. (Karel, receiving technician)

The difficulty of organizing trade unions among such a disparate group

The company does not have a trade union organization and is not bound by a supra-enterprise collective agreement. The drivers tried to establish a trade union in the company, but the foundation of a trade union is very demanding in terms of organization and, what is more, it is conditional on the common representation of majority interests. The nature of the profession, however, makes it difficult for drivers to associate and the idea of establishing a trade union in the company did not come to fruition.

Trade unions? … The drivers did think about it seriously. But, how can I say it, they are a disparate group and they do not meet often, only sometimes in parking lots, one or two at a time… (Igor, lower management)

The company management does not want trade unions in the workplace. It would be expensive for the company in terms of both time and finances. According to the company's personnel manager, the trade unions, for example, do not sufficiently support business growth.

Career and development prospects a possible source of motivation?

Although career development is unlikely for a number of employees due to a flat organizational structure, the company offers possibilities for both personal and qualification growth. The employees may participate in various training courses. A number of compulsory and financially demanding training courses took place upon the establishment of the authorized servicing facility. The company also employs a language teacher holding language courses in which every employee can participate during working hours. Although these language courses might also be available for drivers they are not able to participate due to their sporadic presence on the company premises. Last year, selected employees completed training in individual departments on corporate strategy and corporate culture. The company organizes regular training for its employees on work safety.

Concerning employee benefits, the employer pays a contribution to additional pension insurance. The employer does not offer a boarding allowance or holidays beyond the legal four-week minimum.

Conclusion

The case study provides an exemplary lesson on how the Czech Republic's accession to the EU has brought with it many challenges for employers and thus many significant changes in employees' working lives. The increased volume of orders has increased company profits, but at the same time has increased the intensity of work and brought with it more stressful conditions and so more difficulties reconciling work and family life. Although the company offers some benefits and professional development opportunities to selected employees there are still considerable gaps in terms of the majority of workers, namely drivers. The company does not consider it necessary to invest in less qualified workers as there will be always somebody else at the door applying for that kind of job. Frequent overtime, a reasonable wage only at the expense of quality of life, health and safety risks connected with enforced violation of regulations, reduced opportunities to develop oneself and no family life are all attributes of the driver's profession. Given the company's profits in recent years we might assume that there was some room at least to reduce the working hours of drivers and not force them to violate

AETR regulations, and also to increase personnel to be able to cover the increased volume of orders more easily.

Czech Republic Case Study 2: Vicious circle in a supermarket – labour shortages, fast working rhythms and high turnover

The sectoral context in figures
The trade and repair sector represents 11.5 per cent (2005) of all employees in the private sector, second only to manufacturing; this share has been relatively stable over time. Despite the increasing influence of the big international retail chains the retail sector remains the domain of small and medium-sized businesses.

The trade and repair sector shows positive economic results, registering the biggest sectoral increase in nominal wages since 1993. More recently, however, wage growth in the sector has been slowing down. In recent years the average wage in trade and repair has been approximately at the level of the average wage. According to the statistics, large companies in foreign ownership offer above average wages. However, this does not apply to the company described in our case study.

Collective bargaining is carried out by the Czech Confederation of Commerce and Tourism (SOCR ÈR) for the employers' side and by the Union of Commercial Employees (OSPO) for the workers. The share of employees organized in the OSPO compared to the total number of employees in the sector is 3.5 per cent. The top-level collective agreement was signed for the years 2004 to 2007.

The following case study describes working conditions in an international retail chain operating in the Czech Republic, taking the example of a single grocery store. The study is based on interviews with six employees holding various positions in the store (main cashier, two assistant cashiers, department manager, two department employees), then with the store manager and the chairman of the trade organization. The case study draws also on the materials published by the company and the materials provided by the trade organization.

High staff turnover affects everybody
The company commenced operations in the Czech Republic in 1991 as one of the first investors entering the Czech market from Western Europe after the downfall of the communist regime.

At present, the company operates 290 stores under two names in the form of hypermarkets and supermarkets, which specialize in food. The company employs more than 14,000 people and thus is one of the largest employers in the Czech labour market.

The case study's focus of interest is a single food store. The store employs 30 employees in Prague. The store is organized into six departments: cashiers, groceries, dairy products, bread and pastries, vegetables and delicatessen. Each department has a manager. The administrative work is performed by a bookkeeper and an assistant; the warehouse work is carried out by two warehousemen and the running of the whole store is the responsibility of the store manager.

Women dominate the workforce (70 per cent). The age structure clusters into two groups: one third of the employees are of pre-retirement and retirement age; they have been working for the company for years and represent the core workforce at the store. The other two thirds of employees are young people who have just left school or have no other options open to them. If they find something better, however, they leave, leading to a high turnover among the employees. The intermediate age group is practically absent.

In terms of education, a secondary vocational education without a school leaving certificate prevails (75 per cent), followed by elementary education (25 per cent). No special qualifications or experience are required; elementary education is sufficient for a shop assistant's job.

Moderate representation of employees' interests

The company has a trade union organization, although its representation, activities and visibility are rather moderate. In all, 14 basic trade union organizations have been established, rather a low number given that there are almost 300 stores. These organizations are often very small, with only a few employees: not infrequently there are only three members, the legal minimum for the establishment of a trade union organization. The share of employees organized in the trade union in the grocery store under the study is around 10 per cent. The total number of company employees organized in trade unions is estimated in the hundreds. Although the employer does not particularly welcome trade unions, it behaves towards them correctly and does not prevent its employees from participating actively. Cases of the kind reported in the media concerning sanctions and threats by employers to employees who decided to establish trade unions in another international retail chain have never occurred in this company.

Top management considers the dialogue with the trade union representatives constructive and rates the cooperation as very good. The trade unions evaluate the cooperation as correct, too, but they are not satisfied with the lack of real change, which takes place rarely.

The company collective agreement was signed for 2004–07; the company is also bound by the top-level collective agreement.

The lack of interest in organizing trade unions is the result not only of the attitude of the employers in the retail sector, but also of the high employee turnover: the core of long-term employees is very small.

The basic problems identified by the trade unions in relation to working conditions are as follows: double shifts are worked, unpaid overtime, failure to observe rest times between individual shifts and uneven wage levels: entry level wages of new employees can be higher or at least the same as those of long-time employees.

Unpaid overtime and double record-keeping of working hours

Working hours and overtime represent the key problem identified by employees and their representatives.

Working hours are based on opening hours (the store is open Monday to Saturday, 7.00 to 20.00, and on Sunday from 8.00 to 20.00). The distribution of working hours varies based on the specific type of work and the employee's position. The working hours of most employees, cashiers and regular employees could be characterized as a double-shift operation, one week on, one week off: the first week the morning shift (6.30–13.30) and the second week the afternoon shift (13.00–20.30), combined with Saturday and Sunday work. Every other weekend is thus a working one for employees. The total number of hours a week should equal 40 hours, on average, as regulated by law.

The record-keeping system of working hours and the planning of shifts is not, however, in keeping with the requirements of the law. The recording of hours does not correspond to reality; furthermore, the right to breaks of at least 12 hours between long shifts and the entitlement to one day off after six days worked are not adhered to.

There is a long-term staff shortage in the stores and in combination with such inevitable problems, absences due to illness or other reasons mean that employees often face unexpected requests for overtime on top of their employment contracts. The overtime is not paid and not properly recorded in the official count of working hours.

Employees are compensated by time off in lieu, but this can in turn lead to a shortage of employees on a shift. This situation results from the system of double record-keeping of working hours: one official set of records, stored in the company computer system, and the real records, written in a ledger, where often not only overtime, but also the failure to observe compulsory rest periods between individual shifts appears.

> The whole attendance record is falsified there. There is the time we really come in and there is the time we put on record ... so that they are covered, our bookkeeper must also falsify things somehow. (Iva, shop assistant)

High intensity of work on the one hand and a lack of employees on the other thus leads to a systematic breach of the law.

The Labour Code is not complied with in any store ... well, you can't stick to the Labour Code when you're short of people; nobody forces them [employees] to be here from morning to late at night. You're definitely entitled to time off after working six days in a row, but it just isn't possible. (Olga, store manager)

Compliance with the regulations on working conditions is monitored by the Labour Inspectorate. However, if an inspection is announced in advance usually no breaches of the Labour Code are found, due to the above-mentioned double record-keeping of work attendance.

A typical example of overtime work which meets with strong resistance among employees is stock-taking, which takes place every one to three months. So that the store does not lose sales, stock-taking takes place during the evening until 24.00. The participation of all employees is compulsory and some employees start work the next day on the morning shift at 6.30.

Is there anything that the employees are satisfied with? Almost the only thing employees were satisfied with at work, apart from good relationships with workmates, was the maintenance of the compulsory meal breaks and rest times, which has improved recently.

Staff turnover – a pressing issue for everybody

High staff turnover is a problem affecting the top management of the company, individual store managers and the employees. This turnover is to a certain extent typical of the retail sector, but it is particularly high in this company. The management considers it a serious problem and tries to alleviate it by trying to identify the causes and then launching various programmes. According to company research, turnover results among other things from low wages, a lack of initial on-the-job training and inadequate communication between the management and the employees. Research also proves that young people leave the company most frequently. One problem not mentioned in the research but which is very urgent and definitely contributes to high staff turnover is unpaid overtime and hard time schedules.

The biggest problem is a lack of personnel; we do not have enough people or they are unqualified. Almost every week we hire new employees, then you have to train them, then they might not like the work because of pay conditions, so you keep on hiring employees over and over again. (Olga, store manager)

The trade unions regard staff turnover as a major problem due to the inflow of new, unqualified workers, who work at a lower level of efficiency and often for the same wages, which increases work intensity for other employees. As a result, the trade unions have protested against agency employees and at present they are no longer hired by the company. The store compensates for the ongoing lack of employees with full-time seasonal workers, students or pensioners.

Another common factor in high staff turnover could be the unrealistic expectations of new employees who are attracted by promises of good wages and bonuses which never correspond to reality.

Not only the low wages, but also the lack of appreciation of their work in the broader sense and the attitude of management to the employees contribute to workers' dissatisfaction and high staff turnover. The attitude of the employees towards the employer is illustrated clearly in the following quotation: "They just use people, squeeze them like lemons and they don't give a damn about them. They don't care about people, they just hire new ones" (Anna, cashier).

Work contracts – the idea of flexibility
Most store employees have concluded a work contract for an indefinite period. Prior to enactment of the law, successive fixed-term contracts were used, even over long periods. Apart from full-time employees, the store also employs seasonal workers. Employment agencies are no longer used (see above). The decision of the top management not to use agency employees was also influenced by a change in the law which meant that this form of employment no longer carries such financial benefits for the employer.

The work contracts of regular employees describe the job generally, as a "shop assistant", whether the employee works as a cashier or in individual departments. The reason for this is flexibility: all shop assistants should be able to substitute for one another. However, this does not work out in reality, as employees who do not normally work as cashiers are afraid of making mistakes which they would then have to rectify out of their own pockets.

Low wages
Generally, wages are below average in retail grocery chains. All employees questioned complained about low wages. Extra pay for work on Sundays and holidays are at the level laid down in the law. Overtime is not paid. The starting salaries of regular employees are CZK 60 per hour (EUR 2.11). Regular and qualified employees earn the highest wages, at CZK 63/64 per hour (EUR 2.22/2.26). Lower wages are at the level of CZK 55 per hour (EUR 1.94). Hourly rates are laid down in the work contract. Gross monthly salary is CZK 9,240 (EUR 325.58) for regular employees and up to CZK 18,000 (EUR 634.25) for departmental managers. The low wage level reflects the minimal requirements in terms of level of qualifications and experience. Despite the generally low wage level, starting salaries for less qualified workers have increased in recent years in Prague. The reason is the very low unemployment rate in Prague region (which is different from the rest of the Czech Republic). To be able to find good new employees, department managers have to offer a better salary, although they are not high enough to keep employees in the work for any length of time.

Uneven wage terms occur even among employees doing the same job. Some employees who have been working in the store a long time are disadvantaged. The wages of full-time employees do not increase in step with wages offered to newly hired employees. Thus, a distortion occurs, with the wages of new employees sometimes being higher than, or at least the same as, those of long-time employees.

Wages consist of a basic part, a personal appraisal and bonuses. The personal appraisal is prepared by the manager based on predetermined criteria. Bonuses depend on productivity and sales of the whole store. The store in question is unable to achieve the set targets over a long period and therefore the monthly bonuses are paid only very occasionally (once every six months), which has a very demotivating effect on the employees. Employees do not receive a bonus if they are sick for three or more days in a given month.

Other benefits in addition to the wage
The company collective agreement contains, apart from traditional benefits in the form of luncheon vouchers, 15 per cent discount vouchers given four times a year for shopping in the company stores. The company contributes to travel costs and, apart from the four weeks' holiday stipulated in the law, employees are also entitled to one day off for each year at the company.

Work and family: the impossible reconciliation
Unpaid overtime and working unsocial hours, especially at weekends, cause serious problems in reconciling work and family, especially because the majority of employees are women. The system of shift work also does not suit most women trying to take care of a family. The store manager adds: "Mums with nine- or ten-year-old children could not work such shifts" (Olga, store manager). There are always exceptions: one cashier stated that the double-shift operation enabled her to take care of her children since her husband worked the opposite shift for a different company.

Due to the impossibility of reconciling of work and family life the "middle generation" of employees is almost entirely missing. Only young people without a family and children on the one hand, and older employees on the other, are willing to stay and work under these conditions.

Training: only for managers or for little more than basic tasks
Further training is not offered to most employees. After the short initial on-the-job training, which takes one or two days, employees are supposed to get on with the job. Further training is offered to store managers in the form of language courses or the possibility of completing their secondary education. Managers of individual departments are trained regularly concerning the goods.

Now that the Czech Republic is part of the EU some grocery stores have begun to accept euros. The grocery store under study is a case in point.

Employees were not given any training on how to work with euros at the cash desk, however; they were asked to do so in their free time.

Vulnerable groups

Discrimination at work is at the root of the whole climate in the Czech labour market. Older people on the verge of retirement could be considered a vulnerable group; in the retail sector they are mostly women. They are afraid of not being able to find another job and therefore keep working for the company, even under disadvantageous conditions, such as lower wages than other workers. They have also to carry the burden of permanent labour shortages and thus a very high work intensity.

Another issue is the low proportion of women in management. In the food store in question women make up 70 per cent of all employees, but the gender ratio in management is 2:3 in favour of men. This is a general tendency: even in feminized sectors of the labour market, such as retail, male employees are more frequently represented in management.

Conclusion

This case study tries to look under the surface and reveal everyday practice and working conditions in the highly competitive retail sector. The labour shortages, which are a day-to-day problem in the store, lead to a very high work intensity which, together with low wages and unpaid overtime, result in very high staff turnover. The vicious circle is thus completed.

Wages are low, bonuses are rare and workers are overloaded. All in all, there is little motivation for employees to stay. To attract new employees slightly higher salaries are offered which results in unequal treatment of older employees whose salaries remain almost unchanged over the years. Older workers with longer work experience in the store, especially those about to retire, are thus at risk of unequal treatment concerning their wages.

The second group at risk of bad working conditions and low wages are young, less skilled workers who form two thirds of the employees in the store. Since there are no special qualification requirements to be employed in the store – a completed elementary education is sufficient – workers are easily replaceable. The Company does not invest to increase the human capital of grassroots workers by providing them with training opportunities. The company culture is basically: "If you don't like it, you know where the door is." There is no attempt to make the employees feel that they have a significant role and that they contribute to the company.

Czech Republic Case Study 3 – Hotels and restaurants: are there any regulations at all?

Sector dominated by SMEs and poor working conditions

Hotel and restaurants represent 3.5 per cent of all employees in the "civil" sector of the national economy. The proportion is growing all the time: in 2000 165,590 persons were registered as working in the sector; by 2005 the number had increased to 170,282.

The main characteristic of the sector is the prevalence of small companies: three out of four companies have 0–19 employees. Wages in hotels and restaurants are well below the national average; in fact, they are the lowest of all sectors.

Company 3: Small pub in Prague – trapped in a vicious circle of unfair treatment

The pub owner started his business as a sole trader two years ago with his wife, who has employee status. After a year the owner transformed the business into a limited liability company. They operated without any other employees for the first six months. Currently, they have six employees, working without a contract. Besides two waiters and two waitresses there is a cook and a female assistant (from Ukraine). The owner is still repaying the loan. Turnover has been rising gradually, however, and the owner considers the company's progress as positive.

Distrust of employees leading to work without contracts

> I have bad personal experience of employing people with a contract. I've tried it several times and most of them became lazy after they'd got a work contract. I can fire workers without a contract if they don't work properly. I like to be able to "bring the best out of them" by saying "Either do your job like you're supposed to or I'll show you the door." (Petr, owner)

In the end, the owner came to the conviction that it was better not to conclude any contracts with his employees at all.

Besides the rigid regulations, according to the pub owner the "overgenerous" unemployment security net is also to blame: high unemployment benefits mean that people can afford to be careless about their jobs. On this account, improper employer–employee relations predominantly have their roots in the overall environment of the sector.

> If I ran the business legally I wouldn't be able to compete. (Petr, owner)

High staff turnover as a result

On the other hand, the employers cannot be absolved of their shabby and illegal treatment of their employees, together with considerable work insecurity, leading to disloyalty on the part of employees towards their employer. *We can therefore talk about a vicious circle of unfairness.*

As already mentioned, it is clear that staff turnover is relatively high. This is typical of the sector as a whole, although it is not always down to the employee. Most employees in hotels and restaurants are easily replaceable. Therefore, there is an above average number of people working on fixed-term contracts because employers are perfectly happy to replace employees after two years.[28]

Trapped in high insecurity

Most actors in our case study agree on the following list of the most widespread practices as regards remuneration in hotels and restaurants:

• work contract on minimum wage + tips;
• work contract on minimum wage + fixed supplementary payment;
• no work contract + low daily fixed amount + sales bonus;
• no work contract + fixed amount per hour + no tips;
• no work contract + tips.

Since the employees at Company 3 work without a contract they receive all their money in cash. Their hourly wage is CZK 70 (EUR 2.4). The cook is the only staff member working full time, apart from the owner's wife, and receives CZK 1,000 (EUR 34.5) for a daily shift (14 hours). Currently, the waiters and waitresses work in the pub as a second job; nevertheless, some of them work there more than 30 hours a week on average. For instance, Marian the waiter works his main job as a shop assistant with a contract on the minimum wage: he works seven days a week for 12 hours a day, but has alternate weeks off.[29] He works these alternate weeks in the pub, starting at 3 p.m. and finishing at 1 a.m. Thus, Marian's average working week is 77 hours in total. Marian is single, without a girlfriend. His private life and "free" time are all behind the bar. He says that two jobs are necessary for him to maintain a decent standard of living.

Regarding family and work reconciliation, running a family business also makes higher demands on the pub owner. He and his wife split the time in the

---

28. Labour Code Amendment Act No. 46/2004 sets the maximum total duration of consecutive fixed-term employment contracts at two years.

29. According to the Labour Code §92, Sub. 1 employers shall organize working time in such a way that the employee is assured of continuous rest of at least 35 hours in a week (defined as seven successive calendar days).

pub more or less equally. However, it means that they hardly meet in private because of the long pub opening hours. Moreover, their son has little opportunity to spend time with both parents together.

Employees at Company 3 are reasonably satisfied with their wages. Most of them make a favourable comparison with their previous jobs. They also value the employee benefits they receive as exceptional:

> We get a free meal and soft beverages on tap are also free. On top of that, everything else is half price for staff. I've never experienced these perks before. In my opinion, he [the employer] does not regard employees as trash; I think he's happy that I'm working for him. (Lenka, waitress)

To motivate the employees, the pub owner from time to time pays bonuses when the pub is full and the workload is heavy. He is well aware that he has to encourage the employees somehow. On the other hand, he does not want to have a wage system dependent on tips since it encourages staff to cheat customers.

Because they work without a contract or with a contract but on the minimum wage the employees suffer from high insecurity in times of illness, holidays and future retirement.

> The worst of it is that you cannot survive when something unexpected happens. It happened to me at the bar where I worked two years ago. I had hurt my knee and I had to stay at home for two months. During that time I hardly had enough money to pay the rent and I was kept by my flatmates. (Marian, waiter)

Employees' living standards are very low; they are unable to get loans or mortgages. People in this position are forced, especially in Prague, to pay market rents which are usually higher than mortgage payments would be.

Attempts to resist employer ill-treatment can backfire. The CMTU CHT chair said that "if you have a dispute with your employer you get a bad reputation which can stay with you for the rest of your career." She referred to an informal HR managers' network which blacklists "unreliable" workers. This problem is more striking in small towns than in the capital.

Long working hours to make work pay
The erosion of working conditions can also be seen in the area of working time. The situation can be illustrated on the basis of the pub owner's interview. He was totally vague about his cook's working time, eventually admitting that the cook works 56 hours a week, which is far above statutory working hours. He commented on this by saying: "I would have to introduce a two-shift system, but then the staff wouldn't be able to earn enough." There are no bonuses for weekend work or when employees have to stay longer than opening hours.

Working time appears to be a problem even in bigger companies in the sector. The CMTU CHT chair mentioned no compensation for unclaimed leave and no bonuses for overtime or for work on weekends.

Conclusion
The overall working conditions situation seems very difficult in the hotels and restaurants sector. One might conclude that rules and statutory standards are flagrantly ignored, particularly in smaller companies.

However, the trade unions do not see the employees' future in the sector solely in dark colours. They believe that if they can achieve some success within larger companies they will be able to spread socially responsible behaviour even among small establishments. Regrettably, teaching business ethics is a very slow process requiring great efforts.

REFERENCES

Baštýř, I. 2005. *Selected topical problems of minimum wage application in the CR.RILSA*. Prague. http://www.vupsv.cz/Bastyr_uplatnovani_MM.pdf

Baštýř. I., and T. Kozelský. 2005. Questionnaire for EIRO comparative study on statutory minimum wages – case.

Czech Statistical Office. 2003. AD HOC Module results 2003 on lifetime education. http://www.czso.cz/csu/edicniplan.nsf/p/3119-04.

———. 2004. *Sick leave due to disease and accident in the Czech Republic in 2003*.

———. 2005. *Bulletin*, 6-2005.

Černík, J. 2006. Of clients and chereps: The organizational structures of Ukrainian labour migration. In A. Szczepaniková, M. Čaněk and J. Grill (eds), *Migration processes in Central and Eastern Europe: Unpacking the diversity*.

Fenclová, Z., P. Urban, D. Pelcová, J. Lebedová and L. Edgar. 2003. Occupational illnesses reported in the health and social care sector and in the veterinary sector in the Czech Republic 1996–2003. České pracovní lékařství. *Ročník* 5, č. 4.

Hospodářské noviny. 2004. The number of entrepreneurs is lower than last year – according to statistics the decrease is 31,000. http://www.szu.cz/chzp/rep04/kc05_10.htm.

Kadavá, Ch. 2005. Discrimination against women with children in the Czech Republic (CZ0504101N): http://www.eiro.eurofound.eu.int/2005/04/inbrief/cz0504101n.-html.

Krause, D., and J. Kux. 2004. *Short report on the issue of small and medium size enterprises*. Prague: RILSA.

Kroupa, A., J. Hála, Z. Mansfeldová, J. Kux, R. Vašková and I. Pleskot. 2002. *Development of social dialogue in the Czech Republic*. Prague: RILSA.

Leontiyeva, Y. 2005. *Ukrainians in the Czech Republic*. www.socioweb.cz.

Livínský, O., and R. Kočí. 2003. Profitable job: Trader in workplaces. In *To the Czech Republic to work*, insert in *Lidové noviny*: http://infoservis.net/art.php?id=1069232801.

Machonin, P. 2005. Poverty in the CR – life and the trickiness of the statistics. *Právo* (18 July).

Main Economic and Social Indicators of the Czech Republic 1990–2004. 2005. Bulletin No. 20. Prague: RILSA.

Mansfeldová, Z. 2005. Social dialogue and its future. In Z. Masfeldová and A. Kroupa (eds), *Participation and interest groups in the Czech Republic.* Prague: Sociologické nakladatelství.

Mareš, P., J. Vyhlídal and T. Syrovátka. 2002. *Unemployed on the labour market.* Brno: RILSA.

Maříková, H. (2005) What is the situation and perspective of women in the labour market in the Czech Republic? In *Women in the labour market (instances of good practice from Europe).* EKS.

MPSV. 2003. *Position of women on the labour market, gender inequalities and attitude of the population.* SOÚ AV.

———. 2005. *Men and women: Persecution and sexual harassment in the Czech industrial relations system.*

Polívka, M., and L. Zamykalová. 2000. *Making appropriate conditions to enforce flexible organization of work and working time as part of employment policy.* Prague: RILSA.

RILSA. 2003. *Modern society and its metamorphoses – MS5: Problems of labour market and policy.* Prague: MPSV.

Simerská, L. 2005. Equal opportunities and improving women's status in the context of foreign investment in the Czech Republic. In *The role of equal opportunities for men and women in enterprise prosperity* (A review from the international conference and the final report form the survey). Prague.

Sirovátka,T., and P. Mareš. 2006. Poverty, deprivation and social exclusion: the unemployment and the working poor. *Czech Sociological Review,* 42 (4). Prague: Institute of Sociology, Academy of Sciences.

Sirovátka, T. et al. 2005. Income poverty, material deprivation and social exclusion in the Czech Republic and its comparison with EU countries. Research paper from the project "Poverty Monitoring". Prague: RILSA – Research Centre Brno. http://www.vupsv.cz/Chudoba2004.pdf.

Štěpánková, P. 2003. Czech Republic. In: C. Wallace (ed.), *HWF Research Report No. 3,* HWF Survey: Country Survey Reports (May).

Vašková, R., J. Hála and A. Kroupa. 2005. Possibilities and barriers of the trade union membership. In Z. Masfeldová and A. Kroupa (eds), *Participation and interest groups in the Czech Republic.* Prague: Sociologické nakladatelství.

Vašková, R., and A. Kroupa. 2004. *Quality of working life in the Czech Republic.* http://www.eurofound.eu.int/ewco/surveys/CZ0502SR01/CZ0502SR01.htm

Večerník, J. 2001. *Labour market flexibility and employment security.* Czech Republic. Employment paper 2001/27. Geneva: International Labour Office.

Vlach, J., and I. Baštýř. 2003. *Basic aspects of earnings movement in the period of the Czech Republic's EU accession. Partial report – Summary of analyses.* Prague: RILSA.

Vyhlídal, J., and P. Mareš. 2006. *Changing risks and chances on the labour market. An analysis of position and chances of threatened groups on the labour market.* Prague: RILSA.

5. Denmark: Towards the individualization of working conditions?

Henrik Stener Pedersen, Rune Holm Christiansen and Maj Pagh Petersen

5.1 INTRODUCTION

Trends on possible vulnerability implications of working and employment conditions in Denmark are evolving in the context of the "flexicurity" labour market model, demographic developments, the educational level of the population, and transitions in the occupational structure, as well as the increasing impact of international competition.

The Danish labour market model is most often referred to in terms of the "flexicurity" model. The term "flexicurity" is used to describe the combination of flexibility and security with an active labour market policy. The flexibility is provided by the easy terms on which employers can hire and fire employees in accordance with enterprise performance. The security is provided to employees in case of unemployment by the social safety net. And the active labour market policy makes sure that unemployed workers are offered jobs or further training (Ministry of Employment, 2005). It is widely agreed that this labour market model has enabled Denmark to sustain economic dynamism. The current situation on the labour market is characterized by very low unemployment rates, labour market bottlenecks in some sectors and increasing labour shortages. With the forecast of still fewer potential labour market participants due to an ageing population, labour shortages are estimated to have increasing impact. This situation, paradoxically, both benefits workers and puts them at risk: while the obvious benefit is immediate access to jobs and income, the potential risk is an increased pace and intensity of work as fewer workers will have to work more.

There has been an overall rise in the educational level of the population, accompanied by a transition towards fewer jobs in manufacturing and more in services (Madsen, 2005). This change in occupational patterns has led to an overall improvement in the Danish working environment (Pedersen et al., 2003). This, together with the decentralization of collective bargaining and the trend towards the individualization of work, has paved the way for greater and wider flexibility in work organization. This has put stress, work–life balance and psychosocial work environment on the agenda, representing new sources of vulnerability in modern working life. However, in focusing attention on recent developments, "traditional" sources of vulnerability should not be neglected: gender differences are still striking, part-time work is often associated with lower wages and less favourable conditions of employment, the pace of work is persistently high and occupational accidents and musculoskeletal disorders constitute prevalent risks.

Table 5.1 below presents the potential sources of vulnerability identified by this assessment:

Table 5.1 Working and employment conditions in Denmark

Element	Item	Trends	Risks/Exposed groups
Contracts of employment	Self-employment	Small overall prevalence, but shift towards "new" service occupations Increasing flexibility	Long hours, lack of supplementary education, stress/ Workers who have attended long-cycle higher education
	Secondary employment	Stable	Low income or long hours Low-skilled part-time workers
	Fixed-term contracts	10% of the workforce	Job insecurity, lower income Mostly female workers, also workers at the edge of the labour market or young workers trying to achieve permanent employment
	Temporary agency work (TAW)	Rising, but only 1%–2% of total employment	More accidents (?), lack of social support / Low-skilled workers
Wages	Real wages	Overall increase	Inequality / Women in low pay occupations, on part time or negotiating wages individually
	Gender gap in wages	Wage disparity remains a labour market feature	
	Low wages	A slight trend towards a more unequal distribution of income	Inequality / Immigrants are more exposed to relative poverty
	Concession bargaining	Few instances	Lower income / Unskilled, low-skilled and some types of skilled workers

Working time and work organization	Long hours	Increase anticipated (due to present and future labour shortage)	Stress and less work–life balance / Mostly male self-employed, managers and professionals
	Part time	Decreasing	Involuntary part-time work, lower income and lack of career development opportunities / Female teachers, nurses, care assistants
	Irregular work schedules	Increasing	Working at odd hours against employees' wishes, lack of work–life balance Employees in services
	Flexible working time	Increasing, but significant gender differences	More men have flexible working time, but these arrangements are often accompanied by long hours and/or exposure to stress
	High pace of work	Constant, more widespread	Musculo-skeletal disorders, stress / manufacture, cleaning, etc. and care sector
	"Boundless" work	Sharp increase	Stress, burnout and lack of work–life balance / Especially advanced service and knowledge workers
Health and safety	Accidents	Stable, maybe increasing	Fatalities, disabilities /Male workers in craft and manufacturing. V. high risk of fatal accidents in construction
	Musculo-skeletal disorders	Stable	Disability or pain / Workers exposed to monotonous repetitive work or sedentary work. Especially women
	Psycho-social	Sharp increase	Depression and suicide / Women in personal services and office and admin, and men in low-skill jobs (highest prevalence registered for women)
Access to training	Participation in supplementary training	Reduction in formal vocational training	The development of a two-tier workforce workforce / Risk of young, unskilled male workers being "left behind", while level of education is generally rising
	Work pressure barrier	Possibly increasing	The absence of skills development /Higher educated professionals and self-employed

Work and family	The working family	Very prevalent	Unbalanced work–life/ Managers, teachers, professionals, nurses and care workers most affected
	Double workload for women	Decreasing	Lack of career development/ Women are still undertaking more household work and working fewer paid hours than men are
	Parental leave	Improved conditions	Risk of maintaining the gender imbalance leaving women with fewer opportunities for career development
	"Boundless" work	Increasing	Less of a distinction between work and private life involving more stress / Especially managers, teachers and professionals
Social dialogue and workers' participation	The trade union movement is adapting to change		The trade union is at risk of becoming less influential in the long term
	Decentrali-zation	Enterprise in focus	Sometimes at the expense of working and employment conditions / Labour market participants
	Individuali-zation	Individualization of working conditions	Weakened workplace union members' representative, more difficult to monitor working conditions and protect workers / Labour market participants
	Membership density	Decline, but still high	Weakened collective bargaining system / Labour market participants
The "new" sources of vulnerability	Marginali-zation	Possible emergence of two-tier workforce	Unskilled, male workers and immigrants most at risk
	New forms of work organization, "boundless work", team work, etc.	Teamwork becoming widespread, new management technologies, personal involvement	Stress, psychosocial risks associated with stress, work–life balance problems, burnout, long hours etc. So far, most prevalent among "knowledge workers", but spreading to other groups
	Socio-economic develop-ments	Labour shortage – expected rise in import of labour	Deregulation of working conditions, pressure on workers' rights

5.2 CONTRACTS OF EMPLOYMENT: NEW TRENDS IN A STABLE LABOUR MARKET

At first glance, employment in the Danish labour market could be summarized in terms of low unemployment rates, bottlenecks and labour shortages in some areas. This is related to the success of the "flexicurity" model mentioned in the introduction. Parallel to this development towards a historically low unemployment rate, the national working conditions survey, the Danish Work Environment Cohort Study (henceforth DWECS), last conducted in 2000 at the National Institute of Occupational Health (henceforth NIOH), found that the proportion of employees experiencing job insecurity decreased from approximately 26 per cent in 1990, to 16 per cent in 1995 and 2000 (Borg et al., 2002).

Atypical employment – an overview

In recent years the concept of atypical employment, and its prevalence and impact on the psychosocial work environment, has been widely discussed. Nevertheless, the vast majority of the working population continue to be engaged in traditional permanent employment relationships: the latest estimate is that around 90 per cent of all employees work on permanent contracts (Statistics Denmark, 2004a). As detailed data on employment contracts are not directly available we have to rely on survey results published between 2000 and 2002. There is some discussion on how to measure atypical employment, as it is not self-evident what should be considered "atypical". The point of discussion is whether "atypical employment" should cover workers that cannot be categorized as either employees or traditional self-employed (plumbers, electricians, and so on), or whether the term should only cover workers opting for or exposed to altogether new ways of organizing work. If the first – and broad – definition is adopted the term atypical employment covers an estimated 22 per cent of the workforce; and if the second – and narrower – definition is applied then 2–4 per cent. The 22 per cent include self-employed, temporary workers and employees engaged in more than one employment relationship, whereas the 2 per cent contain the self-employed, excluding traditional self-employment such as hairdressers, carpenters, farmers, and so on (see Table 5.2). Only the 2 per cent may be said to capture the "new" trend of an increased prevalence of what has been coined "free agents". Please note, however, that temporary agency work, which most researchers would consider atypical employment, is not contained in this 2 per cent.

Table 5.2 The prevalence of atypical employment in the Danish labour market

	Percentage	Survey population	Estimation of actual figures, relying on Statistics Denmark data
Total labour force (18–59)	100	5 447	2 559 000
– Self-employed	4	227	102 000
– Self-employed, excluding trad. self-employed	2	104	51 000
All employees	100	4 769	2 385 000
– Temporary employment	9	432	215 000
– Secondary employment	13	611	310 000
Self-employed and temporary employees (% of total labour force)	12	659	317 000
Self-employed, temporary employment and/or salaried workers with secondary employment	22	1 200	563 000

Source: Madsen and Petersen, 2000.

Looking at the development of atypical employment relationships Madsen and Petersen (2000) find that the proportion of self-employed and temporary workers has been relatively stable since the beginning of the 1980s. There are no dramatic increases to be identified. However, as the figures on the aggregate level remain unchanged and new groups of atypically employed can be identified, there is an indication of profound changes in the nature of atypical employment relationships. In industry and among unskilled or less-skilled workers it has diminished, whereas atypical employment has been on the rise in "new" service occupations demanding a more educated workforce, such as consultancy and IT. Atypical employment is not exactly growing, but it has taken a new form and is more widely distributed on the labour market.

Self-employment

Madsen and Petersen (2000) find that of the abovementioned 2 per cent of the workforce who can be categorized as self-employed 53 per cent have attended higher education, 39 per cent can be considered low paid and 55 per cent work more than 38 hours a week. As to wages it is evident in PLS (2001) that self-employment does not necessarily entail lower wages. According to this study, only 7 per cent of the atypically employed have low wages (defined as an income less than EUR 26,845/DKK 200,000 per year, before tax). Furthermore, it is reported that the average workweek for the self-employed is around 50 hours and that skills and competence development are less common for the self-employed than for employees in general. Considering that the self-employed – typically consultants, engineers, lawyers, and so on – most often work in areas where lifelong learning may prove to be crucial in the long term, we may speak of a new risk here. Apparently, the same process of work pressure (that is, long hours) as a barrier to further education as pointed out in the "Access to training" section is at work in the case of the self-employed. On the other hand, the self-employed report that they have more opportunities to learn new things on the job, which may compensate. Moreover, this is just one indication that the self-employed benefit from working conditions involving more human development than do employees in general: the self-employed experience more variation in tasks, more control, are more motivated and more satisfied with their jobs. However, as the better psychosocial work environment apparently compensates for the long hours it is still worth keeping in mind the issues that might emerge from working excessively: stress and other related health consequences and work–life balance problems. Moreover, we may suspect job insecurity to be more likely for the self-employed, although this has not been analysed in depth. Another aspect of the new forms of self-employment to be addressed is whether workers are pushed into self-employment or opt for it. The PLS study (2001) distinguishes between push and pull factors in the decision regarding self-employment. The study shows that most self-employed are pulled into self-employment: an indication that in the current situation self-employment is most often an option and/or a career opportunity. As labour shortages may become even more significant in the near future, the risk of a labour market pushing people into self-employment might diminish.

Secondary employment

Another type of atypical employment is when employees work more than one job. From Madsen and Petersen (2000) it appears, quite surprisingly, that those who have attended higher education are far more likely to maintain more than one job. Most of these employees are men, between 30 and 50 years of age. To identify the reasons why some employees have more than one job we have to distinguish further and take income and working time into consideration. Madsen and Petersen (2000) report that in some cases those with less formal education might be working two jobs for economic reasons and in other cases they might do so because they are employed considerably fewer hours in their main occupations than is the "typical" employee. In this group we might expect to find people at the margin of the labour market and employees on low wages (see "Wages") and/or vulnerable employees trapped in part-time work (see "Working time and work organization").

Fixed-term contracts

Approximately 10 per cent reported being hired on a temporary basis (Statistics Denmark, 2004a). According to Tüchsen et al. (2002), many temporary jobs are the result of the government-facilitated leave-of-absence schemes. The leave period for the permanently employed involves fixed-term employment for another worker, since the job is secured to the employee on leave. Hence, an initiative towards improving conditions for the permanently employed may involve less favourable conditions for others. Figures from Statistics Denmark (2004) reveal that of the estimated 240,000 employees on fixed-term contracts, 86,000 or 36 per cent report they could not find a permanent job. Of these, 62 per cent are women and 38 per cent men (Statistics Denmark, 2004a). The occupational groups most and least affected by fixed-term employment relationships are professionals, social and health workers, childcare workers, but also managers.

Temporary agency work (TAW)

From 1993 to 2004 the number of temporary agency workers increased, quite dramatically, from "virtually none" to somewhere between 16,000 and 32,000 employees. The uncertainty regarding the figures on TAW reflects differences in the conceptions of TAW as well as in the registers from which data are withdrawn. According to ECLM (2006) TAW employment involves 16,000 employees; according to Jørgensen (2006a) approximately 22,000; and according to Statistics Denmark (2004b) around 32,000. However, TAW continues to be relatively limited in terms of the labour market as a whole, making up somewhere around 1 per cent of total employment. Thus, the prevalence of TAW in Denmark is relatively low compared to, for example, the Netherlands and Luxembourg (Storrie, 2002) – an indication of the flexible labour market system: compared to Sweden and Germany, for example, it is relatively easy for employers to hire and fire workers in Denmark. However, in recent years the employers' association Danish Commerce and Service (DH&S) has signed collective and company-specific agreements with a variety of different trade unions, covering general workers in different industries and human service workers (Jørgensen, 2006a). In addition, sectoral agreements for TAW exist for the industry, construction, office and administration sectors and for electricians. Moreover, an agreement for the hotels and restaurant sector bans TAW (Employment Relations Research Centre, 2006). As to the actual effects of these agreements on working conditions at present we do not know very much, but we may assume that this formalization of working conditions has helped reduce the potential risks associated with TAW, such as lower wages, job insecurity and the lack of proper training.

5.3 WAGES: DENMARK IS WELL OFF, BUT DISPARITIES PERSIST

Generally, wages are relatively high and quite equally distributed in Denmark, compared to other countries. Most recently, wage-increase rates have been around 3 per cent and with the current very low inflation wages appear to be increasing steadily and have been doing so since around 1990 (Ministry of Finance, 2005; Statistics Denmark, 2006a). Moreover, inequalities in disposable household incomes have been estimated as fairly low compared to other countries (Ministry of Finance, 2004a). However, some observers point out that such inequalities are rising.

At the intersection of the ILO outline and national debates we are currently able to identify four ongoing, and sometimes overlapping, discussions on wages at the societal level and in different research communities:

1. the persistence of a gender gap in wages;
2. a trend towards greater inequality in income distribution, relative poverty and lower incomes among ethnic minorities;
3. wage concessions in industries affected by international competition.

Wage inequality – the gender gap in wages

A study by Deding and Wong (2004) shows that gender-related pay differences remain a feature of the Danish labour market. Deding and Wong (2004) find that the wage disparity between men and women remains quite stable over the investigated period, with just a small increase observed at the end of the period. Whether the average pay calculations are based on earnings per performed working hours (working hours excluding hours of absenteeism) or earnings per paid working hours (including hours of absenteeism), the conclusion remains: Danish men earn more than Danish women. On average, the pay gap is between 12 per cent and 18 per cent, depending on how pay is calculated. Differences in length of education and work experience are still important determining factors in explaining the gender pay gap. However, these factors have become less important during the five-year period under observation, given the overall rise in educational level among women. This indicates that the reasons for the gender pay gap must be found elsewhere: Deding and Wong (2004) emphasize occupational and sectoral gender segregation as crucial determining factors in explaining the pay gap. Many women work in lower-paid occupations and are traditionally employed in sectors with lower pay and a higher prevalence of part-time work. Furthermore, it is clear that promotion and career advancement influence the level of occupation and pay. In this respect, women in general are more likely to have an interrupted career path. Thus, the determining factors are gender differences in relation to part-time work and childcare leave. However, when the background variables contributing to the gender wage gap are all taken into consideration we still find a part of the gender wage gap to be unexplained. This, as stressed by many, may be a cultural issue of women not being as proactive as men in the still more widespread individual wage negotiations – a possible effect of decentralized bargaining and flexible work arrangements (see section "Social dialogue and workers' participation"). In terms of development towards more flexibility, women as a group may be regarded as in a less fortunate position than men.

Income distribution and low wages

In Denmark, the minimum wage system bargained by the social partners, in combination with the welfare state, is usually perceived as preventing poverty in society at large. Recently, however, the issue of relative poverty and whether there is poverty or a significant degree of income inequality in Danish society has been discussed. This discussion has mainly centred on the conditions faced by groups at risk of social exclusion: senior citizens, the long-term unemployed and others receiving social benefits. In addition, a tendency towards a more unequal distribution of income has been identified. The reason for the slightly increasing rates of inequality is mainly increasing house prices (adding to the disposable income of house owners) and income from interest (ECLM, 2005). The Danish Ministry of Finance (2004b) has estimated that of the 225,000 in the low-income group (the relatively poor) – those with a disposable income less than 50 per cent of median income – 32,000 are salaried workers and 21,000 are freelancers. This equals approximately 2 per cent of the active workforce. Unfortunately, we know very little about this group of workers and thus cannot provide further statistics. No attention has been directed towards the issue of low income as related to the world of work. Instead, the focus has been rather on ethnicity and the employment situation. The figures in Table 5.3 show that the wages of immigrants and descendants of immigrants are much lower that the average wages of Danish workers. The average incomes of descendants of immigrants from non-Western countries appear to be less than half the average income. However, this is partly explained by the differences in age between the different groups presented in the table. The average age is relatively higher for

Danes and wages are normally found to increase with age. Nevertheless, this factor cannot fully explain the differences in income levels.

Table 5.3 Average income (DKK) per year for immigrants, descendants and Danes 16–66 years of age, 2002

	Immigrants		Descendants		Danes	
	Persons	Average income	Persons	Average income	Persons	Average income
Western countries	92 697	208 761	8 174	231 849	–	–
Non-Western countries	185 797	152 317	15 497	115 140	–	–
Western/non-Western countries – total	278 497	171 104	23 673	155 455	–	–
Danes					3 308 806	244 469

Source: Dahl, 2005.

Furthermore, 11.5 per cent of all immigrants are found to live in relative poverty (Table 5.4). Since immigrants make up 21 per cent of the relative poor and only 7.7 per cent of the total population, being an immigrant equals increased risk of exposure to relative poverty (Dahl, 2005). In the case of immigrants and their descendants we may speak of circles of vulnerability as they have relatively lower wages, less education, are more likely to be loosely attached to the labour market and on average are more likely to commit a crime (for statistics, see Dahl, 2005). This vicious circle may be broken, however, as the cleaning enterprise case study in the second part of this report indicates: deliberate efforts to integrate ethnic minorities have been shown to have an effect.

Concession bargaining – what is the trend?

As no statistical evidence exists, we currently know very little about likely developments on concession bargaining – collective bargaining where work-

Table 5.4 Relative poverty – Danes and immigrants, 2002

	Share of total population	Share of ethnic group living in relative poverty	Ethnic group's share of the relative poor
Danes	92.3	3.6	79.0
Immigrants	7.7	11.5	21.0
Total population	100.0	4.2	100.0

Source: Dahl, 2005.

ers accept a wage reduction against employment security in enterprises facing severe competition. One feature appears to be that concession bargaining mainly affects firms in traditional industries employing unskilled, semi-skilled and skilled workers.

Concession bargaining may be considered a "new trend" in two respects:

1. Without the general decentralization of labour market bargaining wage concessions simply could not have taken place as they have – the concession bargaining we have seen so far is agreed upon at enterprise or even at enterprise divisional level (Due and Madsen, 2005).
2. The demands of some employers to cut wages have been substantiated by international competition and the possibilities of relocation.

Summing up, we may conclude that concession bargaining is an emerging potential trend. The question is whether this trend is going to have any significant impact on earnings. This has not been the case up to now.

5.4 WORKING TIME: DOES FLEXIBILITY PRESUPPOSE WORK INTENSITY?

Most collective agreements have laid down a 37-hour week. On average, Danish workers work 39.9 hours weekly and this has not changed significantly in recent years (Jørgensen, 2005a). Denmark has one of the shortest formal working weeks in Europe; only French and German workers have shorter weeks. This is the equivalent of 1,600 hours a year per worker on average against a 1,800-hour European average. Nevertheless, due to the very high labour-market participation rate for women, the Danish population as a whole spends more time in the labour market than any other Western nation, as every third couple/family spends more than 80 hours working a week, and less than 10 per cent fewer than 70 hours (Danish Board of Technology 2005 – see also the "Work and family" section). Moreover, working time arrangements are becoming increasingly flexible, often involving longer hours, part-time work and increased work intensity.

Working long hours, part time and irregular hours

The 37-hour week has been the norm since its introduction in 1990. Since then, working time reduction, or extension, has not been very high on the agenda in collective bargaining (Jørgensen, 2005a). The flexibility of collective agreements, however, in principle opens the way for alternative arrangements, including longer hours. Due to the impact of growing labour shortages, the Confederation of Danish Industries (DI) predicts that an increasing number of Danish companies will negotiate a 40–45 hour week with different groups of employees in the near future (TV2 Nyhederne, 2005). In the DWECS, the only data source operating with a concept of long hours (48 hours or more per week), they find that a total of 15 per cent (22 per cent of men and 8 per cent of women) of workers spend more than 48 hours at work (Tüchsen et al., 2002). The groups most exposed to long working weeks are freelancers, managers, professionals, lorry drivers and, as already mentioned, the self-employed.

Male predominance in terms of long working weeks coincides with a higher percentage of women in part-time work. According to Wehner et al. (2002) there are about three times as many women working part time as men. This is connected with the high frequency of part-time work in professions dominated by female workers, such as schoolteachers, nurses, home care assistants, office assistants and cleaning assistants. Another decisive factor is the socioeconomic status of occupational categories, as the jobs connected with higher income and education levels have a smaller prevalence of part-time work (see also "Wages"). Whether part-time employment constitutes a vulnerability trap or not depends on the reasons employees work part time. Though most employees work part time because they are engaged in training or education and do not want to work more, around 16 per cent – which approximates to 102,000 employees – work part time because they cannot find another job (17 per cent for women and 14 per cent for men) (Statistics Denmark, 2006b). This condition might pose a risk of low wages for some labour market participants. On the other hand, for others part-time work offers much needed flexibility in balancing work with family life.

In 2002, a law on part-time work was passed by the Danish Parliament. The act makes it easier to make agreements about part-time work at the enterprise level, regardless of the collective agreements already in place. The Danish Confederation of Trade Unions (LO) objected to the act since it weakens collective bargaining. However, the act makes it illegal for an employer to lay off employees who refuse to accept part-time work, and thus protects employees against being pressured into accepting a potentially precarious situation (Wehner, 2002).

As to irregular work schedules the percentage of 18–59-year-olds working irregular work schedules increased from 8 per cent in 1990 to 11 per cent in 2000 (Tüchsen et al., 2002). Employees in 24-hour care centres for children and senior citizens and nurses are among those with the most irregular schedules (the implications of this are examined in the care centre case study). It is anticipated that the expanding service sector and the demand for more flexible services will increase the overall prevalence of irregular schedules.

Finally, as regards flexible working time, apparently men are better off than women with regard to the opportunities furnished by positive flexibility: almost one in three male employees have flexible working time as against less than a quarter of females (Andersen et al., 2004).

Work intensity I – the traditional form: pace of work

The traditional form relates most directly to work intensity as it has manifested itself historically in manufacturing, at factories, and so on, in the form of an increased pace of work, achieved, for example, through time studies and scientific management.

Apparently, a decrease in the pace of work overall has not occurred, even though we have witnessed a rolling back of manufacturing industry (where a high work pace is traditionally the norm). This is mainly due to the fact that a higher pace of work has been introduced in other areas as well, especially in human services, for occupational categories such as care assistants and nurses. It has been reported, for instance, that every fourth nurse always/often has to skip lunch break (NIOH, 2005b). The high levels for pace of work thus reflect the persistence of a high work pace in occupations requiring relatively low skills, as illustrated in the cleaning enterprise case study, and the introduction of a higher pace of work in sectors which were traditionally better off, as illustrated by the care centre case study.

Work intensity II – new trend: piles of work under "boundless" conditions

A different kind of work intensity involves work that tends to pile up and work organized so that the workload of assignments and the time available to complete them satisfactorily cannot be reconciled, measured in terms of the tradition and concept of quantitative demands. These conditions relate particularly to knowledge work and lead to symptoms of stress and burnout. On average, 25 per cent experience that they "rarely" or "never" have the time needed to complete their assignments, while 31 per cent state this to be the case "sometimes" (NIOH, 2005a). Typical characteristics of knowledge work are that it is organized by projects and assignments, that it involves the appliance of information and communication technologies (ICT) and that the task of organizing work is left to the employee. This very often coincides with flexible working time arrangements and releases work from the spatial constraints of the workplace (through teleworking), leaving the employee with a chance to decide when and where to perform work – work becomes "boundless". This may be viewed as an achievement and employees performing knowledge work generally report being more satisfied with and dedicated to work.

However, we may point to some negative consequences as well. The use of ICT together with increased employee control often lead to an excessive increase in working time and work outside office hours (Financial Services Union, 2006; see also biotechnology enterprise case study), a potential stress factor which may influence the work–life balance negatively (see "Work and family"). Moreover, knowledge work often entails new management technologies *requiring* the employee to develop both professionally and personally. This may imply difficulties for the employee to insist on and maintain the boundary between work and private life (Danish Board of Technology, 2005; Bovbjerg, 2003).

5.5 HEALTH AND SAFETY: A SHIFT TOWARDS PSYCHO-SOCIAL RISKS

The exposure to different risks varies significantly across different job categories and sectors. In the DWECS the work environment was found to have improved from 1990 to 2000. This improvement, however, had more to do with the changing composition of the labour force than any actual interventions in the work environment. Thus, some risk factors now have less influence as fewer people are exposed to them. Nevertheless, this change also implies a shift in what we have to consider the most important work-related health outcomes.

Accidents – a persistent risk despite overall decline

Since 1996 a steady decline in work-related accidents has been observed. However, for 2004–05 there was an increase in recorded incidents (see Table 5.5). The Working Environment Authority (henceforth WEA) asserts that this

Table 5.5 Reported work-related accidents, Denmark, 2000–05

	Seriousness				Year of accident	
	2000	2001	2002	2003	2004	2005*
Fatal accidents	68	50	57	51	44	55
Other serious accidents	5 343	5 107	4 831	4 763	5 140	4 993
Other accidents	42 852	41 871	39 215	36 151	39 648	39 529
All accidents	48 263	47 028	44 103	40 965	44 832	44 577

Note: Number of accidents in 2005 expected to rise as more were reported that year.

Source: WEA, 2006.

increase is mainly due to the 2004 revision of the Workers Compensation Act (*Arbejdsskadessikringsloven*). As more occupational accidents are now being legally recognized there is more of an incentive for employees to report accidents to the WEA, whose registers have always been subject to underreporting (WEA, 2006). Paradoxically, increased figures in the WEA registers may thus reflect better conditions for injured workers. As to occupational accidents, male workers are more at risk than female. Male workers are involved in 1.6 times more accidents than female workers; and as regards serious accidents, male workers face twice the risk of female workers, and fatal accidents only rarely involve women. This is explained by the high prevalence of accidents in sectors dominated by men, such as construction and farming.

Furthermore, younger workers appear to be more exposed to accidents, presumably because they have less experience in the job (WEA, 2006).

Musculo-skeletal disorders a persistent problem

Musculo-skeletal disorders, which result from the strain of ergonomic factors, remain a prevalent occupational risk for Danish workers. What might appear to be an overall decline until 2003 now appears more as minor fluctuations around an incidence rate which remains quite high.

This decrease is presumably due to wider use of lifting equipment (technology) as well as relatively fewer jobs in the sectors demanding such intense physical activity. On the other hand, the disorders caused by the other main source of musculo-skeletal disorders, monotonous repetitive work, did not decline to the same extent: monotonous repetitive work is still widespread in the labour market, for instance, in the cleaning sector (see the cleaning enterprise case study). Female workers run almost double the risk of men of developing musculoskeletal disorders – with no indications of significant improvements in the near future. The change in occupational patterns towards more service jobs will most likely produce new patterns for the distribution of musculoskeletal disorders.

Table 5.6 Reported musculo-skeletal disorders by gender, Denmark, 2000–05

	2000	2001	2002	2003	2004	2005	Total
All workers	6 851	7 340	6 309	5 511	6 084	7 221	39 316
Men	2 515	2 725	2 436	2 128	2 331	2 896	15 031
Women	4 336	4 615	3 873	3 383	3 704	4 321	24 232

Source: WEA, 2006.

Prevalence of psychosocial diseases rapidly increasing

Though the exact prevalence of work-related psychosocial diseases is very difficult to estimate there are clear indications of an alarming trend. The recent growth speaks for itself. From accounting for only 3 per cent of occupational diseases in 1996, the increase to almost 17 per cent in 2005 is remarkable: while in 1996 there were 453 incidents, in 2005 there were 2,345 (Christiansen and Pedersen, 2005; WEA, 2006). Moreover, the WEA registers for psychosocial diseases are subject to considerable underreporting. It is suggested that the actual figures might be 20 times as high, based on a comparison with the DWECS. In given incidents, the source of the psychosocial disease, and whether indeed it is work-related, may be very difficult to assess due to the complexity of the matter: two individuals exposed to similar conditions of work may not display the same symptoms. The most frequently stated causes are (WEA, 2006):

*   bad relationships with colleagues, clients or superiors (including bullying);
*   excessive volume or pace of work;
*   traumatic experiences (including exposure to violence);
*   working time;
*   lack of job decision latitude.

Many of these risk factors are not single incidents, but working conditions that affect many employees during long periods of their working life. A lot of workers are exposed to these factors, even though they might not enter the statistics or develop an actual disease. Interestingly, male employees are somewhat better off in regard to these last mentioned conditions (Groth et al. 2002), whereas women are overly represented in the WEA registers on psychosocial diseases. Approximately three times as many psychosocial diseases are reported by women than by their male counterparts. This tendency is constant from 1993 to 2005, and partly displayed in Table 5.7.

Table 5.7 Reported psychosocial diseases, Denmark, 2000–05, by sex

	2000	2001	2002	2003	2004	2005	Total
All workers	870	1 213	1 423	1 551	1 955	2 345	9 357
Men	226	287	360	383	455	585	2 296
Women	644	926	1 063	1 168	1 483	1 758	7 042

Note: For 2004 and 2005 there are 17 diseases for which gender is not reported.

Source: WEA, 2006.

An explanation emerges when looking at the sectoral distribution of the incidents: four of the five sectors reporting most psychosocial disorders include human service workers, predominantly women (the fifth sector is office and administration). The underlying reason for this higher level of reporting among personal service workers is the very high emotional demands of care work (Pedersen et al., 2003), an increased exposure to violence and threats of violence – a risk that increased from 11 per cent to 21 per cent from 1993 to 2001 (Christiansen, 2005) and a very high pace of work leading to stress and burnout (see "Working time and work organization" and the care centre case study). Men are also affected. The Copenhagen Psychosocial Questionnaire (COPSOQ) identifies the worst psychosocial work environment among postal workers, slaughterhouse workers, bus drivers, medical secretaries, unskilled electronic equipment assemblers, warehouse workers and wrappers (NIOH, 2005c), of which the first three are jobs occupied mostly by men.

5.6 ACCESS TO TRAINING: HIGH ON THE AGENDA

Lifelong learning and access to training have been high on the agenda recently. In 2004, the Danish Government appointed a tripartite committee on lifelong qualifications development and education for all labour market participants. The committee consists of the social partners at national level and the relevant government ministries. It aims to ensure the continuous skills and competence development of Danish employees in the face of technological development and globalization. In March 2006 the Government and the social partners issued a final declaration calling for improvement in four areas:

1. Motivating more employees to participate in adult and continuing training, while also offering more possibilities for participation. In addition, employees' competences should be acknowledged to a greater degree.
2. Strengthening basic skills, particularly for those who are less well educated and for other vulnerable groups, such as non-nationals who need Danish language proficiency.
3. Ensuring that the different training schemes are attractive, focused and flexible in relation to both individual and company needs. Moreover, there must be an improved framework to ensure that employees can participate in adult and continuing training in their own time.
4. Ensuring that there is adequate financial and regulatory support.

So far, there has been no clarification on who is going to finance these improvements. However, the prime minister has encouraged the social partners to take the financing of the scheme into account in future rounds of collective bargaining (Jørgensen, 2006b).

Employee participation in further training and education

In assessing supplementary training activities in the workplace the Institute for Konjunkturanalyse or IFKA (2004) distinguishes between formal and informal training. IFKA (2004) concludes that there has been an overall reduction in training activities since 2000. This corresponds to the estimate published by the Ministry of Finance (2006), in which the above-mentioned tripartite committee concludes that activity in the field of publicly financed supplementary training decreased by approximately 5 per cent from 1994 to 2004. According to IFKA (2004) about 27 per cent of Danish employees have not participated in vocational training or any informal learning that can be characterized as training, and the group inactive in supplementary training counts more men than women. Moreover, formal training activities have been reduced significantly, when measured by the number of workers who have received education from different suppliers of vocational training. The group in the Danish labour market that is least engaged in formal education is young male workers who work at smaller workplaces in industry or in trade and service. Furthermore, companies with small budgets for training seem to be those with many unskilled workers and in the private sector those in industry, construction, trade and restaurants. For the public sector, residential care institutions are among the workplaces that spend the smallest amount on training per employee. The employees that do receive formal training are mainly top managers, salaried employees, managers of salaried employees and skilled workers. The fact that unskilled workers are passed over with respect to training compared to these groups is not surprising considering the types of education supplied: personal development, education of managers, and communication and teamwork are the most prevalent forms of training.

This unequal distribution of vocational training has led to a debate regarding the plausible development of a two-tier Danish workforce, the lower tier being unskilled or semiskilled workers. Workers who do not receive training are potentially exposed to marginalization, and this problem is reinforced by the development towards the relocation of low-skill jobs in the face of international competition (Madsen, 2005). We must mention, however, that this issue is much disputed and that the current situation of a labour shortage may mitigate such worst-case scenarios.

Pressure of work is a barrier to supplementary training

As part of the work of the tripartite committee mentioned above a survey was conducted mapping the barriers to further training. The survey results revealed that the main barrier was pressure of work: being busy at work and having no one to cover for the employee during training activities (Eurofound,

2006b). Data reveal that pressure of work is most often a barrier to further education for employees who have attended long-cycle higher education.

5.7 WORK AND FAMILY: WORK–LIFE IMBALANCE

Occupational patterns for men and women: the working family

Denmark has the highest employment-to-population ratio in Europe. The age group of 16–66 years old consists of approximately 3.6 million people, and of those, 73 per cent are active in the labour market. Women are only slightly underrepresented in this age group, making up approximately 47 per cent of the labour force and 50 per cent of the 16–66 year old population (Statistics Denmark, 2006a). This occupational pattern of female workers means that the Danish population overall works more than any other Western nation's population (see "Working time"), despite the fact that formal working time is shorter than ever before. This might explain why around 34 per cent of employees experience that work demands the energies of the employee to such an extent that it conflicts with family or private life, and 25 per cent feel that work takes away too much time from family or private life (NIOH, 2006). At first sight, it might seem paradoxical that the highest employment-to-population ratios are found among men and women living in couples with children (Andersen et al., 2004). This is only possible due to the support of a well-developed public childcare system. Figures isolated for Copenhagen show that 63 per cent of children 0–2 years of age and 96 per cent of children 3–5 years of age attend childcare facilities of various sorts (Rostgaard, 2004). Nevertheless, this group of employees is also the group wishing most to reduce time spent at work (Danish Board of Technology, 2005).

Distribution of domestic work – is there a "double workload" for women?

When both partners are working the distribution of domestic work becomes even more important. On the basis of 1987 and 2001 datasets Bonke (2002) shows that the time allocated to paid work, domestic work and primary needs (sleep, hygiene, and so on) has increased, resulting in leisure time being reduced by one and a half hours a day. The gender gap is narrowing in the sense that there is a less distinct difference between hours spent on paid work and hours spent on domestic work by the two sexes. Still, men spend around an hour more on paid work than women, whereas women spend an hour more on domestic work. Though we cannot speak of a double workload for women – since the total amount of working time (paid and domestic) is quite equally distributed between the two sexes – we may say that women are more likely to perform unpaid work than men are.

Parental leave and gender equality

The conditions for parental leave have improved in recent years. A law was passed in 2001 providing parents with the opportunity to take care of their children at home by offering financial support. From 2002, maternity leave was extended by 20 weeks, and now parents have 52 weeks with a per diem allowance at their disposal. It has also become possible to opt for a combination of leave and part-time work. Paradoxically, some observers point out that these initiatives might not promote gender equality. The Confederation of Salaried Employees and Civil Servants in Denmark (FTF) (2004) states that the extended parental leave arrangement is actually adding to this imbalance, as it is women who receive most of the extra leave. Parental leave is also a question of financing in many families. When distributing the leave time between them, couples are often reluctant to give up the man's (usually higher) salary. Indeed, Danish women still take the majority of the leave period. On average, Danish fathers spent 18 days on leave after their child was born, while women took leave for an average of 272 days after giving birth (Statistics Denmark, 2006c). As a result, every third privately employed female engineer, bachelor of commerce or lawyer has experienced negative effects on their career in connection with parental leave, and one in ten report losing their job, despite the law's prescriptions (Danish Society of Engineers, IDA, 2005). The underlying reason for such discriminatory practices is the companies' costs in relation to parental leave. Smaller businesses in particular experience this problem, and it represents another potential barrier for hiring or promoting women. However, there seems to exist a consensus regarding the establishment of a central employer-financed equalization fund for parental leave. This will help ensure equalization of companies' costs in connection with parental leave benefits, according to the Danish Confederation of Trade Unions (LO), as the costs of parental leave will fall on the fund and not directly on the single employer. Most social partners have already agreed to establish such funds, and by October 2006 the part of the labour market not covered by collective agreements will be covered by a fund set up by parliament.

5.8 SOCIAL DIALOGUE AND WORKERS' PARTICIPATION: DECENTRALIZATION

Denmark, together with the other Scandinavian countries, is distinctive in that many fundamental working and employment conditions are defined by a basic agreement rather than by labour law. Historically, this has its basis in the "September Compromise" agreed on by the Danish Confederation of Trade Unions (LO) and the Confederation of Danish Employers (DA) in 1899. The result of this compromise was the founding of the collective bargaining system – although revised several times, still in force – based on the basic agreement (*Hovedaftalen*). The basic agreement covers conditions that apply to all members, such as working time, minimum wages, workers' participation, and so on. The fundamental rules regarding workers' representatives, for instance, have their basis in the basic agreement. The continuing influence of trade unions is reflected by the figures: 77 per cent of the private labour market is covered by collective agreements, leaving the remaining share to private/individual agreements or the protection of the White-Collar Workers' Act (*Funktionærloven*), while in the public sector the coverage of collective agreements is 100 per cent (Jørgensen, 2005b). However, new trade-offs have emerged as a result of the decentralization of the bargaining system and a declining union membership density.

Challenges for the trade union movement in adapting to change

The "traditional" issues of collective bargaining – wages and working time – have always been a focal point in bargaining. However, approaches to the question have varied considerably in recent decades. The reduction of working time has not been on the agenda for some 20 years. Instead, variable working time and, more recently, flexibility have been the central issues. Wages have also lost importance in the central negotiations and are left to be determined locally to a larger extent. The Danish model can be categorized as a *multi-level bargaining system*, meaning that negotiations take place at intersectoral, sectoral and enterprise level, and that these levels are interconnected (Jørgensen, 2005a). Generally, there has been a shift from sectoral bargaining towards more company-level collective bargaining and every aspect of pay and working conditions is now negotiable at company level, as long as management and employees agree to negotiate (Jørgensen, 2005b). This decentralization of bargaining is altering the role of the workplace union members' representatives. They are now engaged proactively in creating higher quality jobs and involved in important company decisions. This certainly provides an opportunity to secure and improve quality of work and employment (see the biotechnological enterprise case study). However, this development includes new trade-offs, potentially exposing employees to the risk of the negative effects of flexibility (see "Working time").

In addition to the decentralization already described, the individualization of work in some areas may prove to usurp trade union representation. As wages in some workplaces are increasingly set according to individual negotiations and work becomes organized more by the "self-managing" individual, employees may come to consider trade union representation as less important. Interestingly, one survey reveals that employees increasingly consult company HR consultants instead of the trade union representatives on questions on wages, parental leave, further training, and so on (Ugebrevet A4, 2005).

These circumstances partly explain the decline in trade union membership. Union membership density declined from 83 per cent in 1996 to 78 per cent in 2005. The fact that many young people choose not to sign up is one important factor. The unions had 471,000 young members in 1993, but this number had fallen by 40 per cent by 2005, when only 284,000 young people were organized. This is mostly explained by demographic changes, smaller birth cohorts, but it does reflect a reduced affiliation. Another explanation is the increased educational level. As more years are being spent in education, fewer are spent in the labour market. This implies that the pool of potential members is being reduced. However, rising educational levels also entail new patterns of distribution of employees among the different trade unions, meaning a relative increase in membership for the Confederation of Salaried Employees and Civil Servants in Denmark (FTF) and the Danish Confederation of Professional Associations (AC), at the expense of the Danish Confederation of Trade Unions (LO). Another development is the flow of new members to trade unions not affiliated to the three official trade union confederations. The 13 unions currently outside the three confederations – unions such as the Christian Trade Union (KF) and unions aiming at very specific occupational groups – now have a total of 151,082 members, or 7–8 per cent of unionized labour (Jørgensen, 2005c). Finally, in the present situation of very low unemployment rates and a general acceptance of the notion of increasing labour shortages, union membership may seem unnecessary to some workers.

CONCLUSION: IDENTIFICATION OF VULNERABLE WORKERS

The task of identifying vulnerable workers is complicated, as the concept of work is becoming increasingly "boundless" in more than one sense. New types of jobs are emerging across traditional professional boundaries and traditional occupations are being redefined by the adding of new tasks. It is of course still possible – and relevant – to pinpoint the cumulative effects of different risks on well-known categories. This is done in the first part of this section. Some new sources of vulnerability are more difficult to assign to specific jobs or sectors. These are aspects of work determined by new ways of organizing work, and their impact transcends traditional labour market categories. The most debated of these issues are presented in the second part of this section.

Vulnerable groups of workers

Considered as a group, women accumulate most risks. Women are more at risk of being lower paid, in a less favourable position regarding individual wage negotiations, trapped in part-time employment and of having fewer opportunities for career development. They are less likely to be able to balance work and family life through flexibility, have less job control, are more likely to enter the statistics for psychosocial disorders and are generally more at risk of developing musculo-skeletal disorders. Nevertheless, men should not be considered a privileged group. Male workers are more at risk from accidents and fatality (this applies particularly to construction workers) and of not receiving enough supplementary training. They are more at risk of working long hours, and of being exposed to the negative impacts of flexible forms of work organization.

If we look at more specific groups of workers, this assessment finds unskilled workers, together with immigrants, more at risk of being left behind as the impacts of international competition and globalization intensify. Highly educated professionals appear more at risk of working long hours with a high intensity of work and poor work–life balance, leading to increased stress and burnout. Finally, human service workers, primarily in the care sector, are at risk of a very high pace of work and stressful conditions.

The "new" sources of vulnerability

The high prevalence of stress among workers is linked to new ways of organizing work. In this assessment, this is in part illustrated by the concept of boundless work. This especially relates to the knowledge work of highly educated professionals, but is spreading to other parts of the labour market as well. Boundless jobs demand a high level of commitment, empowering the "self-managing" employee and typically leading to higher job satisfaction. However, the exact same characteristics are a potential cause of stress, burnout and a less balanced work life.

Self-employment and temporary agency work (TAW) have so far only limited prevalence, but have been discussed widely in the anticipation that it might become more widespread. Apparently, the relaxed regulations on hiring and firing in the flexicurity labour market counteract very dramatic increases for atypical employment. Nevertheless, the two express the significant trend of flexibility in work and employment. The self-employed are typically well off, though working long hours and at risk of not developing enough skills and competences. The TAW may be a professional (for example, a nurse) whose skills are in high demand or a low-skilled worker vulnerable to poor working conditions. However, as more TAW are now covered by collective agreements it would be more appropriate to speak of an integration of TAW into the established labour market than of a return to the conditions of day-labourers.

A final interesting development is the shortage of labour. This is already a serious problem in the construction sector, and bottlenecks are anticipated in other sectors as well. This has so far only resulted in a limited importation of labour, but the presence of Eastern European workers has given rise to heated debates. The trade unions, for instance, are concerned that foreign workers will put pressure on wages and that they will undermine the employment status of Danish workers as secured by collective agreement. It is still too early to predict the future scale and influence of imported labour, but it is plausible that it will have an impact on working and employment conditions.

REALITY AT ENTERPRISE LEVEL: CASE STUDIES

Summary

The case studies presented here illustrate:

• how different working conditions influence each other, taking the local context into account, and how different trade-offs emerge at enterprise level;
• potential cumulative effects or results of specific combinations of risk factors;
• the development trends presented and the different points assessed in the first part of this report;
• the impact of social dialogue and collective bargaining.

As to the more specific criteria of inclusion and the composition of cases, the case study enterprises were chosen in accordance with the risks and exposed groups identified in the first part of this report. The three cases thus illustrate and encompass as many as possible of the sources of vulnerability displayed in Table 5.8.

Table 5.8 Main features of case study enterprises, Denmark

	Case 1 – Novozymes	Case 2 – ISS	Case 3 – Sølund
Main perspectives	Knowledge work and work–life balance – new job characteristics new risks	Traditional jobs in the face of change – labour shortages, employee turnover and job development	Public-sector care of senior citizens – trends in working and empl. conditions as an ageing population increases the significance of public services and work in human services
Sector	Biotechnology	Cleaning	Health care
Location	Suburban area	Large city	Large city
Employment contracts	Permanent	Permanent	Permanent Temporary
Wages	High	Low	Low
Working time	37h/week Overtime, long hours and working time flexibility is prevalent	37h/week Part time Evening and night work Weekend work	37h/week 28h/week (night) Part time Evening and night work Weekend work

	Case 1 – Novozymes	Case 2 – ISS	Case 3 – Sølund
Access to training	Integrated in jobs	Facilitated by the enterprise and increasing	Possible
Health and safety	Stress	Musculo-skeletal disorders Poor psychosocial work environment	Stress and burnout High emotional demands
Social dialogue and workers' participation	Local	Collective agreements	Collective agreements

Vulnerability implications

The case studies reveal the different vulnerability implications inherent in knowledge work, cleaning and care for senior citizens. When considering vulnerability implications the immediate context of the case should not be neglected. It is noteworthy that a contributor to work intensity in one case study may be regarded as a possibility for job development in another case. In Case Study 1, the adding of different tasks to the job of the knowledge worker increases work pressure, whereas it diversifies the job of the cleaning assistant in Case Study 2. This is due to the characteristics of the job already in place by the time of the new development. Moreover, the specific story of the cases should not be neglected when focusing on vulnerability implications. In each case, counterweights and tendencies counteracting worse conditions of work and the negative impacts of occupational risks can be identified.

The vulnerability implications identified as a result of the three case studies are summarized in Table 5.9:

Table 5.9 Vulnerability implications of working and employment conditions, Denmark

Occupational risks relevant – concepts assessed in first part	Contributors to vulnerability – categorized according to case material
Case 1 – Novozymes • Psychosocial risks – stress • Long hours • Flexible working time • Work intensity • Work–life balance	• Stress • Flexibility • Individualized organization of work • Work intensity – shorter deadlines, more tasks • Organizational change • Lack of work–life balance • Flexible working time

Case 2 – ISS	
• Low wages	• High employee turnover
• Musculo-skeletal disorders	• Low wages and status
• Unsocial hours	• Work intensity leading to stress
• Work intensity	and ergonomic exposure
• Psychosocial risks	• Working alone and at odd hours
• Lack of training	• Pace of work bargained by the
	social partners
	• Timeframes fixed in the cleaning contracts

Case 3 – Sølund	
• Gender	• Stress and burnout
• Work intensity	• Work intensity
• Low wages	• Lack of resources for care work
• Unsocial hours – shift work/	• Emotional demands
irregular work schedules	• Increasing demands in care of clients
• Psychosocial diseases	• Lack of work–life balance –
• Stress	due to evening and night work
• Work–life imbalance	

Note: The table only summarizes vulnerability implications and not the specific context and counter tendencies.

Denmark Case Study 1: "Boundless" work in biotechnology

This case presents working-conditions issues related to knowledge work in a modern enterprise heavily dependent on R&D. By knowledge work we refer to employees whose work includes developing or utilizing knowledge. A knowledge worker has typically attended higher education and undertakes tasks related to seeking, analysing, organizing or processing information. Working-conditions issues and risk factors normally related to this type of work include working long hours, stress, work intensity in the form of tight deadlines and work–life balance problems. Nevertheless, knowledge work also typically involves a greater degree of job decision-making latitude than other types of jobs and a lack of traditional health and safety issues, such as physical exposure.

The sector: an infant industry experiencing high growth
The biotechnology industry consists of enterprises whose primary commercial activity depends on either the application of biological organisms, systems or processes or provides specialist services to facilitate the understanding of those things. The products of the industry are utilized for agricultural, environmental and health-care purposes.

The biotechnology industry is an example of an "infant" industry that has experienced impressive growth rates over the last decade. The speed of this process can be discerned in the following figures: in 1988 only nine companies operated in the Danish labour market, but by 2003, 100 companies had been established in the biotechnology industry, as many as 45 in the period 2001 to 2003. In 2003 the sector was estimated to employ 17,329 persons. However, although employment in the sector has risen dramatically, the biotechnology industry still only makes up approximately 0.6 per cent of total employment.

An enterprise under permanent price pressure
Novozymes is a leading international biotechnological company employing 4,068 persons at 39 facilities, on four different continents. In this case presentation we focus on knowledge workers at the Novozymes headquarters, just outside Copenhagen.

Novozymes was founded in 2000 when it was decided to separate Novozymes from the medical company Novo Nordisk in order to concentrate on the new market for enzymes. Novozymes operates in an international market and changes in working conditions may reflect that. For a number of years Novozymes has reported experiencing constant price pressure on its markets. They also face increasing competition in the future from producers in low-cost countries, particularly China and India.

Conditions of work and employment: new opportunities and new risks
Knowledge-intensive production at Novozymes is identified as offering new possibilities for employee development and increased job autonomy. At the same time, however, it is producing new risks for knowledge workers.

Good performance on occupational health and safety
Measured on the basis of such traditional variables as levels of occupational disease and accidents, rate of absence or employee turnover, Novozymes appears a model workplace and displays a high level of corporate social responsibility. Though employee turnover rose from 5.5 per cent in 2004 to 6.6 per cent in 2005, it can still be considered fairly low. In addition, average seniority at Novozymes is nine years. The rate of sick leave fluctuated around 2.5 per cent to 3 per cent for the period 2001 to 2005. In comparison, the Ministry of Employment (2005) estimates the national average to be around 5 per cent.

As to occupational accidents, Novozymes lies far below the national average. At Novozymes the frequency of occupational accidents per million working hours was 7.1 in 2004 and 4.6 in 2005. The national average, according to the Confederation of Danish Employers, fluctuates around 30 accidents per million working hours (Confederation of Danish Employers, 2006). With regard to occupational diseases the frequency was 1.8 per million working hours at Novozymes. This may be considered quite low, though we lack proper data sources for comparison.

Novozymes not covered by a collective agreement

In national debate the decreasing influence and gradually altering role of the trade union movement is a recurrent issue. In this respect Novozymes appears almost as the ideal type of modern enterprise often referred to by researchers in search of development trends. Novozymes is not covered by any collective agreement. This is not because Novozymes does not accept the unionization of employees. On the contrary, there is a long tradition at Novozymes of union–management bargaining. The local unions at Novozymes bargain all conditions related to work and employment. However, approximately only 50 per cent of employees are organized in unions. This (for Denmark) very low percentage does not reflect a decline in union membership at the workplace – it has never been much higher. The relatively low figures for unionization at Novozymes (if compared to the 78 per cent national average) reflect the fact that professionals at Novozymes experience less of a need to organize in unions than employees in other enterprises and sectors. Correspondingly, relations between management and unions are characterized more by open dialogue, mutual respect, close cooperation and compromise, while conflict arises only in relation to particular issues. Also characteristic of this relationship between the two parties is that employees contact managerial staff or the human resource department as frequently as they do the local union representative in various situations calling for clarification in the workplace.

Interestingly, this arrangement does not in itself imply worsening working conditions and increased vulnerability for employees.

Stress at work the most prevalent problem

Through "work climate surveys" carried out every second year Novozymes has identified work-related stress to be a problem which is possibly on the rise. Stress levels, as well as employees' estimate of the importance of the issue, have been recorded for 2001, 2003 and 2005. Interpreting the stress figures as hard data may be somewhat problematic as the three waves of the survey are quite close and the reference period quite short. Interestingly, however, the figures do not reveal significant changes in recorded stress levels, although the importance of the issue in the employees' opinion is increasing. Nevertheless, from interviews with Novozymes representatives it becomes evident that stress is agreed to be a prevalent problem and a key symptom reflecting the intensity and organization of work. It has been possible to identify four, to some extent interrelated, causes of stress:

1. flexibility;
2. individualized work organization;
3. work pressure; and
4. organizational change.

1. The concept of flexibility may be said to encompass the three last-mentioned causes, and should be regarded as parallel to the concept of boundless work as described in the first part of this report. Flexibility may function as a stressor in the sense that it entails less clarity of roles in work organization, leading to insecurity and a need to clarify expectations on the part of employees. From embracing flexibility as the solution to all problems, Novozymes' management has come to realize that flexibility may have negative impacts as well. One way to counteract the negative impacts of flexibility could be a move to less flexibility in work organization. However, such a strategy would imply giving up the increased job decision-making latitude or autonomy of employees also inherent in the flexible organization practised at Novozymes.

2. One aspect of flexibility which deserves to be described at a little more length is individualized work organization. Planning the sequence of work, planning how to perform work, planning working time, deciding the place of work (teleworking) and, to a great extent, deciding the content of work, is undertaken by individual knowledge workers at Novozymes. In this sense, the employee should be seen as self-managing. This way of organizing work should indeed be perceived as empowering employees and contributing to higher job quality. On the other hand, these conditions put great demands on the individual employee's ability to function independently and navigate through work, as well as requiring committed employees to limit their efforts in order not to work excessively. Thus, the psychosocial dynamics resulting from individualized work organization may increase work intensity.

3. In addition, work pressure is reported to arise from flexible ways of organizing work in a more traditional sense. At Novozymes shorter deadlines for work projects, more diverse tasks and more tasks in general have continuously been given to knowledge workers. This means that the knowledge workers now undertake more administrative and practical/technical tasks, tasks formerly undertaken by secretaries and other administrative personnel, building caretakers and technical personnel – all categories of job reduced in numbers at Novozymes. This development is the result of an increasing focus on efficiency in the face of increased international competition.

4. Finally, organizational change is reported as a contributor to stress. This is mainly due to the insecurity concerning roles and the distribution of tasks to be performed, usually following restructuring. The adjustment to new conditions in the workplace takes place only gradually, and employees may encounter stress or insecurity in this process.

As already mentioned, the management at Novozymes is well aware of the issues mentioned above. In recognition of this, the human resource department at Novozymes offers courses in working and stress management techniques, and, after a period of facilitating major projects, is currently focusing strongly on ensuring a continuous clarification of expectations in relations between employee and management by facilitating common procedures for employee–management dialogue.

Work–life balance reflects work organization and working time
Novozymes operates on the basis of a negotiated 37-hour workweek for employees. Still, work–life balance is reported as being an issue. Two main reasons for this can be identified:

1. There are employees who cannot manage to get their work done within the 37 weekly hours; these employees work overtime on a permanent basis, so to speak. Normally, overtime is compensated, but if the hours accumulated exceed 50, compensation is not given for the additional hours, according to a rule passed unilaterally by management.
2. The option of working from home facilitated by Novozymes leads some employees to work additional hours and, in many instances, without recording the hours spent (for example, answering e-mails at night). Private and family life do seem to suffer from these conditions.

The work–life balance problems of many employees have led Novozymes to facilitate tools for ensuring a balance for employees, to provide flexible maternity and paternity leave schemes for employees, provide employees with the opportunity to work from home (this may have opposite effects, depending on the employee), and so on. The persistence of work–life balance problems, however, apparently relates to the distance from top-level management initiatives and programmes to everyday practice in the different departments at Novozymes, as well as the fact that there are no mechanisms incorporated in work–life balance programmes that restrict employees from working excessively. There are two factors that may contribute to improving the possibility of striking a balance:

1. At Novozymes employee representatives and the human resource department have a tradition of working closely together.
2. The HR department strongly emphasizes facilitating dialogue across all levels of the organization.

Conclusion
The present case study illustrates working- and employment-conditions trends for the "academic professional" or knowledge worker in boundless work (as assessed in the first part of this chapter). Due to international competition and an increased organizational focus on efficiency and new ways of organizing work, the Novozymes case study illustrates:

- the lower membership density of trade unions and their altered role, more integrated in the (human resource) policies of the enterprise;
- the diminished influence of traditional exposure factors, as measured by employee turnover, sick leave and occupational accidents;
- "boundless" work: flexibility, individualization of work organization, increased work intensity and constant organizational change; and their negative impacts;
- increased stress levels and problems reconciling work and family life;
- interestingly, however, increased employee control and job satisfaction also proves to be a result of working under boundless conditions.

Denmark Case Study 2: Resolving shortages and turnover through organizational changes and employment of ethnic minorities

Introduction

This case presents the "traditional" job of cleaning in a large-scale enterprise, focusing on developing services. The risks related to working conditions and employment associated with cleaning are typically perceived to be the detrimental effects on employees of monotonous repetitive work, work intensity, low status and wages, and lack of skill development opportunities. However, this case study illustrates significant countermeasures: the integration of ethnic minorities as a means of counterbalancing a high employee turnover and labour shortages, considerable progress in the elimination of risk factors traditionally associated with cleaning and the development of cleaning jobs.

A sector dominated by both large firms and individual self-employed

The cleaning sector in Denmark is characterized by a few very large companies and a vast number of small enterprises, often self-employed. Throughout the 1990s many public institutions decided to give their cleaning contracts to private enterprises instead of employing their own personnel.

Enterprise ISS: growing and diversifying in labour-intensive services

ISS is an international company founded and based in Denmark. The ISS Corporation employs approximately 311,000 employees worldwide, around 13,400 of them in Denmark.

ISS's core business has historically been cleaning services. Over the years the products offered have developed into many different services related to cleaning, thus reflecting the flexibility demanded today. For the time being, ISS has four main business areas: (i) cleaning; (ii) property services; (iii) office support; and (iv) catering.

Moreover, these different elements are offered as integrated services, enabling customers to co-design the product they opt for.

In this case description we focus on the cleaning services provided by ISS. The overall question to be addressed is in what way, to what extent or whether the job of cleaning is being transformed or remains "traditional" in the face of modern management practices and enterprise development.

Cleaning is normally considered a labour-intensive service and a physically hard job. This also holds true in the case of ISS. However, as documented below, interesting changes and tendencies can be identified.

From "cleaning lady" to cleaning professional – from part time to full time
Historically, cleaning was a job undertaken mostly as part-time work by women whose husbands were the breadwinners. This highly gender-specific job profile has changed over the years. Within the last decade or so, cleaning as part-time work has become less common, and less gender-specific. Nevertheless, ISS estimates that today the share of employees working part time in ISS is below the national average of 14–15 per cent (according to Statistics Denmark, 2005). Most of the employees working part time at ISS today are either students or persons holding the job as secondary employment. The main reason for this reduction in part-time work, according to both ISS and the trade unions, is that it is more advantageous to have cleaning personnel working full time. For ISS, the incentive is to inculcate stronger ties to the company in individual workers and to improve quality. For the trade union the incentive is to make cleaning a profession that the employee can make a living out of, and to make the development of higher job quality more likely. The trade union focuses particularly on training as a means of improving wages and job status, as well as a way of reducing monotonous and repetitive work. Moreover, the introduction of service assistant vocational training (endorsed by the social partners and the Ministry of Education) and the training courses facilitated by ISS should be considered an integral part of the process described above.

Shortages pulling up wage levels
The wage of a cleaning assistant at ISS is similar to the industry level negotiated with the general workers' trade union, the United Federation of Danish Workers (3F). Cleaning personnel are paid by the hour at a rate of DKK 112.5/ EUR 15.1 per hour, which is around the average. On the other hand we find two indications that wage levels might increase in the near future. First, the current shortage of labour in the Danish labour market may put pressure on wages to increase. According to the collective agreement, ISS has the possibility of hiring people at less than the agreed minimum wage for the first three months of employment. In practice, however, ISS does not apply this provi-

sion as the result would be a labour shortage. In addition, cleaning has always been a sector in which the better-qualified part of the workforce could find employment if high unemployment should afflict their "own" sector. Typically, in the case of unemployment in building and related trades, cleaning jobs are undertaken by skilled workers. In the current situation, with a general labour shortage, skilled workers are re-employed in their respective trades, leaving ISS with a smaller base for recruiting new personnel. This may contribute to a general increase in wages for cleaning assistants.

Secondly, these days cleaning does not necessarily entail unskilled employment since the introduction of official service assistant training and ISS's efforts to train employees at all levels may point in the direction of higher status and higher wages for cleaning professionals. Although there are examples of higher wages for trained cleaning personnel in public institutions, higher wages for trained personnel are not (yet) integrated in the collective agreements.

Lowering turnover through employment of ethnic minorities and on-the-job training

Like any other company in the cleaning sector, ISS currently faces the problem of high employee turnover and the difficulties of attracting new employees (due to the general shortage of labour in the Danish labour market). Labour turnover is mostly related to newly hired employees; employees who stay in the job for some time tend to continue the occupation of cleaning assistant. Reducing the costs of hiring and training new employees has become a new focus for ISS. Efforts to reduce employee turnover have for the time being taken two forms:

1. socio-experimental projects focusing on the psychosocial work environment in workplaces, conducted and partly financed in collaboration with work environment actors and authorities;
2. public–private partnerships for referral to employment and on-the-job training at ISS for the unemployed on public benefit schemes.

1. As to the first type of project, results show that initiatives to develop jobs characterized by repetitiveness, a high pace of work, lack of development opportunities, working at odd hours and working alone in the direction of more job decision-making latitude, resolution of conflicts and redefinition of job content have reduced employee turnover and sick leave. Moreover, the project "Attentiveness in the workplace" (*Nærvær på arbejdspladsen*) showed that it is possible to reduce employee turnover at workplaces with a high share of ethnic minorities (non-European nationals and descendants of non-European nationals), a group often considered to have only tenuous

attachment to the labour market. At ISS approximately 33 per cent of all employees have a non-Danish ethnic background and are employed under the same conditions as ethnic Danes. In comparison, ethnic minorities constitute somewhere around 10 per cent of the Danish population.

The above-mentioned project also aimed at developing jobs so that employees experience greater involvement in the job, creating shared values for employees and management across different cultures and developing a work culture that involves different ethnic groups. The concrete measures taken to ensure these results included involving employees in the quality assurance of their work, participation in the planning of holidays, Danish courses for the different ethnic groups, contributions to increase efficiency in a context of cutbacks, the creation of a forum for information and consultation, telephone contact with absent employees following up on sick leave, and so on. The project has shown that is possible to improve job quality, as well as contribute to the integration of ethnic minorities through deliberate efforts. Moreover, the "Attentiveness in the workplace" project has shown positive results financially, and in this sense it might raise awareness of the importance of the psychosocial work environment and lead to alternative ways of organizing work on a larger scale.

2. As to the second type of project, programmes designed to upgrade skills and competencies via on-the-job training have managed to move approximately two thirds of those involved from public benefit schemes to regular employment at ISS or elsewhere. ISS is currently involved in approximately 20 different public–private partnerships of this kind. The projects are not identical, but in the case of the suburban municipality of Herlev the project involves the municipal administration referring potential employees to ISS after a first application for social benefits (*kontanthjælp*). At ISS it is assessed whether the person can be hired immediately or should first pass through a course of individually designed on-the-job training. So far, 113 persons have been referred to ISS and 67 per cent have gone from public benefits to gainful employment.

Occupational health and safety – towards the elimination of monotonous and repetitive work?
It is hard to determine whether ISS is different from other cleaning enterprises in respect of health and safety exposures in general, as hard data exist only for occupational accidents. On that count, ISS employees are exposed to approximately 30 accidents per million working hours, which is similar to the sectoral average, according to the Confederation of Danish Employers (DA). On a general note, ISS benefits from being a large enterprise and from the formalization of the management of health and safety at work in the form of the

principal health and safety committee as the main coordinator of health and safety related activities (*Hovedsikkerhedsudvalget*). In terms of improving the chemical and physical work environment, there is a constant search for and development of more environmentally friendly cleansing agents, reducing the risk of exposure to harmful chemicals, and the introduction of a new and ergonomically better mop. Activities such as these have helped considerably to reduce the risks associated with cleaning. As regards safety, ISS seeks to ensure that employees perform their different tasks in such a way as to result in the least ergonomic, chemical, and so on, exposure. This information on the safest possible ways of performing work is provided through the training of new employees and the health and safety representative at the workplace (*sikkerhedsrepræsentant*), inspections and quality control, and the (statutory) annual workplace assessment ("APV").

In the last 15 years much attention has been focused on reducing the prevalence of musculo-skeletal disorders and the negative impacts of monotonous and repetitive work – first, via the rotation of employees to different areas and the variation of tasks performed; secondly, via development, which is currently altering the job profile of cleaning assistants and finds expression in such concepts as "visible service", "visible cleaning" and "facility service". These concepts are offered to customers as additional services as a way of increasing the level of service (for example, distributing mail in the firm, setting up meetings, and so on). The concept aims at having ISS customers outsource more service functions than the cleaning already provided.

Nevertheless, there may still be two obstacles to eliminating repetitive work. First, we may point to the possible discrepancy between the intentions of the principal health and safety committee (*hovedsikkerhedsudvalget*) and everyday practice at different workplaces. Secondly, the specific organizational context may in some instances counteract efforts to promote safety behaviour. Customer demand, price specified in the contract, service level and time use, local management practices and type of cleaning may all put pressure on cleaning personnel and increase work intensity, resulting in a poorer ergonomic environment as safety procedures are set aside. Interestingly, however, the main contributor to intensity of work is the high pace of work fixed in the collective agreements bargained by the social partners. The trade unions accept a high pace of work to ensure that employees can make a living out of a full-time (37-hour) cleaning job.

Problems due to psychosocial work environment and job development
Although the psychosocial work environment may vary to a great extent at the different ISS workplaces according to local circumstances, cleaning jobs at ISS do share some general features:

- Working alone and at odd hours – many do not feel safe working at night and alone. Employees are instructed to cope with the situation and, for example, asked to lock the doors to adjoining rooms to provide some sense of security.
- Job decision-making latitude in relation to the performance of different operations – apart from health and safety instructions and contractual obligations, employees are free to decide how and in what order to perform different operations.
- Job decision-making latitude in relation to working time schedules – in some instances employees are free to allocate working hours as they wish within a certain time interval, for example, between 5 p.m. and 8 a.m.
- Feeling of community among colleagues – this has to be "engineered" to some degree as cleaning is undertaken by individuals working mostly alone. An ISS employee representative reports the introduction of a "log book" in which issues to be discussed can be entered and joint breaks as positive developments.
- Management quality – may vary a great deal according to local circumstances.

There is a shared awareness at ISS that problems in the psychosocial work environment are connected with high rates of employee turnover and sick leave. Sick leave is measured as a regular part of the statutory workplace assessments ("APV") and is reported to the principal health and safety committee as an indicator of the state of the psychosocial work environment. Moreover, discussions are held with employees who have had sick leave to evaluate whether the absence is related to the work environment in any way. These discussions are conducted on the basis of the Work Environment Act (*Arbejdsmiljøloven*) provisions which state that such discussions must be between two equal parties. In addition, problems in the psychosocial work environment may be uncovered through employee satisfaction surveys carried out on a regular basis, and, if the psychosocial work environment at a workplace is called into question, a questionnaire developed by the National Institute of Occupational Health is applied. The figures for sick leave are quite similar to the national average. At ISS the figures for long-term sick leave (*dagpengeberettiget sygefravær*) are around 3 per cent, whereas the national average is somewhere around 2.6 per cent (Ministry of Employment, 2005).

Stress: the conflict between time frame and the wish to do a good job
Stress is also reported to be a problem. In some instances stress is reported to lead to conflicts such as harassment. ISS has a very clear policy on harassment of every kind, and reacts promptly by reporting any incident that may come to its knowledge to the relevant authorities. Stress and related psychosocial

exposures are reported as being caused by the high pace of work and the time allotted for cleaning laid down in the customer contracts: cleaning contracts include a definite time frame for cleaning each area, according to the level of service the customer wishes to pay for. Interestingly, it is reported that stress in some instances may arise as the result of a conflict between the time frame measured for cleaning a given facility and the employee's wish to do a good job. These employees feel that if they perform the work as laid down in the customer contract they do not leave the facilities *really clean*, which they would prefer. However, this depends on individual employees and their notion of work done properly.

Conclusion

In many instances, cleaning is still characterized by the exposure factors traditionally associated with cleaning jobs. Cleaning typically includes: relatively low wages and status, working at odd hours, exposure to the risk of developing musculo-skeletal disorders, working at a high pace, working alone and relatively low amounts of autonomy in the job.

This reflects the fact that the elimination of risks is difficult, given the nature of the job, the demands of customers in a highly competitive market and the pace of work bargained by the social partners.

However, our results show clear indications of job and skills development and increased job quality to face labour market bottlenecks and to adapt to the increasing demand for the training of employees, as job profiles change. At the same time, the integration of ethnic minorities was developed as a way to reduce staff turnover and solve shortage problems.

The trends illustrated by this case study include:

- organizational innovation (socio-experimental projects, public–private partnerships, new service concepts);
- corporate social responsibility (integration of ethnic minorities and unemployed);
- formalization of health and safety activities (systematic development of safer technology; equipment and materials and instructions on working more safely); and
- developing skills and competences (officially sanctioned vocational education, vocational training programmes, courses, and so on).

They contribute to reducing levels of sick leave, increase job decision-making latitude, diversify job content, increase the labour-market affiliation of persons at the margins, reduce ergonomic and psychosocial risks and develop employees.

Denmark Case Study 3: The difficulty of attracting skilled labour in demanding, stressful and poorly funded care centres

The working and employment conditions issues usually considered in relation to the institutional care of senior citizens include: difficulties attracting qualified workers at care centres and recruiting students for basic social and health training (*SOSU-uddannelserne*), the low status and relatively low wages, the high risk of developing musculo-skeletal disorders (especially in the lower back), low job decision-making latitude, high emotional demands, a high pace of work, which is further increasing due to reductions in public expenditure, and, on the bright side, the fact that care assistants value their work as meaningful and that management is supportive of employees.

Sector characteristics: workers' exposure to psychosocial problems
Care of senior citizens is typically undertaken by public institutions or care centres which report to the municipal administration as the directly responsible authority. The care centres vary a lot in terms of size, number of employees, psychosocial work environment and facilities offered to the residents and employees, according to current political arrangements and the budgeting of the municipal authority. Data provided by Statistics Denmark indicate that in 2005 95,899 persons were employed at residential and sheltered homes (primarily for the elderly).

Regardless of the variation mentioned above, there are two things common to working conditions for employees who care for senior citizens at all care centres:

1. The municipalities generally follow a senior citizen policy which entails keeping them in their own homes for as long as possible; the care requested from care centres has thus become more intensive as clients are in general older and more in need of care and assistance.
2. Employees at care centres are covered by and work according to identical collective agreements.

A survey of the psychosocial work environment conducted by the National Institute of Occupational Health in 2005 (National Institute of Occupational Health, 2005) revealed that employees at care centres for senior citizens are significantly more exposed to: emotional demands; the need to hide their emotions; burnout; stress; insomnia; symptoms of depression; somatic stress; and cognitive stress than employees in general. Moreover, the employees at care centres experience less variation in their work and rate their general health as being worse than employees in general.

Sølund, the largest care centre in Copenhagen
The Sølund care centre in Copenhagen is a residential home for senior citizens. Although the centre has its own management it reports to the municipal administration which has overall responsibility for quality of care. The 400 seniors are nursed by around 400 persons (including all personnel at the care centre), of which a substantial proportion work part time. This makes Sølund the largest care centre in Copenhagen. Our focus will be the work performed by employees directly involved in the care of senior citizens (*"Social- og sundhedsassistenter"*, *"Plejehjemsassistenter"*, *"Social- og sundhed-shjælpere"* and *"Sygehjælpere"*). In addition, the care centre employs trained nurses in the care of senior citizens.

Conditions of work and employment: accumulated risks
Most of the psychosocial risk factors outlined previously are also found at Sølund. Sølund has difficulties attracting qualified labour, the occupation of care assistants is reported as being characterized by relatively low wages and a lack of status, a high pace of work and high emotional demands on the employee. Moreover, stress appears as the major problem in the workplace and several incidences of work-related burnout have occurred. However, results indicate that awareness and a willingness to counteract such factors might mitigate the negative effects and point towards potential solutions. However, demographic and economic conditions as well as policy decisions might turn out to indicate developments in the opposite direction.

Occupational health and safety – technology improves working conditions
For the Sølund care centre, the statistics on accidents at work show an increasing trend. In 2003, 12 accidents were reported; in 2004, the number was 18; while for 2005, 26 accidents were reported. At first sight, these figures might appear alarming. However, underlying the increasing number of accidents reported is the fact that work-related accidents became a target area at the care centre during the same period. Thus, the most likely explanation of the increase is the increased focus on accidents: in other words, previously there was substantial under-reporting. Though we are not able to give an exact estimate, the physical work environment has become safer at Sølund. Two reasons for this have been identified:

1. The risk of accidents and ergonomic exposures has been reduced gradually as adequate equipment and technology have been developed. In the care of senior citizens at care centres, the main physical exposure has always been patient transfer. Previously, this task was undertaken simply by lifting the patient. Now, however, employees are not allowed to lift patients

without using the proper equipment: various technical aids have been developed covering the different types of patient transfer. In addition, it is required for all care workers at the centre to attend courses in patient transfer techniques, while transfer technique instructors are employed in all units housing senior citizens at the care centre.

2. The formalization of health and safety activities at the care centre has most likely helped to increase safety, as attention is directed towards existing risks and work environment issues not taken into consideration before.

Working day and night – the need for alternative contracts of employment

As care is required at all hours, Sølund needs to be manned around the clock. Since it is the experience at Sølund that night shifts cannot be fully manned by full-time employees (as a consequence of the difficulties of attracting qualified labour), part-time employees, substitutes and temporary agency workers are used to a great extent. Sølund employs approximately 400 persons, of whom only 260 are full time. This means that as many as 35 per cent of the employees at the care centre work part time – the national average is 14–15 per cent (Statistics Denmark, 2005). However, in the case of Sølund part-time work should not be considered a source of vulnerability, as part-time employees are only used by the care centre as a way of counteracting the labour shortage. The employees working part time can be grouped into two categories. The first group consists of employees hired on a permanent basis, but for personal reasons wishing only to work part time. If such an employee wishes to work more hours the care centre generally responds either by offering more hours of care work or by offering the employee other work (cleaning, cooking, and so on). This is possible mostly because of the size of the workplace. The other group of part-time employees consists of students and others who work at the centre as secondary employment. These employees typically leave the care sector again.

Employees at Sølund work a regular 37-hour week (the national standard). However, for employees working evening and night shifts, 28 hours a week counts as full time. The department manager plans work schedules together with the individual employee. However, this does not completely eliminate the work–family conflict. Work–life balance is reported as a problem for some employees.

Stress and burnout relate to the intensity of work

Stress is the most prevalent and significant work-related health hazard at Sølund. Stress is reported to be the cause underlying most occupational accidents, as employees sometimes neglect safety procedures, typically in situations when the employee is stressed or pressured by work. Similarly, burnout leading to longer periods of sick leave among employees at Sølund is not unheard of. The care centre does not have a specific policy to counter stress and burnout, but is aware of the problem. Initiatives to reduce stress levels include arranging "topic days" where work environment professionals or private consultancy firms are invited to provide employees with the knowledge and tools to cope with a stressful work environment. In addition, stress is discussed frequently at the meetings of the health and safety committee at the care centre (which consists of both management and employee representatives). This means that the subject of stress is not taboo and is discussed openly at the workplace.

Two main sources of stress have been identified: first, emotional demands that may be considered intrinsic to the work, which involves close contact with clients or patients. For care assistants the emotional strain of conflicts arising from impatience or aggression on the part of clients, typically due to waiting, may result in stress. This stress factor has been on the rise since there has been a trend towards more demanding clients at the care centre as the age of the clients has risen due to the policy of providing care in the home for as long as possible. Secondly, at the core of the stress problem lies the high pace and pressure of work. This, again, is reported to reflect the care centre's lack of resources. At Sølund it is estimated that the administration and authorities do not allocate enough workers to cover all care services. This leads to increased work intensity for the existing employees.

The high levels of stress and the general pressure of work are partly reflected in the statistics on sick leave: at Sølund sick leave amounts to 7.7 per cent, somewhat higher than the average national level of approximately 5 per cent (Ministry of Employment, 2005).

Trends for the near future
In the case of Sølund, the current high employee turnover is not an appropriate indicator of quality of work. For employees with a peripheral association with the care centre (students, and so on) a high turnover can be expected. In addition, the average age of employees at Sølund is relatively high and at present many employees are retiring each year. This means that Sølund has a high turnover in parallel with a high average seniority. However, the high turnover is a problem in another respect: it intensifies the difficulties of attracting qualified labour. Above all, Sølund is not capable of attracting social and health care trainees (approved vocational training for the care sector). Another aspect of the difficulties of attracting qualified labour is presented by the relatively low wages for care centre personnel. It seems that there are no tendencies worth mentioning that could mitigate the problem of labour shortage at the care centre. On the contrary, care of senior citizens remains highly gender-specific employment: only 7.5 per cent of employees are male (and there are no indications of a change), and the care needed by the centre's clients is grad-

ually becoming more demanding. If the demands for care increase without a proportionate allocation of economic resources then the task of attracting qualified labour may become even more difficult.

Conclusion

This case study illustrates trends affecting employees at public sector care centres providing care services for senior citizens in the context of an "ageing society". The implication of demographic development in Denmark is that a relatively larger share of citizens will be seniors in the future. This, on the other hand, means that a larger share of the workforce will be employed in the care sector in general, and at care centres for senior citizens in particular. This development underscores the need to focus on working conditions for care workers.

From this case study the main challenges for ensuring and improving the quality of work for employees at public sector care centres are as follows:

- a safer physical work environment; and thus
- a shift from physical to psychosocial work environment risks;
- necessity for evening and night work which applies to care work in general;
- the interrelations of stress, pace of work and resources;
- the problem of an increasing administrative burden for employees;
- the use of peripheral labour to counter the difficulties of attracting qualified personnel; and
- increased pressure on care centre employees to cope with more demanding clients.

The vulnerability issues reflected by this case study are:

- work–life balance problems arising from the need to provide round-the-clock services;
- stress as a result of an increased pace of work;
- burnout resulting in long periods of sick leave for single employees;
- increased emotional demands and conflicts as work pressure increases in the context of human service work.

The existing problems will only be exacerbated by the increased pressure on care services resulting from an ageing population.

REFERENCES

Andersen, M., S.B. Pedersen and V. Skov. 2004. *Køn og arbejdsliv*. Statistics Denmark, Copenhagen.

Bonke, J., and N.T. Meilbak. 1999. *Danskere på fuld tid – deres faktiske og ønskede arbejdstid*. SFI-survey, Copenhagen.

Bonke, J. 2002. *Tid og velfærd*. National Institute of Social Research, Copenhagen.

Borg, V., H. Burr and E. Villadsen. 2002. *Psykosocialt arbejdsmiljø – Arbejdsmiljø i Danmark 2000*. National Institute of Occupational Health, Copenhagen.

Bovbjerg, K.M. 2003. Selvets disciplinering – en ny pagt i arbejdslivet. *Tidsskrift for arbejdsliv*, no. 3.

Confederation of Salaried Employees and Civil Servants in Denmark (FTF). 2004. *Ligestilling mellem kvinder og mænd*, at http://www.ftf.dk/page.dsp?page=6514.

Christiansen, J.M. 2005. *Vold på arbejdet – med særlig vægt på FTF-medlemmernes arbejdspladser*. Copenhagen: CASA.

Christiansen, R.H., and H.S. Pedersen. 2005. *Trends for risk factors in the Danish work environment*. Dublin: European Foundation for the Improvement of Living and Working Conditions.

Dahl, K. 2005. *Margrethe, Etniske minoriteter i tal*. Copenhagen: National Institute of Social Research.

Danish Board of Technology (Teknologirådet). 2005. *Balancen mellem arbejdsliv og andet liv*. Copenhagen: The Danish Board of Technology (Teknologirådet).

Danish Society of Engineers (IDA). 2005. *Barselsorlov koster*, at http://ida.dk/Nyheder/Presseklip+fra+IDA/2005/April/18.04.+Barselsorlov+koster .htm.

Deding, M., and K. Wong 2004. *Mænd og kvinders løn – en analyse af løngabet 1997–2004*. Copenhagen: National Institute of Social Research.

Due, J., and J.S. Madsen. 2005. *Den danske model – revisited*. Copenhagen: Employment Relations Research Centre (FAOS).

ECLM (Economic Council of the Labour Movement – Arbejderbevægelsens erhvervs-råd). 2005. *Indkomstuligheden stiger fortsat*, at http://www.aeraadet.dk/media/file-bank/org/Indkomstulighed-mb.pdf.

———. 2006. *Fortsat kraftig vækst i vikarbranchen*, at http://www.aeraadet.dk/ media/filebank/org/vikarbesk-2006q1-mw.pdf.

Employment Relations Research Centre (FAOS). 2006. *I krydsfeltet mellem fleksi-bilitet og sikkerhed*. Copenhagen: Employment Relations Research Centre (FAOS).

European Foundation for the Improvement of Living and Working Conditions. 2006a. *Outlook for occupational risk trends*, at http://www.eurofound.eu.int/ewco/ 2006/01/DK0601NU05.htm.

———. 2006b. *Pressure of work is main barrier to further education*, at http://www.eurofound.eu.int/ewco/2006/03/DK0603019I.htm.

Financial Services Union. 2006. *Smil du er på – en undersøgelse af arbejdsliv og psykisk arbejdsmiljø i den finansielle sektor*. Copenhagen: Financial Services Union.

Groth, M.V., H. Burr and A. Guichard. 2002. *Køn, arbejdsmiljø og helbred – Arbejdsmiljø i Danmark 2000*. Copenhagen: National Institute of Occupational Health.

IFKA. 2004. Kompetenceløft i Danmark. *Øje på uddannelse* (September). Copenhagen: Danish Confederation of Trade Unions (LO).

Jørgensen, C. 2005a. *Collective bargaining and working time in Denmark 2004*. Forskningsnotat no. 60. Copenhagen: Employment Relations Research Centre (FAOS).

————. 2005b. *Questionnaire for EIRO comparative study on changes in the national collective bargaining systems since 1990 – case of Denmark*. European Foundation for the Improvement of Living and Working Conditions, at http://www.eiro.eurofound.eu.int/2005/03/word/dk0412102s.doc.

————. 2005c. *Decline in union membership continues*. European Industrial Relations Observatory, at http://www.eiro.eurofound.eu.int/2005/08/feature/dk0508103f.html.

————. 2006a. *Temporary agency work in an enlarged European Union*. European Industrial Relations Observatory, at http://www.eiro.eurofound.eu.int/2005/06/word/dk0506104t.doc, 2006a.

————. 2006b. *Unions disagree on financing of continuing training*. European Industrial Relations Observatory, at http://www.eiro.eurofound.eu.int/2006/04/articles/dk0604019i.html.

Madsen, M., and A. Petersen. 2000. Nye ansættelsesformer på det danske arbejdsmarked – bliver de atypiske de typiske? *LO-dokumentation* no. 2. Copenhagen: Danish Confederation of Trade Unions (LO).

Madsen, P.K. 2005. *Udredning om udviklingstendenser på det danske arbejdsmarked, in Bilag til Fremtidens arbejdsmiljø*. Copenhagen: Working Environment Authority.

Ministry of Employment. 2005. *Flecicurity – Udfordringer for den danske model*. Copenhagen.

Ministry of Finance. 2004a. *Fordeling og incitamenter 2004*. Copenhagen.

————. 2004b. *Lavindkomstgruppen – mobilitet og sammensætning*. Copenhagen.

————. 2005. *Økonomisk redegørelse*. Copenhagen.

————. 2006. *Livslang uddannelse og opkvalificering for alle på arbejdsmarkedet - rapport fra Trepartsudvalget* – Bind 2, *Kortlægning og analyser*. Copenhagen: Ministry of Finance.

NIOH (National Institute of Occupational Health). 2005a. *Helbred og trivsel på arbejdspladsen*. Copenhagen: NIOH.

————. 2005b. *Sygeplejerskers arbejdsmiljø, trivsel og helbred* (SATH). Copenhagen: NIOH.

————. 2005c. *Psykisk arbejdsmiljø: Store forskelle på det danske arbejdsmarked*, Nyhedsarkiv, 05-12-2005, at http://www.ami.dk, 2005c.

————. 2005d. *Det grænseløse arbejde i konflikt med familielivet*, at http://www.ami.dk.

————. 2006. *COPSOQ data*, at http://www.ami.dk.

Pedersen, H.S., S. Mahler and C.B. Hansen. 2003. *Danish Work Environment Cohort Study, 2000 (DWECS)*. Dublin: European Foundation for the Improvement of Living and Working Conditions.

PLS. 2001. *Atypisk beskæftigelse i Danmark – Delrapport 2*. Copenhagen: PLS Rambøll Management/Ministry of Employment.

Rostgaard, T. 2004. *Dagpasning skole og ældrepleje* Copenhagen: National Institute of Social Research.

Statistics Denmark. 2004a. Nyt fra Danmarks Statistik nr. 213 – Arbejdskraftundersøgelsen 1. kvt. 2004. Copenhagen.

———. 2004b. Data kindly provided by Statistics Denmark at the request of Oxford Research A/S in June 2004.

———. 2006a. *Statistisk Årbog 2006*. Copenhagen.

———. 2006b. Nyt fra Danmarks Statistik nr. 359 – Arbejdskraftundersøgelsen 2. kvt. 2006. Copenhagen.

———. 2006c. http://www.statistikbanken.dk/socdag10.

Storrie, D. 2002. *Temporary agency work in the European Union*. Dublin: The European Foundation for the Improvement of Living and Working Conditions.

Tüchsen, F., H. Bøggild, H. Burr and E. Villadsen. 2002. *Arbejdstid – Arbejdsmiljø i Danmark 2000*. Copenhagen: National Institute of Occupational Health.

TV2 Nyhederne. 2005. *DI forudser arbejdsuge på 45 timer*, at http://nyhederne.tv2.dk/article.php?id=3222733.

Ugebrevet A4. 2005. Personalekonsulenten fortrænger tillidsrepræsentanten. *Ugebrevet* A4 28-11-2005 – no. 40. Danish Confederation of Trade Unions (LO).

WEA (Working Environment Authority). 2001. *Anmeldte arbejdsskader – Årsopgørelse 2000*. Copenhagen.

———. 2003. *Overvågningsrapport 2003*. Copenhagen.

———. 2006. *Anmeldte arbejdsskader 2005 – Årsopgørelse 2005*. Copenhagen.

Wehner, C., M.M. Johansen and S.E. Navrbjerg. 2002. *Deltidsarbejde i Danmark*. Copenhagen: Employment Relations Research Centre (FAOS).

6. France: Patchwork – tensions between old and new patterns

Philippe Méhaut

6.1 INTRODUCTION

Like every other country, since the beginning of the 1980s France has been facing huge economic changes. However, some have stressed that the pace and scope of these changes has been faster and deeper than in other European countries (Culpepper, 2006). One might point to the rapid and tough industrial restructuring, the withdrawal of the state from most industries, the globalization of the largest French firms, the growth in the share of total employment of small firms, the growing importance of services and good productivity results. The consequences for the world of work are significant and have given rise to a vibrant political and academic debate.

The unemployment rate remains higher than in most north European countries, and one can speak of a "French employment disease": fewer jobs are being created. Employers (and international organizations such as the OECD) are calling for more flexibility in the labour market: the high level of worker protection is said to be undermining job creation. As we shall see, however, despite the high level of protection a lot of flexibility is already available through various forms of atypical employment status.

Internal flexibility, including working time flexibility, is high. France's productivity is also high compared to other countries. However, the main consequence is that work organization and working conditions are perceived by workers as deteriorating. There are doubts about the possibility of further intensifying the pace of work without negative consequences for health and safety at work.

Firms are more and more becoming "entrepreneurs" and less and less "employers". They try to restrict their core workforce and to develop subcontracting, outsourcing and new forms of commercial relations (with individuals, other firms or organizations) in order to transfer the risk of the employment relationship to them.

Table 6.1 Working and employment conditions in France

Element	Item	Trends	Risks/Exposed groups
Social bargaining and workers' participation	Membership density	Very low, but stabilized high rate of coverage by collective agreements	Union's weakness at the firm level, new kinds of concession bargaining Low worker representation in SMEs
	Decentralization	New possibilities for "opt out" clause at the firm level	
Employment status and contracts		Global stability, increasing level of (short) fixed-term contracts and other precarious forms New kind of 2-year "open-ended" contract without protection against dismissal	Young new entrants on the labour market, women, unskilled, > 50 years old
Unemployment		Global rate decreasing (for one year) long term, still very high	Young people, unskilled, shift from unemp. benefits to minimum income benefits, "poverty trap"
Wages	Real wages Wage inequality	Increasing for some years Wage disparity remains stable	Women: –6/–13%
	Low wages	Increasing due to increasing share of household services/ retail, high role of SMIC, incidence of low wages < other countries	Immigrants, young people, single parents
Working time and work organization	Long weeks and long hours	Decreasing (35h regulation), but strong political struggle, could increase again	Self-employed, managers, males
	Part time	Increasing, rather "long part time" (>=50%) Differences between voluntary/compulsory	Females, nurses, home care assistants, more voluntary
	Unsocial hours	Increasing	Women, health services, retail
Work organization, work intensity and working rhythms	Work intensity	Increase, both in terms of pace and quantitative demands, and as a result of new organizational forms	Stress, burnout and work–life balance problems. Affecting all groups of workers, increasing for highly educated workers

Health and safety	Work injuries/ fatal	Decreasing	Construction, transport, blue-collar workers
	Work-related diseases	Increasing (new kinds: cancer)	Expanding not only for blue-collar workers
	Others: TMS and stress	Greatly increasing	Women in retail, hospitals
Further training	Rate of access	High, decreasing	Unskilled, women, part-timers, migrants have the lowest opportunities
	Impact	Low on mobility and flexisecurity Important change in the legal provisions to be implemented	
Work and family		High women's rate of activity, high fertility rate. Working families and unstable families increasing	Single parents
Sources of vulner- ability	Structural		SMEs, retail, building, household services, hotel and restaurant, transport
	Individual		Women, unskilled, blue-collars, part timers, young/old, migrants

New trends, new groups

Most of the "risky" industries are expanding, namely household services; new risks along the chain of subcontractors (top firms without employees, change from an employment relationship to a commercial one reporting the burden on employees in subcontracting firms); increasing barriers between labour force segments? (cumulative risks: unskilled + health problem+ young + part time...); work intensity and health problems increasing for highly-skilled white-collar workers could lead to unemployment and/or downgrading.

Looking at the consequences in terms of vulnerability, three main trends must be distinguished. First, the French model of "good jobs" remains alive. Instability and low wages are expanding and so the model is eroding, but the changes have been incremental and the core of the model (internal labour markets, employment stability for skilled workers, and so on) is still alive. Secondly, this model, which emerged during the Fordist period, is displaying weaknesses: it concentrates most of its protection on "insiders"; the level of flexicurity is low, with gaps in relation to external mobility (low level of unemployment benefits for those on short-term contracts, limited rights to training). Moreover, the model is too much oriented towards the "male" figure of a worker in a large firm. The new trends in employment (female work in retail and household services, the growing share of employment in SMEs) are not in step with the historical model of bargaining, collective agreements and social protection. The result is, on the one hand, growth in the cumulative risks for some groups of workers (unskilled, migrants, women, and so on) who are excluded or at the margin of the labour market, and on the other hand the emergence of new risks for those who, despite their integration in the new "learning economy", must face the consequences of flexibility. Thirdly, despite these numerous and incremental changes, there is still no clear picture of a new model of work and employment relations. Tensions between old and new patterns are strong. The French system is more and more a patchwork, as most of the reforms are partial ones (some additional types of labour contracts added to the many existing ones, some changes in unemployment benefits, but for specific categories and/or situations) with no discernible red thread for its restructuring.

6.2 NEW RISKS OF EMPLOYMENT INSTABILITY?

If non-standard labour contracts are increasing (Amira and de Stefano, 2005), the consequences for employment instability are contradictory (Ramaux, 2006). And, as in other countries, there is a huge debate about the relationship between employment protection (France ranks high in this according to the OECD), the growth of non-standard contracts and the level of unemployment.

Still a high level of employment stability?

As in Auer and Cases (2000), some recent papers emphasize the question of employment stability. The common thesis of growing instability has been challenged (Ramaux, 2006). Based on employment surveys from 1969 to 2002, L'Horty (2004) shows that there has not been a significant increase in instability (defined as the risk of quitting employment from one year to another, either for unemployment or inactivity). The 2002 level is close to the 1969 one. Analysing the risks in greater detail, he divides data according to industry level, job tenure, age and skills, and labour market experience. According to age, there was a higher risk for the over-50s at the start of the period, but this is now decreasing; there is a low level of risk (and very little change) for the 30–50 age group, but a growing one for those aged 20–30; job tenure (more than 5 years) remains a good protection; and more highly skilled employees have the lowest level of instability. Combining all these variables, he concludes that risk has remained stable and that there has been a change in its distribution between various groups of employees. With other goals and methods, but based on similar data, Behaghel (2003) shows that job tenure has been stable (and has even increased slightly) over the past 30 years. Job tenure is the best protection against unemployment for those aged 30–50, but its power is decreasing for the young and for the over-50s.

If the internal labour market remains a strong characteristic of the French labour market, this model is being eroded (Valette, 2005). Moreover, the feeling of job instability is higher among French workers than in other countries. This could be partly due, on the one hand, to a strong commitment to the internal labour market model, and on the other hand to the difficulties and gaps within the unemployment benefit system.

The growing importance of non-standard labour contracts

Self-employment had decreased regularly for 20 years (12.7 per cent in 2002). Among wage earners, the regular (open-ended) contract remains dominant. However, the share of non-standard contracts has increased dramatically (from 3.6 per cent in 1982 to 12 per cent in 2004).

Table 6.2 Employment by status, wage earners, France, 2004

	Private	%	Public	%	Total	%
Temporary	490	2.9	–	–	490	2.3
Fixed-term	1 187	7.0	496	10.4	1 683	7.7
Open-ended	15 000	88.4	4 125	86.2	19 125	87.9
Labour market schemes	288	1.7	166	3.5	454	2.1
Total	16 965	100.0	4 787	100.00	21 753	100.00

Source: Insee labour force survey.

The use of temporary agency contracts is highly concentrated among low-skilled blue-collar workers and young people. It fluctuates along with the economic cycle. In some industries, temporary work is also a screening device for the hiring process (Moncel and Sulzer, 2006). If in most cases temporary work is involuntary, "regular" (voluntary, all year round) temporary work is estimated to constitute 20–25 per cent of the activity of temp agencies, mainly involving skilled workers (Lefèvre et al., 2002).

Fixed-term contracts are more developed in some industries (agriculture, household services, health care and education). They are a tool for quantitative flexibility, as well as for the temporary replacement of employees (in the public sector). However, fixed-term contracts are also more and more the dominant way of entry into the job (70 per cent of recruitment is on the basis of fixed-term contracts in private firms with more than 10 employees). Fixed-term contracts are more frequent in very small firms (14 per cent of employees). Young school-leavers are strongly affected by fixed-term contracts (CEREQ, 2001). Due to the high use of fixed-term contracts in the hiring process (as a screening device), they could be described as a port of entry to regular employment (about one third of workers move from fixed to open-ended contracts from one year to another). But fixed-term contracts also more often end in unemployment.

Recently, debates about the two types of contract and the level of protection against dismissal have been acute. Some proposals favour eventual unification of the two kinds of contract with a larger contribution from the firm to unemployment insurance in case of firing (Cahuc and Kramartz, 2004; Blanchard and Tirole, 2003). On the other hand, employers' associations are calling for a new type of contract (*contrat de mission*). A recent law made available a new kind of two-year contract (*contrat nouvelle embauche*) for firms with fewer than 20 employees. This new contract is theoretically open-ended. As in the United Kingdom, during the first two years the level of protection against firing is very low. Its use is increasing, but evaluations are not yet available. At the beginning of 2006, the government proposed a similar contract specifically for young workers (below 26 years of age). The result was a long strike in the universities and joint protests by trade unions and students. For the students, the new contract was seen as reducing employment protection (few advantages in comparison to a fixed-term contract and a risk of jeopardizing the chances of an open-ended contract). For the unions, the new contract was regarded as yet another step towards destroying the classical employment relationship (firing would have been possible without any explanation required during the two years). On the employer side, this new tool for flexibility was not entirely welcomed either. Some organizations feared that it would discourage young people. Others did not like the legal uncertainty of the contract. There was a risk of judicial proceedings, as the two years could be regarded as contradicting the ILO regulation on fair trial periods. Moreover, employers and unions were strongly opposed to the method: a unilateral governmental act without any discussion with the social partners. The government was obliged to withdraw its proposal.

Employment under labour market schemes also plays a role in the development of non-regular contracts, especially in the public sector. Most schemes are targeted on young unskilled workers and the long-term unemployed. Public employment policy, which since the beginning of the 1990s has emphasized social insurance contribution reductions or exemptions, has led to a decrease in subsidized schemes in the private sector. Recently, however, due to increasing unemployment, schemes have been reshaped and are increasing again.

High level of long-term unemployment

The unemployment rate has fluctuated considerably in recent years. It fell rapidly from 1997 to 2001, and then increased from 2001 to 2005. The first period was characterized by a good economic situation, as well as by a very proactive employment policy. From mid-2001, the poor economic situation and changes in employment policy led to a new rise in unemployment, which halted in 2005. At mid-2006, the unemployment rate was slightly below 9 per cent.

Unemployment distribution is very sensitive to job experience and qualifications. In the four years after leaving full-time education, the risk of unemployment is 10 per cent for the holders of a university degree and up to 40 per cent for those without a degree. For those with longer labour market experience (5 to 10 years), the risk is lower, but the gap is the same (5/6 per cent to 28/30 per cent) Measuring the unemployment of older workers is more difficult; 480,000 older workers are in early retirement schemes or exempted from jobseeking requirements and some invalidity or sick leaves are likely to be disguised early retirement. Unemployment is also high among immigrants (17 per cent in 2004). This is also the case for people from ethnic minorities (with French nationality) and from racially mixed suburb areas (Maurin, 2004). Evidence of discrimination in hiring is copious. A young migrant originating in the Maghreb and with a university degree has a higher probability of being unemployed than a French young person and/or a migrant from the south of Europe (Frickey, Murdoch and Primon, 2004). Recently, the debate about the use of anonymous curriculum vitae has been acute. Some large firms have also signed (sometimes with unions) "diversity bills" to promote minorities.

France has performed badly in relation to long-term unemployment, which is concentrated among the over-50s. Recent changes in unemployment benefits (and new changes are coming into force next year) have increased the requirements for benefit entitlement (longer previous work period) and reduced the duration of benefits. One consequence is a shift from (long-term) unemployment benefit to minimum income benefit (RMI[1]). Young labour market newcomers are most affected by the unemployment benefit "gap". They have difficulty getting enough work experience to qualify for unemployment benefit and cannot benefit from the RMI before they are 25 years old.

6.3 WAGES, REVENUES AND POVERTY

Wage trends, wage structure, wage distribution

Net wages fell from 1992 to 1996 (–0.8 per cent in real terms). This trend was reversed between 1996 and 2000 (+4 per cent). Three principal factors could explain this trend: (i) the rapid fall in the inflation rate, (ii) the improved

---

1. The minimum income benefit is a means-tested income allowed to anybody, taking into account total personal and family income. In some cases, it could be combined with some wage income.

labour market situation, and (iii) the higher level of skilled job creation (Romans and Séroussi, 2005). At the bottom of the hierarchy, wage compression around the minimum wage (SMIC) increased. Since 2000 the trend has been less positive: wage moderation linked with the 35-hour week and the poor economic situation. Wage compression is higher in France than in other European countries (D9/D1 about 3) and stable over the long run if we consider only full-time wage earners.

Recently, wages have come back onto the agenda. On the one hand, the unions are demanding wage increases in light of the significant profit increases of large firms. On the other hand, there is a dispute regarding purchasing power: the rapid increase in energy prices and housing costs are said to be inadequately captured by the official price index. There is also considerable discussion about the SMIC. Employers (and some unions) are calling for a less state-led policy on the minimum wage. Its alleged negative impact on the level of employment is sometimes emphasized (even if there is a high level of national consensus around the principle). Moreover, its negative impact on wage compression has been hotly debated.

Recently, a number of women have won court cases against gender discrimination (glass ceiling or wages). This does not mean that the gender question is behind us. The high concentration of female part-time workers at the bottom of the job distribution pile (part-time, low-wage, dead-end jobs) in some expanding industries (retail, home care and household services) could be a major problem for the future. And for the same job and same individual characteristics, wage differences between men and women can be between 6 per cent and 13 per cent. Moreover, wage differences seem to be increasing for the new generations, but mainly due to part-time work (IRES, 2005).

A low incidence of low-wage work

We here follow the OECD definition of low-wage work (two thirds of the hourly median wage). According to this definition, the average incidence of low-wage work was 12.2 per cent in 2002, falling from 13.7 per cent in 1995 (Askenazy et al., 2006). Gender differentiation, as well as age and educational differentiation, are strong (8 per cent men, 17 per cent women; 26 per cent under 26 years of age). The average incidence of low-wage work is higher for temporary agency work and fixed-term contracts (28 per cent). Part-timers are more affected by low-wage work (about 30 per cent). A higher concentration of low-wage workers appears in agriculture (29 per cent), the service industry and services to households (38 per cent). Exit from low-wage work seems to be easier in France than in other European countries (part of the explanation could be the highest share of low-wage work among young school-leavers and the prevalence of seniority rules) (Askenazy et al., 2006).

Low-wage work is very sensitive to minimum wage regulations. As a matter of fact, since the beginning of the 1970s, the minimum wage has been the driving force behind low-wage work. Recently, increases in the hourly minimum wage (political choice and/or a consequence of the 35-hour regulation) have led to an increasing percentage of workers paid at the minimum wage level (15.6 per cent in 2004 compared with 11 per cent in 1990). As the low-wage threshold and the minimum wage are very similar, the characteristics of workers at the minimum wage level are also quite similar.

A growing number of working poor

In France, the usual threshold for defining poverty is 50 per cent of the median household income (60 per cent in the EU). Table 6.3 shows the trend from 1970 to 2001. The decreasing percentage of households below this threshold is mainly due to the decreasing percentage of retired households (high augmentation of pension and other schemes for old people). At the opposite end of the spectrum, working and/or unemployed households are increasing in number (in keeping with the prevailing economic situation: estimates for 2002, 2003 and 2004 forecast a new increase). The number of working poor is estimated to be roughly 1 million, partly due to part-time work and/or to the structure of the family (number of children).

Table 6.3 Households below the poverty threshold (50% of median revenue)

	Total households	Wage-earning households	Retired households
1970	15.3	3.9	27.3
1990	6.8	4.5	3.6
2001	6.2	5.4	3.8

Source: Observatoire nationale de la pauvreté, 2004.

Analysis must combine the question of the working poor with the statutory minimum income (RMI). On the one hand, there is a strong link between entitlement to the entry under the RMI (*revenue minimum d'insertion*) benefit, the level of unemployment and the unemployment benefit rules. Recently, the shortened duration of unemployment benefit and the increase in long-term unemployment have led to an increase in those entitled to the RMI (882,000 in 1996, 975,000 in 2003 and 1.1 million in 2005). On the other hand, the workfare policy has increased the pressure on RMI beneficiaries to take any kind of job (part-time, public schemes) and makes it possible to combine RMI with wages. Some studies (Guillemot, Pétou and Zadjela, 2002) emphasize that the RMI does not imply an inactivity trap but a higher risk of poverty.

6.4 RETURNING TO LONGER WORKING TIME AND INCREASING WORK INTENSITY

Back to work?

The recent debate about working time could be easily summarized under the political slogan "back to work": French workers and the French population do not want to work. On the one hand, some cultural analyses stress the fact that the French would prefer leisure (including home work) to work and consumption. This could explain why some personal services are less developed in France than in the United States. On the other hand, most studies do not show a clear decline in the value of work in the society. Moreover, when focusing on the unemployed and/or excluded from the labour market, research shows a strong willingness to work. Even when dealing with the classical question of the unemployment trap, research does not provide evidence of such traps (Guillemot, Pétour and Zadjela, 2002) and shows that some behaviours are highly rational in preparing for a good reinsertion into the labour market.

Working time in a life-course perspective
A first issue is the total working time of individuals throughout their life. Two French specificities must be emphasized. At the beginning of working life, the rate of activity for the youngest is very low. The average age of entry to the labour market is 21. Both apprenticeships and regular work during studies are poorly developed. The dominant French model is full-time studies followed by a difficult school-to-work transition. School-leavers are more affected by unemployment than other groups. At the other end of working life, France is also well known for its low rate of activity after 55. The official retirement age (60) with full entitlement has been raised. Gradually, over a number of years full entitlement will be obtained at 65. In the 1980s and 1990s, however, both company and state policy was to favour and finance early retirement schemes, sometimes at 50. If the state is withdrawing from this policy (decreasing public funds to support early retirement), some large firms and industries are still encouraging early retirement (and it remains a union demand when bargaining social plans in the case of plant closures and/or redundancies). Seniority-based wages, as well as skill considerations, play a role in the substitution of older workers by younger ones. And keeping older workers active is an economic and political goal, with a number of new schemes focusing on this age group (specific work contract). However, some analyses underline the fact that work organization and work pace are an obstacle: companies do not know how to reshape work organization. In some cases, subcontracting and outsourcing have led to a lack of job positions for older workers.

Decreasing annual and weekly working time

Annual working time has decreased sharply in the past 20 years. According to OECD data, France has among the shortest annual working hours in Europe. This is due to two convergent factors: on the one hand, the growth of part-time work (see below), and on the other, the 35-hours regulation.

Implemented from 1998 to 2002, mainly as tool for employment sharing, the 35-hours regulation is under great pressure. On the one hand, most analyses agree that it has had a real impact on employment growth (300,000 jobs created), as well as productivity and internal flexibility. Most large firms do not want to return to the previous regime. On the other hand, the impact on workers is more ambiguous. Data show a positive impact on the work/life balance (with high gender differentiation). But it also shows an increasing workload for some categories (blue-collar workers, hospital workers) as well as dissatisfaction regarding the flexibility of working time over the year, mostly for workers with a previously stable weekly or annual hours arrangement (Boisard, 2004; Pelisse, 2002). In contrast, managerial staff and skilled workers declare an improvement in their daily life, even with an increased workload during working time.

Recently, there have been political attempts to abolish the 35-hours regime. Three sets of measures have been adopted (IRES, 2005):

1. Firms are allowed to increase the number of annual overtime hours (from 130 to 220) at lower cost; 4 hours overtime per week is now possible, which could make it possible for firms where working time is 39 hours not to have to change to 35 hours.
2. A new mechanism for social contribution exemption, now based on hourly wages and not on monthly (35h) wages, which favours firms where working time is longer and contributes also to alleviating the cost of overtime.
3. Convergence with the statutory minimum wage (in 2005).

The new regulation (2005) enshrines a kind of opt-out clause (based on the firm's collective agreement) and allows small firms (fewer than 20 employees) to avoid the 35-hours obligation (IRES, 2005). Inequalities in annual collective working time are high (increasing since 1998) between small and large firms and between industries; 50 per cent of employees in very small firms work more than 38 hours (average 37.2h).

In some firms, when difficulties occur the 35-hour week is a matter of bargaining during social plan negotiations: there is a trade-off between a new working time regime and a lower level of redundancies (Bosch, Hewlett Packard).

Significant differences between voluntary and involuntary part-time work

Part-time work is increasing in France, as in most European countries. From 1982 to 2002, the number of part-timers increased from 2 to 4 million; 80 per cent are women (CERC, 2005); 30 per cent of part-timers are underemployed (ILO definition) (Attal-Toubert and Derosier, 2005). The increase has been fostered by public policy (exemption from social contributions, special rules and tax reductions for private households), as well as by the shift in activities (increasing share of services). Part-time work is concentrated among women, low-skilled blue- and white-collar workers, and is more frequent in very small firms (28 per cent of employees, a slight decrease, due to a change in the exemption from social contributions). However, it must be analysed in terms of various dimensions.

Compulsory part-time work is more usual for low-wage/low-skilled workers. It is also more prevalent among women, according to the gender division by occupation and or/industry. Compulsory part-time work (or underemployment according to the ILO definition) is highly developed in retail and household services. As these industries are expanding, the risk of compulsory part-time work is increasing. Compulsory part-time work is also increased by employment policies: most public schemes involve part-time work. The hourly wage of part-timers is lower than for full-timers and often social rights (retirement, unemployment, access to training) are lower or even absent. Short part-time work (less than 50 per cent) is unusual. In most cases, part-time work is 50 per cent or more (increasing since the 35 hours regulation). Again, one can distinguish between voluntary (long) and compulsory (short) part-time work.

Unsocial working hours have not shown a dramatic increase. Working on Saturdays (always or occasionally) is decreasing (46 per cent to 43 per cent). Sunday work and night work are slightly increasing (Sunday, 19 per cent to 20 per cent, night – midnight to 5 a.m. – 12 per cent to 14 per cent, more quickly for women since the ban on night work for blue-collar women was lifted due to the EU regulation). Unions, but also employers (in small independent retail outlets) are fighting against the extension of Sunday work in large retail industry. Evening work (8 p.m.–midnight) is also increasing (15.8 per cent in 1994, 17.7 per cent in 2001, also at a quicker rate for women than for men (Bué, 2005).

Work organization and working conditions: hidden problems

From an EU perspective, particular attention must be paid to trends in work organization and their different consequences for the employment relationship, working conditions and training opportunities. In a comparative perspective, Lorenz and Valeyre (2004) define four types of organizational prac-

Table 6.4 Main indicators on physical risk

	Tertiary		Industry		Construction	
	1991	1998	1991	1998	1991	1998
Remaining long in a difficult posture	26	35	29	37	57	64
Heavy load	28	35	32	37	61	68
Long or frequent walks	27	34	30	39	28	40
Breathing dust	27	30	46	46	73	78
Risk of falling	16	21	21	26	61	71
Short exposure to loud or sharp noise	21	24	47	48	53	55

Source: DARES, enquêtes condition de travail.

tice: (i) the learning organization, (ii) lean production, (iii) Taylorist organization and (iv) "simple structures". They map European countries according to the diffusion of these models. This contrasts the Nordic countries, where learning organizations are more prevalent, with France, with a higher share of lean organizations.

Moreover, most analyses report deteriorating working conditions, a trend that started later in France but has been deeper (Askenazy, 2004). It is commonly linked with new forms of work organization: lean production, just-in-time, client-orientation, job rotation, quality control, and so on. However, a number of other factors are also emphasized in the French case. The level of the minimum wage and decreasing working time are converging on the goal of higher productivity by increasing the workload. Moreover, the very low level of unionization at the enterprise level, and the fact that the French unions are putting greater emphasis on wages and employment than on work content could explain a part of that trend.

The indicators are worst for physical working conditions, despite the growth of the tertiary sector and the fall in the number of blue-collar workers. Service activities are not without physical strains.

A more recent study (Arnaudo et al., 2004) based on a large survey conducted by industrial doctors ("*médecin du travail*") provides a similar picture. It also confirms a change in management styles: less direct and constant control through the hierarchy (for all categories, including skilled and unskilled blue-collar workers), but increasing indirect control through computers (14.5 per cent in 1994, 27 per cent in 2003), also for all categories.

6.5 HEALTH AND SAFETY: FALLING STANDARDS

The survey conducted by the "*médecin du travail*" also provides information about health risks at work. It shows an increase in exposure to noise (+5 per cent from 1994 to 2003), chemical products (+3 per cent, 7 million employees, with a high concentration and increase among blue-collar workers and workers in trade and services). The situation is less clear for biological risks (Arnaudo et al., 2004).

Other sources report a change in the structure and frequency of work-related risks. On the one hand, the rate of work injuries is decreasing in the long run, although it remains higher in France than in other European countries. On the other hand, an increase in work-related illnesses is discernible (+20 per cent per year, rising from 15,000 in 1998 to 40,000 in 2003) with major concerns about cumulative trauma disorders (70 per cent of total illnesses registered) and cancer. Part of this increase is due to better legislation and better information on the part of doctors; but part is also due to new risks, and the increase is coherent with poor indicators on working conditions. Recently, the question of asbestos was put on the agenda again due to the increasing number of deaths. Employers and the government have been declared liable by the courts. The cost of compensation is increasing and will continue to increase. A similar picture is forecast for other occupational illnesses. This situation could bankrupt the insurance system. The government has launched a plan to improve health and safety at work, including an increase in research and new obligations for firms to prepare and present a document reviewing all the risks in the firm. The social partners are also bargaining on the question of working conditions.

However, the French system of control remains weaker than in other countries and costs for firms are not equally distributed. While firms of more than 200 employees bear full costs (compulsory insurance contributions are linked to the level of injuries), this is not the case for small firms (Askenazy, 2004). Moreover, this system is said to induce under-declaration of injuries (estimated at around 20 per cent), as well as subcontracting risky tasks to small firms. It has been proved that 80 per cent of nuclear radiation injuries affected workers in small firms working as subcontractors in nuclear power plants (Thébaud-Mony, 1999, quoted by Askenazy, 2004). The social partners do not appear to have been particularly worried about the problem. As a matter of fact, it took them more than eight years to reach agreement about musculoskeletal diseases. Furthermore, in some industries the trade unions would prefer a wage premium rather than seek to do away with the risk. The fear of unemployment is part of the explanation for this.

Work injuries are more frequent among blue-collar workers and newcomers to the labour market and at SMEs. A recent survey (Coutrot and

Waltisperger, 2005) shows a relationship between poor health situation and rate of activity, mainly for older workers. In the same survey (based on individuals' declarations concerning how they feel, rather than medical or insurance data), 20 per cent of health problems are said to be related to work, with high disparities among social categories (Waltisperger, 2004).

Stress, particularly for white-collar workers and management, is significant. The question of stress at work is increasingly cited as a key issue in service activities with a strong emphasis on customer relations, including retail, as well as in some public services, such as health care, education and the police. White-collar workers and women are increasingly comprising vulnerable labour market groups.

In 2005 a new initiative was launched by the state (*Plan santé au travail 2005–2009*). The aim is to reduce the number of work injuries and illnesses, to strengthen monitoring of firms, to improve knowledge and prevention and to strengthen active company policies. Social partners are also being approached. Implementation of most of the new measures is planned from 2005 to 2006 (Ministère de travail, 2005).

6.6 TRAINING: NEW FRAMEWORK FOR IMPLEMENTATION

At the turn of the century, a number of reports and critical assessments emphasized that the system created by the 1971 Act was running out of steam and was no longer adapted to the new economic and social context.

The limits of the system

If the access to further education is rather high in France, inequalities are strong. Blue-collar workers, unskilled workers, women, workers on short-term contracts, workers in SMEs and migrants have fewer opportunities than skilled workers in large firms (Fournier, Lambert and Perez 2002). As training courses become shorter and shorter, the relationship between training and skill development is said to be declining, as are opportunities to upgrade through training. Moreover, the share of training has been declining in public employment policies. As a matter of fact, opportunities for the unemployed to take up training courses are fewer than for employees (Fournier, Lambert and Perez, 2002).

In 2003 and 2004, a national agreement and a new law brought about a number of changes in the further training system. Examination of the key points of the 2003 agreement and law reveals both a considerable degree of continuity with the past and some major innovations (Méhaut, 2006).

Extension of two basic principles: the employer training levy and industry-level control

The agreement and subsequent legislation confirmed and strengthened the basic characteristics of the system. For small firms (fewer than 10 employees), the training levy was increased significantly: between 2003 and 2005 it rose from 0.15 per cent to 0.45 per cent of the wage bill. At the same time, the position of individual industries and of the bodies that collect the training levies has been strengthened. First, the increasing levies paid by small firms will be paid directly to these bodies. Secondly, their monopoly on the collection of the levy throughout their particular industry has been firmly established in more tightly worded clauses. Finally, it is mainly at the level of the individual industry (and its collection agencies) that the priorities will be decided on (for example, training for unskilled target groups, gender equality, programmes for older workers, and so on) which firms will have to comply with if they seek financial support from the mutual funds.

A more individualized system

The most significant measure is the establishment of a new "individual right to training", midway between a training plan and individual training leave. Employees are granted a theoretical right to 20 hours' training per year, which can be accumulated for up to six years. When they wish to exercise this right, they enter into discussions with their employer about the training they have in mind, which has to enhance their competences with a view to career development, be consistent with the training priorities established at industry level and take place in part outside normal working time. If agreement is reached on these terms, employers bear the direct training costs and pay employees 50 per cent of their normal wage for the hours of training outside normal working time.

A new approach to training based on mobility and career development

Although it bears the title "Agreement on employees' access to lifelong training" the agreement actually puts forward an extended concept of training based on the twin principles of mobility and career development. As early as the preamble and the first article, the agreement puts considerable emphasis on the changes that have taken place in work organization and patterns of mobility and on the need for career plans, to be discussed between employees and their employers and possibly supported by skill assessments and career guidance. It provides for the introduction of individual education and training passports (an idea based on European proposals). "Reskilling contracts" (*contrats de professionnalisation*) have been introduced for workers newly recruited from the unemployment register; these contracts replace the various forms of assistance available to unemployed individuals with low skill levels. And workers most at risk of losing their jobs because of technological change and/or skill obsolescence can take advantage of "reskilling periods". These may include on-the-job training, formal training and evaluation of knowledge and know-how acquired through experience and must lead to a certificate or diploma. Workers aged 50 and over, those with more than 20 years' seniority and/or those regarded as a priority at industry level may claim their right to these "reskilling periods". In this case, the costs are borne by the industry-level organization, which reimburses the employer. This new concept of training fits the development of "competencies-based management" (Méhaut, 2004).

6.7 WORK AND FAMILY LIFE

Despite high and persistent gender inequalities in the labour market (higher risk of unemployment for women, higher incidence of part-time and compulsory part-time work, a glass ceiling for managerial occupations, wage discrimination), some analyses emphasize the changing face of women's employment (and of work–family life conciliation). In the 1970s, the growth of the female employment rate was still based on the model of the "male breadwinner". The second step, during the 1980s, despite the growth of part-time work, was a transitional one: both family policies and employment policies centred on building institutional rules towards more equality. However, part-time work was the main tool for work–family life conciliation. The 1990s (and perhaps beyond) saw a new step forward towards "equality". This was due not only to the development of the labour market, but also to women's improving performance in education and to the changing structure of the family, with an increasing number of single-parent households (Barrere-Maurisson, 2000).

    This does not mean that the global workload (working time plus home work time) is equally shared. Inequalities between men and women remain high; however, in the case of two parents equal in the labour market (full-timers) and/or of single households, the women's model is getting closer to that of the men (see Barrere-Maurisson, 2000). Nevertheless, when comparing the French and the Swedish cases, inequalities between men and women are higher in France: less time is devoted to family activities by French men (cleaning, cooking, childcare), a more significant trend for French women to withdraw from the labour market when they have young children (Anxo, Flood and Kocoglu, 2002).

Part-time work with unstable working time organization (as in retail) or unsocial hours (as in health care), and frequent shifts from employment to unemployment seem to increase disorganization of social and working times and have negative consequences, for example, for children (Millet and Thin, 2005).

As emphasized by Bouffartigue (2005), in France the question of the work–family life balance remains strongly influenced by the "conciliation" approach, the implication of which is that it is a female issue. And if highly qualified women, under the new regime of flexible, autonomous working time (the model of the highly skilled manager, or the creative or intellectual professions) sometimes manage to build a new and more equal balance, it is not the case for those working under new compulsory flexible working time in the field of unskilled or semiskilled services (household services, care work), where unions are also weak and/or male-dominated.

6.8 WEAK SOCIAL DIALOGUE

Unionization is well known to be at a very low level in France. The rate of unionization is about 8 per cent, decreasing over the long term, but stable and slightly increasing in recent years (Amossé, 2004). Major differences exist between the public and private sector, between small and large firms (unionization a mere 3.5 per cent in firms of fewer than 50 employees) and between categories of workers. The highest rates of unionization are for highly skilled workers (managerial staff, technicians, teachers, nurses), the lowest for semiskilled or unskilled white-collar (5.5 per cent) and blue-collar workers (6.1 per cent). Employment status also has a strong impact:

However, the very low level of unionization does not mean that unions are not present: half of the workers report that union representation exists at the level of the firm and 38 per cent at the workplace level. In the last round of elections for employee representatives trade unions won 78 per cent of the votes (71 per cent ten years previously).

A recent national agreement (2001) in the small craft industry tries to promote the activity of trade unions and employer organizations: a compulsory percentage of the wage bill must be devoted to union and employer representatives within all bipartite organizations. Another employer organization, representing another part of the industry, brought a law suit against this agreement. Another way of extending union representation at company level is so-called "*mandatement*", whereby a workers' representative can be appointed by the workers in a firm where no unions are represented. He is not an official union representative, but acts on behalf of a union, representing the workers with some kind of union mandate and protection. Such representatives are protected in the same way as official union delegates. This was used in the negotiations on the 35-hour week, mainly in small firms, and could be a response in other areas in relation to SMEs.

However, the trend may go in another direction: in 2004, the new law on the training system included the possibility of "opt-out" agreements at the enterprise level, thereby breaking down the "hierarchy of norms". It is too early to determine the consequences of this new law. Recent studies (Jobert and Saglio, 2005; Méhaut, 2006) suggest that even employers' organizations are not so keen on this new possibility: it will reduce the power of the industry-level organizations and open the door to labour market dumping.

Analysing the situation in a more global perspective, most observers underline the lack of social dialogue at national level. On the one hand, unions and employers' organizations have difficulty agreeing on and implementing new rules. On the other hand, the government often decides unilaterally (minimum wage, working time, "*contrat première embauche*"). Lallement (2006) suggests a shift in the French industrial relations model. The previous centralized bargaining process with sectoral agreements is eroding. Unions are less representative. They have difficulty taking into consideration at-risk groups, as well as new types of employee. Union representatives are mainly men, older and skilled workers in large firms. Some associations are merging (the unemployed, the homeless), alongside and sometimes against the unions. In the last 10 years many campaigns have been led by informal groupings (nurses, students, artists, and so on). It is a sign of the trade unions' difficulties, their weakness in some areas and growing corporatist movements, far away from the classical "class struggle model".

And recent trends show that the classical organization of French industrial relations (industry-level bargaining) is increasingly finding it difficult to cope with new issues, as well as new structural organization:

- new issues are more global in nature and require a "desegmented" approach (work and housing, work and health);
- new forms of organization of production (HRM at group level, relations between "*donneur d'ordre*" and subcontractors, common issues at local level) and the new organization of public policy-making (increasing power of regional and local authorities) are challenging the actors' organization (Mériaux and Verdier, 2006).

6.9 SYNTHESIS: VULNERABLE WORKERS AND THE NATURE OF WORK

Summarizing the main characteristics of the French model, one can conclude the existence of a very classical model of cumulative risks putting the burden on the weakest part of the labour force.

"Structural factors" (industry and size of firm) seem to play a greater role in France than in other countries. Very small firms (fewer than 10 or 20 employees) in the building industry, retail, transport, household services and in hotels and restaurants can be characterized as follows: higher concentration of non-standard labour contracts, including public schemes, in some industries with a higher incidence of "black-market labour"; lower rate of access to training; fewer career opportunities and no external mobility; and, as a consequence, higher risk of unemployment; higher incidence of low-wage work; and a lower level of social protection in case of redundancies and/or plant closure. Some of these characteristics are also present and expanding in subcontracting industries highly dependent on the wage level and globalization pressure (subcontractors in the second tier of the car industry or in the clothing industry) and/or in industries competing on low-value-added markets. If we cross the structural variable with job/individual characteristics, most unskilled blue-collar jobs and some unskilled white-collar ones (in building, transport, retail, hotels and restaurants, cleaning, household services) are accumulating a lot of negative indicators.

Taking individual characteristics into consideration, most analyses are very similar: level of education, mainly for unskilled workers according to the ISCED scale, gender (women), age group (young school-leavers/dropouts; older workers >55), single parenthood, living in a deprived urban area (Maurin, 2004), immigrant status, bad health are all "factors of risk", especially in combination. Most of these factors are not only produced by and dependent in the labour market and work environment. Bad health is not necessarily the result of bad working conditions. Some young school-leavers with a high risk of labour market exclusion are also in bad health. Dropping out and de-schooling are the result of complex interactions between family situation, school organization, urban policies, and so on. They do not fit into the classical organization of segmented public policy (separated treatment of school problems, housing problems, employment problems, health problems), as well as the segmentation of collective rules and protections built up by the social partners. They also call into question official French "republican" equality (no affirmative action), as shown by disputes concerning policies on immigrants and suburban areas.

However, this process is also giving rise to new risks affecting, though less overtly, other groups of employees.

Analysing the risks from a legal point of view, Dupuy and Larré (1999) carried out the following analysis (see Table 6.5). On the horizontal axis, the authors examine the share of power within the work (organization). Organization symbolises the way the tasks are distributed, the individual's control over his own job and "organizational risks". Vertically, they examine the distribution of risks. Risks (wages and/or employment) depend on the nature of the contract (covered by labour law or not, or moving from standard to atypical employment).

Table 6.5 Matrix of organizational and employment/wage risks

Organization	Risk		
	Individual	Mixed	Collective
Individual	1	4	7
Mixed	2	5	8
Collective	3	6	9

Source: Dupuy and Larré, 1999.

As an example, cell 1 could define the situation of a self-employed individual in handicrafts. He organizes all his productive activity himself, bears the uncertainty of the production process and its result, as well as the economic risk (work, income and employment risk). Cell 9 shows the opposite situation, a Fordist wage earner in a large firm with virtually no control over his job and tasks, with risks collectively regulated and shared.

The other cells describe intermediate situations (all currently existing in France). Cells 3, 5, 6, 7 and 8 could be regarded as atypical wage-earning relationships: cells 2 and 3 have a certain level of organizational dependence but bear a lot of risk (in some trade activities, temporary work: see the hospital case study and the "portage" case study below which could be analysed as a movement from cell 8 to 2 for some individuals, or from cell 1 to 7 for others). Cell 6 could represent the case in which, in classical organizations, part of the wage now depends on results. Cell 5 shows the trend characterizing new forms of labour organization and management: growing autonomy within the job, but more risk on the wage and employment sides (see, for example, the issue of competency-based management (Méhaut, 2004)). In the new forms of production organization cells 5, 1 and 2 are expanding, due both to internal organization and HRM and to the shift from being an employer to being rather an entrepreneur without direct employees (Morin, 2002). This affects mainly managers and specialists in various technical or managerial fields. On the one hand, they must meet performance-related requirements; on the other hand, some of them find their labour contracts being substituted by quasi-commercial contracts. The risk of unemployment is growing for these categories, as well as other risks related to working conditions (stress, burnout). The latter is also expanding among professional white-collar workers, such as nurses, teachers, and so on.

Another area of the debate concerns household services, undergoing something of a rebirth. Most analyses report growth in this kind of activity: home care for the elderly, childcare, cleaning. This growth is also viewed as a solution to unemployment and a way of increasing, through part-time work, the rate of (female, young or old) employment. A solution promoted by employment and tax policy is, on the one hand, to provide tax concessions for households using this kind of service, and on the other hand, to facilitate the wage earning relationship, using a so-called *"cheque emploi service"* which is both a labour contract and a tool for payment. But it could reinforce direct "face to face" relations between employer and employee, the latter often with little knowledge of their rights and strongly dependent on individual employers in a kind of domestic service relationship (Meda and Minault, 2005). The other solution is to promote private (profit or non-profit) intermediate bodies, acting as employers and go-betweens the employees and households, and providing a more classical wage-earning relationship, including the grouping of working hours, training, and so on (see case study). So far, the first solution has prevailed in public policy. If this continues, it could lead to problems with quality of employment (and/or to recruitment problems for firms). In the most recent forecast employment prospects for 2015 (7.5 million recruitments), 1.5 million could be unskilled or semiskilled blue-/white-collar workers in industry, building, transport, and others, of whom 900,000 will be in household services, child and home care, and cleaning (Chardon et al., 2005).

These three issues – (i) the erosion of the old internal labour market and the Fordist system, (ii) the margins of the internal labour market and (iii) the growing importance of new activities – are part of the French patchwork. None can be addressed by a single actor. The problem is not only to reshape the system, but also to reshape the actors.

REALITY AT ENTERPRISE LEVEL: CASE STUDIES

Introduction

All the cases presented here represent small islands in the French employment situation. However, they all reveal the tensions in the French model of employment and contribute to presenting the French "patchwork". They constitute key innovations or experiments which relate to one of the main problems of the French labour market: the relationship between the core workforce and the various groups waiting for a permanent job or seemingly excluded, for various reasons, from the labour market.

In all cases, we deal with vulnerable groups of workers, but in a wide range of senses.

Case 1 provides a good example of the tensions within the public sector between the use of a core workforce and a peripheral one, under significant industrial and budget constraints. It could help us to understand the growth of atypical employment, as emphasized in the first part of this chapter.

Case 2 is in another world. We are here in the high-skill segment of the labour market, mainly involving older workers. The two main issues are: (i) how older specialists can be kept in activity, and (ii) how economic and employment risks can be shared.

Case 3 tells a more classical story within an industry coping with high seasonality and difficult working conditions. The experiment analysed here is an attempt to provide a solution to the high-flexibility requirements by sharing the workforce between several employers. They combine a kind of market-led solution with a kind of social solution.

France Case Study 1: Industrial flexibility and poor working conditions in hospitals: what impact on employment stability?

Introduction

Hospitals, despite belonging among services, concentrate many of the characteristics of traditional factories: working 365 days a year, 24 hours a day, with "just-in-time" requirements for the provision of care and, if possible, total quality. Moreover, these industrial constraints are reinforced by the budget pressures on hospitals. Public funds are becoming more and more scarce, and the new funding rules are pushing towards stricter internal control of costs and, eventually, to an organization based on cost and profit centres.

On the one hand, national surveys on working conditions provide a poor prospect. They report a sharp increase in the (short, hourly) time constraints on doing the work (declared by 24 per cent of workers in 1998 but by 48 per cent in 2003). On the other hand, physical workload indicators (painful physical movements, long or frequent walking, heavy loads) are also increasing. Above all, indicators concerning workplace requirements of mental attention are also increasing (need to look at small lettering, brief signals, and so on).

In this case study of a public hospital, we will try to link the management of the workforce with working conditions.

Characteristics of the hospital
The hospital is located 40 kilometres from a large town, in a highly industrial suburb with a working-class tradition (strong presence of industrial workers and trade unions and a long-term communist municipal council). This public hospital covers a population of approximately 250,000 and although it is in close proximity to a large town with large hospitals of its own, it remains the hospital of choice for the local population, except in cases of highly specific medical needs. It provides general medical care: general medical services, surgery, obstetrics, emergency and resuscitation, dialysis, psychiatry, gerontology (including in partnership with old-age centres), and various outpatient services.

The level of employment has risen slightly in the last few years, partly due to the development of new activities, such as out-patient activity and obstetrics, and partly in compensation (especially for the care staff, particularly nurses) for the reduction in the number of work hours resulting from the implementation of the 35-hour week. With more than 500 beds and a high level of outpatient activity, the hospital is a middle-size general hospital, with 1,100 employees and 180 doctors.

As a public hospital, it is governed by civil service regulations in all matters related to recruitment, remuneration, working time and mobility. The core of the workforce is very stable and could be said to be ruled by classical internal labour market rules: wage increases based on seniority, opportunities for internal (horizontal) mobility between wards and (minor) opportunities for internal vertical mobility (upgrade path through vocational school from unskilled work to nurse's assistant, from nurse's assistant to nurse), strong national regulations regarding working time, various bonuses (night shift, Sunday shift).

Technical and organizational changes, work organization and workload
In common with the French healthcare sector as a whole, the hospital is facing strong pressures: on the one hand, from technical changes: development of new diagnostic and surgical techniques, as well as medical treatments; on the other hand, changes in the demand for services, including home services (care and cure) for old people, local networks with doctors practising in the town.

This has had two consequences for hospital services: first, strong development of outpatient activity (such as daily dialysis, casualty, home services, day psychiatric treatment) with a different kind of organization from traditional wards; second, a reduction in the duration of patient hospitalization: that is, more rapid patient turnover. Despite this decrease, the total number of days of hospitalization remains stable (higher rate of occupation of beds).

The management reports a greater need for flexibility in the workforce to meet the changing and unpredictable needs of the various wards. However, management and employees also report an increasing workload, due to the higher patient turnover. The hospital has attained higher productivity and better funding, but with staff only slightly increasing. Employees say that the work is harder and that they have more "difficult patients" to take care of.

Absenteeism indicators, often regarded as a proxy of bad working conditions, have been quite stable for five years. Official recorded absences represents roughly 10 per cent of total working time, more than half of which comprises sick leaves. The amount of "hidden absences" is said to be significant in some wards, let's say 2 per cent or 3 per cent of total working time. Part of these leaves are normal, if we take into account the share of young women (maternity leave) and the high number of older nurses and unskilled workers. However, the incidence is higher than in the economy as a whole, and higher than average for French hospitals.

Managing industrial constraints and high absenteeism
How is employee replacement organized and internal flexibility handled? The hospital, like industrial organizations, uses a wide range of solutions, affecting the employees in a number of ways.

The first set of solutions could be described as managing internal flexibility within the core workforce. The hospital has organized a pool of replacements (mainly for nurses and nurse's assistants) to cover maternity leaves, training leaves, and so on. Another internal solution is overtime, asking permanent employees to work during holidays or other free days, but permanent employees are reluctant to do overtime and it is expensive for the hospital. A third solution, for part of the workforce (mainly unskilled workers) is compulsory part-time work. Dividing a full-time position into two part-time ones permits more flexible management, according to need (early morning cleaning in parts of the hospital, part-time home care, and so on).

A second set of solutions comes under the heading of external flexibility, drawing on a peripheral workforce, without civil servant status:

• An increase in employment under open-ended contracts, primarily in the case of doctors, nurses and technical staff (managers, IT staff). This represents the first boundary of the core workforce in relation to the technical staff: stable employment conditions, good wages, but without regular civil servant status.

- An increase in the number of employees working under short fixed-term contracts: to temporarily replace employees on leave (short illness, holidays), to comply with statutory constraints (filling a vacant post until a newly appointed civil servant is assigned to the post), to provide a "transition" between the end of subsidized employment and a possible appointment as a civil servant, and to temporarily adjust the number of staff according to increases in the hospital's volume of activity.
- Extensive use of subsidized employment (CES and CEC), particularly of unskilled workers, which has helped to reduce the wage bill and to increase the number of workers without creating new posts; this was also done in response to political pressure (quotas imposed by the state, pressure from the municipal council in this high unemployment area).
- A rise in "forced" part-time work, particularly for unskilled workers who have had to accept 50 per cent part-time positions in order to be granted permanent employment status. Unskilled workers have to weave their way through a veritable obstacle course in order to obtain a position in the hospital as a civil servant.

It is estimated that, at any given time, non-civil servants in precarious employment, employed under fixed-term contracts or subsidized contracts (full-time equivalent) account for 10 per cent of the volume of employment (roughly the level of absenteeism) and 16 per cent of the total workforce. The trade unions have denounced this situation (although they do not oppose CES employment), while the management team ponder the risk of developing a "two-track hospital'.

Some of the workers in the peripheral workforce will never get a permanent job. They will probably move to other jobs or return to unemployment. Length of time on the "waiting list" (before getting a permanent position) could be between 2 and 5 years. The peripheral "reserve army" is becoming highly concentrated on low-skilled, low-wage workers: mainly women between 30 and 50, some of them returning to the labour market after childcare, some as single parents, with a rather low level of education and training. Most have experienced other jobs, sometimes in factories (textiles, clothing) or in cleaning (including for households). They have also often experienced unemployment spells. The attractiveness of the hospital as the main local employer for women, providing good jobs for the core workforce, is high, and explains why they accept belonging to its "reserve army" for a long time.

What are the consequences for quality of jobs? Wages are lower than for permanent employees: the minimum wage is the rule, without any seniority premiums. If some of these employees are able to choose their working time and quantity of working hours, those looking for an entry into the core workforce are obliged to show a high level of working time flexibility according to the hospital's short-term needs. Moreover, they will work in the hardest work-places, shunned by the permanent workforce. According to the interviews, some of these employees are more affected by work injuries than the permanent workforce and they get hardly any training. As they are not public employees, they are less covered by the statute and no other kind of collective agreement covers them. Nevertheless, getting on the waiting list represents a slim chance of later getting a permanent job.

Conclusion

This case study could be regarded as a very traditional portrayal of the French divide between insiders and outsiders in the labour market: strong internal labour markets with a high level of protection of the core workforce, and a flexible peripheral workforce, with casual employment, very short-term contracts and lower wages. A similar situation is found in most hospitals.

However, the situation is more uncertain, on both the demand and the supply side. Some casual workers may prefer, for personal reasons, such status and working time arrangements (for example, nurses wanting to work only part of the year). Others are part-time (or even full-time) workers in other jobs: working on short-term contracts at the hospital is a kind of wage supplement. This probably represents a minority, however, as most of this reserve army come from unemployment. Implicit rules also apply in the case of peripheral workers, as we have already seen for subsidized employment contracts. The waiting list is also organized on the basis of seniority rules. Gaining in seniority within the reserve army, you increase your options concerning working periods, probably work more regularly, and get closer and closer to the port of entry to the core workforce.

France Case Study 2: Portage: a new form of labour market intermediation

Introduction

This case study has been chosen because, in contrast to the previous one, it concerns mainly skilled or highly skilled workers, and the majority of the workforce are over 50 years old. If, as in the previous case, it could be regarded as organizing a kind of outsourcing of some jobs from the core workforce, it is organized in a very different way, providing better social protection than classical fixed-term contracts or temporary agencies. Moreover, this kind of company is rather new in France and could still be regarded as an innovation in the labour market.

The main characteristics of "portage"

The *"société de portage salarial"* or contractor company is a way of organizing a new kind of employment relationship.

Firm A acts as "go-between" between worker B and firm C. Between firm A and worker B there are two kinds of relationship: on the one hand, there is a "permanent" agreement of *"portage'*, by which the worker is linked to A and delegates to A his business relationship with C or others; on the other hand, there is an employment relationship, depending on the business agreement with C, in which B is a wage earner employed by A. The business agreement between A and C describes B's tasks, costs, form of payment and other things (including A's liability in the case of problems).

Initially, portage was developed for two purposes: first, to coordinate the activities of managers and specialists made redundant by their firms but able to perform temporary missions as specialists – through portage they are able to retain some advantages of the traditional wage earner; second, for freelance consultants, who are attracted by the fact that the company deals with all their administrative tasks on their behalf (A does the accounts, pays all social contributions, and so on). A also provides insurance: if C does not pay the bill, A's insurance will cover the risk. Moreover, B will be given a full employment relationship (open-ended – sometimes – or fixed-term contracts) and social protection (health, retirement and unemployment benefits) which are better and cheaper than for independent workers. A pays all taxes and social protection contributions and pays B a wage, according to the amount and duration of the contract with C, including social protection and its own administrative costs.

Today, portage firms[2] are increasingly being regarded as traditional employers and covered by labour law, despite the fact there is no clear subordinate relationship between A and B. B is performing a kind of independent activity. This activity is a direct business relationship between B and C. And A is not regarded as maintaining a business relationship with C. C is the client and private property of B. Moreover, the unemployment administration, despite a number of disputes, now regards portage as providing access to unemployment benefits, if it is not a "hidden" independent activity.

Portage is an expanding activity. There are now something like 100 companies in this field, with between 10,000 and 30,000 wage earners with portage status. No precise data are available, however. It does seem that portage has developed particularly in management consultancy, IT consultancy, education and training ('independent trainers'). One can also find signs of activity in hairdressing and personal care and in some craft and artistic activities.

---

2. Under French law, there is a clear divide between business law and courts and the labour code and courts.

The portage company – based on heterogeneous *"portés"*

The Portage Company (PC) has been operating for three years. With EUR 6 million annual turnover and about 100 *"portés"*, it is not one of the largest portage firms but it is expanding very quickly. It presents itself as one of the best, remaining loyal to the "portage spirit". At national level, five employees work full-time for the portage company, dealing with relations with the "portés", accounting and commercial relations with firms. The portage company gives technical and legal advice to the *portés* during discussions of individual missions. However, in the spirit of portage, it is the *porté*'s own responsibility to design the mission, costs, payments, and so on. The business relationship with the client firm also pertains to the *porté*. The portage company is expanding and now has a number of regional offices. Like other companies in the same line the portage company mainly offers fixed-term contracts, depending on the duration of the mission. However, for some *portés* with a good portfolio of clients, the company may conclude an open-ended contract. This was the case with one of the people interviewed, who works as a computer-systems consultant for a number of large firms. He was previously employed by a large national firm, then started out as an independent consultant (his own firm is still going) before deciding to take advantage of portage (better social protection, less administrative constraints, better opportunities to get loans from a bank due to his full-time open-ended contract). The portage company offers high-quality services to its *portés*, and its charges are correspondingly higher than other companies. Depending on the size of the contract, the portage company will charge between 5 per cent and 15 per cent. However, the portage company will pay wages in advance, independently of the client firm's payment schedules.

As in similar firms, a kind of informal network is developing among the *portés*. They can pass on experiences, clients and openings for specialists. If a minority of the *portés* are rather young, experimenting with a new form of "independent activity', the majority are specialists and managers, aged from 40 to over 60. Most have either been made redundant by their company or have chosen to leave (for example, due to conflicts with higher management). They come to the portage company sometimes through outplacement firms. At the portage company they develop their competencies. They are sometimes placed with their previous firm, but their new position as external consultant is easier. Another group of *portés* is often self-employed, with a good track record at their previous firm. They have joined the portage company because they wanted to offload administrative tasks and devote more time to maintaining their portfolio of contacts.

At the regional level, where our interview was conducted, the portage company had about 10 *portés*. Some were working in high-tech fields such as IT and Internet; others were working as specialists for international shipping firms. Others were more distant from the pure portage spirit (independent, with their own business).

The situations of portage employees and the consequences on their working conditions are very heterogeneous.

If your portfolio of clients and reputation are good enough, you can choose to work only a few weeks a month or for part of the year, as you can charge a high price for your services. As an independent, you can also more easily choose your location. Moreover, your income may be higher than working for a temp agency if your bargaining power with your client is good. For some early retired or retired people, PC offers an opportunity to increase your income, with an additional part-time wage, added to your retirement benefits. It is often the choice of retired specialists with children/students still at home.

On the other hand, as already mentioned, PC provides a kind of wage-earning relationship to formally independent workers. In this case, it could be a more comfortable solution, alleviating the constant stress arising from full independence.

Lastly, for some other employees, PC is a second-best solution: they probably would prefer a classical open-ended contract in a firm. But they are regarded as too old for the labour market.

Between wage earner and independent activity

Among the various sectors and professions covered by portage, apart from the traditional consultancy (technical or managerial), one can find translators and interpreters, artists, and even hairdressers working from home. In this case, and a number of others, portage companies act not only as go-betweens, but also as franchising companies, delivering services and authorizing the employees to work under the brand name of the company. Another frequent field of activity is training. Independent trainers provide services to firms through portage companies with compulsory state registration as training providers. Sometimes, portage is also used by regular full-time or part-time employees who want to undertake additional work in their field of specialization outside their regular job.

Portage is therefore a mixed solution, between the traditional wage-earning relationship and independent activity, or a mixed solution between the independent and the internal specialist of a large firm and/or temporary work.

Conclusion

Portage is rather new and expanding. PC seems to be an example of best practices within the sector. It clearly provides a good alternative to a purely independent position and to a temporary work agency: better income, friendly human resource management, share of the risks. It fits in well with the needs of senior workers wanting to remain in work, and who are discriminated against in the French labour market. However, not all portage companies follow the same model. A quick look at other companies provides a more blurred picture. Some offer very poor services, poor social insurance and only fixed-term contracts, depending on the duration of your commercial contract with the client firm. Your wage will be paid only after the end of your mission. In this case, it is clearly disguised independent work at a lower cost. And, in some cases, the portage company looks like a temporary agency. Depending on the future development of this kind of practice, but also on the way in which it may be regulated (through collective agreements and quality norms at the sectoral level, or by law) it may or may not reduce the vulnerability of employees.

France Case Study 3: Employers sharing the workforce – a flexible but also a social solution

Introduction
The choice of this case study is guided by two considerations. On the one hand, it is the only one in the industry sector. Moreover, it deals with the meat industry which ranks badly in terms of working conditions. On the other hand, as in the two first studies, it focuses on a new structure, the employer's intermediate association, recently created and expanding. But here the innovation is being led by some local employers in order to provide better employment status to precarious employees.

The ham factory
The ham factory is a pork meat factory, specializing in cooked ham, located in a rural area, but close to large towns. Just before the case study the ham factory belonged to an international group of more than 100,000 employees all around the world. But this group was involved not only in the food industry and tried to disengage itself from pork meat activity. The ham factory has now been sold to another international group (50,000 employees), more specialized in the food industry and, moreover, in pork meat. The managers are optimistic that the new group will be able to provide better access and scale economies on the pork market.

The ham factory, with 350 employees, is not a very large plant, but it ranks high among French ham factories. It mainly works for the large retail industry, providing basic products under the brand of the retailers. In this segment of its market, the ham factory enjoys rather a good position, due to the medium quality of its products and its fulfilment of international quality norms. But it faces an unstable economic situation, losing some share of its market or recovering it and being partly dependent on the cyclical variations on both its raw material market (pork) and its consumer market. As a member of an international group, Ham is also under pressure from international norms, benchmarking indicators which often focus on wage costs and staff levels.

Employment and working conditions
Like most of the factories in the food processing industry, the ham factory faces a dilemma. First, the food processing industry (and especially meat) is not very attractive. Although wages are governed by a rather good collective agreement and above the SMIC regulation, working conditions are often seen by workers as bad: bad odours, blood, working in cold areas. Classic Taylorist work organization still prevails. On the production lines, some working postures are very difficult (at the very beginning, for cutting up pork, at the end, for handling). Like other food processing factories, the ham factory faces a number of health problems: work injuries as well as – increasingly – musculoskeletal diseases. Nevertheless, most workers have a long tenure and do not want to quit. This could be explained by the wage level and by the fact that the ham factory is the largest factory in the area. However, the core workforce are rather low-skilled. The ham factory is engaged in a quality improvement process, developing more sophisticated machines. This requires a better skilled workforce. The ham factory is developing an active training policy for its core workforce, trying to upgrade it through training courses and a qualification process, based on qualifications at the industry level. This policy also fits in with higher requirements for the hiring of new employees.

For semi-skilled or unskilled workers, as well as for seasonal and/or replacement needs, the ham factory uses the temporary agency channel. It is expensive, but provides a high degree of flexibility and makes it possible to avoid falling under international benchmarking indicators regarding wage costs. However, on the one hand, it is becoming more and more difficult to recruit young people through this channel and, on the other hand, it conflicts somewhat with quality requirements and norms. Moreover, some temporary workers, who are virtually permanent workers at the ham factory, will come into conflict with the legislation on temporary agencies (temporary contracts of no more than 18 months) and do not benefit from the seniority rules which apply to the core workforce.

For all these reasons the ham factory decided to create an employers' association in order to share part of its workforce with other employers.

The employers' "group": purpose and objectives of this initiative
The employers' group is another way of intermediating between the entrepreneurship relation and the employer relationship, as in the "portage" case study.

Initially, five firms in the local area got together, probably on the basis of previous individual relations between their managers (in employers' associations). The purpose is to share workers, according to the seasonal needs of the various firms, in order to gain both flexibility and security within the framework of the labour laws. The five firms belong to the food processing industry. Three of them experience high seasonality (chocolates, local sweets, olive products). The other two (the ham factory and a related plant) do not face the same seasonality problem, but do have a problem articulating the core and the peripheral workforce. The employers' group was founded at the beginning of 2006. The trade unions were involved in the process. It is a non-profit association and employs the workers shared between the five firms. The labour contract is signed with the group. It then delegates workforce to the firms and invoices the costs to the users. The members of the group also pay an annual membership fee, partly covering overheads. They also pay money into a special account in order to cover the risk of redundancies. The president of the group is a former senior manager of the ham factory, now retired. In his previous work, as a highly skilled white-collar representative, he was a member of many joint committees and other bipartite bodies at the sectoral level. He is very interested in workers' conditions and the growth of atypical employment conditions and is involved in many local bodies advocating active labour market policies. The director (part-time) is a private consultant and has had a lot of experience in the field of HRM.

Employees within the "group": high mobility but greater security?
The group of employers commenced activities in spring 2006. When the interviews were done, it employed 40 people, above the medium size of SMEs. There are two different categories of employees. One includes those working for the ham factory and its related plants, mainly men, who were previously working at the ham factory via the temp agency. Most have moved from the temp agency to the group of employers where they found an open-ended contract, along with other advantages of permanent workers (including some seniority premiums). The group of employers is also planning to develop an active training policy for this kind of permanent worker. The other group is also mainly under open-ended contract, and they work for the three other firms. Some were previously working as seasonal workers, others were hired through the channel of the public employment agency, mainly from vulnerable categories (women, the low-skilled, some migrants, and so on). It is planned that these employees will move from one firm to another, according to the different seasonal peaks of the firms. The group is also developing a new kind of periodic open contract: it is a classical open-ended contract, but covers only a part of the year, fixed in the contract (800 hours). The employees are free to work for other firms during the other periods or they get rights

to unemployment benefits. Nevertheless, the group is expecting to be able to shift these employees to a full-time, open-ended contract later.

Looking at the vulnerability issue, the group provides a better employment situation than a temporary agency or a fixed-term seasonal contract. Wages could also be slightly increased. And, as seen above, the permanent contract opens doors for other opportunities in everyday life (childcare, housing, and so on). In that sense, the group could be an interesting response to growing precarious employment in some activities. If the workers are stabilized within the group they can more easily undergo training. Regarding other dimensions of vulnerability, mainly working time, health and safety, the group does not seem to provide any advantages compared to its firms' members. The workers are delegated to the firms and work under exactly the same conditions as the core workforce. However, one can expect that, gaining in experience, the workers will be less exposed than those on a short-term contract starting from scratch. As the firms have some difficulty recruiting, the group provides a more attractive alternative. And, due to the civil engagement of its members, it is focusing, at this stage, on the weakest part of the labour force, unskilled men or women. The group is trying to develop better job/life quality, for example taking into account the travel difficulties of employees when allocating them to firms.

The group: a story still at the beginning
The group faces the classical problems of multi-employer activity. On the one hand, a single collective agreement must be selected to govern all workers involved in the scheme. In this, they have taken one of the less advantageous collective agreements of one of the member firms as the basic agreement. Most employees start at the level of the minimum wage. However, depending on the firm you work for and/or your job, wages and other related advantages are adjusted according to the enterprise collective agreement. At this stage, the unions are implicitly in agreement with the creation of the group and the director is discussing (not bargaining) at local level with union representatives. They are opposed, for example, to the periodic open-ended contract.

On the other hand, neither the firms nor the employees are fully convinced at this early stage of the experiment. The firms clearly understand the cost advantages (the group is cheaper than a temp agency), as well as the transfer of the employment risk to the group. But they have not yet experimented with the other advantages (workers returning regularly, knowing the work processes and workplaces, with training provided by the group). The employees benefit from the open-ended contract. But they are a little concerned by the flexibility requirements (moving from one firm to another, polyvalence in various positions). But the experiment is just starting.

The managers of the group are quite confident about the future. They plan to increase the number of employees to 80. They are discussing the expansion of the membership with other local firms in the food processing industry. Moreover, they want to develop the group not only in the low-skilled segment of the labour market but also, if possible, among skilled or highly skilled employees.

Conclusion

The group is quite a classical figure in the French labour market. The first employers' groups started in the mid-1980s, and the number of groups is increasing, as is the number of employees involved. Nevertheless, studies have revealed many difficulties. On the one hand, it is not easy to build up long-term cooperation between firms which are sometimes competing in both the product market and the labour market. Equilibrium is difficult to reach and requires a lot of conditions (individual commitment of the leaders, other kinds of relations between the firms). On the other hand, the groups are always in tension between performing a kind of social function in the labour market (that is, focusing on low-skilled workers and providing a kind of transition between unemployment and regular employment) and a broader service to their members (including higher skilled employees and jobs). But it seems a good way of achieving some flexicurity for workers in firms with high seasonal activity.

REFERENCES

Amira, S., and G. de Stefano. 2005. Contrats à durée déterminée, intérim, apprentissage, contrats aidés: les emplois à statut particulier ont progressé entre 1982 et 2002. DARES, Premières synthèses, n° 14.2.

Amossé, T. 2004. Mythes et réalités de la syndicalisation en France. DARES Premières informations, n°44.2.

Anxo, D., L. Flood and Y. Kocoglu. 2002. Offre de travail et répartition des activités domestiques au sein du couple: une comparaison entre la France et la Suède. *Economie et statistique*, n° 352–53: 127–50.

Arnaudo, B., I. Magaud-Camus, N. Sandret, T. Coutrot, M.C. Floury, N. Guignon, S. Hamon-Cholet and D. Waltisperger. 2004. L'exposition aux risques et aux pénibilités du travail de 1994 à 2003: Premiers résultats de l'enquête SUMER 2003, Premières Synthèses, No. 52.1, DARES. December.

Askenazy, P. 2004. *Les désordres du travail, Enquête sur un nouveau productivisme, La république des idées.* Paris: Seuil.

Askénazy, P., E. Caroli and J. Gautié (eds). 2006. *Low wage work in France.* New York: Russell Sage.

Attal-Toubert, K., and A. Derosier. 2005. Enquête sur l'emploi 2004, le chômage augmente légèrement malgré la reprise de l'emploi. *Insee première*, N° 1009.

Auer, P., and S. Cases. 2000. L'emploi durable persiste dans les pays industrialisés. *Revue Internationale du Travail*, 139 (4).

Barrere-Maurisson, A.M. 2000. *Travail, famille, le nouveau contrat*. Paris: Folio, Actuel.

Behaghel, L. 2003. Insécurité de l'emploi: le rôle protecteur de l'ancienneté a-t-il baissé en France? *Economie et Statistique*, n° 366: 2–23.

Blanchard, O., and J. Tirole. 2003. *Protection de l'emploi et procédure de licenciement*. Rapport au Conseil d'Analyse économique. Paris.

Boisard, P. 2004. *Working time policy in France*. Document de travail n° 34, Centre d'études de l'emploi.

Bouffartigue, P. 2005. La division sexuée du travail professionnel: quelques remarques pour une perspective temporelle. *Lien social et politiques*, n° 54, 13–23.

Bué, J. 2005. Travail de nuit et du soir depuis 10 ans, une progression plus rapide pour les femmes que pour les hommes. DARES, Premières informations, n° 40.2.

Cahuc, P., and F. Kramarz. 2004. *De la précarité à la mobilité: vers une sécurité sociale professionnelle*. Paris: La documentation française.

CERC. 2005. *La sécurité de l'emploi face aux défis des transformations économiques*. Rapport n°4. Paris: La documentation française.

CEREQ. 2001. *Quand l'école est finie, premiers pas dans la vie active de la génération 1998*. Marseille.

Chardon, O., M.A. Estrade and F. Toutlemonde. 2005. Les métiers en 2015. DARES, Premières informations, n°50.1.

Coutrot, T., and D. Waltisperger. 2005. L'emploi des seniors souvent fragilisé par des problèmes de santé. DARES, Premières synthèses, n° 08.1.

Culpepper, P.D. 2006. Le système politicoéconomique français depuis 1985. In Culpepper, Hall and Palier (eds), *La France en mutation, 1980–2005*. Paris: Presses de Sciences Politiques, 39–63.

Dupuy, Y., and F. Larré. 1999. Entre salariat et travail indépendant. *Travail et emploi*, n° 77.

Fournier, C., M. Lambert and C. Perez. 2002. *Les français et la formation continue, statistique sur la diversité des pratiques*. CEREQ, Document no. 169 (November).

Frickey, A., J. Murdoch and J.-L. Primon. 2004. Second generation immigrant youths and the French labour market: The case of higher education students. In *International migration in Europe: New trends, new methods of analysis*, 2nd Conference of the EAPS Working Group on International Migration in Europe, Rome. 25–27 November.

Guillemot, D., P. Pétour and H. Zadjela. 2002. *Trappe à chômage ou trappe à pauvreté: quel est le sort des allocataires du RMI?* Matisse, Université Paris I.

IRES. 2005. *Les mutations de l'emploi en France*. Repères: La découverte.

Jobert, A., and J. Saglio. 2005. *La mise en œuvre des dispositions de la loi du 4 Mai 2004 permettant aux entreprises de déroger aux accords de branche*. Rapport pour la DRT, CRISTO, IDHE.

Lallement, M. 2006. Transformation des relations de travail et nouvelles formes d'action politique. In Culpepper, Hall et Palier (eds), *La France en mutation, 1980–2005*. Paris: Presses de Sciences, 109–44.

Lefèvre, G., F. Michon and M. Viprey. 2002. Les stratégies des entreprises de travail temporaire, acteurs incontournables du marché du travail, partenaires experts en ressources humaines. *Travail et Emploi*, n°89.

L'Horty, Y. 2004. Instabilité de l'emploi: quelles ruptures de tendance? *Les papiers du CERC*, n°2004-01.

Lorenz, E., and A. Valeyre. 2004. *Les formes d'organisation du travail dans les pays européens*. Centres d'études de l'emploi.

Maurin, E. 2004. *Le ghetto français, enquête sur le séparatisme social*. La république des idées. Paris: Seuil.

Meda, D., and B. Minault. 2005. La sécurisation des trajectoires professionnelles, DARES, Document d'études n° 107.

Méhaut, Ph. 2004. Competencies based management: what consequences for the labour markets? *Economia et Lavoro*, XXXVIII, 1, 2004, 165–80.

———. 2006. Une scène nationale traditionnelle: l'accord de 2003 et la loi de 2004 sur la formation professionnelle tout au long de la vie, in Mériaux and Verdier (2006).

Mériaux, O., and E. Verdier (eds). 2006. *Les relations professionnelles face aux risques du travail et de l'emploi*, Rapport au CGP, Lest-Cerat, Aix en Provence.

Millet, M., and D. Thin. 2005. Le temps des familles populaires à l'épreuve de la précarité, *Lien social et Politiques*, n° 54, 153–62.

Ministère du travail. 2005. *Plan santé au travail*, www.travail.gouv.fr

Moncel, N., and E. Sulzer (eds). 2006. *L'intégration des jeunes opérateurs chez PSA, Contextes sociétaux, effets de site et identités au travail*. CEREQ, Marseille, Nef n° 22.

Morin, M.L. 2002. L'externalisation du risque, vers de nouvelles figures de l'employeur? Cadres CFDT, Février, 73–80.

Observatoire national de la pauvreté et de l'exclusion sociale. 2004. Rapport national. Paris.

Pélisse, J. 2002. A la recherche du temps gagné: les 35 heures entre perceptions, régulations et intégrations professionnelles. *Travail et Emploi,* n°90 (April).

Ramaux, C. 2006. *Emploi: éloge de la stabilité, l'état social contre la flexicurité*. Paris: Mille et une nuits.

Romans, F., and G. Séroussi. 2005. *La dynamique des salaires et du coût du travail entre 1996 et 2000*. Insee, France, Portrait social, 2003–2004.

Supiot, A. (under the supervision of). 1999. *Au-delà de l'emploi, transformation du travail et devenir du droit du travail en Europe*. Paris: Flammarion.

Valette, A. 2005. *Impacts of internal and external changing conditions on French and British labour market segmentation*. Paper to the IWLPMS, Berlin.

Waltisperger, D. 2004. Le travail responsable d'un problème de santé sur cinq. DARES, premières synthèses, n° 19.1.

7. Germany: Towards a dual labour market?

Akima Hamandia

7.1 INTRODUCTION

For the last three decades, persistently high unemployment (11.7 per cent in 2006), especially long-term unemployment, has been a feature of the German labour market. Since publication of the results of the OECD's large-scale cross-country study on employment in 1996, it has been widely recognized that this problem is attributable not only to slow economic growth, but, more importantly, to the lack of flexibility of the regulations governing employment conditions.

Since the 1990s, however, the pressure to introduce more flexibility into the German labour market has increased as a result of a number of different processes. First, globalization and an intensification of competition among firms bring the need to adjust labour costs to fluctuations in demand. The option of externalizing standardized tasks and relocating production sites to lower-wage countries, especially in eastern Europe, has become easier. Second, an individualization of personal lifestyles and life paths, increasing female labour market participation and the desire to combine work and family life have generated demands for more flexible and atypical work arrangements among the workforce (Beck, 1986). In response to these developments, and with the aim of creating employment, a number of legislative reforms were introduced as early as the 1990s, facilitating the introduction of part-time and temporary work and allowing for greater working time flexibility. The collective bargaining system has been continuously decentralized, the influence of trade unions weakened and collective agreements have provided greater scope for individual deviations from predetermined rules. The main aim of the so-called *Hartz* reforms was to improve employment opportunities especially in the low-wage sector for the most disadvantaged groups on the

Note: I would like to thank Onno Hoffmeister of Hamburg University, Department of Economics, and Joachim Wolff of the Institute for Employment Research in Nürnberg (IAB) for their valuable criticisms.

labour market, in particular the long-term unemployed, low-skilled and older persons (see Box 7.1).

In the wake of these changes, work arrangements deviating from full-time regular employment have become more and more popular. The number of part-time jobs, temporary jobs, marginal jobs, on-call work, flexitime contracts, and so on, has significantly increased. But what do these new forms of work offer employees? Do they serve as a bridge from unemployment to a regular working life? Or do they rather constitute a reservoir of second-class workers, hopping from one precarious job to the next, putting up with inconvenient working times, unhealthy work conditions, low pay and uncertainty about their future income? Is a dual labour market developing, characterized by well-protected full-time employees on the one hand and persistently disadvantaged workers on the other? This report indeed finds strong evidence for an increasing polarization of the German labour market, in all spheres of working life. Despite these trends, considerable transitions and vertical mobility between both forms of employment could be observed.

Table 7.1 Trends in working and employment conditions, Germany, 2006

Element	Item	Trends	Risks/Exposed groups
Social bargaining and workers' participation	Membership density	Strong decline	Weakened collective bargaining system; increased use of derogatory rules within firms, employers and trade unions establishing company agreements.
	Decentralization	Individualization of negs. on working time and wages	Extension of working time, lower wages: increasingly unequal working conditions
Employment status and contracts	Temporary employment	Considerable increase	Low-paid and low-qualified workers, mostly men, but also more and more people of foreign origin, older workers
	Self-employment	Considerable increase	Young and highly qualified persons, increasingly women, are affected by uncertain income flow, long working hours and job insecurity
	Mini-jobs	*Hartz reforms* not expected to have much effect	A growing number of women are single-job low-paid workers, not covered by social security
	Short-term contracts	Light increase but stable	Repetitive, exclusively short-term jobs for low-skilled workers
Wages	Real wages	Modest increase; growth rate lower than productivity growth	Exceptionally lower wages among low-skilled workers not covered by collective agreement, East Germans, immigrants, women

Wages (cont.)	Wage inequality	Increasing wage inequality; workers shift from middle to lower wage stratum	Increasing poverty risk also among full-time workers, job insecurity
	Low wages	Decreasing upward mobility; increase of poverty risk much steeper than for other employment groups	Low-wage earners who are the main breadwinner of the household face a poverty risk of 33%
Working time and work organization	Long hours of work	Increase	Self-employed, academics, workers in public and private services, full-time workers, part-time women
	Part-time	Increase in the number of hours of work for women vs only a few hours for men, migrants	Most female part-timers (especially in western Germany) are low paid. Not always voluntary, male part-timers are more exposed to poverty risk
	Flexible working time	Significant, widespread	Does not necessarily help to better combine work and family duties, working parents
Work organization, work intensity and working rhythms	Work intensity	Increase, in terms of both pace and quantitative demands, and as a result of new organizational forms	Stress, burnout and work–life balance problems, as well as bullying. Affecting most workers' activities in services, production sector, occupations are often exhausting and associated with mental and physical stress.

7.2 CHANGING FORMS OF EMPLOYMENT

Self-employment: a stepping stone to employment

Since German reunification, the number of self-employed people has increased continuously as a proportion of total employment. Between 1993 and 2005, average annual growth in self-employment amounted to 1.6 per cent, compared to 0.2 per cent for the active employed population. The self-employment growth rate has been especially high in recent years (3.8 per cent in 2005, 3.6 per cent in 2004). There were 4 million self-employed in 2005, which represented 10.2 per cent of total employment (Sachverständigenrat 2005: 119). A strong trend towards self-employment can be observed especially in the former GDR, where the proportion of self-employed in the total employed population doubled, from 4.5 per cent to 9.2 per cent between 1991

Box 7.1: The Hartz reforms

In the mid-1990s, a debate got under way about the expansion of the "low-paid sector" as a means of creating new jobs. Finally, in February 2002, the Schröder government established the "Commission for Modern Services on the Labour Market" which was charged with developing measures to reduce unemployment by raising labour market flexibility, while as far as possible preventing cuts in social protection systems. The group – consisting of 15 persons from politics, business, trade unions and academia – was led by Peter Hartz, former human resources executive at Volkswagen. The "Hartz" Commission prepared a set of reform proposals laid down in Agenda 2010, known as Hartz I, II, III and IV. These were implemented in four steps between 2003 and 2005. The Hartz reforms focused on increasing labour market flexibility and creating new incentives for employment, especially in the low-wage sector. The aim was to bring particularly the long-term unemployed and the most disadvantaged groups on the labour market (young people, people without vocational training, women, older workers, migrant workers, and so on) into employment. The reforms consisted of four packages (Hartz I–IV). One part of the reform focused on the transformation of the German Federal Labour Office (*Bundesagentur für Arbeit*) into a modern service provider. Job-placement activities have been improved, and unemployment and social assistance were merged into a new basic benefit scheme at the level of social assistance, so-called "*Arbeitslosengeld II*". In addition, the package introduced the following policy instruments: a new *self-employment grant* for formerly unemployed, the so-called *Ich-AG*, the introduction of "staff services agencies" (PSA), the reform of *mini-* and the introduction of so-called *midi-job*s, and the promotion of employment incentives for older people.

---

and 2003 as a consequence of the economic transition (see Sachverständigenrat, 2005: 115).

The *Hartz reforms* increased the incentives for unemployed people to become self-employed (see Box 7.1). The new business start-up grant (called *Ich-AG* ["Me Ltd."] by Hartz) strengthens the already existing (since 1986) "bridging allowance" (*Überbrückungsgeld*) which capitalizes unemployment benefits entitlements in order to help the unemployed in setting up their own business. Whereas the individual amount of bridging allowance is based on unemployment benefit plus social insurance contributions and is paid for only six months, the *Ich-AG* allowance is paid as an annually decreasing lump sum for three years provided that annual income does not exceed EUR 25,000.[1] For this reason, this allowance is more suitable for those self-employed who do not expect particularly high profits from their self-employment at the beginning and for those who only have low unemployment insurance entitlements (Leschke et al., 2006: 7).

---

1. The *Ich-AG* allowance is a monthly allowance of EUR 600 in the first year, EUR 360 in the second year and EUR 240 in the third year. The beneficiary has to pay a pension contribution. Social security contributions can be paid at a lower rate. After the period of financial support, the newly self-employed are responsible for their own social security. They also have to pay 10 per cent tax.

In 2003, the first year after the reform, around 93,000 previously unemployed benefited from the *Ich-AG* start-up grant. By 2005, their number was already up to 239,000 (see Kritikos and Wießner, 2004; Wießner, 2005). In the same time period 160,800 unemployed started their own businesses with support from the bridging allowance. Both groups together made up about 0.8 per cent of the active labour force in 2005 (Bundesagentur, 2006, cited in Leschke et al., 2006: 7).[2] Since 2005, however, the increase in the uptake of both start-up measures has slowed down, compared to 2004, which is probably the result of a new basic benefit at the level of social assistance allowance, the so-called *Arbeitslosengeld II*.

Ich-AGs were started mainly in services, construction, trade, crafts and IT (Bundesagentur, 2006, cited in Leschke et al., 2006: 8). In 2004, more than 40 per cent of the newly founded *Ich-AGs* were run by women; most work for their *Ich-AGs* on a part-time basis, earning an additional household income. In general, the businesses realized within the scope of *Ich-AGs* are quite small, present low growth potential and therefore do not create a sustainable basis for a livelihood (see Sachverständigenrat, 2006: 125f.). Only a fifth of the *Ich-AGs* founded so far, however, have been terminated. Among these break-ups, 54 per cent returned to unemployment, whereas 40 per cent found a new job. Among the reasons for business failure were insufficient preparation, information deficit and underestimation of the social insurance costs. In one third of the failed cases, the businesses went bankrupt (Wießner, 2005).

As persons switching from unemployment to an *Ich-AG* constitute a significant share in the active labour force (0.8 per cent) the goal of promoting employment can be said to have been attained (see Sachverständigenrat, 2006: 125). It seems to be both a means of better combining paid with unpaid family work and a stepping stone to employment.

Temporary work: strong increase due to state incentives

In 2004, around 400,000 persons were registered as temporary workers in Germany, compared to only 138,451 in 1994. Between 2003 and 2004, the increase in the number of temporary workers was especially strong, at 55,000. Their share in overall employment rose by 8 per cent between 1998 and 2004. However, with a proportion of 1.2 per cent in the total workforce their importance is rather low compared to many other European countries, such as the United Kingdom (5.1 per cent), the Netherlands (2.5 per cent), France (2.1 per cent) and Belgium (2.2 per cent). According to German Federal Labour Office statistics, the share of temporary workers has also grown within the group of

---

2. In 2004, 65.2 per cent of all new start-ups were financed by state subsidies by comparison with 27.3 per cent in 2002.

workers paying social security contributions, amounting to 1.2 per cent in 2003 compared to 0.4 per cent in 1993. In western Germany, the rise in temporary work is mainly due to increasing demand from manufacturing firms, confronted by strong competitiveness and cost pressures, whereas in the former GDR it results from the expansion of demand in services. The employment share of temporary work is higher in eastern Germany than in western Germany (Sachverständigenrat, 2005: 115 ff.; Arrowsmith, 2006: 6; Jahn and Wolf, 2005: 2–3).

Temporary workers tend to be males, foreigners, people without vocational training and young people. Although more than half of them are below 35 years of age (compared to 38 per cent in the whole economy) and the temporary workers' average age is 37.5, Germany has a higher presence of older workers in temporary work than other European countries (Arrowsmith, 2006: 10). Manufacturing, construction, trade (export activities), repairs and services are the major domains of temporary work. By contrast, sectors such as cleaning services, trade and gastronomy do not make great use of it because of their strong reliance on marginally employed workers.

Recent surveys by the Institute for Employment Research (IAB) show that there is a trend of the expansion of temporary work also among higher skilled workers. These include personnel with professional training, such as technicians or engineers, but showing a lack of the complementary expertise required in their area of specialization or having outdated skills (Bellmann, 2004: 137). Regardless of their skills, they are employed at the lowest qualification level in the firm, although increasingly their position is longer-term. Temporary workers' gross hourly wages are on average EUR 11 and thus 30 per cent lower than those of core workers (Schlese et al., 2005: 570f.). The survey by the European Industrial Relations Observatory reports that 15 per cent of temporary contracts last for only a few days. The majority of the assignments terminate after a period of less than three months (see Arrowsmith, 2006: 9).

As a consequence of the Hartz reforms, the 1972 Temporary Employment Act (*Arbeitnehmerüberlassungsgesetz*) was thoroughly amended in 2002.[3] The new regulation extended the maximum assignment duration from one year to two years and also stipulated for temporary workers working continuously for one year at the same company equal treatment and equal pay to the rest of the workforce (since 2004) (see Boemke and Lembke, 2002; Bellmann, 2004: 135). Nevertheless, firms can derogate from the equal-pay principle and introduce below-average wages if this is agreed in a collective agreement.

---

3. Until 2004, temporary work was forbidden for blue-collar jobs in the construction sector because of the strong opposition of the trade unions. It was allowed only as a means of avoiding short-time work and lay-offs if a collective agreement foresees this.

The new reform also introduced "staff service agencies" (*Personal Service Agenturen, PSA*), which are located at local or regional labour offices. Their overall purpose is to reduce hiring barriers, especially for disadvantaged unemployed persons, to diminish bureaucracy and to improve services for employers. PSAs help the unemployed to get a temporary job, thereby complementing the privately organized temporary work agencies (TWA).[4] In some cases, they also deliver training to enhance jobseekers' employability. PSAs are given financial incentives for placement of the unemployed. Private firms can receive bonuses and relief from unemployment insurance contributions if they hire unemployed persons.

Although the exceptionally high growth in temporary work after 2003 can partly be explained by the economic upturn, it is also attributable to the introduction of the PSA (Sachverständigenrat, 2005: 115ff.). Between April 2003 and the end of 2005, 129,000 unemployed (much fewer than expected) entered a PSA. The integration success was lower in eastern Germany than western Germany (see Leschke et al., 2006: 12; Jahn and Windsheimer, 2004a, 2004b). Especially the long-term unemployed benefited from the reform, although they are still underrepresented compared to their share in total unemployment. Also, female and younger workers have been increasingly placed in temporary employment by the reform. However, it is becoming clear that the PSA reaches, on average, fewer lower-skilled people than the TWA did.

From the perspective of workers and the unemployed, the expansion of temporary work can be said to have had both positive and negative effects. On the one hand, this work form offers new opportunities for taking up employment covered by social security and guaranteeing a relatively secure income flow. On the other hand, temporary workers most often represent the lowest category within firms in terms of task complexity, which is also reflected in their pay level due to the derogation rules. Only about a third of temporary workers were able to switch from temporary work to regular employment. The trade unions have frequently complained that firms employing temporary workers often do not respect the provisions of collective agreements (Deutscher Bundestag, 2006a: 123f.).

Short-term contracts: relatively stable

According to GSOEP data, in western Germany 1.6 million people were employed on a short-term contract in 2004. Their share in total employment remained relatively stable between 1995 and 2004 at around 5–7 per cent

---

4. In comparison with already existing temporary agencies, PSAs carry out the placement, not the hire of persons.

(Gieseke and Groß, 2006: 247ff.). This contrasts with countries such as Spain and other European countries and can be explained by the rather rigid German Law on Part-time and Fixed-term Employment *(Teilzeit- und Befristungs-gesetz)*. In Germany it is not allowed to extend short-term contracts after a certain period of time. In some sectors, they can be extended only three times.

In (western) Germany, the incidence of short-term work is slightly higher in services than in industry. It is also more widespread in medium-sized and large companies than in small ones. Workers with low, as well as those with high qualifications are much more likely to work short term than those with intermediate vocational training. This is due to the fact that the incidence of short-term contracts in Germany is much higher in the public sector, independently of qualifications, than in the private sector (Gieseke and Groß, 2006: 247ff.).

What are the prospects of short-term workers entering into regular employment? Gieseke and Groß (2006: 251) report that two thirds of persons previously with short-term contracts got an unlimited contract after three years, while around 21 per cent of men and 15 per cent of women still had a short-term contract at the end of this period. The risk of repeated short-term work is especially high among young workers, the low-skilled and those employed in the public sector.

As part of the Hartz reforms, in 2003 it became possible to limit the employment duration of older workers without explicit reason and without time limit. The age limit was fixed at 52 years. These measures were combined with wage insurance *(Entgeltsicherung)* for older workers, comprising short-term financial compensation comparable to the so-called "combination wage" *(Kombilohn)*, and relief from unemployment insurance contributions *(Beitragsbonus)* granted to firms if they hire a person older than 55. They were aimed at encouraging firms to employ older workers on a short-term basis against the background of exceptionally high unemployment among that group in Germany. Unfortunately, according to recent evaluations, the employment situation of older workers has not been effectively improved by the new legislation (Deutscher Bundestag, 2006a: 128f.). In addition, on 23 November 2006 the German parliament reached agreement on a new bill raising the pension age from 65 to 67 years step by step up to 2012.

7.3 WAGES

Overall development: decrease in real hourly wages

The development of wages in Germany over the last decade has been shaped by the moderate approach of the trade unions in collective bargaining. The growth rate of the wage levels set by collective agreements, which remained at a comparatively low level (around 2 per cent) from 1996 to 2002, diminished even further in subsequent years, standing at 1.6 per cent in 2005 (Schäfer, 2000: 535; Bispinck, 2006: 90). Real wages, adjusted by price increases, has grown on average at a slower rate than productivity since 1993 (Bontrup, 2004: 314; Sachverständigenrat, 2005: 131). Annual real wages have fallen since the beginning of the 1990s, despite increasing hourly wages, expressed in 2000 prices.

Wage inequality: increasing wage differentiation

Between 1992 and 2003, the Gini coefficient[5] of wage incomes steadily increased from 0.38 up to 0.42 in western Germany and from 0.31 to 0.41 in eastern Germany. This increasing inequality stems from a number of different sources: first, the share of full-time employees in total employment diminished (from 42 per cent to 35 per cent) in favour of part-time or marginally employed workers, whose wages typically lay far below the average wage (Göbel et al., 2005: 178f.). Second, the wages of full-time employees themselves have become increasingly differentiated over time. Between 1980 and 1997, the share of full-time employees with monthly wages below 75 per cent of the mean increased in western Germany from 31 per cent to 36 per cent, while the share of those earning more than 125 per cent of the mean increased from 15 per cent to 16 per cent. A similar development can be observed in eastern Germany from 1993 to 1997, with the difference, however, that the comparatively small proportion of employees earning very low wages (less than 50 per cent of the mean) increased, while in western Germany that proportion remained unchanged (Bispinck and Schäfer, 2005: 25).

The increasing wage differentiation is obviously the result of the decentralization of collective bargaining. While previously wages were commonly fixed at branch and regional level, and embedded in agreements between employers and trade unions, they are nowadays increasingly settled at the firm level, or even in individual negotiations.

Low-wage employment on the increase

In international comparisons, low wages are usually defined as wages below two thirds of the median wage. This threshold amounted to EUR 1400 per month, or EUR 9.07 per hour, in 2003, according the German Socioeconomic Panel (GSOEP). The risk of earning a low wage is by no means limited to part-time or marginally employed people. Three out of four employees in this group earn a low monthly wage. Among west German full-time workers, the

---

5. The Gini coefficient can be taken as the average of relative distances between observed wages.

share of workers earning less than two thirds of the all-German median has continuously increased since 1993. Not so among full-time workers in eastern Germany and other employment groups. When focusing on the hourly instead of the monthly wage, the trend is similar (see Table 7.2).

Table 7.2 Share of low-wage earners in different employment groups, Germany, 2003 (%)

	Germany			Western Germany			Eastern Germany		
	1993	1998	2003	1993	1998	2003	1993	1998	2003
Monthly wage below 67% of the median									
Total employed	24.6	24.9	27.6	21.4	22.8	26.5	38.8	33.7	32.6
Full-time employed	8.9	8.2	7.6	3.8	5.0	5.2	29.9	21.6	18.8
Part-time, marginally employed	81.3	80.6	77.7	80.5	80.2	78.3	86.4	82.6	74.3
Self-employed	31.4	23.7	21.5	29.8	20.9	20.7	40.1	35.4	25.2
Hourly wage below 67% of the median									
Full-time employees	12.5	10.9	12.6	5.4	6.2	8.8	41.3	30.5	29.8
Part-time, marginally employed	51.6	49.2	49.4	47.9	47.1	47.3	74.0	60.7	61.2
Self-employed	29.9	32.2	25.8	24.3	27.7	21.5	57.6	48.9	45.6

Source: Göbel et al. (2005), "Mehr Armut durch steigende Arbeitslosigkeit", *DIW-Wochenbericht 10/2005*.

The share of full-time employees falling below this threshold has increased continuously since 1997, in eastern Germany since 1994. Women, east Germans, people without professional qualifications, young persons below 24, foreigners and persons employed in small enterprises are overrepresented in the low-wage sector. Moreover, low wages are widespread among full-time employees in services, especially those related to private households and hotels and restaurants (Rhein et al., 2005: 1–3).

Single low-wage jobs: major determinant of poverty

The poverty risk of low-wage earners, in contrast to other employed persons, has increased considerably since 1993 (see Table 7.3).[6] A more detailed inves-

6. This trend was observable in both eastern and western Germany, although the poverty rates in the eastern part of the country were higher.

Table 7.3 Poverty rates of different employment groups, Germany, 2003 (%)

	1993	1998	2003
Full-time employed	3.9	3.6	4.4
Part-time, marginally employed	12.1	15.8	17.2
Self-employed	6.1	4.8	4.3
Wage < 2/3 of the mean	12.9	17.5	20.4
Wage > 2/3 of the mean	2.7	2.2	2.9
Unemployed	28.7	31.7	39.1

Source: Göbel et al. (2005), "Mehr Armut durch steigende Arbeitslosigkeit", *DIW-Wochenbericht* 10/2005.

tigation reveals that poverty is almost exclusively limited to those low-wage earners who do not share their household with at least one employed person earning more than a low wage. This group of people makes up 47 per cent of all low-wage earners. Every third such person lives in poverty. The members of the remaining part, for whom the low-wage jobs can be regarded rather as an additional than as the major source of income, face a poverty risk of less than 1 per cent. The GSOEP data reveal the alarming trend that not only the proportion of persons with low-wage jobs in the total labour force but also their likelihood of being poor has increased since 1993 (Göbel et al., 2005: 180–3).

According to the IAB Establishment sample, only half the full-time employees who had earned a wage below two thirds of that employment group's median in 1996 were still employed full time five years later. A tenth of them had switched to a part-time job and a third had stopped being employed in a job paying social security contributions. About a third of previous low-wage earners in eastern and western Germany who remained full-time employed had been able to get beyond the low-wage threshold and obtain better pay. In western Germany, this percentage had been much higher ten years earlier: half the employees who earned a low wage in 1986 had ceased to do so by 1991 (Rhein et al., 2005: 3f.).

Mini- and midi-jobs: widespread use of mini-jobs

As in other European countries, jobs paid below a certain monthly wage threshold are granted relief from taxes and social security contributions in Germany. The aim of these measures is to create incentives for the unemployed to take up employment in the low-wage sector. Within the framework of the Hartz reforms these rules were changed in 2003. The wage level below which employees are exempted from social security contributions (mini-jobs) was lifted from EUR 325 to EUR 400. In the wake of the Hartz reforms a mini-job is employment with a monthly wage of EUR 400 or less, regardless of working time. Now, for each mini-job the employer is obliged to pay 25 per cent of the wage to cover social security contributions and income tax.[7] For jobs falling in the zone between EUR 400 and EUR 800 a month – so-called midi-jobs – the employees' social security contributions are not fully levied but gradually increase from 4 per cent to 21 per cent of the wage, and income tax is calculated according to the regular schedule. Employers pay full contributions of 20.85 per cent (Rudolph, 2003). The aim of the mini- and midi-job reform was not only to integrate the unemployed in the low-wage sector but also to increase social protection coverage by lowering incentives for undeclared employment (Leschke et al., 2006: 13).

In June 2005, 6.7 million of mini-jobbers were registered, 2.6 million more than before the reform (Deutscher Bundestag, 2006a: 124). They therefore represent three quarters of all workers with wages below 67 per cent of the median; 17 per cent of all jobs were mini-jobs in 2004 (Schupp and Birkner, 2004). The number of midi-jobs increased by only 100,000 to 720,000 (Leschke et al., 2006: 14). The increase in mini-jobs is particularly due to the growing number of such jobs as a secondary activity (see Brandt, 2006: 447). Nevertheless, for three quarters of mini-jobbers this job was still their sole occupation in 2004, especially married women, who make up two thirds of mini-job workers.

Mini-jobs are also overrepresented in cleaning services, gastronomy, sport and trade (see Case Studies 1 and 2). In these three branches, there are more mini-jobbers than other employees. In the retail trade, vacant workplaces are increasingly being replaced by mini-jobs. Moreover, about 60 per cent of the 83,000 reported domestic jobs in Germany are mini-jobs (Deutscher Bundestag, 2006a: 124ff.; Schupp and Birkner, 2004). Every fourth job transmitted by temping agencies is a mini-job. The share of foreigners among mini-job workers increased by 28 per cent between mid-2003 and the end of 2004 (Deutscher Bundestag, 2006a: 124). Mini-jobs are more widespread in western Germany than in eastern Germany (Sachverständigenrat, 2004: 173; Reinberg and Hummel, 2005: 3; Schupp and Birkner, 2004).

Recent evaluations of the Hartz reforms have shown that mini-jobs have not been the bridge from unemployment to regular employment that was expected. Moreover, mini-jobs seem to have pushed people out of socially protected employment (Deutscher Bundestag, 2006a). They do not provide enough income and social security and are above all performed by persons who already have income security (Leschke et al., 2006: 14). Micro-simula-

---

7. Employees do not contribute to social security benefits, but therefore have no entitlement to social and unemployment benefits or pensions unless they make voluntary contributions.

tions carried out by the German Institute for Economic Research (*Deutsches Institut für Wirtschaftsforschung – DIW Berlin*) confirm that the mini-job reform has had a small effect on labour supply. They reveal that the spouses of wage earners have few incentives to work for more than EUR 400 because the tax-splitting rules create a high marginal tax burden. At the same time, employed persons earning slightly more than EUR 800 have an incentive to reduce their working hours below this threshold (Steiner and Wrohlich, 2005). Others see a lack of knowledge of the midi-job rule as an important reason for its limited use (Leschke et al., 2006: 14).

Another legislative change which has affected the low-wage sector was the introduction of rules for occasional work (so-called *"one-Euro jobs"*) allowing unemployed persons to work for communal and charity organizations for an hourly wage of maximum EUR 2, while not losing their unemployment benefits. According to IAB calculations, the net earnings of an unemployed person working 40 hours per week in a one-Euro job is more or less equal to 67 per cent of the full-time employees' median wage (Cichorek et al., 2005: 3). In the course of 2005, around 200,000 persons were employed in such work (Sachverständigenrat, 2005: 126).

7.4 WORKING TIME AND WORK INTENSITY

Gap between usual and collectively agreed working time

In 2004, the average annual working time of all workers amounted to 1,359 hours. It steadily decreased by 17.2 per cent between 1991 and 2004 (by the same rate for men and women). This decrease was significantly stronger in the former GDR (–32.3 per cent) than in western Germany (–12.4 per cent) because of the labour market situation and the working time reductions after reunification. These were achieved by the reduction of collectively agreed weekly working hours in most economic sectors and of part-time working hours. Moreover, the proportion of full-time positions has considerably decreased: the figure of 23.7 million full-time employed in 2004 was 20 per cent lower than in 1991. This decrease affects both men and women to the same extent and was stronger in the former GDR than in western Germany (38 per cent compared to 13.8 per cent). In 2004, the usual annual working time of full-timers in Germany amounted to 1,679 hours; it was 2.2 per cent higher in eastern Germany than in western Germany, although working times in both parts of the country are converging (see Wanger, 2006: 12, 20).

Usual working times are longer than those laid down in collective agreements. In 2003, west German full-time workers worked 41.9 hours per week (east Germany: 43 hours), compared to the 38.9 hours laid down in agreements (eastern Germany: 39.8 hours). Among part-time workers the usual working time was 21.4 hours a week, 1.2 hours higher than agreed in western Germany. In eastern Germany, the usual working time – 25.8 hours – exceeded that agreed by 2 hours (ISO, 2004 cited in Rürup and Gruescu, 2005: 16).

In eastern Germany, 46.2 per cent of the workers covered by collective agreements had an agreed weekly working time of 40 hours and more, compared to only 6 per cent in western Germany. In western Germany, 23.5 per cent of workers had a collectively agreed working time of 35 hours a week and less, while only 3.4 per cent of eastern German workers had so low an agreed working time. Collectively agreed working hours vary considerably across sectors. In industry, most firms have collectively agreed working hours below 40 hours. By contrast, in services (hotel and restaurants, banking) almost half of all firms show a weekly working time of 39 weekly hours. In large companies, the agreed weekly working time is on average shorter than in small companies (DIHK 2004 cited in Rürup and Gruescu, 2005: 13-14; Bispinck, 2006: 91, 95f.).

Recent research underlines the relationship between working time duration and the skills level of employees. Whereas low-skilled workers have comparatively shorter working hours, technical staff, engineers and managers often work longer. They enjoy higher work identification and are therefore more likely to work longer: 50 to 70 hours a week or even more, for instance in the IT sector (see Haak and Schmid, 1999; Bosch, 2000a).

Furthermore, usual working hours diverge from preferred ones. Gender differences are relevant here. Most full-time male workers want more paid overtime since unpaid overtime may now be found in every fifth firm. By contrast, full-time female workers aspire to a general reduction in working hours (overtime and collectively agreed hours), which are up to 36.3 hours a week for women in the former GDR and 35.7 for women in western Germany. In contrast, most part-time workers would prefer an extension of (agreed and usual) working hours, regardless of gender and region (involuntary part-time) (ISO, 2004 cited in Rürup and Gruescu, 2005: 16f.). The gap between usual working hours and workers' working time preferences underlines the discrepancy between work and family life.

Strong increase in part-time work

Whereas the number of full-time employees has fallen by a quarter of million, the number of part-time workers has doubled since 1991, reaching 24.5 per cent of the labour force in 2005 (Schäfer and Vogel, 2005: 132). 75 per cent of part-time workers are women. In 2005, the female part-time rate amounted to 44.3 per cent, compared to only 7.4 per cent for their male counterparts (Statistisches Bundesamt, 2006). However, part-time work is becoming increasingly popular also for men. Their share in part-time employment has trebled since 1991 (see Wanger, 2006: 15).

The substantial use of part-time work in Germany is primarily attributable to western German women's employment pattern. The female part-time rate in western Germany was 51.1 per cent in 2004, compared to part-time rates of 38.1 per cent among eastern German women, 17.5 per cent of eastern German men and 15 per cent of western German men. Women in the former GDR are more likely to work full time because they were used to doing so before reunification, thanks to the generous childcare provisions (see Wanger, 2006: 7).

More than half of part-time jobs (54 per cent) are marginal, with few hours.

Inconvenient working times very common

Regarding the distribution of working hours, there is a general trend towards the "around-the-clock society", in which night, weekend and shift work are widespread. In 2004, almost half of dependent workers had such inconvenient working times compared to only 38 per cent in 1991 (Seifert, 2005: 479).

Workers in different categories face different kinds of inconvenient working time. The self-employed are particularly affected by weekend and evening

Table 7.4 Share of workers with inconvenient working hours by employment type, Germany, 2005 (%)

	Saturday work		Sunday work		Evening work		Night work		Rotating shifts	
	(1)[2]	(2)	(1)	(2)	(1)	(2)	(1)	(2)	(1)	(2)
Self-employed	46.9	29.3	22.1	28.0	39.8	29.5	6.0	11.8	1.0	0.3
Civil servants	21.2	22.7	16.8	20.3	23.3	27.5	9.9	13.1	10.5	1.4
Blue-collar workers	22.7	24.0	11.4	10.5	26.0	12.7	14.2	5.7	22.8	1.8
White-collar workers	23.1	18.5	12.1	12.3	23.0	19.0	6.4	5.1	10.7	1.0
Others[1]	26.7	13.0	14.1	7.6	17.7	10.2	3.1	3.3	7.5	1.3
Short-term employed	23.9	21.9	14.1	15.3	24.9	19.0	9.0	8.6	14.7	2.0
Permanently employed	22.8	20.4	12.0	12.0	23.9	14.8	9.2	5.6	14.6	1.2
Full-time employed	22.5	22.2	12.7	13.1	25.9	19.5	10.7	6.9	16.7	1.4
Part-time employed	23.9	15.9	10.6	10.0	18.7	11.9	4.9	2.9	8.6	1.1
Total	25.8	21.1	13.4	13.8	25.4	18.5	8.5	6.4	12.7	1.2

Notes:
(1) Often.
(2) Casually.
[1] Apprentices, trainees and workers helping in family business.
[2] Permanent and regular.
Source: Statistisches Bundesamt, National Account Statistics, 2006.

work (half of them regularly work at least on Sundays). Blue-collar workers often need to work rotating shifts. Night work is most common among public employees. White-collar workers appear to have the most convenient working times, according to the categories shown in Table 7.4. All kinds of inconvenient working times occur slightly more often among short-term than regularly employed workers. Interestingly, full-time workers have more inconvenient working times than part-time workers. Particularly, the share of those working rotating shifts is much higher among full-time workers (see Table 7.4).

The German National Statistical Office (*Statistisches Bundesamt*) (2004) reports that 22 per cent of employed mothers with a child younger than 18 usually work on Sundays. Seven years previously, their share was only 20 per cent.

Shift, night and weekend work are useful means for employers to extend production and service times. As services are increasingly demanded "around the clock", the expansion of the service sector has had a strong impact on the growth of inconvenient working hours (Seifert, 2005: 479). The most inconvenient working times are concentrated in transport, communication, trade, gastronomy, public and private services, for instance care (nursing and elderly care) and security.[8] A sector-specific pattern can also be identified: in trade and hotels and restaurants, Saturday and evening work are particularly widespread, while night work is rather concentrated in transport and communication and Sunday work in public and private services. Apart from transport and communication, night work and rotating shifts are also very common in mining and manufacturing.

According to the National Statistical Office, the proportion of employees working rotating shift systems has increased significantly over the last ten years, as in most European countries. In Germany, their share in total employment increased from 9.7 per cent to 15.5 per cent between 1993 and 2003.

7.5 HEALTH AND SAFETY

Health of self-employed and part-time workers most at risk

As employees' health is difficult to capture in surveys, it is often derived from absenteeism rates. Ichino and Riphanhn (2004) analysed GSOEP data and found that German workers, excluding the self-employed and public employees, are on average absent from work one day out of 24. The absen-

---

8. The high concentration of inconvenient working hours in public services correlates with high absenteeism rates (see section 7.5).

teeism rate is thus 4.3 per cent. This rate was significantly higher among public sector employees (4.9 per cent) than in the private sector (4.1 per cent). For comparison, the authors report absenteeism rates in the private sector of Italy ranging between 1.6 per cent and 2.8 per cent, depending on enterprise size.

However, absenteeism rates are strongly influenced by factors unrelated to health, especially by the degree of employment protection (ibid.). An alternative indicator is the share of persons dropping out of jobs for health reasons. On the basis of GSOEP data, Elkeles et al. (2000) found that between 1984 and 1991, 6.7 per cent of all employees changed their employment situation for health reasons. The majority of them (58 per cent) were older than 50, but still 30 per cent were less than 40 years old. Among the persons who switched from one job to another for health reasons, older workers, part-time workers, professionals, clerks and the self-employed were overrepresented.

Workers' health can also be inferred from their likelihood of switching from employment to early retirement or pension schemes for health reasons. Butchers, train drivers and construction workers have a significantly higher likelihood of terminating their career due to threatened health than due to age. By contrast, soldiers and policemen, lower-level managers, "other" technicians and architects have the greatest chance of remaining employed until reaching their statutory retirement age.

Threats to health at the workplace: increasing stress

A number of studies have shown that health threats are directly related to physical and mental stress at the workplace. The data of the BIBB/IAB survey seem to establish an overall trend: the physical hazard, measured as the frequency of carrying heavy loads, has remained constant since 1979, while mental hazard, measured in terms of narrow scope for self-determined action, has increased (Röttger et al., 2003: 593; European Foundation, 2006). It is estimated that nowadays 7 per cent to 9 per cent of all expenditure on health and 50 per cent to 60 per cent of lost working days are attributable to stress at the workplace (Aldana, 2001; European Agency, 2001).

In 2002, 11.3 per cent of the employees interviewed by EIRO reported that they had been victims of harassment or "bullying" at least once in the course of their working life. This occurs in all types of establishments and occupations in Germany. Women are particularly affected by this: their rate is 75 per cent higher than that of men. Some 43.9 per cent of the victims fall ill as a result of bullying. Half of them remain sick for more than six weeks. Disciplinary action undertaken by the employers concerned, such as transfers and dismissals, often affects the victims of bullying more than the offenders (see European Foundation, 2006).

Bödecker et al. (2002) studied the relationship between physical and mental risk at work and health on the basis of health insurance data combined with expert interviews. They estimate that 23 per cent of the risk of becoming ill can be attributed to carrying heavy loads or performing difficult tasks, 14 per cent to narrow scope for self-determined action, 7 per cent to handling dangerous materials, 7 per cent to vibrations, 3 per cent to noise and 2 per cent to coercion.

In the BIBB/IAB survey of 1998/1999, 90 per cent of male blue-collar workers, but only 49 per cent of white-collar workers reported having to carry heavy loads at work. The percentage was lower among female workers (75 per cent of blue-collar, 46 per cent of white-collar workers). Blue-collar workers are also more affected by mental stress than white-collar workers: 97 per cent of male blue-collar workers and 90 per cent of male white-collar workers reported narrow scope for self-determined action. The difference is narrower among their female counterparts: 95 per cent of female blue-collar and 91 per cent of female white-collar workers reported being affected by this kind of stress (Röttger et al., 2003: 593f.).

Surveys on the working conditions of temporary workers (see Schlese et al., 2005; Bothfeld and Kaiser, 2003; Jahn and Rudolph, 2002a, 2002b) emphasize that increased job insecurity, low wages and restricted further training opportunities increase the physical and psychological burden, as well as the likelihood of accidents. Particularly repetitive and exhaustive activities and physical strain are associated with lower motivation at work. Worsening performance at work, a decline in product and service quality, absenteeism and high staff turnover are typical additional effects. The affected workers are seldom informed about the risks at their workplaces and they seldom have an influence on their working conditions (see also Kvasnicka and Verwatz, 2003: 724).

EU legislation on health: low impact

The protection of workers' safety and health in Europe is regulated by the Council Directive of 12 June 1989 on the introduction of measures to encourage improvements in the safety and health of workers at work (89/391/EEC), implemented in Germany in 1996. At the heart of this reform was the introduction of obligatory risk assessments (*Gefährdungsbeurteilungen)*, according to which employers must assess the physical and mental risks at each workplace. In a survey carried out by the WSI in 2004, only 50.1 per cent of the interviewed firms (with more than 20 employees) confirmed that they had conducted a complete risk assessment, while 17.4 per cent reported that they had not; 9.6 per cent of the firms had conducted an incomplete risk assessment; the remaining 18.6 per cent had not heard about it. The implementation rate of risk assessments was positively related with firm size. This might be due to the better developed organizational infrastructure for employment protection and the presence of company doctors at larger firms. Small firms often lack a collective agreement on health protection. Moreover, risk assessments appeared to be most common in raw materials and in communication and transport, whereas in finance, insurance and trade they are seldom carried out (Ahlers and Brussig, 2004; 2005).

7.6 WORK AND FAMILY: A DIFFICULT BALANCE

Germany is faced by far-reaching demographic change, reflected in an ageing population[9] and a birth rate which is one of the lowest in Europe (1.35 compared to 1.85 in France and 1.74 in Denmark). This represents a major challenge for family policy. The main reason for the declining birth rate seems to be women's reluctance to bear children. According to Bertram (2005), the problem is not so much that fewer women have children but rather the tendency towards "one-child families". Against this background, the discussion on the balance between work and family life has gained particular importance in recent years. It has mainly focused on three aspects: (i) the introduction of wage-related parental leave entitlements with the aim of encouraging fathers to become more actively involved in the care of children; (ii) the improvement of childcare utilities for little children from birth to the age of six; and (iii) the promotion of family-friendly working time organization.

The new Parent Allowance Act: a controversial issue

On 14 June 2006, the government agreed on a bill concerning the new Parent Allowance Act (*Elterngeldgesetz*). According to this reform, employed parents who interrupt their career or reduce their working hours by up to 30 hours per week (maximum), are entitled to twelve months' parental leave. During the period of parental leave they receive two thirds of their former net pay, although no more than EUR 1,800 per month. Two more months are paid if the other partner interrupts his/her job for the purpose of childcare. Moreover, parental leave entitlements of EUR 300 per month during a two-year period are also foreseen for unemployed parents (Deutscher Bundestag, 2006b).[10] The purpose of this reform is to increase the participation of men in childcare

---

9. According to estimates of the Statistisches Bundesamt, in 2050 a third of the population will be above 60 years of age. The number of young people under 20 has already decreased from 21 to 16 per cent (see Statistisches Bundesamt, 2003; Henry-Huthmacher and Hoffmann, 2006: 7).

10. Social and family benefits in Germany are among the highest in Europe. In 2004, they made up 4.5 per cent of GDP (Deutscher Bundestag, 2006c).

and to encourage couples to have children by providing some relief from loss of income. There have been successful experiences with a "parent allowance" in Sweden and other Western European countries. The Christian Democratic Party (CDU/CSU) sought especially to support housewives having a second child, whereas the Social Democrats (SPD) criticized that position.

Childcare facilities: lack of infrastructure

In Germany, childcare facilities for children under 3 remain inadequate. As in other European countries with low fertility rates – such as Italy, Spain and Austria – only 10 per cent of children below 3 years of age attend a childcare facility. While all-day schools are fairly common in most European countries, in Germany they only cover 5 per cent (2001) (Kröhnert et al., 2005: 15). Furthermore, education facilities for primary school children are unsatisfying. In western Germany, only 5 per cent of these children attend some kind of childcare facility after school. In eastern Germany this percentage is much higher, at 41 per cent (see Henry-Hutmacher and Hoffmann, 2006: 8). Childcare facilities for children of pre-school age – between 3 and 6 years – vary a lot in Germany. While in western Germany, the majority (80 per cent) of the existing childcare facilities are only half-day nurseries, the overwhelming majority (90 per cent) of eastern German facilities are all-day institutions.

Public childcare utilities in the eastern part of the country also enjoy a much higher attendance than those in the west: 31.2 per cent of east Germans but only 4.3 per cent of west German children between 1 and 2 years old normally go to a public day-care institution; between 2 and 3 years, 77.4 per cent of east German and 16.7 per cent of west German children attend them. For children aged 3–4 years the figures are 93.9 per cent and 72.6 per cent respectively (see Bien, 2005: 3–4; Henry-Hutmacher and Hoffmann, 2006: 8).[11] These differences in childcare infrastructure can be explained by the institutional settings. In eastern Germany it is still shaped by the family policy of the former GDR, according to which all women were supposed to have access to the labour market. For this reason, an extended public all-day childcare infrastructure, as well as education facilities were built up in order to help women combine work and family duties. Although childcare utilities have been severely cut back in the wake of reunification the basic structure remains. By contrast, childcare utilities in western Germany have always been scarce, except in large urban centres.

---

11. In general, in eastern Germany, day care for children younger than six years of age is open longer (7 am–5 pm) than in western Germany, where less than half of the facilities offer this (see Bien, 2005: 8).

The alarming results of the PISA study have led to an understanding that childcare facilities should also be seen as educational institutions (see Schoch and Wieland, 2004: 19). Local governments have already begun to transform primary schools into all-day schools, allowing the better coordination of education and nursery care (see Henry-Hutmacher and Hoffmann, 2006: 9).

Family-friendly working time organization

Firms also play a major role by treating parents and non-parents equitably. The organization of working time plays a key role with regard to family-friendly policies. In firms, family-friendly measures are mainly concentrated on working time flexibility. Day nurseries within companies, as they used to exist in both parts of Germany before 1949, are nowadays almost non-existent (see Höltershinken and Kasüschke, 1996).

Flexible working hours are not necessarily family-friendly
In the 1990s, equal treatment and family-friendly regulations such as parental leave, support for children's facilities and caregiving (sabbaticals), flexible working hours (long-averaging working time accounts), part-time and distance work were concluded in a wide range of collective agreements and company agreements, particularly in sectors in which women were strongly represented and many high-skilled workers needed. Most of these agreements were concluded in large firms, especially in communications and finance. However, the impact of such rules in collective agreements remains minor (Klenner, 2005a: 41ff.).

According to a study by the German Economic Institute Köln (*Institut der Deutschen Wirtschaft Köln*), 46.4 per cent of firms have introduced family-friendly measures. In 29.3 per cent these were laid down in collective agreements and 12.4 per cent in company agreements; 13.5 per cent of the firms had a respective firm directive (see Flüter-Hoffmann, 2005: 8). In 2004, the German Chamber of Commerce and Industry (*Deutscher Industrie- und Handelskammer, DIHK*) interviewed 20,000 firms in respect of working time flexibility. Two thirds of them reported flexible working hours. Flexible weekly working hours and working time accounts on an annual basis were the most widespread and increasingly practised measures. The flexible working time schemes perceived as the most "family-friendly" – for instance, staggered hours and teleworking – were also on the increase. However, it is still unclear which categories of workers benefited most. When these working hours are individually negotiated, they tend to be offered mainly to skilled workers at a higher level in the company hierarchy (see Rürup and Gruescu, 2005: 35). Moreover, not all flexible working time schemes are family-friendly. Time account systems, for example, are linked with the risk of dissociation of work and family life, as compared to standard working hours (see Seifert, 2005: 481).

Inconvenient working hours

A survey by Klenner (2005b) at the end of 2003 among 2,000 workers with children and workers with regular care duties at home reported on their experiences and expectations regarding family-friendly working conditions. Two thirds of the interviewed mothers and fathers said they enjoyed family-friendly working conditions, the other third said they faced unfriendly ones. Regarding the distribution of working hours, some of the workers interviewed criticized their working hours, particularly if they were in the late afternoon or evening, as they overlapped with childcare. For 60 per cent, an increase in inconvenient working hours (evening and weekend work) was a problem, particularly if the distribution of working hours could not be planned. Almost one quarter of parents had to deal with that problem. Concerning the flexibility of working hours, overtime accounts were perceived as positive for the work–life balance because of the resulting days off, in contrast to staggered working hours and working time tuning in a team, which make them much more exposed to the firms' needs; 61 per cent of the respondents had such an overtime account, 43 per cent were affected by staggered hours and only 33 per cent of workers by working time tuning in teams (Klenner, 2005b: 211).

Shorter working hours are family-friendly

The parents' responses were strongly correlated with their usual working hours. Parents who usually work 20 to 29 hours a week were largely satisfied compared to other groups of workers. Fathers' dissatisfaction was above average when they had to work 50 hours or more. For mothers this threshold was reached at 40 hours. These results were not correlated with region (eastern vs western Germany) or level of qualifications. More than a quarter of the fathers and more than half of the mothers would prefer shorter working hours, whereas a quarter of the mothers would like to extend their working hours. In general, it is essential for mothers to have a choice concerning the duration of working time in their work contracts. For fathers the suppression of overtime seems to be the cornerstone.

7.7 ACCESS TO TRAINING: A PRECARIOUS SITUATION

The German dual vocational training system is characterized by in-school education and in-firm training. This system ensures the delivery of precise and practice-oriented technical knowledge combined with work experience. The German dual vocational training system has been seen as an exemplary model for many other European countries as it is considered an important competitive advantage for Germany in international competition and a guarantee of economic performance (see Streeck, 1995: 32 and Sorge, 1997: 36ff.). However, in the last ten years, this system has been confronted with a decline in the number of apprenticeships. The German Government has made every effort to encourage firms to create more in-firm training places.

Decrease in the supply of vocational training within firms

Since the mid-1990s the situation of vocational training within firms has been precarious as a consequence of the transformation process. In 2005, the number of those seeking vocational training increased by 0.6 per cent, whereas the supply of training positions declined by 9.3 per cent. In September 2005, there were 40,900 applicants for 12,600 vocational training positions (Sachverständigenrat, 2005: 120). In western Germany, the excess demand for training positions has increased, while in eastern Germany it has fallen slightly in recent years. This is obviously due to the migration of young people from eastern to western Germany seeking better training places (see Haas, 2002).

Empirical evidence shows that firms' decisions regarding apprenticeship positions depend on many firm-specific factors, such as economic sector, workforce structure, firm size, the required skill level, technical level and expected personnel development (see Dietrich et al., 2004). While the supply of apprenticeships has considerably decreased in traditional handicraft occupations in western Germany, it has grown relative to other sectors in hotels and restaurants. Only a few positions are offered in the public sector. The increase in continuous training opportunities outside firms, which has been observable since 1999, has not been able to compensate for the reduction of training within firms. This situation particularly affects the number of apprenticeship positions in future-oriented professions, such as IT or media, where we can observe a decrease of 15 per cent to 20 per cent.

The low supply of training positions within firms is primarily driven by restructuring and economic downturn. One third of firms consider the costs of training too high, particularly because of the high social security contributions, which amounted to 40 per cent in 2004 (compared to 20 per cent in the 1970s). One quarter of firms are not willing to train due to high economic fluctuations and prefer to hire skilled external personnel on a short-term basis. Such alternative personnel strategies have already been implemented in the IT and media sector, consultancy and publishing (see Dietrich et al., 2004). In addition, firms complain that many school-leavers have poor secondary and intermediate qualifications (see Bellmann and Hartung, 2005).

Unskilled and low-skilled people are more at risk from precarious employment

According to the OECD (2004), training reduces the risk of unemployment and has a positive impact on the expected wage level. It also enhances chances of re-entering the labour market after job loss. The IAB comes to similar conclusions. Older academics, aged between 55 and 64 years, show a low unemployment rate and are almost fully employed (70 per cent). In contrast, people without vocational training have more difficulty finding a job. In 2004, every fifth jobseeker in western Germany and every second jobseeker in eastern Germany without vocational training was unemployed. Reinberg and Hummel (2005: 3f.) estimate that 20 per cent to 40 per cent of all low-skilled employed persons are marginally employed in mini-jobs. They are also overrepresented in the low-wage segments of regular employment. Skills are a more important determinant of unemployment than gender: a man without vocational training (27.8 per cent) has double the risk of being unemployed than a woman with vocational training (10.2 per cent) and his unemployment risk is six times higher than for a female academic (4.7 per cent).

Between 1995 and 1999, the proportion of young pupils, students and trainees in jobs with no connection to their training increased by 89 per cent to 700,000. Most are employed in services, performing simple tasks, such as filling the shelves in self-service shops, cleaning or working as waiters, and requiring high time flexibility and inconvenient working hours. In 1999, among schoolchildren, 76 per cent had low monthly earnings (less than EUR 300). Among students, 27 per cent had a full-time job in addition to their studies. Half the working students had a low-paid job (less than EUR 325 per month). Only 16 per cent earned less than EUR 300 a month, while more than 16 per cent earned more than EUR 1,100 per month (see Voss-Dahm, 2002, and Reinberg and Hummel, 2005).

Less educated workers or workers with low literacy, older workers, women, immigrants, part-timers and temporary workers are less likely to enter employer-paid training compared to those who are already highly skilled or have a good job (OECD, 2003: 239). In June 2004, the government agreed a three-year National Pact on Training and Specialized Apprenticeships (*Nationaler Pakt für Ausbildung und Fachkräftenachwuchs*), in cooperation with the central associations of German industry. This initiative aimed at increasing access to education and training for disadvantaged groups by spreading the costs and benefits more evenly. Companies were encouraged to sign a pact committing them to create more vocational training places and so avoid financial penalties from the government (see Sachverständigenrat, 2005: 120). This pact helped to drastically reduce the shortage in vocational training positions from 2004 to 2005 (ibid.).

7.8 SOCIAL DIALOGUE AND WORKERS' PARTICIPATION

Since the 1990s, there has been a strong and steady decentralization of collective bargaining on wages and working conditions, particularly working time. The difficult situation in the labour market, the far-reaching restructuring in the metal industry and increasing importance of the service sector, a majority of employees not affiliated to a trade union, have sharply changed the industrial relations landscape in Germany.

Trade unions' loss of power

Structural changes in the economy have contributed to the reshaping of industrial and labour relations. Firstly, employment in the service sector, where union density is low (around 5 per cent and even lower), has grown. Secondly, in manufacturing, as in the automobile industry for instance, the importance of SMEs (small and medium-sized enterprises) has considerably increased in parallel with the dismantling of larger firms. The workforce in SMEs is barely unionized. Thirdly, the socio-demographic structure of the workforce has also shaped trade union density: highly-skilled workers and young people are less likely to be in a trade union than low-skilled and older ones. Finally, the change in employment forms – such as the considerable increase in self-employment, temporary and single-job low-paid work – also explains the diminishing support for trade unions. In 2001, trade union density among temporary workers was only 15 per cent (see Schlese et al., 2005: 571). As a result, trade union density was 22 per cent in 2005 compared to 34 per cent at the beginning of the 1990s (see Hamandia, 2005: 63).

Decreasing coverage of collective agreements

In the context of increased global competition, firms are less willing to accept common rules for the regulation of employment conditions. Instead, they seek for wage flexibility and differentiation and differential forms of work organization in order to save costs and thereby increase their competitiveness. For these reasons, in the last decade many employers have left their employers' association. In economic sectors dominated by SMEs the coverage rate of employers' associations is almost zero. This has even further diminished the impact of regional collective agreements. Also, firms with a high proportion of skilled workers, whose wages are laid down in individual employment contracts, are seldom covered by collective agreements (see Ochel, 2005: 10). As a consequence, German trade unions have been forced to accept more concessions since the middle of the 1990s.

Between 1998 and 2004, the share of employees covered by collective agreements has decreased by 8 percentage points to 61 per cent in western Germany and by 10 percentage points to 41 per cent in eastern Germany. Meanwhile, the evidence shows that firms often do not respect collectively agreed rules (Bispinck and Schulten, 2005: 467; Bispinck, 2006: 73f). In this context, regional collective agreements (*Flächentarifverträge*) have lost out in favour of local agreements signed at the enterprise level. Establishment agreements are signed between works councils and employers' representatives, and company agreements are concluded between trade unions and individual companies (Bispinck, 2006: 74). At the end of 2004, 34,000 regional collective agreements and about 27,800 company agreements were in force (see Ochel, 2005). In eastern Germany 12 per cent of firms were covered by company agreements (*Firmentarifvertrag* or *Haustarifvertrag*) compared to only 7 per cent in the west.

Extension of opening clauses in collective agreements: deterioration of working conditions

This decentralization process was accompanied by an increase in the number of opening clauses (*Öffnungsklausel*) in collective agreements. These entitle employers to derogate from the collective agreement at the establishment level. Such opening clauses can cover all aspects of working conditions, and particularly wages and working time. Bispinck and Schulten (2005) note that, in recent years, firms have made fairly extensive use of them. According to a recent WSI works council survey, this applied to three quarters of firms covered by collective agreements in 2005. Half the firms used opening clauses in order to increase working time flexibility, 26 per cent to extend working hours. However, few firms made use of the opportunities for wage differentiation allowed in collective agreements. A fifth introduced wage reductions for beginners (see Bispinck, 2006: 56f.).

However, for employees the standards agreed in opening clauses are most often worse than those fixed in collective agreements. Schlese (2005: 569–72) observes that lower wages were quite commonplace. This development has led to the recent discussion on the introduction of a legal minimum wage in Germany, of the kind practised in France, in order to set a floor for collective agreements. In addition, at a large number of firms (a quarter) agreements dealing with "location and employment security" (*Standort- und Beschäftigungssicherungsvereinbarungen*) have been concluded. These are often coupled with benefit cuts (see Bispinck and Schulten, 2005: 467) (compare Case Study 3).

Moderate collective bargaining

Wage increases in collective bargaining have been quite moderate since the mid-1990s, amounting to around 2 per cent on average. They were even lower in 2005 (1.6 per cent). As a result of gradual reductions in working hours, collectively agreed weekly working hours range between 35 and 40 hours in western Germany and between 37 and 40 hours in eastern Germany. However, since 2004 trade unions have been confronted by massive employer demand for extension of working hours. Public employers have played a major role in this by extending the working time of public employees to almost 42 hours a week. Opening clauses have been introduced in many sectors (such as lacquer handicrafts, construction) allowing companies to extend the number of working hours without financial compensation. This ultimately resulted in a decrease in hourly labour costs. In addition, the distribution of working time has been largely flexibly handled in many collective and firm-level agreements (long hours-averaging periods, flexible staggered hours systems and time accounts).

Nevertheless, in 2003 the metalworkers' trade union *IG Metall* managed to achieve a basis for the introduction in the next few years of new collective agreements on wages, in which wage differences between production and clerical workers who carry out comparable activities will be abolished. In some sectors, the trade unions were forced to sign agreements which guarantee good working conditions for the current workforce, but which do not apply to future employees (at Volkswagen, for instance). In 1996, the "Posting Act" signed in March 1996 (*Arbeitnehmer Entsendegesetz*) enabled the trade unions to set a minimum wage for workers in the construction industry in the collective agreement. This Act was extended by the government to cleaning services in August 2006. By extending collective agreements to the national level, in particular on wage issues, the state attempted to ensure minimum working conditions for workers in different sectors and therefore partly compensate for the weakening of the German collective bargaining system (see Bispinck, 2005: 71f.; 2006: 63).

Furthermore, many collective agreements on old-age provisions were concluded. As a consequence of the 2002 reform of the Temporary Work Act, the collective agreement of 11 June 2003, agreed between two of BZA temporary agency associations (*Bundesverband Zeitarbeit Personal-Dienstleistungen e.V.*) and the DGB trade unions (*Deutscher Gewerkschaftsbund*), laid down employment and wage conditions for temporary workers in Germany. This collective agreement fixes hourly wages varying from EUR 6.85 to EUR 15.50 (see Bothfeld and Kaiser, 2003: 486). This rule was introduced on 1 January 2004. Since then, 99 per cent of temporary work agencies have come to be covered by collective agreements. The trade unions claim that stronger centralization would help to reduce growing wage inequalities. In addition, the promotion of vocational training through collective agreements has also been an important issue in collective bargaining since the mid-1990s (see Bispinck and Schulten, 2005: 470–471).

REALITY AT ENTERPRISE LEVEL: CASE STUDIES

The following case studies are based on substantial interviews conducted in different economic sectors: Case Study 1 in cleaning services, Case Study 2 in the retail trade and Case Study 3 in the automobile industry. These interviews were conducted with managers responsible for personnel policy at national and local levels, workers' representatives and trade unionists. In addition, company documents and national statistics were analysed. The survey focuses above all on large firms running businesses in the national and international environment.

In general, the case studies show a gradual deterioration of working conditions and growing groups of vulnerable workers. These include: migrant women (to a lesser part migrant men) in cleaning services, women and schoolchildren in services, elderly people in industry and the self-employed in general. The choice of enterprises in different sectors (services versus industry) also allows an understanding of how the vulnerability process occurs depending on different workforce structures and labour adjustment needs. In services, mini-jobs and marginal part time are the main instruments used to adjust employment to firms' flexibility needs, whereas in industry temporary work as well as in- and outsourcing gain in importance. The choice of industry has also enabled us to observe how personnel adjustment was conducted under the high pressure of restructuring: the tension between flexibility and employment security was dealt with by compromises offering employment protection to core employees while increasing flexibility of working time, using early retirement schemes, internal mobility of employees, and, to a lesser extent, fixed-term contracts through temporary work.

All case studies show the extension of new forms of labour flexibility and shrinking employment protection, while at the same time job insecurity is increasing. In addition, these changes are accompanied by a decrease in trade union density – among the self-employed unionization is even quasi inexistent – and a weakening of workers' representatives and an increase of labour disputes at the establishment level. In terms of working conditions, the results show a clear picture: the increase of fixed-term contracts with lower wages, irregular and inconsistent incomes, suppression of extra payments and bonuses for inconvenient hours of work. The flexibility of working time in terms of length and distribution of working hours has risen: long hours of work and a higher incidence of inconvenient hours of work in the evening, at night and on weekends. The high labour turnover of employees in some sectors (in cleaning services and in the retail trade) also expresses the worsening of working conditions. According to all case studies, work has been intensified and it has become more difficult to combine work and family responsibilities.

Table 7.5 Case studies: main features of enterprises studied

	Case Study 1	**Case Study 2**	**Case Study 3**
Main features			
Sector	Cleaning services	Retail trade	Automobile industry
Number of employees	14,000	40,000	30,500
Ownership	German	German	Multinational
Main angle	Mini-jobs; temporary work; majority of migrant workers (60%)	Mini-jobs and marginal part-time	Restructuring/ relocation; temporary work and working conditions in suppliers' firms
Main trends			
Employment contracts	60% part-time and 20% in mini-jobs Temporary work; high labour turnover (67–72%)	More than 50% part-time Increasing marginal part-time (26.3%) High labour turnover of mini-jobbers (67.5%)	Temporary work In- and outsourcing
Working time	80–120 hours a month very flexible distribution on different fragments of the day; high incidence of inconvenient hours of work (evening, night and weekend work) risk of total availability	Trend towards long hours; 20 hours a week, resp. 80 hours/ month; very flexible length and distribution and of working time Short-term changes	Extremely flexible
Health and safety	Higher work intensity and risk of burnout; deterioration of work conditions by 60%	Higher work intensity and risk of burnout	Higher work intensity, higher psychological stress because of higher job insecurity

Work and family	Difficult work–family balance because of inconvenient and irregular hours of work	Difficult balance: inconvenient and irregular hours of work; job insecurity	Not discussed
Wages	Low pay: Majority of workers get max. EUR 400 (for 51 hours/month) or EUR 800 in full-time; Wage decrease by 3.63%: lump sum payments, unpaid overtime, low hourly wages	EUR 400-800 on average per month (EUR 1,000 gross salary/ month) Overtime payment avoided by working time flexibility	Strong decrease by suppression of extra payment for overtime or extra bonus Wages of temporary and suppliers' workers lower than those of core workers
Social dialogue and participation of workers	Low union density (10%) Restricted workers' participation	Low union density (5%); almost no works council and restricted application of collective agreements; social dialogue almost non-existent	Relationships between workers and their representatives are more conflictual; increasing opening clauses on wages and working time

Germany Case Study 1: A cleaning service enterprise minimizing costs through temporary work

A is a German multinational company in the services industry. In 2006, the firm employed 50,000 employees in 18 locations in Germany. In cleaning services, the firm employs 14,000 workers in Germany and provides services for 5,000 customers.

Economic development in cleaning services: hard price competition

In 2006, there were 702,828 persons working in German cleaning services, compared to 700,000 (in 6,400 cleaning firms) in 2002.[12] Ten large firms have come to dominate the cleaning services market. The selected company is market leader. In recent years its turnover has been continuously increasing, rising from EUR 1.14 billion in 2000 to EUR 1.20 billion in 2001. Over the period 2002–2004 turnover increased by EUR 60 million and in 2005 by 11.6 per cent. The cleaning services sector is a labour-cost-intensive sector. Competition is hard because cleaning companies have to compete with firms from countries with extremely low wages. For this reason, companies in this branch increasingly look for new ways to reduce personnel costs. In addition, this sector shows a long-lasting tradition of a workforce with foreign origins, in which its share is quite high.

The share of women is very high, at 89 per cent (Schürmann and Schroth 2004, p. 88); 80 per cent of workers in this sector are low qualified and have no vocational training; 26.3 per cent of all cleaners work on a full-time basis, while 26.4 per cent are part-time; by contrast, 47.3 per cent are marginal workers.

The prevalence of mini-jobs and temporary contracts

At the same time, 56 per cent of work positions in cleaning services are mini-jobs (see Kalina and Voss-Dahm, 2005: 1). Gather et al. (2005: 28–38) argue that the Hartz reforms on temporary work and mini-jobs had a deeply negative impact on wages in cleaning services. As a consequence of the Hartz reforms, in 2002 the new regulation on temporary employment extended the maximum assignment duration from one year up to two years and also stipulated for temporary workers, having worked continuously for one year in the same company, an equal treatment and equal pay to the rest of the workforce (since 2004). Nevertheless, firms can derogate from the "equal-pay" principle and introduce pay below the average if this is agreed in a collective agree-

---

12. By contrast, the German Building-Agriculture-Environment Trade Union (Industriegewerkschaft Bauen-Agrar-Umwelt) registered 850,000 workers in the cleaning sector. Most of them (500,000) are not covered by social security.

ment. Further, in 2003 the Hartz reforms stipulated that the wage level, below which employees are exempted from social security contributions (mini-jobs), has been lifted from EUR 325 to EUR 400.

Most of the leading cleaning firms in Germany have founded subsidiary companies in order to make greater use of temporary work and avoid provisions laid down in collective agreements (free-rider strategies). The extension of the earning limit for mini-jobs (from EUR 325 to 400) has led to an increase in the working hours of precarious workers (including cleaners) of 10 hours a month in western Germany (on average 50 hours a month instead of 40.63 hours a month before 1 April 2003) and of 13 hours a month for cleaners in eastern Germany. Kalina and Voss-Dahm (2005) have examined labour turnover in services and show that in cleaning services the labour turnover of workers contributing to social security – 67 per cent – is almost as high as for people working on a mini-job basis (72.1 per cent).[13]

The authors warn that cleaners are increasingly becoming workers at risk because it is becoming more difficult for them to pay their social security contributions given that regular socially protected part-time jobs are no longer offered. That means that instead of new jobs being created the working conditions of industrial workers have deteriorated.

Collective bargaining at branch level and social dialogue at enterprise level

Trade union membership in cleaning services is very low, at about 10 per cent. The trade union is part of a European movement trying to promote workers' interests internationally in this sector. Employers in cleaning services are more likely to be members of the sectoral employers' association (*Bundesverband des Gebäudereiniger-Handwerks*) in the former West Germany and in Berlin than in the former GDR. However, organized firms cover more than 50 per cent (more than 400,000) of all workers (850,000) in cleaning services.

Wages are the "striking point"

In autumn 2003, the employers' association *Bundesverband des Gebäudereiniger-Handwerks* and the trade union *IG Bauen-Agrar-Umwelt* negotiated a new collective agreement. The largest cleaning firms threatened the trade unions with leaving the employers' association because of the wage disputes. The national collective agreement in this sector would as a result have lost its regulatory function. In order to avoid this, gross hourly wages

---

13. By contrast, in the whole economy the annual average labour turnover rate of workers covered by social security is 29 per cent, compared to 63 per cent for people having a mini-job (see Kalina and Voss-Dahm, 2005: 3).

were reduced by 3.63 per cent on average in western Germany in the new collective agreement introduced on 1 April 2004.

In 2004, the trade union Building-Agriculture-Environment and the building cleaners–craft employers' association negotiated two new collective agreements for the cleaning sector: (i) the collective agreement for industrial workers, dealing with working conditions in general, valid since 1 April 2004 until the end of 2007 at the earliest, and (ii) the collective agreement on wages, valid since 1 April 2004. The resulting collective agreements were extended at national level by the previous German Employment Minister, Clement. These agreements are therefore valid for all employees in cleaning services in the whole of Germany, including marginal workers, and regardless of whether the cleaning firm belongs to an employers' association or not. The collective agreements also apply to workers from new EU Member States.

The use of lump-sum payments for specific tasks

The trade union also complained that informal low-paid work is widespread and hidden behind "lump sum" payments. In this case, cleaners are responsible for a building and get a monthly sum to clean it. The work package is fixed independently of the time needed by workers. Usually, these work packages are too demanding and cannot be completed in time by the workers. As a result, workers work longer than they should. The result is unpaid overtime and average hourly wages of only EUR 3–5.

The unions want a legal minimum wage. The employers oppose it because they don't want to depend on or be limited by regulations. They prefer to keep the collective agreement as it is. On 15 May 2006, the fifth negotiation round took place after the previous negotiation round on 5 April 2006. Previous negotiations had not been successful. The trade union organized protest actions with thousands of building cleaners. The main demand of the trade unions is the introduction of a national minimum wage of EUR 10 per hour that would enable workers to ensure subsistence, higher than the lowest wage set by the current collective agreement. The trade union demands two different minimum wages: one for semi-skilled or unskilled workers and another for skilled workers.

In this context, on 28 August 2006, the government in office decided to extend the German Posting Act (*Arbeitnehmer Entsendegesetz*), signed in March 1996 in the construction sector, to cleaning services. This Act obliges all employers (included those not in an employers' association and not covered by collective agreements) to employ workers at a minimum wage via a collective agreement for skilled and unskilled workers and should protect small and medium-sized enterprises from unfair competition from firms from low-wage countries (see Bundesministerium für Arbeit und Soziales, 2006).

Creating a temporary agency to avoid paying regular wages
In the company, most workers are women (80 per cent) and low qualified. They are trained within the firm. The firm employs some apprentices (8 per cent). They are trained in the firm and employed in simple tasks.

High proportion of migrant workers
According to the estimates of managers interviewed, the proportion of cleaners of foreign origin (from Poland, Ukraine, Russian Federation, Turkey) is particularly high (around 60 per cent), above all in large urban areas. Many of them have no vocational training and do not speak German very well. Nevertheless, more and more Germans are joining the firm and taking jobs in cleaning because of the poor general situation in the labour market. In this case, it is their main source of income.

Cleaning contracts are signed for a year and may then be extended. The average contract runs for two or three years. Most employees are blue-collar workers employed initially on a fixed-term basis. Some employees have one-year contracts. The employer would like to increase the proportion of such contracts. If things work out, their contracts are then turned into unlimited ones.

In 2003, the firm has created its own temporary agency (PSA). The share of temporary work amounted to about 10 per cent. It was the goal of the management to increase the number of temporary workers in order to limit personnel costs, but ultimately the customer was not satisfied with the high personnel fluctuation and their uncertain qualifications. One manager said that it was important to have a stable workforce over the whole year.

Working time: flexible but organized to cut costs
The share of employees working on a part-time basis is significant, accounting for 60 per cent of the workforce, whereas only 20 per cent of the workforce is full-time employed; 20 per cent of the whole workforce have a mini-job (marginal part-time). According to the management, a disadvantage of mini-jobs in the past was that such workers were allowed to work only 40 to 70 hours per month because of the previous 15-hours-limit rule, and the firm needs people who work 80 to 120 hours a month (full-time positions include 169 hours), while part-timers work four to six hours a day.

Cleaning services are provided 24 hours a day, 7 days a week. Many employees work Wednesday to Sunday. In general, working time duration varies between 1.75 hours and 8 hours a day, for 5 days. Offices are cleaned before or after opening and working hours. The length and distribution of working hours are fixed and organized according to the customers' needs.

> The customer decides when the cleaning time is, and according to this, we distribute the personnel over the time window. In general, working hours are fixed in the morning or in the evening. (…) The customer wants to spend as little money as

possible, also for night work. It means that work has to begin at five in the morning and end at ten in the evening.

There is a close correlation between working time duration and distribution of working hours. Some customers would like cleaning activities to occur at the limit of the firm's core working hours. An increasing number of customers are demanding that window cleaning be performed between 1 and 5 o'clock in the morning. The employer opposes this customer demand because of additional costs related to night work. The firm limits the number of employees working after 10 o'clock at night in order to avoid paying bonuses for night work.

Night work occurs between 10 o'clock at night and 6 o'clock in the morning. The incidence of night and weekend work depends on the building to be cleaned. Hospitals, homes for the elderly and nursing homes are cleaned 24 hours a day, seven days a week (also during the weekend). Additional pay is foreseen in the enterprise agreement for night and weekend work, public holidays and overtime according to the collective agreement.

For women with children, it seems quite difficult to combine family and work because of inconvenient working hours, irregular hours of work, and being at work during different parts of the day. Most managers interviewed do not show any empathy for such problems.

For the employer it would be perfect (because of cost savings and as a better response to customers' needs) to have flexible people work two hours in a district one day and two hours in another district the next day. Employees are against this practice because of low wages and the need to combine work and family duties. Furthermore, employees say they prefer working regularly at the same place because they can identify with the customer. They attach particular importance to a social attachment to the firm where they work. Employees work hard to keep their jobs, but often complain about inconvenient hours (very early morning, evenings and weekends).

Conclusion
The employment situation is characterized by increased numerical flexibility in terms of working hours and functional flexibility of workers (employed in different locations). There is also a tendency to substitute regular full- and part-time employment by marginal fixed-term part-time employment, students' and pupils' jobs, as well as elderly workers. Marginally employed workers (mostly female migrants) often have to accumulate such employment with other work because of the relatively low wages. Inconvenient working hours, in particular night and weekend work, and usually longer hours of work, are widespread, particularly in cleaning activities within public and private services (hospitals, care). For women, it is difficult to combine work and family duties because of inconvenient and irregular working hours. In general, these occupations are coupled with high labour turnover, which makes

social dialogue more difficult. There is the risk of a deprivation of workers' status and rights through the loss of identification with the firm and the total availability of workers to meet firms' and customers' needs. Nevertheless, the customer often requests a more stable (and thus not temporary) and so qualified labour force, thus contradicting the enterprise's strategy.

Germany Case Study 2: Flexibility through mini-jobs in a retail trade company

Retail company B is a discount store and part of a large German retail group including at least four large firms. Annual turnover of the group in 2005 was EUR 21.5 billion in Germany. It is the fifth largest retail company in Germany. Company B has turnover of EUR 12 billion and comprises 2,500 subsidiaries in Germany, employing about 40,000 workers. Most are women.

Sector with increasing employment but reduced full-time positions

According to the German Statistical Institute (*Statistsiches Bundesamt*), in 2005 the German retail trade experienced a turnover increase of 1.2 per cent, 0.7 per cent points in real terms. In 2004, the workforce increased by 1.7 per cent, followed by a decline of 0.3 per cent in 2005 (corresponding to 7,000 workers). Between 1999 and 2004 the number of full-time positions fell by 11.5 per cent, whereas the number of part-time positions paying social security contributions only increased by 6.6 per cent and the number of marginal part-timers by 20.9 per cent.[14] Marginal part-time positions are low-paid and often associated with few hours. In 2004, about 2.7 million people were working in the German retail trade; 80 per cent of them were women. Around 79 per cent of the workforce has vocational training, whereas in discount shops this proportion is much lower (trade union data). Forty-nine per cent are full-time workers and 24.7 per cent are part-time. The proportion of marginal employees amounts to 26.3 per cent (see Kalina and Voss-Dahm, 2005). In the German retail trade, the turnover of employees in mini-jobs is twice as high (67.5 per cent) as among those contributing to social security (35.2 per cent). This could mean that key tasks are performed by employees contributing to social security, whereas marginal workers only work according to fluctuations in demand in secondary working areas (see Kalina and Voss-Dahm, 2005).

---

14. According to trade union data, this personnel decline in the German retail trade essentially involves a decrease in full-time positions (33,000 positions). By contrast, at the same time the number of part-time workers not contributing to social security has increased by 25,000. Since 2000, the number of marginal low-paid workers has continuously increased, but remains 713,000 on average, whereas the number of part-timers contributing to social security has decreased from 588,000 to 564,000 (Warich, 2006).

The change in the personnel structure between 2004 and 2005 reduced working time volume by 0.9 per cent. The number of hours of work has fallen from 3,241 to 2,791 million hours (Warich, 2006). Nevertheless, both the turnover increase and the workforce reduction have led to an increase in sales productivity (by 1.6 per cent) and in labour productivity (by 2.5 per cent). In 2005, retail trade space increased from 114 million to 118 million square metres.

Conflict over the collective agreement
In the retail trade, four different collective agreements govern the working conditions of workers: (i) the collective agreement on working conditions in general, (ii) the collective agreement on wages, (iii) the collective agreement on the flexibility of wage components and (iv) the employment protection agreement. The collective agreement on working conditions in general was signed on 1 January 2003 and was valid until the end of 2005. In November 2005, it was renegotiated, as was the collective agreement on wages.

Negotiations were very difficult between the trade employers' association for Berlin and Brandenburg, *Handelsverband Berlin-Brandenburg*, which is a member of the main German trade employers' association, *Hauptverband des deutschen Einzelhandels*, and the trade union *ver.di*'s retail trade department in Berlin and Brandenburg. The resulting agreements should serve as pioneer agreements for the retail trade in the whole of Germany. Negotiations lasted six months, including four different negotiation rounds. The last negotiation round lasted eight days. The employer rejected the 3.5 per cent wage increase demanded by the *ver.di* trade union, wanted a 40-hour week and wanted to hire long-term unemployed people who had previously worked in retail at wages 10 per cent below the collective agreement. Furthermore, they wanted to introduce so-called opening clauses – "*Öffnungsklausel*" – which would allow firms to introduce wages 20 per cent under their negotiated level, without the trade unions being able to do anything about it. On 4 January 2006, both parties finally agreed to introduce the former two collective agreements, retrospectively valid since 1 July 2005.

The parties finally agreed on a wage increase of 1 per cent for 7 months only. The union accepted this because of the high unemployment rate in the region.

Employment relations in the firm: no social dialogue
Works councils are almost nonexistent. They can only be found in seven of the 2,500 subsidiaries. It is worth noting that trade union organization in the German retail trade is quite low (5 per cent). Corporate culture is quite authoritarian. The employer is hostile towards workers' representative organizations.

The firm's agreements in all locations fix four to five regular working days a week between Monday and Saturday. At Company B, most employees work 20 hours a week and earn a gross salary of about EUR 1,000 a month, regardless of whether they are in the eastern or western part of the region. Most have no retail vocational training. The employment of workers without vocational training or with only experience of working in the retail trade, is part of the management strategy to reduce personnel costs. According to the collective agreement, workers with a retail trade vocational training have to be paid more than workers without vocational training. In addition, workers without vocational training have to remain four years at the same wage level. The trade union criticizes this policy sharply and complains that these workers have to leave the company after four years, after being bullied, because they become too expensive in the fifth year. For workers, it is also a wage loss, although they do the same work than other employees. They earn EUR 9.75 an hour. In the best case, an employed person with retail vocational training at the highest level earns EUR 12.25 an hour.

New employment contracts: exclusively part-time work (through midi- or mini-jobs)
The employer claims to have created 20,000 new jobs in Germany over the last three years. Most new work contracts have been signed on a part-time basis (+30 percentage points) with lower working time and low pay. Full-time positions are no longer offered. Most new work contracts contain 10, 14, 16 or 18 hours of work per month. There are all kinds of part-time contracts. Some people have a 60-hours contract per month. The length and distribution of working hours are very flexible. Overtime is not paid. Many employees have to take a second or third job to ensure their livelihood. The number of employees earning on average EUR 800 (midi-job) and EUR 400 for fewer hours of work (mini-job) has considerably increased.

Two years ago, the employer decided to externalize the truck vehicle park to reduce labour costs and diminish the firm's risks in general. The collective agreement in the retail trade is no longer valid for these employees, but rather the collective agreement in the transport branch, which means wage losses of up to EUR 800 a month for workers.

Working time flexibility to avoid payment of overtime
The firm is open six days a week from eight in the morning to eight in the evening. The work is organized in two shifts. The morning shift begins at 6 o'clock and ends at 2 o'clock in the afternoon. The afternoon shift begins at 2 in the afternoon and ends at 9 or 9.30 in the evening. Between 6 and 8 o'clock in the morning, workers have to unpack food and non-food articles and put them in the shelves. From 8 on, they sit at the till almost without a break until

2 o'clock in the afternoon (end of shift). After work, employees are really exhausted.

> There are no real breaks. Well, to smoke a cigarette or go to the toilet, I am allowed to leave the till.

Nevertheless, most employees usually work longer, up to 160 hours a month as an annual average. They often have to switch flexibly between different branches. Usually workers have to stay on after closing time in order to tidy up and clean. There is no extra pay for overtime. Although the working plan is prepared two weeks in advance, short-term changes occur constantly, requiring extra staff. In addition, mini-jobs are increasingly taken by schoolchildren, students, women with a working partner, and retired persons and are seen as an "additional earning activity". According to a workers' representative, work has intensified over the last years.

Conclusion

In this case study, there is a general trend to replace regular (protected) employment through marginal low-paid employment, although the firm already has a lot of flexible room to manoeuvre in terms of work organization: high numerical flexibility with the help of varying working hours and functional flexibility through the assignment of polyvalent workers. Further, working conditions are getting worse: the collective agreement is not systematically applied within the firm. Long working hours are usual. For workers, extra pay for inconvenient hours has been suppressed. Most workers are increasingly obliged to accept part-time arrangements such as midi- or mini-jobs – mainly women but also increasingly schoolchildren, students and elderly people. As a result, many workers have to look for an additional job because of the relatively low incomes. For women, all these changes make it more difficult to combine work and family duties, particularly as job insecurity has increased and social dialogue is almost non-existent.

Germany Case Study 3: Automobile company restructuring and relocating to face overcapacity

The company is a subsidiary of the world's largest auto producer, whose parent company is in the United States. In 2006, the German company employed approximately 30,500 people, compared to 41,300 employees in 2001. Car production occurs at four different locations. In the first quarter of 2006 the group achieved a profit of almost EUR 396 million (US$ half a billion). The German company has total production of 520,400 vehicles a year. In 2005, the group sold 389,150 cars and light commercial vehicles in Germany.

The German automobile sector: enormous overcapacity

The automobile industry is Germany's key industry. It is one of the major employers and has been of the few "growth engines" of the Germany economy in recent years. It accounted for 12 per cent of employment and 20 per cent of investments in the German manufacturing sector, and for 23 per cent of all German exports (see Jürgens et al., 2006: 20). The technological research and the manufacture of high-tech products explain its worldwide reputation.[15] EUR 16 billion are invested in automotive research and development – a third of the entire budget spent by the industry on research and development as a whole.

1991 was the year with the highest employment level in the history of the German car industry, reaching a level of 806,000 employees. However, the industry experienced a severe crisis in the first half of the 1990s. Between 1991 and 1994 over 20 per cent of the workforce lost their jobs. Employment fell over the subsequent five years to 682,000 in 1996, before increasing again. By 2004, auto industry employment had recovered to 802,000. Over the last ten years, the automotive industry has created over 90,000 jobs (+16 per cent) in Germany.[16] The growth in jobs in the German automotive industry has been primarily due to employment expansion in the supply industry.

This trend in employment could not be continued in 2005, when business dynamics slowed down considerably. In 2005, there were 7,000 job losses, which came mainly from manufacturers of car and car engines (total workforce 401,400).[17] 329,000 employees are now working for car suppliers, almost half the total workforce in the German car industry.

This increase in domestic production was accompanied by an even higher increase in the value of exports over the same period. The proportion of cars produced by German car makers outside Germany in their total production rose from 27 per cent in 1991 to 46 per cent in 2004 and demonstrates a remarkably strong performance on the part of the German car industry (see Jürgens et al., 2006: 21f; Verband der Automobilindustrie, 2006: 47).

The cost pressures put on suppliers by their customers remain extremely high. This partly explains why the number of production plants owned by German suppliers in eastern Europe has doubled over the last decade. As a consequence, it is expected that, in the near future, more than 50 per cent of all German suppliers will have production plants in these regions. They have created 160,000 new jobs over 300 locations in eastern Europe (see ibid.: 12–20).

---

15. Today, every second car produced in Germany is a premium model compared to only 37 per cent ten years ago.

16. By contrast, the German manufacturing sectors have lost three million jobs since reunification.

17. The chassis and trailers sector and the component supply sector managed to maintain their workforces at a similar level to last year: 328,700 and 36,300 respectively.

Escape clauses to avoid collective agreement provisions

The automobile sector is highly regulated and precarious employment is not typical. The automobile industry is a traditional labour union stronghold; its patterns of industrial relations have a large influence on the manufacturing industries and the German institutional setting of labour regulation as a whole. In 2004, the unionization level was 75 per cent in the German car industry, whereas the unionization rate of the overall economy was an average of only 30 per cent. All automotive OEMs have powerful works councils. Metal-industry collective agreements play a central role (see Jürgens et al., 2006: 20).

In the German metal industry, the collective agreement sets a 35-hour week. This was signed by the German metalworkers union (and the largest union in the country) *IG Metall* and the employers' association of the metal and electrical industry *Gesamtmetall*. In 2004, a wage agreement and the so-called "Pforzheim escape clauses" introduced an option allowing companies to deviate from agreed union wage rates. The 2006 agreement for the metal and electrical industry provides further options for differentiating between pay levels and calls for negotiations on improving flexibility. A 3 per cent wage increase was paid for these flexibility options. The agreement does nothing to increase employment levels in the automotive industry (see Verband der Automobilindustrie, 2006: 18).

Deteriorating conditions to avoid closure or relocations

In 2005, work contracts of workers within the company were extremely flexibilized due to two important restructuring processes in 2001 and 2004, which were closely related.

The 2004 restructuring: significant job cuts

As early as May 2001, and prior to the announcement of the restructuring plan for the entire company, the majority of factory committees signed a new employment agreement which paved the way for the further dismantling of jobs in one of the German production sites by extending shift work and increasing flexibility in the parts shop. This accord granted company management the right to invoke the principle of flexibility to determine for each employee, not only the number of weekly working hours (from 30 to 40), but even the times for clocking on and off (between 6 a.m. and 11 p.m.) and workers had to accept these conditions with only a week's notice. Furthermore, not just one but two Saturday shifts (mornings and afternoons), as well as the introduction of a permanent night shift, are to be arranged in future when the need arises. All these concessions were endorsed by the factory committee in the name of "defending local work sites and jobs" and imposed on workers under the constant threat of further job losses if they failed to comply.

On October 2004, the chief of the company unit responsible for Europe decided to drastically cut staff numbers in order to reorganize production in Europe. The target was to reduce the production duration of the three most important automobile models by 30 to 40 per cent in order to become the most productive automobile producer in the branch: most producers need on average 25 hours to produce a car and the idea was to reduce this duration to 13–17 hours. For this reason, productivity had to be increased and production sites outsourced. The company planned an operating profit of about EUR 168 million (US$ 212 million) in 2006 after a EUR 49 million (US$ 62 million) loss the previous year.

The production manager for Europe said:

> We want to concentrate as far as possible on our key business in order to improve our cost structure and return securely to the profit zone.

By "key" activities the production chief means final assembly, press work, the shell and painting. The German company unit must be a pioneer in this area. It has already begun to look for external suppliers for logistics and transport, final assembly of engines and radiator pre-assembly, as well as axle manufacturing. The success of this plan will influence the decision about the site in Europe for the production of the next automobile model. The different production locations in Europe are therefore in competition with one another. As a consequence, the parent company announced that it was cutting 10,000 of the existing 32,000 jobs at different production sites in Germany by 2007. The closure of an entire assembly plant was also being discussed. The production site in question employs 25,000 workers. The company also intends to cut 2,000 jobs outside Germany from its 63,000-strong European workforce. Executives of the company planned to save half a billion euros (US$ 623 million) by 2006 by cutting jobs and benefits.

Trade union leaders not reflecting workers' views

IG Metall fears significant job losses since the parent company has already cut the staff by 25 per cent in US production sites by offering employees financial compensation and early retirement. In addition, the fear of relocating production towards cheaper eastern countries as well as a degradation of employees' rights through competition between production sites in Europe have led to widespread strikes and protests organized by *IG Metall* in Germany. However, during the unofficial strike called against the parent company's plans to eliminate thousands of jobs in Germany, the workers were confronted with open hostility from the majority on the works committee and from *IG Metall*. The trade union leaders really did want to preserve the company by helping the management to overcome the crisis through greater flexibility, but this position often caused consternation among the majority of workers.

A young worker at the gear assembly plant criticized the way the union and works committee had failed to pass on information:

> We have had no information from the unions and the factory committee. The press knows more than we do. We are the last to find out what is happening. We have also received no information about the situation in Sweden. It would be better if there were a common strategy, then we could make management understand. Our colleagues in another production plant are holding back, we don't hear anything about what is happening there either. There are no direct contacts.

A group of older workers who have worked for 40 years in the axle plant of the German company said:

> The expansion to the east (of the European Union) is being used to destroy well-paid jobs here and introduce radically lower wages. The consequence is increasing unemployment. We cannot compete with wages of 3 to 4 euros. We have to pay our rent and other housing costs, and these amount to more than 100 euros a month. Those at the top aren't bothered about our living conditions, they have their millions.

Difficult negotiations and far-reaching concessions

The management has used the dramatic situation to achieve far-reaching concessions on working conditions. By putting both the Swedish and the German production sites in competition, it is able to use the concessions proposed by the Swedish management to obtain more concessions from the German workers' representatives. Under pressure from the company management, the works committee of the company, chaired by a union leader, proposed making working hours more flexible and increasing the weekly range of working hours from 32–38.75 to 30–40. The union declared that this arrangement could also be extended to other car factories in Germany. The works committee also proposed a wage freeze for a number of years, in which some bonuses would be cancelled and offset by wage increases at a later date.

Finally, the parent company made it clear that the offer of the German works committees did not come close to meeting the targeted savings.

In reaction to the management position, the works committee and *IG Metall* indicated that further concessions could be made to meet the savings targets.

Agreement securing the German location and employment

After five months of negotiations, the management and workers' representatives agreed a contract securing the German location until 2010, including the following points:

- job suppression without dismissal (unless with due notice)
- increased working time flexibility

- increased production flexibility
- future collective agreed wage increase to be deducted from workers' wages
- reduction of Christmas bonus
- employment of 250 temporary workers
- flexible break rules
- reduction in the discussion time within work teams
- displaced firms' closure time
- uniform night-shift premium according to the collective agreement

The flexibility of working hours has increased extremely. A 48-month averaging working hours period was introduced for a five-shift system, including weekend work (now Saturday morning, Sunday night). At the same time, shift duration was reduced from 36.83 to 36.25 hours and short breaks were cut by 9 minutes. The definition of Sunday work has been changed (from Saturday 10 p.m. to Sunday 6 a.m.). Wages have been cut through the suppression of bonuses: workers had to agree to a cut in the Christmas bonus of 30 per cent, to 70 per cent of a monthly wage from 2006 on.

After the job cuts, the management reached agreement with representatives of the factory committee to hire a certain percentage of temporary workers for production activities. These temporary workers are paid EUR 7.03 per hour, which is much less than core workers. As a result of transfers of undertakings and outsourcing, great pressure has been put on wage levels.

Higher work intensity for both core and suppliers' workers
First experiences have shown that the majority of workers were very agitated and complained about the resulting work intensity, although the location secure agreement (*Standortsicherung*) was accepted by the majority. Most of the 2,500 workers, who moved into a newly created employment and retraining unit, said they had very little hope of finding a job afterwards. Moreover, working conditions within car suppliers, whose activities are closely gearing manufacturing within the (customer) company, were largely worse than those of core workers.

Most of these car suppliers offer lower wages, poor working conditions and more working time flexibility than the large auto producers. More generally, they are not covered by collective agreements. At some suppliers, there has been no wage increase in the last seven years. Only half of the firms' workforce is regularly employed, the rest are temporary workers. This situation leads to greater price pressure on larger companies and encourages them to externalize their activities in order to save costs and increase productivity. Finally, most workers hope that volume and model distribution will not be renegotiated in 2007 or afterwards and that the location will survive with almost all current workers after 2010.

Conclusion

The restructuring of the company has led to huge concessions in the field of working conditions (greater working time flexibility coupled with a wage decrease). At the same time, core workers have been replaced by temporary ones, whose employment status is more insecure than core workers (fixed-term contracts, meaning higher job insecurity; greater flexibility in working hours, lower wages and dismissal protection are not necessarily covered by collective provisions). However, in the selected company the working conditions of temporary workers and workers within suppliers are worse than those of core workers. Low-skilled workers (manufacturing) are more concerned by this development. However, there is a growing risk of downwards adjustment of employment conditions of flexibly employed workers to the whole core workforce of the company. In general, the restructuring process has also weakened social dialogue. The strikes and different conflicts have disunited workers and their representatives.

REFERENCES

Ahlers, E., and M. Brussig. 2004. Gesundheitsbelastungen und Prävention am Arbeitsplatz. *WSI-Mitteilungen 57(11)*, 617–24.

Aldana, S. 2001. Financial impact of health promotion programs: A comprehensive review of the literature. *American Journal of Health Promotion*, 5, 296–320.

Arrowsmith, J. 2006. *Temporary agency work in an enlarged Europe*. Dublin: European Foundation for the Improvement of Living and Working Conditions.

Beck, U. 1986. *Risikogesellschaft auf dem Weg in eine andere Moderne*. Frankfurt/M.: Suhrkamp.

Bellmann, L. 2004. Zur Entwicklung der Leiharbeit in Deutschland: Theoretische Überlegungen und empirische Ergebnisse aus dem IAB-Betriebspanel. *Sozialer Fortschritt*, 53 (6): 135–42.

Bellmann, L., and S. Hartung. 2005. Betriebliche Ausbildung: Zu wenig Stellen und doch sind nicht alle besetzt. *IABKurzbericht 272005*. Nürnberg: Bundesagentur für Arbeit.

Bertram, H., W. Rösler and N. Ehlert. 2005. *Nachhaltige Familienpolitik. Zukunftssicherung durch einen Dreiklang von Zeitpolitik, finanzieller Transferpolitik und Infrastrukturpolitik*. Gutachten im Auftrag des Bundesministeriums Familie, Senioren, Frauen und Jugend. Berlin.

Bien, W. 2005. *DJI-Kinderbetreuungsstudie 2005: Erste Ergebnisse*. Durchführung: Deutsches Jugendinstitut, München, in Zusammenarbeit mit der Dortmunder Arbeitsstelle Kinder- und Jugendhilfestatistik Feldarbeit: INFAS Bonn. Förderung: Bundesministerium für Familie, Senioren, Frauen und Jugend August 2005.

Bispinck, R. 2005. *WSI Tarifhandbuch*. Frankfurt am Main: Bund Verlag.

———. 2006. *WSI Tarifhandbuch*. Frankfurt am Main: Bund Verlag.

Bispinck, R., and C. Schaefer. 2005. Niedriglöhne? – Mindestlöhne!: Verbreitung von Niedriglöhnen und Möglichkeiten ihrer Bekämpfung. *Sozialer Fortschritt: unabhängige Zeitschrift fuer Sozialpolitik*, 54: 20–31.

Bispinck, R., and T. Schulten. 2005. Deutschland vor dem tarifpolitischen Systemwechsel? *WSI Mitteilungen 8/2005*, 466–72.

Bödecker, W., H. Friedel, C. Röttger and A. Schroer. 2002. *Kosten arbeitsbedingter Erkrankungen*. Bremerhaven.

Boemke, B., and M. Lembke. 2002. Änderungen im AÜG durch das "Job-AQTIV-Gesetz": fragwürdige Liberalisierung der Zeitarbeit. *Der Betrieb*, 55 (17): 893–99.

Bontrup, H.-J. 2004. Zu hohe Löhne und Lohnnebenkosten: Eine ökonomische Mär. *WSI-Mitteilungen*, 57/2004, 313–18.

Bosch, G. 2000a. Arbeitszeit und Arbeitsorganisation: Zur Rolle von Produkt- und Arbeitsmärkten im internationalen Vergleich. *Arbeit. Zeitschrift für Arbeitsforschung, Arbeitsgestaltung und Arbeitspolitik*, 9 Jg. (200), Heft 3: 175–90.

———. 2000b. Arbeitszeit, Arbeitsorganisation und Qualifikation: Wer begründet eine bestimmte Arbeitsorganisation wählen will, muss das Zusammenspiel von Qualifikation und Arbeitszeit verstehen. *Personalführung*, 33 (10): 52–60.

Bothfeld, S., and L.C. Kaiser. 2003. Befristung und Leiharbeit: Brücken in reguläre Beschäftigung? *WSI-Mitteilungen*, 56 (8): 484–93.

Brandt, T. 2006. Bilanz der Mini-jobs und Reformperspektiven. *WSI-Mitteilungen*, 8/2006: 446–52.

Bundesministerium für Arbeit und Soziales. 2006a. Kabinett billigt Ausweitung des Arbeitnehmer-Entsendegesetzes auf das Gebäudereinigerhandwerk. BMAS Pressemitteilung vom 23.8.2006. URL 4.9.2006: www.bmas.bund.de/BMAS/Navigation/Presse/pressemitteilungen,did=151514.

———. 2006b. http://www.bmas.bund.de-/BMAS/Navigation/Presse-/nachrichten, did=110752.html.

Cichorek, A, S. Koch, and U. Walwei. 2005. Arbeitslosengeld II. Erschweren "Zusatzjobs" die Aufnahme einer regulären Beschäftigung? *IABKurzbericht*, 8/2005.

Deutscher Bundestag. 2006a. Bericht 2005 der Bundesregierung zur Wirksamkeit moderner Dienstleistungen am Arbeitsmarkt. Berlin. Bundestagsdrucksache. URL: http://www.bmas.bund.de/BMAS/Redaktion/Pdf/hartz-evaluation-volltext, property=pdf,bereich=bmas,sprache=de,rwb=true.pdf.

———. 2006b. *Gesetzentwurf der Fraktionen der CDU/CSU und SPD. Entwurf eines Gesetzes zur Einführung des Elterngeldes* (20.06.2006). Berlin.

———. 2006c. *Antrag: Flexible Konzepte für die Familie – Kinderbetreuung und frühkindliche Bildung zukunftsfähig machen* (05.04.2006). Berlin.

Dietrich, H., S. Koch, and M. Stops. 2004. Lehrstellenkrise: Ausbildung muss sich lohnen – auch für die Betriebe. *IABKurzbericht 62004*.

Elkeles, T. 2000. Erwerbsverläufe und gesundheitsbezogene Statuspassagen: Empirische Ergebnisse zu Determinanten begrenzter Tätigkeitsdauer. *Arbeit*, 9 (4): 306–20.

European Agency for Security and Health at Work. 2001. *Stress lass nach! Bewusster Umgang mit Stress*. Bilbao.

European Foundation for the Improvement of Living and Working Conditions. 2006. *2004 Annual Review for Germany.* European Industrial Relations Observatory online: http://www.eiro.eurofound.eu.int/2005/01/feature/de0501201f.html.

Flüter-Hoffmann, C. 2005. *Familienfreundliche Regelungen in Tarifverträgen und Betriebsvereinbarungen. Beispiele guter Praxis.* Gutachten im Auftrag des Bundesministeriums für Familie, Senioren, Frauen und Jugend. Institut der deutschen Wirtschaft Köln.

Gather, C., U. Gerhard, H. Schroth and L. Schürmann. 2005. *Vergeben und Vergessen? Gebäudereinigung im Spannungsfeld zwischen kommunalen Diensten und Privatisierung.* Hamburg: VSA-Verlag.

Giesecke, J., and M. Groß. 2006. Befristete Beschäftigung. *WSI Mitteilungen,* 5/2006: 247–54.

Göbel, J., P. Krause, and J. Schupp. 2005. Mehr Armut durch steigende Arbeitslosigkeit. *DIW-Wochenbericht,* 10/2005.

Haak, C., and G. Schmid. 1999. *Arbeitsmärkte für Künstler and Publizisten ? Modelle einer zukünftigen Arbeitswelt?* Berlin: WZB.

Haas, A. 2002. Regionale Mobilität am Arbeitsmarkt: Wohin nach der Berufsausbildung? Die Ost/West-Mobilität von jungen Fachkräften. *IABKurzbericht,* 7/2002.

Hamandia, A. 2005. *Arbeitszeitgestaltung in Deutschland und Frankreich: Ein Vergleich der Aushandlungsprozesse am Beispiel multinationaler Unternehmen.* München und Mering: Rainer Hamp Verlag.

Henry-Huthmacher, C., and E. Hoffmann. 2006. Familienreport 2005. *KAS-Arbeitspapiere* 151/2005. Sankt Augustin: Konrad-Adenauer-Stiftung.

Höltershinken, D., and D. Kasüschke. 1996. *Betriebliche Kinderbetreuung in Deutschland.* Opladen: Leske & Budrich.

Ichino, A., and R.T. Riphahn. 2004. Absenteeism and employment protection: Three case studies. *Swedish Economic Policy Review,* 11 (1): 95–114.

Jahn, E.J., and H. Rudolph. 2002a. Zeitarbeit - Teil I: Auch für Arbeitslose ein Weg mit Perspektive. *IABKurzbericht,* 20/2002.

———. 2002b. Zeitarbeit - Teil II: Völlig frei bis streng geregelt: Variantenvielfalt in Europa. *IABKurzbericht,* 21/2002.

Jahn E.J., and A. Windsheimer. 2004a. Personal-Service-Agenturen ? Teil I: In der Fläche schon präsent. *IABKurzbericht,* 1/2004.

———. 2004b. Personal-Service-Agenturen ? Teil II: Erste Erfolge zeichnen sich ab. *IABKurzbericht,* 2/2004.

Jahn, E.J., and K. Wolf. 2005. Flexibilität des Arbeitsmarktes: Entwicklung der Leiharbeit und regionale Disparitäten. *IABKurzbericht,* 14/2005.

Jürgens, U., M. Krzywdzinski and C. Teipen. 2006. *Changing work and employment relations in German industries – breaking away from the German model?* WZB discussion paper, sp iii 2006-302. Berlin.

Kalina, T., and D. Voss-Dahm. 2005. Mehr Minijobs = mehr Bewegung auf dem Arbeitsmarkt? Fluktuation der Arbeitskräfte und Beschäftigungsstruktur in vier Dienstleistungsbranchen. *IAT-Report* 2005-07. Gelsenkirchen: Institut Arbeit und Technik.

Klenner, C. 2005a. Gleichstellung von Frauen und Männern und Vereinbarkeit von

Familie und Beruf – Eine Analyse von tariflichen Regelungen in ausgewählten Tarifbereichen. In R. Bispinck (2005), *WSI-Tarifhandbuch*, 41–64.

———. 2005b. Balance von Beruf und Familie. *WSI Mitteilungen*, 4/2005: 207–13.

Kritikos, A., and F. Wießner. 2004. Existenzgründung: Die richtigen Typen sind gefragt. *IABKurzbericht* 03/2004.

Kröhnert, S., N. van Olst and R. Klingholz. 2005. *Emanzipation oder Kindergeld? Wie sich die unterschiedlichen Kinderzahlen in den Ländern Europas erklären.* Diskussionspapier. Berlin-Institut für Bevölkerung und Entwicklung.

Kvasnicka, M., and A. Werwatz. 2003. Arbeitsbedingungen und Perspektiven von Zeitarbeitern. *DIW Wochenbericht* 70 (46): 717–25.

Leschke, J., G. Schmid and D. Griga. 2006. *On the marriage of flexibility and security: Lessons from the Hartz-reforms in Germany.* WZB discussion paper 2006-108. Berlin.

Ochel, W. 2005. Dezentralisierung der Lohnverhandlungen in Deutschland – ein Weg zu mehr Beschäftigung? *Ifo-Schnelldienst*, 58 (5): 7–18.

OECD. 2003. *Employment Outlook*. Paris.

Reinberg, A., and M. Hummel. 2005. Vertrauter Befund: Höhere Bildung schützt auch in der Krise vor Arbeitslosigkeit. *IABKurzbericht*, 9/2005.

Rhein, T., H. Gartner, and G. Krug. 2005. Niedriglohnsektor. Aufstiegschancen für Geringverdiener verschlechtert. Bundesagentur für Arbeit. *IAB-Kurzbericht*, 3/2005.

Röttger, C., H. Friedel and W. Bödeker. 2003. Arbeitsbelastungen und gesellschaftliche Kosten – Fokus und Perspektiven der Prävention. *WSI-Mitteilungen*, 56 (10): 591–96.

Rudolph, H. 2003. Mini- und Midi-Jobs: Geringfügige Beschäftigung im neuen Outfit. Bundesanstalt für Arbeit. *IAB-Kurzbericht*, 6/2003.

Rürup, B., and S. Gruescu. 2005. *Familienorientierte Arbeitszeitmuster? Neue Wege zum Wachstum und Beschäftigung.* Gutachten im Auftrag des Bundesministeriums für Familie, Frauen und Jugend.

Sachverständigenrat zur Begutachtung der gesamtwirtschaftlichen Entwicklung. 2004. *Erfolge im Ausland? Herausforderungen im Inland.* Jahresgutachten 2003/04.

———. 2005. *Die Chance nutzen? Reformen mutig voranbringen.* Jahresgutachten 2004/05.

———. 2006. *Arbeitsmarkt: Den Reformkurs fortsetzen.* Jahresgutachten 2005/06.

Schäfer, C. 2000. *Geringere Löhne – mehr Beschäftigung?* Hamburg: VSA-Verlag.

Schäfer, A., and C. Vogel. 2005. Teilzeitbeschäftigung als Arbeitsmarktchance. *DIW Wochenbericht*, 7/2000.

Schlese, M., F. Schramm and N. Bulling-Chabalewski. 2005. Beschäftigungsbedingungen von Leiharbeitskräften. *WSI-Mitteilungen*, 58 (10): 568–74.

Schoch, F., and J. Wieland. 2004. *Aufgabenzuständigkeit und Finanzierungsverantwortung verbesserter Kinderbetreuung.* Stuttgart–München: Richard Boorberg Verlag.

Schürmann, L., and H. Schroth. 2004. Brot und Kröten? Die Liberalisierung der Leiharbeit und ihre tarifpolitischen Folgen im Gebäudereinigerhandwerk. *femina politica* 2/2004: 87–90.

Schupp, J., and E. Birkner. 2004. 'Kleine Beschäftigungsverhältnisse: Kein Jobwunder – Dauerhafter Rückgang von Zweitbeschäftigten? *DIW Wochenbericht* 34/04. Berlin: Deutsches Institut für Wirtschaft.

Seifert, H. 2005. Zeit für neue Arbeitszeiten. *WSI-Mitteilungen* 8/2005, 478–83.

Sorge, A. 1997. *Mitbestimmung, Arbeitsorganisation und Technikanwendung.* Expertise für das Projekt "Mitbestimmung und neue Unternehmenskulturen" der Bertelsmann Stiftung und der Hans-Böckler-Stiftung. Verlag Bertelsmann Stiftung. Gütersloh.

Statistisches Bundesamt. 2003. Im Jahr 2050 wird jeder Dritte in Deutschland 60 Jahre oder alter sein. Pressemitteilung 6.6.2003: www.desatis.de/presse/deutsch/pm2003/p2300022.htm

———. 2004. 22% der Mütter mit Kindern unter 18 arbeiten an Sonn- oder Feiertagen. Pressemitteilung 7.5.2004.

———. 2005. *Mikrozensus 2001–2003*. Bonn.

———. 2006. *Mikrozensus 2003–2005*. Bonn.

Steiner, V., and K. Wrohlich. 2005. Minijob-Reform: keine durchschlagende Wirkung. *DIW Wochenbericht* 8/2005S, 141–46.

Streeck, W. 1995. German capitalism: Does it exist? Can it survive? In Crouch and Streeck (eds), *Y a-t-il plusieurs formes de capitalisme?* Paris: Editions La Découverte.

Verband der Automobilindustrie. 2006. *Auto annual report 2006*. Frankfurt am Main.

Voss-Dahm, D. 2002. Erwerbstätigkeit von SchülerInnen und Studierende nimmt zu: Bildung und berufliche Praxis laufen immer häufiger parallel. *IAT-Report*, 2002-06.

Wanger, S. 2006. Erwerbstätigkeit, Arbeitszeit und Arbeitsvolumen nach Geschlecht und Altersgruppen: Ergebnisse der IAB-Arbeitszeitrechnung nach Geschlecht und Alter für die Jahre 1991–2004. *IAB-Forschungsbericht*, 2/2006. Nürnberg: Bundesagentur für Arbeit, 52p.

Warich, B. 2006. *Branchendaten Einzelhandel – Prognose 2005*. W&A.B.E–Institut Berlin.

Wießner, F. 2005. Neues von der Ich-AG: Nicht jeder Abbruch ist eine Pleite. *IABKurzbericht*, 2/2005.

8. Hungary: Employment instability due to fixed-term contracts

Beáta Nacsa and János Köllő

8.1 INTRODUCTION: FREQUENTLY CHANGING PATTERNS AND POLICIES

The macroeconomic indicators evidence a growing economy for 2005,[1] which had a favourable impact on the labour market. Labour force participation, which has been low since the transition, increased somewhat, though only by below 1 per cent in 2005. Job-search activity also rose, resulting from a small increase in unemployment. Real wages were on the rise, driven by the wage increase in the public sector. These tendencies continued during the first half of 2006, but unfavourable changes were forecast for the rest of the year: a decrease in labour force participation and in real wages, for political and financial reasons. As regards industrial relations the most significant change was the continuous improvement of the network of sectoral consultation forums.

Employment-related risks shifted onto workers

The major labour legislation of 1992 established the system of three-pillar employment relationships,[2] providing for a range of different working conditions, job stability and wage systems for workers in different sectors. While job stability, employment-related rights and relative wages of civil servants showed a tendency to strengthen, workers' protection in the commercial sector has been progressively weakened. By 2006, this frequently-changing legislative framework[3] had resulted in substantial

---

1. In 2005 GDP growth was about 4.3 per cent, industrial productivity grew by 10.7 per cent while inflation was as low as 3.6 per cent according to the consumer price index.
2. Act No. XII of 1992 on the Labour Code, Act No. of 1992 on Civil Servants, Act No. of 1992 on Public Employees (employees of publicly owned hospitals, schools, libraries, and so on).
3. The Labour Code has been modified 48 times since its enactment in 1992.

Table 8.1 Working and employment conditions, Hungary

Element	Item	Trends	Risks/Exposed groups
Industrial relations	Trade union membership	Low (approx. 17%) and showing a declining tendency	Weakened interest in representation of workers at all levels
	Coverage of collective agreements	Moderate (approx. 33%) and decreasing	Weakened protection of workers, especially blue-collar workers
Labour market	Low level of labour force participation	Continuously low level of economic activity (54.5% of working age population), even in years when the economy is growing	People lacking marketable skills, living in underdeveloped regions, usually in small settlements, with no proper transport to the neighbouring urban labour markets Young people and Roma seem affected above average
	Unemployment	Slightly increasing (2005: 7.1%), but considered to be a good sign of improving labour force participation The share of long-term unemployment shows a growing tendency (2004: 40%, in 2005: 41.6%)	Less-educated work force (with/without elementary schooling and vocational training) are most exposed to risk. Women and young people seem increasingly affected
	Regional inequality	Stable but high	Especially the less-educated workforce living in northern and eastern regions, in villages
Employment status	Fixed-term employment	Low level, but increasing	About half of employment contracts concluded with new hires and ex-unemployed are fixed-term
	Illegal undeclared work	High, but presumably decreasing	Employees of small domestically owned firms, especially in industries such as agriculture, construction, tourism, retail trade and real-estate services. Considerable regional differences

Wages	Real wages	Decrease in 2004 (−1%), increase in 2005 (+8.8 %) and in Q1 2006 (+5%). For the rest of 2006 a decline was forecast	Workers in agriculture, hotels and catering, and construction are paid far below average Blue-collar workers in manufacturing are also paid below the industrial average wage
	Wage inequalities	Regional differences are considerable, and slightly increasing	Workers in northern and eastern part of the country
		Gender inequalities remain considerable especially among graduates	10% is average gender wage gap, 20% for university graduates and almost 30% for college graduates
Safety and health	Serious and fatal work accidents	After a peak in 2004 (+30%), number of serious or fatal work accidents started to decrease again (15.6% in 2005)	Construction workers (especially employees of subcontractors), and and workers with considerable driving duties
Working time and work organization	Overtime	Still the most frequently applied means of flexible use of workforce	For blue-collar workers: extra hours or extra shifts are usually remunerated. For service workers an extra 1–2 hours seems usual, with a great risk of being unpaid, especially for female workers. In case of white-collar employees: massive overtime, of which only half is paid, especially among managers and professionals
	Working time frames	Moderately increasing	Workers working two or three shifts, and seasonal workers
	Working intensity	On the basis of sporadic information (case studies), it seems to be high	Blue-collar workers working on assembly lines; managerial and professional employees
	Work-related stress, the pressure to adapt	Since the transition period, it remains high regardless of regardless of gender though male workers turn out to be less adaptable	Managerial and professional employees

variance across social groups in terms of employment stability, job protection, working conditions and wages. In the commercial sector, employment-related risks have largely been shifted onto workers, which has created a considerable vulnerability factor for wage labour. The regulatory framework of the Hungarian labour market has become very flexible and provides only extremely weak labour protection for workers (Cazes and Nesporova, 2006). The contracts made with newly hired workers are increasingly fixed-term. The regulation of working hours and rest periods is very liberal (Fodor, 2004). Wages are predominantly set at enterprise level, through mainly on an individual basis, not by collective bargaining (Koltay and Neumann, 2005). The minimum wage, despite its twofold increase in 2001–02, is still rather low compared to the EU average. Job protection is continuously decreasing (Kulisity, 2004). Fixed-term contracts can be terminated by the employer on the day of expiry without any obligation to pay any form of compensation, and open-ended contracts can be terminated almost at zero cost in the first three years of tenure.[4] According to the available data, employers also manage to find ways of avoiding or minimizing the financial burden of dismissing workers with longer tenure (Köllő and Nacsa, 2004). Job protection is mainly provided in the form of procedural rules, to be followed in case of transfer of undertakings or mass redundancies, or in the form of an obligation to provide written reasons for dismissal which can be challenged in unfair dismissal litigation.[5] Unemployment benefits are not generous and only limited labour market services are available in labour offices.

Mapping the various aspects of vulnerability

The less-educated segment of the workforce seems to be at an intersection of different employment-related risks.[6] The transition process and detrimental changes to social and labour policies worsened the employment-related prospects of several social groups, including the Roma minority (Kertesi, 2005), older workers (from 40 onwards) (Adler, 2004), young people (Galasi and Varga, 2005), and mothers with young children (Koncz, 2004). The combination of any of the above-mentioned risk-generating factors with a low level of education (or lack of skills in demand) exposes individuals to a very harsh labour market position, especially if they live in underdeveloped regions (in small settlements in south-west, north-east or south-east Hungary).

---

4. See Labour Code §86 c, §92, §95.

5. See, respectively, Labour Code §85/A–85/B, §94/A–94/G and §89.

6. The labour force participation of the less-educated work force is far below the Hungarian and European average in which regard Hungary shares the fate of other Central European countries. The withdrawal of the less-educated workforce from the labour market into economic inactivity seems to be a Hungarian speciality, however (see Köllő, 2005).

This chapter explores the so far neglected phenomenon of fixed-term contracts among new employment contracts, one of the most important dimensions along which new types of social inequality are emerging. We shall give an account of the incidence of fixed-term contracts in various social groups, and its relation to job stability, working time and wages. We shall show the enormous differences between social groups along these dimensions and identify the groups most affected. Our research has been limited to a certain extent because of lack of data.[7] Virtually nothing is known in Hungary about a number of important aspects of the employment relationship, such as work intensity, certain types of working conditions, especially of a physical and psychological nature, work-related stress and other aspects of workplace health and safety. We address some of these areas in the case studies.

8.2 EMPLOYMENT STATUS: LOW LEVEL OF LABOUR FORCE PARTICIPATION

Continuously high share of economically inactive persons

During the early transition years, Hungary opted for rapid reduction of the state sector, while a generous social safety net was provided in order to soften the change of regime. These policies, though providing shelter for several social groups during the harsh years of transition, contributed to almost half a million people being permanently pushed out of the labour market into economic inactivity. People losing their jobs in 1989–91 *and* remaining permanently inactive are unlikely to return to employment, including those below retirement age. In the first quarter of 2006, 2,603,700 people were economically inactive, of whom 60 per cent were women and 27 per cent belonged to the 15–24 age cohort. More than 400,000 inactive persons have no lawful income whatsoever. The ratio of inactivity fell slightly compared to the same period in 2005, by 51,000, of whom 36,000 were men (CSO, 2006). In recent years several measures have been introduced to increase the level of employment: providing wage subsidies for employers creating new telework jobs and for public administrative bodies in case of transforming regular jobs into telework jobs; supporting seasonal employment; and allowing non-profit organizations to provide temporary agency work. Several types of subsidies have been made available for employers providing work for different vulnerable groups of workers: disabled, new graduates, unemployed over 50 years of age, and mothers returning from childcare leave (Frey, 2005, 2006).

---

7. The microdata we have are available up to the end of 2003, due to the fact that researchers have access to CSO microdata only after some years of delay. Nonetheless, we have no reason to believe that the trends and cross-sectional differences have changed significantly since then.

Part-time employment: relying on two sources of income

Part-time employment has only a marginal presence in the Hungarian labour market. In the second quarter of 2006, among the employed the vast majority were employed on a full-time basis (3,772,000), while the number of workers in part-time jobs was relatively low, at 162,300, among whom the proportion of women was 63 per cent. According to LFS, it is usually not women with young children attending nursery school who work part time. Significant proportions of part-time employment are observed among females below 20 years of age and, more importantly, workers above retirement age. It seems that part-time employment is a form of employing workers who receive some form of state-provided benefits: almost half of part-time workers receive either a pension or childcare allowance. Consequently, it is not surprising that the hourly wages of part-time workers receiving a pension or childcare allowance is only marginally higher than those paid to full-time employees: they work 51.7 per cent less and earn 47.3 per cent less than full-timers. By contrast, workers not receiving any form of pension/benefit seem to accept part-time jobs conditional on relatively high hourly wages: they work 48.9 per cent less but earn 31.7 per cent less, a margin of 34.9 per cent above the hourly wage rate paid to an observationally similar full-timer (Köllő and Nacsa, 2004). The proportion of part-timers is 2.5 times higher in fixed-term contracts than open-ended contracts.

Decreasing number of self-employed

In Hungary, the number of independent earners, as defined by the ILO, fell in the transition years. Specific groups show different development tendencies, but only the number of small proprietors increased, before stabilizing at around 378,000 from 1992. In the second quarter of 2006, 476,000 were considered to be self-employed or members of a partnership, 19,000 were unpaid family workers (among whom 72.6 per cent were women), and 5,100 were members of cooperatives. The majority of self-employed opted for a vulnerability-reducing life strategy similar to what we observed among part-timers: among sole proprietors the proportion of main job holders was relatively low, while that of pensioner entrepreneurs and, especially, second job holders was high (Laky, 2005). In 2003–05, the Parliament and the Ministry of Employment Policy and Labour introduced several measures to curb the practice of entering into fake civil law contracts with quasi self-employed persons (as a way of avoiding employing them) by strengthening the Labour Inspectorate, and through the establishment of the National Employment Register (Frey, 2005, 2006).

Undeclared work: can be legal or illegal

Working in the black/grey economy results in extreme vulnerability: no legal protection is available against any breach of employment rights and no service period is accumulated for the purpose of social security entitlements. Nonetheless, not all undeclared work is 'black', as Teréz Laky pointed out. In Hungary, under specific conditions, some working activity can be carried out without declaring it to the state, while still being lawful: the work of small agricultural producers and students doing temporary work under the auspices of student cooperatives.[8] It is estimated, however, that illegal undeclared work is substantial. The most comprehensive surveys of the size of the informal economy estimate that between 15 per cent and 20 per cent of Hungary's GDP is generated in the informal economy (Lackó, 2005). Undeclared work seems to be concentrated mainly in small firms in agriculture, construction, tourism, retail and real-estate services, with strong regional variations.

There is a statistically significant inverse relationship between employment (as well as labour force participation) and indicators of the informal economy: regions with a sizeable informal economy have lower employment rates. Nonetheless, the data suggest that the grey economy and grey/black work are an effect rather than a cause of low formal employment, and provide some sort of living for those who fall out of the official labour market and social safety net (Köllő and Nacsa, 2004).

In order to combat undeclared work, several administrative measures have been introduced: the establishment of a National Employment Register; strengthening the powers of the Labour Inspectorate; stepping up the investigation of the construction industry by the tax and labour authorities; making the criminal consequences of undeclared work more severe. In Q1 2006, the Labour Inspectorate found illegal black-market work at almost every third employer included in the investigation campaign aiming to catch those employing undeclared workers.[9] The continuously high share of undeclared work exposes a substantial group of workers to an unpredictable future with its detrimental economic, social and psychological consequences,

---

8. Work is considered to be legally undeclared when the working activity and the income generated by it do not have to be declared under the social security and taxation law. In Hungary, income generated up to a certain amount from sales by agricultural small producers was practically tax-free until 2006. According to CSO's agricultural survey conducted in 2000, almost half the households in the population aged 15–74 (46.8%) were engaged in agricultural production, and almost one third produced some income-generating sales. This is also supported by the data of Microcensus, 2005. According to the estimates, some 150,000–200,000 students work more or less regularly (Laky, 2005).

9. The firms to be investigated were not selected on a random basis but based on whether undeclared work was probable. Therefore, the results of the investigations cannot be treated as being in any sense representative.

and also reduces the employment-related revenues of the state and social security funds.

8.3 PRECARIOUS WORK IN FOCUS: FIXED-TERM CONTRACTS

Growing proportion of fixed-term contracts among new hires

As discussed in a comparative study by Cazes and Nesporová (2003) employment contracts have typically been of indefinite duration in Central and Eastern Europe. This holds for Hungary, too, as far as the totality of employment contracts is concerned. According to the Labour Force Survey for the second quarter of 2006, the vast majority (3.2 million) of the employed population (3.4 million) are employed under an employment contract of unlimited duration. Although the number of fixed-term contracts is still relatively low overall (233,500 employees in Q2 2006), there is a high and increasing rate of fixed-term contracts among *new hires*, particularly new hires from unemployment. More than 30 per cent of newly hired workers are given only fixed-term contracts, while the ratio for new hires from unemployment is even higher: more than 50 per cent, despite the fact that in the workforce as a whole only about 6.5 per cent of employment contracts are fixed-term. Table 8.2 shows that the proportion of fixed-term contracts increased by less than 1 per cent in relation to all contracts, but by more than 12 per cent in relation to new contracts.

Table 8.2 Fixed-term contracts as a percentage of total and new employment contracts, Hungary, 1997 and 2003

Year of interview	All employees	New employees
1997	6.30	40.09
2003	7.19	52.34

Note: New employees: hired within 3 months prior to the interview. LFS, N=517,200 quarterly employment spells.

We use the pooled LFS sample to study how the probability of being given a fixed-term contract was affected by worker and enterprise characteristics, overall and in the case of new hires.[10]

---

10. The estimates are based on a sample of 517,000 quarterly employment spells pertaining to 149,000 workers aged 15–64. Type of contract was coded as a dummy, with 1 standing for all types of fixed-term contract. In the period as a whole, an average of 6.7% of employment contracts were fixed-term.

Major differences by age, occupation and enterprise size

A number of conclusions could be drawn from this analysis. We observe relatively high shares of fixed-term contracts among younger and elderly workers and those with only a primary education. There are also some groups – such as employed pensioners, parents engaged in childcare and unemployed people involved in public works – with a very high probability of having fixed-term contracts. More importantly, differences by occupation seem to be substantial. Workers in elementary and traditional skilled blue-collar occupations are much more likely to have a temporary job than drivers, tertiary-sector workers and white-collar workers. The ratio of unskilled workers among fixed-term contracts holders is more than 80 per cent (Laky, 2005).

Interestingly, small and medium-sized employers tend to avoid fixed-term contracts:[11] frequently it cannot be foreseen how long the firm will need a particular employee, and terminating a fixed-term contract before the expiry date would put a substantial burden on the employer. If the proper length of contract cannot be determined with high probability, the employee is provided with an open-ended contract with the maximum possible probationary period of three months. If employment is terminated during this period, there would be no obligation to pay and there is practically no room for litigation claiming unfair dismissal. If the contract is terminated during the first three years of tenure, no severance payment need be paid, only 30 days' notice, of which half is paid without an obligation to work. In the letter of dismissal following the end of the probationary period, the reason for dismissal has to be indicated and it can be challenged in an unfair dismissal claim. On the other hand, if the duration of a fixed-term contract was miscalculated and the worker becomes superfluous before the expiry date, the contract can be terminated only if the employer pays the worker's average salary for the remainder of the contract. Therefore it is very rare that SMEs conclude a fixed-term contract, preferring open-ended contracts which are easy and cheap to terminate, especially during the first three years of tenure. Data on the number of severance payments indicates that terminations are strongly biased towards workers with short tenures and the burden of dismissal is not as heavy as one might think on the basis of the Labour Code regulations (Köllő and Nacsa, 2004).

---

11. Unpublished interview with an HR professional providing HR services for SMEs (at the time of the interview: 19 firms). The interview was prepared by Beáta Nacsa. Available from the author (in Hungarian).

Will fixed-term contracts gain further ground?

The future of fixed-term contracts can best be approximated by having a closer look at their incidence in age groups, cohorts and years. The fact that a relatively high fraction of young workers are employed on fixed-term contracts may indicate a pure age effect: all cohorts start with a high share of fixed-term contracts, and gradually move to permanent jobs as they grow older, no matter where we are in calendar time. Alternatively, the age patterns may follow from a calendar year effect: the labour market moves from permanent to temporary employment relationships by increasingly concluding fixed-term contracts with young labour market entrants. Table 8.3 helps to disentangle these scenarios in cohorts older than 16 and younger than 36.

Table 8.3 shows the proportion employed with fixed-term contracts by single year of age and calendar years.[12] We observe, first of all, that the proportion of fixed-term contracts fell with age in all calendar years, and

Table 8.3 Proportion employed on fixed-term contracts by single year of age and year, Hungary, 1997–2003 (%) (LFS)

Age	1997	1998	1999	2000	2001	2002	2003
17	31	28	24	21	24	34	29
18	17	21	23	28	26	24	29
19	20	14	20	23	24	22	30
20	13	15	14	19	21	22	22
21	12	11	13	17	16	15	15
22	9	10	8	13	16	15	16
23	8	8	9	10	11	13	12
24	8	10	8	10	10	10	13
25	7	9	8	9	8	8	10
26	7	7	8	7	8	9	11
27	7	8	7	7	8	7	8
28	5	6	8	9	8	7	8
29	7	8	5	8	8	9	10
30	7	8	8	7	8	8	9
31	5	5	6	7	7	7	7
32	7	6	6	7	7	7	8
33	5	9	6	7	6	5	7
34	6	5	5	7	8	6	6
35	6	8	6	6	10	10	7

---

12. Reading the table row by row shows how the FTC share changed at a given age. By reading the table by column one can see how the cross-sectional age/FTC profile changed over calendar time. Finally, by moving south-east along a diagonal line we can follow the path of a particular birth cohort. We have over 1,500 observations in nearly every cell of the matrix, allowing reliable estimates, although smaller random-looking fluctuations do occur.

8.5   WORKING TIME PATTERNS: SLOW MOVE TOWARDS FLEXIBLE WORKING TIME

Overtime rather than flexible working time

In Hungary the majority of employees (approximately 71 per cent) work a normal daytime work schedule without shifts. No gender pattern could be observed in working time arrangements. According to case studies carried out in 2004, despite the modification of the Labour Code flexibilizing working time arrangements, the demand for flexible use of manpower is usually met through overtime rather than different forms of working-time frame (Neumann and Nacsa, 2004). As far as length of working time is concerned, according to the data of Microcensus 2005, one third of managers and professionals and of employees in the service sector usually work longer hours than the generally applicable 40 hours working week.[15] The data on overtime could also indicate intensive use of manpower. According to the L FS in 2004, 5.5 per cent of workers worked overtime during the week preceding the survey, 10.1 hours on average. There was no major difference in length of overtime between blue- and white-collar workers. The most overtime had been worked by senior officials and managers (11.7 hours) and they worked the most unpaid overtime hours (5.4 hours: average unpaid hours for non-manual workers were 3.6 hours and for manual workers 1.8 hours) On average, about a quarter of overtime (2.6 hours) was not remunerated. The most unpaid overtime hours were in services. Women are more exposed to unpaid overtime than men (CSO, 2005).

Fixed-term workers more exposed to unpredictable working time

Table 8.6 looks at the differences between open-ended contract and fixed-term contract jobs in terms of working time using the 1997–2003 LFS panel. It seems that fixed-term contracts are more often associated with unpredictable work schedules than open-ended contracts, and this remains true after controlling for demographic, human-capital and contextual variables. The usual weekly working time of those with a predictable schedule does not vary widely across type of contract; nor does the proportion of those working long hours. By contrast, the proportion of part-timers is 2.5 times higher in fixed-term contracts than in open-ended contracts.

---

15. Agricultural employees work even longer: half of them work more than 40 hours a week, but this is justified at the peak of the season, KSH 2005. évi *Mikrocenzus*. 3. A foglalkoztatottak helyzete (Budapest 2006).

Table 8.6 Working time in jobs with open-ended and fixed-term contracts, Hungary, 1997–2003

	Open-ended	Fixed-term	Difference Raw	Difference Controlled
Working time unpredictable (%)	5.6	9.3	3.7	3.3
Usual weekly working time				
(if predictable, hours)	40.7	39.6	–1.1	–0.8
(Coefficient of variation)	(.195)	(.234)		
Less than 36 hours a week (%)	4.4	11.1	6.7	5.3
More than 40 hours a week (%)	15.8	15.4	–0.4	0.3

Notes:
Pooled LFS 1997–2003, N=517,136.
'Controlled' shows legit marginal effects after controlling the equations for the variables in Table 8.2.

8.6 SAFETY AND HEALTH: POOR RECORD IN CONSTRUCTION

In the first quarter of 2006, the Labour Inspectorate investigated 6,659 employers suspected of breaching health and safety regulations: more than 93 per cent of them had committed some breach of the law. In this period there were 4,896 accidents at work, of which 28 were fatal. In the same period in 2005 the respective numbers were 5,529 and 36 (change in 2006: –6.4 per cent and –22.2 per cent) which indicates that the trend regarding work accidents is improving. Most fatal accidents happen in construction and inland transportation. In construction, employees of smaller companies (at the end of the subcontractors' chain) are particularly exposed to accidents. The employers, especially in the construction sector, neglect their health and safety obligations. In terms of gender differences, men are much more exposed to workplace accidents (69.6 per cent), and especially serious work-place accidents (151 out of 160 cases), due to the gender segregation of physical work (Report, 2005). The proportion of non-EU subjects among those suffering a serious workplace accident in Hungary is relatively high (7 cases out 160, 4 of them in construction) (Report, 2005).

Jobs created by large manufacturing companies (mainly multinationals, but also some domestic companies) expose workers to heavy physical and psychological stress; automation and computerization do not protect the health of workers any better than older technology (Adler, n.d.). High labour intensity may lead to early damage to health and (partial) loss of working ability, as suggested by one trade unionist during an interview prepared for Case Study 1. Multinational firms, however, tend to take health and safety regulations seriously and, in order to compensate for the hard work requirements and to preserve the working ability of their employees, provide excellent recreational and leisure services and to some extent health care as well (Adler, n.d.).[16] At domestic employers working conditions tend to be worse and the environment less comfortable than in foreign-owned firms. Work intensity in the latter is lower, the working regime is less strict and the individual needs and problems of the workers are taken into consideration to a greater extent (Adler, n.d.).

8.7 ACCESS TO TRAINING: MAINLY FOR EMPLOYEES WITH OPEN-ENDED CONTRACTS

Access to training is available primarily to the employed. We have calculated employed workers' probability of participation in (re)training (of any kind) in the four weeks prior to the LFS interview, by type of contract. We use data from 2003 when more detailed data gathering on retraining started in the LFS.[17] It results from this analysis that fixed-term contracts are associated with *less* retraining in the case of young low-skilled workers and *more* retraining in the case of young high-skilled workers. For older workers we find negligible differences by type of contract and generally much lower training participation rates. It seems that for high-skilled young people fixed-term contracts often mean a way of combining work and further studies (the retraining rates are as high as 30–40 per cent), while for the low-skilled it unambiguously means the end of (or at least a break in) skills accumulation.

8.8 WORK AND FAMILY

Attitude change concerning gender roles

Survey data collected on attitude changes on gender roles revealed that in the wake of the political transformation the male-breadwinner model became more

---

16. These research findings are fully supported by our Case Study 1.

17. Since participation in retraining depends heavily on age and education, particularly in eastern Europe, we use a flexible functional form – with the participation dummy on the left hand and years in school, age and their interaction on the right-hand side – of a probit equation aimed at predicting the probability of retraining separately for FTCs and OECs. According to the International Adult Literacy Survey of 1994–98 only 19 per cent of Czech, Hungarian, Polish and Slovenian adults attended a retraining course in the year preceding the interview, as opposed to 38 per cent in 17 other participating countries. The respective data were 7 and 18 per cent for low-skilled adults (0-11 years in school) and 5 and 14 per cent for low-skilled people older than 35 (authors' calculations using the IALS files).

acceptable than during the 1990s. The revaluated concept of female homemaker provided a new and apparently attractive form of identity to many women who had lost their employment during the transition. After the first shock of transition, however, the attractiveness of traditional gender roles decreased again somewhat in most segments of society (with the exception of young men) and became similar to what had been observed in the late 1980s (Blasko, 2005).

Who bears the burden?

Data on men and women with care responsibilities show that long-term family care is mostly performed by women, while men share only short-term responsibilities.[18] About 15 per cent of women under 45 years of age receive child benefit, rising above 30 per cent at age 27–28. Men are also eligible for assistance but account for only 2 per cent of recipients. As a rule, mothers on child benefit withdraw from the labour market, with only about 7 per cent of them being employed by ILO–OECD standards and 1 per cent actively seeking work. Out of ten mothers on child benefit only four believe that they can continue working in the same workplace as before pregnancy (SCO, 2005). Labour market conditions have a strong impact on how long a woman stays on child benefit. Women living in high-unemployment regions are more likely to have children and, once they have children, are more likely to stay long-term on child benefit than their counterparts in low-unemployment districts. The estimated difference between the 'best' and 'worst' regions amounts to about 6 percentage points. Level of education, another proxy of labour market prospects, is closely correlated with the probability of having children but has no strong impact on the conditional likelihood of being on child benefit. However, the decision to both have children and receive child benefit is more frequent among less-educated women, particularly those with only 0–7 years of education. Child benefit schemes continue to provide a recourse for mothers with poor employment prospects, and may probably encourage the choice of non-participation rather than employment and job search. Socially useful and popular as they are, some argue that three-year childcare leave may also tend to curb labour supply as well as labour demand.[19] In 2004–05, the government introduced several measures to ease the way back to employment for mothers: women on GYES (childcare allowance, equal to the minimum old-age pension) can establish an

---

18. 341,000 women and 5,000 men took parental leave to take care of children; 28% and 22% of men took time off work for family reasons without using holidays (SCO, 2005).

19. The cost of these schemes is low compared to expenditure on health, education, public administration, budget-financed investments and public debt payments but they do contribute to high payroll taxes (Köllő and Nacsa, 2004).

employment relationship without losing eligibility for GYES. As the lack of day-care facilities seems to be one major employment barrier for mothers with young children, since 1 July 2005 every settlement with more than 10,000 inhabitants is obliged to provide nurseries for children below the age of 3.[20] Only 4 per cent of nurseries are located in small settlements, while about 15–20 per cent of the relevant cohort live there. The local self-governments can meet this obligation by financing family day-care services, as well (Frey, 2006).

8.9 COLLECTIVE BARGAINING: LOW COVERAGE OF COLLECTIVE AGREEMENTS

Much lower trade union membership and collective agreement coverage than estimated

Both institution-based and survey-based indicators hint at substantially lower levels of unionization and coverage by collective agreements than the expert estimates used in international comparative research.[21] In light of the recent data, both estimates seem exaggerated. Trade union membership is constantly declining: in 2003, there were 906,000 union members, according to the data provided by the unions themselves (23.2 per cent of the workforce). The data provided to the tax authorities also shows a declining trend: 600,000 workers paid union dues directly from their wages.[22] According to the Labour Force Survey of 2004, the unions had 549,000 members. Between 2001 and 2004 the proportion of union members fell from 19.7 per cent to 16.9 per cent (by 2.8 per cent). In 2004, union members were found primarily in the 50–59 age group (23.3 per cent), while only 8.5 per cent of young workers between 15–29 years of age had a union card.

Decentralized collective bargaining system

The Hungarian system of collective bargaining is highly decentralized, in contrast to the system in the majority of EU-15 countries: the vast majority of agreements are concluded at company level, and only a few sectors are

---

20. Women raising children in villages said that they do not return to work because of lack of nurseries or other day-care possibilities.

21. Authors rely on ILO and OECD estimates as high as 60% for union membership and over 70% for collective agreement coverage in the mid-1990s. See, for example, Cazes and Nesporova (2003).

22. If union dues are deducted from wages and transferred to the account of the union by the employer, they must be included in the personal income tax return. See Koltay and Neumann (2005).

covered by sectoral or extended collective agreements. National-level collective bargaining is typical only of public-sector employees. Analysis of the issues regulated by collective agreements shows that the majority of enterprise collective agreements cannot be considered workplace-level regulations strictly prescribing the conditions of individual employment for everyday workplace practice. As far as the content of regulations laid down by collective agreements is concerned, they often merely repeat the provisions of the Labour Code and the issues in question are not always dealt with on their merits. Case studies on enterprises indicate that union confederations and employers' organizations do not provide much support for local bargaining; only a few sectoral trade unions give adequate support for enterprise negotiations by sending experts or well-prepared 'negotiating partners' (Neumann and Nacsa, 2004). Case Study 1 is among the exceptions. Since 2000, several measures has been taken by the State to promote collective bargaining, especially at sectoral level (Ladó and Tóth, 2006).

Dilemma for the social partners: which risk to take?

Case studies and further anecdotal data reveal that trade unions and employers' organizations are continually facing pressure to choose between two options: (i) to make a stand against violations of labour and tax law by employers but thereby contribute to job losses, or (ii) to side with them in order to preserve the status quo.[23] For smaller employers the question is whether to employ black or legal labour, or how large the payment 'under the table' should be. Larger employers seem to follow the regulations more strictly, though in many cases overtime is manipulated or unpaid, alongside other wage supplements. Trade unions are increasingly forced by their members to side with the employer in breaking the law when the employer threatens to leave the country altogether or to shift employment abroad because of high labour costs. In light of comparative data indicating that Hungarian labour costs are far from high (labour costs in the EU-25 are 3.7 times higher, while in Austria and Germany they are 4.5–5 times higher) this threat seems to be exaggerated (CSO, 2004).

---

23. See Labour Inspectorate data given above on black-market employment at investigated employers (almost 30%).

8.10 MAPPING THE INTERRELATED FORMS OF VULNERABILITY

Inactivity and low education

Most of the economically inactive belong to the less-educated population. The employment level of less-educated workers began to fall alongside the transition and there has been no major change in their labour market participation since then. Less educated people, especially those with only primary education or non-marketable vocational training (or not even that) have very poor prospects of finding a job which would provide them with stable employment and a decent income, probably because Hungary lacks a sizeable small-firm sector employing low-skilled wage labour (Köllő, 2005).

Roma minority hardest hit

The social group hit hardest by the transition was Hungary's sizeable Roma community, accounting for about 5 per cent of the population. While in the 1980s Roma men enjoyed full employment, surveys conducted in 1993 and 2003 estimated that the employment level of Roma men had dropped sharply to only 39 per cent, and that of Roma women a mere 20 per cent in both years, which is surrealistically low in comparison with the employment level of the total population of around 50 per cent. The employment level of the Roma is far below what would be expected on the basis of the skill composition and spatial distribution of the Roma population (Kemény and Janky, 2004). Kertesi points out that the quality and social prestige of work done by the Roma is extremely low (usually dirty and degrading work that is not done by others), and their workplaces are unstable. Most Roma are employed in public works programmes, and their rate of losing their job is three times that of the non-Roma population of comparable education level (Kertesi, 2005). Growing ethnic segregation in schools and growing relative deprivation of the regions with a high Roma density, together with continuing discrimination, threaten to deepen the severe ethnic divide (Havas, Kemény and Liskó, 2002). The public works programmes contribute to consolidate the underclass status and segregation of the Roma population as they provide only unpredictable, short-term and low-quality, degrading work. Organized at the level of local municipalities, public works undermine the normal functioning of geographically wider natural local labour markets which usually are fixed by commuting possibilities. Kertesi suggests the reorganization of the system of public works in order to provide longer-term, predictable, sustainable, non-segregated and non-degrading work to the Roma population in order to break the vicious circle of underclass status. He emphasizes the importance of regional level coordination (by regional labour offices and/or regionally organized non-profit organizations), the need for the utilization of special knowledge and skills in setting up new projects, the participation of Roma leaders in reorganizing work and the role models of Roma and non-Roma participants and members of local communities.

Different aspects of vulnerability among older and upper-middle-aged workers

The labour market participation of older workers has been improving in the past two years: the employment rate of workers above working age is higher than that of the workforce as a whole. Further improvement can be expected in this regard, since targeted policy measures have been introduced to smooth the process of retirement (a programme called 'premium years') providing well-paid and subsided part-time employment for older workers in both the state and private sectors. It seems, however, that workers above 45 years (or even over 40) are more vulnerable than those over 55 because (i) they are not covered by specific regulations providing protection against dismissal on the basis of approaching eligibility for old-age pension; (ii) if they lose their job, it is very difficult for them to find a new one because employers tend to employ them only if there is no other applicant; (iii) their representation is high in upper or managerial positions which results in higher work-related stress; (iv) a high proportion of these cohorts do not have a marketable education and usually are not motivated enough to participate in lifelong learning (Adler, 2004).

Diminishing prospects for less-educated young people

By the second quarter of 2006, the youth unemployment rate had reached 17.3 per cent, which is almost three times higher than that of the 15–64 age group (7.2 per cent.) The influence of the baby-boom of the second half of the 1970s ('Ratkó's grandchildren'[24]) is still important: many could not obtain a proper education before being pushed out of the labour market permanently. The proportion of young people among the economically inactive (neither in education nor receiving child benefit) is rather high: 160,000 persons (17 per cent) in the 15–24 age group and 68,000 (35 per cent) in the 25–29 age group.[25] Most are undereducated, with little cultural capital and living in

---

24. Anna Ratkó, 1949–53, Minister of Health. Her policy on strictly prohibiting contraception led to returning peaks in birth (Ratkó's children, and grandchildren). These peaks are causing serious and recurrent problems in childcare, education, health care, employment, housing, etc.

25. LFS, ad hoc module on youth employment, 2004.

villages mostly in disadvantaged regions. Preferences regarding employment status, job permanency and working time reveal that more flexible forms like self-employment, part-time jobs, temporary jobs or telework are not popular among young people at all, which reduces their overall employability.[26] A higher level of education does not protect from vulnerability either. The employability of higher education graduates increased dramatically between 1997 and 2002, while their wages increased moderately in 1994 and 1995, and considerably between 1996 and 1998. Afterwards, a falling trend in employability and wages started due to the fact that the demand and supply of graduates balanced out in the second half of the 1990s (Galasi and Varga, 2005). By 2003 the number of new workplaces for professionals stopped increasing, while the output of higher education was still on the rise. Consequently, in the last two or three years graduates have started to "invade" types of job previously filled by secondary school graduates as an alternative to unemployment. We track this trend in Case Study 1.

Women with children away from the labour market too long?

The generous child-benefit system, which provides three years of leave per child for mothers, results in serious difficulties when the women try to re-enter the labour market. About 9–10 per cent of women are on childcare leave in Hungary. CSO Surveys have kept track of them, concluding that their re-employment is becoming more and more difficult. Hiring and career development practices limit equal opportunities for women. Although women's educational level is higher than that of men, the employment position of women is gradually deteriorating: professional and educational segregation are pushing women to the margins of the labour market where the possibilities for advancement, level of income and job security are worse than for men, and the chances of being poor are greater (Koncz, 2004). Income differences have not been reduced (Kollonay, 2004; Czuglerné, 2004). Women from the Roma minority and those with low education are especially vulnerable.

Major regional differences

Regional differences in terms of employment rate and wage level remain substantial. Less-educated people living in remote settlements and/or belonging to the Roma minority are severely vulnerable. The growing poverty of children is worrisome: the poverty risk of the 0–15 age group is 142 per cent of the national average (CSO, 2006).

---

26. Ibid.

Different aspects of vulnerability of fixed-term workers

Those employed on fixed-term contracts in Hungary tend to be young blue-collar workers or, to a lesser extent, older workers, irrespective of educational attainment. Gender, education, ownership and sector do not matter nearly as much as age and occupation in determining who is employed on fixed-term contracts. Temporary employment seems to be spreading among prime-age workers and nearly all blue-collar occupations. Workers employed on fixed-term contracts are more likely to work irregular hours and/or do part-time work. They earn lower wages, particularly at older ages and low levels of education. We found evidence that the wage differential is not explained by contract-specific skills differentials. Few of the fixed-term contract workers are covered by collective wage agreements. Among young educated workers temporary employment and further studies are often combined, while young unskilled workers in temporary jobs get virtually no retraining. Fixed-term contract workers are exposed to very high risks of job loss but do not face particular difficulties finding new jobs compared to their observationally similar counterparts losing permanent jobs. The age-cohort-year patterns of fixed-term contracts forecast further shifts from indefinite to temporary employment in the coming years. This may add to unemployment, but the major expected impact will be a marked deterioration in job stability, mostly reducing the welfare of young blue-collar workers.

REALITY AT ENTERPRISE LEVEL: CASE STUDIES

All the case studies presented here revolve around a typical scenario: Case Studies 1 and 2 focus on the flexibilization of working time, while Case Study 3 is concentrated around a major reduction in labour force. Regarding their outcomes, none of our Case Studies corresponds fully to the stereotypes. In Case Study 1 the trade union has been able to protect the collective agreement, due to the support enjoyed by the union from its workers, the national confederation and some western European unions. In Case Study 2 the employer, which opted for extensive use of temporary agency work, started to cooperate with another manufacturing firm with a different peak season in order to reduce the vulnerability of their agency workers. In Case Study 3, beyond the lay-off procedure, efforts to improve the employability of vulnerable groups are also discussed.

Hungary Case Study 1: Negotiations at automobile supplier on the limits to fixed-term work

An affiliate of a multinational

The automobile supplier is a foreign-owned company, an affiliate of a multinational which has been operating in Hungary for more than a decade. Its main field of activity is the production of electronic control systems, mainly for cars, which is subject to unpredictable changes in demand. As for financing, all contracts are drawn up by the European office of the company, which supplies the Hungarian affiliate with a sum to cover costs + 1–2 per cent. The plant is located in an industrial park, next to a small town of 15,000 inhabitants, in Fejér County. The neighbouring factories employ altogether about 6,000 workers. The automobile supplier transports its employees by bus from its own and two neighbouring counties, about 30 settlements in all. Recently, production has been fairly steady: a major product was introduced 1–2 years ago and will be sold presumably for the next 6–7 years. Production is organized according to the multinational company's production system, the just-in-time model.

Distribution of employees

The company employs 3,250 workers: 65 per cent are production workers, 25 per cent non-production physical workers, and 10 per cent white-collar workers. The proportion of male and female workers is 35 per cent/65 per cent. Most jobs are unskilled: standing jobs, along a conveyor. Among assembly workers only 5 per cent can work in a sitting position. Most production workers are women. The average age of employees is 36–37 years. The employer seems to follow a policy of employing workers at an age at which less-educated women are unlikely to have more children. The company has never experienced problems finding unskilled workers for the assembly line; there is, however, a shortage of certain types of skilled metal-workers. According to the trade union secretary, the educational level of those doing semi-skilled and unskilled jobs varies: some are functionally illiterate, some are skilled workers (hairdressers, cosmeticians, bookkeepers, retail assistants, and so on). A smaller proportion has a college degree, especially among the younger ones. Her conclusion that a growing proportion of new graduates must start their working life in very low-level jobs corresponds to research results.

The process of hiring and firing workers
A hiring session lasts for two weeks and leads to the hiring of 20–30 new employees at a time. Written and practical tests are applied to measure the necessary skills for unskilled/semiskilled jobs. On-the-spot training lasts for about two weeks. The company has the policy of ending the employment contract by mutual consent in order to avoid possible unfair dismissal claims. If the company initiates the separation, they offer a severance payment and notice period which would be due in the case of ordinary dismissal. They followed this strategy even against a worker whose constant mistakes led to a situation in which the automobile factory had to stop production for some days because all parts supplied by the automobile supplier were defective. Violence in the workplace is an instant sacking offence, as is coming to work under the influence of drugs or alcohol. Other offences, especially first-time, lead only to disciplinary procedures. Two years ago there were collective redundancies: 350–400 workers were dismissed, but when the new product was introduced, many were reemployed. There is no obligation in the collective agreement in this regard. The fluctuation rate is 1 per cent per month.

Workers' representation
Forty per cent of the workers are trade union members. Two trade unions have representation: the larger one (with 860 members) is affiliated to an alternative trade union confederation; the smaller one (with 400 members) is affiliated to a major union confederation. A works council also operates in the company, affiliated to the company's European Works Council. The trade union's personal contacts, obtained through the European Works Council meetings, helped the unions to protect the workers from a major and rather detrimental modification of the collective agreement. This will be discussed later. Relations between employer and unions seem satisfactory. The hiring

process also includes a lecture delivered by the union which creates a personal connection between union leaders and new hires. To resolve sensitive issues (such as absenteeism, temporary production halts, and so on) the management seeks the cooperation of the union, which it usually gets.

Remuneration
Blue-collar workers are paid on hourly basis, white-collar workers on a monthly basis. Payment is calculated according to wage grade: the basic salary is determined on the basis of work title and seniority. It determines a fixed amount which is not to be modified by the employer in any direction. The company's collective agreement has not increased wage bonuses for shift work, overtime, weekend shifts, and so on, above the rate laid down in the Labour Code. In 2005, the average salary for production workers was gross HUF 93,000 (EUR 338: EUR 1 = HUF 275 +/–15 per cent) (HUF 103,000/ EUR 374 including overtime), HUF 113,000/EUR 411 for non-production workers (HUF 127,000/EUR 462 including overtime),[27] and HUF 250–270,000/ EUR 909/982 for white-collar workers. Because the firm experiences serious absenteeism, a wage supplement (bonus for being present) has been introduced, rewarding those workers who work the whole month (HUF 15,000/EU 54 a month).

The collective agreement also provides:

- meal vouchers – HUF 4,500/EUR 16 (the maximum tax-free sum);
- private healthcare fund contribution – HUF 5,500/EUR 20 per month;
- vacation vouchers – to be distributed by the Works Council;
- allowances – for births and deaths;
- Women's Day present;
- seniority bonus after 5, 10, etc. years' service;
- recreation facilities (for example, swimming, gym);
- company healthcare services, including massage, psychologist, screening, and so on.

Collective agreement provisions
The company has an open-ended collective contract, and wage agreements are renewed on an annual basis. Workers enjoy the benefits of the collective agreement in the following regards:

- stipulation of 40 hours' weekly working time and three-shift work schedule – which prevents the employer from introducing a flexible

---

27. The data on average salary might indicate wage discrimination: male and female workers are rather segmented, and female workers working on the conveyor earn lower rates than male workers in non-production jobs.

working-time frame, not even for the two months permitted by the Labour Code (for longer periods, the agreement of the union is required);
- the proportion of fixed-term employees is limited to 5 per cent;
- a disciplinary procedure;
- 40 minutes of breaks which form part of the daily 8 hours' working time: 2 x 10 minutes, and 1 x 20 minutes;
- strict wage grades; gives no room for individual bargaining and keeps the workers organized;
- a social package (for details see above);
- overtime must be announced at least 48 hours in advance. This enables workers to organize care for smaller children.

Negotiations on modifying the collective agreement
During and immediately after the introduction of a new major product the company's labour needs rise significantly. The company cannot rely on inner flexibility because of the working time limitations of the Labour Code, the three shifts in the collective agreement and the limitation of fixed-term employees to 5 per cent.

Two years ago the company won an extra order during the summer which could not be met because the workers refused to interrupt their holidays. The owner investigated and found that it was the fault of the management: some managers had a 25 per cent salary cut for six months.

To improve its room for manoeuvre, the management formulated a proposal for modifying the collective agreement, requesting:

- a raising of the limit on fixed-term workers from 5 per cent to 25 per cent;
- the introduction of a new flexible working time frame;
- a shortening of the 48-hour notice period before overtime, and the right to initiate disciplinary measures against workers who do not comply.

The union successfully rejected all these demands. It received powerful assistance from its national confederation, including good legal advice on how to argue against a flexible working time frame. Also, the deputy president of the confederation participated in the negotiations. He suggested consulting the unions of other European affiliates on what kind of regulations they had on these issues. The union utilized the personal contacts gained through European Works Councils meetings and the international connections of the confederation. On the basis of the data provided by other unions, the union could argue that no European affiliate has such rules on working time organization. The union also threatened a strike. Finally, the company gave in.

Ad hoc agreement on the reduction of working time

In 2005, however, the problem of flexible working time arose the other way around: the company wanted to halt production for an extra week. The original management plan was to send the workers on holiday for five working days. After the negotiations with the union, the agreement was as follows: they reduced the speed of the conveyor so that the workers were employed one day more without producing more. Those who had several vacation days left from the previous year were sent on holiday, but for those who had very few vacation days the management found other tasks in the factory for two working days; they also received two days paid standstill.[28]

Health and safety issues

The automobile supplier is not a particularly dangerous workplace (there is no heat, no dangerous chemicals, no significant noise, and so on). The work along the conveyor is rather tiring because it is done in a standing position, and overburdens the shoulders and the waist. Alongside the conveyor there is a special carpet to protect joints and relieve tiredness. In the assembly room everyone must wear protective glasses. It was difficult for the workers to get used to this. Workers wear work clothing (women: a wrap and a mantle in different colours for assembly and quality control workers; men: overalls) and additional protective clothing if needed: special boots and visibility waistcoat.

The health and safety issues are divided into 17 areas, each area being taken care of by a designated manager. Every month a meeting is held to deal with health and safety issues. Health and safety representatives are elected from among the workers. According to the HR manager, no workers have suffered a work accident or from a work-related illness. According to the trade union secretary, however, many workers have become disabled as a result of working on the assembly line. She also referred to a number of legal cases.

Summary: a typical multinational – atypical balance of power

This case study involves a typical assembly plant of a multinational firm: it employs unskilled workers on assembly lines, paid just above the minimum wage for working hard in three shifts. Though the work provided by this firm is not sophisticated, and the wages are not high, still this type of employer plays an important role in the Hungarian labour market (which struggles with a low employment participation rate resulting mainly from the low economic

---

28. The Labour Inspectorate investigated the agreement, and found it to be a good example of a workplace settlement. During the investigation, however, it was also found out that the previous year some workers had worked 16 hours on some days (two shifts in a row) and now the company is expecting to be fined because of it. The company has already been fined by the Labour Inspectorate for exceeding the weekly working time limit (48 hours including overtime) and violating the prohibition on working on national holidays (1 May).

activity of unskilled labour) by providing work and income for those lacking skills in demand.

As production depends on unpredictable changes in demand, the employer has to use its workforce flexibly. The management's room for manoeuvre is very limited because the collective agreement stipulates a three-shift system, 40 hours a week working time, setting a limit on the use of fixed-term contracts at 5 per cent of the workforce and requiring 48 hours' notice before overtime, and so on. Under such conditions, the management can use the workforce flexibly only by paying overtime extra shifts or extra hours. To change this the management pushed for a modification of the collective agreement. The union, which enjoys strong support among the workers and has a charismatic leader with good national and international connections, was able to protect the status quo and maintain the comparatively good position of the workers. The employer will probably recommence negotiations because the regulations of the collective agreement prevent the employer from introducing internal or external flexibility.

Hungary Case Study 2: Reducing agency workers' vulnerability: working for two companies with different peak seasons[29]

Consumer electronics firm
The subject of this case study is a major multinational competitor in the household appliances (consumer electronics) market.[30] This study focuses on one manufacturing plant in central Hungary, established in 1991. Like other multinational companies, the management was attracted by the savings offered by a low-cost skilled workforce and the favourable tax regime offered by the local government, including tax holidays and duty-free zones. The plant manufactures high-tech consumer electronic devices for both export and the local market. During its 15 years of operation, the product profile has changed several times, according to changing consumer and market demand.

Fluctuations in productivity
One of the main characteristics of consumer electronics is the seasonality of production: before Christmas the demand for consumer electronics rises to a considerable extent. In production terms this means working at full productivity for at least five months before the holiday. There is no other peak period like this during the year. From the human resources point of view, the

29. Case study and original text prepared by Ágnes Fiedler.
30. The company invested EUR 216 million in Hungary in 1989–2001.

periodic fluctuations in production are among the main problems. They have to find appropriate solutions to adapt to production, using flexible employment and working time. Though the company is eager to reduce the negative effects of seasonality, it still remains a big risk factor for the workers.

Flexible use of manpower
According to demand, the total number of workers fluctuates over the year between 76 per cent and 130 per cent of the average annual number. In 2005, the average total number of employees was approximately 1,800 between January and July, and approximately 2,900 from August to December. The number of employees with open-ended contracts remained more or less the same during the year, at approximately 1,300 workers. They represent the "core group", including administrative staff and workers indispensable to maintaining productivity in the low season. When the company faces a change of profile, some open-ended contract workers are dismissed, too. The number of agency workers was around 500 in the first half of the year, and 1,600 in the second half of the year.

Fixed-term workers: temporary agency workers
The main way of dealing with the seasonality of production is fixed-term employment. All the fixed-term workers are hired by a recruiting agency.[31] The plant has been using temporary agency work since 1997. The number of temporary agency workers reflects production fluctuations. Contracts do not usually last for more than 6 months; the average duration is 3–4 months. These workers tend to be unskilled and the work requires no expertise; during the 3–4 months of employment there is little time to 'waste' on training. Many temporary agency workers return year after year to save up some money for Christmas; in the other half of the year they do other seasonal or rural jobs. If the management is satisfied with a particular temporary agency worker, they can ask the recruiting agency to hire them again. In some cases, the company itself can hire the temporary agency worker and sign an open-ended contract. But the vast majority of fixed-term workers have to leave the plant after Christmas and wait for another possible assignment.

Two companies sharing the same workforce at different peak seasons
Fruitful cooperation has developed between two plants and a recruiting agency, thereby bringing some continuity into the lives of more than 100

---

31. According to the Hungarian temporary agency work model, the agency is the employer and the employee has an employment contract. The duration of the contract is determined independently of the duration of the assignment. This way the company (assembly plant) can avoid all the costs caused by the termination of contracts since the worker remains employed by the recruiting agency and can be assigned other work in another plant.

temporary agency workers. The consumer electronics firm tried to find another plant with seasonal production in the region with different peak seasons so that the flexibility demands could complement each other. The 'partner' plant is located 40 kilometres away, and transport is fairly good (by Hungarian standards) between the two towns. The workers (approximately 120) are employed by the same recruiting agency: in the first six months of the year they work at a food manufacturing plant, and in the second half of the year they work at the consumer electronics assembly plant. This cooperation has been going on for two years and has received positive feedback, so the company is trying to find other partners to share the workforce with.

Different aspects of workers' vulnerability
The permanent workers have experienced many changes in production: back and forth from three-shift to four-shift work, annualization and time frames. The real difficulty is getting used to the strict routine of the assembly work itself; if adaptation is successful the changes between shifts and other work organization issues do not represent such a problem. The annualization efforts did not receive negative feedback from the workers; most would prefer to work every day of the week (even holidays) and have a longer leave period when they can take care of private matters. Young parents in particular experience the negative side of the rapidly changing shifts and work routine; especially in families where both parents work in the assembly plant. The most vulnerable group of workers is definitely temporary agency workers. They seem to do the same work at the same place like 'normal' employees but legally they are employees of another company. If the assembly plant does not need them any more, they can be easily sent away from one day to another, without any obligations and costs. They get paid by their legal employer (recruiting agency) and they are not entitled to receive bonuses or other premiums (discounts on the company's products, for example) like regular employees. The attitude of agency workers is not helped by this: working only for a couple of months and knowing beforehand they will be fired sooner or later is not motivating. Towards the end of their period of employment such workers often just stay at home rather than going to work. The management cannot really do anything about it: the workers are going to be dismissed anyway.

Relative weakness of the union
One union represents the workers' interests in the plant. The union does not belong to a union confederation at national level, and does not represent the workers in the other plant of the company either. The first, company-level, collective agreement was in 1993. It applied to all three plants of the company in Hungary (since then, the company has closed and relocated one plant).

Since 2002, however, when the company withdrew from this agreement, there has been only a plant-level collective agreement. The management and the union negotiate the collective agreement every year when they set wage levels and discuss other important issues. During 2001–2002 relations between management and union reached rock bottom because the union refused to agree to the annualization of working time (instead, the company introduced an eight-week time frame which can be imposed by the management unilaterally – by way of comparison see Case Study 1) and because the union did not agree to the growing proportion of temporary agency workers. Following the tensions in 2002 and due to some personal conflicts, the management tried to fire one of the union leaders. The union leader successfully sued for unfair dismissal and the court reinstated him.

Do temporary agency workers undermine the position of workers with open-ended contracts?
Temporary agency workers are in the lowest wage category and, because of their status, cannot pursue a higher wage. In fact, they help the management to keep wage levels very low: if they are satisfied with low wages, the other employees have to accept it as well. The use of temporary agency workers weakens the union: temporary agency workers theoretically have the right to join the union but in fact they do not do so because it is not worth it for a couple of months. As the number of temporary agency workers keeps rising, the union is losing its strength: the proportion of union members among the employees is decreasing.

Improving relations between union and management
Despite the continuous problems, the parties have moved away from playing a zero-sum game and learnt to cooperate and respect the other's standpoint. Collective bargaining is continuing, the agreement is revised each year and the parties meet monthly in order to discuss current issues, for example, number of overtime hours, leaves. There are still problem issues, but relations between the parties have improved considerably and both are optimistic about this tendency.

Summary: who bears the costs of flexibility?
When production is seasonal in its nature, companies have to find suitable measures to accommodate annual fluctuations or adjust to changing market conditions. They combine various forms of non-conventional employment and the basic units of work are no longer the working day or week, but monthly time frames. The assembly plant has found a way of achieving greater flexibility through temporary agency work, though there is also a negative side: the workers hired by a recruiting agency are much more

vulnerable than employees with an open-ended contract. These negative effects form the core of the union's concerns. Temporary agency work is a way of achieving flexibility, although it favours companies. The company has made attempts to compensate the negative effects of temporary agency work: it shares the workforce with another seasonal business with a different peak period, so making the future more secure for these 120 workers. This can serve as a good example of how to find better flexible solutions, though there remains a lot to do with regard to vulnerability if we want to reduce the differences between groups of workers – who, after all, are doing the same work.

Hungary Case Study 3: The role of collective bargaining in maintaining workers' employability

The company is one of the major employers in Hungary. It is state owned, and its main function is to provide a specific type of service. The company is continuously in debt. How to manage the company's debt and the burden it puts on the state budget are major economic issues. Recently, the company underwent major restructuring, including a massive workforce reduction (20 per cent of workers). The company launched programmes to take care of workers laid off, and to maintain the employability of workers identified as vulnerable groups (elderly, upper-middle-aged, mothers on childcare benefit).

Industrial relations
There are 12 trade unions at the company, of which five are representative. Works councils are elected in accordance with the Labour Code. Company-level interest reconciliation councils have been organized to provide the social partners with a forum to negotiate on strategic issues and to conduct collective bargaining. The collective agreement was negotiated in 2001 for the period 1 January 2002–31 December 2006. The social partners and the company reached this long-term agreement after experiencing wage strikes on a yearly basis. Top trade union leaders are criticized by lower-level trade union leaders and rank and file workers for losing contact with the shopfloor, being too integrated in the company's structure and enjoying managerial salaries paid by the company due to their membership in participation forums (for example, works councils).

Decision on collective redundancies
The Government decided that a major redundancy programme had to be instituted at the company, resulting in a 20 per cent reduction in the workforce over three years (2004–06). The trade unions used every possible means to

undermine this decision (mass demonstrations, litigation claiming that their participation rights had been violated by the management in the course of making the decision on mass lay-offs, obstructing related management decisions, and so on). The unions, having been unable to get the government decision cancelled or modified, started to cooperate with the management in the course of implementation. After almost four months of negotiation in the company interest reconciliation council, the management concluded an agreement with the representative unions on methods of softening the harmful effects of the lay-offs on individual workers.

The process of collective redundancy
The strategy was to dismiss first of all those for whom some sort of income could be secured in the future, and to deal with each employee according to their needs. In the period 1 January 2004 –31 December 2005, 3,100 employees were dismissed (28 per cent), 2,500 employees retired (23 per cent), 2,800 employees were transferred to other companies (25 per cent) and 2,200 employees (24 per cent) left the company in another way (by mutual consent, termination by the employee, extraordinary dismissal by the employer). During the mass lay-off, the hiring of new employees was severely curtailed. Towards the end of 2006, at the final stage of collective redundancies, most employees, even university graduates with several years' professional experience, felt in danger of being selected for dismissal. At this stage, the employees had the impression that the management was determined to reach the workforce reduction target under any circumstances, regardless of whether it promoted medium to long-term organizational aims. The three-year-long lay-off process has exposed employees to an extreme level of work-related stress since none of them could be sure of keeping their job.

Taking care of those laid off
The company has relied on three ways of taking care of those laid off:
1. The *transfer of workers* took place under the regulations on transfer of undertakings. In 2004 the new employers undertook not to dismiss transferred employees for one year, and during 2005 for one-and-a-half years. The transferee companies – according to the management – are economically stable, providing services partly to the company. According to the unions, these companies are not stable enough economically to provide continuous employment for those who have been transferred, and will not be able to maintain working conditions in the longer run. In 2006 a strike was been organized in protest against the deterioration of working conditions.
2. The company set up three types of *early retirement scheme*. The schemes were designed to encourage the workers to join the programme as soon as the opportunity arises in order to prevent the dismissal of other

workers who would not be eligible for any of the retirement schemes, and therefore would be at risk of being left without any source of income: for example, joining the programme resulted in a payment of 7 months' average salary for those who joined in January, but only 2 months' average salary for those who joined in December.

3. Those not transferred or retired received a generous *severance payment* package based on the collective agreement (for those with 30 years' service, 6 months' pay in accordance with the Labour Code plus 8 months' pay in accordance with the collective agreement). Every worker dismissed for company-related reasons received an additional 3 months' average wages. The average gross payment (including taxes and social security contributions) for one laid-off worker was HUF million (EUR 10,700).

Establishment of a foundation to provide individual care for dismissed workers

The company established a foundation to support workers' efforts to find new employment. The foundation provides counselling for employees (psychological, career, and so on) according to individual needs. It is also engaged in matching supply and demand in the company's internal labour market.

According to the management, the foundation has developed a number of novelties in its services: it seeks to identify the competencies of dismissed workers on which a new life and employment strategy could be based (instead of primarily focusing on the needs of the local labour market). The competencies of workers are mapped by means of interviews by focusing on employment experience, formal education, possible work in the informal economy, hobbies, and so on. On this basis a personalized plan is designed for all workers who join the programme. For dismissed workers with marketable experience and/or in-house training, and only lacking a formal certificate to find a new job, the foundation provides possibilities for obtaining formal qualifications (usually after attending refresher training for a number of days). The foundation has established close links to civil organizations (rather than state labour services) engaged in providing services for the unemployed. This cooperation has proved especially fruitful with a network of former unemployed people.

Special programmes for specific vulnerable groups

To improve the employability of specific vulnerable groups, the company has designed special programmes:

For *older workers*, belonging to the 54–57 age cohort with 25 years of employment. Instead of dismissal, the employment contract is modified to a fixed-term contract, and the employee receives average wages for a period equal to the notice period, severance pay and possibly an extra payment stemming from the collective agreement or the collective redundancy programme (3 months) without the obligation to work. If the employee finds new employment during this period, the employment relationship is terminated by mutual consent and the employee gets the remaining sum of money.

For *upper-middle-aged workers,* targeting women above the age of 45, and men above the age of 50.[32] These categories of workers are protected by the collective agreement: they can be dismissed only if there are serious grounds for dismissal. The main purpose of the programme is to keep them employed by finding jobs in the company's internal labour market, and to enable them to fill these gaps through training and retraining. The success rate is 50 per cent.

Another target group of company employment policy is *persons on childcare leave.* It has been recognized that it is difficult to re-employ women after long years of childcare leave, partly because the relevant gaps have been filled by others, and partly because the knowledge and skills of such mothers become outdated. Through a questionnaire the workers' needs were mapped (100 out of 400 workers answered). After matching individual and company demands, training for occupations sought by the company, software courses, language courses, and other forms of retraining were provided to interested workers.

The company is continually seeking new employment policy measures. Now it is considering the best way of supporting dismissed workers seeking to set up their own business. In this regard a preliminary investigation has already been carried out in order to identify possible forms of stable and profitable company-linked small enterprise. The other targeted policy is formulating ways and means of organizing and supporting the relocation of workers from one part of the country to another in order to keep them employed.

Summary: identifying the vulnerable groups within the company and providing special employment services

The company has introduced employment policy measures to provide individualized services for workers not only in the event of collective redundancy, but also with the aim of maintaining the employability of the members of vulnerable groups. For redundancy counselling, the company's methodology focuses strictly on the actual skills and competencies of the individual, and designs a workable strategy on this basis, instead of starting to

---

32. The division of workers by gender and age indicates possible age discrimination.

design the individual strategy according to labour market requirements. The company's other focal point is working out programmes to maintain the employability and current employment of vulnerable groups, such as mothers on childcare leave, older or upper-middle-aged workers.

Despite the skilfully structured employment policy of the company, serious unfavourable tendencies could be identified. The three-year collective redundancy plan exposed workers to extreme work-related stress due to their personal insecurity, which has still not been addressed by the company. Relying on the national pension fund to secure the future livings of one quarter of the dismissed workers seems an improper strategy from a national perspective[33] – first of all, because economic inactivity has already reached a troubling level; secondly, because the pension fund is already in serious financial crisis; thirdly, because a reduced amount of old-age pension will not support a decent life. The solution could be to integrate these workers into the employment programmes of the company and provide services for them in order to improve their employability. Transferring workers to other firms does not seem to be a real solution since these employers are financially dependent on the company (owned by the company or its services sold to the company), therefore the transfer of workers seems only a formal solution which also exposes the workers to much less safe and predictable working conditions.

---

33. Sending into retirement all eligible workers is a frequently applied method of redundancies in both commercial and state sectors.

REFERENCES

Adler, J. 2004. A 45 éven felüliek foglalkoztatása és továbbképzése [Employment and training of the over 45s]. *Munkaügyi Szemle* 7–8.

———. n.d. *Meeting the labour needs of investors in human resource development*, Research Report published by OFA Kht. Available: www.ofakht.hu

Berki, E. 2005. Minimálbér [Minimum wage] 2001–2002. In László Pongrácz (ed.), *Foglalkoztatást elősegítő kutatások*, OFA Kutatási Évkönyv. 3.

Blaskó, Zs. 2005. Dolgozzanak-e a nők? [Should women work?]. *Demográfia*, 2–3, pp. 159–86.

Cazes, S., and A. Nesporova. 2003. *Labour markets in transition: Balancing flexibility and security in Central and Eastern Europe*. Geneva: ILO.

———. 2006. 'Labour markets of CSEE countries: from transition to stabilization', lecture delivered at Sub-regional Seminar on Balancing Flexibility and Security in the Labour Markets of Central and South Eastern European Countries, 11–12 May, Budapest.

———. 2007. *Flexicurity. A relevant approach in Central and Eastern Europe*. Geneva: ILO.

CSO. 2004. *Labour costs in Hungary*. http://portal.ksh.hu/pls/ksh/docs/hun/xftp/idoszaki/merokoltseg/merokoltseg04.pdf.

———. 2005. *Working time arrangements*. http://portal.ksh.hu/pls/ksh/docs/hun/xftp/idoszaki/pdf/muszakrend05.pdf.

———. 2006a. *Labour Report* (January–March 2006). http://portal.ksh.hu/pls/ksh/docs/hun/xftp/idoszaki/munkero/munkero062.pdf.

———. 2006b. *Laeken indicators*. http://portal.ksh.hu/pls/ksh/docs/hun/xftp/idoszaki/pdf/laekindikator.pdf.

Czuglerné, J.I. 2004. Munkaértékelés, bérezés, in *Nemek esélyegyenlősége*, pp. 87–91.

Fodor, G.T. 2004. A magyar munkajogi jogalkotás 21. század eleji kihívásai, EU Tanulmányok 3. köt., pp. 617–37.

Frey, M. 2005/2006. Changes in the legal and institutional environment of the labour market, annual essays. In K. Fazekas and J. Koltay (eds), *The Hungarian labour market*. Available in English at http://econ.core.hu. [http://econ.core.hu/doc/mt/2006/en/legal2006.pdf]

Galasi, P., and J. Varga. 2005. *Munkaerőpiac és oktatás* [Labour market and education]. MTA KTI.

Havas, G., I. Kemény and I. Liskó. 2002. *Roma children in primary school* [in Hungarian], Oktatáskutató Intézet. Budapest: Új Mandátum.

Kemény, I., and B. Janky. 2004. *Hungary's Roma population at the onset of the 21st century* [in Hungarian]. Mimeo.

Kertesi, G., and J. Köllő. 2001. *Ágazati bérkülönbségek Magyarországon* [Sectoral wage differences in Hungary]. Final study of the OFA-supported research. Budapest.

————. 2003. Market concentration, collective agreements and industry wage rents [in Hungarian]. *Közgazdasági Szemle* (October–November).

Kertesi, G. 2005. *Roma foglalkoztatás az ezredfordulón* [Roma employment at the millennium] (in Hungarian). MTA KTI Munkagazdaságtani Füzetek 2005/4.

Köllő, J., and B. Nacsa. 2004. *Flexibility and security in the labour market: Hungary's experience.* Flexicurity Paper 2004/02, ILO-CEET, p. 29.

Köllő, J. 2005. A nem foglalkoztatottak összetétele az ezredfordulón. Budapesti Munkagazdaságtani Füzetek BWP. 2005/2. Magyar Tudományos Akadémia Közgazdaságtudományi Intézet. Munkaerőpiaci Kutatások, Budapesti Corvinus Egyetem, Emberi Erőforrások Tanszék.

Kollonay, Cs. 2004. Szabadság és kötöttség – egyenlősítő szabadság, a munka 'elnőiesedése' – avagy a globalizáció torz 'egyenlősítő' szerepe. In *Kertész István-emlékkönyv*, pp. 211–29.

Koltay, J., and L. Neumann. 2005. In focus. Industrial relations in Hungary. In K. Fazekas and J. Koltay (eds), *The Hungarian labour market.* http://econ.core.hu/doc/mt/2006/en/infocus2006.pdf

Koncz, K. 2004. A nők munkaerő-piaci helyzete az ezredfordulón Magyarországon [Women's labour market situation at the turn of the twenty-first century in Hungary]. *Statisztikai Szemle* 12.

————. 2004. A nők munkaerő-piaci helyzete az ezredfordulón Magyarországon [Women's labour market situation at the turn of the twenty-first century in Hungary]. *Statisztikai Szemle* 12.

KSH. 2006. *2005. évi Mikrocenzus. 3. A foglalkoztatottak helyzete.* Budapest.

Kulisity, M. 2004. A munkaviszony megszüntetés rendszeréről. In R. Rácz and I. Horváth (eds), *Tanulmányok a munkajog jövőjéről* [Essays on the future of labour law]. Budapest: FMM.

Lackó, Mária. 2005. A *'shocking'* sector. Budapest: TÁRKI and KTI-IE (March).

Ladó, M., and F. Tóth. 2006. Sectoral level – efforts and trends. In K. Fazekas and J. Koltay (eds), *The Hungarian labour market*, pp. 92–109. Available at: http://econ.core.hu/doc/mt/2006/en/colofon_toc2006.pdf

Laky, T. 2005. *The Hungarian labour market.* http://en.afsz.hu/engine.aspx?page=en_full_afsz_en_labour_market_information

Neumann, L., and B. Nacsa. 2004. A rugalmas alkalmazkodást elősegítő szerződéstípusok, különös tekintettel a Munka Törvénykönyve 2001. évi módosításának hatásaira. *Munkaügyi Szemle*, 5–6.

Report by the Minister on Employment Policy and Labour to the Government on Workplace Safety and Health for 2004. 2005. Available: www.ommf.hu.

SCO. 2005. *Reconciliation of work and family life.* http://portal.ksh.hu/pls/ksh/docs/hun/xftp/idoszaki/pdf/visszamunkaero05.pdf.

9. Poland: Vulnerability under pressure from unemployment

Stéphane Portet and Karolina Sztandar-Sztanderska

9.1 INTRODUCTION

Low wages are the main source of vulnerability in Poland but also the main vector of cumulative vulnerability. Because of the low wage level, employees are more inclined to accept vulnerable employment and even dangerous working conditions. Indeed, employees frequently trade off higher income against longer working time, unsocial hours, hazardous working conditions and precarious employment. However, besides this vulnerability relating to working conditions, another major source of vulnerability is the low employability of certain social groups: women, particularly women with babies, young people, disabled and older people.

Table 9.1 Working and employment conditions in Poland

Element	Item	Trends	Risks/exposed groups
Social bargaining and workers' participation	Membership density	Decline (14%) but not in new sectors (retail, security) Implementation of Directive 14/2002/EC soon	Low collective bargaining system at enterprise level
	Sectoral, regional, national collective bargaining	Development of sectoral commissions within the tripartite national commission Regional tripartite commissions Very few interfirm collective agreements	Increasing disparities among workers (public/private, large and SMEs)

359

Employment status and contracts	Temporary employment and self-employment	Self-employment stable Fixed-term contracts increasing despite European directive on fixed-term contracts Temporary agencies, increasing but still marginal Self-employment, stable, even slight decline but increase in disguised labour relationships	Increasing vulnerability of labour contract Groups at risk: 15–24-year-olds Workers in individual farms, construction, retail, hotels and restaurants individual households Workers working part time More frequent in SMEs and private sector
Wages	Real wages	Lower increase since 2001 Hiring salary tends to be lower because of unemployment	
	Wage inequality	Wage disparities remain stable	Women still earn less than men. People aged 15–24 are in a worse position than a few years ago
	Low wages	4% of full-time workers are earning just the minimum wage but 14.3% of all workers earn less Increasing poverty, 59% of the population living below social minimum	Groups at risk: Women Children in large families Young people aged 15–24 Lowest wages are found in small firms
Working time and work organization	Long weeks and long hours	Increasing	Prevalent for such groups as self-employed and managers as well as workers in individual farms, retail, hotels and restaurants, construction Very long hours in case of supplementary jobs Very difficult work–life balance and difficult for women to choose motherhood. In consequence, very low fertility rate

Working time (*cont.*)	Part time	Stable over the last 15 years and at a low level	Part time is less feminized than in other EU countries and affects above all retired and disabled people
	Flexible working time	Increasing. Very important share of shift working Flexibility schedule mainly decided by the employers	More men have flexible working time. Very high level of flexible working time in hotels and restaurants and retail sector
Work organization, work intensity and working rhythms	Working intensity	Increasing	Stress and difficult work–life balance. Burnout of young people reaching top positions
Safety and health	Fatal and serious accident	Declining	Fatal accidents have increased most in transport, communication and storage
	Accident at work	Increasing	High increase in manufacturing, decrease in construction due to more frequent checks by the Labour Inspectorate, but construction remains a sector at high risk
Access to training		Low level	Access more limited for workers on short-term contracts and part-time jobs
Work–life balance		Increasing difficulty because of longer working hours and increasing demand for availability from the employers	Main risk: demographic sustainability
		Very few good practices Non-observance of the legal provisions on maternity and parental leave Lack of collective childcare facilities	Low level of occupational activity of women with young children
Access to occupational activity		Low level of occupational activity High outflow from unemployment to inactivity Deep geographic inequality	Groups at risk: Women with young children Men over 45 Disabled Young

9.2 EMPLOYMENT CONTRACTS

The main characteristics of the Polish labour market in this respect are the high level of short-term contracts and the frequent use of civil contracts.

Fixed-term contracts

Whereas in 1987 only 4.5 per cent of employees worked on a short-term contract, in recent years the proportion has risen significantly: in 2001, 12.7 per cent (Q4); in 2002, 16.8 per cent; 20.9 per cent in 2003, 24 per cent in 2004, 26.5 per cent in 2005 and 25.3 per cent in 2006 (Q1). Between the first quarter of 2001 and the first quarter of 2006, the number of employees working on short-term contracts increased by 110 per cent. In the first quarter of 2006, 2,781,000 employees were on short-term contracts. Poland has the second highest rate of short-term contracts in the EU-25, after Spain.

The short-term contract is developing above all in the private sector. Its development is due to very permissive legislation which between 2002 and 2004 provided for neither a maximum duration of fixed-term contracts nor a number of possible renewals. Article 25 of the Polish Labour Code, according to which three successive renewals of a short-term contract transform it into a permanent contract, was postponed until Poland's accession to the EU. Since that date, Article 25 has been in force which is in accordance with Article 12 of Directive 99/70/EC of 28 June 1999 concerning agreements on fixed-term contracts. Since this date, a third fixed-term contract is automatically transformed into an open-ended contract. If one takes into account the increase that occurred after May 2004, it does not appear that the new regulation has hindered the development of short-term contracts in Poland. Indeed, between the second quarter of 2004 and the first quarter of 2006, the number of fixed-term contracts increased by 19.1 per cent and the share of workers having only a fixed-term contract increased by 12.4 per cent.

The proportion of people working on a fixed-term contact in a given population seems a good indicator of their overall vulnerability on the labour market. If women less frequently work with a fixed contract (22.4 per cent)[1] than men (25.3 per cent), fixed-term contracts are more frequent for workers aged 15–24 (63.4 per cent) and tend to decrease with age (apart from post–working age groups: 28.8 per cent). This could be explained partly by the fact that in older age groups people are still working on the basis of contracts signed during the former regime. However, taking into account the fact that a lot of workers have changed their workplace since 1989 this could explain only a small part of the difference in terms of age. Younger age groups have fixed-

---

1. The following figures concern the fourth quarter of 2004 (authors' calculations).

term contracts more often because they tend to be employed for trial periods more often, but also because of the lack of permanent employment. Fixed-term contracts attributable to a lack of permanent contracts affect 47 per cent of men and 57 per cent of women. In terms of economic sectors, the share of workers having only a fixed-term contract is highest in sectors with cyclical production (small farms, construction, hotels and restaurants) or in sectors with significant staff turnover, such as retail (33.3 per cent). In the latter case one should note that fixed-term contracts underline the low level of commitment of the employer as well of the employee, which is confirmed by the relatively low level of involuntary fixed-term contracts in that sector (50 per cent).[2] Fixed-term contracts are more frequent among people with a lower level of education and occur more frequently in small enterprises (38.5 per cent in enterprises of less than 5 workers) where the employer's commitment to job stability is limited.[3] The share of fixed-term contracts is three times higher in the private sector than in the public sector, testifying to an increasing dualization of the labour market.

Fixed-term contracts shorter than 6 months are worked by 9.9 per cent of employees. These workers must be regarded as very vulnerable. Very short contracts occur mainly in the private sector, in small firms (18.6 per cent) and in economic sectors with cyclical activities (construction, hotels and restaurants, small farms). They are also more frequent among part-time workers (23.9 per cent) than full-time workers (8.8 per cent).

According to employers the main reason for offering mainly fixed-term contracts is the legal framework. Indeed, in the case of fixed-term contracts an employer need give only two weeks' notice whatever the length of the contract, and does not have to give any reason for dismissal.

Self-employment and disguised employment

One of the main issues in Poland is the use of civil contracts instead of employment contracts. This involves encouraging employees to become self-employed and then hiring them on the basis of a civil contract to perform the same work. In this way, employers avoid paying social security contributions. It is only fair to point out that a proportion of employees do this voluntarily, working on the basis of a civil contract in order to pay lower social contributions and lower income tax. The self-employed, having registered their one-person company, can freely decide the level of their social contributions at a lower rate based on 75 per cent of the national average wage and pay a flat-rate income tax of only 19 per cent, the lowest level; they are also entitled to

---

2. See Case Study 2.
3. See Case Study 3.

reimbursement of VAT and to subtract from their income costs linked to their business activity.

The Central Office of Statistics does not collect data on this kind of work relationship in the labour force survey, but two surveys published in 2005 enable us to make some kind of estimate. A survey issued by CBOS (CBOS, 2004a) confirmed a previous estimate (Portet, 2005). According to it (N=996), 6 per cent of the employed are working on the basis of civil contracts. Given an employed population of 14 million in 2004, the total number of people working on the basis of a civil contract was 840,000 – the majority of them could be employed on the basis of a labour contract. Finally, research conducted by Juliusz Gardawski in 2006 gives similar results: 5.5 per cent of the working population had only a civil contract.

The second survey was conducted by the Central Office of Statistics in 2004 (Główny Urząd Statystyczny, 2005b). This COS survey focused on the autonomy of the self-employed. Among the 2,892,000 self-employed, 88 per cent declared that they could freely decide their working time schedule and how they should complete their tasks. This was the case for 92.2 per cent of men and 81.3 per cent of women. Thus, 12 per cent of the self-employed are dependent. The highest levels of dependence are in health care and social services, where only 58.8 per cent of the self-employed can be regarded as independent; in financial intermediation, where 71.4 per cent of the self-employed are independent; and in transport and communications, where only 72.7 per cent of the self-employed are independent – the most independent self-employed are in the agricultural sector (95.6 per cent). The relatively high level of dependency of the self-employed in health care and social services, transport and financial intermediation must be linked to the widespread use of civil contracts in place of employment contracts among nurses, doctors, drivers, insurance agents and so on. According to the survey conducted by COS among the self-employed with fewer than 9 employees, 5.6 per cent were working for only one client and 4.7 per cent for mainly one client. Without figures broken down by the number of people employed by a firm it is difficult to estimate the proportion of self-employed in a real employer–employee relationship. However, it is interesting to note that only 63.1 per cent of the self-employed working for only one client could be regarded as independent in terms of working hours and ways of approaching tasks. These self-employed should be regarded as a very vulnerable group because they are totally dependent on one employer and the framework of the relationship is less secure than an employer–employee relationship.

Employment of temporary workers

According to the Ministry of Labour and Social Policy, in 2005 the number of temporary workers reached 374,968, while in 2004 it was 206,665 (Brodowski and Flaszyńska, 2006, 23). In 2005, men accounted for 53 per cent of this group. Temporary work typically does not require high qualifications. In 2005, the largest group of temporary workers was labourers performing simple tasks in industry (57,344); they are followed by store men (17,983), machine operators in metal working (11,967) and office staff (10,892). Because of the lack of relevant data, no long-term analysis of temporary work is possible.

The legal situation of temporary work and interim agencies in Poland was regulated in 2003[4] by a basic law on protection and equal treatment of temporary workers, especially in terms of health and safety. The law also seeks to make it more difficult to replace permanent contracts with temporary ones by specifying the conditions under which companies are allowed to make use of temporary work. For instance, firms that have implemented mass redundancies during the latest six months cannot sign temporary contracts at all. Furthermore, a temporary worker cannot replace employees dismissed less than three months ago (unless it was for negligence, misconduct and so on) nor replace striking workers. Finally, it is forbidden to sign a temporary contract with a worker previously permanently employed in the company.

In 2005, the Labour Inspectorate reported that in relation to temporary workers the law was not being respected, with the following suffering particular neglect: proper drafting of contracts (62 per cent), working time records (no overtime paid – 10 per cent, no five-day working week – 20 per cent), safety and health conditions (no obligatory medical examination, no information about professional risk – 20 per cent).[5] The last problem could be reduced if the law was more precise about the responsibility for providing safe and hygienic conditions at work. Currently, responsibility for this matter depends on a free agreement between employers and interim agencies. The Labour Inspectorate emphasizes that the working and employment conditions of temporary workers are no worse that those of other workers.

Despite the Ministry's aim of defining temporary contracts as labour contracts, the final version of the law makes it possible to employ temporary workers on the basis of a civil contract (a contract concerning a particular task, a mandate contract). In consequence, a significant number of temporary workers remain vulnerable as civil contracts do not specify working time limits or a minimum wage and do not always entitle workers to social insurance. Fierce competition between interim agencies causes them to favour this profitable solution. However, the Interim Agencies Association (ZAPT) has

---

4. This law was passed on 9 July 2003 (Dz. U. Nr 166, poz. 1608 z późn. zm).
5. *Sprawozdanie Głównego Inspektora Pracy z działalności Państwowej Inspekcji Pracy w 2005 r.*, Państwowa Inspekcja Pracy, www.pip.gov.pl.

launched a campaign "Fair Temporary Work" against this practice: *The aim of the project is to counteract the abuse of mandate contracts by dishonest agencies that seek to save money and force workers to sign disadvantageous civil contracts.*[6] This campaign seeks to address the issue of the increasing use of civil contracts instead of working contracts. The share of temporary workers signing a civil contract is still slightly increasing, reaching almost 36 per cent in 2004 and more than 38 per cent in 2005.[7]

9.3 WAGES AND INCOME VULNERABILITY

In the second quarter of 2006, the average gross wage was PLN 2,427 (EUR 619, for full-time workers in firms with more than 9 employees), the minimum gross wage was PLN 889 (EUR 227). For employees, the average net wage in 2004 (Q4) was PLN 1,216 a month, the median wage being PLN 1,000. The gap between men and women was 17 per cent; 14.3 per cent of employees had a wage lower than the monthly net minimum wage; and 17.6 per cent had a wage less than 60 per cent of the mean average.[8] Females are overrepresented among the working poor, as are younger workers. Wages are exceptionally low in small-scale agriculture, where 51.4 per cent of workers earn less than the minimum wage. In order to understand this figure one has to take into account the high level of part-time jobs in that sector. Low wages are particularly frequent in small firms and among workers with very short-term contracts. Because of the low level of other incomes such as property incomes, for working people the wage is the main source of income. Low wages could be regarded as the main source of poverty among workers. This is particularly the case of part-time workers who are in a very vulnerable situation: 77.5 per cent of part-time workers have wages under 60 per cent of the mean wage.

Our case studies show that bonuses make up an increasing proportion of wages. For example, in hypermarkets the "attendance bonus" often accounts for more than 30 per cent of total salary. This is leading to increasingly fluctuating wages and increasing vulnerability of workers. Interviews at the enterprise level revealed numerous cases of sick workers going to work because they did not want to lose their crucial bonus. Low wages are also a powerful incentive for trade-offs, whereby workers agree to worse health and safety conditions in return for higher wages. This also applies to employment contracts. Many workers accept work on the basis of a civil contract, receive

---

6. Source: www.zapt.pl
7. *Raport z działalności agencji zatrudnienia w 2005 r.*, p. 18.
8. Authors' own calculations on the basis of 2004 (Q4) Labour Force Survey data.

Figure 9.1 Wages according to working time, Poland

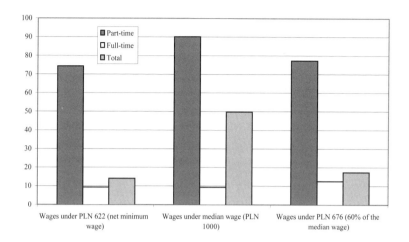

Source: Authors' calculations based on Labour Force Survey 2004 (Q4).

"envelope payments" or work without any contract at all just to increase their net income. Low wages force workers to have multiple jobs, as well as to work overtime. For 59 per cent of Poles, the most significant thing about work is the wage; for 57 per cent the stability work provides. Only 43 per cent attach particular importance to the content of work, for example, in terms of self-realization opportunities. Having interesting work and work in keeping with one's qualifications is rated only twelfth on the scale of essential values. Reasonable schedules are a significant factor for only 22 per cent of Poles, and the absence of stress and pressure is a significant criterion for only 47 per cent (CBOS, 2004b). Wages are the most important factor because most wages are low.

Wages are generally defined at the local level; there are relatively few collective agreements. Wage negotiations take place only in firms with workers' collective representation. In small firms, wage negotiations are generally on an individual basis. This is the main reason why wages are lower in smaller firms where 37.8 per cent of the workers earn less than 60 per cent of the minimum wage. Wages are the main reason for industrial action: in recent years wages have increased more slowly than productivity and inflation, but also many workers have suffered delays in wage payments (around 10 per cent).

The year 2006 might be a turning point in terms of wage policy. The massive emigration of Polish workers (anything between 600,000 and 2 million, depending on the source), mainly to the United Kingdom and Ireland after those countries opened their labour markets to the new Member States, led to a major shortage of workers in several regions and branches (construction, industry). In order to retain their workforce many employers have recently been forced to offer high wage increases (30 to 50 per cent).

Gross wages are very low, and at the same time the social contributions paid by employees are very high (18.71 per cent of gross wage). Welfare support and public services provide only for a safety net targeted on a limited group of people. Education and health care are always more a commodity. Prices are increasing faster than wages. Also, if low wages must be regarded as the main source of poverty among workers one must also take into account the cutting back of welfare support to obtain an overall picture.

Polish GDP per capita (PPP) represented only 48.2 per cent of the EU-25 average in 2004. Poland, with Latvia and Lithuania, is among the poorest European countries. Close to two thirds of Polish household budgets are used to meet basic needs: food, housing and clothing. Health care accounts for only 5 per cent of expenditure, leisure for 6 per cent (Główny Urząd Statystyczny, 2005a) Only 32 per cent of households have a computer, 16.9 per cent have access to the Internet, 29 per cent a dishwasher, 11.7 per cent a DVD player and only 46 per cent a car.

Since 1998, poverty has been increasing after a relative decline between 1994 and 1996.

In 2003, 12 per cent of the population declared expenditure lower than the subsistence minimum. This is a threshold of extreme poverty below which a person is no longer able to satisfy their basic biological needs. The same year,

Figure 9.2 Increasing poverty, Poland, 1994–2003

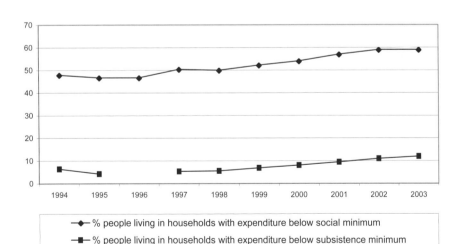

Source: Główny Urząd Statystyczny (2004).

59 per cent of the population lived below the social minimum calculated on the basis of a basket of goods and services enabling them to satisfy their elementary biological, cultural and social needs. Other indicators confirm this progression of objective poverty. Thus, the share of the population living below the level at which one becomes entitled to social assistance increased from 15 per cent in 2001 to 19 per cent in 2003 (Główny Urząd Statystyczny, 2004). The same year, 20 per cent of the population had expenditure lower than 50 per cent of average household expenditure. In 2001, this rate was 17 per cent. A large majority of Polish families have financial difficulties: 42 per cent of families restrict their expenditure on leisure, 38 per cent on clothing or shoes and 37 per cent on health care, 27 per cent do not have money to buy enough food and 22 per cent had to abandon the idea of studying. Only 28 per cent of Polish households do not have financial difficulties (CBOS, 2005). This situation is a direct result of low wages but also of the fact that working people are responsible for a growing number of inactive people not only at a collective level (through taxes and contributions) but also at the household level. More than half of the population over 15 is inactive and because of the low level of welfare support these persons are mainly dependent on working people within the family.

In 2003, for the first time in many years, there was a decrease in the number of inspected employers who had breached regulations on wages (falling from 68 per cent in 2002 to 62 per cent in 2003).

In 2004 there was a further decrease in the percentage of inspected employers infringing wage regulations, to 58 per cent. Despite this falling trend, however, the scale of problems in this area must be considered disturbing.

9.4 WORKING TIME

Long working time and unsocial hours

Working time tends to be long in Poland. In 2006 (Q1), the average working time of the active population was 39.9 hours a week: 37.3 hours for women and 42 hours for men. For employees, average working time in 2004 was 39.43 hours:[9] full-time employees worked 41.53 hours a week, while part-time workers worked an average of 19.93 hours. The highest average working times occur in fishing, retail, transport and construction. Size of enterprise is not really a factor in average working time. Form of ownership is far more important. Workers in the private sector work 4 hours more than those in the

---

9. Authors' own calculation on the basis of 2004 (Q4) Labour Force Survey data.

public sector, whereas part-time work is less frequent in the latter. Managers work on average 43.48 hours a week.

Twenty-seven per cent of workers work more than 40 hours a week in their main employment, and 16 per cent more than 48 hours (17.5 per cent in the case of full-time workers). In terms of long working hours men are more vulnerable than women: 21.6 per cent of men work more than 48 hours a week, whereas this is the case for only 9 per cent of women. Long working hours occur in individual farms, fishing, retail, hotels and restaurants. The bigger the enterprise, the lower the share of workers having long working hours. In firms with fewer than 10 workers 22.1 per cent of workers work more than 40 hours a week, whereas this figure is 19.5 per cent in firms employing more than 100 persons. The longer working hours occur in individual firms where 43.6 per cent of people work more than 40 hours a week and 32 per cent more than 48. These longer hours can be linked with the substantial use of overtime, which is very often unpaid (Portet, 2005).

Working time is on the increase, but there is also a trend towards intensification: 50.8 per cent of employees are subjected to permanently high rates of work and in Poland employees have limited control over their working time. Stress, unknown before 1989 for the majority of employees, has become an important characteristic of labour relations, as testified by the frequent requirement for a "strong resistance to stress" in job offers (Portet, 2005).

Long working hours are associated with unsocial working hours: 6.9 per cent of employees usually work Sundays, 16.1 per cent usually work Saturdays, 7 per cent usually work at night, 12.4 per cent usually work evenings and 25.9 per cent work shifts. In terms of unsocial working hours, women are in a better position than men, primarily because they are poorly represented in industry; they therefore work less at night and in the evening. Basically, the workplaces characterized by a significant number of unsocial hours are the same as those with long hours, indicating areas of significant vulnerability in terms of health and safety. The only major difference concerns construction where unsocial hours are less frequent than the average, and manufacturing, where the level of unsocial hours contrasts with a lower proportion of longer hours. An interesting figure concerns the high level of unsocial hours in the case of disabled people, who should normally be offered more convenient working hours. This raises the question of the reality of disability in the case of some workers, for instance in the security sector where a lot of people are employed by so-called sheltered firms and their employment subsidized. One of our case studies concerns this sector. Our interlocutors confirmed that a lot of people officially counted as disabled people do not have a real disability, and not only do they work full time but also work overtime and often have supplementary jobs.

Supplementary jobs

In order to get a realistic idea of the length of working time in Poland, one has to take into account multiple jobs: 8.8 per cent of workers have a supplementary job. People with supplementary jobs work an average of 48.52 hours a week, and 56.4 per cent of them work more than 48 hours. Men have more opportunities than women to find a supplementary job because of their qualifications and type of work, but also because of their lower domestic commitment. The rate of supplementary jobs increases with age. Public sector workers more often have a supplementary job, particularly in education and health care where wages are very low and workers tend to boost their basic income by a supplementary job in the private sector.

Part-time work

In 2006 (Q1), 1,452,000 people worked part time, that is, 10.2 per cent of the employed population; 13.5 per cent of women and 7.6 per cent of men were working part time. The share of part-time work (2004, Q4) is higher among self-employed (13.9 per cent) than among employees (7.2 per cent) and compared to other European countries part time is slightly feminized. Women count for 58.1 per cent of part-time workers. Part-time work occurs more often in agriculture (concentrating 45.2 per cent of total part-time workplaces), retail and real estate, affects mainly workers in small firms and is particularly widespread among workers with very short-term contracts and disabled people.

Until 2004, part-time workers were discriminated against. However, the implementation of the European directive on part-time work improved their situation. They are now entitled to be paid overtime, including a supplement, but by contract employers can freely decide the upper limit of working time that can be regarded as the basis for overtime. Part-time work became a right and employers have to look at every request from employees to work part time.

The working time of part-time workers is on average 22.3 hours per week (23.3 hours for employees). Poland is thus among the countries with rather long part-time work. In 2004, only 14.5 per cent of part-time workers worked fewer than 15 hours per week and only 13.6 per cent worked more than 30 hours per week. There was no really difference between men and women, apart from the higher share of men (15.3 per cent) than women (12.7 per cent) working more than 30 hours per week.

Beyond the financial vulnerability already mentioned, part-time work appears to be a vulnerable form of employment mainly in terms of employment stability. Part-time workers have the highest level of fixed-term contracts (53.8 per cent), underlining that part-timers are not regarded as full members of the enterprise staff but more often as supplementary workers and do not have a stable commitment to the enterprise.

At the same time, whereas in most of European countries part-time work is a very flexible form of employment and often involves unsocial working hours, in Poland – with the exception of Saturday and Sunday work – part-time work is more respectful of workers' private life.

9.5 HEALTH AND SAFETY: RECENT DEVELOPMENTS

Generally speaking, during the last three years health and safety conditions in Poland have improved. In particular, progress is noticeable as far as number of accidents and occupational diseases are concerned. However, the data on health and safety, collected mainly by the Labour Inspectorate, exclusively concern people working on the basis of a labour contract. Basing on information from case studies, it is clear that workers with civil contracts or without any contract at all are more vulnerable. The Labour Inspectorate does not analyse conditions of work for this category of worker. During field research several persons and even employers mentioned that the labour inspectors did

---

Box 9.1 Results of labour inspections

According to the Labour Inspectorate, the occupations most exposed to accidents at work in 2005 were construction (13 per cent), driving (8.4 per cent) and mining (5.9 per cent). The dominant group among those killed in work accidents in 2005 were drivers (18 per cent). Another phenomenon to be noted is a significant percentage of people working at a company less than one year among persons injured in accidents at work: in 2005, one in three of those injured had been employed at their company less than one year.

In 2005, labour inspectors examined the circumstances and causes of 2,515 accidents at work, which had resulted in 3,172 persons being injured, including 1,029 individuals with serious injuries and 549 fatalities. Collective accidents constituted over 16 per cent of the total number of those investigated. Analysis of the types of events indicates that the most frequent causes of accidents in 2005 were: loss of control of a vehicle (21 per cent), fall from a height (12 per cent) or being hit by a falling object (7 per cent).

As far as types of factors related to work accidents are concerned, their share was similar to that in the years 2002–04. Technical causes were a leading factor in 12 per cent of accidents, organizational causes in 39 per cent and human factors in 49 per cent.

not address the question of self-employment because it goes beyond the Labour Code. At the same time, the Labour Inspectorate does investigate whether civil contracts are in place to disguise a labour relationship.

Accidents at work

According to Central Statistical Office data for 2005, 84,402 persons were injured in accidents at work. This constitutes a fall of 3,114 (3.6 per cent) compared to the previous year. There was also a decrease in the number of persons killed in work accidents (from 490 in 2004 to 470 in 2005 – 4.1 per cent) and in the number of persons with serious bodily injuries (by 7.7 per cent).

Most vulnerable are manual workers, particularly people employed in mining, industrial processing, agriculture, hunting and forestry, and construction. In recent years, there has been a significant increase in the number of deaths in agriculture, hunting and forestry, and construction.

Safety

The annual analysis of working conditions conducted by the Central Statistical Office covers entities with 10 or more workers. In 2005, the analysis covered 60,800 enterprises, employing 4,819,200 workers, that is, 45.6 per cent of the working population, excluding private farming. Among this group, 576,500 individuals (that is, 12 per cent of all those working in the examined companies) worked in conditions of occupational hazard.

The level of hazards to employees' health (number of those employed in hazardous conditions per 1,000 employees) fell slightly, to 119.6 (a fall of 1.3 per cent in comparison with the previous year). This rate was the lowest since 1990.

According to the Central Register of Occupational Diseases, run by the Occupational Medicine Institute in Łódź, in 2005 the number of diagnosed occupational diseases in Poland was 3,249, 541 (14.3 per cent) fewer than in 2004.

In recent years there has been a clear falling trend in the sickness rate (that is, the number of occupational diseases per 100,000 employees): in 2006 it was 34.8, in 2004 41.0, in 2003 46.6 and in 2002 53.6). This falling tendency has been observed since 1999.

For several years the Labour Inspectorate has conducted a large number of detailed inspections, focusing on particularly difficult sectors and on firms employing fewer than 10 workers. The results of their inspections indicate that the main form of gross negligence common to a number of sectors and typical of small enterprises is the lack of hazard identification. In some case occupational risk assessment is even not revised after accidents. Other problems in firms employing fewer than 20 workers include the lack of obligatory health and safety training and improper use of electrical equipment and wiring.

9.6 WORK–LIFE BALANCE

Work–life balance is not a central issue of Polish political debate. Nevertheless, the decrease in the number of births has started to worry politicians and some voices are now addressing the question, but mainly as regards women with young children who must be regarded as a very vulnerable group.

In a very harsh labour market, women with children start with a real handicap. To get a job, to keep it, to pursue a career is very often incompatible with the parental project. Women often have to choose between work and children: 62 per cent of Poles declare that the principal reason for the falling birth rate is the fear which women have of losing their job (CBOS, 2006); 19 per cent of workers report a refusal to re-employ women at their company after parental leave; 12 per cent report cases of dismissal of women because of absences related to childcare; 6 per cent cases of dismissal of pregnant women (CBOS 2006). Admittedly, Poland is not alone in this, but because of the demands of employers and the precariousness of the labour relationship, the situation of women with young children is among the most difficult there. Many women decide to postpone maternity. According to a survey carried out by IPiSS in 2001, 14.7 per cent of women postpone having a child (Graniewska and Balcerzak-Paradowska, 2003, 301–3). The average age of mothers was 27 in 2003, a stable figure since the 1990s, but the average age for the first child is increasing (24.7 years in 2003). The fertility rate is only 1.23 children per woman. However, the desire for children remains high: only 4 per cent of Poles do not want a child (1 per cent in 1996), 12 per cent want one child (8 per cent in 1996), 49 per cent two children (50 per cent in 1996) and more than one third of Poles would like to have at least three children.

Analysis of the activity and employment rates of women according to the number and age of children allows us to measure the impact of motherhood on occupational activity. These rates strongly decrease for women with children below three years of age. This illustrates the social norm promoting the deactivation of mothers with children of that age.

As a result of a traditional model of the family women have to cope with long hours of domestic work.

Employers, with a few exceptions – mainly managers in high-tech companies – do not provide specific working time arrangements aimed at improving the working time balance. In the public debate there have been many calls for the development of part-time work. In fact, this could not be regarded as a satisfactory solution, not only because part-time work involves very low wages but also because it does not meet a real demand from workers, even among women.

The model of career interruption for childcare is strongly supported by a family policy mainly based on parental leave (Portet, 2004). Only 2 per cent of children under 3 go to nurseries and only 41.6 per cent of children aged 3–6 attend pre-school.

9.7 SOCIAL DIALOGUE

Social dialogue in Poland is relatively poor. The new departure in 2002 of a tripartite commission, bringing together employers' organizations, trade unions and government representatives, hides a low level of collective bargaining. In 2004, there were 163 branch or sectoral agreements among 4,350 companies and 1 million employees.

The trade union presence is relatively small. According to a survey conducted in 2006 by Juliusz Gardawski, the global rate of unionization among employees is 17.1 per cent. Trade unions are mainly active in the public sector, where 28.4 per cent of employees are unionized – in the private sector the figure is only 6.2 per cent. Freedom of association is often not respected.

In 2006, Directive 14/2004 on worker's information and consultation was implemented in Poland. Until 2008, only firms employing more than 100 workers have to organize a works council, but after this date firms with only 50 workers will also be affected. This regulation could provide a new democratic space for social dialogue within enterprises; it will all depend on whether employers and trade unions build a new kind of relationship. The employers do not really support this new regulation, even though the National Tripartite Commission supports it, and it constitutes the first agreement of its kind between the social partners. In fact, at the firm level most employers tend to restrict the right to information and consultation.

9.8 VULNERABILITY TO UNEMPLOYMENT

The most vulnerable populations are people with low qualifications and people whose temporal availability and productivity are limited. Young people, disabled people and people with dependent children are most vulnerable.

The principal characteristic of the Polish labour market is the existence of mass unemployment. Poland has the highest unemployment rate in Europe. In

July 2006, the unemployment rate in Poland was 15.7 per cent. This impacts on the labour market at both the macro level (legislation, economic policy, tax policy, social policy, collective action), and the individual level (form of employment relations, wages, respect for the rights of employees).

Polish unemployment has a structural dimension: only a quarter to a third of unemployment can be regarded as cyclical (Góra, 2004). Vulnerability to unemployment is very different among different social groups: the impact of place of residence, age and gender is considerable.

Figure 9.3 Rate of unemployment by regions, Poland, June 2005

Vulnerability in terms of place of residence

The areas most affected by unemployment today are the same as at the beginning of the economic transformation, and are found particularly in the west and north of the country. One significant factor is the importance in the regions of state farms under the former regime. The rate of Polish unemployment varies thus from 6.3 per cent in Warsaw to 40 per cent in the commune of Łobeski (Zachodniopomorskie). Only the large cities have a relatively low rate of unemployment: 6.7 per cent in Poznań, 7.2 per cent in Cracow and 7.4 per cent in Katowice.

Vulnerability towards unemployment in terms of gender

Women are more affected by unemployment than men, even if the gap has tended to decrease in recent years. In June 2005, women accounted for 53.4 per cent of the unemployed. Unemployed women have a 30 per cent lower probability of getting a job and a 57 per cent higher probability of moving into inactivity (Bukowski 2005). The main group of female unemployed is in fact re-entrants (from inactivity), accounting for 46 per cent of total female unemployment. Women tend more to move from inactivity to unemployment and vice versa: once excluded from the labour market it appears to be harder for them to return.

Vulnerability towards unemployment on the basis of age

The principal unemployment problem in Poland is the high level of young people without a job. In June 2005, 601,100 people below 25 years of age were registered in Labour Offices, accounting for 28.1 per cent of total unemployed. In the fourth quarter 2004, 38.9 per cent of 15–24 year olds were unemployed. This figure hides an even more worrying reality: the increase in the unemployment of young graduates and of young people without a higher education. Thus in the fourth quarter of 2004, 80 per cent of young people leaving school with a basic vocational diploma were unemployed; this figure was 29.2 per cent for graduates with tertiary education.

Apart from young people aged below 29, a higher unemployment rate affects people aged 40–44 (15.1 per cent, Q IV 2004). This is due mainly to the high level of female unemployment for this age group (17.8 per cent). For men over 30 the highest level of unemployment occurs in the age group 50–54 (15.4 per cent), with an increase in the unemployment rate starting at age 40. However, this figure hides a second phenomenon: the increasing deactivation of workers older than 45. This deactivation is partially based on generous pre-retirement programmes. In Poland, these workers are particularly vulnerable because of inadequate qualifications and because they can easily be replaced by younger workers who are more competitive in terms of labour costs. Once unemployed, these workers face real difficulties in returning to the labour market. The average duration of unemployment is 18.9 months for the age group 35–44 and 19.8 months for the age group 45–54 (Q IV 2004).

Vulnerability of disabled people

Generally speaking, the participation of disabled people in the Polish labour market is far from satisfactory. Comparative surveys in 19 OECD countries

Figure 9.4 Differences in employment rates between disabled people and total population, Poland, late 1990s

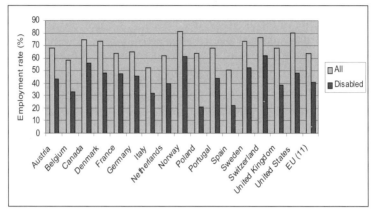

Source: *Transforming Disability into Ability*, OECD, Paris, 2003, p. 35.

show that Poland is in last place with regard to both the relative employment rate and the absolute employment rate of the disabled (OECD, 2003: 33–35).[10]

Poland remains an exception since the main reason for the extremely low employment rate is not a relatively higher unemployment rate for disabled people, but rather a significantly higher inactivity rate in this population.

Similar to other countries, the activity rate and the employment rate of disabled persons in Poland vary with the level of disability.[11] For instance, in 2004 the activity rate for all disabled people in the age group 15 and over was 16.2 per cent, while the equivalent ratio for the *severely* disabled was only 4.7 per cent. Furthermore, at the same time and in the same age group 13.1 per cent of all disabled were employed, but only 4.3 per cent of the *severely* disabled. This proves not only that the disabled form a vulnerable group on the labour market, but also that their status is considerably differentiated depending on disability level.

Among the working disabled in Poland special employment programmes prevail, particularly employment in sheltered enterprises (*zakłady pracy chro-*

10. One should note that as a consequence of different national definitions of "disability" comparative studies are always exposed to some inaccuracies.

11. Polish law provides three categories of disability: mild, moderate and severe. The level of disability influences the amount of social benefits received by a disabled person and defines his or her privileges, such as a working time limit of 35 hours a week for moderately or severely disabled (40 hours a week for mildly disabled) or the right to extra holiday – 10 days a year. Other privileges concerning the disabled population include: the right to work in specially adjusted conditions, no overtime.

nionej). The disabled in real employment constitute only a small part of the working disabled (Golinowska, 2004: 239). The research conducted by the National Fund for the Rehabilitation of Disabled People (PFRON) indicates that the causes of this phenomenon include: unfavourable attitudes of employers towards disabled persons and lack of knowledge about the law concerning their employment (Golinowska, 2004: 239). Specialists also point out that disability benefits do not oblige disabled people to undertake vocational rehabilitation (Golinowska, 2004: 242).

With the exception of sheltered enterprises receiving funds from PFRON, Polish policy towards disabled people is based on a mandatory employment quota. This means that enterprises with over 25 employees are obliged either to employ disabled persons (6 per cent of the workforce) or to pay a special monthly contribution to PFRON. Smaller enterprises might receive back part of the wage costs of the moderately and severely disabled. Also, all enterprises creating a new post for a disabled person directed to them by the Employment Office (*urząd pracy*) may be reimbursed part of the costs (the amount depends on the working hours, level of disability and wages of the disabled person) (Szylko-Skoczny, 2004). Moreover, disabled people may receive special credits in the case of self-employment.

CONCLUSION

Vulnerability in Poland is characterized by the high level of unemployment and inequalities in terms of unemployment risk. The social groups that have the greatest difficulty in finding a job are also the most vulnerable within enterprises. This is particularly the case for unskilled workers, young and older people and people (mainly women) with children under school age. Disabled people appear to be a very vulnerable group, too.

The main cause for concern as regards the Polish social model is the fact that the weakest members of society are also those subjected to the most vulnerable forms of employment. Labour market competition keeps wages low and allows employers to offer very unstable and often unsatisfactory forms of employment (short-term contracts, civil contracts, and so on).

Low wages must be regarded as the second source of vulnerability. In order to increase their current net income workers often accept poorer social protection by entering into a civil contract or no contract at all, and they have to work long hours to earn a wage sufficient to cover their basic needs. Low wages mean that poverty is widespread even among those in work; this maintains a vicious circle where some workers accept anything to increase their earnings. The minimal welfare provisions (other than for the disabled) also push workers to accept any job.

In some extreme cases, workers take the whole risk, while their employers give virtually nothing in return. The labour relationship is regarded as essentially short and the notion of mutual commitment seems on the way out. The weakness of social dialogue does not help.

The long working hours, the difficult work–life balance, the poverty and the precariousness of the labour relationship challenge the sustainability of a social model also suffering from a sharp decrease in the fertility rate, which might also be regarded as a sign of people's doubt about the future.

REALITY AT ENTERPRISE LEVEL: CASE STUDIES

We have chosen three enterprises in the service sector: in security, retail and cleaning. These three firms offer different views of the Polish world of work and the various sources of vulnerability. The various vulnerable groups, sources of vulnerability, practices and types of management share a number of common characteristics: they involve mainly low-skilled or less-experience workers, people with lower productivity, such as the retired or disabled, or with lower availability, such as workers with young children, who are also the most vulnerable on the labour market. But vulnerability is also a matter of concern for employees belonging to middle management and even small employers.

These case studies show that in a context of labour-cost reduction it is not enough to address the question of labour regulation. What is needed above all is to define a new regulatory framework for activities in which clients (often public organizations) are in a powerful position and impose prices at which it is scarcely possible to make a profit. In these three case studies we see how the companies use all the freedom given by the labour regulations – and even sometimes break the law – to reduce labour costs. This has a price: more vulnerability for workers in terms of lower wages, lower social protection, precariousness of the labour relationship and an impossible work–life balance.

Table 9.2 Case studies, Poland

Features	Nickel Group	Large	Small
Sector	Security services	Retail	Cleaning
Location	Mainly large towns and cities. Case study – Wrocław	Warsaw	Warsaw
Ownership	Polish – Private	French – Private	Polish – Private
Number of employees	30 000	460	20
Turnover	High	High (30% a year)	Low
Profits	Increasing	–	Increasing but low
Employment contracts	Mainly fixed-term contracts 12 000 persons with civil contracts 33% of subsidized workplaces for disabled people	Fixed-term contracts and part-time work in the case of cashiers	Unlimited duration, fixed-term contracts and illegal employment (mainly)

Working time	40 h/week but can be more on civil contract Weekend work and night work, long working hours. Total working hours with supplementary job: 260–280 h/month	40 h/week ½ or ¾ time for cashiers Long working hours and permanent availability for management staff	Unregulated and seasonal. During snow period can be 20 hours a day
Wages	Minimum wage With supplementary jobs: 1,200 PLN/month (EUR 300)	Minimum wage and premium (30% of basic salary)	PLN 1,200 net (EUR 300) In case of legal work just PLN 860 (EUR 215) declared – the rest "under the table"
Health and safety	Good	Lack of transport Break in working time not observed	Bad. Not taken into account. Physically very hard work
Social dialogue and workers' participation	Trade union relatively weak but regarded by employer as partner in social dialogue	Trade union relatively strong but no real social dialogue	No trade union
Main problems identified by employers	Low wages Conditions of public tender Changes in the law on sheltered companies Turnover and absenteeism	Regulation on working time – Rigidity Regulation on health and safety (too restrictive)	High social contributions Low wages Harsh competition
Main problems identified by employees	Low wages Long working hours Civil contracts Fixed-term contract organization (management)	Low wages Irregular working time Fixed-term contracts Bad work	Low wages
Main positive feature identified by employers	Good contact and social dialogue with the trade union	Low level of wages	Flexibility of the legal framework of the labour relationship Reliability and motivation of workers
Main positive feature identified by employees	Freedom of unionization	None	Honesty of employer Wages paid on time Individual arrangement with the employer on topics, such as working time, annual leave

Poland Case Study 1: Nickel Group: Using every legal opportunity in terms of disabled, temporary and civil contracts

Introduction

The Nickel Group is Poland's largest group of outsourcing companies providing services to enterprises and financial, health care, welfare and public administration institutions.

The Group's operations are divided into four main segments:

1. cleaning services: interior and exterior cleaning services and specialist cleaning services for institutional customers;
2. security services: services related to manned and electronic security, alarm systems, CCTV (Closed Circuit Television), fire protection and CIT (cash in transit and cash in processing services);
3. catering services – preparation and delivery of food;
4. other: supplementing key areas with other services for institutional clients (temporary work shows the most significant sales growth), such as facility management, medical services, clothing rental and services, laundry services, personnel and payroll services, and temporary employment services.

Nickel is using all legal opportunities to decrease labour costs, above all in terms of social contributions and paid overtime: employment of disabled and retired people, use of civil contracts instead of labour contracts, supplementary contracts. At Nickel, the legal framework is respected but used in all its complexity.

Security services in Poland

In this case study we mainly focus on the security services company belonging to the Nickel Group.

At present, approximately 3,600 companies, employing a total of 200,000 people (including both licensed and unlicensed guards), operate in the Polish security services market. It is estimated that as a result of a tendency to replace manned security with electronic security, employment levels in the security sector are set to fall approximately 40,000 – 20 per cent – in the next five years.

The Polish market for personal and property security services is very fragmented, and there is no leading company controlling the market. The key players' market shares vary from 2 per cent to 11 per cent. Nickel Group is one of the leaders.

Companies offering security services concentrate on manned security services (MSS), electronic security services (ESS), monitoring (MON) and cash-in-transit and cash-in-processing services (CIT).

The exact number of people working for Nickel Group is rather difficult to measure. Because of the frequent use of civil contracts, the figures relating only to workers on employment contracts are not really reliable. During the field research two trade unionists reported the number of workers as close to 30,000.

In 2005 Nickel Group employed 20,128 workers, up from 15,343 at the end of 2001. Nickel Group's security company employed 9,000 workers in 2005, accounting for 37.44 per cent of total Group sales.

A new leitmotiv: increasing labour productivity
As labour expenditure accounts for 69.1 per cent of total production costs, workers bear the brunt of the pressure for greater profitability.

This new business policy seems to be quite efficient: in 2005, Nickel Group increased sales by 8.6 per cent and returned to the black after a long period of very bad financial results. The new business policy was based on the separation of the different areas of activities, each of them being supervised independently, and general cost-cutting policy. This consisted in a wage freeze, the generalization of flexible forms of employment, including the use of civil contracts for supplementary tasks in order to avoid the surcharge of paid overtime. But a major source of labour productivity increase since May 2004 has been massive layoffs with lower productivity with, on the top of that, the most disabled workers.

A creative human resources policy
Nickel Security (NS) employs various categories of people, including many retired and disabled people, as well as workers working mainly for other firms. In order to continue to enjoy the status of sheltered employer, Nickel Group has to employ 40 per cent disabled people in its workforce. Taking into account the structure of employment in terms of part-time and full-time contracts, Nickel Group currently employs exactly 40 per cent disabled, just enough to continue receiving subsidies but no more, since the focus is now on increasing labour productivity and reducing costs.

Retired people are mainly former military personnel or policemen entitled to retirement after 15 years' service. These are particularly attractive to employers because they do not need a work contract, being already insured on the basis of their retirement status. The same applies to people working for other firms and disabled people being paid an allowance by the social security system. Beyond the issue of social protection, these workers also have a valuable asset; they are ready to work for low wages, as they have another source of income.

Fixed-term or civil contracts as a rule
At Nickel Security (NS), the rule is the fixed-term labour contract or the civil contract. Only a few workers enjoy a permanent contract: they are often work-

ers who were formerly employed on that basis by a former employer who has decided to outsource security activities and has given the contract to NS. In this case, the contract with NS often lays down that NS will employ the former employees on the same basis for a determinate period of time. The overwhelming majority of NS' employees work on fixed-term contracts. These contracts are generally of three or five years. The main reasons for opting for a fixed-term contract are the 14-days notice period, the fact that in case of dismissal no reason need be given and there is no obligation to consult with the trade unions, but also because the contracts with clients are generally signed for a period of three years.

Among the 30,000 employees around 12,000 are employed on the basis of a civil contract. As mentioned below, this form of employment is the rule for retired people, people having already a contract with another company, and recently disabled people. According to the trade unionists we talked to, the Labour Inspectorate has not addressed the issue of the massive use of civil contracts: they dismiss the issue by saying that it is a "not a contract relating to the Labour Code so we are not interested in it". The owner of the cleaning company – the third firm we analysed – reported exactly the same behaviour on the part of Labour Inspectorate.

Low wages and long working hours: a vicious circle

Wages at NS are among the lowest in Poland and often workers receive no more than PLN 500 net (EUR 125). The average gross wage of a full-time worker (including management) at NS was PLN 1,530 in 2005 (EUR 382), that is, 40 per cent below the average wage in Poland. The majority of blue-collar workers earn the legal minimum gross wage of PLN 869 (EUR 217) a month but only if they work full time. Someone employed on a labour contract is paid PLN 3.79 (EUR 0.9) net an hour. In fact, wages are dependent on the contract with the client and so for the same work people do not always receive the same amount of money. Most contracts are subject to public tender. Price is generally the deciding factor (normally 70 per cent of the decision criteria). A sum of PLN 5.20/hour (EUR 1.3) is frequent, lower than the minimum wage, and the only option is to employ people on the basis of a lump-sum contract regarded as complementary to other sources of income. In this case, disabled and retired people are perfect employees. The main firms on the market tried to reach agreement on a common lowest price (PLN 7) but there is always one firm, usually a smaller one, which is willing to offer a lower price than the one offered by the cartel.

The low wages imply very long working hours. NS Group, as a large company and a sheltered employment firm, is submitted to frequent checks by the Labour Inspectorate. This situation makes it impossible to avoid paying overtime. With a view to making cost reductions, employers thus try not to use overtime at all, preferring to employ workers on civil contract. People working on the basis of a civil contract are not entitled to paid overtime, as they are not subject to legal regulations on working time.

To disabled and retired people one must add another group of workers "valued" by employers, namely those who work primarily for other companies. These workers are mainly employed under particular circumstances or at weekends. They work for PLN 4.2/hour. They come under two categories:

1. People working part time at another firm. They are generally employed on the basis of a labour contract, but NS need pay only a small part of total social contributions because the rest is paid by the other employer. They are employed on the basis of a labour contract because a civil contract below the limit of the minimum wage in their first employment would oblige NS to pay social contributions in their entirety.
2. People working full time at another firm. They are employed on a civil contract. They are "perfect" workers, according to the human resources director. However, it seems quite difficult to find workers with all the necessary skills and qualifications (including licences): hence the employment of people working part time elsewhere.

In this sector, most workers combine jobs, and a monthly working time of 260 hours is regarded as normal. In fact, all firms lease workers to one another. Workers also work during their "holidays".

Vulnerability of disabled workers
Nickel Group enjoy the status of integration firm for the disabled. Since 2004 and EU accession Poland has had to comply with Art. 88 of the Treaty on public aid to private firms. Within the framework of these new legal constraints – and also of the political will to reduce welfare expenditure – the law on subsidies for integration firms has been modified several times since May 2004. Not only has the amount of subsidy decreased, but also plans are in preparation to transform lump-sum subsidies into subsidies based on real extra expenditure on the employment of disabled people. Before May 2004 Nickel received PLN 6–7 million in subsidies for an estimated extra cost due to disabled workers of only PLN 1–2 million.[18] As a result, there was a risk that the group's business model would be too dependent on these subsidies. Such a situation is regarded as hazardous by the Nickel board. Anticipating a further decrease of subsidies from the government, Nickel decided to develop a new business model and in 2004 decided to limit the proportion of subsidies in

---

18. This estimate is made mainly on the basis of expenditure related to adaptation of workplaces for disabled people.

total sales revenue. The share of subsidies declined from 21.6 per cent in 2003 to 8.6 per cent in 2005 and the Group was planning a further reduction to 7.5 per cent in 2006. In 2005, the share of state subsidies in this company's sales revenues was 8.8 per cent.

In May 2004 the firm launched a double restructuring process: on the one hand, it separated the different activities into several specialized units; on the other hand, it reduced the number of disabled workers by 32 per cent between the beginning of 2004 and the end of 2005, while the total number of employees remained stable. The ratio of disabled to non-disabled in full-time equivalents decreased from 42.5 per cent to 33 per cent. As their employment depends mainly on subsidies, disabled workers appear to be particularly vulnerable. Whereas Poland has the lowest level of employment for disabled people in Europe, the case of Nickel shows that the new reform might have a negative impact. The least productive workers – that is, the most clearly disabled – are made redundant. At the same time, many disabled workers are not really disabled. Many have a phoney certificate they obtained by bribing doctors. This certificate entitles them to social benefits depending on their level of disability and above the level of the subsidy paid to the employer. This gives the employer the opportunity to offer them lower wages (because workers have another income source) and to employ them on the basis of a civil contract (no social insurance contributions are paid for disabled employees). Such a scenario is frequent in the security sector. Practices which have given rise to abuse are in the background of the public debate on the reform of subsidies aimed at supporting the employment of disabled people. In the case of Nickel, however, it seems that the genuinely disabled have been dismissed, while the "fake disabled" have kept their jobs because they are profitable to the firm, combining high productivity with all the advantages of disabled workers in terms of labour costs.

Before the implementation of the new company strategy, disabled people were mainly employed on the basis of a labour contract (on a part-time basis), entitling the employer to subsidies from the state. Within the framework of the new business plan involving a reduction in the share of subsidies in group revenue, the disabled workers the company would want to keep are being offered a change in their labour contract, transforming it into a civil contract in order to reduce social contributions.

The role of the clients
Another problem with transforming labour contracts into civil contracts, however, is that clients demand people employed on a labour contract because they believe they are more committed and more reliable. Some clients agree to pay more than the minimum because they want only workers with experience and a labour contract. By demanding this they express their desire to

have the best workers. Reliability is an important issue in the security sector and workers with a labour contract are regarded as more reliable. In fact, only a minority of clients express this kind of demand and most are concerned above all with the lowest price. In this case, the form of employment does not matter and civil contracts are the rule.

In the case of public tenders it is often hard to win a contract when workers are employed on a labour contract. In fact, only a law aimed at regulating the market would be able to hinder the development of civil contracts.

Conclusion

NS serves as a good illustration of the general trends in the security sector, at least of the biggest firms where work without any contract is very rare but where all the sources of flexibility given by the law are used by the employers. The main problems in the sector are: long working hours; low wages; and the precariousness of the labour relationship

These issues are closely linked. Workers are used to working long hours to boost their very low basic wages. NSZZ Solidarnosc is demanding hourly pay of PLN 10 (EUR 2.25). Trade unionists report monthly working time above 300 hours as a frequent figure. Workers in the sector suffer from difficulties in balancing work and family life. Taking into account the stress of certain workplaces, the fatigue due to long working hours and the precariousness of their labour contracts, workers in this sector must be regarded as really vulnerable. The security sector is rapidly developing. More and more companies are outsourcing their security division. Often, security companies like NS employ the former workers of the firms they are contracting with. But while for the first few years these workers often keep their labour contracts and level of remuneration, that generally changes with time and they join the other workers, working on the basis of a civil contract and lower wages.

Poland Case Study 2: BIG (hypermarket, Warsaw) – playing within the legal boundaries

BIG is a hypermarket in Warsaw. It employs 460 workers. This case study seeks to describe how companies can benefit from keeping their activities legal and how opportunities for flexibility and cost-cutting are numerous. BIG must be regarded as representing best practice in the sector. In this company each worker has a contract (labour or civil), is paid on time and has the freedom to join the trade union. Nevertheless, working conditions still demand improvement, particularly regarding the long and unsocial working hours, low wages and work–life balance. The retail sector has been under scrutiny by the Labour Inspectorate recently and the case of BIG allows us to determine whether the checks carried out by the Labour Inspectorate have led to any improvement in working conditions. It seems that the impulse to investigate Polish hypermarkets came from the press and public criticisms of working conditions.

Supermarkets under close supervision by the Labour Inspectorate

The Labour Inspectorate has made the retail sector a special target since 1999, conducting frequent intensive checks. Supermarkets and hypermarkets are the object of harsh criticism in both the media and political debate. Retail establishments – known as hotbeds of "exploitation" and "slavery" (journalist in *Gazeta Wyborcza*, 21 February 2005, 28 April 2005) and as "forced labour camps" – have come to represent extremely bad working conditions.

The main problems reported in 2004 by the Labour Inspectorate concerned working time and compliance with health and safety regulations (45 per cent of all offences). In particular, retail outlets did not respect paid leave (67 per cent), did not keep accurate records of working time (52.5 per cent) and failed to pay overtime (47.5 per cent). These general tendencies have been confirmed by detailed inspections carried out at three chains: *Biedronka*, *Kaufland* and *Lidl*. Although it is very difficult to obtain detailed and reliable figures on these issues in the case of BIG, during interviews workers mentioned false records of working time and unpaid overtime as frequent in this hypermarket.

Constant action by the Labour Inspectorate, trade union efforts and media attention have resulted in a gradual improvement in working conditions. BIG's human resources manager confirmed that media criticism has had a positive impact.

Table 9.3 BIG, Poland: Number of retail outlets checked by the Labour Inspectorate, 1999–2004

	1999	2000	2001	2002	2003	2004
Number of inspected retail outlets	22	52	67	58	139	66
Number of employees of whom:	10 984	21 237	19 695	23 260	35 765	10 705
Women	7 480	13 335	12 818	9 654	22 235	6 861
Junior workers	94	160	362	112	342	44

Source: Labour Inspectorate Report (*Przestrzeganie przepisów prawa pracy w supermarketach, hypermarketach i sklepach dyskontowych w latach 1999-2005*, Państwowa Inspekcja Pracy, Warsaw, 2005).

According to Labour Inspectorate data, the number of offences has been falling in the establishments which have been systematically inspected and re-inspected and which have been in the sector for more than six years. It also seems that meetings with the foreign owners of the three frequently inspected chains – Biedronka, Kaufland and Lidl – might indicate that they were not fully aware of working regulations in Poland.

BIG is certainly not a constant law-breaker. In the opinion of a trade union-ist who works there: *generally speaking, the law is respected.* However, as he also points out, there is still a lot of work to do, particularly in the use of fixed-term contracts of short duration, the payment of overtime and the improve-ment of the work–life balance.

Labour contracts but of shorter duration

In comparison with other hypermarkets, the advantage of BIG is that people are hired on the basis of labour contracts. Despite the fact that civil contracts are more profitable for employers, for the reason that there are no working time limits and lower social contribution costs, the labour contract remains the rule for almost everybody, apart from seasonal workers (at Christmas, for example). According to the human resources director this solution is widely accepted by management and there is no pressure to cut expenditure at all costs. Moreover, she would only reluctantly resort to solutions regarded as attempts to circumvent the law, which, apart from anything else, would com-plicate human resource management.

At BIG, people are initially hired on the basis of a probationary contract, which may legally last no more than three months. Typically, what follows is a one-year short-term contract. The third step in a hypermarket career is another fixed-term contract, this time for a longer period – 3 to 5 years. Currently, per-manent contracts constitute approximately 15 per cent of all labour contracts with general workers. Both the trade unionist and the human resources man-ager remarked that the avoidance of permanent contracts is currently much stronger than it used to be. Advantages for employers are clear: two weeks' notice, no reason required to fire an employee and the possibility of using this uncertain employment situation as a means of motivating workers. The human resources manager underlined the importance of motivation: *We have fre-quently observed, particularly in the case of lower-ranking workers, a large deterioration in work quality when an employee has a permanent contract.* As we shall see later, the form of the contract is almost the only instrument that the human resources department has at its disposal to motivate workers.

Working time: surfing on the border line

BIG is open 8.30 to 22.00 Monday to Saturday and 9.00 to 20.00 on Sundays. The working time of general workers is organized in two shifts, so they can work full-time contracts. The first starts at 6 o'clock in the morning, the last finishes at 10 o'clock or 11 o'clock in the evening during the week. General staff are equipped with electronic cards recording the number of working hours, which theoretically should exclude abuse. However, the trade union indicates that there are still two systems of counting working time: one "official", one "real". As he says: *every two months the employer refrains from recording overtime*. The trade union tries to combat gross abuses in this area. According to the human resources manager, an improvement in the general situation of workers is already noticeable because of the fear of labour inspections and thanks to trade union action.

Unsocial hours at normal hourly rates

Supermarkets and hypermarkets are open on Saturdays and Sundays. Some restrictions on weekend opening hours have been introduced at the local level in one Polish town, Radom. However, this regulation is not observed since fines are much lower than turnover from weekend days. The current government will probably try to limit working hours on Saturdays and Sundays in future. For the moment, employees of BIG, like those of other retail outlets, have to work unsocial hours at normal hourly rates. It is perfectly legal to give them two days off in mid-week. Since 2004, the Labour Code has provided for "weekend" work. When an employee works only the weekend he/she is not entitled to higher hourly rates. Only people working during the week and on Sunday are entitled to higher hourly rates or extra free-time. In practice, higher hourly rates are never paid and extra free time is rarely given.

Impossible to plan leisure with over-flexible working time schedules

The second problem is the availability requirement. We have already mentioned this in relation to middle management, but it affects other staff too. It means that working hours are never fixed. A third group of workers, cashiers, all of whom are part time, are also affected. The cashiers' department is exceptional because it has its own computer system making it possible to plan individualized timetables. Generally speaking, the availability requirement means in practice that workers cannot plan their leisure time in advance. Working timetables are always being changed due to the constant lack of staff. Workers are often informed of changes the day before and sometimes even the same day. In the case of absences or additional work the working plan is modified from one day to the next. The practice of keeping employment at the minimum is common among supermarkets and hypermarkets, and because of the high turnover and absences, changes in working time schedules are the rule. The Labour Inspectorate regards this as one of the main causes of infringements in the retail sector. According to the law, workers should have stable working hours and in case of changes must be informed in advance.

A new category at risk: middle management

The human resources director drew our attention to a vulnerable group that has never aroused public interest, middle management:

> The real problem is middle management overtime, since in many shops there is no record of working time, but only a signature on a list. ... I've always thought that middle management in a hypermarket is a "handicapped elite". Everybody says "that's cool, you're a manager", but in fact there is such a lot of work and extreme stress connected to it ... Availability in the case of managers ... means that they must always be available ... even if they are not at work and a problem comes up it's their fault because they haven't organized things properly.

No recorded overtime in the case of middle management can lead to the paradoxical situation that their real hourly rate of pay is the same or lower than that of a general worker. Middle management often work more than 12 hours a day, 6 or 7 days a week. The stress is permanent because of pressure from higher management, the benchmarking of their activities and the high turnover of workers, whereas wages are just over the national average. An experienced human resources director earns less than PLN 4,000 a month (EUR 1,000).

Health and safety regulations: the Labour Inspectorate between employers and employees – different truths

Beyond low wages and unsocial working hours, health and safety in the retail sector is a real issue. This concerns above all the lack of equipment for lifting heavy weights. In the course of the media's campaign against health and safety violations in hypermarkets, one journalist used a comparison which caught the imagination of those unaware of working conditions in the retail sector: "*Female shop assistants as Hercules*" (*Gazeta Wyborcza*, 2 May 2005–3 May 2005, "Sprzedawczyni jak Hercules"). This problem of workers being required to exceed restrictions on lifting heavy weights is particularly urgent, according to the trade union. Our informant said that it is still possible to see women having to push 400-kg trolleys instead of the 80 kg laid down in the law. On the other hand, a human resources manager who does not approve such extreme violations drew our attention to the fact that the 80-kg limit for women is unrealistic:

> Trolleys alone weigh 50 kg and so 80 kg would only allow on top of that, say, 30 packets of sugar. It is not much for a woman. So the limits are not reasonable at all. ... Luckily the inspectors have common sense ... They do not measure everything ... We even started talking about having to serve notice to all the women and employ only men. Rules of this kind may lead to such extreme situations.

She added that if the Labour Inspectorate interpreted all the rules to the letter they would be forced to close the shop. However, such "common sense" rule interpretation is not favoured by the trade unions.

Conclusion

Hypermarkets in Poland are often regarded as employers which seek to circumvent the law, exploiting their workers and taking advantage of the high level of unemployment to offer low wages and bad working conditions. In fact, only part of that picture is true. On the one hand, hypermarkets, mainly because of their fear of the media, try to respect the law, even if working time violations are frequent. On the other hand, they offer very low wages and precarious work contracts. Because of this, they face very high turnover which, according to the human resources director we met, is a permanent source of disruption. In large cities, such as Warsaw, where unemployment is lower than in the countryside, hypermarkets have a problem in filling their vacancies. The wages offered are not sufficient to provide for the needs of the family. Workers in hypermarkets belong among the working poor. Because of the low wages, this kind of job is mainly for people with a supplementary income, such as a pension or supplementary job, or young people still living with their parents. Beyond low wages, unsocial and unstable working hours are a matter of concern.

Because of the low wages, those working at BIG come mainly from small towns around Warsaw where housing costs are lower. They often commute for hours. This travel time, associated with flexible, night and weekend working, tends to destabilize family life. This must be regarded as one of the main issues in the sector and constitutes a barrier to the employment of people with family responsibilities.

Poland Case Study 3: An extreme employer–employee coping strategy (cleaning sector, Warsaw)

A negotiated illegal route

The case of the Small Company (SC) illustrates the situation of SMEs in Poland. In SMEs labour law is often less important than local "agreements" between employees and employers. Employers often breach the law, impose their rules on their employees and frequently negotiate illegal strategies with them. These local agreements aim mainly at avoiding the payment of social contributions. But by going down this illegal route employers and employees put themselves at risk. Employers risk inspection; employees run the risk of a low retirement pension and a lack of social insurance.

Small enterprises: when the law does not apply

The Labour Inspectorate conducted several checks between 2001 and 2003 at small enterprises employing fewer than 20 workers. The main problems concern health and safety breaches and lack of working time records. In 70 per cent of cases, occupational risk is not correctly evaluated; at 40 per cent of enterprises there is no obligatory health and safety training before starting work; and in a third of companies, electrical equipment and wiring were not properly used. In comparison with the Labour Inspectorate's findings the situation of the employees at SC in our case study is rather positive and they did not mention any concern in terms of health and safety. Compared to other sectors, such as construction, transport, and so on, the cleaning sector is less dangerous. Moreover, all employees had participated in health and safety training before starting work. Nevertheless, the employer's duties of course do not cover illegal workers or people employed on the basis of a civil contract, who at SC constitute more than 70 per cent of all workers.

The second problem mentioned by the Labour Inspectorate in their report on small enterprises– lack of reliable working time records – is also a serious problem at SC, especially for men, who work extremely hard during the winter when they are responsible for snow clearance. It is interesting to note that even when SC was inspected by the Labour Inspectorate, the latter did not question the falsified working time records presented by the employer.

Generally speaking, workers at small companies like SC are more vulnerable than those at large enterprises, such as those described in Case Studies 1 and 2. The sentence "*the law is generally respected*" does not apply to their situation. In contrast to large enterprises, small ones are less frequently inspected. Moreover, the high level of unemployment makes employees keen to hang on to their jobs, so they are less likely to report offences committed by their employer. Notifications of law-breaking are more likely if there is a conflict between employer and employee, for instance following a dismissal.

The flexibility cocktail: labour contracts, civil contracts, no contracts...

At SC there are three categories of workers. The first consists of five employees with a permanent labour contract. They have worked for the SC for quite a long time and are called *trusted workers* by the boss. All of them have a legal contract but from time to time some of them ask the employer to dismiss them on paper: they continue working without a contract and at the same time receive unemployment benefit from the local labour office. In the second group there are 10 workers who most of the time are employed illegally: because of the danger of labour inspections they sign a daily civil contract related to a specific task (*umowa o dzieło*); if there is no inspection this civil contract is destroyed, but if there is, it gives the labour relationship the appearance of legality. Workers with civil contracts are the most vulnerable group since they have no social security or other benefits which come from labour contracts (such as prospects of a retirement pension after a number of years of work). The last group – four people receiving state pensions – do not want to work legally at all because they would lose their benefits. Their social insurance is paid by the state because they are retired.

Extreme work conditions organized in accordance with seasonal needs
In summer all employees work about 8 hours a day. Eight men start at 6 in the morning and finish at 2 p.m. in the afternoon. Eleven women begin at 7 a.m. and end at 3 p.m. They work in different housing cooperatives scattered throughout Warsaw and its suburbs. Tasks are divided between men and women. Men work outside (sweeping up, watering and mowing lawns) and in the garages. Women work inside on the staircases (sweeping up and cleaning the floor). In winter, men work much longer hours: according to the contracts signed with the housing cooperatives, the Small Company is responsible for snow clearance from 6 a.m. until 10 p.m. When it snows, men can work as much as 16 hours a day. Overtime is not paid because there is no additional money from clients for the winter season. But extra hours of work are recorded and compensated in the form of days off during spring and summer.

As already mentioned, holidays are generally respected, even for people not employed on the basis of a labour contract. If one worker is on holiday, the others are responsible for doing their work. This form of work organization excludes the possibility of frequent absenteeism. One worker who was asked whether it was difficult to take a day off answered there was no problem, but in practice it was exceptional. *Are they often ill? –* we asked the boss. *– No. Not even after this hard winter* [snowfalls lasted until the end of March]. *Everybody was complaining but everybody came to work.*

Minimizing official wage payments?
All those working 8 hours a day at the SC have the same real incomes, paid without delay: about PLN 1,200 net (EUR 300). But legally employed workers have in their contract the minimum wage (in 2006, PLN 899.10 gross – EUR 225) or part of it if they are officially employed half time: the rest is given "under the table". According to the boss it is the only possible solution. He does not want to distinguish between those with contracts and those without: it would lead to tensions between the workers. What matters is their work. The rule is: if they do the same work, they earn the same.

The Small Company's wage system differs from that of the Nickel Group or BIG. The Nickel Group's strategy is to find a cheaper workforce for lower-paid contracts (former policemen and military men on pensions, disabled people who agree to work for less) or to keep down costs by using civil contracts. BIG offers very low wages but with a labour contract. For BIG, the recruitment costs are not important and even if the high turnover is a problem, BIG copes with that and sticks to its low-wages policy. SC chooses to pay people more than the minimum wage, but saves on employment costs (labour contract, civil contract or no contract at all) and on official income declaration (actual income is never declared). Three factors can explain these differences. First, as a large and protected enterprise Nickel is often inspected and cannot run the risk of illegal employment; the same applies to BIG. Second, it is difficult to find people to work in the cleaning sector because it is demanding, physical work with low prestige. There is no potential cheap workforce for cleaning, unlike in the case of hypermarkets (students, who pay less social contributions, look down on cleaning work and most of the pensioners who work at SC live outside Warsaw and cannot earn less because of transport costs). Finally, work at SC requires cooperation between employees working on different sites (for instance, in case of absence, holiday or snow clearance), which would be more difficult if there were visible differences in incomes.

An employer at risk
In the case of SC the employer is not in a much better situation than his workers. Competition in the cleaning sector forces him to break the law. According to him, if he obeyed the law he would not be able to win any tenders. In fact everybody in the sector is breaking the law. According to his calculations he would have to get four times as much from his clients to employ everyone legally at the current level of social contributions and other expenses. He considers this situation extremely stressful, but sees no prospect of improvement since no client will agree to increase its costs. Despite all the difficulties, relations between the employer and his employees are reasonable: the two sides seem to understand one another's situation. SC is typical of those small firms where the employer works with the employees, suffering the same bad working conditions and not earning much more than his employees on an hourly-rate basis. The boss does not hesitate to expose himself to risk (say, by employing somebody illegally) if it benefits the worker. Often the demand for illegal work or fake dismissal comes from the employees themselves. He also tries to provide his workers with paid leave, even when they are not legally employed. His positive attitude towards his workers may be also caused by the fact that it is difficult in these conditions to find people to do such hard, physical work.

Conclusion
SC is typical of how small companies circumvent the law because of competition. This creates a vicious circle where illegality calls for more illegality and offers no chance to whose who want to respect the law. In the case of SC, the employer does not respect the law but does offer his workers basic rights.

The most important thing in the "deal" between the employer and the employees is the level of net wages. Everybody has a very short-term horizon, employees and employers alike. Employees are well treated and paid on time, but are very vulnerable, notably toward illness, lay-off and firm bankruptcy. Only those with a labour contract and retired people have social insurance. Moreover, this paternalistic management comes at a price for employees. As in their situation no written rules structure the labour relationship they often have to ask for things that other workers regard as a right, such as paid holidays. By asking they put themselves in a position in which their hands are tied when the employer demands unplanned overtime or unpaid help. In an enterprise like SC there is no workers' collective, but solidarity exists between the employees and the employer which hinders legal proceedings in case of what could be regarded as breaches of the agreement. For example, a worker who has been dismissed or wanted his worker status recognized by the Labour Inspectorate or a court would not be able to count on the testimony of the other workers. In fact, beyond the equal treatment of workers (apart from the privileged "trusted workers") the individualization of the labour relationship must be regarded as a source of vulnerability for workers who thereby only benefit from rights the employer accepts.

Conclusion

These three case studies illustrate the main sources of vulnerability in Poland:

- low wages
- long and unsocial working hours
- precariousness of the labour relationship
- poor social protection

Low wages lead to an increase in the number of working poor and put workers in a position where they have to accept legal or illegal solutions to increase their net income. This is the case of overtime and unsocial hours as in the case of Nickel, civil contract or moonlighting in the case of SC and Nickel. It is interesting to note that even respect for the legal framework does not give workers total protection (as at Nickel and BIG). The main source of concern is that part of the working population is accumulating these sources of vulnerability. These people, as shown in the first part of this chapter, are the most vulnerable as regards unemployment and inactivity: low-skilled workers, young and older workers, women with young children. But the case of BIG shows that vulnerability goes well beyond this population and concerns also people with a high level of education and experience, as in the case of middle management and even small employers, as in the case of SC. These people are subjected to very long and unsocial working hours and permanent stress. A Polish sociologist wrote 10 years ago that "in Poland there are people with time and people with money". Ten years later this is still true, but one must add that for some people having money also comes at the cost of social protection and job security.

REFERENCES

Brodowski, M., and E. Flaszyńska. 2006. *Raport z działalności agencji zatrudnienia w 2005 r.* Warsaw: Ministerstwo Pracy i Polityki Społecznej.

Bukowski, M. 2005. *Employment in Poland 2005.* Warsaw: Ministry of Economy and Labour.

CBOS. 2004a. *Polacy o swoim zatrudnieniu.* Warsaw: CBOS.

———. 2004b. *Praca jako wartość.* Warsaw: CBOS.

———. 2005. *Oceny sytuacji materialnej.* Warsaw: CBOS.

———. 2006. *Polityka państwa wobec rodziny oraz dyskryminacja w miejscu pracy kobiet w ciąży i matek małych dzieci.* Warsaw: CBOS.

Główny Urząd Statystyczny. 2004. *Sytuacja gospodarstw domowych w 2003 r.w świetle wyników badań budżetów gospodarstw domowych.* Warsaw: GUS.

———. 2005a. *Sytuacja gospodarstw domowych w 2004 r.w świetle wyników badań budżetów gospodarstw domowych.* Warsaw: GUS.

———. 2005b. *Typowe i nietypowe formy zatrudnienia w Polsce w 2004. r.* Warsaw: GUS.

Golinowska, S. (ed.). 2004. *W trosce o pracę: Raport o rozwoju społecznym. Polska 2004.* Warsaw: UNDP, CASE.

Góra, M. 2004. Trwale wysokie bezrobocie w Polsce. Refleksie, próba częściowego wyjaśnienia i kilka propozycji. In M. Boni (ed.), *Elastyczny rynek pracy w Polsce: jak sprostać temu wyzwaniu? Zeszyty BRE Bank-CASE, 73.* Warsaw: CASE, 123–44.

Graniewska, D., and B. Balcerzak-Paradowska. 2003. Praca zawodowa – rodzina w opiniach respondentek, in B. Balcerzak-Paradowska (ed.), *Praca kobiet w sektorze prywatnym – szanse i bariery.* Warsaw: IPiSS, 123–52.

OECD. 2003. *Transforming disability into ability: Policies to promote work and income security for disabled people.* Paris.

Portet, S. 2004. La politique de la 'conciliation' entre vie professionnelle et vie familiale en Pologne. Le cas du travail à temps partiel (1970–2003). *Nouvelles questions féministes*, n° Vol. 23, 49-70.

Portet, S. 2005. Poland: Circumventing the law or fully deregulating, in D. Vaughan-Whitehead (ed.), *Working and employment conditions in new Member States: Convergence or diversity?* Geneva: ILO, 273–338.

Szylko-Skoczny, M. 2004. *Polityka społeczna wobec bezrobocia w Trzeciej Rzeczpospolitej.* Warsaw: Instytut Polityki Społecznej UW.

10. Romania: Labour market under external pressure

Alina Surubaru

10.1 INTRODUCTION

Romania has been under increasing pressure during its accession process to catch up in terms of both economic development and harmonization with EU regulations. At the same time, impressive flows of inward investment have been the most influential factors in terms of working and employment conditions, not always positively, whilst Romania has begun to be confronted by a serious emigration problem.

Romania and EU enlargement

It was finally in 2000 that the first encouraging statements were made about Romania: "after years of disappointing Romanian economic performance, macroeconomic trends and prospects ... improved ... as investment accelerated and private consumption boomed, pulled by rising real wages and income" (European Commission, 2002). The privatization process reached its final stage and Romanian exports to the EU grew significantly, particularly in clothing. At the same time, EU enlargement became a key issue in Romania. The political agenda was strongly influenced by this process and the government worked hard to implement new laws to facilitate Romania's integration in the EU.

More than ever, the public debate is focusing on working and employment conditions. In 2003, Parliament passed the first post-communist labour regulations and since then, labour legislation has been actively discussed by various social actors (political parties, business organizations, trade unions, lawyers, economists, and so on). On 5 July 2005, after long discussions with the most representative business organizations and trade unions, the government modified the Labour Code. But some business organizations are not entirely satisfied, considering this law "far too generous", and continue to lobby for additional changes.

The constantly changing legal framework is an important characteristic of the Romanian economy, particularly during the last decade. Paradoxically, EU enlargement has helped reinforce the instability of the legal framework: on the one hand, the EU aims to stabilize the Romanian political and economic situation by imposing a coherent legal framework, the *acquis communautaire*; on the other hand, the plethora of new laws, promulgated according to the *acquis communautaire*, can in the short term generate more uncertainty. In the case of the Labour Code, the ambiguity concerning part-time contracts, civil contracts and working time has often been underlined in the public debate, but its effects have not been fully analysed, either by the authorities or by researchers.

Table 10.1 Elements of the world of work, Romania

Elements	Item	Trends	Risks/Exposed groups
Employment status	Self-employment	Stable	Men living in rural area, accumulating two jobs
	Contributing family workers	Decreasing	Women with low education living in rural areas
	Temporary work	Not developed	Young people in agriculture, retail, energy and construction
	Part time	Decreasing	Women from rural areas; young people
	Underemployment	Slightly decreasing	Young people
Wages	Real wages	Increasing	Lowest-paid workers in agriculture, retail, garment manufacturing and hotels and restaurants
	Wage inequalities	Increasing	Lowest-paid workers; women
Working time	Long hours	Increasing	Employers in service; Self-employed in agriculture; Employees in constructions, hotels-restaurants and retail
	Overtime	Not paid	All sectors
Occupational safety	Injured at work	Decreasing	Employees in coal mining
	Satisfaction with working environment	Decreasing	Employees in coal mining, manufacturing, construction, transportation

Access to training	Technological training	Very low	All sectors
Work and family	Work flexibility	–[1]	Women; young people
	Parental leave	–	Women
Social dialogue	Trade union membership	Decreasing	Young people; employees in retail, public administration and garment industry
	Collective agreement	Widespread	Employees in public administration, financial intermediation, garment industry and hotels
	Social conflicts	Decreasing	Employees in coal mining, transportation, energy, chemical industry, and garment industry

The influence of foreign capital flows and labour migration

Against this general background, the main labour market trends are as follows: demographic decline, gradual development of the service sector, regional discrepancies in employment and increasing real wages. As a matter of fact, Romania appears nowadays to be under pressure from two types of mobility: *"immigration" of foreign capital* and *emigration of low-paid workers*. As risk progressively diminished from 2000 and production costs remained very low, many foreign investors came to Romania and contributed actively to the improvement of national economic results. In spite of this, regional discrepancies in employment were maintained and workers living in rural areas, especially young people and women with low education, suffered particularly. As a result, migration abroad became a significant phenomenon and reinforced the general trend of demographic decline.

Demographic decline has been extensively analysed by Romanian statisticians who have repeatedly pointed out the ageing of the active population. However, demographic decline is also related to the decline of industrial employment in the late 1990s. While 4.7 million persons worked in the industrial sector in 1990 (mining and quarrying, manufacturing, electric and thermal energy), in 2003 there were only 2 million. In 1997, the privatization pro-

---

1. There is only one available statistical survey about reconciliation between work and family life.

cess accelerated and, as a result, large masses of industrial workers were laid off. Some of these workers left the cities and moved to rural areas, others migrated to western Europe (Italy, Spain and Greece). When the Schengen visa was no longer necessary for European travel, external migration became the best way of escaping poverty: in 2002, the active population decreased by 7.4 per cent in urban areas and 16.3 per cent in rural areas.

According to the data made available by the National Labour Office for Labour Migration, around 45,000 persons migrated legally in 2004, with another 8,300 being processed during the first quarter of 2005 (Ghinararu, 2005a: 23). However, no statistics are available concerning migration abroad, since migrants generally leave the country as tourists, set up more or less temporarily in destination countries and then work in the informal sector (house cleaning, baby sitting, elderly care, construction, restaurants, and so on).

External migration has had a strong impact on employment in agriculture. In 2000, agriculture was the main employment sector, with 41.4 per cent of total employment, and representing 23 per cent of those of working age. In 2003, it represented only 34.7 per cent of total employment and, for the first time since 1989, the service sector became the main sector of employment (35.7 per cent of total employment).

Despite this decline, Romanian agriculture, dominated by subsistence production, remains an important sector of the economy. In terms of occupational status, agriculture concentrates the bulk of the self-employed (peasant–farmers/proprietors and contributing family workers).

The last important trend in the Romanian labour market concerns increasing real wages. In 2000, an OECD report criticized the Romanian government's arbitrary decision to increase wages (OECD, 2000: 14), especially in the public sector. However, this has been justified by economic growth, sustained by a dynamic private sector. Moreover, from a 40 per cent rise in December 2000 as against December 1999, inflation then fell by around 10 per cent every year, finally reaching a single-digit figure for the first time in 14 years, at 9.5 per cent in December 2004 as against December 2003.

In June 2006, average nominal net wages were RON[2] 835 per month, which represented an increase of 15.7 per cent on the average nominal net wage of June 2005.[3] Despite this trend, the Romanian real wage is one of the lowest in Eastern Europe and, as already mentioned, many western European companies, especially from manufacturing and computer engineering, are relocating or subcontracting there. As the second part of this chapter will explain, the impact of foreign investors on employment has been mixed. On

---

2. From 1 July 2005, the domestic currency the leu (ROL) was revalued and 10,000 lei in circulation on that date were exchanged for 1 new leu (RON). In January 2006, RON 1 was worth EUR 3.6.

3. *Press Release*, No. 40, 7 August 2006, Bucharest: National Institute of Statistics.

Figure 10.1 Civil employment, by main activity of national economy, Romania, 1998–2003

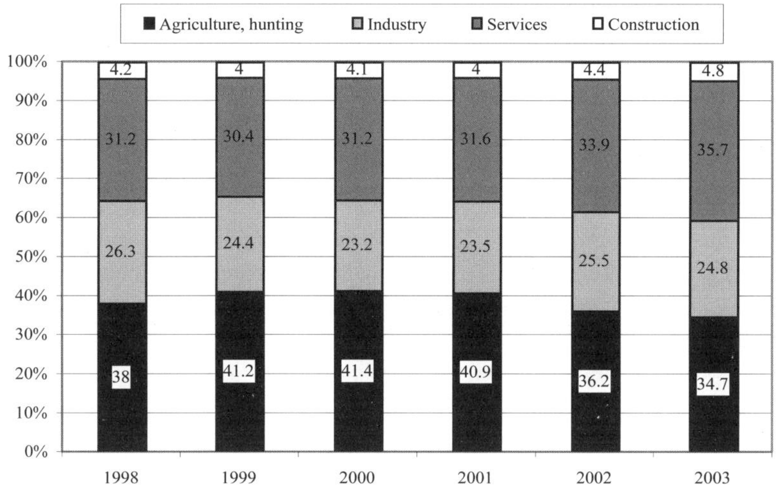

Legend: ■ Agriculture, hunting ☐ Industry ■ Services ☐ Construction

Data by year:

Year	Agriculture	Industry	Services	Construction
1998	38	26.3	31.2	4.2
1999	41.2	24.4	30.4	4
2000	41.4	23.2	31.2	4.1
2001	40.9	23.5	31.6	4
2002	36.2	25.5	33.9	4.4
2003	34.7	24.8	35.7	4.8

Source: National Institute of Statistics, 2004

the one hand, these companies have improved working conditions by offering their employees better training (see case study 3) or a safer working environment (see Case Study 2). On the other hand, employees began to be aware that these large enterprises which possess significant resources do not pay them fairly – on the contrary. Thus, Romanian workers feel justified in mobilizing for better wages (see Case Study 2) or leaving the company in order to seek more money elsewhere (see Case Study 1).

Low wages represent the most important source of vulnerability for Romanian workers. When combined with other sources of vulnerability (lack of social dialogue, insecure working environment, and so on), low wages become a real trap, especially for agricultural and manufacturing workers.

10.2 EMPLOYMENT STATUS: INCREASED VARIETY OF CONTRACTS

Today, the employed and the self-employed represent the dominant types of employment. Since 2000, the proportion of self-employed in total employment has remained relatively stable, whereas the percentage of employees in total employment has increased substantially, by 6.1 per cent.

In the third quarter of 2005, 63.5 per cent of working persons were employed, 20.0 per cent were self-employed, 14.7 per cent were contributing family workers and 1.7 per cent were employers (National Institute of

Statistics, 2005a and b). Women made up the highest proportion (68.4 per cent) of the contributing family workers category and represented 29.0 per cent of self-employed persons.

As regards distribution of employment by level of education, 55.4 per cent of employees were high-school graduates, including vocational school, 12.7 per cent were university graduates and 4.7 per cent were graduates of technical schools; persons with a low level of education (primary, gymnasium and no education) represented 27.2 per cent. Most working persons with a low level of education lived in rural areas (83.9 per cent) and carried out economic activities as self-employed (42.5 per cent) or contributing family workers (36.0 per cent). Among persons with a low level of education, women worked more frequently than men as contributing family workers (26.0 per cent as against 9.7 per cent).

Self-employed and contributing family workers are mainly involved in subsistence agriculture and for this reason are rather excluded from the classical labour market. Women with a low level of education and young people (15–24 years) are particularly vulnerable and, as a result, they often migrate to western Europe to find better job opportunities (Ghinararu, 2005a: 22–26).

As compared to the self-employed and contributing family workers, employees benefit from more secure employment. Unlimited contracts prevail (97 per cent) and "black work" represents only 1.3 per cent. However, in order to increase the flexibility of the Romanian labour market, the recent work regulations introduced a greater variety of work contracts: fixed-term contracts, part-time contracts and temporary agency contracts.

The law states that individual employment agreements for a determinate period cannot be concluded for more than 24 months. The period can be extended no more than three consecutive times, and the accumulated period cannot exceed 24 months. For the time being, fixed-term contracts are not widespread. In the third quarter of 2005, 1.84 per cent of employees had a fixed-term contract, of whom 34 per cent had a fixed-term contract of 0–6 months and 29 per cent had a fixed-term contract of 7–12 months. Most were young people (35.56 per cent were aged 25–34 years old and 26.9 per cent 15–24 years old) and worked for private companies in agriculture, retail, energy and construction. The highest number of fixed-term contracts were signed by skilled workers in agriculture (13.3 per cent) and retail workers (6.6 per cent). Nevertheless, the number of fixed-term contracts of skilled workers in agriculture significantly decreased from 22.3 per cent in 2002 to 13.3 per cent in 2005. Women working in these two sectors are more vulnerable as they signed fixed-term contracts more often than men.

The law is more ambiguous on part-time work than fixed-term contracts. Before 2003, part-time work was usually governed by a civil contract (a formal agreement between an employer and an authorized legal person).

Although the law has created a new type of part-time labour contract, it does not mention what should happen in relation to existing civil contracts. In practice, the Labour Inspectorate has encouraged the substitution of civil contracts by part-time contracts (Stoicescu, 2003: 17), and as a result civil contracts fell from 1.1 per cent of employed persons in 2002 to 0.3 per cent in 2005.

Despite the introduction of the part-time contract, the percentage of persons working part time declined from 17.3 per cent in the third quarter of 2000 to 10.5 per cent in the third quarter of 2005. Most of these persons (87.8 per cent) came from rural areas. As compared with other sectors, agriculture, construction, retail and transportation make more regular use of part-time contracts.

Most part-timers (70.3 per cent) work a regular number of hours daily. Another 11 per cent work fewer days per week but with a number of daily hours equal to full-time work (National Institute of Statistics, 2004a). Generally speaking, persons in part-time jobs could not find full-time work (49.8 per cent), while 36.1 per cent did not want a full-time job. Surprisingly, a willingness to work more hours was expressed by only 5.6 per cent of employed persons. Most were men (69.9 per cent) and living in rural areas (56.4 per cent); in this category, 17.1 per cent were actually seeking another job.

Concerning gender differentiation, women worked part time more frequently than men did. In 2000, 18.5 per cent of women worked part time as against 14.2 per cent of men. However, in 2004 the situation changed and 11.25 per cent of women worked part time as against 10 per cent of men. Because statistics do not explicitly study this population across time, it is difficult to explain the decline of part-time work. One can only assume that migration abroad is a partial explanation: some recent sociological studies confirm that the rural population is the most affected by the rush towards western Europe (Bleahu and Anghel, 2005: 160–94).

With regard to underemployment, in 2005 this phenomenon affected 9.1 per cent of working persons, which represented a slight decrease from the previous year (9.8 per cent). In 2003, 8.2 per cent of working persons declared that their job did not correspond to their vocational training. The categories of occupation most affected by underemployment are agriculture, retail and services. In 2005, after an increase in 2004, underemployment of workers in agriculture declined by 3 per cent and remained stable for retail and services.

Young people are the most underemployed category (16 per cent of persons belonging to the age group 15–24 as against 7 per cent of persons aged over 50). The percentage is constantly growing: in 2003, 12.5 per cent of youngsters were underemployed and in 2004, 15.3 per cent. The survey presented in the second part sought to explain this phenomenon, making the assumption that students work to finance their studies and more easily accept jobs that do not correspond to their training or qualifications. The results confirmed this hypothesis and demonstrated that for the graduates under study underemployment concerned only their first jobs.

In conclusion, with regard to employment status there are several categories of vulnerable workers. First, self-employed and contributing family workers in the agricultural sector have more insecure employment than employees. Within these categories, women with a low level of education and young people aged 15–24 are particularly at risk. Second, although fixed-term contracts are not widespread, young people belonging to the age groups 15–24 and 25–34 more frequently have fixed-term contracts than other age groups. Moreover, youngsters are the most underemployed category of workers and thus accumulate risk. Finally, despite the recent decline of part-time work, women from rural areas represent a vulnerable group because they encounter real difficulties in finding a full-time job and, in consequence, migrate to western Europe.

10.3 INCREASING WAGE DIFFERENTIATION

Like other eastern European countries, former socialist Romania had very low income differentiation. In terms of monetary income, an engineer did not earn much more than a skilled worker. Ten years after the fall of the communist regime, the situation dramatically changed as income differentiation sharpened and real wages decreased progressively. This trend stopped only in 2001 when real wages began to increase slightly (see Table 10.2) (National Institute of Statistics, 2004b). In June 2006, real wages increased by 8 per cent as against June 2005 and thus the average nominal net wage reached RON 835. However, workers on low incomes remain particularly vulnerable and, despite government efforts to establish a minimum wage (Wage Act, 1991), this population group has suffered most from the transition's economic problems.

Information made available by the European Commission and the Romanian government suggests that wage differentials between sectors increased during the 1990s (the standard deviation of inter-industry wage dif-

Table 10.2 Net nominal and real wages, Romania, 1995–2004 (1990 = 100%)

	1995	2000	2001	2002	2003	2004
Indices of net nominal wage	6 219.8	66 412.2	93 741.8	117 640.5	150 253	185 854
Indices of real wage	66.5	59.4	62.4	63.9	70.8	78.3

ferentials increased by three times, from 16.2 in 1990 to 48.9 in 1998) (European Commission, 2002: 9). Today, financial intermediation registers wages more than twice the national average. Coal mining, telecommunications and energy all have nominal average net wages more than 50 per cent higher than the national average. On the other hand, several sectors have wages below the national average: hotels and restaurants (–31.3 per cent), retail (–26.7 per cent), agriculture (–19.4 per cent) and health care (–13 per cent).

By type of ownership, wages in the public sector remain much higher than in the private sector. In 2004, wages in the public sector were 23.9 per cent higher than the national average, which represented an increase of 23.8 per cent as against 2003. This situation may be partly due to the under-reporting of wages by private companies. As Case Study 3 illustrates, many employers declare paying the minimum wage in order to reduce their social contributions. On top of that, however, they pay employees so-called "envelope payments" which of course do not show up in the statistics.

Income varies significantly by both sex and region. In 2005, women earned 16.1 per cent less than men, regardless of ownership type: women's net wage was 91.8 per cent of the national average, all sectors included. The highest discrepancies between men and women were detected in retail (28.2 per cent), manufacturing (26.2 per cent) and hotels and restaurants (22.7 per cent). By regions, in 2005 the average wage was below the national average in 31 out of 42 counties. On the other hand, in Bucharest, the average wage was 23.7 per cent higher than the national average. However, income variation by regions has a limited impact on internal migration because the lowest-paid workers prefer to leave the country altogether rather than try to find a better job elsewhere in Romania.

One surprising reason for income differentiation, underlined by some Romanian researchers (Popescu, 2003: 35–37), is the luncheon voucher. Luncheon vouchers benefit from particularly favourable tax provisions (Law 142/1998) which allow employers to make savings on their social contributions. Luncheon vouchers can be issued to employees up to a value of EUR 30 per month and represent a common way of paying in supermarkets. When companies do not offer them, workers on low wages are hardest hit affected. For instance, the garment workers from Case Study 1 saw their incomes fall by as much as 50 per cent when their employer decided to cut luncheon vouchers and travel reimbursement.

These data describe a rather paradoxical situation. While real wages are increasing and the service sector is booming, a large part of the workforce is not benefitting from economic growth as their incomes remain very low. Although trade unions intervene frequently on this subject, especially by annually negotiating the national collective agreement and by mobilizing reg-

ularly for better wages, their demands are not always met. When social dialogue is absent, workers are even more at risk and, as a result, low wages
become the main reason for leaving a job or the country.

10.4 LONG HOURS

In 2003, the Labour Code established a weekly working time of 40 hours for
adults, and 30 hours for teenagers. For adults, the maximum weekly working
time (including overtime) is 48 hours. Supplementary hours, therefore, cannot
exceed 8 hours per week, and the employer is required to inform employees
in advance and in writing. There are 20 days' minimum annual paid holidays.

The Labour Code allows workers to have several contracts and, as a result,
working time can be accumulated. For instance, Madam Escu may have an
unlimited contract with company X and a part-time contract with company Y.
She may work from 8 a.m. to 4 p.m. for company X and then from 7 p.m. to
10 p.m. for company Y. Her weekly working time would be 55 hours but still
she would not be breaking the law.

In the debate on accumulated working time a number of Romanian experts
pointed out a crucial anomaly: a person could also have several contracts for
the same period of time (Grigorie-Lacrita, 2005: 15–27): on paper, Madam
Escu could work from 8 a.m. to 4 p.m. for both companies. In other words,
this situation facilitates unjustified fraud and corruption, as one person cannot
be in two separate places at the same time.

Nevertheless, the share of persons with several jobs remains low. During
July–September 2005, only 3.3 per cent of employed persons had secondary
jobs, a fall of 3 per cent against the previous quarter. Most of them lived in
rural areas (80.8 per cent), worked in agriculture (88.9 per cent) and were men
(64 per cent). They generally had a first job as a regular employee and were
self-employed as a secondary occupation: only 4.1 per cent of these persons
were employees for their second occupation. The average working time in the
secondary occupation was 15.6 hours per week.

However, since 1996 the number of persons working more than 40 hours
has grown constantly and as a consequence long hours became an important
vector of vulnerability in Romania, especially because overtime is not usually paid.[4] While in the third quarter of 2005 the average working week was
41.3 hours, the number of persons who worked more than 40 hours per week
was very high (26.3 per cent). Within this, 18.9 per cent worked between 41

---

4. There are no relevant statistics regarding unpaid overtime. The survey described in the second part of this chapter, however, provides some information about this major problem of the
Romanian labour market.

and 50 hours, 6.1 per cent worked between 51 and 60 hours and 1.3 per cent worked more than 60 hours.

Among persons working full time, employers constituted the highest proportion of persons working more than 40 hours per week (63.3 per cent), followed by the self-employed (48.3 per cent), contributing family workers (37.5 per cent) and employees (22.8 per cent).

In 2004, the longest working week was recorded for employers working in services (48.4 hours) (National Institute of Statistics, 2004a: 32). In 2005, the longest average working weeks were recorded in construction (44 hours per week), agriculture (43.6 hours per week), hotels and restaurants (43 hours per week) and retail (42.4 hours per week).

With regard to location, persons from rural areas work longer than those from urban areas. Thus, in 2005, 28.6 per cent of persons living in rural areas worked more than 40 hours per week as against 23 per cent of persons living in urban areas.

On the subject of atypical work (working evenings, nights and weekends), recent surveys indicated that in the third quarter of 2005, 64.5 per cent of workers were affected, an increase of 4.7 per cent from the previous quarter. The most striking outcome of these surveys is that 93 per cent of atypical employment included work on Saturdays. Shift work is recurrent in mining (48.7 per cent), hotels and restaurants (48.6 per cent), health care (42.4 per cent), transport (34.3 per cent), manufacturing (29.8 per cent) and retail (24.4 per cent).

To summarize, with regard to working time, several categories of workers are at risk. Together with employers from the service sector, the self-employed and contributing workers in agriculture accumulate the longest working hours. Moreover, employees from construction, hotels and restaurants and retail are particularly exposed to stress because overtime is not always paid.

10.5 OCCUPATIONAL HEALTH AND SAFETY: GAPS BETWEEN SECTORS

Theoretically, Romanian legislation on occupational health and safety is already in harmony with EU legislation and lays down all the relevant occupational health and safety requirements. In reality, occupational safety and health is not always a priority for employers and several industrial sectors still possess old equipment that represents a real danger to workers. Coal mining and textile manufacturing are particularly affected by this problem since investment in new technologies is expensive and these economic activities are no longer competitive. In addition, working conditions in agriculture appear to be particularly tough as this sector is acutely lacking in modern equipment (for instance, the majority of peasants/farmers do not even possess a tractor).

On the other hand, significant sectors of Romanian economy have made efforts to improve occupational safety and, as a result, European standards are now being implemented. First, there is a recent trend of introducing lunch breaks, and employers, especially foreign ones, offer their employees meals at company canteens. Second, although garment producers continue to delay the installation of clean and sanitary conditions in their factories, they are already introducing new machines, better lighting and air conditioning (see Case Study 1). Tyre manufacturing is another example of successful upgrading because its modernization has engendered a significant fall in the number of those injured at work (see Case Study 2).

At national level, the number of those injured at work has also fallen in recent years. The total number of injuries fell from 48 in 1999 to 28 in 2003. Nevertheless, the number of fatalities did not decrease significantly (445 persons in 1999, 414 in 2003). The highest rate of labour injuries was still registered in coal mining (22.8 per cent) (www.insse.ro).

With regard to work discomfort, in 2005 more than half of all employees declared that their working conditions were not satisfactory. As compared with the previous year, the percentage of persons suffering from heat, cold, humidity, dust and painful postures remained relatively stable, while the percentage of persons complaining about dirtiness, noise and uncomfortable postures slightly increased (see Table 10.3) (National Institute of Statistics. n.d.).

In 2005, working conditions in mining were the most uncomfortable: 37.1 per cent suffered from heat, 21.1 per cent from cold, 15.3 per cent from excessive humidity, 56.6 per cent from dust and pollution, 35.9 per cent from dirtiness, 36.5 per cent from noise, 10.6 per cent from painful postures and 26.6 per cent from uncomfortable postures. Manufacturing, construction and transportation were other sectors characterized by uncomfortable working conditions.

Table 10.3 Employees experiencing uncomfortable working conditions, Romania, 2002–05

	Heat	Cold	Humidity	Dust	Dirt	Noise	Painful postures	Uncomfortable postures
2002	30.6	10.8	3.5	18.8	12.0	18.6	1.9	14.0
2003	38.0	13.8	3.7	18.2	12.7	17.7	2.9	14.1
2004	31.0	12.6	3.8	21.1	11.4	18.5	2.2	13.5
2005	30.5	12.3	4.1	20.7	13.3	19.8	2.6	15.0

The percentage of workers not satisfied with a number of aspects of their working conditions (stability of employment, working time, working environment and wages) slightly increased in 2005 as compared to 2004. If working environment ranks second, the main reason for discontent remains wage level (see Table 10.4) (National Institute of Statistics. n.d.: 60).

Table 10.4 Working population not satisfied with working conditions, by main ownership type (public and private), Romania, 2004–05

Ownership type	Stability of employment		Working time		Working environment		Income	
	2004	2005	2004	2005	2004	2005	2004	2005
Public	9.8	10.5	7.8	9.3	18.9	21.3	43.9	45.7
Private	20.2	20.2	21.8	23.1	32.0	34.1	54.2	57.2

Thus, with regard to occupational safety and health, there is a gap between sectors in Romania. Foreign investors pay special attention to occupational safety and health and as a result, some workers benefit from better working conditions. On the other hand, workers in agriculture, coal mining, textile industry, transportation and construction continue to carry out activities in a difficult environment and therefore suffer the most from unsatisfying working conditions.

10.6 A NEGLECTED ISSUE: ACCESS TO TRAINING

Although branch collective agreements and the Labour Code contain training clauses, training is neglected by most Romanian employers. In 1999, only 11 per cent of enterprises provided continuing training. Participants represented about 8 per cent of all employees and 20 per cent of total staff of enterprises providing training. Participation rates were at their highest in small enterprises. In terms of sector, apart from financial intermediation, the highest participation rates were observed in community, social and personal services and transport (Joint Assessment Priorities, n.d.: 15–16).

Six years later, the situation had not improved. Training was still not a priority and a recent study revealed that the large majority of employees had never received any form of training (Ghinararu, 2005b). Some 53 per cent of employees had to train themselves to keep up with technological developments in their company, and only 25 per cent of companies had offered training in the past two years. Besides, according to the Workforce Survey from the third quarter of 2005, workers aged over 34 are even absent from training statistics.

Considering this situation, companies which provide training are considered as the best career choice and graduate students favour joining multinational companies in order to acquire specific skills. For instance, in computer engineering multinational companies offer individual intensive training – including abroad – and thus Romanian employees can become globally competitive (see Case Study 3). However, in other industrial sectors dominated by foreign capital (car component manufacturing, food processing, beverages, and so on) training remains more occasional.

In conclusion, it should be underlined that continuing training is a neglected issue in Romania and for this reason the social partners should make more effort in financing, monitoring and evaluating training programmes.

10.7 WORK AND FAMILY LIFE

In the second quarter of 2005, 14,634,000 persons of working age were surveyed for the first time in an ad hoc module attached to the Household Labour Force Survey (National Institute of Statistics. 2005). The main purpose of this survey was to obtain information on the reconciliation of work and family life, especially through the analysis of the work flexibility of employees with dependent persons (children up to 15 years of age or sick, disabled or elderly relatives in need of care).

Over a third (34 per cent) declared they had to take care of dependent persons, living in or outside the household. Out of 4,981,000 persons with family responsibilities, 53.5 per cent were women, 53.3 per cent lived in urban areas and 73.9 per cent were 25–44 years old.

A breakdown of the working age population by labour status showed that 60.5 per cent were employed, 4.9 per cent were unemployed (ILO standards) and 34.6 per cent were economically inactive.

According to this survey, working time flexibility presupposes the ability to vary the start and end of the working day by at least one hour in order to fulfil family obligations. Generally, 46.7 per cent of working age persons have this possibility. In rural areas, flexibility in adjusting working time is higher (64.2 per cent of persons). In contrast, in urban areas people usually have fixed working time: over two thirds (67.2 per cent) of employed persons living in urban areas could not vary the start and end of the working day by at least one hour.

Out of 4,131,000 persons who generally could vary the start and end of the working day for family reasons by at least one hour, 1,859,000 (45 per cent) had to take care of dependent persons. Under normal circumstances, 4,725,000 persons were unable to benefit from working time flexibility, although 37.4 per cent of them declared responsibilities for dependent persons.

The distribution of employment by economic sector shows a high level of working time flexibility for workers in agriculture (81.5 per cent) in comparison with only 27.1 per cent in industry and construction; 36.7 per cent of employees in services could vary their working time, especially in trade (42.5 per cent), health care and social assistance (38.2 per cent).

Forty-nine per cent of employees could generally take one or more days off for family reasons, without using holidays, unpaid leave or other special leave. Of these persons, 54 per cent could be absent from work only occasionally; 64.1 per cent of persons aged 55–64 could benefit from this, in comparison with 45.7 per cent of younger people.

Out of employees with responsibilities for dependent persons, 46 per cent could not take one or more days off for family reasons, without using holidays, unpaid leave or other special leave.

The highest flexibility in relation to absence from work was recorded for persons engaged in agriculture: 81.5 per cent in comparison with 35.7 per cent for non-agricultural workers. Among the latter, the share of those who can take days off varies from 45 per cent for hotels and restaurants to 30 per cent for manufacturing.

In the last 12 months, 5.2 per cent of workers were absent from work, without using holidays or other types of leave, for reasons of sickness or other emergencies related to dependent persons: 6.9 per cent of women but only 3.9 per cent of men experienced such situations. The rest were either not absent for such reasons or, although facing emergency situations, were not obliged to ask permission (because they were on maternity or childcare leave).

In unpredictable cases (accidents, severe sickness, and so on), 20.7 per cent of absent persons benefited from special permission from the employer, fully or partially paid. The period of absence was not paid in 22.9 per cent of cases. Other special types of agreement did not exist for 56.4 per cent of cases.

An unexpected result of this survey was that out of 4,981,000 persons aged 15–64 who take care of dependent persons, 94.7 per cent were not willing to change their work because of family responsibilities. Among those who did not wish to change, 94.6 per cent took care of children, 13.5 per cent took care of dependent adults and 8.1 per cent of both adults and children. Of those persons willing to reorganize their working life 84.5 per cent would prefer not to work or to work less in order to have enough time for children or care of dependent persons. Most of these persons were employees (68.2 per cent) or women (73.5 per cent) and live in urban areas (58.5 per cent).

Women are entitled to 126 days of maternity leave regardless of their tenure with the company. During this time, they are paid 85 per cent of the average wage earned in the six months before the maternity leave. Upon request, either of the two parents may be allowed further paid nursery leave to take care of children under two years old, with an allowance of 85 per cent of the gross average salary. In 2005, the number of persons who benefited from this type of leave over the 12 months preceding the survey was 17.3 per cent of those entitled. The overwhelming majority of these persons were women (92.2 per cent). The women who benefited from parental leave represented 30.1 per cent of all women entitled to it; 54.9 per cent of those who did not benefit from parental leave indicated as the main reason non-fulfilment of the relevant conditions – 23.1 per cent of the latter declared they were not entitled because their partner had asked for this type of leave and only 7.2 per cent because the person preferred to work.

In conclusion, the first Romanian survey on the reconciliation of work and family life shows that over a third of employees have significant family responsibilities. Despite the hypothetical work flexibility of employees, a very small percentage of persons (5.2 per cent) in fact took time off work for family reasons. Furthermore, one may assume that family life may also be affected by long working hours (see section 10.4). In sectors where overtime is recurrent, reconciliation of work and family life is rather difficult and workers caring for dependent persons, especially women in manufacturing, represent an at-risk group.

10.8 SOCIAL DIALOGUE AND WORKERS' PARTICIPATION

Like other European countries, Romanian social dialogue is organized at national, branch and enterprise level. The recent debate on work regulations revealed that at national level, as compared to business organizations, trade unions were very active. In addition, the development of collective labour agreements indicates that Romanian trade unions are also active at branch level. However, at enterprise level, social dialogue is absent and trade union membership, after a dramatic fall from 90 per cent in the early 1990s to 44 per cent in 2002 (Preda, n.d.), continues to fall.

Concerning collective labour agreements, only 14.2 per cent of employees are not covered. The sectors which do not have a collective labour agreement for all sub-sectors are public administration, financial intermediation, textiles, garment manufacturing, communication, publishing and hotels (Preda, n.d.). Workers in textiles, garment manufacturing and hotels are particularly exposed to economic hazards because they accumulate risks (low wages, long working hours, unsafe working environment, lack of training, and so on) and the absence of social dialogue increases their vulnerability.

In contrast, workers in construction benefit from the most successful collaboration between the social partners. In 1997, trade unions and employers' organizations in the construction sector established a Social Fund to pay workers during the winter. Then, confronted by a lack of skilled workers, the social partners decided to create a Special Commission charged with employees' training. In the future, they also intend to create a Pension Fund. Unfortunately, this type of initiative remains the exception.

To summarize, it should be underlined that even if the trade unions are now aware of the importance of lobbying for government regulation, they are still reluctant to act or interact at enterprise or local level, and more generally there is no institutionalization of social dialogue.

CONCLUSIONS: VULNERABLE WORKERS IN A CHANGING ROMANIA

While EU enlargement is strongly influencing the Romanian public agenda, two important processes are shaping the labour market. On the one hand, foreign investors have become important economic actors and consequently are to a certain extent able to impose new rules (safer working environment, better training, and so on) which correspond to international standards on working conditions. In addition, successful Romanian entrepreneurs are following this example and progressively improving working conditions, too. However, many sectors of the economy are still excluded from this trend and a large proportion of employees are low paid. As a result, the most vulnerable of these workers leave the country and settle down more or less illegally in western Europe. The social effects of Romanian illegal immigration, even if not urgent, are likely to require public intervention in the not too distant future.

Apart from low-paid workers who emigrate to escape poverty, women and young people accumulate several risks and therefore need particular attention. Women are traditionally a vulnerable group. In Romania, women with a low level of education living in rural areas are particularly at risk. Most are active as contributing family workers in agriculture, and because they do not have experience as employees, their access to the labour market is limited.

Young people's access to the labour market is also difficult. Their unemployment rate is very high (18.5 per cent) and in urban areas reaches 27.8 per cent. When they do find a job, 15.3 per cent of them declare themselves underemployed and more than a third accept a fixed-term contract. Finally, youngsters have difficulties reconciling work and family life since they cannot change their working programme for family reasons.

The case studies provide empirical information on young people's working conditions and how they manage to find their first job. The three enterprise case studies illustrate how several problems (low wages, insecure working environment, envelope payments, lack of social dialogue, and so on) interact to produce worker vulnerability.

REALITY AT ENTERPRISE LEVEL: CASE STUDIES

The empirical evidence of working conditions in Romania is based on several interviews with managers who agreed to participate in the ILO study. An original statistical survey completes our analysis and provides unique information about a new vulnerable group on the Romanian labour market: graduate students.

Table 10.5 summarizes the main features of the three enterprises under study. Firm 1 and Firm 2 are old socialist factories privatized in the 1990s. Firm 1 has Romanian capital, while Firm 2 and Firm 3 belong to multinational companies.

Reality at enterprise level reveals a rather mixed world of work in a changing Romania. Industrial sectors making extensive use of unskilled workers are more exposed to the race towards lower labour costs and, as a result, the need to remain competitive is constantly eroding workers' rights (*see Firm 1*). Nevertheless, other economic sectors are managing to improve working conditions and workers' rights are beginning to be more respected than in the past (*see Firms 2 and 3*).

Table 10.5 Main features of enterprise case studies, Romania

Features	Firm 1	Firm 2	Firm 3
Sector	Garments	Chemicals	New technologies
Location	Small town located in rural area	Two small towns located in two different rural areas Capital city	Large town located in developed urban area
Ownership	Romanian	French	Austrian
Number of employees	2 077	228	151
Turnover	Stable	Increasing	Increasing
Profit	Stable	Increasing	Increasing
Employment contracts	Unlimited duration	Unlimited duration	Unlimited duration Fixed-term (generally substitute for probation period), trainee
Working time	40h/week Two shifts Occasional weekend work	40h/week Shift work Weekend work Night work	40h/week Occasional long working days Occasional weekend and holiday work

Wages	Lower than other Romanian garment firms	Workers: higher than average	Level similar to other firms in software sector (EUR 500/month), but considered to be better as there are no "envelope payments"
	Minimum wage for workers, EUR 90–100/month	White-collar workers: level similar to other firms	Project-based bonus Profit-based annual bonus
Restaurant vouchers and transport	No restaurant vouchers No travel reimbursement	Restaurant vouchers Travel reimbursement	Restaurant vouchers Travel reimbursement
Health and safety	Very bad condition of toilets	Work injuries diminished significantly since the company was bought by the French group	Risks related to desk work Increasing work intensity
	Better lighting and heating of workrooms than 5 years ago	Increasing intensity at work	
Social dialogue and workers' participation	Powerless trade union	Active trade union	No trade union Individual and annual collective bargaining concerning working conditions
Main problems identified by managers	Fluctuating low-qualified workforce Low wages	Fluctuating high-qualified workforce	Unfair competition ("envelope payments") Fluctuating high-qualified workforce

Romania Case Study 1: The need to remain competitive eroding workers' rights

The Romanian garment industry: pressure towards low wages

The garment industry is one of the most important branches of Romanian industry. In recent years, this sector has contributed more than 5 per cent to GDP, 10 per cent to GNP and over 35 per cent to Romanian exports. The recent development of Romanian garment exports took place in an economic environment characterized by slow privatization, deep crisis in the textile sector and an increasing number of garment enterprises.

The privatization of light industry started in 1991 and finished in 2002. In 1998, only 67 per cent of enterprises were privatized (Romanian Trade Ministry, 1998). The majority of textile enterprises did not survive this process and as a consequence Romanian garment enterprises rely massively on fabric and other imports (Marin, 2003). In the meantime, the number of garment enterprises has grown significantly since the fall of communism. In 1989, there were 544 enterprises; in 1997, 5,761; and in 2005, more than 8,000. Small and medium-sized enterprises are preponderant, but their life expectancy ranges from 1 to 3 years. The largest enterprises (usually former socialist enterprises) continue to be the most important players in the sector and generate the major part of both exports and employment.

However, the increasing number of garment enterprises has not generated real employment growth; on the contrary, employment in the garment industry has fallen by 50 per cent since 1989. At the same time, while in 1989 employment in the garment industry represented 13 per cent of employment in industry as a whole, in 2005 it represented 22 per cent (Mirciu, 2004).

In 1998, the international organization Clean Clothes carried out a study on working conditions in the Romanian garment industry[5] and noted several problems. First, the minimum wage guaranteed by the collective national agreement did not reach the subsistence minimum. At that time, inflation was very high and increased rapidly every month. Because the minimum wage was negotiated once a year at national level, the consequences of inflation were negative, especially for low-paid workers. Second, the real working week was longer than the legal working week, with many workers reporting more than 50 hours per week (10 hours per day). Third, Clean Clothes underlined the bad working environment of some factories which lacked good lighting, air conditioning or clean washrooms.

Eight years later, working conditions have improved slightly, although low wages and working time remain hot issues. During the investigation, it appeared that Romanian managers had made some efforts to improve lighting,

---

5. http://www.cleanclothes.org/publications/easteuroma.htm

but air conditioning is still absent in the majority of factories. Some companies have tried to modernize their washrooms, but many continue to ignore the problem. Firm 1 seems representative of recent developments in working conditions in the Romanian garment industry.

Firm 1: An outsourcing company for a multinational's goal operations

Firm 1 is one of the largest Romanian garment producers. Established in 1971 in a small town, the company enjoyed special treatment under the centralized economy because it was the main subcontractor of a large French company. Despite the usual constraints of the centralized economy, Firm 1 was allowed to develop a close relationship with the foreign company. Production was therefore organized in accordance with French quality standards and French technicians frequently visited the factory. A few years after the establishment of this company, another Romanian factory (2,500 employees) began to work for the same French company.

Despite this particular situation, the managers of these factories knew nothing about international costs. They were mainly charged with monitoring production and reporting to the Ministry of Light Industry on economic or political problems. Moreover, like many Romanian garment factories, these two factories were located in rural areas and recruited generally peasant-farmer women. The average wage, including that of white-collar workers, was lower than the average wage of other branches of industry.

After the fall of the communist regime, these factories continued to be the main subcontractors of the French company. Firm 1 was privatized in 1995, but the shareholders were extremely diffused and corporate control was never transparent. In fact, the managers (who now have 8 per cent of the shares) run the company and decide general company policy.

Difficult working conditions

Although Firm 1 has a close relationship with a western company, organization of production has never really developed since the 1970s and the managers seem uninterested in making changes. For instance, the computerization of the company was carried out as late as 2002, and only because the French partner asked for it. Furthermore, the general organization of the factory is to a certain extent obsolete, as production takes place in a building with several floors, which involves some carrying by hand. The toilets are very dirty and apparently there are no changing rooms or showers. The workshops are well illuminated and ventilated, but this is a recent investment.

Increasing uncertainty

If the strong relationship with the French company protected Firm 1 against the most common problems of the transition, the liberalization of the Romanian economy in the 1990s raised significant challenges. Most important were the proliferation of small Romanian factories and the arrival of other European garment producers. For this reason, Firm 1's managers faced two problems.

First, after liberalization the French company established new subcontracting relationships with other Romanian factories. The new subcontractors agreed to work for lower prices and therefore obliged Firm 1 to sign new contracts on worse conditions. The number of orders diminished and, as a consequence, the cost of a working minute dramatically fell, too.

Second, several European companies offered Firm 1 other subcontracting contracts. However, unlike the French company's contracts which lasted 5 years, the new contracts lasted 3 or 6 months. Moreover, the number of orders was considerably lower and quite sporadic.

This situation generated a lot of uncertainty for the management. Although turnover has remained stable over recent years, profits have fallen slightly. In order to maintain the same level of profit, the management took the decision to improve competitiveness by reducing workforce costs.

The race to the bottom for unskilled workers

No alternative for older workers

In 1989, Firm 1 employed approximately 3,000 workers. Over 90 per cent were women who started their professional life at 16 or 17 years old, earlier than other industrial workers. They learnt their trade on the job and sometimes they managed to get better jobs within the company: for instance, the production supervisors and most team leaders are former workers who have been working at Firm 1 for 30–35 years. Usually rural women, this type of worker is very loyal to the company and even if working conditions deteriorate, she thinks she has no other choice but to accept them:

> I've worked here all my life; I know everything about this company. I started with the basics and nowadays, although I didn't complete my secondary education, I've managed to get a better job as team leader. After privatization, some people in the company managed to buy some shares, but of course they already had a good position: they were engineers. Nowadays they are the real owners of the company and decide about our future. Unfortunately, I think that they are not really interested in improving the company's economic situation. Instead of modernizing the company or raising wages, they invest the profits in all kinds of businesses (medical engineering, retail, and so on). As a worker, I have no say, I accept everything because I don't have any other choice, the rate of unemployment is quite high in our region and for an older woman like me, there are no jobs!

High mobility among youngest

Besides this category of worker, there is another important one: workers who do not hesitate to leave a low-paid job for a better one. In the case of Firm 1, this kind of worker has led to a significant reduction in the total number of employees: in 1999, the company employed 2,500 workers but only 2,007 in 2004. Mostly young women (18–30 years old), these low-skilled workers are more reluctant to accept bad working conditions. They complain about shift work and the long unpaid hours. As a result, they move more easily from one company to another and are ready to experience unemployment for a short period of time. Since 2002,[6] some of these workers have been emigrating (more or less legally) to Italy and Spain and work particularly in house cleaning, for a wage five times higher than they can earn in Romanian garment enterprises.

As one manager put it, young workers come and go because:

> they do not accept working for EUR 100 per month; there is a big difference between the loyalty of ageing workers and the young workers. Sometimes, the young workers have a child because the state pays them an allowance of EUR 200–230 per month, which is twice their salary.

Long commuting time leading to work–family imbalances

At present, over 40 per cent of the workers are aged between 45 and 55 years old and almost 25 per cent are aged between 20 and 35 years old. In 2004, 12 per cent of the workers were on childcare leave. The majority of employees, 65 per cent, are still rural women who commute between residence and workplace. Because they are also engaged in farming, the working day for commuting women is particularly long (12–13 hours) and tiring.

Moreover, days off for family reasons are not encouraged. When an unexpected event occurs (accident, death of a close parent), workers benefit from unpaid leave. As a worker put it:

> When you are single, everything is fine. When you are married with children, it becomes really difficult to work and take care of your family, too. For instance, my children can't count on me because I am never at home. When they are sick, my boss doesn't care. She always says that unpaid leave is reserved for exceptional cases...

Declining social dialogue and powerless trade unions

At the beginning of the 1990s, a trade union was created and the majority of workers were unionized. The trade union negotiated wage rises annually and asked for travel reimbursement and luncheon vouchers. The managers agreed to give workers luncheon vouchers and partly reimburse travel costs (30 per cent of an average wage). However, when competition sharpened between Romanian subcontractors, the managers stopped the distribution of luncheon

---

6. Since 2002, Romanian citizens no longer need a Schengen visa to travel to western Europe.

vouchers and travel reimbursement for commuting workers. As a result, workers' real income fell by more than 50 per cent and the trade union could do nothing about it. Moreover, some trade union leaders left the factory and nobody took their place. The organization continued to exist, but the trade union had no real negotiating power.

In the meantime, work intensity has accelerated. In order to maintain low production costs, the management imposed higher standards and called for unpaid overtime if the daily target was not reached. Considering the rural area's unemployment rate, the workers had no choice; they had to work harder for less money. The absence of a strong social partner facilitated the implementation of management decisions and workers continued to think that *"they have no say"*.

Conclusion

As identified in the first part of the chapter, low wages are one of the most important sources of vulnerability in Romania. When combined with long working hours and powerless trade unions, low wages become a real trap for workers. The case of Firm 1 illustrates that the increased economic competition and the race toward lower labour costs in a traditional sector have severe consequences for unskilled workers, especially for older women living in rural areas. Older workers are at risk because they have little opportunity to find another alternative job. But young workers also suffer from other types of risks: the bad working conditions they have to face persuade many of them that migration is the best solution and, as a result, they are leaving Romania on a large scale.

Romania Case Study 2: Modernization and social compromise in chemicals

Romanian chemical industry in a new era

The Romanian chemical industry has a long tradition in oil and petrochemicals. Communist economic policy was oriented towards the development of heavy industry and, as a result, the chemical sector benefited from significant investment. Because Romania was until recently the leading European oil provider, the state built many refineries and tended to focus on the production of basic chemicals.

However, from 1990 on, the industry experienced dramatic falls in output and employment fell by more than 60 per cent.[7] Privatization was slow and large enterprises proved difficult to sell as technologies were obsolete and

---

7. By 2005, the Romanian chemical industry employed only 90,000 workers.

expensive upgrading was needed. Only in the late 1990s did some foreign multinationals become interested in the potential of the Romanian chemical industry and invested massively. However, oil production and distribution remained surrounded by controversy and many political scandals shook the sector.

As compared to the garment industry, the chemical industry employs few unqualified workers (only 1–2 per cent). Manual workers are preponderant (74.1 per cent), and skilled specialists represent almost 18 per cent (Université Catholique de Louvain, 2005). Most workers graduated from technical schools and afterwards received on-the-job training.

Trade unions are quite active in this sector, even though the membership declined slightly after privatization. At national level, the most representative organizations participate in tripartite discussions and at branch level negotiate collective agreements. Occasionally, trade unions take strike action which can turn out to be particularly violent if there are lay-offs. However, as the President of the Federation of Free Trade Unions in the Chemical and Petrochemical Industries (FSLCP) told us, wages are the most common cause of conflict:

> Although general working conditions have improved lately (i.e. work-related injuries fell from 3 per cent in 2003 to 2.2 per cent in 2004), the average wage has not really increased. In 2006, the real average monthly wage is only RON 1119 (EUR 313.62).

The importance of wages is illustrated by the mobilization of a trade union in tyre manufacturing (Firm 2). The analysis of this conflict reveals the dilemmas of social dialogue at enterprise level and the problematic reconciliation between the local dimension of workers' demands and the multinational's global strategy.

Tyre manufacturing is particularly interesting because it has become one of the most dynamic chemical sub-sectors. Dominated since 2000 by a small number of well-known global companies, it represents 3.5 per cent of the chemical industry's production and employs around 6,100 persons. The sub-sector has progressed spectacularly over the last five years: exports have grown by 100 per cent and labour productivity indices have increased by more than 50 per cent since technological investment became a priority for the foreign management (Chamber of Commerce and Industry of Romania, 2005).

Nevertheless, for the multinationals who decided to purchase old tyre factories, significant organizational changes were necessary and Romanian workers had to adjust their skills to international standards. This process was a real challenge for the foreign investors who, despite some local resistance to change, including from the trade unions' side, managed to maintain their leading market position.

Restructuring tyre manufacturing

Firm 2 was created at the end of the nineteenth century and since the beginning has specialized in rubber. The development of the automobile market gave it a real boost and Firm 2 rapidly became a leading manufacturer of tyres for all kinds of vehicles. Nowadays, the company has more than 130,000 employees, including 4,000 research engineers, owns six natural rubber plantations, 74 plants situated in 19 countries and sells tyres, publishes maps and operates a number of digital services in more than 170 countries.

After the fall of communism, eastern Europe became a market for expansion. Car sales boomed and, in consequence, tyre sales too. Poland and Hungary were the first countries to receive attention from tyre producers, but Romania started to be an attractive destination only in recent years.

The first foreign investors arrived in Romania in 2000 and immediately opened a new plant. A year later, Firm 2 became interested in tyre manufacturing, but had a different strategy. Instead of building a new factory, they bought two old ones from a local businessman. Both in rural areas, the plants employ more than 3,000 persons and produce tyres for cars and trucks.

Privatized in the 1990s, these factories had already experienced several changes, including a number of lay-offs. However, the organization of production remained unaffected and workers were never forced to adopt international standards. Many economic activities were not externalized (maintenance, transportation, cleaning, catering, and so on); managers were reluctant to subcontract these tasks. Furthermore, injuries at work were frequent because technologies were outdated and poorly maintained.

Firm 2 made safety at work a priority. As investment in new technologies was costly (more than EUR 150 million) and took a lot of time, the company had to wait five years before its first profits in Romania. However, as a manager at Firm 2 told us, one of the most important consequences of this strategy was *the fall in injuries at work*. The plants were transformed into secure workplaces and European quality standards were implemented successfully.

Mobilization and compromise

However, in 2005 workers were not entirely satisfied with their working conditions. Even if their wages were higher than the local industrial average wage, workers considered that management should pay more attention to this issue. Therefore, during the negotiation of the annual collective agreement the trade union asked for a wage rise of 30 per cent. At that time, the average wage in this plant was ROL 10 million (EUR 270.45), three times the national minimum wage. The average wage was not considered relevant by the trade union because of the firm's internal wage differentials, especially between manual workers and administrative staff. In fact, while manual workers earned around EUR 200, members of the administrative staff earned much more.[8] Moreover, the factory's modernization made workers aware that they belonged to a strong company with significant financial resources. For this reason, they felt justified in asking for higher wages.

Because the management rejected their demands, the trade union decided to strike. First, they went on a two-hour token strike, but the management agreed to a wage rise of only 3.5 per cent. Judging this offer unacceptable, the workers went on an all-out strike which lasted 12 days.

During the strike, workers demonstrated peacefully in the courtyard of the company and their action never degenerated, apart from when they loudly called for the plant manager's dismissal. The trade union continued to negotiate but the management did not give in. Only after two weeks of strike action was an agreement finally reached to increase wages by 8 per cent.

This conflict was a unique opportunity for each party to test the other's limits. The workers discovered that the trade union may speak out, but its power is relative. The management learned how to maintain the company's position and to explain the financial situation more clearly. The compromise was a lesson for future negotiations and, as a result, the next collective agreement was signed without a problem.

If the wage problem remains unresolved, the workers appreciate working for Firm 2:

> Since Firm 2 took control, our working conditions have changed a lot. They have paid attention to ergonomics and we are grateful – we had never seen that before ... of course, we work harder and we only have one free weekend per month, but this is a price worth paying. What is reassuring for us is that Firm 2 is a serious investor. This means that the law is respected and workers don't have to worry about the future. Because Firm 2 is a leading tyre manufacturer, clients and orders must never be late! (Male manual worker, 2006)

Conclusion

As compared to Firm 1, Firm 2 reveals a different reality in Romanian traditional industry. For this reason, the second case provides a more complex picture of workers' vulnerability and helps us underline some positive trends already outlined in the assessment. First, the modernization of Firm 2 proves that efforts have been made in improving health and security at work. Second, despite the generalized race towards lower labour costs, Firm 2 remunerates rather fairly (although not meeting employees' demands): overtime is paid and shift work is compensated according to the law. Finally, trade unions are active and management encourages social dialogue.

But this case is also a good illustration of two negative trends not sufficiently highlighted by statistics: extent of unsocial hours, and increasing work

---

8. Information on the wages of Romanian administrative staff is not available.

intensity. Although shift work is legally compensated, rare free weekends suggest a difficult reconciliation of work and family life. Moreover, the race towards higher productivity leads to increased intensity at work, especially at multinational companies. The next two cases confirm these findings and suggest that highly skilled workers (IT engineers and other graduates) are particularly affected by these negative trends.

Romania Case Study 3: Fighting against "grey work" in IT

The Romanian IT sector: the growth of multinationals
The IT sector has existed only since 1989. Sixteen years later, more than 8,000 companies are now registered and Romania is considered an "emerging software exporting nation" (Romanian Business Association of Software Producers, n.d.). Nowadays, software and services exports dominate the Romanian software market (almost 97 per cent).

The industry is highly concentrated: 63 per cent of turnover is realized by companies situated in the capital. Bucharest also employs 45 per cent (11,300 persons) of IT workers, whereas Timisoara, the second largest software centre, employs only 10 per cent (ILO, 2002). Despite this, the structure of the Romanian IT market is constantly evolving. In 2002, there were very few large companies: more than 3,000 had no employees and had turnover below US$ 1,000 per month, while around 600 small and medium-sized enterprises had turnover between US$ 100,000 and US$ 1 million.

At present, small companies are still numerous, but the multinationals (Alcatel, IBM, Hewlett-Packard, Microsoft, Oracle, Siemens, and so on) have become much more important and have given a new impulse to local production. Apart from greatly increased turnover, the recent arrival of these companies has had two other major consequences. First, by offering new job opportunities and better wages to highly skilled Romanian IT workers, the multinationals have helped to stop the brain drain which characterizes the sector in central and eastern European countries (Cojanu et al., 2003: 7). Secondly, their direct investment in Romania has to some extent modified the local employment pattern, dominated by "grey work".[9] The case of Firm 3 illustrates this trend and explains why some highly skilled workers think that multinationals are the best career choice.

The company: diversification and outsourcing
Firm 3 is a hierarchical independent research and development unit within an Austrian multinational (MNC). The Austrian MNC was established in the sec-

---

9. Usually, Romanian students graduate from university when they are 22 years old.

ond half of the nineteenth century and is one of leading companies in electronics and communication engineering. Nowadays, the company has a diversified portfolio and offers worldwide business solutions for automation and control systems, communication services, medical equipment, transportation, and so on. MNC also has products for private consumers: car navigation systems, computers, fixed-line phones, mobile phones, hearing instruments and home appliances.

In Romania, the Austrian MNC has several independent units which produce and sell different kinds of software, home appliances, computers, motor systems, automotive electronics and mechatronics. Firm 3 was established in 2001 in a large town located in a well-developed urban region, and offers services and business solutions in information technology, communications and company organization. For instance, the company exports software for industrial automation, energy management, hydroelectric plant monitoring systems, data acquisition and transmission systems, and so on.

Since 2001, Firm 3 has grown constantly and has recruited more than 150 highly skilled workers. However, the company is currently at a crossroads and is looking to relocate to another Romanian large town, situated in the northwest of the country. Workers have not been informed about this project and most of them think that management seeks to develop a subsidiary company. In order to explain this decision, the human resource manager said that "*local authorities are obstructing Firm 3's activities*". However, he did not directly complain about local corruption and only suggested that "*bad relations with the local authorities are frustrating for an honest company*". Nevertheless, during our interview, he underlined that Romania is changing and gave the example of excellent cooperation with central government concerning a particular legislative matter.

Job security but hard work
Firm 3 has no difficulty recruiting. Because it has a good reputation, many young graduate students (with or without professional experience) apply spontaneously online. One candidate out of five is invited to an interview with an engineer who evaluates their technical skills. Then, a psychologist submits the candidate to a psychological test and, if the candidate passes this last examination, the company offers a fixed-term contract (three or six months). The fixed-term contract is considered a probationary period and, as a result, the wages of new entrants are generally lower than those of other employees. After the probationary period, the fixed-term contracts are replaced by unlimited contracts and wages progressively increase to EUR 500 per month.

Firm 3 is organized in teams. Each team is in charge of a particular project and is relatively autonomous in organizing its working schedule. Working time is flexible, but the team leader may call for overtime when necessary. If the team delivers the software earlier than planned, the team members receive a bonus. Weekend work is strongly encouraged, but not compulsory.

Training: the main asset

All employees benefit from intensive training, especially abroad. The high level of technology requires a minimum of six months' training. Usually, training is provided by highly experienced foreign technicians and is regarded as an essential step in improving an employee's skills and performance:

> Before training, employees are not really productive for us. Training is a big investment for the company, but it is absolutely necessary. ... Students think that we need experienced people, but they are wrong: we certainly need highly skilled persons, but above all we are looking for open-minded, innovative and reliable people. (Human resource manager)

Thus, the average employee is rather young (under 35 years old), highly educated and living in an urban area. Women are well represented, but men are slightly preponderant. All employees speak good English and most speak German or French as well.

The management fights against "grey work"

Despite the positive aspects of Romanian software engineers, the human resource manager thinks that they have one "*disturbing characteristic*" generated by the "*bad business environment*". The Romanian software market is dominated by small companies which make extensive use of "*envelope payments*". Every month, the employees of such firms receive the minimum wage and also an "*envelope payment*" of approximately EUR 300–400. Generally, the employees have no choice and are forced to accept this arrangement, even if it prejudices their retirement pension. Before working for Firm 3, 75 per cent of its experienced employees were receiving "*envelope payments*".

The human resource manager believes that these practices have a distorting effect on the labour market: the employee becomes (against their will) a cheat. Since fraud is part of everyday life, Romanian workers can be easily "corrupted". For a company for which business confidentiality is very important, "*stabilizing its business environment and respecting its employees become crucial tasks*".

For these reasons, Firm 3 has a strong communications policy. First, the management is open about the problem of "*grey work*" and demands government action. They use the mass media to make the public aware of the importance of honesty at work and are seeking to draw the attention of the business community to this matter. Second, they have established long-lasting cooperation with several universities. Every year, Firm 3 offers 100 scholarships (EUR 100 per month) and encourages summer internships (EUR 250 per month). The declared purpose of these actions is to "*advertise respect at work. If Romanian employees understand that some firms really respect them, then it will be harder to corrupt them.*"

Trade unions not encouraged

Nevertheless, no trade union represents the workers. Like many companies recently established in Romania, Firm 3 is not against trade unions, but it does not encourage them as regular social partners either. However, although wages are negotiated individually, a number of general working conditions are discussed collectively. Every year, the employees are asked to write down their demands. Then, the management makes a list of the ten most frequently mentioned problems and, after consulting all the employees at a collective meeting, he agrees to address some of them. Last year, the employees asked for a canteen and this year they talked about a kindergarten. As the human resource manager explained:

> Providing decent working conditions by building a canteen or a kindergarten is part of our strategy of advertising respect at work. We don't need a trade union to help us understand human dignity.

Although the canteen and the kindergarten are important issues, the absence of a trade union, including at branch level, prevents the workers from transparent wage evaluation and thus may encourage discrimination. Moreover, if Firm 3 decides to change location, the workers are not necessarily informed rapidly and risk having only minimal social protection.

Multinationals: the best career option?

Despite the lack of social dialogue, the young highly skilled employees of Firm 3 are quite satisfied with their working conditions. They consider themselves as "*privileged*" and think that working for a well-known Austrian multinational is the best career option.

Alex (male, 27 years old) has recently joined Firm 3. Born in a large town, he graduated with a Masters degree in engineering and found his first job as a graphic designer in a small company in his home town. His first employer did not make extensive use of "*envelope payments*", but wages were far below the market level. When the company started to have financial problems, Alex decided to leave immediately. He heard through a friend that Firm 3 was recruiting and he applied. Now he works there as a graphic designer and, after a three-month fixed-term contract, the company offered him an unlimited contract, though without increasing wages. Although disappointed at earning only EUR 300 per month, Alex still believes that:

> Firm 3 is the best thing that has happened to me. I really enjoy being here; I like the working environment, my colleagues and our corporate culture. Like everybody

else, I work under stress because of the deadlines, but this is nothing compared to the other companies. My girlfriend is working as web designer for a small American company and every month she has to argue with her boss because of the envelope payments!

Ion (male, 29) works for another IT multinational, in Bucharest. He thinks there is a profound gap between multinationals and small and medium-sized companies:

I know the IT sector quite well because I have had several IT jobs. Envelope payments are a bad Romanian habit and we can't do anything about it. Only the big companies are honest, they have their own internal rules and envelope payments are not one of them. … Another important thing about multinationals: they offer high quality training and for this reason, working for them is well worth it!

Apart from the good working conditions, the optimism of the young IT engineers can be also explained by the short history of these companies in Romania. Established only at the end of the 1990s, the MNCs have a strong human resource strategy because they want to stabilize the Romanian workforce. To some extent, they have succeeded since the brain drain has diminished.

Conclusion

While this case exposes positive trends in increasing wages and improving training, several negative aspects of the IT labour market are also highlighted. First, "grey work" continues to represent an important problem and workers from small companies suffer the most from unpaid overtime. Second, despite job security provided by multinationals, stress at work is rapidly developing and may have severe consequences for young engineers. Third, because trade unions are not encouraged by IT multinationals, workers do not benefit from social dialogue and may be exposed to economic hazards.

Romania Case Study 4: Graduates: a new vulnerable group?

Statistically, youngsters have the highest rate of unemployment in Romania and for this reason they may be considered a vulnerable group. However, one category of youngsters constitutes an exception: *graduate students*. They have the lowest rate of unemployment among youngsters and they are generally considered rather "privileged" on the labour market. Speaking foreign languages, nowadays graduate students grow up in an open society strongly influenced by Western culture. Their knowledge and skills recently acquired at university are far better adapted to capitalist enterprise than the socialist professional experience of older people. In consequence, a number of managers think that the dynamism of graduate students contrasts with the lack of interest of some older workers and thus consider high skilled juniors as the best employees.

Nevertheless, reality is more complex. Graduate students too may have serious difficulties finding a job. They sometimes work without a legal contract and, as the case of Firm 3 reveals, they usually receive "envelope payments". It therefore seems important to address more specifically the question of *graduate students' access to employment* and to examine their *vulnerability* more closely.

Graduate students under the microscope

The survey presented in this section was conducted by e-mail in May 2006. The participants were selected according to three general criteria. First, they had to be aged between 22 and 36 years old; second, they had to be graduate students; and third, they had to have had at least one job during their lifetime. Initially sent to 100 persons, the questionnaire was finally completed by 80 persons. The distribution by age group and sex is presented in Table 10.6:

Table 10.6 Graduate students by age group and sex, Romania

Age	Women	Men	Total
32–36	4	4	8
27–31	24	13	37
22–26	27	8	35
Total	55	25	80

Family: a diversified background

Originating mostly in urban areas,[10] the participants in this study come from different social backgrounds. Their fathers' occupations include: engineer (26.25 per cent), worker (22.5 per cent), teacher (12.5 per cent) and executive director (8.75 per cent). Their mothers' occupations include: worker (18.75 per cent), teacher (17.75 per cent), engineer (11.25 per cent) and executive director (11.25 per cent); 43.75 per cent are the only child and 10 per cent come from a family with minors. Only 5 per cent said they had a brother/sister without a university degree.

In order to round out their social background, we asked if they took any private classes when they applied to the university. This is because in Romania private classes are common and we assumed that many poor stu-

10. For instance, 38.75% were born in Bucharest, 12.5% in Brasov, 3.75% in Constanta, 3.75% in Timisoara, and so on.

dents do not attend university because they cannot afford to do what is necessary to prepare for the entrance exams. This survey confirmed the importance of private classes: 70 per cent of participants stated that they had taken more than one private class when they applied to the university. However, one unexpected result is that workers financed the private classes of their children as frequently as engineers and teachers. This leads us to conclude that, regardless of parents' occupation, graduate students benefited from significant family support during their secondary education.

Studies: main preferred fields

Seventy per cent of our respondents graduated in Bucharest. Most graduated in business studies (27.5 per cent) and political science (18.75 per cent); the others graduated in foreign languages (12.5 per cent), law (8.75 per cent), science (7.5 per cent), journalism (6.25 per cent), psychology (6.25 per cent), medicine (3.75 per cent), arts (3.75 per cent), sociology (2.5 per cent) and architecture (1.25 per cent).

Forty-five persons obtained at least one short-term scholarship while at university.

Methodology

The survey was structured in two parts. The first part raised the issue of the graduate student's first job (see *Box 10.1*). The second part was dedicated to the same topic but in relation to current job; one supplementary question requested a brief description of all the graduate student's jobs. The main pur-

---

Box 10.1 First job before graduation

1. What was your first job before graduation? What were your responsibilities?
2. How did you find your first job (family members, friends, connections, university employees, an interim agency, newspapers or the Internet)?
3. What type of contract did you have?
4. How many employees did the company have?
5. How many hours did you work per week?
6. How often did you do extra work?
7. Was extra work paid or compensated with free time?
8. Were employees unionized?
9. Were you unionized? Please give reasons for your decision.
10. What do you think about social dialogue at branch and national level?
11. Are you still working for the same company? If not, why did you leave this company?

pose of this survey was to give a dynamic picture of graduate students' working conditions from their first job until the current (or most recent) one.

Job and work before graduation: often hard with "grey" conditions

The data indicate that, despite family financial support during their secondary education, the majority of respondents (62.5 per cent) decided to work before graduation. Moreover, 60 per cent of students interviewed who benefited from a short-term scholarship while at university also had a job.

The working conditions of this category of youngsters are particularly difficult. Access to employment is arbitrary and depends mainly on social networks. "Black work" is not predominant, but "grey work" and "envelope payments" are frequent. Moreover, working time is very long and overtime is generally unpaid. Social dialogue is regarded as "inefficient" and young workers are rarely unionized.

The first job: not reflecting university qualification

As Table 10.7 indicates, most students at business school, political science school, journalism school and the school of psychology had a job before graduation. However, jobs were less frequent among students at law school, medical school and the school of sciences.

Before graduation, 23.75 per cent worked in the retail sector and 13.5 per cent had a job as executive secretary or secretary-receptionist. Except for the journalism undergraduate, none of the working undergraduates had a first job in keeping with their university qualifications. Thus, we can assume that this category of young people is particularly vulnerable in the labour market as they probably have part-time jobs and accept working without a contract more easily because they do not yet have a university degree.

Table 10.7 First job before graduation

University	Yes	No	Total
Foreign languages	6	4	10
Journalism	4	1	5
Political science	11	4	15
Business	15	7	22
Science	1	5	6
Law	1	6	7
Psychology	5	1	6
Medicine	1	2	3
Arts	3	0	3
Sociology	2	0	2
Architecture	1	0	1
Total	50	30	80

Employment status: surprisingly, full-time jobs

The results concerning employment status before graduation did not confirm our assumptions because the majority of students worked full time (68 per cent) and had an unlimited contract (48.75 per cent). Twenty-two per cent signed a civil contract and 13.75 per cent had a fixed-term contract. As a matter of fact, few graduates (15 per cent) did not have a contract for their first job. "Black" work is particularly widespread in the retail sector, especially in small enterprises (less than 20 employees). Almost 90 per cent of undergraduates without a contract worked part time and declared they left this first job because of the low wages.

Most respondents found their first job through their social network: 20 per cent through connections, 18.75 per cent through friends, 15 per cent through university employees and 11.25 per cent through family. Only 33.75 per cent found their first job using traditional strategies: 20 per cent through newspaper advertisements, 7.5 per cent through the Internet, 5 per cent applied spontaneously and 2.5 per cent found it through an agency. This leads us to conclude that access to the first job is particularly difficult and the traditional strategies of finding a job are less effective for undergraduates.

Working time: long hours

Before graduation, 31.25 per cent worked fewer than 20 hours per week; 41.25 per cent worked 40 hours per week (the legal working time) and 27.5 per cent worked more than 40 hours per week. Surprisingly, 21.25 per cent worked more than 50 hours per week, of whom 29.41 per cent worked more than 60 hours per week.

Overtime is very common: 81.25 per cent frequently did overtime and 45 per cent more than 10 times per month. Undergraduates are usually not paid for overtime, especially when working as executive secretaries.

Social dialogue: not close to the trade unions

Ninety-six per cent of respondents were not unionized. When asked to explain their motives, they mentioned three main reasons. First, some graduate students think that Romanian trade unions defend, not the workers', but the employers' interests:

> In Romania, trade union members actively participate in the executive board of the company. Therefore, they usually defend their own private interests.

> Trade union leaders talk a lot, but do nothing. They are concerned with their own career. The well-being of Romanian workers is marginal for them.

Second, some young employees openly criticize the trade union's political commitments:

There is too much politics inside trade unions. I don't think that politics should be involved in social dialogue.

I was never interested in trade unions because for me, these organizations are like the political parties. They defend obscure interests and I don't want to be involved in their schemes.

Third, other respondents declare that trade unions are not welcomed in small and medium-sized enterprises, especially in the retail sector. As a consequence, all workers, including undergraduates, suffer from arbitrary management decisions:

When I was a student, I worked for a retail chain. It was a rather disastrous experience because workers' rights were not respected. Nobody defended our interests, trade unions were forbidden and if somebody complained, this person was quickly fired.

Job and work after graduation: still difficult conditions
Despite the fact that the overwhelming majority of undergraduates worked full time, this situation did not prevent them from obtaining a university degree. Moreover, almost 90 per cent of our respondents currently work in their university field of competence. Despite this, their working conditions have not improved since graduation.

Even though "black" work, part-time work and civil contracts tend to disappear, access to employment continues to be difficult. Thus, connections became the most important way of finding a job (35 per cent), while other social resources (family, friends and university employees) considerably decline. At this point traditional strategies become more frequent: 27.5 per cent found their current job through newspapers, 7.5 per cent through the Internet, 7.5 per cent applied spontaneously and 1.25 per cent found it through an agency.

After graduation, the few persons working fewer than 40 hours per week are those with an independent profession (freelancers, doctors, translators). Most respondents work 40 hours per week (55 per cent), which represents an increase of 13.75 per cent as compared to working undergraduates. However, the percentage of persons working more than 50 hours also increased, from 21.25 per cent to 35 per cent, of whom 32.14 per cent work more than 60 hours per week.

Long working hours seriously affect family life and, as a result, most respondents are single (77.5 per cent). Moreover, overtime is generally not paid: 93.75 per cent of graduates frequently do overtime, but 50.70 per cent of them are never paid nor receive any compensation. If the wage issue was not directly addressed by our survey, the answers to question 11 (*see Box 10.1*) indicate that unpaid overtime and unsatisfactory income represent the main reasons for quitting a job. Because graduates continue not to trust trade unions, they consider that social dialogue cannot really improve their working conditions. Thus, 75.5 per cent of graduates had changed their job more than twice and 10 per cent had had ten different jobs.

Conclusion
We saw in this case study that graduates accumulate risks and therefore need more attention. Undergraduates are particularly exposed as they more frequently have atypical employment status, accept "black" work and are not paid for overtime. Since social dialogue is absent at enterprise level, graduates continue to ignore trade influence on working conditions and, as a result, they consider that switching jobs is the only solution. Even though this survey did not explicitly study graduate migration to Western countries, we presume that many young highly skilled persons confronted with poor working conditions may decide to leave the country.

REFERENCES

Bleahu, A., and R. Anghel. 2005. Migratia romaneasca in Spania; Milano Centrale. Statut ilegal, piete de munca si practici transnationale la migranti romani din Milano, *Sociologie romaneasca* [Romanian sociology], 3 (2).

Chamber of Commerce and Industry of Romania (CCIR). 2005. The Romanian national export strategy. Bucharest (October): http://www.ccir.ro/ ccirweb/resources/menuDespreNoi/uploads_dpos/SNE_document_final.doc.

Cojanu, V., R. Butnaru and R. Lazar. 2003. *Analysis of competitive clusters: The software and ship building industries.* SOREC: http://www.sorec.ro/pdf/ OEcoN3/05_V.Cojanu.pdf

Competitiveness of the chemical industry sector in the CEE candidate countries. 2001. http://ec.europa.eu/enterprise/chemicals/docs/studies/comp_nat_ reviews.pdf

European Commission. 2002. *Joint assessment of employment priorities in Romania.* Brussels (October).

Ghinararu, C. 2005a. *Youth employment in Romania: Trends, developments and issues under debate.* Bucharest: National Labour Research Institute of Romania (December).

———. 2005b. *Studiul explorativ asupra cererii de formare profesionala continua,* Bucharest.

Grigorie-Lacrita, N. 2005. Codul Muncii pe intelesul tuturor. *Tribuna economica*, 37.

ILO. 2002. *Information and communication technologies and decent work: Finding solutions in the information society* (April).

Joint assessment of employment priorities in Romania. 2002. Brussels: European Commission (October), p. 2.

National Institute of Statistics. 2004a. *Work organization and working time arrangements, second quarter.* Bucharest: National Institute of Statistics.

———. 2004b. *Castigurile salariale si costul fortei de munca,* Bucharest.

———. 2005a. *Reconciliation of work and family life, second quarter,* Bucharest.

———. 2005b. *Forta de munca in Romania. Ocupare si somaj in trimestrul III 2005.* Bucharest.

———. n.d. *Conditiile de viata ale populatiei Romaniei.* Bucharest.

OECD. 2000. *La politique sociale et la politique du marché du travail en Roumanie.* Paris: OECD (February).

Popescu, N.N. 2003. Cresterea veniturilor salariale prin tichete de masa. *Tribuna economica*, 1–2.

Preda, D. n.d. Sindicate si patronate in Romania, http://www.ugir1903.ro/download/ sindicate_si_patronate_in_Romania.pdf.

Romanian Business Association of Software Producers. n.d. IT Outsourcing in Romania, http://www.anis.ro/

Stoicescu, D.L. 2003. Inlocuitorul conventiilor civile: contractul de munca cu timp partial. *Tribuna economica* [Economic voices], 17.

Université Catholique de Louvain. 2005. *Monographs on the situation of the social partner organizations in the chemical industry: Bulgaria, Romania and Turkey* (December), http://www.uclouvain.be/cps/ucl/doc/trav/documents/Chimierapport-candidat.pdf

11. Spain: The paradox of job insecurity alongside high employment growth

Rafael Muñoz de Bustillo Llorente

11.1 INTRODUCTION

The purpose of this chapter is to study the evolution of work and employment conditions in Spain, paying special attention to what we will call *vulnerable workers*. From the perspective adopted in these pages, workers face at least three major sources of vulnerability: (i) those related to low pay and poverty, (ii) those resulting from the physical and psychical hazards of their work and (iii) those related to losing the job. Together with these sources of vulnerability, other aspects of work contribute to the (adverse) quality of employment, including: length of working time, disparity between actual and preferred working time, flexibility of working time schedule, intensity of work, working environment, chances of promotion and, related to this, existence of training, and workers' voice in work design and organization. This chapter will also survey those matters more closely related to quality of work and working conditions.

To what extent are Spanish work and employment conditions different from the European average? And if so, what are the underlying causes that explain such differences? According to our analysis (see Table 11.1), there are a number of characteristics specific to the Spanish model concerning conditions of work and employment, probably related both to the lower level of economic development of the country relative to the EU-15, and to the two significant and long-lasting episodes of high unemployment suffered by Spain in the last two decades of the twentieth century that made the fight against unemployment the major objective of economic and social policy, almost leaving behind everything else. Together with these, the late and relatively poor development of the Spanish welfare state has also contributed to the relative lower quality of work and employment conditions in Spain.

In the review presented over the next few pages, as well as in the case studies, the high level of temporary employment stands out as the major problem of the Spanish labour market from the perspective of "quality" of work. As job

Table 11.1 Working and employment conditions in Spain

Elements	Item	Trends	Risks/Exposed groups
Social bargaining and workers' participation	Membership density	Comparatively low (17%) although high participation in trade union elections (57% of employees)	Temporary workers, employees in small enterprises, immigrants
	Decentralization	Decreasing level of firm collective agreements (CA). Decreasing percentage of workers covered by CA in construction and services	Potential risk of decentralization in future reform of CA system. Difficulties in monitoring the effectiveness of CA
Employment status and contracts	Temporary employment	Highest level of temporary work in the EU despite incentives given for permanent contracts	All workers affected but young workers with low education, females and immigrants are overrepresented
	Self-employment	Self-employment above the EU level but declining. Countercyclical behaviour	Self-employed working for single firms
Wages	Real wages	Wage moderation. Long-term deterioration of minimum wage	Women, workers with elementary education, working in micro-firms
	Wage inequality	Wage disparity roughly stable in the last decade (Gini Index around 0.29). Growth of employment in sectors with wages lower than average	More women in lower pay sectors and occupations. Immigrants
	Low wages	Higher comparative level. High risk of alternating low wage/unemployment	Temporary workers and immigrants more exposed to relative poverty. New phenomenon, no statistical data available
Working time and work organization	Long weeks and long hours. Part time. Flexible working time	Relatively long week and working hours. Low comparative level. Insignificant	The whole work force. Highly involuntary. Trade-off between long hours and flexi-time

Elements	Item	Trends	Risks/exposed groups
Work organization, work intensity and working rhythms	Work intensity	No statistically discernible trend Bad comparative working conditions Growing work–life balance problems	Women
		High level of accidents at work	Temporary workers, construction workers

stability is a good in itself, a high percentage of temporary employment has a direct negative impact on workers' well-being. However, the implications go beyond this direct effect, as temporary workers have lower wages, lower probability of participating in training schemes and higher risk of accidents. Furthermore, the insecurity associated with temporary contracts has had a significant negative impact on the process of emancipation and family life and on the fertility rate. Lastly, from a macroeconomic point of view it can be argued than temporary work has a negative impact on productivity growth, one of the major problems of the Spanish economy nowadays. The coincidence of a high rate of temporary employment and an unusually high rate of employment growth could lead to the wrong conclusion that the latter is, at least partially, driven by the increase in labour flexibility allowed by the use of temporary contracts. This is a conclusion not granted by the data if only because the Spanish labour market has suffered such a high rate of contingency at least since the end of the 1980s.

A second major issue of the Spanish labour market, with a clear and deep negative impact on working conditions, is the high rate of labour accidents, even after taking into consideration the peculiarities of the Spanish economic structure in comparison with other European countries.

Third, the last decade has witnessed a stagnation of real wage growth in a context of very high employment growth, the major achievement of the Spanish economy. However, most of the employment growth has taken place in sectors with lower than average wages. In 2004 around 14 per cent of workers were on low wages (less than 60 per cent of the median wage) making low wages an important source of poverty. With wages stagnant, it seems that the high rate of employment growth has not been enough to improve the financial situation of a significant proportion of Spanish households. For a quarter of Spanish families, wages (or the combination of wages and other income) are not high enough to meet their needs, especially in a context of a very high increase in housing costs. This probably explains why, although Spanish workers on average work longer hours than their European colleagues (something usually considered negative in the literature in terms of job quality) working time reduction is not as high on the workers' agenda as in other European countries, and also why the relatively low proportion of part-time jobs are to a large extent involuntary.

The potential negative impact of long working hours on the work–life balance is increased by the low percentage of workers with flexible working time. This type of working time organization is still a rarity in Spain, where most workers have fixed entry and exit times from work (especially in the private sector). Furthermore, working time is fixed by someone else for a majority (93 per cent) of Spanish workers, leading to a situation in which more than one quarter of workers end up having problems reconciling their working and non-working lives, the second highest percentage in the EU-15.

In relation to training, the proportion of firms with institutionalized training programmes is much lower in Spain than in the rest of the EU: 36 per cent compared to the EU average of 62 per cent. As a result of this, only around one quarter of the employees receive training. In contrast, the "chosen ones" dedicate more time to training than the European average. In this respect we can talk of the existence of a skewed training model in which a majority receive no training and a minority get more than the European average. Lastly, in relation to self-employment – Spain has one of the highest self-employment rates in the EU-15 – the lack of data prevents us seeing whether there has been a "denaturalization" of self-employment in the sense that work that used to be performed by employees is now performed by self-employed people as part of firms' strategy of outsourcing. The self-employed work longer hours and have a higher poverty risk than employees. This points to the existence of a two-tier self-employed labour market, with both very high and very low productivity.

11.2 THE EROSION OF SPANISH WORKERS' PRIORITY: JOB SECURITY

According to the Spanish Barometer of May 2005 (CIS, 2005), to the question "Which of the following aspects of a job do you value most?", 74 per cent replied "Stability", followed at some distance by "Wages" (50 per cent). Using this indicator of the importance of job stability for Spanish workers as a guideline, our review of quality of work will start with an analysis of job security in Spain. The major difference between the Spanish labour market compared to rest of the European Union (and the OECD) is the abnormally high percentage of workers with fixed-term contracts. According to the Spanish Labour Force Survey (EPA) in 2005, 32.5 per cent of employees had a fixed-term contract, more than twice the average of the EU-25 (13.7 per cent). Furthermore, of the EU-15 Member States only Portugal, with 19.8 per cent, comes close to the Spanish level of contingent workers; among the accession countries, for example, only Poland, with 22.7 per cent, has a relatively high percentage.

The major change of the early 1980s: the promotion of fixed-term work

This characteristic of the Spanish labour market is not something recent and can be traced to the first major reform of the Spanish Labour Code of the democratic era.[1] In 1984, in a context of high and growing unemployment (21 per cent), it was considered that the high level of worker protection through redundancy payments was hindering the hiring of new workers. In order to reduce this disincentive, the hiring regulation was liberalized, creating a system of hiring *à la carte* with several types of fixed-term contracts with no redundancy payments. The impact of the reform on the structure of employment is clear and long-lasting: in 1987 the percentage of workers with fixed-term contacts was 15 per cent, three years later it was 30 per cent.

This high level of employees with temporary contracts and its negative implications for the economy led to four labour law reforms. The first, in 1994, eliminated the general applicability of short-term contracts, leaving this type of contract to apply to specific groups. The second took place in 1997, making available a new type of open-ended contract with lower dismissal costs for specific types of workers. The third was in 2001, extending the 1997 reformed open-ended contract to new groups of workers and making fixed-term contracts less attractive for employers by introducing a small redundancy payment of 8 days' wages per year at the end of the contract. The last, in May 2006, aimed at reducing the use of temporary contracts with a programme of transforming temporary into open-ended contracts. These reforms have so far had little impact in the contingency rate of the private sector, which has fallen from 39 per cent to 33.3 per cent (2005), although paradoxically the overall impact of this change was masked by the increase in the use of short-term contracts by the public sector, where the percentage of contingency went up from 15 per cent to 24 per cent. In any case, in 2005, 91 per cent of the 17.1 million labour contracts signed (in a country with 15.5 million employees) were temporary contracts (down from 95.6 per cent in 1996).[2]

---

1. In the *Estatuto de los Trabajadores*, the major labour law code in democratic Spain, approved in 1980, labour contracts were assumed to be for an indefinite period. Only under specific circumstances, related to the characteristics of the activity performed (due to seasonal reasons or to substitute another worker with a permanent contract) could firms use fixed-term contracts.

2. For an example of a firm with all its production workers on temporary contracts see Case Study 4 in part two of this chapter.

Changes in self-employment

Spain, in accordance with its lower income per capita relative to the EU-25, has one of the highest indexes of self-employment compared with the richer members of the Union. It is normally accepted that self-employment decreases along with economic growth (partly due to the shrinking share of agriculture where self-employment is high). Nevertheless, the proportion of self-employed shows a decreasing trend over time as the Spanish economy has converged in income with the more advanced European economies: in 1970 self-employment was 30 per cent of total employment, while three decades later it was 18 per cent (16 per cent if we exclude agriculture, where the self-employment rate is 50 per cent). These numbers do not reflect, at least not yet, the supposed *renaissance* of self-employment related to the birth of the New Economy and the reduction in transaction costs allegedly associated with it.

A longitudinal analysis of self-employment shows that in Spain it follows a countercyclical pattern. During recessions the rate of change of the self-employment index usually turns positive (first half of the 1980s and 1992–95), to regain its long-term falling trend when the economy recovers (Muñoz de Bustillo, 2002). This behaviour can be interpreted in terms of the existence of a group of self-employed workers to whom self-employment is second best to being employed by a firm: these workers use this alternative only when they cannot find a job in the labour market due to the economic situation.

Although in Spain aggregate data do not show any indication of a change in trend in the percentage of self-employment, the process of outsourcing that has characterized the production strategy of firms in the last decade has given rise to the question, especially among trade unions, of whether this tendency could lead to a denaturalization of self-employment, as many self-employed could end up working solely or mainly for a single firm but without the protection offered by a labour contract. If we leave aside anecdotal evidence, one of the few available sources of information on this subject is the 2004 special module of the LFS on the organization of working time. This module includes information about whether the self-employed work for a single client, a situation that could be interpreted in terms of a denaturalized labour relation (a labour relation formalized through a civil contract). The result indicates that, so far, only a minority – 15.6 per cent – of self-employed workers (without employees) work for a single client. This average hides important differences among regions, however, rising to 53.6 per cent in Islas Baleares (Balearic Islands). By sector, this circumstance is relatively common in agriculture where one in three self-employed workers works for a single client, but much less common in industry (14 per cent), services (11 per cent) or construction (7 per cent). Aware of the specific vulnerabilities of self-employed workers, in September 2006 the government presented a draft aimed at increasing the social protection of this group of workers.[3] Among other things, the draft includes a section on the improvement of health and safety at work and another considering the possibility, under certain circumstances to be evaluated, of extending unemployment benefits to the self-employed.

Impact on quality of work

In a world where security is valued, lower job security due to fixed-term contracts can be interpreted as constituting lower quality of work. But the impact of this direct job insecurity is different depending on (i) how short contracts are, (ii) the groups affected by it and (iii) the chances of getting a permanent contract after having a temporary contract with the same or a different firm. In relation to the first item, in 2004 as many as half the contracts of definite duration were for less than one month. In fact, this type of very short-term contract has gained importance since the mid-1990s (in 1995 it was 20 per cent). Temporary contracts in Spain are generally of relatively short duration.

In relation to the second point, in general temporary workers are younger, less educated and tend to be in agriculture and construction, but this type of working contract is not limited to these groups of workers. Although fixed-term work is concentrated in younger age groups (61 per cent in 2005 among workers 20 to 24 years old), the contingency rate is quite high even among older workers (29.6 per cent of 30–39 year olds). The education level plays a different role as workers with secondary education or higher show a lower probability of temporary work, although the probability does not decrease with level of study – that is, those with university studies do not in general show a lower probability of fixed-term contracts.

In relation to the third item, the very low number of permanent contracts signed every year in Spain – a mere 9 per cent in 2005 – seems to support the interpretation of temporary contracts as a dead-end for many workers. Güell and Petrongolo (2005) illustrate clearly the low level of conversion of temporary into permanent workers: the transformation from temporary to permanent is highest for workers employed for 9–12 quarters (2–3 years), that is, for workers about to reach the maximum time allowed by law for a temporary contract, and still only a fifth of workers get a permanent job. Furthermore, according to these authors' estimates, the rate of conversion of fixed-term contracts into permanent contracts decreased monotonically from around 18 per cent in 1987 to 6 per cent in 1997, increasing slightly since then.[4] These

---

3. For example, the draft presents the picture of "economically dependent self-employment" (sic), when on a permanent basis 75 % of the work load depends on a single firm.

4. This result is coherent with that obtained by Alba (1998) for the period 1987–96, according to which the probability of transition from a temporary to a permanent job decreased markedly from 1987 to 1995.

results are coherent with the very low conversion rates obtained by Amuedo-Dorantes (2000).[5] Summing up, temporary employment is also the main entrance to a permanent job, but this conclusion is trivial: due to the dominance of temporary hiring by firms only 1.18 per cent of permanent contracts were signed by workers not employed in the previous year.[6]

11.3 WORKING TIME AND WORK ORGANIZATION

Working time is an important component of the quality of work for several reasons. Workers face constraints in terms of the availability of jobs with a working time that suits their needs, both as regards length and distribution of working time. Jobs are usually offered on the basis of fixed blocks of time (Martinez-Granado, 2005), leading to two different kinds of problems: people working more or less than they would choose, and people working different hours than preferred. This can affect workers' ability to lead a satisfying life outside work.

Preference for longer working hours

The average weekly working time of Spanish full-time workers is 41.6 hours, close to the EU-25 average of 41.7, and the third highest of the EU-15 after the United Kingdom and Greece. The usual working week is one hour shorter for full-time employees, and almost 5 hours longer for the self-employed. Looking at total employment rather than full-time employment alone, due to the low proportion of part-time workers in Spain – unlike in, say, the Netherlands – does not change the working time picture very much, reducing the average working week by only one hour.

In terms of quality of employment, the type of working schedule and the degree of convergence between working schedule and workers' preferences in relation to the distribution of the different parts of the day between work and other activities is as important as the overall length of the working day. In this respect, the distinctive feature of working schedules in Spain is the high percentage of workers with split shifts: 56.4 per cent. This situation is at odds with workers' preferences, as shown by a survey conducted by the CIS in May 2005, in which only 19.2 per cent of workers showed a preference for this

---

5. The relation between workers' characteristics and conversion rates is explored in Casquel and Cunyalt (2004) from a different perspective, using data from the demand side. See Amuedo-Dorantes (2001) and Hernanz (2003), Chapter 3.

6. Period 1987–2002, percentage of workers with permanent contract in year *t*+1 not employed in year *t* – Güell and Petrongolo (2005), p. 26.

type of working arrangement.[7] It looks as if the distribution of working time in Spain is still dominated by the traditional way of organizing work, with a long break in the middle of the day in which workers go home for lunch and a short siesta. This schedule is probably quite practical for workers living close to home, but it is clearly impractical in large cities with long commuting times.

In Spain until recently the debate about working time was mostly driven by the high and persistent level of unemployment. The reduction of working time was mostly defended in terms of its allegedly positive impact on employment, and not so much in terms of the existence of longer than desired working hours. In fact, according to the 1999 EU ad hoc labour market survey the preferences of Spanish workers for a shorter working week (at a given hourly wage rate) is lower than in other European countries, something partially explained by its relatively lower GDP per capita. There are other indicators that point in the same direction, for example only 9.5 per cent of collective agreements (covering 13 per cent of employees) include a clause eliminating overtime.[8] Still, the available information on actual versus preferred working time shows that although there is a high correlation between the two, the correlation is far from perfect. In Spain, for example, preferred weekly working time was 12 per cent lower than actual working time, while for the EU-15 it was 10 per cent lower. In contrast the difference for the Netherlands was under 1 per cent.

Between part time and long hours

To get a better view of working time in Spain it is important to look at both extremes of its distribution: those working long hours and those working part time. Starting with the former, as already mentioned, part-time employment in Spain is relatively low compared with other EU countries. At the end of 2005 part-time employment was around 12 per cent. In the first half of the 1990s there was an increase in the proportion of part-time employees, from 4 per cent to 8 per cent, but the percentage remained roughly constant until 2005, where we can see an increase in part-time employment to 12 per cent, probably due to changes in the methodology of the Labour Force Survey. As usual, part-time employment is mostly female – 78 per cent in 2006 (2nd quarter). One of the reasons advanced to explain the low utilization of part-time employment in the Spanish economy is the use of temporary work instead. In fact, according to Muñoz de Bustillo and Fernandez (2006), in Spain part-time

---

7. 64% of workers showed their preference for working only in the morning, 3.4% in the late afternoon and 1.1% at night (CIS, *Barómetro, May, 2005)*.

8. MTAS, Estadística de Convenios Colectivos, Cuadro 24.A(1). Total collective agreements registered until May 2006.

work is mainly used by firms with low operating hours and not as a way of increasing operating hours beyond the average working day/week.

From a policy-makers' perspective, the promotion of part-time employment is usually a way of increasing employment-creation capacity and reducing the unemployment rate. But is part-time work a desirable arrangement for workers? In the Spanish case it does not seem so: in 2005 the main reason given by those working part time was that they could not find a full-time job. In fact, only around 12 per cent of part-time workers declared that they did not want a full-time job. The rest mentioned other reasons, including family duties, sickness or education as the main reason for working part time.

In relation to the working time of part-time workers, according to the Encuesta de Coyuntura Laboral there has been a narrowing of the difference between average working time of full-time and part-time workers due to the increase in the average annual working time of part-time workers (11 per cent from 1996 to 2005) and the slight decrease in annual working time of full-time workers (–2 per cent in the same period). As a result of these trends, annual working time of part-time workers at the end of 2005 was 58.9 per cent of the equivalent of full-time workers (from 52.6 per cent in 1996).[9]

The other end of the working time spectrum is occupied by workers with long working hours and workers with multiple jobs, of whom 70 per cent work 40 or more hours a week (10 per cent more than 50 hours). In 2006, 2.5 per cent of Spanish workers were holding multiple jobs, a small percentage, but twice the 1.25 per cent of the early 1990s. Therefore, it seems that there is a small but growing percentage of workers who feel they need to have more than one job in order to make ends meet. In total, around 20 per cent of workers have a weekly working week of more than 40 hours.

Lack of working time flexibility

Another important issue related to working time is the flexibility of working schedules: often more important than the overall length of the working day or week is the possibility of organizing – up to a point – one's working schedule. According to the Encuesta de Calidad de Vida en el Trabajo (ECVT) of 2004, 64 per cent of blue-collar workers (and, interestingly, 68 per cent of women) and 73 per cent of white-collar workers never or almost never have flexibility in relation to their working schedule (when to start and finish work), a percentage slightly higher than in 2000 when it was 60.3 per cent (70 per cent in the case of white-collar workers). It is interesting that workers who enjoy this type of flexibility also have a higher probability of prolonging their working day (27 per cent vs 15 per cent of workers with fixed entry–exit times), and

---

9. This process of convergence has been especially intensive in manufacturing, where the average working time of part-time workers is 64.5% of the annual working time of full-time workers.

to change the number of hours worked depending on the needs of the firm (27.6 per cent vs 12.1 per cent of workers with fixed entry–exit times). There is also a positive relation between flexitime and duration of working week, although not as intense as in other countries, such as the United States (Muñoz de Bustillo et al., 2004). In this respect it looks as if flexibility of working time is not a free lunch, but compensation from firm to worker in return for greater working time availability. Furthermore, this fixed working schedule is almost always (93 per cent of cases) fixed by the employer. Only 5.7 per cent of employers fix the schedule in consultation with their workers, too limited a percentage to favour a good fit between working and non-working life.

11.4 WORK–LIFE IMBALANCE?

In 2002, 92 per cent of Spaniards considered that both men and women should contribute to the family income,[10] but, as Macinnes (2005) reminds us, 15 years earlier a majority of adults agreed with the male-as-breadwinner principle: "A man's job is to earn money; a woman's job is to look after the house and family." This change in opinion reflects the huge transformation in the conception of the role of women in the family that has taken place in Spain in the course of less than two decades.

Under these new circumstances the work–life balance faces three important negative restrictions of a different nature. The first restriction is the product of the specific pattern followed by the incorporation of Spanish women into the labour market; the second is related to the lack of a prompt response on the part of public policy; and the third to the employers' policy, with the low level of compliance or adaptation of Spanish firms to the new situation created by the incorporation of women into the labour market.

Although in Spain the percentage of households with two working adults – 43 per cent in 2000 – is the lowest of the EU-11, it increased very rapidly in the 1990s (12 percentage points from 1992). This change has outpaced the institutional and cultural changes needed to confront the new challenges to work–family balance posed by dual-earner households. Furthermore, in Spain, in contrast with all other EU countries except Greece, in most dual earner households both partners work full time. This puts extra pressure on the ability of working couples to balance their family and working lives, especially if they have children.[11]

---

10. CIS Barómetro, February 2002.
11. The proportion of dual participation households is roughly the same for those with and those without children. In 2000, 35.4% of households with no children and at least one partner at work were couples where both had full-time jobs; the proportion for couples with children was 35.6% (Franco and Winqvist, 2002).

There is very little public provision to facilitate a proper work–life balance: Spanish social expenditure on family protection as a percentage of GDP – 0.5 per cent – is the lowest of the EU-25. State and regional provisions to improve the work–life balance is also very modest in comparison with other EU countries (Lopez and Valiño, 2004). This increases the burden of parents with full-time jobs as they cannot rely on a satisfactory supply of social services to facilitate the reconciliation of work and family obligations. For example, while the percentage of children attending nursery school between 3 and 5 is practically 100 per cent, from 0 to 3 years the percentage is only 11 per cent due to the lack of public nursery schools and the high cost of private services (in 2000, 56 per cent of nursery schools were private).[12]

As result of the combination of a high percentage of full-time workers, low provision of public services and the high price of private formal childcare for the under-threes, in Spain there is a general reliance on informal care, usually within the family: in 2004, 21 per cent of people aged 65 and over were taking care of their grandchildren, and 39 per cent had taken care of them at some time in the past.[13] It is reported (Fundación Encuentro, 2004) that around 30 per cent of women under 30 with dependants would not be able to work without the support of their relatives (mainly their grandparents). This system of informal care is under threat due to population aging and the rise of a new form of dependency related to old age. In Spain, the formal system old-age care is very limited, with only 6.5 per cent of the elderly population receiving formal public social care. This means that most of the elderly dependent population are under the informal care of their relatives, usually their daughters.

As a result of all these circumstances it will become increasingly difficult to reconcile work and family duties, impacting the capacity of workers (once again mostly women) to meet standards both at home and at work. In this last respect, according to two different surveys conducted by the Autonomous Regions of Madrid and Cataluña, difficulties reconciling family and work lead to absenteeism and a reduction in work capacity. In Cataluña, for example, between 11 per cent and 25 per cent of those interviewed considered that these tensions often affected their capacity to work. In Madrid, 20 per cent of women interviewed acknowledged that they had arrived late to work in the last quarter more than once due to family reasons, 24 per cent had had to leave early and 20 per cent had on occasion not showed up at work at all for the same reason.[14]

---

12. In order to compensate for the high cost of formal childcare provision, in 2003 a EUR 100 monthly subsidy for working women with children under 3 years was approved. In the first 18 months around 700,000 women benefited from the measure.

13. In fact, support for the family was not confined to grandchildren, as almost 10% helped in food preparation for their family and 6% took care of adults (IMSERSO, 2004).

14. Fundación Encuentro (2004) Chapter IV.

Neither the administration (through changes in labour regulations) nor firms have developed a consistent and well-functioning body of practice aimed at easing the reconciliation of work and family duties. According to the recently released *Establishment Survey on Working Time 2004–2005* (Riedman et al., 2006), Spanish firms rank low on almost all indicators related to improving work–life balance, whether it be flexible time arrangements (43 per cent of firms vs 48 per cent in the EU-21), existence of firm-specific parental leave programmes (17 per cent of firms vs 30 per cent in the EU-21), phased retirement schemes (19 per cent of firms vs 37 per cent in the EU-21). The expected shrinking size of the Spanish labour force associated with the reduction of the fertility rate and the increase in life expectancy of the population[15] will probably force firms to put into practice work–life balance policies in the future. Until now an abundant labour force and the above-mentioned gender specialization have allowed Spanish firms to forgo systems to improve the work–life balance of their employees.

A good index of the low development of practices helping to improve the work–life balance is what collective agreements have to say on the issue. In this respect, in collective agreements the work–life balance is identified with the work–family duties balance and the right to leave and sabbaticals, only one of the potential ways of reconciling work and life. Very few collective agreements include clauses dealing with working time agreements for workers with dependants. For example, of the few collective agreements that include flexible time, only 2.7 per cent do so for work–life balance reasons. In relation to leave, most collective agreements limit themselves to covering the same reasons considered in Spanish labour law giving the right to leave (for marriage, for example), and often giving the same number of days. For example, only 2.3 per cent of collective agreements include the right of leave in case of divorce (and only to an average of 1.5 days), a common contingency but not regulated by law. The same applies to other contingencies: only 8.4 per cent of collective agreements regulate the right to take a child to the doctor, and only 1.15 per cent include time off to attend training courses for those with a handicapped child. In relation to unpaid leave, 3.45 per cent include leave to "take care of family business", 2.3 per cent in case of the sickness of a child and 1.15 per cent to take care of a relative with a terminal illness.[16] As we can see from these examples, corresponding to 87 collective agreements published from September 2003 to February 2004 and analysed in the *Informe Randstand* (2004), in practical terms Spanish firms seem to attach little

---

15. 89% of men born between 1956 and 1960 will reach the age of 50 (93% in the case of women) and life expectancy at that age will be almost 33 years for men and 38 for women (Pérez Díaz, 2003).

16. For a more detailed analysis see *Informe Randstan* (2004) pp. 100-116.

importance to the reconciliation of work and family life, although it is recognized that these difficulties are one of the reasons behind work absenteeism,[17] especially among women.

11.5 WAGES: IS WORK ENOUGH?

Wages are an important part of what makes a good job, as they constitute the main source of income for a majority of families. For the purpose of our analysis four items are relevant in relation to this issue: (i) how wages have fared in the past, (ii) the level of wage inequality, (iii) the type of employment created during the employment boom and (iv) the proportion and characteristics of low-wage workers.

Wage moderation

In relation to the first question, during the last decade Spanish real wages have been stagnant: from 1996 to 2005 real wage costs per worker (the index we will take as a proxy of average wages) rose 0.47 per cent. In fact, if we take 2000 as the starting year for the comparison, total real wage costs fell by a total of 0.45 per cent.[18] Thus, in aggregate terms we can say that during the last decade improvements in the Spanish labour market have been limited to the much needed generation of new jobs: in the same period total employment increased by 53.6 per cent (from 12 to 19 million), but in a context of an aggregate wage freeze. This wage moderation, backed by the two main trade unions, is for many analysts one of the key elements behind the huge employment growth experienced in Spain.

Wages influenced by type of employment created

Ten sectors of activity contributed 89 per cent of the growth in employment from 1996 to 2006, 99 per cent if we include manufacturing (EPA and SES, 2002). Out of these ten sectors, six (restaurants and hotels, retail, real estate, entrepreneurial activities, construction and domestic service) – accounting for two thirds of total employment created – have an average wage significantly lower than the overall average. In 1996, 41 per cent of all employees worked

---

17. According to a survey conducted among 2,216 human resource managers in different countries (CREADE 2001), while 90% of human resource managers believe that a good work–life balance improves productivity, and 95% believe that it is possible to offer working time flexibility without impairing the productivity of the firm, still only a minority of firms offer flexibility (excluding part-time and flexible holidays). This is especially true of Spanish firms.
18. Quarterly Labour Cost Survey (Encuesta Trimestral de Coste Laboral) and Wage Survey (Encuesta de Salarios en la Industria y los Servicios), constant €.

in these sectors; in 2004 the percentage was 53 per cent. Therefore we can say that in the last decade a significant part of Spanish employment creation has been concentrated in sectors of economic activity with lower than average wages. This characteristic is behind both the low wage growth and the low productivity growth experienced recently in Spain. If one of the desirable characteristics of a job is a "reasonable" wage, and if we identify a "reasonable" wage with the average wage in the economy, then we can say that the employment recovery of the Spanish economy has to a large extent been based on low-quality jobs.[19]

Low-wage workers on the increase?

In 2004 the percentage of low-wage workers (with wages under 60 per cent of the median) was 13.8 per cent. Analysis of the evolution of low-wage work (Muñoz de Bustillo and Anton, 2006b) shows that there has been a decreasing trend in the percentage of low-wage jobs in the Spanish economy. It seems, though, that the huge increase in employment, even though concentrated in sectors of activity with wages lower than average, has not contributed to a relative increase in low-wage work. The intensity of low-wage work is nevertheless very different among different groups of workers, higher for those aged 16–24 (35 per cent), women (25.6 per cent), part-time workers (70 per cent), workers with temporary contracts (26 per cent) and private sector (17 per cent). As regards education, the percentage of low-wage work has the usual negative relationship with the level of education of the workers, being lowest for workers with a university degree, although it is interesting that in the last two waves of the survey there was a surge of low-wage work among this group of workers. Small and medium-sized enterprises show a much higher percentage of low-wage work: the rate of low-wage employees among those working in firms with 1 to 4 employees was 36.6 per cent, while only 1.7 per cent of those working in large firms (500 or more employees) were low-wage workers. Finally, the type of contract could have a significant impact on wages. According to the Structure of Earnings Survey (SES), the average wage of workers with temporary contracts is 60.6 per cent of the wage of their colleagues with an open-ended contract, with a greater difference for men (59.5 per cent) than for women (63.5 per cent). As we can see, the wage gap related to type of contract is huge, especially if we consider that

---

19. This connection between wage and productivity growth is valid on the assumption of constant distribution of income between wages and profits and among different types of workers. Otherwise the increase in productivity does not warrant a correlative increase in wages. This was the case, for example, in the United States from 1996 to 2001, where most of the huge productivity increase was absorbed by the richest decile of income distribution, leaving little for the other 90% (Dew-Becker and Gordon, 2005).

the SES does not cover agriculture and the public sector, and only establishments with 10 or more workers, leaving out small firms, where lower wages tend to be concentrated.

Having established the intensity and characteristics of low-wage employment in Spain, the next step is to analyse the extent to which having a low-wage job leads to poverty risk for workers. As expected, employment is the most effective way to secure oneself against the risk of poverty: the poverty rate of those employed is 11.2 per cent in contrast with an overall poverty rate of 19.9 per cent. Nevertheless, workers (including low-wage workers but also other employees and the self-employed), after inactive people, constitute the largest population group at risk of poverty (27 per cent) . The rate of poverty risk among the self-employed, 32.8 per cent, is particularly high.

Focusing on the relation between employment, low wages and poverty in the subset of low-wage workers, the percentage of working poor during the period fluctuates around 5 per cent, rising from 4.8 per cent in 1994 to 5.8 per cent in 2004. In 2004 almost one third of the working poor had low wages as defined in this chapter, and the rest were workers with wages over the low-wage line but with household characteristics that pushed them under the poverty line. In this respect, there has been an important reduction in the percentage of working poor with low wages during the period. This reduction is shown clearly in the evolution of the correlation coefficient between poverty and low wages: from 0.290 in 1994 to 0.179 in 2004. Finally, in 2004 almost one fifth of low-wage workers lived in poor households. The rest of low-wage workers lived in households with other sources of income (or lived alone) allowing the household unit to push itself above the poverty line.

The last question to be addressed in this section concerns the extent to which low wages constitute only an episode suffered by workers who in due course are then able to rise to better paid jobs, or alternatively constitute entrapment in the lower segment of the labour market. In this respect, according to Ramos-Díaz (2005), in Spain the *stepping stone hypothesis*, by which low-wage jobs are entry doors to the labour market to be followed by better paid jobs, has to be discarded in favour of the *durable trap hypothesis* by which low-wage workers either remain as such ("low-wage persistency"), or they became unemployed only to be hired again as a low-wage worker ("revolving door effect").

11.6 HEALTH AND SAFETY: THE POOR RECORD OF THE SPANISH ECONOMY

Health is a key element of human well-being, therefore a vital element of working conditions is the risk of suffering an accident at work or an occupational disease. According to the theory of compensating differentials, the existence of undesirable characteristics associated with certain jobs, such as a higher risk of accident, should be compensated in the market by higher wages (or shorter hours). If this were the case, we could argue that ultimately workers would choose between different combinations of wages, other positive characteristics and accident (or occupational disease) risk, according to their own preferences. Unfortunately, in general the data do not seem to back this hypothesis (Pita and Dominguez, 1998). To give an example, in Spain construction has the highest rate of work accidents (10.5 per cent in 2004), but its wage is 15 per cent lower than the average.

A reverse trend compared to other EU countries

Spain has a clear negative record in relation to other European countries. First, Spain has a higher rate of both fatal and non-fatal accidents at work, even after taking into consideration the different economic structure of Spain, and the different proneness to accidents of different sectors of activity. In 2000 the standardized Spanish rate of non-fatal accidents at work (with more than three days' absence) was 7,052 per 100,000 persons in employment, compared with an EU-15 average of 4,016.[20] The index for fatal accidents (excluding road traffic and transport accidents) was 4.7 per 100,000 workers, compared with 3.2 for the EU-15. Second, although in the last few years Spain has managed to reduce its rate of accidents at work, the reduction has not been strong enough to compensate the increase in the accident rate at the turn of the century, leaving the Spanish rate for serious accidents in 2005 at a similar (and comparatively high) rate to a decade ago. In contrast, the EU-15 shows a decreasing trend throughout the period: in terms of standardized rates, the EU-15 went from 111 in 1994 to 94 in 2001, while in Spain the index went up from 88 in 1994 to 108 in 2000, and down slightly to 106 in 2001 (base year = 1998).

The Spanish context

The causes commonly adduced to explain the high level of accidents at work in Spain include the growing share of construction in the Spanish economy, the increasing reliance on outsourcing,[21] the higher percentage of temporary workers and the higher proportion of small firms.[22]

---

20. Eurostat (2004), p. 115.

21. Of the 332 fatal accidents studied by INSHT (2003), one third of the deceased workers worked in subcontracted firms: 54% of the accidents studied were in construction, 19% in services and 14.4% in manufacturing.

22. See, for example, the report of the UGT on work accidents in Spain 1996–2002: Comisión Ejecutiva Confederal UGT Salud Laboral y Medio Ambiente. *Evolución de la siniestralidad en España 1996–2002* http://www.ugt.es/slaboral/siniestralidad96-02.pdf

According to type of contract, 52.6 per cent of the employees who had an accident were on fixed-term contracts, much higher than the percentage of employees with this type of contract (32.5 per cent). This high difference in the rate of accidents at work by type of contract could be the result of differences in the characteristics of the economic activities performed by temporary and permanent workers, or different personal characteristics of the workers themselves. In this respect, it is well known that certain economic activities are more prone to accidents than others. Although personal and job characteristics are crucial to explaining the probability of accidents at work, it seems the duration of the labour relation is also important, both for its impact on job efforts and specific investment in training by the firm.

Nevertheless, according to a detailed analysis of fatal accidents made by the National Institute of Security and Health at Work, INSHT (2003), most fatal accidents are the result of multiple causes of very different natures, ranging from deficient work organization to the actions of the workers themselves: among the former type of cause, this study highlights the lack of proper work practices and training, as well as the lack of systems of risk evaluation at firms; among the latter, workers' failure to comply with health and safety rules and their refusal to use safety equipment. The design of work (inadequate organization of work and prevention) is behind 64 per cent of the cases studied. For example, significant causes of fatal accidents include workers having to carry out "non-usual tasks" and coordination problems when more than one firm is involved in the production process. Another risk factor is the small number of health and safety inspectors on Spain: 1 per 25,000 workers in the Region of Madrid, for example, compared with a European average of 1 per 7,000.

According to the data collected by the European Working Conditions Survey, Spanish workers on aggregate perceive their jobs as more risky in terms of both poor working environment and injurious physical activity. Only in relation to pace of work do Spanish workers offer a rosier picture of their working environment. Finally, by way of counterpoint, it is important to be aware that the relatively poor working conditions for many workers described so far is only part of the picture. Workers in general consider relations with their fellow workers to be very satisfying and show a relatively high (7.3 on a scale from 1 to 10) level of pride in their work.[23]

---

23. According to the 2004 ECVT, 72% of workers consider that their relations with their fellow workers are good, compared to only 2.5% who have bad relations. It is interesting, however, that only 58% consider their relations with their bosses to be good (24% indifferent).

11.7 TRAINING FOR CONVERSION TO HIGHER-QUALITY JOBS

According to the EU, the key to more and better quality jobs is training, and more specifically lifelong learning, as the ever-increasing rate of technological change can render today's knowledge useless in a short time.

A few key indicators of the quality of education

It is outside the limits of this chapter to analyse in detail the quality and level of the education completed by Spanish workers, so we will focus on only a few indicators that will help us in our study of training. As a starting point, in comparison to the rest of Europe, Spain – along with a few other southern countries such as Italy and Greece, and especially Portugal and Malta – has an unusually high percentage of the workforce in the lower educational categories (ISCED 0–2).[24] The workforces of all other EU countries have a pyramid-like educational profile. For these five countries, however, the profile is quite different: in all cases a majority (or close to it) of workers are in the group with low levels of educational attainment. However, what makes Spain different from the rest of the countries included in this group is that in Spain the percentage of the population with a tertiary education is slightly above the EU average. Therefore in Spain there is a high level of work force polarization in terms of level of educational attainment: a relatively high proportion of workers at both ends of the educational spectrum and a low percentage in the middle. In fact, Spain has the highest index of workers with a tertiary education in relation to workers with an upper secondary education in the EU-25 (ISCED 5–6 relative to ISCED 3–4).

This situation is important for two reasons. First, as the economic structure of Spain is not oriented to the production of high-tech high-human-capital goods and services, the combination of a high percentage of workers with tertiary education and a low percentage of workers with secondary education can lead to the underemployment (in terms of skills) of part of the group of workers with higher educational attainment, who can find themselves overqualified for the type of job they end up doing. On aggregate, in 2004, 17.4 per cent of employees considered themselves over-skilled in relation to their job, a proportion higher than in 2000, when it was 14.4 per cent. The percentage is higher for women (20.7 per cent), workers aged 20–29 (24.5 per cent and 27.6

---

24. According to the International Standard Classification of Education, ISCED, designed by UNESCO in the early 1970s, education is divided in 6 different levels: 0 = pre-primary, 1, primary, 2 = lower secondary education, 3 = (upper) secondary education, 4 = post-secondary non-tertiary education, 5 = first stage of tertiary education and 6 = second stage of tertiary education. For more details see (http://www.unesco.org/education/information/nfsunesco/doc/isced_1997.htm)

per cent, respectively) and for those with temporary contracts (27.5 per cent). (ECVT, 2004). This fact could also explain the lower unemployment rate of workers with tertiary education.

The second implication of the skewed distribution of workers according to their level of education is that, *ceteris paribus*, training is both more important for the proper preparation of the labour force for the challenges of the new age of technological change (the compensatory role of training), and more difficult, as for those with a lower educational level the process of learning will probably be more problematic.

Lack of training

Unfortunately, according to comparative EU data (Eurostat, LFS, 1999) it seems that Spanish firms do not attach much importance to the training of their workforce: Spain is once again at the lower end of European countries ranked by relative participation of employees in training courses: 25 per cent compared with the EU-25 average of 39 per cent. In contrast with this lower participation of workers in training, those workers who participate in training courses do so for a longer period of time: 42 hours compared to the EU-25 average of 30 hours. Thus, in this respect we find another polarization of workers: most workers do not have any training at all, but the few who have on average spend more time at it. This polarization also shows up when we look at the distribution of training according to workers' educational status, as participation in training is positively correlated with level of education: it is almost six times higher for those with a university degree than for those with basic or no education (Fundación Tripartita para la Formación y el Empleo, 2003). Those with more education (and younger) profit more from continuous training, thereby hindering the compensatory role of training and increasing the risk of already vulnerable workers. In addition, according to the ECVT 2004, the proportion of temporary workers receiving training in firms with formal training is 55 per cent, compared with 62.5 per cent in the case of workers with a permanent contract.[25]

The low priority given to training is also indicated by the small number of firms with training programmes for their workers: only 36 per cent compared to the EU-25 average of 62 per cent. This difference is especially important in small firms: the percentage of small firms (with less than 50 employees) with training programmes in Spain is half the European average. The difference narrows as we increase the size of firm. Finally, this lower priority given to

---

25. *Encuesta de Condiciones de Vida y Trabajo*, 2004, Table 4.1B, http://www.mtas.es/estadis-ticas/ECVT/Ecvt2004/IN4/index.htm)

training is also visible in the low proportion of training in the total labour costs of Spanish firms: a mere 0.36 per cent in 2004.[26]

Summing up, if we consider that a good job is a job that allows workers to continue learning, then we have to say that a majority of Spanish jobs do not meet this criterion. This circumstance is probably related to the high percentage of temporary work and a culture of hiring and firing (see section 11.1), as well as the high proportion of small firms in the Spanish economy and the greater difficulty faced by small firms in organizing training on a continuous basis.

CONCLUSION: A CLOSER LOOK AT VULNERABLE WORKERS

We have reviewed the main challenges characterizing work and employment conditions in Spain: high rates of temporary employment and accidents at work, longer working hours, stagnant wages, growing problems in reconciling work and life, and low levels of on-the-job training are among the most pressing problems of a significant portion of Spanish workers. On the bright side, in the last few years Spain has witnessed a huge growth in employment alleviating the chronic curse of unemployment suffered by the country since the early 1980s, and the most recent measures taken by the government – achieved through social dialogue – to incentivize the transformation of temporary into permanent contracts seems at last to be producing a small but discernible change in the tendency of employment creation.[27]

The average lower quality of Spanish employment conditions in comparison with European standards is the product of several factors, among which we would like to highlight: the lower level of economic development, with an economic structure still focused in sectors with lower productivity and less room for the improvement of working conditions without jeopardizing profits; the high level of unemployment and its impact on the negotiating power of employees; the lower affiliation rates and the relative weakness of trade unions derived from it; the concentration of collective agreements, at least until relatively recently, on wage-related issues (forgetting other issues with important implications for quality of work); the lack of an established culture of partnership within the firm;[28] and the late development of the welfare state, still to this day weaker than in most EU-15 Member States. These factors explain

---

26. Comparative data for 2000 was 2% in the EU-15 versus 0.42% in Spain. (Eurostat, labour cost survey, 2000).

27. *Acuerdo para la mejora del crecimiento y el empleo* (Agreement for the improvement of employment and growth), 9 May 2006.

28. For example, in Spain 62% of employees can discuss changes of work organization with the firm, compared with an EU average of 71% (85% in Finland).

why firms do not face much pressure, apart from the pressure deriving from government regulations or their own moral standards, to improve the working conditions of their employees. On the other hand, the priority given to the fight against unemployment has led to a watering down, in terms of labour market regulation and enforcement, of public intervention in this area. Finally, the facilitation of temporary employment (adopted as early as 1984) as a means of increasing flexibility without reducing the protection (through redundancy payments) of workers with permanent contracts has led to the segmentation of the labour market and the growth of a contingency labour force with very little power to demand improvements in their working conditions.

To conclude, we will focus on those groups of workers who, due either to their personal characteristics or the characteristics of their jobs, are especially vulnerable to the changing nature of the labour market. First, we will define the different sources of vulnerability.

A first source of vulnerability (υI – see Table 11.2) is the risk of losing one's job, weighted by the cost of losing it and the duration of the unemployment spell. For example, in Spain young workers with temporary jobs have high vulnerability because they have an expiry date to their contracts (therefore their probability of losing the job is high), and the unemployment rate is high and therefore the risk of remaining unemployed is high too, while the percentage of workers qualifying for unemployment benefits is relatively low –23.6 per cent for unemployed aged 20–24 in 2006 (2nd quarter).[29] But those with a better education and continuous training will probably have a lower chance of losing their job, as they will be more flexible and even if they do lose it the time spent unemployed will probably be less due to their greater versatility.

In this framework, the first category of vulnerable workers is clearly those with temporary contracts, and within this group those with less education and training, as their chances of finding a permanent job are lower and the probability of suffering longer unemployment spells higher. At some distance behind the first group are workers with permanent jobs and a high salary, but working in sectors with high volatility due to the changing situation of their markets: foreign competition, relocation abroad, outsourcing, and so on. This is clearly a new type of uncertainty that now affects groups of workers formerly protected from market fluctuations. For this group of workers as a whole, the risk overall is still considerably lower, but the cost in terms of forgone earnings can be considerably higher as their chances of finding a similar job once past their prime working age is low.[30] Furthermore, as pensions

---

29. It can be argued, however, that if the risk of losing a job is high, the chance of young workers building up years of tenure will be low, negatively affecting their future wages.

30. For example, according to Arranz and Garcia-Serrano (2003) the wage penalty associated with a lost job ("wage scare" in their terminology) is much higher (almost twice as high) for workers over 45 than for younger workers.

Table 11.2 Incidence of different types of vulnerability, Spain

Type	Source of vulnerability	Comparative level	Workers affected		Trend
			'000	%	
υI	Job insecurity[1]	Very high	4 777.2	32.4	+/– stable
υII	Discontinuities in working life	High	n.a.	n.a.	growing
υIII	Disabilities[2]	Depends on criteria used	793.3	4.2	n.a.
υIV	Lack of training[4]	High	11 541.1	78.4	Slowly decreasing
υV	Accidents at work[3]	High	871.7	4.8	Slowly decreasing
υVI	Low wages[5]	Average	2 134.5	14.5	Slowly decreasing

Notes: [1] 2004, EPA; [2] LFS Special module 2002, employed + unemployed with disabilities; [3] 2004 ECVT, Table 4.2; [4] 2004, *Estadisticas de Accidentes de Trabajo*, EPA, includes all workers; [5] 2002 rate applied to 2004 employees SES and EPA; n.a. = not available.

usually depend disproportionately on wages earned in the last few years of work, the financial impact of losing the job at a late stage of working life can affect the size of the pension.

There are two instruments of economic policy that can compensate for this source of vulnerability: improving unemployment protection, and education and training to improve the employability of workers. In the Spanish case, any effort in the direction of equilibrating the permanent–temporary distribution of employment towards the European average would also reduce vulnerability.

A second source of vulnerability, υII, is related to the discontinuity of working life, imposed this time not by the normal working of the labour market (hiring and firing), but by the restrictions faced by certain groups of workers in terms of having less time available for work in their life cycles. As we have seen, a growing number of workers, usually women, have to engage in other time-intensive activities, such as taking care of children or elders, leading either to breaks in their careers, to part-time work or to overwork (market work + household work). This situation can lead to a deterioration in the performance of the (usually female) workers, both at home and at work, to a reduction of their chances of promotion and well-being and to an increase in the risk of losing or quitting their job. In all cases, this will lead to a reduction of future wages. In this respect according to Gutierrez-Domènech (2005) the main impact of maternity on Spanish working mothers is a reduction in the employment rate: only 60 per cent of women employed one year before giving birth were employed one year after, with a lower permanency rate for those with fixed-term contracts (50 per cent versus 78 per cent).

A third source of vulnerability, υIII, is related to the impact of disability on the chance of having, and keeping, a job. At the time of the last Spanish national survey on disabilities, deficiencies and health (1999), there were 1.3 million persons of working age with different degrees of disability (mentally handicapped, visually impaired, and so on). This group of citizens has both a lower labour force participation rate, 32.2 per cent, and a higher unemployment rate, 26 per cent. Thus a majority (76 per cent) were either unemployed or inactive. Although half of the non-active disabled population mentioned their incapacity to work as the reason for not being engaged in jobseeking, adding the unemployed and those not looking for a job because they think it is useless due to their disability, the corresponding unemployment rate (unemployed plus hidden unemployed) is 50 per cent, confirming the particular vulnerability of this group of citizens as workers. This type of vulnerability is usually addressed by the state through special employment programmes, although they seldom reach the desired level. In Spain, only 15 per cent of disabled workers benefit from these type of programmes.

A fourth source of vulnerability, υIV, is a lack of training, especially when combined with low human capital. If we consider that workers with high human capital and access to lifelong learning are in a better position to successfully face the labour market changes associated with changes in demand and technology, then lack of training can be considered an important source of vulnerability. As we saw in section 11.7 the workers most vulnerable in this category would be those who have not completed upper secondary education. In 2004 among 18–24 year olds, 30 per cent abandoned education before obtaining an upper secondary education certificate (compared to 18 per cent in the EU as a whole). This group, with low formal human capital, will face higher constraints when adapting to the expected technological and organizational changes of the future. Other groups subject to this source of vulnerability are temporary workers, employees of small firms and older workers.

A fifth source of vulnerability, υV, is related to the risk of having accidents at work. As we have seen, some workers – especially temporary workers – and some sectors (construction for example) are especially prone to accidents at work. The dilution of health and safety responsibilities in firms subcontracting part of the production process (very common in construction) – a practice that has increased lately across the whole spectrum of the economy – is also an important source of accident risk. Therefore the employees working for subcontracted firms are also subject to this source of vulnerability.[31]

---

31. For example, in one of the most serious labour accidents of 2005 that resulted in the death of six construction workers (in Almuñecar, Andalusia), five of the deceased were employees of a Portuguese firm subcontracted by a Galician firm that was doing construction work for a third firm (in fact a temporary union of three other firms) hired by the regional government.

The last source of vulnerability, ʋVI, is related to low wages. Low-wage workers are vulnerable in a different sense from sources I to V. Low-wage workers can be found in permanent jobs with a low health risk: the vulnerability is not related to the work itself, but to the inadequacy of the income derived from work to meet the needs of the worker and his/her family. This low level of income will increase the cost of episodes of unemployment as it can be expected that low-wage workers will have lower levels of savings than average workers to face spells of unemployment or other unexpected expenditures. According to the *Encuesta Continua de Presupuestos Familiares* (Household Survey), there has been an increase in the percentage of households that find it difficult or very difficult to make ends meet, from 21 per cent in 2001 to 26 per cent in the last quarter of 2005. Considering that for 69 per cent of Spanish households their major source of income is labour, and for 31 per cent social benefits, and considering that in the last few years social transfers (mostly pensions) have increased in line with the Consumer Price Index, it is reasonable to assume that for an important group of Spanish families, wages (or the combination of wages and whatever other income they might get) are not high enough to meet their needs.

From our analysis we can say that Spain has a comparatively high proportion of vulnerable workers. A rough estimate of the volume of workers affected by each period of vulnerability is offered in Table 11.2 on page 461.

In interpreting Table 11.2 it is important to notice that we cannot add the workers affected by different sources of vulnerability to come up with an estimate of the proportion of vulnerable workers, as many workers suffer from more than one type of vulnerability. In fact, we can say that one of the characteristics of vulnerable workers is that they suffer from vulnerabilities from many different sources. For example, as we have seen, the rates of accidents at work and the rates of low-wage work are higher among those with temporary contracts, while their probability of receiving training is lower. Furthermore, the different types of vulnerabilities have different implications, and even if we could add up the numbers, the aggregate would be meaningless, as we would be dealing with heterogeneous items. In any case, the numbers show that a relevant proportion of Spanish workers face one or another type of risk in terms of their vulnerability to a changing labour market.

Before concluding this section it is important to call attention to a new population group which is highly vulnerable to several of the previously mentioned sources of malaise. Three decades ago Spain was a source of emigration with up to three million workers abroad. Ten years ago Spain was one of the EU countries with the lowest proportion of immigrants (around 1.4 per cent). In contrast, in 2005 the percentage of immigrants was close to 9 per cent, making immigration one of the major concerns of Spaniards. Focusing on extra-EU immigrants, this group is characterized by a higher unemployment rate, and although with a level of education roughly similar to Spanish nationals (and higher if we do not take into consideration the different age composition of the two groups), they are overrepresented in low qualification–low-wage jobs, and mostly work in small firms in construction, agriculture and services. Their rate of temporary employment is also higher (59 per cent). Finally, the poverty rate among immigrants is twice the rate of the non-immigrant population[32] (including EU residents in Spain). Immigrants therefore are more prone to suffer from at least four out of the six vulnerabilities considered in Table 11.2: I (insecurity), IV (lack of training), V (accidents), and VI (low wages).

---

32. For more details see Muñoz de Bustillo and Antón (2006c).

REALITY AT ENTERPRISE LEVEL: CASE STUDIES

General context

Compared to other European countries, Spain is characterized by a high proportion of small and medium-sized enterprises. In fact, half of Spanish firms (excluding agriculture) have no employees whatsoever, and of those with employees, 87 per cent have fewer than 10, and 98 per cent fewer than 50. Thus, we can say that large firms are *rara avis* in the Spanish economy as only 0.11 per cent of firms with employees have 500 employees or more. This will have implications in terms of training and wages since large firms usually pay higher wages and have better training facilities. Furthermore, trade unions are more present in large firms, while small firms usually rely on informal systems of labour relations.

From the perspective of employment distribution the situation is slightly different: according to the ECL (*Encuesta de Coyuntura Laboral*) 55 per cent of employees worked at firms with 50 employees or less, while almost one quarter of employees worked at firms with more than 250 employees. This duality in terms of firm size is the first aspect to be taken into consideration when selecting the case studies. Furthermore, although with only four case studies we cannot expect to cover all the relevant types of firms in the Spanish economy, we have tried to include firms with different competitiveness strategies.

Spain Case Study 1 – Employment stability through training in a printing company

The first firm selected belongs to the publishing and printing sector. The size profile of the sector is quite similar to the aggregate size distribution of firms according to employment, with three differences: lower self-employment, slightly higher proportion of firms with from 5 to 50 employees, and only 1 firm over 1,000 employees (0.004 compared to 0.021 per cent). In 2004 the share of the sector in total employment was 1.47, down from 1.59 in 1996. This reduction in relative employment was nevertheless compatible with employment growth over the period of 65 per cent. The sector is characterized by an average wage 19 per cent higher than the national average and by average wage dispersion. This sector has experienced significant technological changes in the last decade as a result of the digital revolution in the handling of images and text. In this context there is a clear divide between firms according to size: small firms usually have older vintage capital and are not able to compete in terms of quality with bigger firms, their survival strategy being to compete on price.

Firm 1 is a family firm created in 1980 with little investment (just a photocopying machine) in a service city not far from Madrid. It only has one establishment, although there is an affiliate firm, fully owned by Firm 1, in Madrid. This firm was acquired 9 years ago in order to have a foothold in the capital, one of the most important markets in the country. The firm has 98 employees (plus 17 in Madrid). Employment has increased in the last few years, and the tendency is expected to continue into the future (especially in the Madrid branch). The firm competes in national and international markets (mostly Portugal). In sharp contrast with the high percentage of temporary workers that characterizes the Spanish labour market, 98 per cent of the employees of Firm 1 have a permanent contract. This corresponds to the highly specific training of the workers. Women are underrepresented in the labour force (25 per cent). Only two persons have part-time contracts, in both cases as result of the workers' desire to better reconcile work and family life, and two more are on part-time retirement, used by the management to bring forward the retirement age, especially in the case of more physically demanding workstations. The average age of the employees is around 30. The firm works on a three-shift basis five days a week, although some processes only work on a two-shift basis. According to the HR managers the shift system night–afternoon–morning is well accepted by the workforce. Only 13 per cent of the workforce has flexible working time. The system of shifts makes flexitime impractical for most production workers. The firm seldom resorts to overtime.

As already mentioned, the firm offers training on a regular basis (external and internal) to make up for the relative scarcity of workers with the necessary training. Most training is directed towards new employees, some of it using publicly funded FIP courses (*Formación Inserción Profesional* (vocational insertion training). The hiring rate – by the firm itself – for the last course was 50 per cent. Workers also participate in chain training (one worker trains his/her colleagues after receiving specific training in new processes or machinery), and there is also training in other areas, such as health and safety. The firm collaborates with local vocational schools in order to improve the local supply of workers with specific knowledge. According to the manager one of the reasons for setting up in Madrid is that it is much easier to find workers with specific skills there. The system of job promotion is still the traditional one, with workers starting at the bottom and advancing with the passing of time and training. The HR manager is himself an example of this promotion system. According to the ISO 9001[33] norm applied by the firm, each

---

33. ISO 9001 and ISO 14001 are generic management system standards. Firms with ISO 9001 accreditation meet certain criteria in terms of quality management such as (*cont. on next page*)

work post has a specific educational entry level, and the firm sticks to it: design employees require a university degree in fine arts, and the rest either vocational training (usually supplied by the local public vocational school) or specific training courses organized by the firm.

The firm does not practise functional flexibility (changes in the tasks performed by workers) as a norm due to the specificity of each workstation. The firm has quality circles and has taken advantage of the introduction of the ISO 9001 and 14001 norms to reorganize the work process. The firm has a web page, although it is merely ornamental. The Internet is used as the major system of communication only with some institutional clients.

The firm contracts out auxiliary activities (accounting, maintenance, and so on). In relation to production, the firm would like to subcontract a number of activities but is not able to do so due to the small size of local industry. The firm is forced to retain machinery with very low capacity utilization in specific side-production processes. This is an significant inconvenience of being located in a tertiary small city.

Relations with the trade unions are characterized as cooperative; wages are above average; and there is a continuous process of reinvestment that gives workers confidence in the future of the firm.

The firm's low – almost zero – temporary employment rate is especially interesting as printing firms have an important feature in common with services: they produce on demand. The need to synchronize production and demand is frequently mentioned as an important reason behind the high rates of temporary work (in order to reduce fixed costs), but Firm 1 does not rely on this type of contract. The reason offered by the management is that the skills required impose the use of permanent contracts.

This case highlights the importance of training in explaining the low rate of temporary work. Spain is still to a large extent dominated by the production of low- and medium-skilled goods and services, and so temporary contracts can be a cost-saving option for firms. In contrast, temporary work is not always an option for firms producing highly skilled products or using capital-intensive production methods that demand specific (and scarce) skills from workers. Furthermore, such firms usually have higher productivity and are thus in a better position to pay the wage premium usually obtained by permanent workers. In fact, the higher productivity, especially when the production process is controlled and intermediated by labour, is very much dependent upon the level of effort and the degree of identification of the labour force

---

satisfying customer's quality requirements, complying with regulations or enhancing customer satisfaction. ISO 14001 is specifically concerned with environmental management. ISO itself does not assess the conformity of quality or environmental management systems to ISO 9000 or ISO 14000 standards. The certification is carried out independently of ISO by more than 720 "certification" or "registration" bodies active nationally or internationally (www.iso.org).

with the firm. This identification is much easier in firms with good working conditions and that show an interest in their workers (not least by investing in upgrading the firm's capital).

Spain Case Study 2 – The impact of public regulation on out-sourcing business services

Business services has had above average employment growth in Spain over the last decade as firms (and the public sector as well) concentrated on their core production activities and externalized many auxiliary activities, such as security, maintenance and cleaning. As a result of this outsourcing there has been both an increase in employment and an increase in the number of firms operating in the sector (by 30 per cent between 1999 and 2005). It is also a very polarized sector in terms of firm size: almost two thirds of firms are individual self-employed persons, while at the other end of the scale 17 firms (0.004 per cent of the total) have more than 5,000 employees.

Firm 2 is one of the major firms in this sector. It has more than 50,000 employees in both Spain and abroad (25 per cent of the total workforce, mostly in Latin America). The firm was established in the early 1960s as a small family firm specializing in cleaning. Over time the firm extended its operations to security, environmental services (gardening and so on), socio-sanitary services, maintenance, temporary employment, logistics and telemarketing. Nowadays the core business in Spain in terms of employment is cleaning and environmental services (63 per cent), followed at some distance by security services (14.6 per cent).

The firm is present in every Spanish province. The data reproduced in these pages refer to a range of activities covering all the different lines of business (excluding the temporary employment agency), although the bulk of the business is made up of cleaning, environmental services, security, socio-sanitary services and auxiliary services in one of the Spanish provinces. The firm faces both local and national competition depending on the line of business. Employment in the local branch fluctuates annually between 400 and 500 workers, due to the existence of strong seasonal fluctuations in demand in some of the services provided by the firm (for example, maintenance and management of swimming pools). There has been significant growth in employment in the last five years (around 25 per cent). Over the next few years employment growth of 8–10 per cent is expected.

In sharp contrast with the firm's sector of activity, where the contingency rate is 44 per cent, most employees of Firm 2 have permanent contracts (around 85 per cent), due to a policy of conversion of temporary employment into permanent employment applied by the firm over the last two years. This policy can be explained, among other things, by the heavy reliance of the firm on public administration contracts in their major business activities (due to the public administration's recent policy of externalization of many auxiliary activities) and the firm's obligation to hire the workers previously performing the outsourced activities for the company that lost the contract (compulsory hiring of workers). Therefore there is little difference between permanent or fixed-term contracts from the point of view of flexibility of employment, because if the company loses the contract, its workers will automatically start working for the new company that won the outsourcing contract. The proportion of women is around 40 per cent, although the percentage is much higher in some activities (cleaning) than in others (gardening or security). The firm uses part-time contracts in certain activities, such as swimming pool management (1,425 annual hours) and auxiliary activities and cleaning, but sparsely, according to the manager. There is a difference of opinion between the firm and the employee representatives concerning what should be considered overtime. The latter consider that for those working part time, overtime is any time worked over contractual working time, while the firm insists that overtime is only time worked above the contractual hours of full-time workers. Interestingly, the workforce is divided on the issue, too, as there is always a group of workers willing to work overtime in order to increase take-home pay, even if overtime is paid less than it should be according to the collective agreement. Working time is strongly determined by type of service, and only workers in administration (3 per cent) have flexible working time.

The view expressed by the employee representatives is much less rosy. According to them, temporary contracts are used in all possible areas, such as swimming pools or "early risers" (a programme financed by the regional government to allow parents to leave their children at school before the start of the school day in order to allow for better reconciliation of work and family responsibilities). This specific line of business uses part-time and temporary contracts with very low hours (90 minutes per day) and low wages. In the case of swimming pools, for example, according to the employee representatives there has been a process of transforming open-ended contracts into fixed-term contracts, together with a "deprofessionalization" of the work: for example, the firm has opted for turning lifeguarding and supervision into little more than summer jobs for college students. This alternative was preferred as a means of reducing the expectation – and demands – of the workforce.

According to the firm, there is an ambitious training programme. In 2004 over 1,500 courses were organized at the firm level. Around 13,000 workers participated in training courses involving a total of 200,000 hours. The firm has its own training institute in charge of all training courses for workers at all levels, although due to the relatively low qualifications of the workforce, the firm has no significant problems filling its vacancies. The employee representatives take a completely different view, however. According to them, the company's "ambitious training plan" is more a public relations device than a system for improving workers' skills. Real training hours are below those stated; most of the time training courses take place out of working hours and are of little practical use. Often courses are approved but never take place. The firm uses both seniority and merit as systems of promotion (hiring every year 30 or 40 workers, mostly with university degrees, from outside), although according to the employee representatives the average worker seldom benefits from promotion and most are stuck in dead-end jobs. One of the few positive things that the employee representatives had to say about the firm is that it honours seniority bonuses and pays wages on time, which tells us something about this firm, but much more about the rest of the firms in the sector.

The manager considers that trade union relations are fairly good, although the situation is different in each branch of the firm, both locally and by sector. The employee representatives believe otherwise. According to them the firm has from the very beginning taken a very antagonist approach to labour relations. In this respect their experience is completely negative. Negotiations are always held on the basis of "blackmail": for example, when the employee representatives ask that one or other of the clauses in the collective agreement be honoured, the firm counters by saying that that clause (the 15-minute snack break, for example) would increase costs and force the firm to lay off workers in order to compensate such an increase.

The firm has the 9001 and 14001 certificates, and has systems of worker participation in work organization, although the intensity of the collaboration differs considerably depending on branch.

Although Firm 2's main business derives from the outsourcing of auxiliary activities by firms and the public administration, it is itself now in the process of externalizing a number of non-core activities, including book-keeping and wage administration. The main reason for this is cost cutting.

This case illustrates the impact of regulation on conditions of employment, highlighting how the compulsory transfer of workers in the case of service outsourcing contracts can lead to a significant increase in job security without negatively affecting the performance of firms providing services to business and public administration. This is particularly important in a context in which a firm's presence in a sector is subject to administrative decisions which can have a dramatic impact in a very short time. This can lead to a culture of contingency among firms: they specialize in providing services in general, rather than specific services, something that can have a detrimental effect on relations between firm and employees.

In contrast with other firm interviews where the opinions of workers and management were very similar, we found a strong conflict of opinion between employee representatives and management. This in itself is a good indicator of conflictual labour relations, and can be interpreted in the general context of the sector as an indirect indicator of bad employment conditions.

Finally, this case is a good example of how job stability, as important as it can be in the Spanish context, is only one of the items that defines what makes a good job. Wages, working conditions, working environment, and so on, are also important. In this respect, the sector of services to firms, especially in firms providing low-value-added services – such as cleaning – due to the nature of the job, usually offer very basic working conditions in comparison with the working conditions of workers performing the same jobs before externalization. When a firm performs a given auxiliary process internally, it only has to cover the labour costs – and what little capital cost is involved. But when the firm externalizes the process, on top of the production cost it has to pay the profit obtained by the firm providing the service. This process will not bring about a deterioration in working conditions unless there is a significant increase in productivity after externalization. In those cases where the gains in productivity are low (due to technological or organizational reasons), the pressure on the workers will probably increase after externalization, leading to a deterioration of working conditions.

Spain Case Study 3 – A hotel: combining fixed-term and agency workers

Firm 3 is an hotel belonging to a chain of 21 hotels, mostly in Spain. The firm has 750 employees nationwide and the establishment where we conducted our interviews has 30. The firm was founded in 1999, and the establishment was inaugurated in 2002; the level of employment has remained roughly constant since then. It is worth noting that the hotel's opening coincided with a major celebration that attracted a large number of visitors to the city. Since then the hotel has experienced a small reduction in turnover and profits, although nowadays it is in the process of regaining its former capacity utilization. Due to the short history of the establishment the labour force is reasonably young, with an average age of around 32 years; 43 per cent of the employees are female, and only two have part-time contracts (in both cases due to worker requests for a better balance between work and family). Although nationally this sector has a high proportion of fixed-term contracts, at Firm 3 the proportion is lower than average, at 14 per cent. The reason is that the firm uses agency workers to cover peaks of demand. In fact, from May to September the firm makes extensive use of this type of worker. In most cases, the agency workers come on a regular basis so the establishment has access to "known" workers but without the need to hire them directly. In order to improve their performance, the establishment gives agency workers training courses.

So far the establishment only gives training to middle-level and skilled personnel, although according to the hotel manager there are plans to extend training to the rest of the workforce. The establishment has different working schedules for the different types of worker: receptionists work on a three-shift basis; kitchen personnel and waiters have split shifts; and room maids continuous morning shifts. As the hotel is open 24 hours a day, seven days a week, holidays and Sundays worked by employees are accumulated into a two-week vacation at low season. Although workers at this establishment know their working schedule in advance, that is not common in many of the firms in the sector, whose workers very often only know their working schedule at short notice. The hotel seldom uses overtime. Planned overtime is remunerated normally, while overtime due to unforeseen circumstances is rewarded informally, with time off. At other establishments in the sector overtime, for fiscal reasons, is often paid "under the table". The sector, as well as restaurants, is also known for making extensive use of unremunerated overtime. That is not the case in Firm 3, which offers in this respect a good example of how policy matters, and how firms in the same sector have degrees of freedom in implementing their own human resource policies. The reason given by Firm 3 for not using overtime is a preference for resorting to agency workers in order not to negatively affect the performance of the employees as a result of overwork. According to the manager, absenteeism is nonexistent. The firm has a policy of functional flexibility within the different categories of worker. In its three and a half years so far the firm has had a turnover rate of almost two workers per post: in all cases the workers either quit or were promoted to other establishments within the firm.

The wages of entry-level workers follow the local collective agreement for hotel workers, while workers with supervisory responsibilities receive a bonus. There are no trade union representatives at the firm, and there is little interest on the part of the employees to organize. According to the manager, the relatively low number of workers and the informal system of worker participation allows good communication between manager and workers. In his opinion, the workers identify well with the firm (and vice versa), leading to a good working environment. The lack of absenteeism is taken as an indicator of a good working environment by the manager.

Although the firm subcontracts some activities, such as laundry, maintenance, and cleaning, their importance in relation to total output is small, and there are no plans to increase it.

A trade unionist familiar with the sector told us that the picture painted by the hotel manager is quite representative of the situation in the part of the sector represented by hotel chains, which usually have higher productivity, a higher occupation rate and therefore higher margins, enabling them to provide better working conditions. This situation is in sharp contrast with other, usually small establishments, which due to their lower productivity are only able to survive by "squeezing" their workers. This is a good example of the "firm cultures" mentioned in the introduction: compromising on "good service", especially in a sector where there is face-to-face contact with the client, is probably not compatible with good working conditions. In this case, the use of agency workers is fully justified, as temporary workers are hired to do temporary jobs and under comparable working conditions. Even if it may lead to a sort of employment segmentation of the firm's labour force it is difficult to find alternative ways of handling the high seasonal changes in demand faced by hotels without resorting to some kind of temporary work.

Spain Case Study 4 – A call centre operating with fixed-term contracts in their purest sense

The last case study is an example of fixed-term employment in its purest form. Telemarketing is a new business activity in Spain, as well as in the rest of the world, a by-product of the telecommunications revolution and a growing strategy for outsourcing information and technical services not long ago handled within firms. In a few years telemarketing has grown to an estimated 50,000 jobs (two thirds of them women). Among the traditional demands of workers in this sector is the equalization of their wages and working conditions with workers performing the same jobs in the firms that have outsourced part of their telemarketing activities. Firm 4 was established in 1998. At that time it was a pioneer in the area of telemarketing, but now it encompasses three different activities: call centre, web servicing and contact centre. Nowadays the firm has eight establishments in four cities with over 2,200 workstations, manned by many more workers. For example, in the establishment analysed, 1,800 employees serviced 400 workstations.

Most employees manning the workstations (tele-operators) have temporary contracts, although according to the collective agreement in force in 2006 30 per cent of temporary contracts should be converted into open-ended contracts. This agreement is not being honoured by the firm due to problems between the firm and the works council concerning the process of selecting workers to profit from the programme of contract conversion. The confrontation is the result of the opposition of the works council to using absenteeism as a variable in the rating of workers. There is a significant problem with absenteeism at the firm, which the works council attributes to the lack of possibilities for taking time off for personal or family reasons.

Focusing on the tele-operators – and leaving aside administrative staff – most workers are on temporary contracts: 10 per cent work full time and the rest part time (30–35 hours, three shifts), although frequently hours are increased according to the needs of the firm. Full-time annual working hours total 1,746. Workers are selected after an unremunerated training course and go through a one-month trial period. Afterwards they usually get a two-month contract. This contract can be renewed, although the firm usually waits for a period of 20 days before signing the new contract to avoid the accumulation of seniority. The advantages of this type of contract are lower dismissal costs and probably greater discipline on the shop-floor. The high turnover of workers also has an indirect impact on opportunities to organize the workforce. A good example is a strike organized at the local branch in Madrid a few years ago that succeeded because at the time the firm had a contract with a local cable provider that lasted for two years, making it possible for the workers to get to know each other. In this respect, in many establishments workers do not even have a fixed workstation, sitting at whatever station is free at the time they get to work. That means that usually they end up sitting with different colleagues, making it more difficult to build up working relationships and socialize. Workers also complain about the lack of space and of good health standards. For example, in a different establishment of the same company it took the workers two years to get personal headphones, even if in the end workers were just given interchangeable ear pads.

There is an automatic monitoring system from which workers have to log out the moment they leave their workstation. The time spent on each call is also monitored, and sometimes illegally recorded (not in this firm) and performance statistics are produced to rate the workers. All this leads to a high level of pressure (controllers and supervisors make up almost 10 per cent of the workforce). Workers believe that the intensity of work does not allow them to perform properly in terms of customer satisfaction. The job itself is also very stressful as the tele-operators have to deal with problems for which very often they are not equipped and questions – such as on quality of services – that are outside their competence. The firm is currently working for two telephone and communications firms, a sector with a very high rate of customer complaints. Workers are also worried about the lack of specific training for campaigns. In the words of one tele-operator: "it is very different to be in charge of telemarketing, attending a medical emergency number, or calls related to domestic violence. For the firm there is no difference at all: there are no specific protocols for these more sensitive jobs" ("Sin el mute: deriva por el trabajo de telemáketing", in *A la deriva por los circuitos de la precariedad femenina,* http://www.sindominio.net/karakola/precarias_tele.htm.). In fact, one of the implications of this lack of training and tools to solve the problems is that workers, as in Daniel Pennac's novel *Au bonheur des ogres*, become scapegoats of the angry customers.

In this context of extremely tight controls and stress, with wages under the national average (under EUR 13,000) and few chances of promotion (promotion to team coordinator is contingent on the campaign being run by the firm at the moment and usually is not maintained afterwards), tele-operators face the extra burden of working in a sector prone to delocalization.

The whole business of tele-operation is currently in the process of off-shoring in search of lower costs, so the workers have the extra pressure of knowing that their jobs might be shifted to a different continent in the near future.[34] This is the ultimate demand-side factor that allows the firms in the sector to continue their labour practices. The difference in tele-operators' wages between Spain and other Spanish-speaking countries is large enough to make the off-shoring threat credible (for example, compare the hourly wage in Spain of EUR 6.55 with EUR 3.5 in Argentina). On the supply side, a high unemployment rate (especially among young and female workers) makes it possible for the firm to offer rigid working conditions and low wages and still be able to cover its labour needs. Also, by many workers, especially university students or recent university graduates, telemarketing is considered just a transitory occupation while looking for something else, an attitude leading to more complacency in relation to working conditions. In fact, recently there were 3,000 candidates for 100 tele-operators' jobs advertised on a Spanish jobseekers' web page. This indicates how much working conditions are a factor to jobseekers.

Summary and conclusions

First, although firms very often face a common set of restrictions: technological change, globalization, regulations, and so on, they still have significant degrees of freedom when it comes to setting their working and employment conditions, and the case studies show they make use of that freedom. For many sectors, there is a high road and a low road, and firms can go either way. For firms that base their competitiveness on a skilled workforce, good working conditions go hand in hand with high productivity. Both the publishing company and the hotel are good examples of such a competitive strategy.

On the other hand, the existence of a significant pool of unemployed workers and the possibility of hiring *à la carte* offered by very permissive temporary employment legislation has generated negative incentives to Spanish

---

34. Recently Jazztel (a telecommunications company) dismissed 800 telemarketing workers in Galicia (Spain), after deciding to provide the service from Argentina. In fact, Jazztel didn't fire a single worker, it just ended its outsourcing contract with two firms, Stream and Teleperformance, operating from Galicia. This is a good example of how this business works. What makes this example even more interesting is that the same firm was having similar problems in Argentina (htto://www.sindicatode teleoperadores.com/Jazztel.html), where there is a very active tele-operators' trade union.

firms to take the low road of contingency, low productivity and low wages. Some firms have a culture of contingency in accordance with which having a loyal labour force is no longer an asset worth paying for. It seems that this culture of contingency also pays in profit terms, at least in the short term. Firms 2 and 4 are examples of such an approach to labour relations. The lack of attachment to a workforce or a community, the excess labour supply and the new ITC technologies that make supervision cheaper compared to traditional systems (Firm 4), together allow firms to reach their targets with a contingent, dissatisfied and probably underpaid workforce.

Second, in this context, public policy has a significant role in improving working conditions (Firm 2). The regulation of outsourcing services in Spain, according to which it is compulsory for the firm getting the outsourcing contract to hire the workers employed by the firm which previously provided the service, has important implications in terms of job stability, and without it the growing market related to the outsourcing of services would be much more insecure. In fact, with this regulation the employee is more secure than the firm itself.

Third, although productivity is not everything, it is an important restriction when setting working conditions. It has been argued – and both the printing company and the hotel are good examples – that good working conditions and a satisfied workforce can lead to an improvement in productivity, which in turn would finance an improvement in working conditions in a kind of virtuous circle. But that is not necessarily the case in all activities. The nature of some production processes is such that it is very difficult to increase productivity. Industrial cleaning in Firm 2, or telemarketing in Firm 4, are two different examples of such processes. In telemarketing, the only way of increasing "measured" productivity is by increasing the number of attended calls, that is, by worsening working conditions. In this context only regulation or the need to "bid for workers" in a context of low unemployment would lead to an improvement in working conditions. But if this is the case, that policy would probably lead also to an increase in prices. That would not be a direct problem for Firm 2, whose activities cannot be off-shored, but certainly it would be a problem for Firm 4, or more precisely, for the employees of Firm 4, as the firm could move its operations to Latin America in search of lower labour costs.

Summing up, good working conditions are the result of many different factors: labour and health and safety regulations, productivity increases, collective bargaining, technological changes, social norms and firm culture. Although some forces operate across sectors and regions (such as public policy) others, such as collective bargaining, technological changes or productivity increases, have different impacts in different sectors of activity, generating differences in employment conditions across sectors and across firms within a given sector.

REFERENCES

Adserà, A. 2003. Changing fertility in developed countries: The impact of labor market institutions. *Journal of Population Economics*, vol. 17: 17–43.

Ahn, N., and Mira, P. 2000. *A note on the changing relationship between fertility and female employment rates in developed countries.* Working Paper No 99–09. FEDEA. Madrid.

Alba A. 1998. How temporary is temporary employment in Spain. *Journal of Labor Research,* 19: 695–710.

Albert C., García-Serrano, C., and Herranz, V. 2005. Form-provided training and temporary contracts. *Spanish Economic Review*, vol. 7: 67–88.

Albrecht, J.W., Edin, P., Sundström, M., and Vroman, S.B. 1999. Career interruptions and subsequent earnings: A re-examination using Swedish data. *Journal of Human Resources*, vol. 34 (2): 294–311.

Amuedo-Dorantes, C. 2000. Work transitions into and out of involuntary temporary employment in a segmented market: Evidence from Spain. *Industrial and Labor Relations Review*, vol. 53: 309–25.

———. 2001. From 'temp-to perm': Promoting permanent employment in Spain. *International Journal of Manpower*, vol. 22 (7): 625–47.

Arranz, J.M., and C. Garcia-Serrano. 2003. *Non-employment and subsequent wage losses.* Instituto de Estudios Fiscales. P.T. N° 19/03. Madrid.

Arranz, J.M., M.A. Davia and C. García-Serrano. 2005. *Labour market transitions and wage dynamics in Europe.* ISER Working Paper, 2005-17. University of Essex.

Auer, P., J. Berg and I. Coulibaly. 2004. *Is a stable workforce good for the economy? Insight into the tenure-productivity employment relationship.* Employment Analysis and Research Unit. Employment Strategy Department. Geneva: ILO.

Baizán, P. 2001. Transitions to adulthood in Spain. In M. Corijn and E. Klijzing (eds), *Transitions to adulthood in Europe*, pp. 279–312. Dordrecht: Kluwer.

Becker S.O., Bentolila, S., Fernandes, A., and Ichino, A. 2005. *Youth emancipation and perceived job insecurity of parents and children.* http://www.iue.it/Personal/ Ichino/ichino_insecurity_12.pdf.

Blakemore, A., and Hoffman, D. 1998. Seniority rules and productivity: An empirical test. *Economica*, vol. 56: 359–71.

Blanchflower, D.G. 2000. Self-employment in OECD countries. *Journal of Labor Economics,* vol. 7: 471–505.

Casquel, E., and Cunyat, A. 2004. The dynamics of temporary jobs: Theory and some evidence for Spain. http://team.univ-paris1.fr/espe2005/papers/ casquel_paper.pdf.

CES (Consejo Económico y Social). 2002. *La emancipación de los jóvenes y la situación de la vivienda en España.* Informe 3/2002. Madrid.

CIS. 2005. Monthly barometer survey (May).

CREADE–Arbora-Global Career Partners. 2001. *Work & life balance: International survey.* Available at http://www.work-and-life-balance.com.

De la Rica, S., and F. Felgueroso. 1999. *Wage differentials between permanent and temporal workers: Further evidence.* Mimeo. Universidad del País Vasco.

De la Rica, S., and A. Iza. 2004. *Career planning in Spain: Do fixed-term contracts delay marriage and parenthood?* Mimeo. Universidad del País Vasco.

Dew-Becker, I., and R.J. Gordon. 2005. *Where did the productivity growth go? Inflation dynamics and the distribution of income.* NBER Working Papers 11842.

Dolado, J.J., García-Serrano, G., and Jimeno, J.F. 2002. Drawing lessons from the boom of temporary jobs in Spain. *Economic Journal*, vol. 112: 270–95.

Dolado, J.J., Felgueroso, F., and Jimeno, J.F. 1999. Los problemas del mercado de trabajo juvenil en España: Empleo, formación y salarios mínimos. *Economiaz*, vol. 43: 136–57.

Eurostat. 2004. *Work and health in the EU: A statistical portrait. Data 1994–2002.* European Commission.

Franco, A., and K. Winqvist. 2002. Women and men reconciling work and family life. Eurostat, *Statistics in focus*, Population and social conditions, Theme 3 – 9/2002.

Fundación Encuentro. 2004. *Informe España 2004.* Madrid.

Fundación Tripartita para la Formación y el Empleo. 2003. *Consolidación y desarrollo de la formación continua en España.* Madrid: FTFE.

Golsh, K. 2003. Employment flexibility in Spain and its impact on the transition to adulthood. *Work, Employment and Society*, vol. 17 (4): 691–718.

Greeg, P. 1998. Impact of unemployment and job loss on future earnings. In H.H. Treasure, *Persistent poverty and lifetime inequality: The evidence.* Occasional Paper No. 10.

Guadalupe, M. 2003. The hidden cost of fixed-term contracts: The impact on work accidents. *Labour Economics*, vol. 10: 339–57.

Güell M., and B. Petrongolo. 2005. How binding are legal limits? Transitions from temporary to permanent work in Spain. http://europa.eu.int/comm/employment_social/employment_analysis/docs/040212_petrongolo.pdf.

Gutierrez-Domènech, M. 2005. Employment transitions after motherhood in Spain. *Labour,* 19 (Special Issue): 123–48.

Hernanz Martín, V. 2003. *El trabajo temporal y la segmentación.* Consejo Económico y Social. Colección Estudios 147. Madrid.

Hernanz V., and L. Toharia. 2004. *Do temporary contracts increase work accidents? A microeconometric comparison between Italy and Spain.* FEDEA Documento de Trabajo 2004–2.

IMSERSO. 2004. *Encuesta de condiciones de vida de las personas mayores en España.* MTAS. Madrid.

Informe Randstad. 2004. *Calidad del trabajo en la Europa de los 15: Las políticas de conciliación.* Barcelona.

Instituto Nacional de Seguridad e Higiene en el Trabajo (INSHT). 2003. *Análisis cualitativo de la mortalidad por accidente de trabajo en España.* Madrid. http://www.mtas.es/insht/statistics/mortalidad2002.htm.

Kramarz, F., and S. Roux. 1999. *Within-firm seniority structure and firm performance.* Centre for Economic Performance Discussion Paper 420. April. London.

López, M.T., and Valiño, A. 2004. *Conciliación familiar y laboral en la Unión Europea.* Madrid: CES.

Macinnes, J. 2005. *Work–life balance in Europe: a response to the baby bust or reward?* Mimeo. http://www.ihs.ac.at/pdf/soz/macinnestext.pdf

Martinez-Granado, M. 2005. Testing labour supply and hours constraints. *Labour Economics*, vol. 12: 321–43.

Ministerio de Trabajo y Asuntos Sociales. 2004. *Encuesta de Calidad de Vida en el Trabajo* (ECVT). Madrid.

Muñoz de Bustillo, R. 2002. *Spain and the neoliberal paradigm.* January 2002. CEPA Working Paper 2002–02. Center for Economic Policy Analysis. New School University. New York. http://www.newschool.edu/cepa/papers/archive/cepa200202.pdf.

Muñoz de Bustillo, R. et al. 2004. *Nuevos tiempos de actividad y empleo.* Ministerio de Trabajo y Asuntos Sociales. Madrid.

Muñoz de Bustillo, R., and Fernandez, E. 2006. Operating hours, working times and employment in Spain. In L. Delsen et al., *Operating hours and working times: A survey of capacity utilisation and employment in the European Union.* Heidelberg: Springer.

Muñoz de Bustillo, R., and Antón, J.I. 2006a. *Low wage work in Spain (1994–2004).* Mimeo. University of Salamanca.

———. 2006b. *Inmigración y estado de bienestar. Una aproximación al caso español.* Mimeo. University of Salamanca

Pérez Díaz, J. 2003. *La madurez de masas.* Imserso, Colección Observatorio de las Personas Mayores No. 12, Madrid.

Pita, C., and Dominguez, B. 1998. Los accidentes laborales en España: La importancia de la temporalidad. *Documentación laboral*, N0. 55: 37–64.

Ramos-Díaz, J. 2005. *Low-wage employment: 'Stepping stone' or 'durable trap'.* Universidad Pompeu Fabra. Barcelona.

Riedman, A. et al. 2006. *Working time and work–life balance in European companies: Establishment survey on working time 2004–2005.* Dublin: European Foundation for the Improvement of Living and Working Conditions.

Simó, C., Castro, T., and Soro, A. 2001. *Changing pathways in the transition to adulthood in Spain: Labor market, marriage and fertility patterns of young people in the last decades.* Globalife Working Paper Series, No. 18. University of Bielefeld.

Simó, C., Golsh, K. and Steinhage, N. 2000. *Entry into parenthood in Spain and the process of globalization.* Globalife Working Paper Series, No. 8. University of Bielefeld.

Torrini, R. 2005. Cross-country differences in self-employment rates: the role of institutions. *Journal of Labour Economics*, vol. 12: 661–83.

12. Sweden: From permanent to temporary employment relationships

Jenny Lundberg and Emma Cronberg

12.1 INTRODUCTION: THE DOMINANT INFLUENCE OF THE EMPLOYMENT CONTEXT

Employment conditions in Sweden should be seen in the light of labour market developments. While the economic growth of the last couple of years has been strong, employment growth has been weak and there is a high rate of absence from work.

According to Eurostat the unemployment rate in Sweden was around 7.8 per cent in 2005, around average in comparison with the EU-15. However, historically Sweden has always had significantly lower unemployment than most EU countries. Today, unemployment is particularly high among young people: in April 2006 the unemployment rate in this group was 27.5 per cent (Statistics Sweden, 2006a), among the highest in Europe; only Poland has a higher unemployment rate among young people. The most recent unemployment figures show unemployment of 6.6 per cent in August (jobseeking students included) (Dagens Industri, 2006).

Immigrants constitute another group whose unemployment is high. In comparison with native Swedes, first generation immigrants are twice as likely to be unemployed. The situation on the labour market with a high unemployment rate affecting certain groups is certainly a contributory factor to the trends in working and employment conditions in Sweden today, where many people only have temporary work or would like to work more hours than they are offered. In search of means to reduce unemployment, especially among young people, the Danish flexicurity model has been benchmarked and widely debated in Sweden. Commonly the debate centres on the consequences of reducing some of the security that the legislation offers workers today in favour of making it easier for employers to hire.

The shift in power due to the centre-right alliance winning the recent election will certainly influence labour market policies. Sweden will certainly see new policies implemented, for example with the aim of creating more jobs and reducing unemployment. There is speculation that there will be some amendments to the Employment Protection Act, making it easier for employers to hire (and fire) and to offer longer temporary contracts. In addition, the new government is expected to reduce the level of unemployment benefits for the long-term unemployed. These expected amendments will surely impact on the Swedish labour market in one way or another if implemented. On the positive side, it can generate more jobs if employers are more willing to hire; on the negative side, it can put unemployed persons in a more financially unstable situation, while at the same time providing less security to those who are employed (less security in the Employment Protection Act).

Table 12.1 summarizes the main trends described in this report, as well as potential groups of vulnerable workers and/or workers at risk.

Table 12.1 Working and employment conditions, Sweden

Elements	Sub-elements	Trends	Risks/Exposed groups
Collective bargaining and worker participation	Membership density	Still high but indications of a slow decline	Young workers who are not unionized
	Decentralization	Collective agreements at sectoral level Wages and working time issues at company level	It is becoming more difficult to monitor wages and working time as they are dealt with at company level
Employment status and contracts	Part-time jobs	Continuous growth and many involuntarily have part-time jobs	Young women with a lower than average income. Sectors: Hotels and restaurants, transport, trade and municipalities
	Interim agencies	Continuous growth but still limited use	Stepping stone for some. However, doesn't always guarantee a certain income and workers are not entitled to compensation from social security agency
Wages	Wage inequality Low wages	Wage disparity remains stable Relatively small differences compared to other OECD countries No legislated minimum wage in Sweden	Women and immigrants are affected More women than men on low wages Main difference in the private sector Lowest wages: restaurant and kitchen assistants and cleaners

Elements	Sub-elements	Trends	Risks/vulnerable groups
Working time and work organization	Working time	10% lower than EU average, but compared to Denmark and Norway it is higher	Men work more hours than women, though more women than men have part-time jobs
	Unsocial working hours	Increasing	Young workers Manual workers
	Overtime	Slight decrease	More men than women work overtime, 45–54-year-olds above all
Work organization, work intensity and working rhythms	Working intensity and rhythm	Increase in working rhythm and too much to do. Could be a result of downsizing and more flexible and decentralized organizations	Women are more affected by increased working rhythm than men are Women have the highest degree of stress-related disorders
Safety and health	Work-related diseases and accidents	Decreasing	Highest in manufacturing Commonest cause of work-related diseases: ergonomic factors
	Work-related disorders	Decreasing	Strenuous postures, monotonous, repetitive work main causes of work-related disorders
Training	Staff training	Positive trend, more people being trained	Less training in the private sector and in small organizations Temporary workers: less access to training
Work and family	Allocation of unpaid work	No significant change in the allocation of paid and unpaid work	Women do more unpaid work while men do more paid work
	Parenting	Age increase of first-time parents. Increase in fathers' parental leave though major share still taken by mothers	
New sources of vulnerability	Contract forms	Increase in part-time work and temporary contracts	Results in some groups of workers, mainly women, being underemployed, as well as making them unstable financially
	EU enlargement	Low-wage workers from the 10 new Member States	Sectors affected are: construction, forestry, hotels and restaurants

12.2 EMPLOYMENT STATUS – THE "RIGHT TO A JOB" DEBATE

Some workers turn to interim agencies or become self-employed in order to find work; others are offered a part-time job or a temporary contract. With continuing growth of fixed-term employment and a high share of part-time workers in Sweden there are concerns and an ongoing debate about job security and the "right to a job", in particular the right to full-time employment.

Attempts to reduce long-term temporary employment

In 2005, 14 per cent of all those employed had some kind of temporary contract (49 per cent women, 51 per cent men). Temporary contracts have experienced significant growth, approximately 4.5 per cent from 1990 to 2005 (Statistics Sweden, 2005e). Temporary work is more common among immigrants than native Swedes. First-generation immigrants are more than one and a half times as likely to have a temporary position as native-born Swedes (National Institute for Working Life, 2003).

A specific type of temporary employment is project-based employment: that is, hiring people to work on a specific project. This kind of employment has doubled since 1990. Comparing the three largest employee organizations – TCO (Swedish Confederation of Professional Employees), LO (Swedish Trade Union Confederation and SACO (Swedish Confederation of Professional Associations) – project-based employment is more common in SACO where 32 per cent of all temporary employees had project-based employment, compared with 12 per cent in TCO and LO respectively (Nelander and Goding, 2005).

To overcome the problem of people being stuck in a temporary position for a long time the parliament (Riksdag) recently voted to make changes to the Employment Protection Act. The changes will come into force from 1 July 2007 and limit temporary/fixed-term contracts to 14 months in any five-year period. Thereafter the job becomes permanent. Since the centre alliance won the election there has been speculation that the amendments will be revoked in order to make it easier for employers to employ on a temporary basis, thus getting more people into the labour market.

Part-time workers: victims of underemployment

Part-time jobs continue to grow in Sweden and there are indications that many people have such jobs involuntarily: that is, they would like to work more.

Twenty-four per cent of all employed had a part-time job in the first quarter of 2005: 37 per cent of women and 12.5 per cent of men (Eurostat, 2005a).

In comparison with 2002, when 21.5 per cent had a part-time job, the total number of employees with this kind of employment has grown (Forssell and Jonsson, 2005).

Sweden has the highest share of both female and male involuntarily part-time workers among the EU-15, as a share of all employed women and men, according to Eurostat's Labour Force Survey of 2002. Around 22 per cent of all part-time workers in Sweden are involuntary part-time workers compared with around 14 per cent on average among the EU-15 (Eurostat, 2003).

A study conducted by the Swedish Trade Union Confederation (LO) shows that many people who have a part-time job would like a permanent contract, primarily for financial and security reasons. Approximately 180,000 working women are underemployed and would like to work more hours (Statistic Sweden, 2005e). Among LO members, young women without children aged 16–25, on lower than average income, are most likely to find themselves in this situation. Thirty-three per cent of this group would like to work more hours, compared with 14 per cent of all LO women (Nelander and Goding, 2005). In 2002, 23 per cent of all part-time working women were involuntary, while for part-time working men the figure was 20.5 per cent (Forssell and Jonsson, 2005). Part-time jobs are particularly prevalent in health care. Part-time employees who do not have a permanent contract are an at-risk group since they are not entitled to unemployment benefits to financially compensate for the lack of a full-time position, which part-time employees with a permanent contract are. This can put them in a difficult financial position. The case study on part-time work illustrates this problem and also how some municipalities have worked actively to overcome the problem.

Prior to implementation of the Part-Time Work Directive it was not uncommon for Swedish collective agreements to provide different employment conditions for part-time and full-time workers by means of thresholds that exempted part-timers.

A form of part-time employment that has grown particularly in the past 15 years is stand-by employment, where one works only when there is a need for extra labour. The number of people affected grew from 40,000 in 1990 (1 per cent of all employees) to almost 145,000 in 2005 (4 per cent of all employees). Many women in hotels and restaurants, transport, trade and the municipal sector have contracts on this basis. Empirical studies conducted by the Swedish labour organization LO show that this type of employment rarely leads to a full-time job (Nelander and Goding, 2005).

Working for an interim agency – stepping-stone or trap?

According to the Swedish government, approximately 60 per cent of those hired through an interim agency end up getting employment at the interim agency's client company. Hence it could be seen as a stepping-stone to a more secure employment contract. As a result, the government has a positive attitude towards interim agencies and their ability to provide a higher employment rate, thus preventing further unemployment in Sweden, according to the former Minister of Employment.

According to the interim agencies themselves, they account for less than 1 per cent of employment. It is worth noting that the majority of employees with the agencies are younger than 30 and there are slightly more women than men (Stjernberg and Walter, 2005). The Swedish Association of Staff Agencies reported in 2004 that 60 per cent of the employees in interim agencies are women, and 62 per cent are within the age group 21–40 (Andersson and Wadensjö, 2002). Immigrants are an overrepresented group among the agencies. Interim agencies are sometimes seen as a possible entrance point for immigrants, who often have difficulties getting into the labour market in Sweden. Our case study neither confirms nor disproves this since the two interviewed interim agencies had different opinions on the matter. But a study conducted by the Swedish Institute for Social Research has revealed that 13 per cent of the immigrants employed by interim agencies in 1998 had employment outside the interim agency two years later (Andersson and Wadensjö, 2004a).

It should also be noted that there could be an element of insecurity working for an interim agency, since this kind of work rarely guarantees a certain income each month. For example, an employee who is not a permanent employee of the interim agency and does not get the equivalent of full-time work is not entitled to financial compensation from the social security agency (which regular part-time workers are), even if they wish to work full time (Andersson and Wadensjö, 2002). This puts workers at risk of ending up in financial difficulties especially if the workers remain in this status on a permanent basis.

Self-employment: higher among immigrants

It is slightly more common to be self-employed among immigrants than among native Swedes. According to a study conducted by the Swedish Integration Board it is not possible to determine whether this is connected to immigrants' difficulties finding jobs elsewhere. In recent years studies have shown that there can be several reasons why immigrants become self-employed. According to one study, the most common reasons are a desire to be independent, to avoid unemployment or to realize a dream or an idea (Brundin et al., 2001).

Among employed immigrants, almost 12 per cent of men and 5.4 per cent of women were self-employed in 2004, compared with approximately 10 per cent of men and 4.5 per cent of women among native Swedes. Almost 20 per cent of all employed men from Asia are self-employed. Self-employed immigrants often work in communications, personal services and trade (Swedish Integration Board, 2005).

Foreign seasonal workers at risk

Every year about 7,000 seasonal workers arrive in Sweden – mainly from Thailand, Poland, Ukraine and Russia – to work as berry and cucumber pickers. The media has on several occasions brought to light the fact that many seasonal workers have to work under unacceptable conditions, with low wages and long working hours. Their Swedish colleagues, often organized in trade unions, work under completely different conditions. For example, the Swedish national newspaper *Dagens Nyheter* in August 2006 described how berry pickers from Thailand work as many as 15–16 hours per day. Furthermore, in June 2006 Swedish Radio reported that migrant berry pickers risk getting paid half as much as Swedish workers.

Since many foreign seasonal workers are not hired under the same employment and working conditions as Swedish workers they ought to be considered a vulnerable group. Although poor working conditions have been highlighted they still exist to a great extent even today and still pose a problem on the Swedish labour market.

12.3 WAGES: GROWING INEQUALITIES

Wages in Sweden are slightly above the EU average, though notably lower compared to Norway and Denmark (Larsson, 2003).

During the past two years Swedish wage increases have remained at the same level, after falling for two years in a row. The rate of increase at the moment is about 3 per cent and is expected to remain at that level over the next couple of years. Figure 12.1 illustrates the wage increase rate from 1996 to 2004 for manual and non-manual workers in the private sector.

Inflationary pressure in Sweden is still low: in August 2006 the inflation (CPI) was 1.6 per cent. The CPI has developed weakly since the beginning of 2004, mainly due to low wage increases and strong productivity growth (National Institute of Economic Research, 2006a). In 2005, the nominal wage increase was 3.1 per cent and the real wage increase was 2.66 per cent for the economy as a whole. The increase was 3.2 per cent for manual workers and 3.1 per cent for non-manual workers (Confederation of Swedish Enterprises). The nominal wage increase has remained fairly stable since 1997 and 1998, with some fluctuations, while the real wage increase has decreased slightly (National Institute of Economic Research, 2006b).

Figure 12.1 Wage increase rate in the private sector, Sweden, 1996–2004

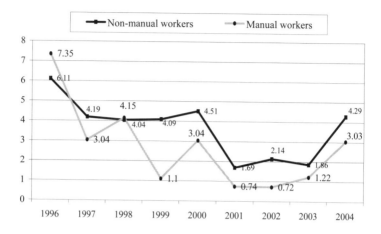

Source: Statistics Sweden.

Although wages are predicted to experience stable growth over the next few years, there is an ongoing national debate concerning the trend towards greater inequality in income distribution (see Figure 12.2).

Figure 12.2 Trends in real wages and inflation rate, Sweden, 1976–2004 (%)

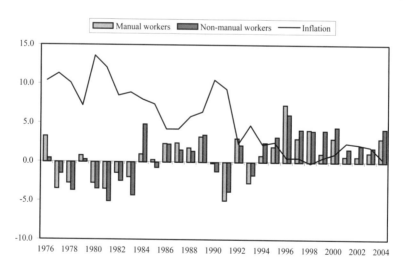

Source: Statistics Sweden.
Note: The figure shows the change in mining and manufacturing.

Another hot issue in the last couple of years has been the threat of wage competition due to low-cost labour arriving in Sweden from abroad. This has particularly affected sectors such as construction, forestry and hotels and restaurants. Sweden has no legislated minimum wage; instead, sectoral minimum wages are commonly regulated through collective agreements. This can be said to have started the so-called "Vaxholm dispute" which involved a Swedish trade union wanting a Latvian employer (with assignments in Sweden) to sign a Swedish collective agreement to avoid wage discrimination and ensure competition on equal terms. The Vaxholm-Laval case is still not settled, but pending in the European Court of Justice. However, today the debate concerning low-cost labour has faded since no major wave of low-cost labour has occurred.

Single-parent households still have a lower standard of living

The living standards of Swedish households grew by almost 2 per cent in 2004, despite the increase in the unemployment rate. In fact, the standard of living has grown every year since 1995, resulting in a 25 per cent higher standard in 2004 compared to 1995. However, a closer look at single-parent households shows a different picture. Single-parent households have a significantly lower living standard than others, although differences are also to be found within the group.

During 2004, single women with children had a standard of living 18 per cent lower than single men with children, and 32 per cent lower than cohabiting parents (Statistics Sweden, 2005c). The total number of single-parent households has increased considerably since the 1990s. In 1991, around 187,000 women and 40,700 men were living in a single-parent household, compared to 229,500 women and 63,100 men in 2004 (Statistics Sweden, 2005d).

Wage inequality and wage discrimination still a hot issue

Wage inequality and discrimination is still a hot issue in Sweden, despite legislation on "equal wages for equal jobs". Though inequality and discrimination have been highlighted and attempts have been made to improve the situation, statistics show little improvement. Generally, women have lower wages than men (on average 18 per cent lower). The difference, expressed as a percentage, has been the same for almost 20 years. Whether the wage gap between men and women depends on discrimination or not has been analysed by Statistics Sweden, where different variables (for example, age, level of education, profession, and so on) were tested. The results showed a reduction in the unexplained wage-gap of 10 per cent, from 18 per cent to 8 per cent.

The main explanation of the inequalities, according to the survey, seems to be choice of profession, with women more than men choosing (or sometimes compelled) to work in low-wage professions (Statistics Sweden, 2004a).

A study conducted by the Swedish labour organization TCO indicates that immigrants have lower wages compared to Swedes with a similar education. On average the wage of an immigrant is 88 per cent of a Swede's. For immigrants from Western countries the wage inequality between Swedes and immigrants is reduced the longer the immigrant has been in the country. No such trend is noted for immigrants from other countries.

Sectoral differences explain more or less 70 per cent of today's wage differences in Sweden, the main differences being found in the private sector (Statistics Sweden, 2004a). However, compared to other OECD countries the differences are relatively small. Occupations in the private sector with the lowest wages are restaurant and kitchen assistants and cleaners, with an average monthly income of approximately SEK 16,300 (EUR 1,757), around 30 per cent lower than the average monthly income (SEK 23,700, or EUR 2,554) in Sweden in 2004.

Thirty-six per cent of employed women and 16 per cent of employed men are considered to be on a low wage. How many of these can be classified as working poor is difficult to estimate, since a low wage, according to Swedish standards, is not a determining factor in itself (Statistics Sweden, 2004b).

12.4 WORKING TIME UNDER CHANGE

Collectively agreed working time per week is 40 hours for full-time workers. Approximately 80 working hours over the year correspond to public holidays; whereas the average amount of hours actually worked is 38.5 (Eurofound, 2005). In the second quarter of 2005 actual average weekly working time in Sweden was 36 hours (around 39 hours for men and 33 hours for women) (Eurostat, 2005b). Working time per year and employee is approximately 10 per cent lower than the OECD average, but higher than in Denmark and Norway (Ericsson, 2005). In the first quarter of 2005, 12.5 per cent of employed men and 37 per cent of employed women worked fewer than 35 hours per week, which is considered to be a part-time job (Eurostat, 2005a).

In 2003, 76 per cent of employees worked during the day, a fall compared to the early 1980s when 83 per cent of men and 81 per cent of women worked during the day. Naturally, daytime work is more common among non-manual workers (88.5 per cent work daytime) than manual workers (59 per cent work daytime). Moreover, with age daytime work becomes more common (Statistics Sweden, 2005g). Along with decreasing day work, nightwork and unsocial hours have increased.

Overtime and unsocial working hours

While the number of daytime workers has decreased, the number of employees with unsocial working hours continues to increase. Unsocial working time is more common among men than women. A survey conducted by Statistics Sweden in 2003 showed that almost 63 per cent of the men interviewed had unsocial working hours at least once a week, and 23 per cent every day, compared to 56 per cent and 12 per cent respectively among the women (Statistics Sweden, 2005g). The development of unsocial working hours is often inter-linked with evening work.

In 2003 evening work was relatively more widespread among young workers: 9 per cent of men and 10 per cent of women worked evenings, compared to 2 per cent of all employed. This difference could probably be related to the fact that many young people take evening jobs to support their studies.

Night work, or shift work that includes night work, was more common among manual workers. For example, shift work was relatively common in manufacturing: almost 30 per cent had this kind of working time, among whom 12.5 per cent had night work (Statistics Sweden, 2005g). Other sectors worth mentioning are health care and social work: almost 42 per cent of employees work by a rolling timetable (meaning that they have different schedules for different weeks) and 13 per cent had nightshifts.

Work during weekends is just as common among men as it is among women. According to a survey by Statistics Sweden in 2002 and 2003, 16 per cent had worked the Saturday, and 15 per cent the Sunday of the week before participating in the survey (Statistics Sweden, 2005g).

While unsocial working hours continue to increase, a slight decrease in overtime can be noted. More men than women work more than 45 hours per week, perhaps not surprising considering that women work part time to a larger extent than men. However, in recent years a decrease may be noted: between 2001 and 2003 the number of men working overtime declined by 6 per cent. It is mainly managers in various professions who work overtime every week: least frequent is overtime in professions without any educational requirements (Statistics Sweden and the Work Environment Authority, 2004). Of all age groups, 45–54 year olds work most overtime: almost 30 per cent of men and 15 per cent of women had worked more than 45 hours during one or more weeks in 2003.

Flexible working time: widespread but not always positive

About two thirds of all companies in Sweden offer flexible working time arrangements, which places Sweden among the top three countries in Europe in that connection (European Foundation for the Improvement of Living and

Working Conditions, 2006). Hence there is no active national debate on the issue since the phenomenon is fairly common. There have been studies of its effects, but the results provide no uniform view of its impact. The possibility of combining family life and work is believed to result in positive health effects; however, some surveys claim that it can result in more stress-related disorders. The results from a study of two large Swedish companies with flexible working hours were presented in 2004, which showed that 28 per cent were – during a two-year period – diagnosed with various kinds of stress-related disorders. This was compared to workers with fixed working times, of whom 6–8 per cent had similar diagnoses. Those with flexible working time worked 52 hours per week on average, compared to an average of 42 hours per week (overtime included) among workers with fixed working time. Furthermore, according to the same study it is mostly women aged 30–47 who are negatively affected by flexible working hours, among whom 38 per cent were (within a period of 2–3 years), diagnosed with some stress-related disorder not identified before the change of working time.

Paradoxically, in relation to the believed positive effects of working time flexibility, the above-mentioned study found that 69 per cent of participants felt that their private time had decreased after changing their working time from fixed to flexible (*Dagens Nyheter*, 2004).

12.5 INCREASED WORK INTENSITY ALONGSIDE DOWNSIZING

In the past 15 years the trend has been to focus on core activities by, for example, outsourcing support functions and operations to meet increased competition. Though economic growth has been strong in Sweden in recent years job creation has been weak. It has also become more and more common not to replace workers who for different reasons have taken time off work or who are absent for some reason. Naturally this puts increased pressure on the other employees.

The public sector went through some structural changes during the 1990s, the consequences of which are still being felt. Some services or areas of services were transferred to the private sector, while at the same time the workforce was downsized. This was the case in health care and social work. However, the downsizing of the workforce was not entirely related to the proportion of work being transferred to the public sector, which again contributed to increased work intensity.

Intensified working rhythms seem to be relatively widespread in the Swedish labour market: 56 per cent of women and 64 per cent of men who have had the same occupation for at least five years consider that their working rhythm has accelerated compared to five years ago, according to the national Work Environment Survey. Furthermore, around 12 per cent at or over the age of 50 did not think that they would be able to work until retirement age: half considered a change in working rhythm necessary to make it possible (Statistics Sweden and the Work Environment Authority, 2004).

Taking a gender perspective, women appear to be more affected by intensified working rhythm than men. According to a survey conducted by Statistics Sweden (Statistics Sweden and the Work Environment Authority, 2005), women have the highest degree of reported stress-related disorders. Women are generally still performing most of the unpaid work within households: in combination with higher workloads, this is likely to have a more negative impact on their health compared to men.

Having too much to do or too much responsibility could be another indication of an increased work rhythm or workload. Relatively high numbers of employees in Sweden feel that they are under pressure at work. The 2003 Labour Force Survey shows that over half the employees in Sweden feel that they have too much to do at work. After increasing during the 1990s the number is now decreasing to the same levels as in the mid-1990s, however. Professions in which more than 70 per cent report that they have too much to do are: teachers, childcare instructors, people in managerial positions, health care staff, administrative professions within social welfare, customs and tax assessment.

Furthermore, 28 per cent reported that they have too much responsibility, and 20.5 per cent of all workers did not consider that they got enough support from their colleagues and/or superiors. One explanation of this seems to be workforce reductions, where employees are expected to perform work previously done by more than one person. Extended responsibility, which often goes together with increasing flexibility, has a stressful impact on employees, at least if they do not feel they get enough support.

12.6 HEALTH AND SAFETY: THE CHANGING NATURE OF RISK

The number of reported work-related diseases, accidents and work-related disorders continues to decrease. Between 2003–05 the number of work-related diseases decreased by 18 per cent and work-related accidents by 14 per cent. The most common types of work-related diseases are suspected to be due to ergonomic factors and they account for 58 per cent of all reported work-related diseases (Work Environment Authority and Statistics Sweden, 2005a and b).

Work-related disorders: a trend-break

According to the Work Related Disorders survey (Statistics Sweden and the Work Environment Authority, 2005a and b), almost one in four employees in Sweden suffered some form of disorder related to their work during the previous 12 months. The disorders may be physical or of some other type (related to other factors such as stress, mental strain, and so on).

Strenuous working postures and monotonous and repetitive work are the main causes of work-related disorders: during 2004 almost 6 out of 10 work-related disorders were caused by this. The second most common work-related disorders are due to organizational factors, where three out of four report that the disorder resulted in problems of a psychological nature (Work Environment Authority, 2005).

In the period 1996–2003 the share of both physical and other disorders due to work rose significantly for both men and women. In 2003, the number of disorders peaked, followed by a decrease in 2004 and 2005. This constitutes a trend-break.

After several years of increasing work-related disorders affecting the neck, a decrease was noted in 2004. The trend-break among women was particularly evident with less work-related disorders in all parts of the body, whereas the decrease among men only concerns disorders of the neck. However, seen over a longer time period there has been an increase in back disorders among women, and of shoulder and arm disorders among men (Statistics Sweden and the Work Environment Authority, 2005a and b). Stress-related disorders and other types of mental strain disorders are the most common disorders among women. Since 1996 these types of disorder have doubled among women; however, since 2004 a decrease can be noted. Large numbers of people with stress-related disorders are reported in social work (almost 28 per cent), schoolteachers (24.6 per cent), upper secondary schoolteachers (21.8 per cent) and production and operations managers (20.1 per cent).

The most common cause of disorders among men is strenuous working postures, which have increased since 1996. Approximately 23 per cent of painters, lacquer workers and chimney sweeps report such disorders, 21 per cent of construction workers and around 18 per cent of motor vehicle mechanics and vehicle repair workers and building and related electricians.

Fatal accidents in decline

Statistics show that the self-employed run a higher risk of being in fatal accidents in comparison to regular employees. The relative frequency of work-related deaths among the self-employed was 5.8 (8.0 for men and 1.3 for women) per 100,000 in 2005. The most common cause of work-related deaths is lost control over vehicle/means of transport (Work Environment Authority, 2005).

On a general note, fatal accidents at work have decreased dramatically in Sweden: the number of fatal accidents in 2005 was around 9 per cent of what it was in the 1950s (although between 2004 and 2005 the number of accidents increased from 56 to 67). The relative frequency of fatal accidents was 1.6 (2.8 for men and 0.3 for women) per 100,000 inhabitants in 2005 (Work Environment Authority, 2006). There are no clear explanations of why fatal accidents are decreasing but one reason could be the increasing focus on systematic work environment management in workplaces.

Sick leave due to work-related disorders

Since the 1980s, sick leave has been significantly higher in Sweden in comparison with, for example, Denmark, Germany and Finland. Although there was a decline in the proportion of those on sick leave because of work-related disorders in 2004 and 2005 it is still more common than in 1996. A closer look at sick leave and work-related disorders reveals that one in ten employed persons reported having had work-related disorders leading to sick leave during the past year. Work-related disorders as a result of accidents more frequently lead to sick leave than other forms of disorder (Statistics Sweden and the Work Environment Authority, 2005a and b).

Almost one in five female cooks, machine operators and transport workers reported having taken sick leave, more than half for five weeks or more. Among men, sick leave is most frequent among mechanical machinery assemblers, various occupations in construction and engineering, and among motor vehicle mechanics and vehicle repair workers. Within most of these occupations more than 1 in 10 men had been on sick leave because of work-related disorders (Statistics Sweden and the Work Environment Authority, 2005a and b).

When an employee has been absent from work for more than four weeks because of sickness, or their work has suffered frequent interruptions due to shorter periods of sickness, employers are required by law to conduct a rehabilitation study. Among the respondents in the survey conducted by Statistics Sweden (2005h) 60 per cent of the women and 48 per cent of the men who met the above-mentioned criteria stated that a rehabilitation study had been conducted. Hence, it is evident that many employees are still not offered a rehabilitation study.

12.7 ACCESS TO TRAINING: A POSITIVE TREND

There is a positive trend regarding staff training in Sweden. In 2003, 2.7 million employees were registered as having had some kind of staff training, the highest number since 1986, when the first staff training statistics were produced (Statistics Sweden, 2003).

During the first two quarters of 2003 employees receiving training attended 1.39 courses on average, slightly below the number of courses during the first two quarters of 2000 (1.44 courses). Furthermore, slightly more women than men attend training: 48 per cent of working women compared to 44 per cent of working men attended training in the first two quarters of 2003 (Statistics Sweden, 2003).

Staff training is more common in the public sector; since women predominate in the public sector they are necessarily overrepresented among those receiving training. During the first two quarters in 2003, 6.0 per cent of working time was spent on staff training at county councils, compared to 2.6 per cent in the labour force as a whole. Furthermore, approximately 90 per cent of all staff training takes place during working time, and about 66 per cent of training is company-specific (Statistics Sweden, 2003).

A correlation between company size and training can also be noted. In companies with at least 1,000 employees 3.4 per cent of working time was spent on staff training, and 55 per cent of the employees attended. In companies with nine employees or fewer 1.6 per cent of working time was spent on staff training and 26 per cent of the employees attended (Statistics Sweden, 2003).

Training is often considered necessary if employees are to remain attractive to employers. In many situations training opportunities (such as paid training during working hours and recurrent training) are limited for temporary workers, or they do not have the same training possibilities as permanent employees (Wikman, 2002). There are no precise figures on the basis of which to compare training opportunities for temporary workers with permanent workers since there are many background variables that ought to be taken into consideration (such as the need for training and previous level of training, and so on). However, to give an indication of the differences, 23 per cent of people employed on a needs basis (professions with lower-level education, dominated by women and young people) received paid training during working hours, compared with 49 per cent of full-time workers who did not work overtime and 62 per cent of full-time workers who worked overtime. The figures for project-based employees and substitute employees were 37 per cent and 38 per cent respectively. If background variables are taken into consideration the difference between temporary workers and permanent workers decreases, though the figures are still significantly lower for temporary workers (Wikman, 2002, figures from the Labour Force Survey and the Work Environment Surveys in 1999).

Hence, temporary workers can end up in a disadvantageous situation as regards training, compared to permanent employees, which can often be due to an unwillingness among employers to invest in training for temporary workers.

People without a job, and people at risk of losing their jobs can, if they are jobseekers through the Swedish employment office, apply to attend so-called labour market education and training aimed to prepare workers for the labour market. One of the goals of labour market education is to increase the possibilities for the unemployed to get a job by offering training/education within sectors/professions where there is a labour shortage (the National Labour Market Administration, 2005). In September 2005, 6 per cent of all unemployed participating in labour market programmes attended labour market education (Swedish Social Insurance Agency, 2005). According to the National Labour Market Administration (2005) 7 out of 10 people participating in such education in 2004 had a job six months after the training was completed. Currently, there is an ongoing government investigation whose purpose is to review labour market training initiatives in order to make adjustments to better fit supply and demand. In addition, the Swedish National Audit Office – Riksrevisionen recently criticized the National Labour Market Administration for lack of efficiency in matching jobseekers with available jobs.

12.8 WORK AND FAMILY: NEEDS AND CHALLENGES

Although 80 per cent of Swedish employees are content or very content with their current job, 70 per cent feel that their work is stressful and would like to have more time with family and friends (International Social Survey Program, 2005). In comparison to 30 years ago today more women are working: this is indicated by, among other things, the increase in the number of children in municipal childcare. In 1972, 12 per cent of children aged 1–6 years were in municipal childcare, compared with 83 per cent in 2003 (Statistics Sweden, 2004c). Hence, balancing work and family life can be challenging, especially with the increasing number of single-parent households or households with dual-income earners.

Age increase among first-time parents

Over the last 30 years the average age at which women have their first child has increased by five years, from 24 years in 1974 to 29 years in 2004. Men on average are two years older than women when they have their first child. Among other reasons people wait longer before having children because it has become more usual for young men and women to get a higher education and more common among women to invest in their career (Statistics Sweden, 2005a). In addition, another likely explanation is that the share of people with fixed-term employment has increased since the 1990s among people of child-bearing age. Consequently, people wait to have children until their situation (hopefully) stabilizes (LO, 2005).

A decrease in working time after parental leave

Recently, the Swedish Trade Union Confederation (LO) proposed that one third of parental leave should be allocated to the father. Parental leave taken by fathers is increasing in Sweden, though mothers still take the major share. In 2004, mothers took 81 per cent and fathers 19 per cent of total parental leave. This is equivalent to 14.3 months for mothers and 1.7 months for fathers. For fathers this is an increase of 7 per cent since 1994, although 20 per cent of fathers did not take parental leave at all (LO, 2005). A survey conducted by the Swedish Tax Agency in 2003 revealed that 20 per cent of both parents said that the father's work determined the parental leave allocation, compared to 5 per cent who said that the mother's work was the determining factor (Bygren and Duvander, 2004). Hence it is often economic reasons that will determine allocation of parental leave, which in many cases puts women in a disadvantaged position from a work perspective. LO's proposal was intended to provide a more equal allocation of parental leave, thus strengthening women's position on the labour market. This proposal has met with varied responses among the political parties, and also among the Swedish population in general.

Furthermore, a study conducted by the Swedish Trade Union Confederation (LO, 2005) reveals that part-time work among women is often connected with the family situation. Female non-manual workers have the highest decrease in working time after parental leave, though female manual workers work part time to a greater extent than all other groups, both before and after parental leave.

Allocation of unpaid work

For decades there have been campaigns in Sweden to try to get men to do a larger share of household tasks. However, no significant change has been noted. According to Statistics Sweden, mothers of young children spend twice as much time taking care of the children and doing other forms of household work as fathers do (Statistics Sweden, 2004c).

The most recent statistics on how much time is spent on household work date from 2000–01. They indicate that men and women on average work the same sort of hours but the distribution of paid and "unpaid" work differs considerably (weekends included). Women did just as much paid as unpaid work (4 hours of each), whereas men did twice as much paid (5.5 hours) as unpaid (2.5 hours) (Statistics Sweden, 2004c).

12.9 SOCIAL DIALOGUE AND PARTICIPATION: UNDER CHALLENGE

Though labour market legislation has increased in recent years – for example, due to the implementation of European directives – collective agreements remain an important instrument in Sweden for regulating working and employment conditions. In many cases, parts of labour market legislation may be amended, wholly or partially, by collective agreements. Collective agreements between the social partners are voluntary and not based on statutory rules, however, as in many other countries. The most important collective agreements are concluded at sector level, while wages and working time issues are increasingly dealt with at local/company level (as result of the Industrial Agreement of 1997). This decentralization of negotiations has created more flexibility in the bargaining system by allowing some agreements to be concluded between the employer and either local union representatives or the employee directly (Bruun and Malmberg, 2005). It has also resulted in many sectoral agreements being framework agreements instead of detailed regulations.

Despite strong collective agreements and a high level of protection of workers through regulations Sweden has in the past ten years made some amendments to existing legislation in order to implement EU directives. The implementation of some EU directives has not only impacted workers (and employers) directly but also to some extent indirectly through flexibility in collective agreements (through implementation of EC benchmarks). Furthermore, the implementation of the Part-Time Work Directive has, for example, given part-timers better working conditions/protection. Prior to implementation of the directive it was not uncommon for Swedish collective agreements to provide different employment conditions for part-time and full-time workers through thresholds that exempted part-timers. Unionization is high in Sweden: approximately 80 per cent of all workers are affiliated to a union and approximately 90 per cent are covered by collective agreements. Being affiliated to a union gives workers protection, support and advice, if needed. However, today is it becoming more and more common to be affiliated only to an unemployment fund, that is, to only have unemployment insurance but not protection by the union. This trend is primarily apparent among young workers. Swedish unemployment insurance is administered by 38 unemployment funds which are formally autonomous, private organizations. Workers who are affiliated only to an unemployment fund, however, could be putting themselves at risk (by choice) since they are not offered the same protection and advice as unionized workers; that is, they do not have the support and back-up of a union.

The recent merger between the Swedish Industrial Workers' Union and the Swedish Metalworkers' Union could be an indication of falling membership among unions. The merger is a way for the two unions to strengthen their negotiating positions.

Concession bargaining

The few studies available make it difficult to determine whether concession bargaining is on the increase. However, the recent debate concerning low-paid workers arriving in Sweden from abroad, in combination with enterprises considering moving their production to low-cost countries, could indicate that there is an increased risk of concession bargaining.

One case of concession bargaining that has received attention in the media is Scandinavian Airlines. The company was losing market share due to fierce price competition. In order to remain competitive, they threatened to cut the employees' wages and working conditions as an alternative to redundancies. This threat led to concession bargaining between the SAS board and the trade unions. The outcome was a wage freeze, and for some workers even a wage cut of up to 10 per cent (*Dagens Industri*, 2004).

CONCLUSION: IDENTIFICATION OF WORKERS AT RISK

This chapter indicates that there are a number of vulnerable groups of workers in the Swedish labour market. On a general note, two traditional groups of workers appear more vulnerable than others; women and immigrants. However, new labour market trends indicate that other, more specific groups might also be at risk, often relating to type of employment contract.

For instance, types of employment and/or types of work contract such as *temporary work* can put people in a very unstable situation. With more people having temporary contracts – such as fixed-term contracts or project-based contracts – we could be witnessing a growing group of vulnerable workers. Some of these temporary workers are also working for interim agencies. These workers can be unstable financially, not knowing whether they will find a new job after their current contract ends or how long they will be on temporary contracts. They generally do not get the same training opportunities as people with permanent contracts.

Another group of vulnerable workers are the underemployed, that is, *part-time workers*. Although attempts are being made to overcome the problem of involuntary part-time work – illustrated in the case study – part-time workers still constitute a growing group. The group of part-time workers without a permanent contract are most at risk since they are not entitled to unemployment benefits (which part-timers with a permanent contract are).

Furthermore, in connection with work-related disorders, some groups of workers and sectors could be singled out. Although work-related disorders are decreasing overall many workers are still at risk. *Manual workers* and *workers in services* stand out: many people in these sectors report that they have work-related disorders or have been on sick leave for more than five weeks.

Women have traditionally been identified as an at-risk group, and there are multiple factors that make them vulnerable as a group. Women predominate in the lowest-paid employment in Sweden, often to be found among sectors that have suffered from downsizing in recent decades – for instance, health care and social work. We have seen that this has also resulted in higher work intensity. Another issue is involuntary part-time work where young women on low incomes are overrepresented. Furthermore, women in single-parent households have a considerably lower standard of living than men in the same situation. Studies also show that more women than men are negatively affected by flexible working time and that stress-related disorders are more common among women than men.

Traditionally, *immigrants* have also been recognized as a group at risk and there are still factors that make them vulnerable. For instance, many immigrants have difficulties getting into the labour market. Some find work through interim agencies, which can put them in a vulnerable situation if they cannot get a full-time job, although for others it can be a stepping stone. Others become self-employed, not always from choice. Statistics also show that immigrants are often discriminated against as regards wages, adding to their vulnerability. There are also indications that immigrant households have a much lower standard of living than native Swedish households.

In summary, the groups of workers in Sweden that have the highest probability of accumulating risks are traditionally immigrants and women. However, these groups also dominate in terms of types of work contract such as temporary work or part-time work. From a safety and health perspective manual workers and workers in services stand out since many report work-related disorders.

REALITY AT ENTERPRISE LEVEL: CASE STUDIES

The three case studies in this section have been selected to highlight some of the main sources of vulnerability identified in the first part of this chapter, such as involuntary part-time work, work for an interim agency and work-related disorders. The purpose of the case studies is to highlight some of the main risks, but also solutions to specific problems.

Sweden Case Study 1: Work-related disorders in a call centre

Approximately 104,000 people in Sweden work in call centres[1] at which work-related disorders and other work-related problems have been observed, not just in Sweden but internationally. Time pressure, demanding customers, few opportunities for the employees to develop within their job and little physical and mental variation at work are typical problems in call centres. High frequency of sick leave and high staff turnover, as well as difficulties with recruitment, have also been reported. Studies have also revealed that workers at call centres have worse working conditions than other computer-based occupations, with longer spells in front of the computer and employees experiencing more physical pain. A study of 16 Swedish call centres (2003) revealed that almost 25 per cent of the participants were stressed at work; about 50 per cent felt as if they were being controlled; and nine out of ten had felt physical pain during the last month, usually headaches or pains in the neck/shoulders or arms/hands. One hundred and fifty-nine of the participants went through a health examination: 50 per cent had health problems that fully or partly could have been caused, or worsened, by the nature of their work. Common solutions to the problems are a change of equipment and/or changed working methods (National Institute for Working Life, 2003).

This case study sets out to observe the problem of work-related disorders in a call centre and to find out whether any measures have been taken to overcome such problems. The case company was selected because of the problems they have with work-related disorders, but also because they are working to prevent such problems.

Case profile

The selected company is a call centre with approximately 1,200 employees in six European countries: the Swedish division of the company has approximately 500 employees in four offices. This case study is based on one of the four offices in Sweden, office A, which has a total of 256 employees: 55 per cent are women and 45 per cent are men. The employees in office A handle both incoming and outgoing calls.

---

1. Sveriges call center förening (www.sccf.se).

The employees work in an open office environment, which is assumed to be beneficial to psychological well-being. The office has wall-to-wall carpeting to keep the sound level down, and twice a year the sound level is measured to make sure that it is acceptable. A majority of employees in office A sit in front of their computers all day (except during the lunch break). The company is aware of the problems that constrained sedentary work might have on the employees' health, such as pains in the neck and shoulders, and have taken some countermeasures to minimize such problems.

Work contracts: the prevalence of part-time work

In office A, 158 employees work full time and 98 work part time (38 per cent): 83 of the part-time workers (85 per cent) are students who only work a few hours per week. It is not known whether any of the part-time workers are involuntary part-timers but one can imagine that most of the students who work part time are voluntary since they primarily work to make some extra money for their studies. In comparison to the study conducted by the National Institute for Working Life (of 16 call centres) this has a very high share of part-time workers. The share of part-time workers in this study was between 2 per cent and 4 per cent (depending on type of call centre) of all employees (National Institute for Working Life, 2003).

The staff turnover is around 10 per cent, which is normal for the industry according to the manager.

Working time: permanent worker availability

Office A is open between 8 a.m. and 9.30 p.m., 365 days per year. These are the maximum opening hours, but they can sometimes be less dependent on customer demand, that is, in some periods the workload is less, hence they can close earlier. It tends to be students in the sales department who work evenings and weekends.

Wages: also performance-based

Employees at office A receive a wage considered average for the sector. The wage is split into two parts: one fixed and one based on performance. Performance-based wages or bonus systems are common in call centres. According to a report based on work environment inspections carried out by the Work Environment Authority in 112 Swedish call centres, a majority had some kind of bonus system. In those call centres where bonuses were linked to quantitative performance (based on speed in carrying out tasks such as number of calls, length of calls, and so on) the bonus system was a stress factor and a barrier to cooperation. In call centres where the bonus system was based on both qualitative (quality of customer contact) and quantitative performance the bonus system was more often seen as a motivating/stimulating factor (Work Environment Authority, 2004).

Wages are regulated through a collective agreement with SIF, the second largest trade union for employees in the private sector. The collective agreement regulates the minimum wage and also allows the employer to individualize the wage system on the top of the minimum wage, based on wage negotiations between the employer and the employee.

Job satisfaction: difference between full-time and part-time employees
Office A carries out job satisfaction surveys among its employees. Altogether, 67–70 per cent of the workers at office A are pleased with their workplace. The survey has shown that part-time workers (mostly students) are most satisfied; this is owing to the fact that these workers spend only a small part of their time at work, and are not subject to the same demands as full-time workers. The least satisfied are full-time workers in customer services.

Means of decreasing sick leave
Sick leave in office A presently affects around 6 per cent of the employees – normally it is approximately 4 per cent, which according to the manager is a satisfactory level. Full-time employees are on sick leave more often than part-time employees. At the moment, office A has four employees on long-term sick leave, of whom one is reported to have a work-related disorder affecting neck and shoulder.

Recently, the procedure for calling in sick was changed. The employees used to give notice to a central secretariat, but now the manager closest to the employee must be notified directly. This practice is believed to reduce the number of sick days and is also supposed to create a closer relationship between manager and employee. Furthermore, employees who call in sick more than four times have a "feel-good" conversation with their manager, that is, they discuss the issue and try to address whether there is anything they can do to make the employee feel better.

This is believed to have a positive effect on short-term sick leave. This initiative has been taken in order to help managers get a better insight into what they can do to make employees feel better.

Work-related disorders: a problem to be solved
As already mentioned, work-related disorders due to incorrect postures have been highlighted in office A. According to the manager, many of the younger employees complain about pains in their neck and shoulders. The employee interviewed believes that work-related disorders are not a bigger problem at the call centre than in any other industry she has worked in, although she confirms that the monotonous work there often results in physical pain.

To minimize the risk of pain and disorders the office has taken several preventive measures. One measure is regular visits by physiotherapists who check that the employees have correct working postures. The employees must also use a so-called roller mouse (located in front of the keyboard) to prevent pains in the arm, shoulder and neck, and the chairs have support for the lower part of the back. Furthermore, the employees are encouraged to exercise. The employer gives all employees a yearly allowance towards gym membership or similar. Another measure is pause programs installed on the employees' computers. These programs can adjust the computer to give a signal when it is time for the user to take a break, during which the employee is supposed to perform special neck and shoulder exercises. This initiative has not been very successful, however, since the employees still complain about pains in their neck and shoulders, although this can depend on infrequent use of the program, according to the employee interviewed.

Office A has invested in adjustable desks to enable employees to vary their working postures throughout the day. The desks were purchased after pressure from the trade union and the employees. According to the manager, the investment was a waste of money since the desks' full functionality is used by a mere 3 per cent of the employees.

The office also has two safety representatives. If employees need some kind of equipment to prevent work-related pain and disorders the safety representatives are delegated to tell the manager, who makes the final decision. Equipment for preventing work-related disorders is purchased only on an individual basis. This approach has been more successful, in terms of both use and cost efficiency, than, for example, the adjustable desks. The employee interviewed has personal experience of work-related pains. The company solved her problem by investing in equipment on her behalf; as a result she has a positive attitude towards the system of buying equipment individually.

Concluding remarks
Office A's activity is characterized by performance-based work, high work intensity and high staff turnover. Typical of this office in comparison to many other call centres is the high share of part-time employees (38 per cent). There is also considerable stress at work, especially for full-time employees, as also witnessed by health and safety disorders and sick leaves. The payment system, partly linked to performance, may also add to the workers' stress.

In terms of work-related disorders, the office has taken several good preventive measures to minimize their occurrence. However, the aids installed do not appear to be fully utilized. It is not enough to have the right equipment; employees must also know how to use it and then actually use it. This discrepancy could also be connected with the lack of instructions on how to use the aids. With high staff turnover and a large share of part-time workers it is probable that information on how to use the equipment is not given frequently enough.

The high percentage of part-time work – a particular feature of office A – has also brought about a sort of dual labour market within the enterprise, with two different types of employees who are facing different types of risks: full-time employees benefit from employment security but suffer from high stress at work and health and safety disorders, and are thus much less motivated; part-time workers have less employment security but enjoy more freedom in terms of time organization, work and family or work and studies, thus leading to greater motivation. One challenge for the company will be to reconcile the interests and needs of these two types of workers in a context dominated by time pressure, rapid delivery and high competition.

Sweden Case Study 2: Possible solutions to part-time unemployment

"Part-time unemployment" is a term often used in Sweden to refer to part-time employees who would like to work full time but are not given the opportunity (involuntary part time). The part-time unemployed are a vulnerable group in the labour market since they are often in a precarious financial situation and their job security can often be low.

Registered (with the Swedish Employment Service) part-time unemployed can receive unemployment benefits for the period they are not working, to supplement their income to the level of full-time employment. To receive unemployment benefit as part-time unemployed you must have a permanent contract. Those working part time but without a permanent contract cannot receive unemployment benefit. It can sometimes be more difficult for the part-time unemployed to find an additional job to provide them with equivalent hours to a full-time job than it is for a person who is fully unemployed since the additional job has to fit with the working hours of the first job.

Part-time unemployment is a problem often found in the healthcare sector. To study part-time unemployment in Sweden a public unit providing care for the elderly within a municipality has been selected. In the last couple of years this municipality has participated in a project to overcome the problem of part-time unemployment. This case study focuses on the problems of part-time unemployment and also the results of their efforts to find a solution.

Case profile
The case profile is a public unit providing care for the elderly at a municipality in the northern part of Sweden. In this municipality approximately 480 people had a part-time job in 2002: 150 were registered with the employment service as part-time unemployed Two thirds of those were employed in the public unit providing care for the elderly. In addition to the 100 registered

part-time unemployed who are working for the care unit there are other part-time workers working for the unit on a temporary basis. Many of these temporary workers would like to work full time, but due to their situation are unable to register as part-time unemployed (since they are not permanent employees); hence they do not receive unemployment benefits.

The majority of employees in the care unit are women. A contributory factor in their difficulties recruiting men is believed to be the unavailability of full-time employment. In one department of the care unit a mere 7 per cent of the employees are men.

In 2002, the municipality joined a project called HELA (HELA refers to full time), which started as a cooperation between five government authorities to reduce part-time unemployment. In short, the HELA project involves implementing individual work schedules and offers full-time positions to those who want to work full time but also with the possibility of flexibility in terms of increasing or decreasing working time at chosen time periods.

Working time: limiting unsocial hours

The majority of work within the division is carried out during the daytime but there are also employees working nights. Work at evenings and weekends is also common, but it is distributed among the employees, who take turns. Prior to the HELA project, part-time employees worked more evenings and weekends in comparison to full-time employees; this was often a way for them to get extra hours (but ignored their work and family imbalances)

Prior to the project, employees worked on a rotation basis according to a schedule set by their supervisor. It was the responsibility of the supervisor to make sure that there were no gaps in the schedule.

Wages: part-timers in low-paid professions

Generally, wages are fairly low in most professions within the healthcare sector, and in particular in those professions where part-time work is common, such as care for the elderly. Wages are regulated through collective agreement and the whole country more or less follows the same wage structure, which helps to prevent wage discrimination within the sector.

Sick leave: the tip of the iceberg of a demotivating system

Sick leave has been an increasing problem in recent years. In August 2002, 22 per cent of all those employed within the division were on sick leave, approximately 50 per cent of whom were long-term sick. Lack of resources is believed to be one reason for the high percentage of sick leave, that is, the employees are often under pressure. In addition, sick leave could also be connected with work-related disorders, due to the nature of the work (home-based care for elderly people), where heavy work is common. According to a report by the Work Environment Authority and Statistics Sweden (2005a and b) 68 per cent of females in such professions are exposed to heavy work. Professions where heavy work is common generally have a higher percentage of people on long-term absenteeism due to work-related disorders compared to the percentage of all employed.

Part-time unemployment: solving it through flexible working time
As previously mentioned, involuntary part-time workers are a vulnerable group in the labour market since they are often in a precarious financial situation and their job security can often be low, particularly temporary part-timers.

The main reason given for not being able to offer all employees full-time employment was financial structures, in combination with a rigid structure of working schedules which follow a given pattern that do not take individual needs into consideration. Working schedules were inflexible, and the employees were not given much opportunity to choose their working times. Employees who wanted to work more were not given extra hours and employees who wanted to reduce their working time were told that this was not possible.

The main reason for wanting a full-time job was financial. Many employees with a part-time job found it hard to cope financially, especially single parents. Having a part-time job was seen by many as insecure, since they did not always know how much extra work they would be offered from month to month, making it difficult to plan. Many part-time employees who wanted to work full time were on stand-by in case extra personnel were needed. This only occurred if someone was off sick or on annual leave. Being constantly on stand-by meant that the part-time employees were rarely able to plan their time off, that is, they did not always know in advance if they were going to be off or if they would get extra working hours.

Hence, bearing the above in mind, the municipality, and in particular the care unit, saw a need to solve the problems by introducing flexible working times. To do this the municipality decided to participate in the HELA project.

Changes made: built-in flexibility
Since then, new routines have been implemented. In short, the concept of part-time unemployment has disappeared. All employees within the division have been given the opportunity to decide how much they want to work, that is, flexibility has been built into the system. As a result, some have increased their working time and others have reduced it. More employees from the "older generation" have chosen to cut down on their working time while more employees from the younger generation have chosen to increase theirs. Hence, the working time problem appeared also to be an intergenerational issue, which was not only centred around working more but also on giving an

opportunity for people who felt that they were working too much to cut down on their working time.

The possibility of choosing offers flexibility for both full-time and part-time employees. The new system gives the employees a sense of security and increased influence over their working time, since their choices do not have to be permanent. Employees can decide to increase or cut down on their working time during a given period. For example, it provides a sense of security for those who today are working part time to know that they are allowed to work full time if they choose. This has, for instance, proved valuable for some women who had gone through a separation. After the separation they found it difficult to manage financially with a part-time job. Thus they were able to increase their working hours. At the same time, some older employees who have increased their working hours for financial reasons have also experienced the downside in the form of physical strain.

Furthermore, those working full time are given a sense of freedom, knowing that they can reduce their working time for a couple of months or even permanently. Knowing that you can influence your working time gives an increased level of comfort in your work. Some women have, for example, taken this opportunity to cut their working hours during periods when they have felt under pressure in order to reduce their level of stress; others have used the opportunity to spend more time with their family – for instance, by taking care of grandchildren, and so on.

The only downside with the new way of organizing working time is that it is not possible for all employees to work full time, with the current number of employees. However, this is not a problem at present since not all employees want to work full time.

More motivated employees

In addition, the new system has given employees much more responsibility to coordinate their working time and to make sure that there are no gaps in the schedule, while also complying with working time regulations. As a result, schedules today are not standardized but individually adjusted. The increased involvement of the employees is believed to have increased their motivation since they are given more responsibility. Furthermore, the employees' understanding of the finances and administration of the division have also increased.

Social dialogue as a means

The trade unions have been involved throughout the project and have been very positive about the changes. According to one of the key persons responsible for the project, it has been very important that the trade unions were in favour of the project. Without their support it would have been difficult to implement in practice. The municipality's strategy was agreed together with the trade unions, and they participated in communicating the changes to their members in the municipality.

Concluding remarks

This case study describes (prior to the changes) a typical care unit dominated by female employees, as well as part-time and temporary work. The care unit has actively worked to overcome problems with involuntary part-time work by implementing flexible working schedules. These efforts have proven successful. By adapting working time to different workers' needs, a more flexible organization has been created, giving the employees more freedom in terms of influence over their working time. Since the workers are able to influence their working time they are better able to control their financial situation as well as create a work–life balance better suited to their individual needs. To some extent it also allows the employees to influence their own health by adjusting working time to a level at which they feel comfortable.

Sweden Case Study 3: Interim agencies – a way into the labour market for immigrants?

The number of workers with temporary employment has grown by 4.5 per cent over the last 15 years in Sweden; in 2005, 14 per cent of all employed had some kind of temporary contract (Statistics Sweden, 2005h). An industry often associated with temporary work is interim agencies. Between 1993 and 2000 the number of employees with these agencies increased tremendously: from approximately 5,000 in 1993 to 42,000 in 2000 (Nelander and Goding, 2005).

One explanation of the growth of such contracts is that they offer increased flexibility to the employer. Laws and regulations in Sweden can make it difficult for employers to hire on a temporary basis. The growth of this industry has resulted in a large supply of labour being made available for temporary hire. Hiring through an interim agency is believed to give increased flexibility, especially if extra staff are needed during shorter time periods.

We can point to a number of characteristics of people with temporary employment. Many articles and reports have revealed that young people, women and immigrants are overrepresented among employees with temporary employment contracts, and within interim agencies in particular there is overrepresentation of immigrants.

This case study focuses specifically on immigrants working for interim agencies. Immigrants are identified as a vulnerable group in the labour market: apart from their difficulties finding a job, they usually also face wage discrimination. However, studies have also shown that unemployed immigrants who get employment at an interim agency have relatively good prospects of finding employment in other industries (Andersson and Wadensjö, 2004a and b). Hence, working for an interim agency can be seen as a possible entrance point to the labour market for immigrants, at the same time as being involuntary if no other options are available. At the same time, it can put the immigrant in a financially insecure situation if the interim agency cannot guarantee a certain number of hours of work per week.

Case profile
This case study is based on interviews with two different interim agencies, agency X and agency Y. The two agencies differ in their set-up and views about immigrants' opportunities on the labour market.

Agency X has 43 employees whom they contract out to client companies, among whom a third are immigrants; all the employees are on temporary contracts and work across all industries. The agency is bound by a collective agreement.

Agency Y provides personnel to the hotel and restaurant industry, mostly cleaning and dishwashing staff. It has a pool of approximately 100 potential employees, of whom nearly 98 per cent are immigrants. The agency operates without fixed contracts/agreements, and the agency has not signed a collective agreement.

Insufficient working time
Neither of the two agencies can guarantee workers a specified amount of working time, since this depends on the hours offered by the hiring company, which of course varies. This clearly puts the interim workers in a particularly vulnerable position. It clearly has an effect on the type of working conditions they are ready to accept.

Wages: discrimination against immigrants
Both agencies interviewed acknowledge the existence of wage discrimination. One explanation given is that immigrants, generally speaking, are more willing to accept lower wages since it can be difficult for them to get a job at all. A study by the Swedish Confederation for Professional Employees (TCO) confirms that immigrants have lower wages compared to Swedes with a similar education. On average the wage of an immigrant is 88 per cent of that of a Swede.

According to agency X, wages in interim agencies that are bound by collective agreements are the same for native Swedes and immigrants. However, agency X believes that interim agencies without collective agreements pay immigrants less than natives. Agency Y has noticed that many immigrants are overqualified for many of the jobs they are offered but are forced to take them in order to get a job at all. Agency Y confirms that immigrants are often paid less than native Swedes; according to the agency this is because the agency's clients pay less when hiring immigrants.

Work contracts: either temporary contracts or oral agreements
Agency X offers temporary contracts to their employees but without a guaranteed number of working hours. Thus they are employed by the agency for a limited period. Agency X's clients have the right to dismiss hired personnel without notice during the first three months. In such a case, agency X is not obliged to offer the employee another job or compensation for the loss of working time.

Agency Y, on the other hand, has no contracts, neither with their clients nor with the workers; instead the agency operates on an ad hoc basis with a pool of workers that they can contact when needed. Agency Y expects the workers to be on stand-by, waiting to be called in when needed. No guarantees of work are given so the owner of the agency does not mind the workers having other jobs. However, he does expect the workers to be available whenever he has a client.

According to both agencies, immigrants are more willing to accept such contracts and the jobs the agencies can offer. This is believed to be a result of the difficulties immigrants have getting other jobs.

The positive role of collective agreements
Of the approximately 500 interim agencies in Sweden, about 375 are bound by collective agreements. The agreements are effective when it comes to preventing the agencies from employing immigrants at lower wages than Swedes. Agency X is bound by a collective agreement, whereas agency Y is not. Agency Y says that it could not comply with such agreements since their wages are sometimes lower than the minimum wages set by collective agreements. For agency Y it comes down to a trade-off between wages and competition: offering their clients lower than average rates is the only way for the company to survive, according to agency Y. Of course, this is related to the sector (hotels and restaurants) that agency Y operates in.

Advantages and disadvantages of work at interim agencies
The agencies express different views on the pros and cons, from the employer's and employees' perspectives, of working for an interim agency. Advantages of working at an interim agency may include:

- great flexibility (for the employer);
- the possibility of working at different workplaces (for employees);

- the opportunity to get permanent employment at one of the hiring companies (for employees).

Furthermore, agency X believes that working at an interim agency is a stepping-stone to the regular labour market, although more so for Swedish workers than for immigrants. However, according to agency X, it is not unusual for immigrants to get permanent jobs at a client company. A couple of years ago, agency Y observed a tendency among client companies to employ hired personnel on a permanent basis. Today, this tendency appears to be in the opposite direction, with an increased demand for hired personnel but an unwillingness to take on hired personnel permanently.

Disadvantages, according to the agencies, concern:

- insecurity – workers are not guaranteed a certain number of working hours or even any work at all. Not knowing from day to day or month to month how much work they will get, and so what their income will be, puts the workers in an insecure situation;
- wages are sometimes lower than the industry average, especially for immigrants.

Concluding remarks

The descriptions of these two interim agencies indicate a very vulnerable position for the workers they employ. However, even when comparing the two agencies, agency Y puts its workers in a more vulnerable position than workers at agency X, since the former only operates with oral work agreements and is not bound by a collective agreement. The question is whether an agency that operates with oral work agreements takes proper legal responsibility for its workers, especially on safety and health issues. In comparison with agency Y, agency X appears to offer somewhat better working conditions for its employees, putting them in a less vulnerable situation, considering that wages are agreed though collective agreements and work contracts are formalized. However, compared with major players such as Adecco and Manpower which often hire their consultants/workers on a permanent basis (the workers who are contracted out to clients are permanent employees of the agency), these two agencies provide little protection for their employees.

REFERENCES

Andersson, P., and E. Wadensjö. 2002. Vem arbetar I bemanningsbranschen? *Arbetsmarknad & Arbetsliv*, 8.

———. 2003. En arbetslöshetsförsäkring för alla sysselsatta? *Arbetsmarknad & Arbetsliv*, 9 (3–4) (fall/winter). National Institute for Working Life.

———. 2004a. *Egen försörjning eller bidragsförsörjning*, SOU: 21.

———. 2004b. Hur fungerar bemanningsbranschen? [How does the temporary work sector work?], Report 2004:15, Institute for Labour Market Policy.

Arbetstidslagen. 2005. 165.

Bergström, F., and R. Hellner. 2005. *Rätt till heltid.* Handelns Utredningsinstitut.

Bruun, N., and J. Malmberg. 2005. The evolution of labour law in Denmark, Finland and Sweden 1992–2003. In *The evolution of labour law*, vol. 2: *National reports, employment and social affairs.* European Commission.

Brundin, E., D. Bögenhold and E. Sundin. 2001. *Invandrares företagande – fakta och implikationer, i marginalisering eller integration: Invandrares företagande i svensk retorik och praktik: en forskarantologi.* Stockholm: Nutek.

Bygren, M., and A-Z. Duvander. 2004. *Många pappalediga inspirerar.* Statistics Sweden.

Confederation of Swedish Enterprises. 2006. *Fakta om löner och arbetstider 2006*, 2006 information available at http://www.svensktnaringsliv.se/frameset_wa.asp? NewsId=2573505&CatId=-1&LangId=1, 2006.

Dagens Industri. 2004. Mer än hälften av SAS-avtalen klara (3 March).

———. 2006. Fler arbetslösa med alliansen (10 September).

Dagens Nyheter. 2004. Flexibel arbetstid leder till utbrändhet (13 September).

———. 2005. Lettiskt företag hyr ut billig personal i Sverige (4 July).

———. 2006. Plockning bär sig olika bra (20 August).

Ericsson, H. 2005. *Svensk arbetsmarknad i ett internationellt perspektiv.* Statistics Sweden.

Eurofound. 2005. *Working time/Working hours*, available at http://eurofound.europa.eu/emire/SWEDEN/ANCHOR-ARBETSTID-SE.html.

Bruun, N., and J. Malmberg. 1992–2003. *The evolution of labour law*, vol. 2: *National Reports.* European Commisson.

European Foundation for the Improvement of Living and Working Conditions. 2006. *Working time and work–life balance in European companies.* Dublin.

Eurostat. 2003. *Labour Force Survey Results 2002.* European Communities.

———. 2005a. *Population and Social Conditions* 16/2005.

———. 2005b. *Labour Market Latest Trends*, 20/2005.

———. 2006. Online database – Employment.

Forsell, J., and I. Jonsson. 2005. *Deltidsarbetslöshet och deltidsarbete i Europa.* National Institute for Working Life.

Hansson, M. 2004. *Det flexibla arbetets villkor – om självförvaltandets kompetens.* National Institute for Working Life.

International Social Survey Program (ISSP). 2005. Umeå University.

Larsson, M. 2003. *Internationella Löner 2003, Löne- och arbetskraftskostnader för industriarbetare i 30 länder.* LO.

LO. 2005. *Arbetsmiljö 1991–2003 – Klass och kön*: http://www.lo.se/home/lo/home.
nsf/unidView/A3EBD74533CD22BDC1256E4E0050FC65, 2006.

National Institute of Economic Research. 2006a. Press release (30 August).

———. 2006b. Statistics on nominal and real wages.

National Institute for Working Life. 2003. *Arbetsförhållanden och hälsa vid ett urval
av callcenterföretag i Sverige* [Working conditions and health in a selection of call
centres in Sweden].

National Labour Market Administration, Arbetsmarknadsutbildning. 2005. *The
Swedish Employment Service.*

Nelander, S., and I. Goding. 2005. *Anställningsformer och arbetstider.* LO.

Primärvårdens nyheter. 2005. Nytt EU–förslag om arbetstiden: Inaktiv jourtid kan
komma att räknas bort, no. 3.

Statistics Sweden. 2001. *Lönestrukturstatistik.*

———. 2003. *Staff training January to June 2003.*

———. 2004a. *Löneskillnader mellan kvinnor och män.*

———. 2004b. *Lönestrukturstatistik.*

———. 2004c. *På tal om kvinnor och män.*

———. 2005a. *Beskrivning av Sveriges befolkning.*

———. 2005b. *Economic welfare of young people – Income, employment and wealth.*

———. 2005c. Hushållens ekonomi (HEK) (2004A01).

———. 2005d. *Income distribution survey 2003.*

———. 2005e. Labour Force Survey, Stockholm (April).

———. 2005f. *Labour market tendency survey for 70 training categories in 2005.*

———. 2005g. Levnadsförhållanden rapport 109 – Sysselsättning, arbetstider och
arbetsmiljö 2002–2003, Örebro. http://www.scb.se/templates/Publikation____
168918.asp

———. 2005h. *Labour force survey.* Stockholm (April).

———. 2006. Press release (2006-07-04 09:30), No. 2006: 172.

———. 2006. Press release (2006-08-22 09:30), No. 2006: 206.

Statistics Sweden and the Work Environment Authority. 2004. *Arbetsmiljö 2003* [Work
environment 2003]. Stockholm.

———. 2005. *Work-related disorders 2005.*

Stjernberg, T., and L. Walter. 2005. *Conference Arbetslivsforum.* Växjö.

Svenska Dagbladet. 2005. Sverige kvar i botten på inflationsligan (28 November).

Sveriges Radio Ekot. 2006. Utländska bärplockare kan få hälften i lön (28 June).

Swedish Integration Board. 2005. *Statistic rapport, statistisk uppföljning av Rapport
Integration 2003.* Norrköping.

Swedish Social Insurance Agency. 2005. *Arbetslivsfakta*, No. 3 (October).

Swedish Trade Union Confederation (LO). 2005. *Föräldraledighet och arbetstid – hur
mycket jobbar föräldrar som varit hemma med barn.*

Tullberg, M. n.d. *Flexibel arbetstid – en ny kvinnofälla?* Göteborg.

Von Otter, C. 2003. *Ute och inne i svenskt arbetsliv.* National Institute for Working
Life.

Wikman, A. 2002. *Temporära kontrakt och inlåsningseffekter.* National Institute for
Working Life.

Work Environment Authority. 2004. *Arbetsmiljö på callcenters* [Working environment
in call centres], Report No. 3.

————. 2005. *Work-related disorders 2005.*

Work Environment Authority and Statistics Sweden. 2005a. *Occupational accidents and work-related diseases 2004.*

————. 2005b. *Heavy lifting and other physically heavy work*, Information on education and the labour market, 1.

13. United Kingdom: Persistent inequality and vulnerability traps

Damian Grimshaw and Lorrie Marchington

13.1 INTRODUCTION

At a time when the UK economy is often used as a model of relatively strong country performance within the European Union it is a valuable exercise to chart recent trends in work and employment conditions in order to identify the extent to which all groups of workers have benefited from the fruits of economic growth and stability. The idea that certain jobs may be associated with features of vulnerability, or that certain groups of workers experience vulnerability traps (see chapter 1), responds to current policy and academic concerns to understand the quantitative and qualitative dimensions of job creation. The Lisbon Agenda famously expresses the need to create "more and better jobs" within the EU. And the United Nations has now followed the ILO's lead with a new Ministerial Declaration in 2006 on "full and productive employment and decent work for all" as a fundamental component of a nation's development strategy (UN, 2006: article 6). Running parallel to these policy ambitions is a growing concern among social scientists to understand trends and characteristics of "job quality". There is new evidence of a polarized pattern of job expansion in the 1990s in the United States, between low-paying and high-paying jobs (Wright and Dwyer, 2003) and separate studies (utilizing different definitions) suggest that up to one in seven jobs are "bad" in the United States (Kalleberg et al., 2000) and one in ten in the United Kingdom (McGovern et al., 2004). Moreover, building on a longstanding concern to identify features of labour market segmentation that distribute the risks of entering vulnerable jobs unevenly among different groups of workers (for example, Wilkinson, 1981), recent studies have usefully identified variation in exposure to "bad jobs" among workers and find that risk is significantly higher for those in non-standard forms of employment (Kalleberg et al., 2000; McGovern et al., 2004).

This chapter seeks to contribute to policy and academic debates on job quality. The first section reviews employment trends in the United Kingdom

Table 13.1 Summary table of job features, employment trends and patterns of vulnerability, United Kingdom

Job features with a potential risk of vulnerability	Trends (2002–05)	Job and workforce patterns of vulnerability
1. Employment contract		
Part-time work	Low share, rising (men); high share, stable (women)	Multiple penalties, mainly affecting women, including low pay, low-skill work, weak bargaining power, weak control over "core hours", and problems of undervaluation
Temporary work	Stable	Heterogeneous group. On average, vulnerable in terms of job insecurity, weak bridge to permanent work, pay penalty and low job satisfaction
Migrant labour	Rapid increase	Heterogeneous group. Evidence in agriculture and food sector that "gangmasters" provide low pay, job insecurity and difficult work conditions
2. Pay		
Pay inequality	High and stable	Marginal improvement in position of lowest decile, but persistent gender pay gap and major disparity between male full-time and female part-time pay
Low pay	High incidence especially for women. Stable until 2002, then decline	90% of low-paid work in just four sectors. Large numbers still paid less than minimum wage. Problem of undervaluation of women's work
3. Working time		
Long hours	High share, small fall (men); medium share, stable (women)	Causes include results-based control of hours and employer-led flexible scheduling. Consequences include health risks, job dissatisfaction and erosion of temporal norms (home–work imbalance)
Shift work	Medium, stable	High use in certain sectors. Nightshift work involves long hours and carries twice the risk of illness or disability. Many workers do not enjoy proper rest breaks
4. Work organization		
Work intensity	Strong increase (all occupations)	Evidence of health risks from overwork and spillovers of stress from work to home

Job features with a potential risk of vulnerability	Trends (2002–05)	Job and workforce patterns of vulnerability
5. Health and safety		
Fatal and major injuries	No change	Higher risk among men than women
Work-related illnesses	Decline	Highest risk in health and social work; new risk of abuse and bullying
6. Training at work		
Vocational training provision	Continued problems of employer support	High share of jobs with no or low skills required. Partial erosion of internal job ladders in large organizations. Weak employer demand for intermediate skills
7. Worker voice		
Trade union representation	Low and falling (men); low and rising (women)	Women now make up the majority of union members (50.2%). Overall, limited opportunities for collective representation and a higher risk of exclusion among the low paid and Asian workers
Coverage by collective bargaining	Low and marginal decline	Majority of workers are not covered and depend on unilateral employer policy for their terms and conditions

and identifies those features notable for their vulnerable character – with attention both to the character of work and the workforce groups at most risk. The second section reports the findings of three case studies – a non-profit organization providing elderly care, a multinational food manufacturing firm and a medium-sized IT services company with offshore operations in India – each selected to illustrate key trends in employment and vulnerable work. The evidence sheds light on four key aspects of vulnerable work, drawing on the views of some vulnerable workers in the United Kingdom:

1. The United Kingdom's highly flexible labour market has downsides, including loss of opportunities to earn enhanced pay during unsocial hours of work and the strong role of gangmasters in supplying migrant workers to fill minimum wage jobs in the food manufacturing and packing industry.
2. Insecurity takes many forms and affects the employment experiences of varied groups of workers, including insecure employment duration for low-skilled agency workers and career insecurity among IT workers in fast-changing IT firms.
3. Many women workers are trapped in undervalued work, and care work is a classic example of this where requirements for credentialized training, along with dedication and responsibility of the worker, are not matched with an appropriate level of pay.
4. Poor working conditions are experienced by many, including hard physical work in the provision of elderly care and in food manufacturing, as well as unreasonable environmental conditions and psychological strains.

Quantitative estimations of the proportion of "bad jobs" have focused on three or four characteristics, such as relative pay, access to health insurance, pension and sick pay benefits, and career prospects. Here we provide a more wide-ranging overview and include seven features of jobs that may carry a risk of vulnerability. For each feature we draw out the implications for different groups of workers where appropriate. Table 13.1 provides a summary.

13.2 EMPLOYMENT CONTRACT

During the 1980s and 1990s there was a strong interest in the proliferation of non-standard forms of employment contract – part-time, temporary, fixed-term and agency contracts – as employers responded to cost pressures and the flexible demands of new forms of production and services delivery.

Part-time work in the United Kingdom is often short-hand for vulnerable work. This is demonstrated in recent studies drawing on both qualitative data

(Jenkins, 2004; Rubery et al., 2005a; Smithson et al., 2004) and quantitative evidence. Results from the *Working in Britain 2000* survey show that part-time workers were more likely than full-time workers to have a "bad job"; on average, a part-time job has 2.2 out of 4 bad characteristics compared to an average score of 1.3 for full-time workers (where a bad job is defined as low paid, no sick pay, no pension and no career ladder) (McGovern et al., 2004). However, there was only a marginal increase in part-time employment during 2001–05, with 26 per cent of workers employed part-time in 2005. But this pattern reflects diverging trends among men and women, with a rise among men from 9 per cent to 11 per cent and a drop among women from 44 per cent to 43 per cent (*Labour Market Trends*, July 2006: Table B1). Of the 1.6 million men in part-time jobs in 2005, 232,000 could not find a full-time job and 507,000 were students or still at school.

To a large extent the vulnerability of part-time work reflects its concentration among low-paid and low-skill employment. Because of the high share of women in part-time jobs, the Equal Opportunities Commission has funded research to investigate the issue. The findings include that:

- part-time workers receive 40 per cent less training than their full-time counterparts (Francesconi and Gosling, 2005);
- for each year of part-time employment, hourly wages decrease by 1 per cent, compared to an annual increase of 3 per cent for full-time workers (Olsen and Walby, 2004);
- there is a large penalty on lifetime earnings among women who always remain in part-time work, and even those who switch to full-time work after just one year in part-time work suffer a 10 per cent penalty after 15 years in employment compared to a similar worker in continuous full-time work (Francesconi and Gosling, 2005);
- part-timers are more likely than full-timers to be hired on fixed-term, seasonal or casual contracts (Francesconi and Gosling, 2005);
- part-time workers have less bargaining power than full-timers: 21 per cent of part-timers are trade union members compared to 32 per cent of full-timers (Hicks and Palmer, 2004);
- while white workers are overrepresented among female part-timers, among male part-timers black, Pakistani and Bangladeshi workers are overrepresented (Francesconi and Gosling, 2005); and
- case studies (Grant et al., 2005) and survey results (Darton and Hurrell, 2005) suggest that four in five part-timers work in jobs "below their potential", either because they held previous jobs where required qualifications or skills were higher, or are employed in jobs that do not use their latent potential.

Jobs defined by a temporary employment contract are also at risk of vulnerability. Following growth during the 1990s, from a share of 5 per cent to 7 per
cent of the workforce, the share has dropped to 6 per cent in 2005 (*Labour
Market Trends*; July 2006). Nevertheless, survey data and case studies suggest
temporary work is an important form of entry into the labour market. Persons
out of work in the previous year are three times more likely to be in agency
work than those in other work, holding all other characteristics constant
(Forde and Slater, 2005: Table 2). A further characteristic is the growing use
of agencies. In 1992, agency employees made up 7 per cent of all temporary
workers, yet by 2000 this had risen to 16 per cent – mostly found in low-to-
mid-level skilled occupations (op. cit.: 257).

   But is temporary work more vulnerable than permanent work? Compared
to permanent workers, temporary workers in the United Kingdom have, on
average, lower job satisfaction, receive less training and are lower paid (Booth
et al., 2002). But the type of temporary contract matters: compared to the
average permanent employee pay of £8.81 in 2000, agency workers earned
£6.84, fixed-term contract workers earned £9.37 and other temporary workers
earned £5.99 (Forde and Slater, 2005).[1]

   Finally, one area that has witnessed expansion during the early 2000s is the
use of legal and illegal migrant labour. In the food and farming sector, organizations that provide casual labour are defined as "gangmasters" under a new
Gangmasters Licensing Act (2004). Investigation of gangmasters' use of
migrant workers in this sector[2] reported an estimated 420,000–611,000 casual workers employed to harvest and pack produce in farm factories in the
United Kingdom, of which around one in three were non-EU nationals and
one in four non-UK EU nationals (DEFRA, 2005). However, while many
British temporary workers were employed directly by the farm enterprise (42
per cent), this was hardly ever the case for migrant workers for whom the
gangmaster was the main source of employment; only 10 per cent of EU
nationals and 16 per cent of non-EU nationals worked directly for the farm
enterprise (DEFRA, 2005: Table 1.7, own calculations). Notably, firms with
supermarkets as customers were far more likely to hire temporary workers
from gangmasters than through direct employment (op. cit.: 26). Also, the
study shows that employment conditions are generally poor and that turnover
is high; nearly half of all gangmaster workers in the sector (48 per cent) stayed
for less than one month. In an effort to combat these problems the government
introduced a new Licensing Act which seeks to increase the visibility of gang-

---

   1. Controlling for personal and job characteristics the wage gaps with permanent workers are
smaller but still substantial: from 22% to 9% for agency workers and from a positive 6% gap to
0% for fixed-term contract workers (Forde and Slater, 2005: Table 3, own calculations).
   2. The definition of the sector is agriculture, horticulture and co-located packhouses and primary food processing (DEFRA, 2005).

masters. From October 2006 it will be an offence to provide labour in the agricultural and food sectors without obtaining a gangmaster's license from the newly established Gangmasters Licensing Authority.

13.3 PAY

Two aspects of the pay structure in the United Kingdom generate a potential risk of vulnerability: wide pay differentials between low and high paid, men and women and full-time and part-time workers; and a high incidence of low pay.

Pay inequality is high compared to many other industrialized countries. However, recent trends suggest a flattening off. The inter-decile measure of pay inequality fluctuated between 3.96 and 4.03 between 2000 and 2005 (ASHE pay data). Above-average gains at the top were balanced by a slight compression of pay differentials among the bottom half of wage earners. More detailed data confirm this picture. During 2000–04, earnings increases up to the 12th percentile were higher on average than the median increase, and so too were earnings increases from the 86th to the 99th percentile (Low Pay Commission, 2005: Figure 2.11).

Underpinning the high pay inequality is a wide gender pay gap. In 2005 mean earnings of all women were 79 per cent of men's (ASHE gross hourly earnings data). The trend over 2000 to 2005 shows only a very slow closing of the gap – of just three percentage points. Women experience higher pay in full-time work, where the gender pay ratio was 83 per cent in 2005. However, women's position in part-time work is especially poor, at just 62 per cent of men's average full-time pay in 2005 (see above for the variety of explanatory factors, and Grimshaw and Rubery (2006) for a review of evidence of undervaluation of women's work in the United Kingdom).

The UK pay structure is also notable for its high incidence of low-wage work. Table 13.2a suggests that around one in three adult employees were low paid during each of the years 1998–2004. Among women the share is higher – around two in five – than among men (around one in five). A key reason is the high share of women in part-time jobs. Estimates by Howarth and Kenway (2004) show that female part-time employees account for more than one third of all low-paid employees; restricted to full-time employees only, the share of low paid is roughly equivalent among men and women.[3]

---

3. Note that Howarth and Kenway (2004) define low pay as gross hourly earnings less than 60% of the full-time median wage.

Table 13.2 The incidence of low pay and very low pay among all employees, United Kingdom

a) Share paid less than 2/3 of median hourly pay for all full-time employees

	Median hourly pay for full-time employees	Percentage low paid		
		All	Male	Female
1998	£8.16	32.2	21.6	43.3
1999	£8.50	33.9	23.4	44.9
2000	£8.76	32.5	22.2	43.4
2001	£9.21	33.1	22.9	43.7
2002	£9.63	33.3	22.5	44.3
2003	£9.96	32.0	22.2	42.1
2004	£10.47	30.0	20.8	39.3

b) Share paid less than 1/2 of median hourly pay for all full-time employees

	Median hourly pay for full-time employees	Percentage very low paid		
		All	Male	Female
1998	£8.16	12.0	6.1	18.2
1999	£8.50	13.8	7.4	20.4
2000	£8.76	12.3	6.5	18.4
2001	£9.21	12.1	6.3	18.2
2002	£9.63	11.7	5.8	17.8
2003	£9.96	10.2	5.3	15.2
2004	£10.47	9.6	5.5	13.9

Notes: Gross hourly pay for full-time and part-time employees, aged 22+ and excluding overtime and other bonuses; 1998–2003 data are partly based on LFS data and 2004–05 data solely on ASHE data; own estimates of percentage low paid are accurate only to the nearest 10 pence.

Source: Median hourly earnings data from the Office for National Statistics, ASHE data (http://www.statistics. gov.uk/downloads/theme_labour/ ASHE_1998_2004/ Table1.xls); own calculations of low pay derived from gross hourly earnings distribution data from ONS.

Surprisingly, the National Minimum Wage, introduced in 1999, had little impact in reducing the incidence of low pay. The main reason is its relatively low level. Expressed as a percentage of the average full-time wage (excluding overtime), it fluctuated around the 36 per cent level during 1999–2004.[4]

---

4. As a percentage of the mean, the National Minimum Wage was introduced at a level of 36.7% in 1999. It then actually fell to 34.2% in 2001 and subsequently increased slowly back to 36.7% in 2004. As a percentage of the median it increased slightly from 47.6% in 1999 to 48.5% in 2004.

Since 2001 increases have been slightly above the annual increase in average earnings, but these increases are yet to make a significant difference to the incidence of low pay. Nevertheless, it appears to have had a more significant impact on the incidence of very low paid (Table 13.2b). The share of all employees very low paid dropped from 12 per cent to 10 per cent between 1998 and 2004. Overall, therefore, while the minimum wage has boosted the earnings of many very low-paid workers, it has not generated a larger spillover effect further up the earnings distribution. The result is a spike at the bottom of the wage distribution, resulting in little change in the overall number of low-paid workers.

13.4 WORKING TIME

Results from the *Working in Britain* survey show that the hours of work required by employers were associated with the greatest decline in job satisfaction during 1992–2000; satisfaction with hours worked dropped from 35 per cent to 20 per cent among men and from 51 per cent to 29 per cent among women (White et al., 2004). Moreover, the results were common across all occupations, with highest levels of dissatisfaction occurring among higher level professionals and managers at one end and semi- and unskilled manual workers at the other end (op. cit.). Trends in the use of part-time work were considered above. Here we discuss the issues of long-hours working and shift work.

Average full-time working hours have fallen in recent years (from close to 39 hours per week in 1998 to 37.4 hours in 2004), but long hours (45+ per week) persist for many: 29 per cent of men and 9 per cent of women in 2005, although these shares dropped slightly during 2000–5. The *Working in Britain* survey reveals that of those working long hours 83 per cent did so because of pressures to meet deadlines and 75 per cent because it was a job requirement, compared to just 39 per cent who worked long hours to earn extra money. Such reasons differ by occupation, with high-level professionals most likely to blame deadlines (90 per cent), technicians/supervisors the job requirement (76 per cent) and skilled manual workers by far the most likely to work long hours to earn more money (81 per cent). The United Kingdom retains its opt-out from the European Directive on Working Time. A survey undertaken in 2001 of workers' experiences of the Working Time Regulations shows a significant share (13 per cent) usually work more than 48 hours per week (DTI, 2004). Three in four of these workers had signed a written agreement with their employer to opt out of the Directive and nearly 60 per cent said they would be happy if their employer limited their hours to 48 per week. The same survey also revealed that where a long-hours worker had experienced a problem with their hours, in 50 per cent of cases this had not been resolved (White et al., 2004).

What these data reveal is a weakening of the standard hours-based approach to full-time work towards a results-based definition, where full-time working is whatever is required to complete the allocated tasks or reach a target performance level. Research shows employers are adapting working time to secure greater effort from workers, either through intensifying work (increasing the mix of "active" to "non-active" periods) or prolonging hours of work (Rubery et al., 2005b).[5] The result is a growing disconnect between the temporal order of working life and family/social life (Dex, 2003). Intrusions into family and private life are experienced by many workers, but there appears to be a sense of inevitability about such changes towards working more unsocial hours and a diminishing ability to organize one's private life (Bunting, 2004). In the context of a radical weakening of trade union power, managers appear relatively free to exercise their prerogative in the deployment of labour.

Data on shift work show that the proportion of workers who work shifts sometimes or most of the time increased slightly during 1993–2003, from 16 per cent to 18 per cent (*Labour Market Trends*, Jan. 2004). Shift work is most common in the transport and communications sector, where more than one in four workers work shifts (30 per cent of men and 19 per cent of women in 2003). And change has been greatest (for both men and women) in the distribution, hotels and restaurants sector; a rise from 11 per cent to 17 per cent for men and from 10 per cent to 15 per cent for women. Of the different types of shift working (for example, three shifts, two shifts, night shifts, weekend shifts, and so on), the most common type is the double day shift, with two shifts of eight hours each, alternated between early (for example, 6 a.m.–2 p.m.) and late (2 p.m.–10 p.m.) over weekly or longer periods. Around one in three shift workers worked this system in 2003.

The night shift is a particular cause of vulnerability. A 2001 survey of night workers found they are more than twice as likely as the general workforce (12 per cent and 5 per cent, respectively) to suffer from an illness or disability (DTI, 2004: Figure 4.9). Their working hours tend to be long, with 22 per cent working 12–14 hours on average per shift (op. cit.: Figure 4.8). Unsurprisingly, therefore, 48 per cent of night workers said they would prefer to work fewer hours and 39 per cent said they would still be willing to work fewer hours even if this meant less money. The same survey also found that 15 per cent do not enjoy proper rest breaks (DTI, 2004: 41).

---

5. Several strategies can be identified, including flexible scheduling to match hours worked with consumer demand, reduction of "core hours" of part-time workers with additional hours contingent upon consumer demand and extension of operating hours with no increase in staffing (Rubery et al., 2005b : 99).

13.5 WORK ORGANIZATION AND WORK INTENSITY

Surveys find significant evidence of an increase in work intensification during the 1990s, and a levelling off between the late 1990s and early 2000s. Data for 1998 show that more than 60 per cent of employees claimed to have experienced an increase in the speed of work and/or effort during the previous five years, compared to only 4–5 per cent who reported a reduction (Burchell, 2002). Green (2002) shows a significant rise in the share of employees agreeing or strongly agreeing with the statement "my job requires me to work very hard" between 1992 and 1997, but no change between 1997 and 2001.

Work intensification has ramifications for a worker's health. Wichert reports a strongly significant negative relationship between work intensification and psychological well-being, as well as a negative relationship with hours of sleep (Wichert, 2002: Table 5.2) – findings that are confirmed in the larger European Survey on Working Conditions where employees working at speed were more likely than other employees to suffer every single illness included in the survey. Also, Nolan finds a strong positive correlation between measures of work pressures (especially the "sheer quantity of work") and job-related tensions experienced in the home (Nolan, 2002: Figure 6.3). A notable aspect of much of the research into work intensification is the finding that this is experienced by a wide range of workers in both high and low-skilled occupational groups.[6] Also, much research has been undertaken to understand the causes and consequences of intensive work effort in the call centre workplace (for example, Bain et al., 2002; Thompson et al., 2004). Work effort in call centres is characterized by limited employee control and autonomy; one study found 46 per cent of employees surveyed in two call centres reported no control, or only a little, over their pace of work, and 61 per cent had no, or only a little, control over the timing of breaks (Taylor et al., 2002: Table 2).

Finally, intensified rhythms of working life can cause "spillovers" of negative emotion from the workplace to the household. The risk of conflict between work and family is increased by lengthened time at work (reducing time and energy available for family life), work stressors (which cause psychological strain at home) and dysfunctional behavioural traits adopted at work (such as aggressive or political styles). Among employees facing high

---

6. Qualitative data reveal work intensification among managers: "Jobs built up that I felt I had no control over completing and I wasn't able to – as hard as I worked and I worked all the hours under the sun – but every day things would be added to my list that would never get done. So I ended up, well, I got stressed" (Account Manager in a utilities company, cited in Wichert, 2002: 101). "My manager said last week. 'Don't take your work home with you'. I just thought that was the most stupid thing you could ever say … because you do. I know I'm stressed and I kick it out on the wife, the kids, the cat and just about anything really" (Manager in a financial services company, cited in Nolan, 2002: 121).

pressures from quantity of work, parents are found to experience greater tensions in the home than non-parents (Nolan, 2002: Figure 6.6).

13.6 HEALTH AND SAFETY

In its role in monitoring injuries at work, the UK Health and Safety Commission (HSC) set a target to reduce the incidence rate of fatal and major injuries by 10 per cent between 2000 and 2010, with half the progress (5 per cent) to be achieved by 2005. This target was not met. Rather, the incidence rate has been stable, fluctuating around 111–121 reported injuries per 100,000 employees (HSC, 2005).

The number of fatal injuries has fluctuated around 200–300 since 2000 (with 220 deaths in 2004–05), following a steady decline from around 500 in 1981 (HSC, 2005). Causes include falling from heights and being struck by a moving object or vehicle. Construction accounted for almost one third of all fatalities in 2002–03 and 39 deaths occurred in agriculture, hunting, forestry and fishing (*Labour Market Trends*, Feb. 2003). The rate of major injuries stood at 118 per 100,000 employees (and 33 per 100,000 self employed) in 2004–05 (HSC, 2005: Figures 1 and 2). Among men there were 167 cases of major injuries in 2004–05 compared to 66 among women, and 665 over-3-days injuries compared to 265 cases among women (HSC database).

By contrast, the risk of ill health caused by work has declined since 1999–2000. The HSC set a more ambitious target than that for accidents, aiming for a 20 per cent reduction of the rate of work-related ill health between 2000 and 2010 – again with half the progress to be achieved by 2005. The 2005 target was met: the rate fell from 2,200 per 100,000 cases in 2001–02 to 1,800 in 2004–05. Nevertheless, numbers of workers affected are still high. Two million people reported ill health due to work reasons in 2004–05. Half of the complaints were related to musculoskeletal disorders The second most common problem was stress, depression or anxiety, affecting more than half a million people (HSC, 2005). Sectors with a high risk of work-related ill health include health and social work, public administration and education, jointly with construction (HSC, 2005: Figure 8).

Finally, a new focus of academic and policy attention is work-related violence – both physical and non-physical (for example, abuse and bullying) – arising from colleagues, managers or customers. The UK Home Office recorded 655,000 incidents in England and Wales in 2004–05 – an uneven declining trend from 922,000 in 2000. Occupations most at risk include protective service occupations, managers and proprietors in agriculture and services, transport and mobile machine operators, leisure and personal service occupations and health and social welfare associate professionals (Home

Office, 2005: Table A27). But physical violence occurs across a range of sectors. In retail, incidents increased by 14 per cent between 2003 and 2004 and verbal abuse rose by 35 per cent (British Retail Consortium crime survey). In public administration, 329 cases of physical violence were recorded in 2004–05 compared to 203 in 2002. And in the airline and rail industries, research has found high levels of physical and verbal abuse among employees (Boyd, 2002).[7] Moreover, the major UK trade unions have issued advice to members on how to deal with non-physical bullying at work, and in November 2005 the TUC called for new legislation to outlaw bullying at work.

13.7 TRAINING AT WORK

Government reforms in the early 2000s were designed to address the long-standing skills gap in the UK labour market. A "Skills for Business" network was launched in 2001 and consists of 25 Sector Skills Councils and the Sector Skills Development Agency, which funds, monitors and supports the Councils. Each Council is an independent body licensed by government and represents a particular sector.[8] The Agency is governed by a Board of Employers. Part of the remit of each Council is to facilitate a Sector Skills Agreement which identifies the skills needed in each sector to improve productivity and to plan the provision of skills through education and training. It is officially described as "a collaboration between the supply-side and the demand-side" (www.ssda.org.uk, accessed July 2005). Employers lead the process, along with trade bodies and employer associations (no trade unions), and consult with organizations that supply and fund education and training. Final agreements, the first of which were launched in 2005, are brokered with the Departments for Education and Skills and for Trade and Industry.

To date, the result is a series of highly detailed reports on the skill needs within each sector and a heterogeneous set of initiatives. For example, employers in the film industry have agreed a collective training levy to fund technician training (a £50 million fund for a network of Academies within universities and colleges). The Council for construction employers agreed a £1 million collective sponsorship fund to support 120 university students per

---

7. Boyd (2002: 161) cites the following interviewees: "I was attacked on the train when I was on duty. The man who attacked me was arrested but I haven't slept for six months since and I am afraid to go to work but I never speak about it" (Railway Customer Operations Leader, male). "I have had a drink thrown over me. I have been spat at and pushed over" (Cabin crew, male).

8. Examples of Councils include E-Skills UK (IT industry and telecommunications), Improve Ltd (food and drink manufacturing), SEMTA (science, engineering and manufacturing technologies) and Skillsmart Retail (retail sector).

year through their studies (www.ssda.org.uk). And IT employers have embraced a new national IT Diploma for youth aged 14–19 years, a new undergraduate degree in "IT Management for Business" (intended to be run in 22 universities by 2008) and a simplified qualifications structure (the "ITQ/e-skills passport") to rebuild employers' confidence with public training provision (Donnelly et al., 2006).

These employer-led initiatives run alongside new government policy. A Skills White Paper in 2005 outlines what appear at first sight to be a range of relatively innovative policies, including: a new National Employer Training Programme which establishes the right, and funding, for every adult to acquire NVQ Level 2 skills (from spring 2007); a commitment to provide Level 2 training to people out of work; a new network of 12 employer-led Skills Academies which are intended to provide a centre of excellence in key sectors (following the model of the Fashion Retail Academy set up by the Arcadia retail group); and an increase in the number of trade union learning representatives (from 8,000 to 22,000) with funding for a Union Academy providing training for trade unions. For some, this latest raft of initiatives represents a sea change in Britain's approach to vocational training:

> Britain is on the verge of establishing a comprehensive system of lifelong learning that will transform its skill base and the lives of ordinary people. (Will Hutton, *The Guardian*, 1 May 2005)

At the time of writing, it is too early to comment on the impact of these reforms, or to assess whether they provide an innovative institutional response to a longstanding problem, or merely represent the latest in a short-termist, stop-go approach to revision and reform that prevents the maturing of the institutional architecture for vocational training provision. What can be said, however, is that it is very likely that more needs to be done. A fundamental obstacle is the absence of conditions that would enable employers to introduce innovative demand-side shifts (in work organization, product market strategy, and so on). For example, studies exploring the impact of the National Minimum Wage on employer investment in skill development found little change among the bulk of firms (Arulampalam et al., 2002; Heyes and Gray, 2003; Miller et al., 2002) and no discernible impact on UK productivity (Forth and O'Mahony, 2003; LPC, 2003: 56–57). Also, instead of providing on-the-job training matched with incremental steps up a job ladder, some large organizations have weakened internal labour market structures, posing a serious challenge for non-graduate entrants, especially (Grimshaw et al., 2002).

Moreover, evaluation of the Modern Apprenticeship programme suggests a government emphasis on achieving volume instead of improving content, as well as problems in service sectors where take-up is high but achievement is low; just one in ten leavers completed a Level 3 qualification compared to four in ten in engineering (Fuller and Unwin, 2003). It seems that services firms in the United Kingdom do not, as yet, display a genuine demand for intermediate skills. They lack a tradition of apprenticeship programmes and often lack the required institutional infrastructure (op. cit.). Jobs remain poorly designed with narrowly specified and repetitive tasks, close supervision and minimal discretion (Beynon et al., 2002).

13.8 SOCIAL DIALOGUE AND WORKERS' PARTICIPATION

Following trends established in the early 1980s, the landscape of British industrial relations is now characterized by a much weakened trade union movement. Union membership density declined throughout the 1990s, but then bottomed out at around 29 per cent during the early 2000s. However, the trend differs for men and women. Among male employees, union density dropped from 35 per cent in 1995 to 28 per cent in 2005, yet among women it remained relatively stable, around 28 per cent–30 per cent. Strikingly, women's density drew level with men's in 2003 and for the first time ever overtook men's the following year. Because women's labour market participation is almost on a par with men's, there are now more women trade union members than men; women accounted for 50.1 per cent of all union members in 2005.[9]

Opportunities for worker voice within UK workplaces are also increasingly restricted. Data from the Workplace Employment Relations Survey (WERS, 2004) show that only 27 per cent of workplaces recognized one or more unions in the negotiation of pay and conditions for some workers – a decline from 33 per cent in 1998. The decline was strongest among small firms – from 28 per cent to 18 per cent, compared to a marginal change from 41 per cent to 39 per cent among workplaces with 25 or more employees.

The pattern of change in coverage of collective bargaining depends upon the definition used in different surveys. The Labour Force Survey shows only a marginal decline in the proportion of employees whose pay was affected by collective bargaining over the period 1996–2005, from 37 per cent to 35 per cent. However, WERS data, which measure the proportion of workplaces that set pay for some workers through collective agreements, show a sharp decline from 30 per cent in 1998 to just 22 per cent in 2004. Mirroring the pattern of

---

9. The main reason is women's overrepresentation in the heavily unionized public sector: union density in 2005 was 59% in the public sector and just 17% in the private sector. Disaggregated by sex we have: public sector 57% of females and 61% of males, and private sector 14% of females and 20% of males (Grainger, 2006: Table 11).

union density, use of collective bargaining is more common in larger work-places (40 per cent), and there are major differences between the public and private sectors, with 77 per cent of public-sector workplaces using collective bargaining, compared to just 11 per cent of private-sector workplaces (Egan, 2005: Table 1).

Finally, union membership is weakest among the low paid. Estimates for 2004 show that among workers at the upper end of the wage distribution, earning £10–20 per hour, more than 40 per cent were union members. By con-trast, among workers earning less than £6 per hour, only 15 per cent were members (Howarth and Kenway, 2004: Figure 10). Also, union density among employees varies somewhat by ethnicity; 2004 data show that it is 29 per cent among whites, 24 per cent among Asian or Asian British and 33 per cent among black or black British employees.

REALITY AT ENTERPRISE LEVEL: CASE STUDIES

Three case studies were selected in order to provide a real-world view on some of the key trends in employment and vulnerable work. Drawing on interviews with managers and employees in each organization, our aim was to show how economic and regulatory conditions in different sectors interact with a variety of employment policies to shape working conditions. We do not intend to provide a representative portrait of the state of employment and vulnerable work in the United Kingdom. Rather, the aim is to complement the above review of research and survey data to show how the characteristics of vulnerable work – especially flexibility, undervaluation, insecurity and poor working conditions – are realized for particular groups of workers in different working environments.

Three sectors are represented in our research, namely elderly care, food manufacturing and packaging, and software services. Table 13.3 shows the additional details of organization size (annual revenue and workforce), ownership structure, performance and key employment issues explored. Size of organization varies from the medium-sized software services firm, with 210 employees (10 in the United Kingdom and approximately 200 in India) to the

Table 13.3 Summary details for case study organizations

	CityCare	KwikFood	OffshoreIT
Sector	Elderly care	Food manufacturing & packaging	Software services
Annual revenue	£14.6 million	€1,600 million	n.a.
Total workforce	1,200	9,000 approx.	210 approx. (200 in India, 10 in the UK)
Ownership structure	Not-for-profit company and registered charity	Multinational, Irish-owned company	Private company
Performance	Significant growth	Sudden decline since 2005	Very rapid growth since established in 1998
Key employment issues	• Tight funding and strong regulations • Undervalued work • Positive opportunities for training • Flexible hiring	• Low pay and poor working conditions • Taylorized work • Flexible hiring with gangmaster agency	• Global coordination of skills and expertise • Dedicated to work, but career insecurity and stress

multinational food manufacturing firm with more than 9,000 employees worldwide. Ownership structure also differs, as do performance trends, with CityCare and OffshoreIT experiencing rapid growth in recent years and KwikFood stable until 2005 when it experienced a sudden drop in product demand at the workplace visited. The key employment issues highlighted in Table 13.3 provide an indication of the main issues related to vulnerable work examined in the discussion below.

United Kingdom Case Study 1: CityCare – dedicated workers but undervalued work

CityCare is a not-for-profit company, registered as a charity, with a voluntary board of six directors. It provides residential care and home care services for the elderly in and around a major UK city. Established in 1991 via the transfer of local authority care homes (and local authority staff) for older people, over the years it has become increasingly independent from the original single local authority. Notably, it has entered the market for homecare (and crisis care) services and regularly bids for contracts issued by a range of local authorities in the region around the city.

It expanded quickly over the period 2000–06, largely by growing the market for homecare (or domiciliary care) services, and generated an annual turnover of £14.6 million in 2005. It employs more than 1,200 people and is one of the largest independent care providers in the region. It provides care to over 2,000 service users across the following range of services:

- 13 residential care homes – permanent care or short-term (respite) care for older people;
- homecare services – personal care and domestic assistance for people in their own homes;
- intermediate care – rehabilitation after hospital discharge or support to prevent hospital admission;
- extra care – for people in supported housing schemes;
- carers' support services – offers breaks to people who are carers.

The switch of focus to homecare services reflects government policy, which recognizes the high costs of residential care, a consumer preference for independence and changed attitudes towards institutionalization, and also a political and economic imperative to reduce demand for hospital beds (requiring local authorities to pay a penalty to hospitals if they delay the discharge of patients) (McClimont and Grove, 2004). CityCare is also one of hundreds of new independent care providers (for-profit and non-profit private sector organizations) that have developed since the 1980s following a string of policy initiatives around community care. Importantly, however, local authorities still purchase the bulk of care (estimated at around 70 per cent).

Tight funding and strong regulations
Like other organizations in the care sector, CityCare faces strong conflicting pressures from, on the one hand, ambitious regulations stipulating minimum standards of accommodation and the scale and composition (skill-mix) of staffing and, on the other hand, restricted funding for patients reliant on local government subsidy. The cost of maintaining large, often very old buildings is added to the cost of renovations to meet minimum standards of accommodation, requiring minimum-sized rooms, a majority of private rooms (only 20 per cent of residents authorized to share rooms by 2007) and en-suite bathrooms (Netten et al., 2001). Yet because the majority of residents and care users are funded by local authorities, CityCare lacks the power to increase fees to cover rising costs.

The manager responsible for human resources claimed that this issue of finance was the most important challenge facing CityCare "because social care across the country doesn't get the funding it ought to get". Many of the problems in managing staff would be eased if the funding situation could be addressed, she argued, including problems of recruiting and retaining good quality staff caused by low pay (she claimed she "would like to pay £8–9 an hour") and the need to improve financial incentives for staff to undertake programmes of skill development. The funding shortfall was exacerbated, in the manager's view, by the short-term uncertainty of the contracting arrangement with the local authorities. Cost-cutting pressures from bidding against other homecare providers destabilized the relationship between managers and workers. Moreover, there was typically very limited information about the next round of tenders for homecare services which made forward planning difficult. In response, CityCare has become involved in a consortium of care providers to improve funding for care by lobbying central government.

On the other hand, the care sector is governed by a "thick" set of institutions, in the form of government regulations, to ensure quality of care to users. The National Care Standards Commission was established in 2002 under the Care Standards Act (2000). It is responsible for ensuring all care homes meet a range of minimum standards covering individual accommodation, hygiene, social activities, meals and staffing needs (DoH, 2002). Staffing needs, for example, require that a minimum of 50 per cent of non-managerial care staff (including agency staff) are trained to NVQ (National Vocational Qualification) Level 2; that the recruitment process includes two references and police checks on candidates; that all staff require induction training and foundation training that meets National Training Organization specifications, as well as three paid training days per year; and that all staff receive formal supervision (at least six times per year) covering career development. At CityCare, there is regular independent monitoring to check on the proportion of staff with NVQ Level 2 qualifications and reports are produced and circulated on the performance of each activity of the business.

The consequences of the institutional and cost pressures at CityCare are three-fold: (a) strong downward pressures on pay; (b) positive opportunities for skill development for care workers; and (c) a flexible approach to finding new recruits. We explore these apparently contradictory principles of employment organization in the following sections.

Undervalued work

The assumption at CityCare, and this is true throughout much of the sector, is that care workers can be relied upon to provide a higher quality of labour for a given wage. In other words, contrary to mainstream economics, pay does not equate with productivity (or service quality in this case); instead, the wage paid signifies an undervaluation of the quality of care work (see Grimshaw and Rubery (2006) for a wide-ranging analysis of definitional issues of undervaluation).

The work of the care assistant is undeniably hard – physically and psychologically – despite specialized moving and lifting equipment. The care assistant we interviewed told us she lost a lot of weight in the two years working in the care sector and now "doesn't need to join a gym!" She also described a stressful working environment ("like chisels in the head"), with pressures to complete paperwork for each resident before handing over to the care worker covering the next shift, and difficulties dealing with agitated or temperamental residents. Nevertheless, she described the work as rewarding, especially being able to give people back their dignity by keeping them clean, tidy and comfortable.

But pay rates are undeniably low for most of the 1,200 staff. When the minimum wage was introduced in 1999, CityCare had to uprate most staff's wages to bring them in line and since then has only sought to pay at, or slightly above, the minimum wage. There are different pay rates for staff working in residential care and those providing home care services (Table 13.4). The rates shown were uprated in line with the increase in the minimum wage in October 2005 to the hourly rate of £5.05. New recruits to the lowest paid groups of catering and laundry assistants earned the minimum wage for their first year and this increased with one year's experience to £5.20. No further pay increments are included in the pay structure. Compared to the low wage threshold, only the higher grades of care officers, care coordinators and managers escape low pay.

What is striking is the very narrow pay differential between the care assis-

Table 13.4 Hourly pay rates for workers at CityCare, United Kingdom, Oct. 2005–Sep. 2006 (UK£)

Position	Residential care		Home care	
	Starter	1 year +	Starter	1 year +
Home Administrator	6.75			
Care Coordinator			6.85	
Care Officer	6.40	7.15		
Night Care Officer	7.40	7.55		
Care Assistant	5.20	5.50	5.75 (practical/personal) 5.25 (domestic care)	
Night Care Assistant	5.40	6.15		
Cook	6.00			
Catering assistant	5.05	5.20		
Cleaner	5.05	5.20		
Laundry assistant	5.05	5.20		
National Minimum Wage	5.05 (Oct 2005–Sep 2006)			
Low wage threshold (66% of median for all employees)	6.37 (April 2005)			

tant and the cleaner. Both jobs involve hard work, but the demands of personal responsibility and social skills are higher for the care assistant than for the cleaner. Yet, the differential is just 15 pence between the starter hourly rates of £5.20 and £5.05, respectively, and just 30 pence for the more experienced workers. This demonstrates the problem of a non-recognition of the skills and job demands of care work. It is also likely that these pay rates are strongly delineated by gender. Evidence from another study exploring responses to the introduction and subsequent upratings of the National Minimum Wage found some care homes narrowed the pay differential between female-dominated groups (for example, care assistants and cleaners), but maintained differentials enjoyed by male-dominated groups (such as cooks or gardeners). One of the laundry workers in the study described her discomfort at earning the same wage as a care assistant:

> [The minimum wage] is not enough though, is it, especially for the carers, for the job they do? ... The girls here, they get the same as me but they do a damn sight harder work. I mean my job compared to their job is a doddle and they are on the same pay as me. They should be on more. ... For me to stay on £4.10 and the girls on, say, a fiver an hour. To me that would be quite fair. (cited in Grimshaw and Carroll 2002)

The care officer and the care assistant interviewed in this study both recognized the low rates of pay they earned for the job. The care officer told us her colleagues often compared their pay with the higher rates offered at nearby supermarkets and questioned their decision to stay at the care home. And the care assistant put it more bluntly:

> We are not paid enough. Everyone says that for what we do. We are vastly under-paid and the union cannot do anything about it. (CityCare, female part-time care assistant)

Indeed, trade unions played little role at CityCare. There was a reduction in premiums paid for unsocial hours working and trade unions had not inter-vened, despite the fact that a union representative sits on the Board of Directors (according to the care officer interviewed). CityCare managers were thus able to abolish premiums for working Saturdays (time and a half) and for Sundays (double time) and replace them with the basic rate. Overtime is also worked at a basic rate of pay. Only night-shift staff retain a small premium (see Table 13.4). In our interview, the HR manager defended this situation and argued for the need to improve the basic rate of pay.

Not all pay rates are shown in Table 13.4 since while care assistants in care homes all earn the same, in home care the pay depends on the contract. CityCare has been seeking to merge pay rates to reduce confusion between groups of workers, but without success. Also, some staff are still on protected rates following their transfer from the city local authority in the early 1990s. For example, night care assistants are on frozen rates of £6.55, far higher than the CityCare rate of £5.25; their pay will remain frozen until CityCare rates catch up – a process that is likely to take more than seven years at current rates of increase in the National Minimum Wage.

Positive opportunities for training
In response to the national regulations on quality of care, CityCare must meet a forthcoming target of half its care staff acquiring National Vocational Qualification (NVQ) Level 2 by 2007. This means levels of training provision at CityCare far outstrip levels found at organizations in other sectors in the low-wage economy, such as food retail or hotels and restaurants, for example. CityCare provides in-house classroom training, as well as on-the-job training, to all care assistants and care officers. Induction training lasts around one week and includes manual handling, infection control, challenging behaviour, health and safety, and so on. Staff are then expected to undertake NVQ train-ing, which involves release for classroom training, although the frequency of training is subject to staffing levels within the particular area of services. The content of training programmes differs for home care workers and workers in residential care homes.

Both care workers we interviewed spoke positively about the training opportunities. The care officer had started work with CityCare as a kitchen assistant 13 years previously, then progressed to a care assistant and then to the post of care officer. She subsequently passed the NVQ Level 3 in Caring, which involved classroom work at CityCare headquarters, assessment on the job and personal study at home. The care assistant had undertaken the introductory training – first aid, fire safety, food and hygiene, essential care practice and moving and handling – and had completed NVQ Level 2. In fact she had completed the NVQ Level 2 twice, once at a previous care organization and again at CityCare since CityCare did not recognize NVQ qualifications from other organizations – a typical problem in the United Kingdom reflecting the bias of NVQs towards organization-specific content over national standards.

The main problem, however, was the absence of clear linkages between skill development and progression. In part because of the tight cost pressures on the organization, the pay structure included very little financial incentive for skill development. On completion of NVQ Level 3, care officers (and night care officers) in residential care homes receive a very small increment to their pay – £0.15 per hour for starters and £0.25 for staff with one year experience or more. Also, care assistants were unlikely to be offered the chance of completing NVQ Level 3 training unless there was a vacant position as care officer. Thus, the potential to progress beyond NVQ Level 2 was obstructed by the pyramidal structure of the job ladder.

Flexible hiring
Because pay is so low and the work so hard (and unattractive to many young jobseekers), CityCare has established two flexible recruitment policies in a context of high staff turnover and strong competition from hospitals, supermarkets and shopping malls. The first involves strengthened links with local sources of potential recruits. Examples include links with local Job Centres (government agencies run by the Department of Work and Pensions), as well as the organizing of Open Days in local non-governmental community centres to reach out to otherwise excluded groups of people (the long-term unemployed and inactive). The CityCare HR manager described this policy as "a strong focus for the company".

The second policy involved establishing an in-house list of temporary agency workers within all 13 care homes in January 2006. Prior to this arrangement, CityCare had relied upon external temporary work agencies, but costs had escalated too high. The HR manager also stressed that since the quality of care strongly depended upon the commitment and long-term attachment of the carer, CityCare wanted to shift away from relying on external staff to deploying only staff that "have been recruited by us and trained by us, to give residents that comfort level" (HR manager). Curiously, however, CityCare was unwilling to extend a similar comfort level to these temporary workers. Although CityCare manages the in-house list of agency staff, these staff are not employees of CityCare; instead they are defined as casual workers. Each casual worker is attached to a base care home but is expected to travel to any of the 12 others. While the distances are not great (up to around 10–15 miles), poor public transport in the city means that travel times can be long for these casual care workers.

Unlike residential care, in homecare services the HR manager argued there was no need for agency staff since appointments of users can be shifted to adjust to staffing problems. By contrast, in care homes there are strict regulations on the ratio of staffing to service user so that vacancies caused by absence, sickness or staff turnover have to be met with temporary cover. However, CityCare does employ some staff on zero-hours contracts in home care services. Also, Care Coordinators in homecare services are expected to fill in when needed, in addition to their weekly workload. Problems of working-time limits are avoided by requiring all staff to opt out of the Working Time Directive "to cover us if someone goes over the maximum hours threshold" (HR manager).

United Kingdom Case Study 2: KwikFood – Poor work and exploitation of migrant workers

Our second case study, KwikFood, is part of a multinational Irish-owned company that manufactures and packages a range of convenience foods and drinks, and also manufactures and trades a range of basic food ingredients. It expanded from a sugar refinery plant in Ireland and now has manufacturing sites in four European countries. It is a market leader in sandwich making and sauce manufacture. Annual revenue totals more than EUR1.6 billion and the workforce numbers over 9,000.

Our case study focused on one manufacturing plant in the north of England. The plant was acquired by KwikFood in 1995 and has subsequently specialized in the manufacture and packaging of chilled ready-made meals. In 1998, it entered into a co-financing arrangement with Tesco, the leading supermarket chain in the United Kingdom, to build a second, more modern factory on the site. However, the arrangement included a commitment by KwikFood to dedicate 100 per cent of its production to supply own-brand products to Tesco. The arrangement was successful for six years, with stable orders and profitable KwikFood business. However, a rapid drop in orders from Tesco in 2005 caused significant losses and this was the financial situation that prevailed at the time of our interviews. Production had collapsed by

30–40 per cent, from around 1 million packaged meals per week in 2000 to just 600–700,000 per week in 2006. Workforce numbers had also been cut, from 900 to 774 over the same period. Remarkably, however, because of the very high level of staff turnover – averaging 25 per cent – KwikFood has not yet had to resort to redundancies.

The collapse was largely caused by KwikFood's dependence on just one customer. Lack of freedom to move into new markets (new products and/or new customers) meant that KwikFood was unable to adapt to a sudden swing in customer attitudes towards manufactured foods. The senior manager we spoke with argued that two incidents had sparked this sudden drop in demand. First, in February 2005 there was a public scare caused by the finding of Sudan 1 – an illegal food dye linked to an increased risk of cancer – in a chilli powder that was used to make a brand of Worcester sauce, which, in turn, is used as an ingredient in thousands of manufactured foods. Secondly, a media campaign during 2005 by a celebrity chef against packaged meals used in school dinners had had a wider impact on people's views regarding the need to purchase fresh food. At the time of the interviews, KwikFood was in discussions with Tesco to request permission to diversify into other markets, but the senior manager believed it highly unlikely they would be able to provide own-brand products to competing supermarket chains. Also, confidential discussions among managers were under way debating how best to improve profits, including the option of making some workers redundant.

The workforce is predominantly male and full time. Among the 614 shopfloor workers, only 33 (5 per cent) work part time, and only 11 (7 per cent) of the 167 are white-collar workers. Also, the age profile is skewed because of the high staff turnover. Among shopfloor workers, one in three are younger than 30 years old. Moreover, a substantial minority have very short tenure: some 31 per cent had been employed for less than two years and only 8 per cent for 10 years or more.

Low pay and poor working conditions

The work tasks at KwikFood are organized in a Taylorist fashion with narrow tasks divided among different groups of workers, very limited job rotation and job titles reflecting the actual task – such as "extruder" or "sauce dropper" or "pasta cooler". The production is organized into four major areas, from mixing of ingredients to the final packaging of the product. In area 1, "preparation and sauces", workers weigh ingredients into huge pans, cook the sauces and then drop the sauces into enormous plastic bags which are tumbled until cool. Area 2 involves the cooking of pasta. Here, extruders make pasta shapes and work with pot boilers to cook the pasta. The production lines are housed in area 3. This is where the different elements of the ready-made meals are combined: depositors drop the sauce and operatives add garnish or flat pasta by hand as meals pass by on a conveyor belt. At the end of the line, the meals are sealed. The final area is the packing area.

Conditions of work at KwikFood are, in the words of the HR manager, "not good". It is cold and employees must wear hair nets, wellingtons and several layers of clothing. The cold temperature is the main reason explaining the difficulties attracting younger recruits; "Kids don't want to do it [work here]. They don't like the cold" (HR manager). And the conditions also explained the fact that most recruits came from out-of-work status: "You wouldn't give up a job to work here" (HR manager).

We talked with a woman in her 50s employed as a packing operative, who had experience of working in different areas of the factory. As a basic operative she is paid marginally above the minimum wage. The cold temperature – between 5 and 10 degrees – is a feature of work throughout the factory, even in the packing area. She wears five layers of clothing – her own two, KwikFood's fleece, her own sleeveless jacket and then one or sometimes two overalls together with thermal gloves. She told us she is sensitive to the cold and "I never get used to the cold". Apparently, during one particularly cold winter, there were icicles in the factory and workers were given special breaks to warm up with hot drinks. She said she "is not allowed to sit down" during the shift, and tries to lean against the line when it stops for whatever reason.

Table 13.5 Hourly pay rates for shopfloor workers at KwikFood, Apr. 2005–Mar. 2006 (UK£)

Position	Morning shift	Afternoon shift
Supervisor	7.61	8.14
Second in command	6.82	7.22
Engineer	6.44	–
Night hygiene chargehand	–	9.18
Night hygiene operative	–	8.32
Warehouse/despatch	6.65	6.71
Controller (e.g. cook)	6.33	6.94
Sealer operative	5.76	6.29
Chargehand (e.g. sauce dropper)	5.76	6.29
Weighers/fillers	5.58	6.10
Grade one	5.34	5.89
Basic operative (e.g. packer, pasta cooler)	5.22	5.78
Probation rate (first 13 weeks)	5.05	5.54
National Minimum Wage	4.85 (Apr.–Sep. 2005)	
	5.05 (Oct. 2005–Mar. 2006)	
Low wage threshold (66% of median for all employees)	6.37 (Apr. 2005)	

The poor conditions of work are not compensated for by higher pay in the way that Adam Smith might have argued. Most shopfloor workers are paid between the minimum wage and the UK low wage threshold (Table 13.5). A small premium is awarded to workers employed on the afternoon shift, since this requires working unsocial hours (3.30 p.m. to midnight). The highest paid manual workers are the 50 or so workers employed (permanently) on the night shift, who receive a shift premium.

The firm is forced to adjust pay annually in line with the minimum wage. It paid rates below the minimum wage when it was first introduced in 1999 and in each year since it has had to uprate its lowest rates to follow the minimum wage. In preparation for the October 2006 uprating of the National Minimum Wage to £5.35, the new April 2006 agreement will need to increase rates paid to basic operatives and to grade one workers. With limited prospects of moving up to the posts of supervisor, second-in-command or engineer, shopfloor workers are faced with a very narrow range of basic pay, from the probation rate at the minimum wage (£5.05) to the rate of £6.94 for controllers on the late shift. The rate of pay is determined according to the employer's conception of the skills required for the bundle of tasks in each job and does not reflect the characteristics (age, work experience or education) of the employee, or differences in performance among workers undertaking the same job.

Taylorized work
Work in the factory is organized along a traditional Taylorist assembly line. Jobs involve a narrow range of simplified tasks and these are repeated in a highly standardized manner. There is virtually no interchangeability of posts among workers. According to the HR manager, this is because "employees don't like [job rotation]". Clearly, a large-scale survey of employees would be required to corroborate this claim.

Training provision is very limited. All new employees undertake an induction programme that includes basic food hygiene and health and safety. All other skills are learned on the job by shadowing a more experienced colleague. Many of the higher-paid jobs are filled internally and the HR manager claimed that all current supervisor and department managers had risen through the ranks.

The nature of work undertaken by the cook we interviewed is illustrative of how technology has been implemented in the factory in a manner that eliminates a great deal of employee discretion and autonomy. No special qualifications are required of cooks recruited at KwikFood (HR manager) and they are paid at a low rate of pay (as a "Controller", see Table 13.5). Nevertheless, they are acknowledged as having a disproportionate level of responsibility. As the HR manager put it, they have "quite a responsibility, because if you put in the wrong ingredients you can waste up to £1 million". In fact, there was a recent case where the KwikFood employer took a worker through the disciplinary process because of a costly mistake. However, the union argued strongly that the pay ought to reflect better the responsibilities of the job and apparently won a pay rise.

After working 13 years in a timber-yard as a labourer, the cook started work at KwikFood with no previous experience in kitchens. After a brief basic induction he worked alongside a senior cook for 13 weeks to learn the basics of the job. His daily work starts at 7 a.m. He checks the cleanliness of pans, sets the paddles (stirring tool) in place and then downloads the ingredients from the computer screen, referring to specific batch codes for each sauce. Once he has obtained the correct spices, he follows instructions on the computer. It will say, "add butter", then "add cheese", "add spices" and so on. As the cook told us, "The computer is in charge of the whole process". The cook works in a team of four and they handle ten pans together, sharing the work according to the different start and finish times of each sauce. Six to seven sauces per pan are cooked during the early shift. Accidents and mistakes do happen, sometimes because the weighing scales are not calibrated correctly, or the computer system goes down, or the seal leaks; in each case, engineers are on site and can be called to correct the problem. Compared to the timber-yard, the cook liked the less physical nature of the work (he had hurt his back previously). He was also satisfied with the regular shifts since these combined with his wife's regular late-shift working (6 p.m.–10 p.m.) so that they could take turns looking after their children; a practical situation, albeit far from ideal in terms of sharing family time together – "We see each other about one hour during the week and more of each other at the weekend."

Flexible hiring with a gangmaster agency

KwikFood faces a very competitive labour market. The local rate of unemployment is low. The factory location is not easily accessible by public transport and the nearest train station is half an hour's walk. Also, it is housed on an industrial estate and other firms pay more for low-skilled workers. According to the HR manager, these conditions, combined with the poor working conditions in the factory, makes it very difficult for KwikFood to attract English workers. Instead, use of a gangmaster agency "is the main way to relieve the pressures". As she put it, "the English wouldn't get out of bed and turn up [for work]".

KwikFood relies on just one agency, which is referred to as a "gangmaster" since it provides agency temps sourced from another country to the food industry. It used to supply English workers, but over time English workers moved to areas of employment that offered more attractive conditions. Since the mid-1990s, the agency has contracted an international workforce, whose composition "reflects what's going on in the world at a point in time" (agency manager), with migrants fleeing from war (Iraq, Afghanistan) and, more recently, travelling from the new EU Member States to seek better employment opportunities. At KwikFood, workers were largely from Latvia and Poland. The agency manager described these migrant workers as "polite, very polite" and, moreover:

[They] do the work we don't want to do. They work on the line – high risk – and in packing. (Agency manager)

Recruits to the agency are charged a £70 fee and typically the worker pays this by allowing the agency to deduct £10 per week. Staff are sourced through word of mouth and the agency organizes buses to transport groups to the KwikFood factory. Often this involves an entire family and distances can be large, requiring long commute times (a return trip of up to two hours). Temporary posts are only confirmed within 24 hours by KwikFood, nevertheless the agency manager seeks to provide a steady stream of income to what he referred to as "a pool of dedicated staff". Curiously, because many workers are grouped in families, and since families are typically more likely to be able to pool income to purchase their own means of transport, the agency manager said he tried very hard to distribute the available work in such a way that each family receives a sustainable level of income. He thus pursues a "needs-based approach" to organizing the agency work.

We have a pool of dedicated staff for the a.m. and p.m. shifts. Some weeks I can promise a week. At the moment it's hit and miss. I'll try to give members of each family three days per week – [since] a family will share a car. (Agency manager)

The agency also takes responsibility for helping the migrant worker assimilate and typically arranges for a new bank account (with TSB/Lloyds Bank since it is more flexible with foreign workers, according to the agency manager), writes letters to set up National Insurance payments, and translates documents (for example, in one case the son of a temp had to have an operation and required translated medical documents); unlike other gangmasters, this agency does not arrange accommodation. On hiring, the agency runs a one-hour induction and one of the more senior agency workers acts as translator.

When economic conditions were better at KwikFood, there were some favourable prospects of winning permanent work with the firm. KwikFood used to operate a temp-to-perm scheme. At any one time, 20 people out of around 100 agency workers would be selected following a 13-week "screening" period. However, this practice was abolished following the collapse of profits at KwikFood in 2005. The number of agency workers is around half its peak level of 120 per day during the late 1990s.

Pay rates are poor for these migrant agency workers. All are employed as basic operatives and all receive the same basic rate – the minimum wage. The agency charges KwikFood a higher rate (£6.70, compared to the minimum of £5.05) to cover its own costs, as well as holidays and sick pay.

United Kingdom Case Study 3: OffshoreIT – Managing an international division of labour

OffshoreIT is a medium-sized IT services company that provides IT consultancy and software services in the United Kingdom. It was established in 1998 with the objective of growing the offshore market with a small managerial office in the United Kingdom and a rapidly expanding base of OffshoreIT employees in Mumbai, India. Consultants in the United Kingdom work with a range of client organizations to promote offshore relocation of IT operations to their office in India. Offshore operations are then implemented with the help of a project management team in the United Kingdom, typically composed of Indian and UK staff. This "unique, integrated approach to the delivery of software services" (company website) is said to combine the knowledge and expertise of a high-quality UK professional team with the flexibility and cost efficiencies of the offshore office in Mumbai. The offshore office is said to be cost-effective not only due to the lower labour costs, but also due to the Indian culture of working hard and the time difference of being seven hours ahead.

In 2006, between 10 and 12 staff were employed permanently in the UK office, including the managing director, two company directors and the operations director. Several agency and freelance staff are also employed (in secretarial and technical posts). In India, OffshoreIT employs more than 200 permanent employees and they provide full support for the UK clients. Indian project managers spend a minimum of three months working in the United Kingdom with the client to familiarize themselves with the specific project. In some instances, this period may be extended at the client's request. At the time of fieldwork there were 25 secondees based in the United Kingdom, but in the past there have been as many as 125. Secondees receive a UK salary while working in the United Kingdom.

By organizing the offshore services through a directly employed workforce in Mumbai, rather than subcontracting to an Indian firm, OffshoreIT claimed to be able to respond to the concerns of many UK firms about poor working conditions. It has developed a corporate social responsibility framework, which includes the goal of providing UK terms and conditions to its Indian workforce; examples include holiday entitlement, sick pay and job security. It also commits the firm to donating 10 per cent of its profits to sustainable development and poverty reduction projects in India. In a press release, the managing director is quoted as stating:

> [OffshoreIT] strives to adhere to the principles of fair trade. As a UK-based company we can offer improved employment terms to those in India and a great opportunity for personal development.

Global coordination of skills and expertise

Our interviews with IT project managers illuminated new types of problems concerning the coordination of production activities across developed and less developed economies. First, because of the recent rapid development in the IT market in India, most "senior" IT project managers have very limited experience – typically two to three years. Added to this are issues related to the lack of tacit understanding about business practices in the UK economy, which is argued to be central to expertise in developing business-friendly software packages.

One IT project manager we interviewed was part of a large team developing and implementing a new software system for a multinational car hire firm. This 18-month, £2 million project is the largest in the history of OffshoreIT. However, at the time of fieldwork it was over-cost and over-time. Of the team, 35 were based in India and 8 were on the client site. Three out of four Indian employees were said to be recent graduates with "no professional experience".

> One of my big reservations ... [with] the IT market in India at the moment – it is very hard to find anyone with any level of skill. ... There is a pool of a lot of people with IT degrees. But the value of those degrees is questionable.

The project manager told us this had "always been a problem at [OffshoreIT]" and that the skills required for testing the new software in the Indian office are "not good at all". This is partly because testing is characterized as a low-value job and attracts the worse candidates. Also, there are doubts about the higher education system in India which varies considerably in quality.

Because of the problems in the Indian office, there were said to be insufficient resources dedicated to the team of analysts working on the client site in the United Kingdom. Typically projects comprise a split of resources consisting of 30 per cent analysis, 40 per cent build and 30 per cent testing, yet this project only has three people undertaking the analysis and 35 people in the build and testing stages. To address the continuing problems, OffshoreIT wants to extend the period of time managers from the Mumbai office visit the client site in order to transfer the tacit knowledge, but it faces difficulties in arranging visas beyond the six-week stay allowed for travel to the United Kingdom for the purpose of meetings. In the opinion of the project manager we spoke with, while offshoring may have been cost-effective in the past, it now carries too many risks and no longer generates large cost savings.

Dedicated to work but career insecurity and stress

Accepting the obvious limitations of the scale of our fieldwork, our impression from talking to two project managers at OffshoreIT was that UK-based employees tended to be dedicated to their work; in particular, they largely found the IT project work fulfilling. However, they suffered from a great deal of insecurity regarding career prospects and experienced stress caused by the complexity of intra-team and inter-country interactions and coordination of work.

Both project managers generally liked their job. One told us, "I just love my job. I love being busy". "Being busy" involves a great deal of travel. A project can be located anywhere in the country since the work is undertaken on the client's premises and this can demand a great deal of time away from home and family. A recent project in London meant that one of the managers only spent weekends at home with his family in the north of England during a period of two-and-a-half months. This caused problems:

> I love the job but at the same time my wife is suffering here. She is alone. My wife sometimes gets lonely. It's a pain travelling and being away from my wife.

Work as a project manager may require up to nine hours a day, 45 hours a week. However, while hours are logged and collated at the end of each month, there is no additional pay for overtime. The more junior project manager we spoke with – paid a basic salary slightly higher than the national average – did not believe this was a problem since, as he put it, "I love this job, so I don't mind spending time on it."

However, an identified problem concerned insecurity over future prospects. For the more senior project manager, the issue was how to avoid the negative reputation effects of being involved in a high-profile project failure. The client had recently stopped making monthly payments to OffshoreIT and project problems had escalated. The manager in charge was on sick leave, suffering from stress. Our interviewee was seriously considering quitting before it was too late. The other project manager was concerned about the lack of transparency in possible career options:

> One thing missing is the career progression. If you lose a customer, ... I'd like to see a review of what is going to happen next – "What is your role going to be in the next 6–12 months?" ... I don't know what's the next step for me here. ... I'd love someone to explain things to me, to say, "Okay, this is your next step". It doesn't happen.

The senior project manager had few ties to OffshoreIT in part because of the absence of a company pension, which he decried as "probably illegal" and noted the contradiction with its promotion of an ethic of corporate social responsibility in India. With the rapid expansion of the company, he seemed less confident of his place among the senior tiers of managers and said he did not want "to rock the boat" by pressing for a company scheme; he had instead made alternative individual arrangements.

While the more senior project manager appeared outwardly stressed when discussing the problems associated with his current failing project, the junior manager had recently been medicated with stress and had taken medication for depression and stomach problems. He blamed his illness on a combination of factors – he was responsible for liaising with the project team in India, but lines of communication were disrupted by his UK line manager which caused a considerable amount of interpersonal tensions. The need for intra- and inter-team coordination was also blamed as a source of tension by the senior project manager. He pointed to tensions not only between OffshoreIT UK staff and the OffshoreIT team in India, but also with managers from the client firm and other IT freelance workers hired both by the client and by OffshoreIT.

CONCLUSION

The evidence in this chapter suggests that despite its relative success as a motor for job growth, the UK employment model also fuels key elements of vulnerability – in the job and for the worker. Our review of secondary data in the first part of this chapter revealed several areas of vulnerability. It showed that part-time work, dominated by women, remains strongly marginalized in the UK employment model. Moreover, the poor character of part-time work explains the high concentration of women in low-wage work, as well as the fact that nearly half of all low-wage workers are employed in the retail sector. Temporary work is more heterogeneous in character, but the rising use of "gangmasters" for placing agency workers in the agricultural and food sectors has been associated with exploitative practices. Long-hours working is on the decline, but it still adds up to 29% of men and 9% of women working more than 45 hours per week on average in 2005. So policy debates still centre on the disconnect between work and family life, and while working mothers have a new right to request reduced hours, more radical policy is urgently needed. Too many workplaces are characterized by outdated, Taylorized work organization – in the old manufacturing sectors (for example, footwear and textiles), but also in the new service sectors (call centres). Inability, or unwillingness, to innovate and develop enhanced forms of job design acts as an obstacle to improved training provision, which, despite the promise offered by new Sector Skills Councils, remains an area of underinvestment. For workers, the result is limited career opportunities, especially for those entering the labour market without higher education qualifications.

The results of the three case studies shed light on the nature of vulnerability at the level of the workplace, given the very tainted empirical data collected. The evidence is only intended to offer a snapshot view and is not representative of other firms in each sector, or of other sectors. Together, the evidence points to four dimensions of vulnerability, which cross sectors and are experienced in different ways by different workforce groups. Table 13.6 provides a summary.

Table 13.6 The character of vulnerability in three case study organizations

	CityCare	KwikFood	OffshoreIT
Flexibility	Abolished unsocial working hours premia	High use of "gangmaster" agency to place migrant workers	The risk of providing IT services with an Indian workforce is displaced to UK project managers
Insecurity	In-house list of casual workers – some on zero-hours contracts	Migrant workers' income security tied to family participation with gangmaster Risk of redundancies due to slump in product demand	Career insecurity caused by change in contracts and limited information from senior managers
Under-valuation	Very low wage rates Narrow differential between cleaner and care worker	Majority paid between minimum wage and low wage threshold	n.a.
Poor working conditions	Hard physical work and psychologically demanding (as well as rewarding)	Taylorist work organization Cold and wet environment	Stress and work–family balance problems

A first element of vulnerability is flexibility. Not all flexible employment policies generate vulnerability, but some do and the UK government's pride in its flexible labour market needs to be tempered by recognition of some of the downsides. At CityCare, a more flexible approach to working time necessitated the abolition of unsocial hours premia, but this removed an important addition to the weekly pay packet for the largely female part-time workforce. The full-time workforce at KwikFood faced a different risk from flexible employment practices, through the company's reliance on a "gangmaster" (temporary work agency) to fill basic operative positions at the minimum wage. And at OffshoreIT, the innovative, flexible use of an offshore Indian workforce carried a number of risks which were largely displaced to project managers responsible for contracts with clients in the United Kingdom.

While the contemporary goal of policy-makers is flexicurity, poorly designed flexible employment practices in our three case studies were accompanied by substantial evidence of insecurity. The three case studies displayed particular variants. At CityCare and KwikFood, insecurity was experienced by agency workers, organized as an in-house list of casual workers at CityCare and recruited by a gangmaster at KwikFood. But the high-paid IT workers at OffshoreIT also experienced insecurity with regard to their future prospects with the firm, reflecting both the uncertainty of a future stream of contracts and the limited trickling down of information from the senior management team.

A third characteristic of vulnerability is undervaluation of the work. CityCare had struggled to keep up with annual increases in the National Minimum Wage and as a result offered very little difference in pay rates between unqualified cleaners and care workers, from whom managers required considerable responsibility and dedication in their work. Indeed, the highly feminized occupation of care work would seem to be a classic case of undervalued work (Grimshaw and Rubery, 2006). At KwikFood, despite the hard work, fast pace and poor working conditions, most workers were paid below the low-wage threshold. There were no efforts to recognize the value of the different jobs through credentialized training or transparent job ladders, for example.

Finally, workers were vulnerable to poor working conditions. The conditions varied from the physical – the very cold temperature in the KwikFood factory or the difficulties of heavy work at CityCare – to the psychological (the stress of managing complex project teams at OffshoreIT and the demands from mentally ill patients at CityCare). Older workers are especially vulnerable to poor working conditions and there is clearly an urgent need to redesign jobs so that physical demands on individuals are reduced, thereby establishing a more sustainable lifecycle of work.

REFERENCES

Arulampalam, W., A.L. Booth and M.L. Bryan. 2002. *Work-related training and the new National Minimum Wage in Britain.* Mimeo. Institute for Social and Economic Research, University of Essex.

Bain, P., A. Watson, G. Mulvey and G. Gall. 2002. Taylorism, targets and the pursuit of quantity and quality by call centre management. *New Technology, Work and Employment,* 17 (3): 154–69.

Beynon, H., D. Grimshaw, J. Rubery and K. Ward. 2002. *Managing employment change.* Oxford: Oxford University Press.

Booth, A., M. Francesconi and J. Frank. 2002. Temporary jobs: Stepping stones or dead ends? *Economic Journal,* 112: 480: F189–F213.

Boyd, C. 2002. Customer violence and employee health and safety. *Work, Employment and Society,* 16 (1): 151–69.

Bunting, M. 2004. *Willing slaves: How the overwork culture is ruling our lives.* London: HarperCollins.

Burchell, B. 2002. The prevalence and redistribution of job insecurity and work intensification. In Burchell et al. (eds), *Job insecurity and work intensification.*

Burchell, B., D. Ladipo and F. Wilkinson (eds). 2002. *Job insecurity and work intensification.* London: Routledge.

Cully, M., S. Woodland, A. O'Reilly and G. Dix. 1999. *Britain at work: As depicted by the 1998 workplace employee relations survey.* London: Routledge.

Darton, D., and K. Hurrell. 2005. *People working part-time below their potential.* Report for the Equal Opportunities Commission. Manchester: EOC.

DEFRA. 2005. *Temporary workers in UK agriculture and horticulture.* London: Department for Environment, Food and Rural Affairs.

Dex, S. 2003. *Families and work in the twenty-first century.* Bristol: Policy Press.

DoH (Department of Health). 2002. *Care homes for older people: National minimum standards care homes regulations.* London: The Stationery Office.

Donnelly, R., D. Grimshaw and M. Miozzo. 2006. *The UK computer services sector: Market conditions, employment and work organisation.* Report for the European project DYNAMO, available at www.mbs.ac.uk/ewerc.

DTI (Department of Trade and Industry). 2004. *A survey of workers' experiences of the working-time regulations.* Employment Relations Research Series, No. 31. London: The Stationery Office.

Egan, J. 2005. Evolution, not revolution – the changing face of the workplace. *IRS Employment Review* 832 (September): 8–15.

Forde, C., and G. Slater. 2005. Agency working in Britain: Character, consequences and regulation. *British Journal of Industrial Relations,* 43 (2): 249–72.

Forth, J., and M. O'Mahoney. 2003. *The impact of the National Minimum Wage on labour productivity and unit labour costs.* Research Report for the Low Pay Commission.

Francesconi, M., and A. Gosling. 2005. *Career paths of part-time workers.* EOC Working Paper Series No. 19. Manchester: EOC.

Fuller, A., and L. Unwin. 2003. Learning as apprentices in the contemporary UK workplace: creating and managing expansive and restrictive participation. *Journal of Education and Work,* 16: 4: 406–427.

Grainger, H. 2006. *Trade union membership 2005 – employment market analysis and research.* London: DTI.

Grant, L., L. Buckner, K. Escott, P. Fisher, A. Suokas, N. Tang and S. Yeandle. 2005. *Low paid part-time work: Why do women work in jobs below their potential?* EOC Working Paper Series. Manchester: EOC.

Green, F. 2002. Why has work effort become more intense? *Studies in Economics,* 0207, Department of Economics, University of Kent.

Grimshaw, D., H. Beynon, J. Rubery and K. Ward. 2002. The restructuring of career paths in large service sector organisations: 'Delayering', upskilling and polarisation. *Sociological Review,* 50 (1): 89–116.

Grimshaw, D., and M. Carroll. 2002. *Qualitative research on firms' adjustments to the minimum wage.* Report for the Low Pay Commission (September).

Grimshaw, D., and J. Rubery. 2006. *The undervaluation of women's work.* Report for the Equal Opportunities Commission. Manchester: EOC.

Heyes, J., and A. Gray. 2003. The implications of the national minimum wage for training in small firms. *Human Resource Management Journal,* 13 (2): 76–86.

Hicks, S., and T. Palmer. 2004. Trade union membership: Estimates from the autumn 2003 Labour Force Survey. *Labour Market Trends* (March): 99–101.

Howarth, C., and M. Kenway. 2004. *Why worry any more about the low paid?* London: New Policy Institute.

HSC (Health and Safety Commission). 2005. *Health and Safety Statistics 2004–2005.* Office of National Statistics.

Jenkins, S. 2004. *Gender, place and the labour market.* London: Ashgate.

Kalleberg, A.L., B.F. Reskin and K. Hudson. 2000. Bad jobs in America: Standard and non-standard employment relations and job quality in the US. *American Sociological Review,* 65 (2): 256–78.

Low Pay Commission. 2003. *The national minimum wage: Building on success.* Fourth Report of the Low Pay Commission, Cm5768. London: The Stationery Office.

———. 2005. *National minimum wage: Low Pay Commission report 2005*, Cm 6475, London: The Stationery Office.

McClimont, B., and K. Grove. 2004. *Who cares now? An updated profile of the independent sector home care workforce in England.* Sutton: UK Homecare Association. Accessed from www.ukhca.co.uk/pdfs.

McGovern, P., D. Smeaton and S. Hill. 2004. Bad jobs in Britain: non-standard employment and job quality. *Work and Occupations,* 31 (2): 225–49.

Miller, L., J. Hurstfield and N. Stratton. 2002. *The national minimum wage and employers' training decisions.* Research Report for the Low Pay Commission.

Netten, A., A. Bebbington, R. Darton and J. Forder. 2001. *Care homes for older people: Volume 1 – Facilities, residents and costs.* PSSRU, University of Kent, Canterbury.

Nolan, J. 2002. The intensification of everyday life. In Burchell, B., D. Ladipo and F. Wilkinson (eds), *Job insecurity and work intensification.* London: Routledge.

Olsen, W., and S. Walby. 2004. *Modelling gender pay gaps.* EOC Working Paper Series, No. 17, Manchester: EOC.

Rubery, J., K. Ward and D. Grimshaw. 2005a. The changing employment relationship and the implications for quality part-time work. *Labour and Industry,* 15 (3): 7–28.

Rubery, J., K. Ward, D. Grimshaw and K. Beynon. 2005b. Working time, industrial relations and the employment relationship. *Time and Society*, 14 (1): 89–111.

Smithson, J., S. Lewis, C. Cooper and J. Dyer. 2004. Flexible working and the gender pay gap in the accountancy profession. *Work, Employment & Society*, 18 (1): 115–35.

Taylor, P., G. Mulvey, J. Hyman and P. Bain. 2002. Work organization, control and the experience of work in call centres. *Work, Employment and Society*, 16 (1): 133–50.

Thompson, P., G. Callaghan and D. van den Broek. 2004. Keeping up appearances: recruitment, skills and normative control in call centres. In S. Deery and N. Kinnie (eds), *Call centres and human resource management*. Basingstoke: Palgrave.

United Nations. 2006. Draft ministerial declaration of the high-level segment submitted by the President of the Council on the basis of informal consultations. UN Economic and Social Council, Agenda Item 2, 5 July.

White, M., S. Hill, C. Mills and D. Smeaton. 2004. *Managing to change? British workplaces and the future of work*. Basingstoke: Palgrave.

Wichert, I. 2002. Job insecurity and work intensification: The effects on health and well-being. In Burchell, B., D. Ladipo and F. Wilkinson (eds), *Job insecurity and work intensification*. London: Routledge.

Wilkinson, F. (ed.). 1981. *The dynamics of labour market segmentation*. London: Academic Press.

Wright, E.O., and R.E. Dwyer. 2003. The patterns of job expansions in the USA: A comparison of the 1960s and 1990s. *Socio-Economic Review*, 1: 289–325.

Index

Note: Page numbers in *italic* denote tables, figures or boxes. A subscript numeral appended to a page number denotes a footnote. Page numbers in **bold** indicate major treatment.